28	FRANCIS BACON	43	HEGEL	56	POINCARÉ
	DESCARTES		KIERKEGAARD		PLANCK
	SPINOZA		NIETZSCHE		WHITEHEAD
					EINSTEIN
29	MILTON	44	TOCQUEVILLE		EDDINGTON
					BOHR
30	PASCAL	45	GOETHE		HARDY
			BALZAC		HEISENBERG
31	MOLIÈRE				SCHRÖDINGER
	RACINE	46	AUSTEN		DOBZHANSKY
			GEORGE ELIOT		WADDINGTON
32	NEWTON				
	HUYGENS	47	DICKENS	57	VEBLEN
					TAWNEY
33	LOCKE	48	MELVILLE		KEYNES
	BERKELEY		TWAIN		
	HUME			58	FRAZER
		49	DARWIN		WEBER
34	SWIFT				HUIZINGA
	VOLTAIRE	50	MARX		LÉVI-STRAUSS
			ENGELS		
				59	HENRY JAMES
			TOLSTOY		SHAW
					CONRAD
			DOSTOEVSKY		CHEKHOV
			IBSEN		PIRANDELLO
					PROUST
			WILLIAM JAMES		CATHER
					MANN
			FREUD		JOYCE
			WILLIAM JAMES	60	WOOLF
			BERGSON		KAFKA
			DEWEY		LAWRENCE
			WHITEHEAD		T. S. ELIOT
			RUSSELL		O'NEILL
			HEIDEGGER		FITZGERALD
			WITTGENSTEIN		FAULKNER
			BARTH		BRECHT
					HEMINGWAY
					ORWELL
					BECKETT

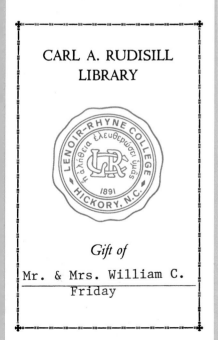

"Thomas Jefferson," by Rembrandt Peale, 1805.

The Great Ideas Today

1993

Encyclopædia Britannica, Inc.

CHICAGO
AUCKLAND • LONDON • MADRID • MANILA • PARIS
ROME • SEOUL • SYDNEY • TOKYO • TORONTO

Drawings in "The Jeffersonian City" are used with permission
of the author.

Library of Congress Number: 61-65561
International Standard Book Number: 0-85229-589-8
International Standard Serial Number: 0072-7288

A NOTE ON REFERENCE STYLE

In the following pages, passages in *Great Books of the Western World* are referred to by the initials "*GBWW*," followed by a roman numeral (indicating the first edition of 1952 [I] or the second edition of 1990 [II]) with volume and page number. Thus, "*GBWW* I: 5, 100; II: 4, 112" refers to a passage from Sophocles' *Oedipus the King*, which is on page 100 in Volume 5 of the first edition, and on page 112 in Volume 4 of the second edition. Sometimes only one reference will be given, since the contents of the first and second editions differ. Also note that passages quoted in an article may differ from the translation of that passage in either the first or second edition, since newer translations of some works are included in the second edition.

Gateway to the Great Books is referred to by the initials "*GGB*," followed by volume and page number. Thus, "*GGB* 10, 39–57" refers to pages 39 through 57 of Volume 10 of *Gateway to the Great Books,* which is James's essay, "The Will to Believe."

The Great Ideas Today is referred to by the initials "*GIT*," followed by the year and page number. Thus, "*GIT* 1968, 210" refers to page 210 of the 1968 edition of *The Great Ideas Today.*

Contents

Preface

Reflecting on the contents of this year's issue of *The Great Ideas Today*, one senses the usual variety of concerns to be found in our volume, which is no easier to summarize than it ever has been. Taking things from the top and going partway through the table of contents, here is Thomas K. Simpson, our regular contributor, writing about space and its dimensions in both philosophic and mathematical terms; here is René de Costa, who last year undertook a survey of contemporary Latin-American literature, finishing what he began; here is a new presence in our pages, Jon Elster, discoursing on what he calls egonomics, which suggests a new science incorporating old ones; here is Otto Bird, also a regular contributor, writing on the subject of infinity, which turns out to be more than one thing, if it is anything at all; and here is Bruce Venable, from whom we heard the year before last on music as a liberal art, and who now continues with what on the face of it must seem an esoteric discussion of song in the Orthodox Christian Church, though this turns out to be an expansion of the views on music that proved so interesting in his original article.

If something common, something shared, is nevertheless to be found among these opening pieces, it seems to be the notion of boundaries and how in each case they need to be expanded. This is not to say eliminated. "Boundary," with its connotation of confinement, is an unpopular conception in these postmodern, deconstructionist days— a late, perverse interval, though one hopes not the last, in the rush of freedom that reaches back as far as the Renaissance—and our first response to any mention of the term may be to think of it as denoting what ought to be removed. But of course the implication is also one of definition, and when we think of enlarging boundaries, or pushing them out, we can mean the enlargement of an idea, the addition to it of meaning which it was not thought previously to have—which it was not realized it had already, if we had only thought.

Certainly Mr. Simpson takes such a view of boundaries as this implies. Some time ago he became interested, he tells us, in the claim of Henri Poincaré that nothing in principle prevents consistent intuitions of non-Euclidean geometry, including those with dimensionality greater than three. There is nothing inherent, that is to say, and as Kant supposed, in our sense of space as having three dimensions—nothing in the nature of our minds that requires this to be so or makes us incapable of perceiving that it is not so. The habit of thinking we live in three-dimensional space is long established, of course, and our sense of reality is rooted in it. But why cannot our sense of reality be enlarged to include, say, a fourth dimension, or to think of space itself as having even more dimensions than that? This is the question to which Mr. Simpson addresses himself, and to which he provides some answers that are the more impressive for arising from experiments of his own with a computer. It is not surprising that he offers us in his discussion of these matters an account of Edwin A. Abbott's little classic called *Flatland*, which anticipates Mr. Simpson's argument, though the anticipation could not have been discerned without such an acute reader of the book as Mr. Simpson shows himself to be.

Professor de Costa has a different extension of our sense of reality in mind. He is concerned to teach us, as he did last year, that there is an extraordinary literature in the Western Hemisphere which most of us until quite recently knew nothing about—which is itself recent, if it comes to that, being a phenomenon of the twentieth century, much of it in the past fifty years or so. It is the literature—the fiction and poetry, chiefly—of Latin America, which we know through Borges, Neruda, García Márquez, Vargas Llosa, and Allende, among others, and which has revealed possibilities in fiction, particularly, beyond anything that Europe or North America have realized.

For his part, Professor Elster is concerned with psychology, in particular motivational conflicts within the person, and how we manage these—but with an extension of his own that recognizes our desires as being far from always rational and self-interested, that sees us as often irrational, non-selfish, and above all non-fixed: we change, Mr. Elster points out, as we get older, and in many situations as they develop— change so much that it is necessary, he argues, to talk of us as having multiple selves. While some pages farther on Mr. Venable, who writes of the Fathers of the Church and the music that made its way into their liturgy, asks us to consider a still further kind of expansion—that whereby music, now wholly secular where it is thought to be serious, was once conceived and may still be recollected as a medium by which men have sought transcendence and communion with a living God.

These articles, together with the one by Mr. Bird, comprise the first two sections of this year's book. In the "Special Features" section, Part Three, we find an old friend, Maurice Cranston, writing on the subject of nationalism, which especially in the Balkans is of such painful interest these days. The roots of nationalism are in the eighteenth and nineteenth centuries, Mr. Cranston reminds us, and conflicts or ambiguities in the meaning of the term are still around to haunt us. After this, Professor George Anastaplo, continuing his series on non-Western cultures and religions, takes up the North American Indians, whose ways of life have long since been shattered by European (and African, and Asian, and Latin-American) settlement, but who have still something to teach us, as we, in overwhelming them, gave lessons, some better than others, of our own. And as chief among these was the thing called civilization—literally, the culture of cities—it is appropriate that the American city, or at least its development, is the concern, later in this part of the book, of Peter D. Paul, an architect and student of urban planning. His account of the subject starts with the urban ideas of Thomas Jefferson in *Notes on Virginia,* the wide-ranging, prophetic work that contains so much of Jefferson's thought as to the United States of America emerging in his time.

Last in this same section is something quite new—something called "A Philosophical Problem to Be Solved," that, as its title indicates, asks for the solution, by some reader, of what Mr. Adler, who conceived it, calls a philosophical problem, namely, how high mental capacity can be transmitted from one generation to the next, as seems to be the case, if the mind is immaterial. Of course, if the mind is not immaterial, the problem does not exist; but then there is the further problem of how a material thing—that is, the mind—can exist when there is no material evidence of it. We invite a solution of the first problem, with rules which readers will discover when they turn to that part of the book.

The remaining portion of this year's issue, Part Four, consists as usual of "Additions to the Great Books Library." First among these is an essay that J. S. Mill wrote about Jeremy Bentham, the great expounder of Utilitarianism, whose influence on Mill was early and permanent, but whose mind he nevertheless thought limited and deeply flawed, so that the essay has as much of doubt in it as praise. This is followed by some essays by Ralph Waldo Emerson, Mill's American contemporary, that reveal an intelligence too restless for ideas yet often strangely productive of them—we are made to think by glancing thoughts, off-hand remarks. There are also comments made on various occasions by Louis Sullivan, the great architect who was not only a planner and designer but a theoretician in his field—very different, of course, from Jefferson. And coming at the end of the volume are three tales by Guy de Maupassant, dead now a hundred years but still a world master in the short story where we know him best—where Ball-of-Fat weeps silent tears among the sanctimonious hypocrites packed close about her, Rachel in "Mademoiselle Fifi" performs her lightning act of courage, and Toine (poor Toine!) makes something strange and tender, while utterly helpless, from his wife's terrible rage.

PART ONE

Current Developments in the Arts and Sciences

Space and Dimensionality

Thomas K. Simpson

Thomas K. Simpson is a frequent contributor to *The Great Ideas Today*. Until 1990, when he retired, he was a tutor at St. John's College in Annapolis, Maryland, and Santa Fe, New Mexico. Recently, under a grant from the National Endowment for the Humanities, he has prepared an edition, scheduled for publication by Rutgers University Press, of three papers on the electromagnetic field by James Clerk Maxwell, designed to make Maxwell's text accessible to readers without special training in mathematics. Other projects include his current role as president of a small corporation, Paraspectives™, Inc., which holds a patent application on a commercially interesting technology for placing the human eye directly into non-Euclidean spaces, making possible, for example, four-dimensional Cartesian graphing in a wide variety of applications. It has led as well to the present article in which representative "paraspective" images are published for the first time.

Mr. Simpson's education was at the Virginia Polytechnic Institute, at St. John's College, at Wesleyan University, and at Johns Hopkins University, where he earned a doctorate in the history of science and technology.

Taken in its pure form, a discussion of "space" might well seem the emptiest of projects: the very caricature of the concerns of the philosopher whose head is "in the sky" and who has time for idle speculation while others attend to the moral and political questions which urge themselves upon us. Those who have attempted a reading of Plato's *Parmenides* know something of the burden associated with the discussion of the largest and most open of questions; Parmenides, as an aging thinker who has covered his ground many times, sighs heavily at the prospect of resuming the discussion of the "One" yet another time. He agrees, it would seem, out of a sense of heroic responsibility to those others present—notable among them the young Socrates, to whom the task of dialectic inquiry must be passed on. The issue, to the end of the dialogue locked in what would seem inconclusive antilogy, is whether Being is One or Many. The mystery which lies behind this question is not only that of the origin of unity but of the unfathomable relation between the inclusive One and the individuals, specific to time and place, which constitute the Many. [1] The issue is not quite so remote as it at first sounds, for each of us, at any moment or through a lifetime, is a living instance of the Many in question. We have real reason to wonder, are we also in some way One? Somewhere in the depths of this question lie the concerns for meaning, purpose, or divine foundation which cannot altogether escape us—at least at moments of crisis in our lives.

Our topic of "Space" and Parmenides' question of the "One" are thus themes ultimately closely related. In each, the difficulty is to confront in speech and thought a concept which contains at the same time all and, seemingly, nothing. It is important that such questions be addressed because we are understandably suspicious that we live in a world which no longer holds together; "Space" or the "One" may be names for that missing principle of coherence which seems to cry out for our attention. No matter if the prospect of success in such an investigation is slight: to have attended to the question of wholeness or coherence of Being is worth the effort.

Nothing *is* except as it is One and Whole; aggregations of parts which are not bound by such a principle of unity have only accidental coherence, indifferently coming to be and passing away, leaving no trace.

Unless the Whole is in some formal way respected, the foundation must be lacking on which respect for any substance or person might be built. Unless we are in some way One before we are Many, members of a single community, why should we respect the rights of our fellow creatures, or care about their suffering or demise? Everything and everyone might then be freely cashed out or traded off, one for another, without the appropriate sense of bereavement at the loss of that which was worthy to be saved. Such words may be applied as any reader wishes: to those plant or animal species the world regards as not worth saving, to an environment which may be exchanged for current gratification, to a nation or a city which, Edmund Burke says, must be more than the sum of its members, to traditions there is not time to listen to or read, to peoples sacrificed to political interests or uninhibited markets. [2]

I pose the question here in terms of "Space," rather than "Being" or the "One," because space is a fascinating mirror in which we may catch this question, and it is after all a term with vast currency among us today. With its great variety of applications, ranging from the most abstract to the most practical, technical, military, or commercial, it seems to cry out for review. At one extreme we have the fabulous formal spaces of the mathematicians; on the other, the space industry associated with that acronym of drama and power, NASA. "Space" is evidently capable of vast imaginative, human, and aesthetic appeal: when we think about them, we tend to care about our spaces, we love to move in them, in their manifestations as deserts, canyons, skies, forests, oceans, and lakes. The challenge and even perhaps mystery of "space" is flourishing in our time, as we become capable of venturing "into" it—though in truth we live our daily lives in outer space, clinging to our tiny planet attached to one commonplace star wandering among hundreds of millions no better or worse in size or situation.

There may be little apparent thread in these diverse uses of our term. Clearly something fundamental has happened to the concept of the One when we find ourselves speaking of spaces in the plural, as our mathematicians, engineers, and even politicians have taught us to do. [3] Evidently, we are involved with a metaphor which has gotten out of hand and is spreading weedlike among us, loosestrife taking over our garden of discourse. All this confusion is at the least a sign of lively interest, and my own sense is that there are deep connections through it all back to its roots, somewhere in Parmenides' antilogy, the mystery of the Many and the One.

A thought which has encouraged me as I first considered this topic is the recognition that even when we do try to conceive of "Space" in its most austere fashion, as an empty box without walls, we find that it is full of surprises and fraught with consequences. Classical geometry is after all, in one understanding, the very study of that empty box, and readers of Euclid's *Elements* know the richness of that text and the mysteries into which it leads. Out of this empty box of Pandora's ultimately emerge the regular solids. They process, one by one, dramatically in Euclid's Thirteenth Book; and Euclid closes by demonstrating to us that there is room in the world for just these five, and no others. Readers who go on to explore the reaches of our spatial intuition by reading a book such as David Hilbert and Stephan Cohn-Vossen's *Geometry and the Imagination* can track the argument in which the possible close-packing of the box with spheres unfolds; we can see this turn into crystallography, and then—lo and behold!—into the structures of the materials of which our world, and we ourselves, are composed. In a sense, it is we ourselves who emerge, body and mind, from that empty box of Euclid's. [4]

It is out of some such sense that I have come to a proposal about the root meaning of the word "space," which I would like to offer as a leading thread through the present discussion. I do not claim that it in fact binds together all the disparate usages of the term, but I think it may point to certain important implications of the concept. Space, it seems to me, is most interesting when understood as a *source,* and I propose to characterize it as *the domain of all possibilities.* Its emptiness signifies not so much blankness as potentiality: it is loaded, or charged, with prospect. [5] On the one hand, this is what we see in Euclid or Hilbert: a world emerging before the wondering eye of our minds. On the other, it is this wonder at unknown and inexhaustible prospects which has always energized the mythology of space—in the diverse forms given it in Genesis or the poem of Lucretius, or by Homer, Virgil, Dante, Newton, or a Native American creation story; by Euclid, Nikolai Lobachevsky, or Einstein, or now, by Steven Spielberg or the Space Agency. There is no simple agreement among these adventurers, certainly, but perhaps some common spirit moves them all. If so, I believe it has something to do with an ultimate coherence of all things, a single source of all possibilities. One might say that this is to take the term "space" primarily in its sense as "cosmos," even if that cosmos seems at times to be nothing more than the arbitrary construction of the purest of formal mathematicians. [6]

Spaces are measured by their dimensionalities, and if indeed the concept of space is as fundamental to our being as I claim here, then the companion question of dimensionality must be of corresponding importance. In one way or another, we move in spaces, and the dimensionality of a space speaks to the fundamental richness or poverty of the motions it permits us. If we think in geometric terms, we may say that these elemental axes or directions of motion, in terms of which all the more complex motions may be analyzed, are the determinants of our freedom. We are bound in spaces which have few dimensions or released into those which have many. For this reason a technical term for these dimensions, "degrees of freedom," may serve us well.

Applied first by engineers to the motions of wheels and levers permitted under mechanical constraints, it seems to work well more generally: the dimensions of a space of any kind measure the degrees of our freedom to move in it. Taking a space as a domain of possibility, we will want in each instance to ask about a space, what are the fundamental axes of empowerment it affords? What activity—physical, mental, or spiritual— does it open to us? The answer must take the form of a count, literal or figurative, of its dimensions.

If "space" is the locus of possibility, it will have a dialectical history which tracks mankind's sense of what is and what might be. I have spoken somewhat boldly in linking a variety of authors and texts, ancient and modern; a corrective is appropriate, which would assert on the other side of the balance that there is in some sense no "space" in Euclid, while Aristotle in the *Physics,* if he really entertains the idea at all, does so only to refute it. [7] Euclid's figures seem to exist simply in themselves and in their relations to one another; they do not appear in a preexisting "space." For Aristotle it is very important to reject any notion of a time or space which preexists, for nothing preexists; existence is what it is precisely because it comes first, timelessly, while time and place are measures of it. "Space" and "place" are very different concepts for Aristotle. Place is relative; in place things are connected to one another in an organic net of substances whose very definitions generate real and essential relationships. Space, on the other hand, if there were any, would be a distinct thing, a preexisting vessel within which all the entities found their locations. Homer too gets along without space. In a world of places, Odysseus travels without a map: he encounters the beings of his mythical world simply as the events of the voyage deliver them to him, or him to them. Story is the surrogate for space in Homer's world. When the world is intact and complete, as it seems provisionally to Homer and finally to Aristotle, there is no need to add the concept of space. It is when the mythical world fractures that space must be invented, to give the pieces coordinates in which to be.

In earlier essays for *The Great Ideas Today,* devoted to the sciences, I have considered by contrast the way in which Genesis and the idea of the Creation seem to transform such questions as this of space. [8] The Lord is that source of being, beyond the created existence we know, who makes it possible to speak of space and time as preceding, as containers into which existence as we know it may be put. It is this sense of space and time which Newton ratifies as "absolute," and on which he is able to found his mathematical philosophy of nature (*GBWW* I: 34, 8; II: 32, 8). In this sense, the conceptual absoluteness of Newtonian space makes mathematical science possible, and even though with Einstein and relativity space-time has supplanted "space" per se, the sense of an ultimate, measurable, and calculable framework survives and flourishes. Where we can thus measure and calculate we can also contrive, and in this way the great dialectical transformation of this idea, from "place" to "space," has brought with it the cornucopia of our modern technological world. Modern "space" as the ground of a scientific world has indeed proved the fount of unbounded possibility.

We conclude that space has thus its own dialectical history. Once there was no space: as we have seen, there is none in Euclid, who has too little distance from the figures he makes and contemplates to need any vast container to put them in. This is indeed at once Euclid's excellence and his irrecoverable innocence: if existence is coherent and single, one may live with it in intimacy and without apology. Thus no word in the lexicon of ancient Greek, it seems, quite means what we have come to mean by "space." [9] The real need for such a term arises only with the advent of radical options: a Creation, suggesting the intellectual thought of a vessel in which to put the new work; or geometries with other postulates, out of which arise thoughts of alternative worlds, one "space" for Euclid, another for Lobachevsky, yet a third for Riemann, whose geometry has no parallel lines. Spaces such as these quickly breed metaphor, and we find, now, spaces to hold what we call systems of all sorts: spaces of opportunity in all fields, political spaces, personal spaces, economic spaces—color space is one instance which we will look at as exemplar later in this essay. Such spaces, as we have seen, all have their dimensionalities, delineating the degrees of freedom which they offer. Our freedoms, once single and conceptually simple, now seem contingent, functions of the dimensionalities of the spaces we are able to devise or claim.

I. Space lab experiments

It would appear in this consideration of space that we are proposing to think very hard about *nothing*, an endeavor if not self-contradictory, at least exceptionally demanding and on its face unpromising. To sharpen our wits, let us undertake the rather elementary experiment of the Empty Box. Think of a box—as ordinary as possible, for we are not to be distracted by it, yet large enough to move one's mind around in. Now remove its contents, utterly. There is to be absolutely nothing left inside. It is important to classify this as a mental, and not a physical, experiment; we are not to labor over approximations to the physical vacuum, nor to be troubled about the problematic exclusion of persistent intruders such as magnetic fields, photons of rare radiations, or elusive and unstoppable neutrinos. Mentally, we simply empty the box. Images of the back side of the box, its corners, color, and so on, should no longer distract us. Now the cleared content of the box is all we have, and it is the very image of nothingness. This is conceptual—let us call it mathematical—space.

7

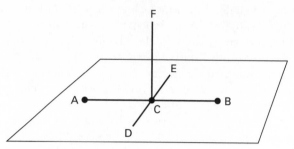

Figure 1. An image on paper of one person's version of "Space Lab Experiment No. 1."

Experiment 1

The first experiment will probably not present any difficulties for you, particularly if you use pencil and paper. It consists in rigorously carrying out the following steps: (1) choose any point; (2) choose a second, distinct point and draw the straight line joining your two selected points; (3) choose any third, distinct point on this line between the two original points; (4) through this point, erect a line perpendicular to the original line; (5) mentally construct the plane which is determined by the two intersecting lines; (6) through the original intersection point, construct the line perpendicular to this plane.

So far, so good. If you faltered at any stage in your construction process, you need only turn at that point to Euclid, whose propositions will empower you to carry out the necessary constructions—for is not the domain of possibility for this emptiness precisely the content of Euclid's *Elements?* [10] The lines which you have drawn, hung with or without his help in the space housed in your mind, should look something like our figure 1. Retain this mental structure, unaltered, for use in the next experiment.

Note that we have made an excursion through a realm of successive dimensionalities. We began in step 1 with the point—that figure, Euclid says, which "has no part," which is only to say that it contains no scope for motion whatever. It is the prison of zero dimensionality. In step 2, by adding another point and joining the two with a straight line, we added as well our first degree of freedom—the line (whether straight or not) is a domain of dimensionality one. Step 3 took us to the plane and dimensionality two, allowing two directions in which we may move (as we do when we travel by compass on the surface of our oceans). Step 4 completed the world as we know it, by adding the third dimension. If we travel to the full limits of each of these dimensions, we may assert with confidence that we can reach any point in the world of Euclid's geometry. Any move beyond would take us outside the universe.

Experiment 2

To the construction of the previous experiment, add the following step: (7) through the original intersection point, construct a line perpendicular to both the original plane and to the line of step 6.

Did you succeed in carrying out step 7? If so, you would have constructed, at one point in your space, four mutually perpendicular lines, which means that you would presumably have ventured outside the universe, into four-dimensional space. Euclid, who has empowered all the previous steps, grants us no power to do any such thing. Our step 7 stands as a Euclidean impossibility. [11] On the other hand, we know now that a four-dimensional geometry is by no means a conceptual impossibility: postulates may be written for it, and propositions formally deduced which delineate in detail the amazing properties of four-dimensional figures. [12] These, however, appear as merely logical constructions. Whether we are capable of truly seeing a four-dimensional figure in that laboratory of our imaginations, which we may call the "mind's eye," is a distinct and fundamental question.

Why should it not be possible to construct four mutually perpendicular lines at a point in one's empty mind? Admittedly it would no more occur to Euclid to speak this thought than it would for him to speak of space, for the idea of the alternative has never arisen. For him the cosmos is in no sense an optional object. But for us, inheritors of the probing spirit of Descartes and confronted with a far more complex tradition, the question cannot be avoided. It may be that we are, after all, creatures entitled to spaces of higher dimensionality than we thought. Might we, by some act of contrivance or will, after all carry out the construction of Experiment 2 and enter a world of four dimensions? Were we to do that, many figures, such as M. C. Escher's, which are tantalizingly "impossible" in three-dimensional space, would become "possible" in four. [13] Figure 2 depicts the failed effort of our second thought experiment.

Figure 2. The failed Experiment No. 2. In three-dimensional space, it seems, there is nowhere for the second perpendicular, CX, to go.

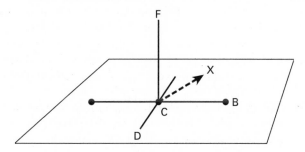

Are we sealed in a human "nature" which will not permit us license to hunt in four dimensions? It is always possible that we have stopped too short, thus early in the history of mankind, in taking stock of the possibilities ultimately open to us. There was a time, prior to the invention of human flight, when we traveled as essentially two-dimensional creatures, crawling about on the surface of the earth and attaining to three-dimensional heights only by virtue of even greater efforts at crawling, in the ascent of mountain peaks. With the dawn of the era of flight, mankind first took command of three-dimensional space. The question of our possible entitlement to claim yet a fourth dimension may serve as paradigm of all such questions: in all the spaces in which we carry out our lives, the same question of the essential bounds of possibility, of the ultimate degrees of our freedom, lurks. We may move forward, exploring new geometries and, indeed, stepping out of the old universe and into the fourth dimension, taking our old human nature into new spaces with us as we go. For those of us who wish better things for mankind's long political future, the analogy to geometry must bring encouragement.

The failure of Experiment 2 may serve as a paradigm which I propose we follow through our investigation of the turns and twists of the concepts of space and dimensionality. We have concluded that a *space,* in the bosom of its very void, is on the one hand charged or loaded with an expanse of *possibility,* while on the other hand, this field of possibility is fenced with walls of impossibility, which strictly delimit its scope. If space is thus loaded or charged, its "possibility" is not the blank of a mere tabula rasa but "possibility" in its strong, etymological sense as *potential* or *power*. [14]

The foundation of every geometry is in its postulates, which are the seeds or keys to the empowerment it grants us. Euclid sets out the few foundations of his work, as requests for our concurrence, at the outset of his work. [15] As we turn to the fruition of his work in Book XIII, we meet the harvest of this seeding, for those postulates planted at the outset yield there the abundant symmetries of the regular solids. We say, as he does not, that these are the fruits of a three-dimensional space; a space with exactly three degrees of freedom. Euclid matches his demonstration of *possibility* with a corresponding writ of *impossibility,* proving not only that there are five regular solids, but that there cannot be a sixth. [16] Yet we can break that mold: figure 3 depicts a regular solid in four-dimensional space, which cannot exist in three, made visible to us now, with the aid of the computer, in an altogether new mode of seeing. These exactly five regular solids are emblems of that measure of the old freedom. Probably all freedoms are consequences of such laws, which empower and delimit at once. And most spaces are, like Euclid's, so silent and invisible that we take them to be the world itself, empty of any commitment, and, like Euclid, do not notice them

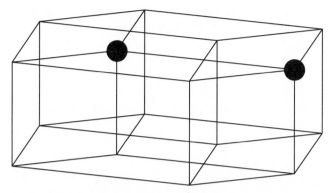

Figure 3. Liberated by the computer from our familiar world, we are now in a four-dimensional space, and find ourselves looking directly at a figure, the hypercube, which would no more fit into three dimensions than a cube would fit into two.

at all. Geometry, Plato claims, is the way to political and philosophical thought. If so, the possibility that we may after all succeed in carrying out Experiment 2 is heartening in a most fundamental way.

An experiment with parallels

Let us now return to reconsider our empty box. It seems that we have, after all, some power to *change spaces,* to expand or alter our geometric commitment. If we are to consider switching spatial allegiances, we must invoke the authority of new postulates, spelled out by a new text. For the moment, let us turn our attention from the question of dimensionality to that of the behavior of parallel lines, a talisman to the entire structure of figure and space. For this purpose, let our author now be Lobachevsky, and let the empty space of our visual imagination be his. [17] We must repeat our first steps carefully and traverse the switching point of spaces quite explicitly. At the root of this alternative is Euclid's Fifth Postulate, the "parallel postulate," which assures in effect that through a given point only one parallel to a given line may be drawn. [18] Lobachevsky discovered that a new geometry was possible in which this restriction did not apply. Our moment of decision, then, between geometries, is the Fifth Postulate: to join Euclid's world, turn it on; to join Lobachevsky's, turn it off. To track this transfer of allegiances, we experiment with drawing parallels; we do so first under the aegis of Euclid, then switch to that of Lobachevsky.

Experiment 3(a) (Euclidean)

Retain the postulates of Euclid's *Elements.*
1. In the original space, erase the earlier figures and draw a single, infinite line. Outside this line, choose any point.

11

2. Through this point, construct a parallel to the original line—that is, a line which does not meet the first when extended infinitely in either direction. Success is assured by Euclid's Proposition 31, Book I, which relies ultimately on his Postulate 5.
3. Through the same point, construct another line, distinct from the first, and similarly nonintersecting in either direction. In Euclid's geometry, failure is assured by the same proposition: one and the same proposition constitutes both avenue and wall.

Experiment 3(b) (Lobachevskian)

Now, change spaces; switch authorities. Cancel Euclid's parallel postulate and thereby invoke the space of Lobachevsky.

Repeat the steps of 3(a).

What was Euclid's wall has now become Lobachevsky's window: step 3 may be accomplished as readily as the first two—in fact, through a point outside the chosen line any number of distinct, nonintersecting lines may be drawn; Lobachevsky calls the boundaries of this bundle of nonintersecting lines the "parallels," one to the right, and the other to the left. Figure 4 represents the failure of Experiment 3(a) and the success of 3(b). [19]

It might seem that a spatial alternative of the sort we have just described concerns only a small talisman of the space, the parallel. But this is in fact key to much else, and these two emptinesses become homes to worlds—each whole, but each utterly strange to the other. As an example of this, we may pursue the Lobachevskian option and carry out an experiment in photographic enlargement.

Figure 4. (a) Another failed experiment: we can find no place in our familiar Euclidean world to fit a second line, PQ, which will never intersect with line AB. By contrast, (b) depicts success. Abandoning the stricture of Euclid's "parallel postulate," we are free to construct as many lines as we wish within the bounds of PQ and PR, none of which will intersect AB—however far we extend them.

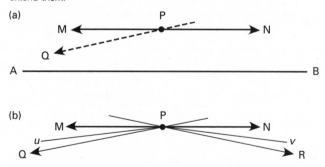

Experiment 4

Invoke the Lobachevskian postulates. (1) Choose a finite line segment, and on it as base, construct a triangle of any arbitrary shape. (2) Now, double the base and construct a triangle of the same shape as the first.

Lobachevsky demonstrates the impossibility of step 2. [20] We have met a wall: triangles in his world cannot change size without changing shape. Similarity of figures is impossible; there can be no slide projector or photographic enlarger in such a space. [21]

The case of Lobachevsky and the issue of the behavior of parallels may lead us to reconsider an assumption we made on entry into our space lab. I emphasized that these were to be exclusively "mathematical" experiments and that we were not to worry about intrusions of such physical objects as photons. But is not the issue between Euclid and Lobachevsky deeply related to alternative possible behaviors of just those photons which were to be excluded? For what is a straight line but the path of a ray of light? [22] As we peer into infinite distances in our mental spaces to determine whether "lines" meet or not, are we not inquiring about, or perhaps prescribing for, the patterns of rays of light? And again, as Poincaré and Einstein emphasize, when we move geometric constructions about in our minds to determine their congruences, or set the sum of the angles of a triangle to determine whether it is Euclidean, Lobachevskian, or Riemannian (respectively, equal to, less than, or more than 180°), are we not demanding behaviors of rigid bodies and thus implicating a physics at the same time and, by the same token, as a geometry? Poincaré emphasizes, speaking of a geometry as "convenient" to a physics, that if we watched as a regular matter left shoes turning into right ones by a certain twist of the wrist, we would find it natural to say that they existed in a four-dimensional world, and he adds that a mathematician skilled in group theory could readily imagine the details of such a process. [23] Since we are now embarked upon views of four-dimensional space, there is no difficulty, substituting a computer for the skill of the practiced mathematician, in depicting the shoe-transformation Poincaré alludes to (fig. 5). These insights, first on the part of Poincaré, and then of Einstein, have led to a new acknowledgment of the intimate relation of these two fields and, from the scientific point of view, the geometrization of physics. It is in this spirit that Einstein in the general theory of relativity comes to speak of the motion of light rays, under the action of gravity, as their passage along trajectories in a curved space. [24]

We have moved by way of these elementary experiments from the notion of space as a blank or empty container, a mere void into which all existences may be placed, to something very much richer. The sense of the field of all possible existents remains, but with a new twist: not a passive field, but the ground of all empowerment, with implications

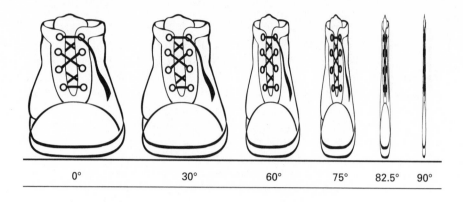

| 0° | 30° | 60° | 75° | 82.5° | 90° |

Figure 5. "Poincaré's Left Shoe." In a world Poincaré invites us to imagine, a left shoe can always be turned into a right shoe by an appropriate twist of the wrist.

for a physics as well as a mathematics. In the inner constitution of the admittedly still "empty" space lie the seeds of all potentiality, of authority and power. When we speak of the degrees of freedom of a space, we may think first of the limitations and entrainments of so many channels of confinement. But when we think of "freedom" in a more constructive sense, the dimensions of a space become so many parameters of possibility, and each new dimension becomes a new entitlement with implications for populations of possible figures which follow in its train. Victor Zuckerkandl in another context has remarked that "The emergence of a new dimension is always the greatest of miracles," for it takes us into a space of power and freedom we had never known. [25] From the habitual commitment to any one space, it is nearly impossible to imagine the opportunities latent in another. But it is our modern way to stretch our minds and to speak of many spaces, or to speak of our one space in its many aspects, as if these shifts were matters of will—as indeed the reader was invited to do, in "switching spaces" in Experiment 3. Ultimately we will have to insist that some larger space contains them all.

II. The Flatlanders

As a truly magic mirror in which to explore these questions of space and its dimensionality, we may turn to Edwin Abbott's remarkable fantasy *Flatland* [2nd ed., 1884], a vision of a world which can only appear to us as ludicrously constricted. [26] With delightful powers of invention, Abbott contrives to fit a complete physics, a social order, and a cast of characters into a space of only two dimensions. Conceiving the geometric limitations of life without height or depth would seem

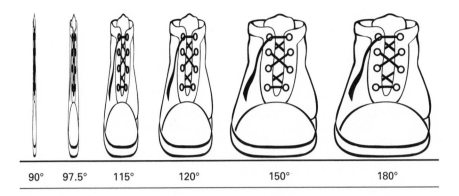

| 90° | 97.5° | 115° | 120° | 150° | 180° |

sufficiently challenging, but for Abbott this is only the beginning. It is rather the metaphor of flattened minds and deprived imaginations that interests Abbott most, and by way of a small but effective plot, he manages to measure the human meaning of space and dimensionality and to test the significance of the denial of one of our accustomed degrees of freedom.

Flatland explores the range of possible dimensionalities of our Experiment 1: dimensionalities zero, one, two, and three, in the forms of Pointland, Lineland, Flatland, and Space, as a succession of increasing "degrees of freedom." To use this phrase is to suggest the metaphoric power of the spatial image, which *Flatland* in its few mischievous and incisive chapters explores. If each dimension of a space adds a degree to the freedom it affords its occupants, then a new dimension is indeed an empowerment, while the denial of a dimension is a radical confinement. As we indulge in mocking or pitying the Flatlanders in their entrapment in what seems to us a mere sheet of paper, the barbs of Abbott's satire return to trouble our confidence in the presumed amplitude of our own world, which is imaged in Abbott's text as a closed box (fig. 6). The special glee Abbott conveys in observing the foibles of Flatland has something to do with the moral and social implications of a life confined to a realm of too few dimensions.

Every reader of the present essay who has not already met Abbott's tale is advised to stop at this point, contrive to obtain a copy, and in half an afternoon join the widespread community of enthusiasts for this quietly sparkling work. For the benefit of others whose lives do not at the moment allow this degree of special freedom, I will attempt to summarize its remarkable investigations.

Flatland is an epic in the manner of Swift, except that our narrator, by name A Square, is a resident of Flatland who has been privileged to escape, if only for a few hours, and thus has gained insight enough into the ways of Space to be able to address us in ways we will understand.

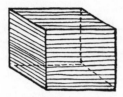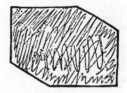

Figure 6. Edwin Abbott's image of a cube generated by stacked-up cards (left). If we see the Flatlanders' lives as ridiculously confined to a sheet of paper, we are analogously committed to life in a very large 3-D "box." The same box (right) as it appears to a Flatland eye, not yet practiced in perspective vision.

In a final irony, we learn that it is written from a Flatland prison cell out of which the reader could extract the incarcerated author with no effort at all, merely by reaching in from above his plane space. The work is infused with such secret ironies.

It is written in two parts. In the first, we are given a sober account of the physical situation and social arrangements of life in Flatland. In the second, we are treated to the narrative of an adventure the counterpart of which we can only pray will not befall us: A Square, on the occasion of the eve of a millennial New Year's Eve in Flatland, is mysteriously visited by a stranger, Sphere, who materializes in Flatland from the third dimension. Square is swept out of his universe for a brief, breathtaking revelation of the truth underlying geometric relationships which, from within Flatland, could be made out only by inference and were thus veiled in ineluctable obscurity. How, after all, could we construe the structure of a pentagon when seen exclusively from within the sheet of paper on which it is drawn? Rendered dithyrambic by the ecstasy of his sudden liberation, Square urges his new mentor to go yet farther into the fourth and higher dimensions, a suggestion which infuriates Sphere, who is satisfied with his resources in three dimensions. In anger, he hurls Square, like Satan out of Heaven, back into the now unbearable constraint of Flatland. Here Square is imprisoned by the authorities for his dangerous audacity in preaching the gospel of three dimensions to the citizenry. It is clear that word of a new degree of freedom looms in the minds of the priests as a threat to the peace and good order of Flatland. A special anathema, now forbidden by special legislation, has been a persistent attempt on the part of scholars of Flatland to address the question, "Whence cometh the light?"—which mysteriously and without shadow illuminates their world, as we can understand, though Flatlanders cannot, from "above."

Edwin Abbott had taken holy orders at Cambridge, and certain of his other works are overtly theological in character. The notion suggests itself that with Square's revelation, Abbott is hinting at Christian liberation, while the mystery of the illumination alludes to the incidence in religious painting of light from another world. [27] There is no limit to the suggestive metaphoric reach of this work, whether entirely intended by its author or not. Abbott presents in the mode of nightmare what is in effect his hero's visit to Hades, in the guise of Pointland—the sealed totality of ego itself, at once the sole occupant and entire extent of a domain of dimensionality zero. That image teems with suggestion and allusion, possibly to Odysseus' interview with the shade of Achilles, or to the ultimate vision of Dante's *Paradiso*, but in any case it certainly becomes a failed attempt to communicate with Aristotle's Unmoved Mover (*GBWW* I: 8, 602; II: 7, 602).

With this hint of the layout of Abbott's work, which is at once too brief and too long to warrant summarizing, let us now return to a consideration of the inhabitants and mores of Flatland.

Dimensionality as ruling principle

As Square's description of the nature and affairs of Flatland unfolds, we see that life in a spatially binding world is pervaded by a corresponding constraint projected into matters social, political, and moral as well. (We leave aside here all questions of Abbott's ingenious projections of the limitation to a planar universe onto the physical world, where we find, for example, that rain always falls from north to south, while a force of gravity, mild in temperate regions but stronger elsewhere, draws all matter southward. Figure 7 gives us a glimpse of a Flatland

Figure 7. Floor plan of a typical Flatland house.

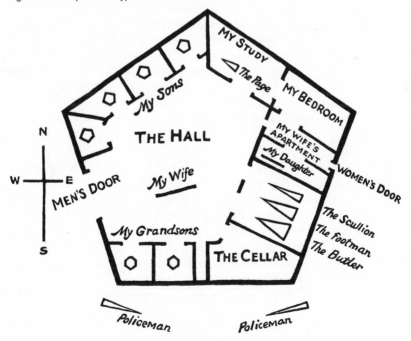

house, its roof peaked to the north to deflect the prevailing rain.) Two-dimensional figures serve as the primary organizing principle of society, with symmetry as the unquestioned mark of aristocratic distinction. Thus, women are mere straight lines; soldiers and workmen, isosceles triangles; the "middle class" are equilateral triangles; professional men (to whose ranks Square himself belongs) are squares or pentagons; while the nobility are hexagons or regular polygons of greater numbers of sides. The fullest symmetry, intensely sought after but perhaps never in Flatland quite achieved, is that of the circle, hallmark of the priest. Irregular figures of any sort are hardly tolerated.

There is, blessedly, a progressive principle at work by which families may hope to advance through successive generations—Square's own grandchild, who reveals his excellence of mind by proposing on his own initiative the question of the existence of a third dimension, is a perfect hexagon. There is a committee (the "Sanitary and Social Board") to certify angles as a matter of public record for admission to higher ranks, and devices of all sorts, including the fiercest of surgeries, are employed for the sake of prospective advancement. In effect, the concept of dimensionality becomes an obsessive principle: women, as straight lines, hardly enter the second dimension, while successive levels of isosceles figures gradually occupy the second dimension. [28]

There is, running through this, a strange and perhaps telling inversion. Though the greatest possible vertex angle is taken with confidence as prima facie evidence of intelligence, it is the women who—with no vertex angle whatever—are by the same token the most *acute,* while the sought-after obtuseness of the aristocracy is hardly reassuring as a metaphor for wisdom. In a hundred such ways, Abbott, we might say, needles his Victorian readers to delight in a perverse self-recognition.

The limited one-dimensional retinas of Flatland eyes have little power to discern the figures which are the ruling principles of their society; Square demonstrates the effect to his readers by asking them to view two-dimensional figures edge-on. Only the fog, pervasive in Flatland, [29] makes their structure of refined social distinctions tenable, the linear images dimming in proportion to the relative distances of portions of the objects. None of this is taken by Flatlanders as an unnatural restraint, of course, but rather as a perfectly obvious fact of life—just as we do not normally suffer as we should from our equally ridiculous inability to contemplate the back walls of our houses as we, locked in our space, approach them from the front. From a decent standpoint in a fourth dimension, we ought of course to be able at once to see the whole house, just as they, from a decent standpoint outside their sheet-of-paper world, would for the first time catch the image of an entire square. It is difficult to grant the evident truth that we are as handicapped in our inability to grasp what a whole cube really looks like as they are to grasp the image of a square.

We are perhaps a century late in getting Abbott's fundamental point—only now are we prepared to use our skills and imaginations to liberate ourselves from this abject confinement inside a three-dimensional space, utilizing the computer and a dawning command over alternative realities we call "virtual," to see for the first time three-dimensional figures in their true forms. We have, it has been discovered, the technical power to do that, and we are now finding strategies to escape the space we once thought was our lot by irreversible decree of nature (fig. 8). [30] We note that even Abbott, summoning us to think more boldly of our own case, gives us no hint as to any way in which Square would have been able to exploit his new standpoint in space and catch on his merely linear retina the new picture *in extenso* of two-dimensional forms. But that problem we can in fact now address. What we lack is the courage of our convictions to use these new resources to challenge such apparent dogmatists as Kant, who would confine us by the supposed nature of our spatial intuition to Euclidean three-dimensional space. [31] Having set himself the question, "How is science possible?"—Kant answers, in the paradigmatic case of Euclidean geometry, that we are able to assert with certainty the propositions of our geometry precisely because in so doing we are merely explicating the relations which belong to our inherent mode of spatial intuition. According to Kant, it is not the external world of which, let us say, the Pythagorean theorem can be asserted as a simple truth; indeed, we know nothing of that world of the things-in-themselves, which is conditioned by neither space nor time. Rather, geometry is the science of the domain of our own spatial intuition.

To do Kant justice, we must acknowledge that he would surely not have written in just this vein if he had met the findings of Lobachevsky before he wrote. Russell has proposed that, had Kant been familiar with the ability of the mind to range freely over the alternative, non-Euclidean geometries, he would readily have granted that our spatial intuitions could not be confined to just the Euclidean sort and referred instead, as the necessary mode of human spatial intuition, to a topology uncommitted to any choice among the Euclidean, Lobachevskian, or Riemannian options—that is, whether one nonintersecting line, many nonintersecting lines, or no nonintersecting line could be drawn through a point outside a given line. [32] It may be that the inherent space of our visual intuition has no metric at all—images are ordered, but if a measuring stick is to attach number to them, we must supply such a ruler and may decide for ourselves what form the metric will take. The space of the visual intuition Kant was relying on may have just the rubber-sheet structure of topology—order and continuity, but no concept of length, no rigid bodies, distances, or measuring sticks at all. Any two forms that can be stretched to fit one another are congruent, which is to say, identical to perception.

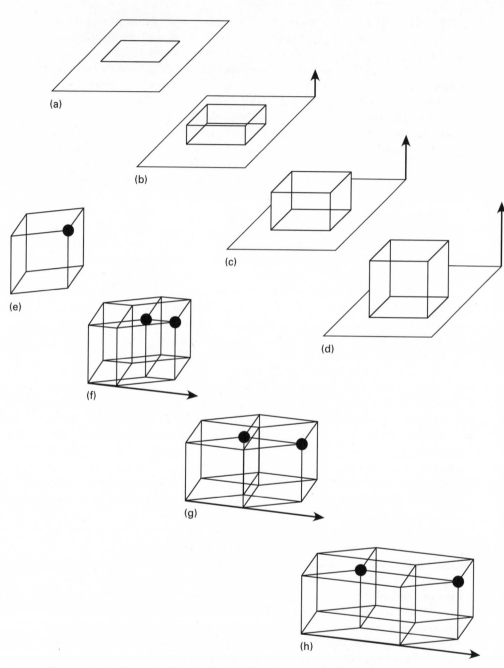

Figure 8. Just as Square in Abbott's tale is privileged to stand outside his space and watch a square develop into a cube (a–d), we are here lifted outside of our world and, from a new platform in four-dimensional space, watch a cube move out along the fourth axis and grow into a hypercube (e–h). The content of the hypercube is not volume, but is as different from volume as volume is from area.

We recall that as we surveyed the results of our initial experiments on figures in space, we reflected that some space might include all of the options—as each space is a world of possibility for its proper figure, so the greater space would house the possibility of each of the lesser spaces. Since we were able to shift spaces in our minds, is not this broader view of Kant's proposition persuasive? Our visual intuition, exercised in imagination, is topological. Uncommitted in itself to any one metric, it admits them all; there is no one metric in our heads. And yet for all this freedom, it may be only a three-dimensional space that we can sense unaided. We might have to resort to a new order of technically assisted vision to get free of the limitations of the three-dimensional box we have always lived in. [33]

Abbott is at his devastating best as he turns to the question of the spirit of revolt which this dimensional constraint, carried as it is into a tyrannical social order, invites. His *Flatland* turns quickly into a veritable handbook for revolutionaries of any era, for with a dry wit and unerring discernment he points out a catalog of methods used to quell revolt. Unlike Charles Dodgson (Lewis Carroll), whose *Through the Looking-Glass* is unmistakably the work of a mathematician eager to work into fiction perceptions of a four-dimensional geometry, Abbott does not approach his work as a mathematical theorist. Perceptive though it is, his geometry is but a device for attacking narrowness of mind and spirit, for which his spatial dimensionality is in turn food for metaphor. Constraint of dimensionality in Flatland is like imprisonment, the preoccupying principle of a pervasive degradation. It is quite evident that Abbott is speaking, through the vehicle of his paper-thin creations, of the mind and society of Victorian England and then, beyond his own time, of narrowness of vision in any era. In terms of the concept which is the topic of the present essay, we may say that the "space" he is speaking of is that domain in which the human spirit dwells: in its amplitude, it empowers freedom of spirit, but in its narrowness, it locks spirit into confinement and repression.

Flatland, Square confides, is dull—spiritually as well as geometrically "flat"—and it is this dullness, founded in fear and dogmatism, from which he would liberate our psyches with his penetrating satire. The degrees of freedom of space in this larger sense measure the possibilities of motion in thought even more than in action. It is particularly significant that the arts of social interaction, founded in an intricate classification by geometric rank, are extremely refined. "Feeling" of one another's angles, which we must remember are never to be seen as such on linear retinas, becomes the very foundation of sound personal relations. The technique is implemented with such philological graces as the prescribed introductory formula, "Permit me to ask you to feel and be felt by my friend Mr. So-and-so," abbreviated by custom to "Let me ask you to feel Mr. So-and-so."

Though recourse to touch, this lowest in the ranking of the human perceptions, serves the purposes of the lower levels of society, the aristocracy has recourse to highly cultivated subtleties which are, we are assured, accessible to linear vision. Lower orders of society learn their basic feeling in the ordinary elementary schools, but "recognition by sight," an art based on the most subtle gradations of figure when viewed artfully from a variety of viewpoints, is attainable only at the best schools and appears to be the principal accomplishment of those who are able to complete successful academic careers at the best universities. We would not dare mock the Victorians from our standpoint in the late twentieth century, knowing as we do that, among us, neighborhood, financial standing, dress, house and automobile, speech, school, and race interweave to certify one's status and fate, perhaps as surely as any more candidly acknowledged refinements of social grace England ever produced. These together open or close the doors on *possibility*, which is the crux of any social space.

Flatlanders are sure that just as it is a work of nature that the world be two-dimensional, so it is a fact of human nature that society be organized according to the symmetries of two-dimensional figures. Thus it is by nature that, with exceptions sufficient only to prove the rule, the more obtuse angles of the figures of higher symmetry, such as the hexagon and octagon, are associated with higher intellectual powers, while the acute angles of the lesser isosceles signify gross and unrefined intellects. Such dogmatic convictions concerning human nature are matched in our own time by comparable claims that humans are by nature acquisitive, warring, or unable to plan reasonably for common actions in groups. Defenders of "human nature" in any age close the doors on any suggestion of higher possibilities. We are bound within the restricted horizons of those who have limited vision.

Flatland, where repression, though as artfully managed as in most modern societies, is nonetheless constantly provocative of rebellion, is described by Square as having to suppress a disturbing number of uprisings. There is a rather straightforward dialectic of space in this sense: as soon as one becomes aware of the confinement within one's limited dimensionality, the thought of a more ample social space, with higher dimensionality, insistently suggests itself. This certainly occurs in Flatland, for special legislation is passed prohibiting any talk of a possible higher space. It is under just this legislation that Square is given what would appear to be a lifetime sentence.

It appears that small-scale disturbances are routinely controlled in Flatland through standard methods such as the co-optation of leaders, while the anger of women leads primarily to a disturbing thread of domestic mayhem, including destruction of intimate relatives in the manner of Euripides' *Bacchae*. However, though they are constantly motivated to revolt, it appears to be only rarely, at most, that women are able to conspire in effective revolutionary actions on the pattern we might associate with *Lysistrata*. This is interesting, as Square seems unyielding in his scathing denigrations of women; yet we detect a current of fear, respect for powers, and, quite possibly, admiration. Women are indeed very special members of Flatland society. They have, as we have seen, extreme "acuity." Though this is distinguished, by way of one of the tongue-in-cheek inversions incorporated in the account of Flatland society, as an absence of mental power, it nonetheless certainly entails the power to wound physically, and one suspects mentally as well. It brings with it a certain "cap of invisibility," since seen end-on, women's needle shape offers little to the eye. Evidently, what they introduce most threateningly is passion itself. After all, they embody Cupid's arrow in their very linear shape, while their invisibility is evidently symbolic of a power to evade the normal defenses of reason. They are in consequence subjected to severe constraint and repression. A large body of draconian regulations, architectural as well as social, is designed to keep women in check. It has, of course, at the same time the opposite effect, provoking the spirit of revolt and that scarce-suppressed domestic mayhem to which we have already alluded.

What is, finally, Abbott's attitude toward women, how does it relate to his theme of restricted dimensionality, and what does it have to teach us? What is this telling us about ourselves? It is not so easy to fathom the double take of Abbott's teasing satire. Constrained as we are to a space which is as narrow in its way as Square's own, we may think like a square, or if we think like a cube, the difference may not be that great. If we are thus lured into at least flickering agreement with Square in a denigrating misjudgment of woman, as it is quite likely we will be, then we have fallen victim to the trap Abbott's satire has laid for us. Square, after all, claims here to speak only as "historian," recounting the attitudes current in Flatland, while noting that report has it they are not so different in Space. [34] By way of the afterimage, latent logic of satire, Abbott praises the "acuity" of woman—we sense that he means an unacknowledged, superior mental ability. If they alone are swayed by passion, then they are the sole hope of a land too dull to endure: passion is an otherwise missing, suppressed dimension of that flattened world. And it is only the women who give any evidence of a saving sense of humor, as they rather gleefully imagine the havoc a revolt on their part might bring to the unbearable good order of the polygons. [35] Having no angle whatever, having no place in the hierarchy of polygonal figures, they are blessedly exempt from the whole game of social advancement. The female and the male realms are thus remarkably separated, like two independent variables of the society, and if they are excused from the opportunities afforded by membership in the male polygonal order, it seems the advantage may be altogether on the women's side. Square's sober account of measured advantage and accomplishment induces a jocular, laughing, counter-text, in a voice which has a distinctly feminine ring. Dimensional depravation means clamping a sober male symmetry and Apollonian order on a far more spirited, if dangerous, Dionysian psyche. Abbott's satire lets Dionysus wear the mask of Apollo. The book becomes a joyous revolt against the strictures of a male-dominated society, and there is some satisfaction in the thought that

> . . . the whole male population of a village has been sometimes destroyed in one or two hours of simultaneous female outbreak. [36]

The great Color Revolt

It is apparent that an inclusive definition of a social space would include modes of motion which are not geometric or, in a literal sense, "spatial." This is illustrated by Square's account of the great Color Revolt.

A leader of memorable status in the annals of Flatland was "Chromatistes," described as a Prometheus who discovered the immense power of the art of color as a release from the intolerable limitations of life in Flatland. Any fresh direction that sense and activity may take is a new "dimension" of life, and the sheer delight of Chromatistes' new art brings new spirit to Flatland; enthusiasm spreads wildly. [37] But this new aesthetic dimension brings political consequences as well: the new degree of freedom becomes a portal for the introduction of democracy. Delight in the many-colored image accompanies democracy, we recall, in Plato's *Republic*—and we may at this point acknowledge that much of Abbott's satire aims at the censorship, arrangements for weddings and governance of births, and mathematically founded social and political hierarchy of *The Republic*. [38] Distinctions of rank, which had to be "felt" out or derived by the art of "sight recognition" in the old order, can now be made by labeling figures with identifying colors, which thereafter anyone might read. Social distinction had been so remote from the lower classes under the old dispensation that its members were barred from even making judgments concerning rank. Only graduates of the great universities were able to draw these distinctions, altogether necessary for maneuvering in the upper class and wielding power. Now, figures which are to be systematically identified by color will be manifest to the least of the laborers, and the cork has come out of the container in which the citizens of Flatland are bottled up. A democratic Color Act is promulgated which will ensure institutionalization of this breakthrough. The whole passage rings of the spirit of the Renaissance, as its suppression, to follow, will suggest the strictures of Protestantism.

In a crafty, duplicitous move tolerable only if indeed ends justify Machiavellian means, the representative of the rulers lures Chromatistes to his doom and, in a speech which is the counterpart of Mark Antony's eulogy of Caesar, quickly brings the new democracy to ruin. From that time, the use of color is forbidden in Flatland (like the reading of Homer in *The Republic*), except to select scholars whose spirits are presumed to be proof against its attractions.

Flatland and cosmic space

For Flatlanders, the physical cosmos is their sheet-of-paper world; for Lineland, the infinite cosmos is their straight line. Neither is aware of a lack of anything a cosmos should afford. Only from without can we apprehend, as observers privileged through the operations of Abbott's satire, that the life of each is as constricted as the physical space, while the most crucial constraints are never spatial.

Can we imagine an opening out of our vast three-dimensional box, into a space greater than ours, in the way our Space is greater than Flatland? We have seen that we can now take a position in four-dimensional space and look upon figures there, as we could in earlier figures. But the question is evidently larger. Can we open our minds to new dimensionalities and recognize the limitations and possibilities of the world in which we live? One clue is the sense in which the vision of our physical cosmos is more ample today than it was a few centuries before. Now that we have come to know ourselves as residents of a star in the unimaginable expanse of a galaxy, and that galaxy just one of an unimaginable multitude in the total cosmos, we begin to get a fuller perspective on our own existence, a little as Abbott's hero did through his brief escape from Flatland.

The trick is to escape from one's own cosmos far enough to be able to get a view of it. If we have grasped the likelihood that life and intelligence are common in this cosmos of the multitude of galaxies— that intelligence and the organization of life are almost surely much larger concepts than we have yet witnessed, and that our own existence is a product of time and the circumstances of our own evolution—then we may open our minds to that space which includes all of this as a domain of unbounded possibility. We will not again listen readily to assertions that "human nature" is fixed in its powers, nor will we take our society's customary measures of rank, success, and progress as other than questionable and provisional. Abbott's satire lifts us laughingly out of our cosmos as we conceived it, and as well out of the mental space we thought sufficient to dwell in. Above all, the orders of our societies, dictated by the narrowness of this space, are seen for a moment in their arbitrariness and artificiality.

III. Color space

Cramped into the limited physical dimensionality of their two-dimensional world, the Flatlanders shaped for themselves a world of mind and spirit correspondingly petty: it was their minds that were flattened by the denial of a dimension of physical movement. If the implications of Abbott's satire trouble us, it is the measures of our world of mind and our human experience that we must look to. We see ourselves now as dwellers in cosmic space, what we tend to call our "physical" universe. What we must turn to now is the consideration of "space" in another, seemingly more immediate sense, taking conscious experience as the domain of primary concern. Whether to speak of this as a "space" is metaphor, once again merely borrowed from our geometry, or whether in fact we have found our ways to a more fundamental and quite literal meaning of the term, we need not decide at the outset.

I propose we look at a realm to which the concept of "space" has, in fact, long been applied—the domain of our conscious experience of color. Taking "space" according to the premise of this essay as *possibility*, we recognize that color, as one fundamental ground of our conscious experience, brings a richness which is one of those we treasure most. Abbott's account of the great Color Revolt reminds us of the power of color in our own lives: as Chromatistes revealed to the Flatlanders, the term *colorless* characterizes a life which, however ordered or rational, is dull and drab.

Although they coordinate and intertwine deeply to constitute that larger world of an individual consciousness, each of the senses is separable in thought and in some way well known to us as distinct. Sight indeed relates intimately to sound—it is crucial to our overall spatial sense that we can "place" a sound as intuitively and almost as surely as we place an image—but we do not confuse them: sight constitutes one perceptual world, a cosmos of color, which is entire in itself. Within sight, we have little doubt that we mean something quite specific, and similarly entire, when we speak as well of "color" as distinct from gray-scale vision. Thus as a form of preliminary exercise, which will prove to contain complexities enough in its own right, it is reasonable to try our hand at taking the measures of what we may call "color space." What are its constitutive elements and its dimensions, and what is the structure of their inherent relations?

One of the philosophers of nature most interested in tracking the relation between domains of conscious sensation and the physical domains to which they refer—one who never in fact retreated from a conviction that it is the subjective experience which is necessarily and always primary in the pursuit of the sciences—was James Clerk Maxwell, better known for his theory of the electromagnetic field than for his dedicated investigations of color perception. His guidance, expressed in a classic paper "On the Theory of Compound Colours," [39] will be most helpful here. In that paper, he emphasizes the fundamental distinction between the study of *color* and the study of *optics*. Speaking of the results of mixing colors, he says:

> We may express this by saying that two compound colours may be
> *chromatically* identical, but *optically* different. The *optical* properties
> of light are those which have reference to its origin and propagation
> through media, till it falls on the sensitive organ of vision; the *chromatical*
> properties of light are those which have reference to its power of
> exciting certain sensations of *colour,* perceived through the organ of
> vision. [40]

Let us specify at the outset, as the point is elusive, that it is color—
these "chromatical properties"—and not optics of which we will be
speaking. We are the immediate, and in some sense solitary, witnesses
to the being of those properties and their measures.

We humans have evolved in such a way that whereas other species
know the world best by way of some form of hearing or smelling,
we flourish in our visual cortex. We grasp things best when we can
"see" them, and in particular, we understand the relationships of other
domains when we are able to project them onto the visual, in a process, taught us by Descartes, we call "graphing." [41] In exploring
the domain of color, then, it is very natural to undertake to make a
spatial graph of its extent and structure; in fact, there is a long and
quite practical tradition of doing so, by way of the construction of the
"color atlas." The first step must be to identify if possible just those
fundamental ways in which color can vary, to ask whether the range of
possible colors can in fact be analyzed into a set of independent degrees
of freedom. It seems in fact that color can be so analyzed, and that
there are just three underlying ways in which color as such can vary.

We may follow the practice of one long-established color atlas, that of
Albert Henry Munsell, and use his terms: *hue, chroma,* and *value.* Hue
first of all identifies a color and to a first approximation corresponds to
the "colors" of the rainbow; we must add immediately, however, that
consciousness knows more hues than are found in the rainbow. Chroma
refers to the degree of the color's "saturation"—it may be faint, or it
may be strong, thin or intense; we may think of this in terms of degrees
of dilution with white. At one end of the chroma scale is the fully intense
color, the color (if it is a spectral color) as it appears in the spectrum
produced by a prism or, better, a diffraction grating. Once these two
coordinates have been established, the third is a question of more-or-
less of the light itself, ranging on a gray scale from white to black.

Now, since by the power of imagination we can assemble in our
minds' eyes any combination of these three factors—choose a hue
from the range of the rainbow, select a saturation from palest tint to
full coloration, and then adjust the mental light level—we have three
independent variables. Mapping this space as we have suggested onto a
Cartesian geometric graph, we have here an example of a "space" with
three orthogonal coordinates. Munsell takes this as a vertical cylinder
wrapped around a globe of the world, with hue as its longitude, as if

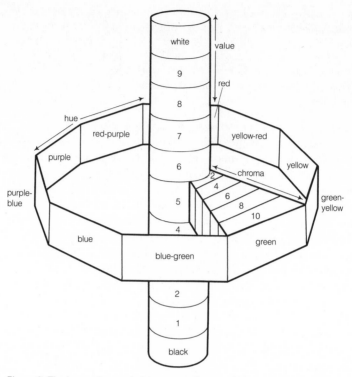

Figure 9. The hue, value, and chroma coordinates of Munsell's color space.

wrapping the spectrum around the equator. The vertical axis of the cylinder then measures value, from white at the north to black at the south poles, while the radial direction measures chroma, from zero on the central axis to one as full chroma at the extreme of total saturation (fig. 9). Munsell locates the equator at degree five on his scale. Range in imagination over the whole world of Munsell's atlas, and you have explored the total reservoir of possibility in the cosmos of color. Every imaginable color finds its place in this three-dimensional color space. Here the *possibility* implicit in the idea of space can be located: it is the power of the imagination to call up the sensation of a color. In hue, we are empowered to traverse the spectrum.

We cannot, however, go beyond it. Though we know that this is only a tiny sample of the total electromagnetic spectrum, which continues unabated into the ultraviolet at one end, and infrared at the other, try as we may we have no power to think a violet beyond the short-wavelength end of the rainbow, nor can we conjure a red beyond its long-wavelength end. Whence are these edges, and why is it unthinkable that consciousness extends beyond? Why cannot we bring ourselves to see the color of heat, or in imagination, to conceive the possibility of perceiving ultraviolet? These are children's questions; they are too serious to allow answers. Here we touch the question of the extremely limited, guarded tuning of our conscious psyche, our tiny sampling of the processes of cosmic space. Can we begin to imagine the ways in which other species and other intelligences might entail consciousness of other sorts, sampling the cosmos in alternative psyches with, for example, awareness of a different range of "colors"? We cannot, of course, ensure that each of us, even when equipped with altogether standard physiological apparatus of vision, "sees" the same "blue" when presented the same spectral hue. [42]

Thus far, though we have spoken of scales, we have given no ground for thinking of this domain of consciousness as having more than topological, rubber-sheet arrangement. Is it a metric space as well? Psychologists, led in the last century by pioneers such as Helmholtz, Ostwald, and Wilhelm Wundt, have not hesitated to measure these phenomena of the psyche, asking only that we be prepared to judge identities by way of color matches and a metric of "equal steps" along each of the axes. Allowing for some adjustment for consensus among the judgments of a group of investigators, meaningful scales can thus be attached to each of these axes, and in this way we find ourselves in the presence of a full-fledged metric perceptual space in which each color can in principle be represented by a vector with three components. That is, each color is designated by a set of three numbers, its measures according to the formalities of Munsell's color space.

Munsell's atlas was conceived in terms of a completely descriptive role and was published as in effect a stipulative dictionary; he writes of the system as *A Color Notation*. [43] This presents an interesting problem of standards and definition. One would like to be able to place, at well-defined, equally spaced points of the color atlas, exemplars of the appropriate colors as definitions and standard referents, and that indeed was Munsell's practice. This, however, raises interesting questions, familiar to some extent in any area of the sciences in which physical standards must be established. Since here the exemplars are physical substances, pigments or dyes with the desired colors, publication becomes a matter of chemical art. The available colors depend on the organic chemist's skill and the luck of the Creation—samples exist of high chroma at some hues, but only weaker examples are available at others. Moreover, since it is not possible to extract these exemplars altogether from the physical cosmos, they are subject to inevitable processes occurring in time. No seals will altogether preserve them; they must fade and degrade.

It is, then, the chemical prescription rather than the substance itself which occupies the place in the atlas, and Munsell's construction becomes a formulary, requiring replaceable standard substances accurately made and verified. There remains the intriguing possibility that organic chemists will later come up with new dyes or pigments, pressing out along each radius toward its junction with the rainbow. But production of the atlas is work for the physical world, and its function is only as a book to be read by the psyche. The colors we are speaking of preexist in the imagination, in a metric color space there; its cylindrical image and the exemplars belong to a different, physical world, to serve as referents and reminders. The real atlas is a thing of the mind.

All of this has been described to this point by way of Munsell's atlas in terms of publishable dyes and pigments and may thus be thought of as the "subtractive" method for producing colors. The pigment in each sample subtracts from the incident light, by absorption, its anti-color, that part of white which it will not reflect, and therefore, exactly that which it is not. This is the tuning of a molecule to the incident radiance. The viewing light must of course be equally standard and indeed was presupposed when we spoke earlier of "white" as a pole of color space. What is white? Star-dwellers as we are, we are tempted to refer to our star as standard and reply, "daylight." We are aware now what a transient, chance choice this is: our star was once blue and is headed for red; we are catching it at mid-color. Other stars have other whites. Yet for human purposes, ours, to which evolution has keyed our consciousness, will do quite well. For Maxwell, daylight was the crucial referent in all optics; designing the original Cavendish Laboratory, he was careful to include light-pipes throughout for delivering daylight to the laboratory benches. Whenever it was available, it was captured and transmitted by a clockwork heliostat, tracking the sun. Maxwell worked with mixtures of pigments by means of a "color top" (fig. 10). [44]

But is the sun's light—by which we mean the totality of the solar spectrum, incorporating all the colors as they occur there—*conceptually* white? From an optical point of view, a conceptual "white" might have equal energy at each color and so would be whiter than daylight, whiter, we might say, than "white"—though it might not look so. Such "equal energy white" becomes a cosmic referent and, in practice, a working technical standard. But Munsell meant daylight, and his pigments were tuned not to conceptual white but to daylight. Pigments are optically very complex: they produce strange spectra that only *look* to the eye like the colors they mean to represent; they will not do so in other lights. So with Munsell's book comes daylight as standard illuminator: it is a star-based book, and not just *any* star but our own at this halfway house in the declining history of its daylight.

Alternatively, a sample can be constructed out of colored lights, which combine to form in principle exactly the same required points in color space. To experiment in this way, Maxwell took samples from a spectrum of daylight, adjusting magnitudes by manipulation of cali-brated slits; the distribution of intensities within the solar spectrum and the confusion of colors involved in widening the slits were problems inherent in this method of lights. Today, however, light of any intensity and color can be generated with precision, and it is possible in principle

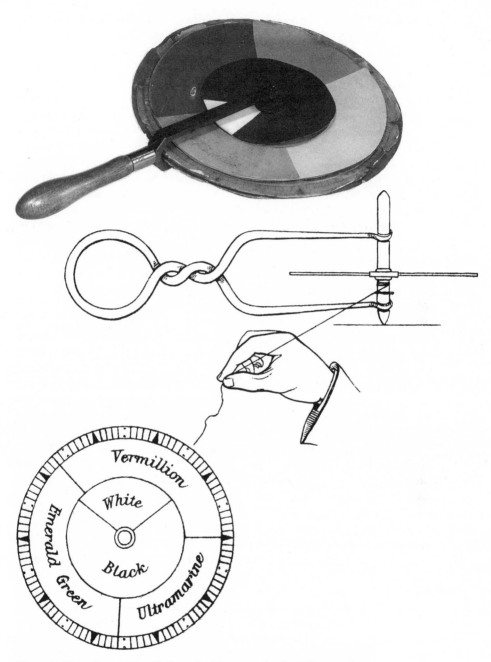

Figure 10. Maxwell's color top. Photograph of the apparatus (top). Diagrams from his paper on "Experiments on Colour, as Perceived by the Eye" (1857) (center and bottom). To match a given color, three adjustable color segments of the outer circle permit mixing in hue, while the white and black segments of the inner circle mix to form the appropriate gray.

to achieve an atlas of pure color. "Purity" of color has become an attainable goal in the sense that the light be, as exactly as required, of a single hue—where "hue," defined by way of the spectrum, translates in its physical counterpart to light of a (virtually) single wavelength. Finally, in this mode there is no longer dependence on the chemist, as the light can be produced as required, mixed at will with equal-energy white and increased in intensity or diminished to black.

Technology thus makes it possible to explore the regions of color space with full exploitation of its three degrees of freedom. It is important to add one caveat: as indicated earlier, though the spectrum suggests the idea of hue, and most hues are found in the spectrum, some are not; these must be produced by the combination of spectral colors. Since pure spectral colors can be produced and combined at will, however, our generalization concerning the technical mastery of color space remains valid. Note that this means that the chemists, and all the technologists of the color industry working with practical colors and dyes, have a fully mapped and available perceptual space within which their products can be located, standardized, and evaluated.

The theory of compound colors

Thus far, we have mapped color space, taking the measures of its extent and degrees of freedom. Of course, it still holds many structural secrets. Behind the apparent simplicity of the pure hues lies a deeper structure in terms of primary colors, elements into which these apparent simples can be analyzed. Further, we all know that colors admit complementarity: pairs can be combined to produce white. This knowledge we owe to Newton; its explicit development was carried out by Maxwell and reported in 1860 in the paper "On the Theory of Compound Colours" to which we referred above. Maxwell makes clear his recognition that he is in some way completing the work Newton's work.

Newton in the *Optics* described a then breathtaking experiment in which, by means of a prism, white light had been decomposed into the colors of the spectrum, and then these again, by passage through a symmetric prism, had been recomposed into the original white. [45] Out of this process Newton arrived at a general theory of the combination of two colors to yield a third, which was related to the two diagramatically as their center of gravity. That is, if the two component colors were present in the intensities A and B, then the combination would be located at a point P such that

$$(A)\ AP = (B)\ BP.$$

Newton worked out a theory of color based on this method of combination and on a conviction of the relevance of the musical octave— a reasonable but unsuccessful hypothesis. Maxwell builds on Newton's

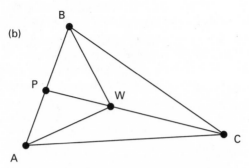

Figure 11. Maxwell's principle of geometrical color combination. (a) Colors A and B combine, as do weights, at their "center of mass" P. (b) When a third color is added, the three colors balance at the combination of color W.

method of the center of gravity and combines this with hypotheses of Thomas Young and David Brewster to show—Maxwell points out that it was implicit in Newton's figures—that all colors can be constructed by mixing combinations of just three, taken as primary. It is a further principle that for each color there will be a complement which, when mixed with the first in the proper proportion, will produce white. Thus, if the two above have produced an equivalent P, there will be a third, C, the complement of P, such that

$$C(CW) + P(PW) = W$$

or, all told,

$$A(AW) + B(BW) + C(CW) = W \qquad \text{(fig. 11)}$$

white now lying at the center of gravity of the system of three.

To put this to the test, Maxwell devised a color box (fig. 12). [46] Without pausing to explain the details of its ingenious optics, let us remark simply that the effect is as if a spectrum were spread on the left of the instrument along the line AB, from which adjustable slits at X, Y, and Z permit variable amounts of three selected colors to combine at the eyepiece at E. There, the combination is to be matched against a sample of white light (daylight) introduced at BC. It is an elegant aspect of the experimental procedure, very characteristic of Maxwell's skill in instrumental design, that it is not necessary to match

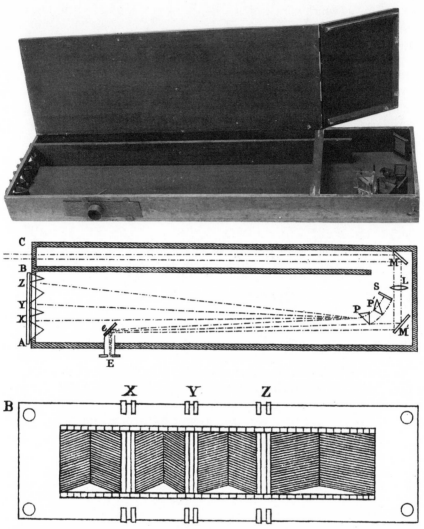

Figure 12. Maxwell's color box. Photograph of one form of the apparatus (top). Diagrams of the box from his paper "On the Theory of Compound Colours" (1860) (center and, in detail, bottom). In effect, the adjustable slits X, Y, and Z select measured samples from the solar spectrum at AB; these combine in the eyepiece at E.

the colors themselves. In every case, white is to be matched against white. Thus the actual procedure will be to choose a slit, and then to find the combination of two others with which it will produce white. From this information, the triangular diagram that takes the three primary colors as its vertices can be constructed. It happens occasionally that the intensity for one of the colors will be negative; since there are no negative colors, this term is simply transposed to the other side of the equation, in which case white plus one of the primaries will equal the sum of the other two. The general theorem of primary colors must be modified to include this possibility.

In practice, in using Maxwell's instrument, two experimenters work as a team, one at the eyepiece and the other managing the slits. The observer, we can infer from Maxwell's report, must be keenly navigating color space, intuitively finding that course of adjustments which, conveyed as commands to the slit-operator, will bring the combination safely to part with a standard white. [47] Maxwell reports to the Royal Society, in their *Philosophical Transactions,* the results of a long and disciplined series of experiments which he and "another observer" had carried out. The report includes the first maps of this new, combinatorial color space, in the form of diagrams Maxwell labeled "J" and "K." "J" is Maxwell himself; "K," one can make out from the text, is Katherine, his wife. His biographer describes with a certain satisfaction the dismay stirred by the Maxwells among their neighbors when on fine days these two could be seen peering for hours into a large box, the size and shape of a coffin, projecting ominously from an upper-story window in Kensington. [48]

The diagram that results (fig. 13) reveals the structure of the resulting color space. White lies at the center, while the hues of the spectrum lie at the numbered points. The interior of the triangle con-

Figure 13. Maxwell's color triangle, representing quantitatively the three-color theory of vision. The triangular space encompasses a range of many, but not all, possible combinations of chroma and hue.

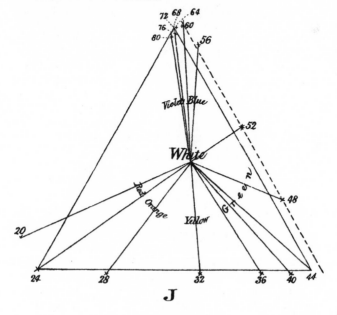

sists of the range of visible color, varying in hue and chroma. Intensity (from light to dark) remains to be represented in the vertical direction, above the plane.

As Maxwell himself remarks, it is unfortunately not the case that all colors lie inside Maxwell's triangle. In current practice, this is remedied by extending the triangle, as shown in figure 14. [49] Here, certain "ideal" colors have been chosen as primaries, beyond the bounds of Maxwell's triangle in such a way that the entire visible domain is mapped as the tongue-shaped region, whose perimeter is the expanse of the spectrum itself. White is shown as a point within the tongue, and complementary colors can be found in all cases by choosing a color such as *D,* and passing a line through *W* to meet the periphery on

Figure 14. Modern version of the color triangle. The tongue-shaped space now encloses all possible visible colors, while the "ideal" primary colors at R, L, and I are invisible! The spectrum lies on the perimeter of the tongue, and any two complementary hues D and E mix to form white at W.

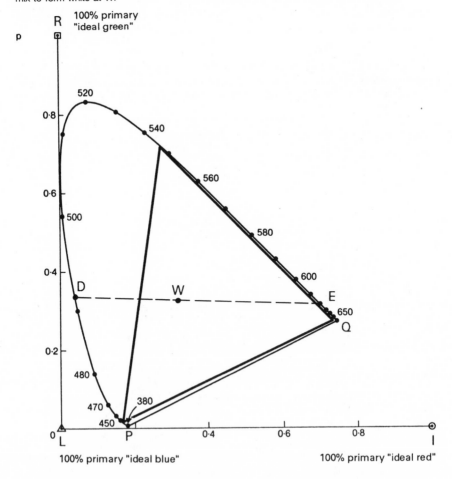

the opposite side, at *E. D* and *E,* combined in the correct proportions, with intensities inversely as their distances from *W,* will produce white. Along the line *PQ* lie those colors which are part of color space, but which are not part of the spectrum, as mixtures of extreme violet and extreme red. We have no clue, of course, as to the meaning of the "ideal colors," though we can see that as they lie beyond the spectrum, they seem to point to an "ideal green," an "ideal blue," and an "ideal red"—each beyond the limits of anything imaginable to consciousness. We shall see in a moment what significance these clues might have. All the phenomena of color, everything in our colorful world, apart from the variable of light-level or value, has its place somewhere in this space, together with the geometric information necessary to concoct it from other colors or, ultimately, from the ideal primaries.

Figure 15. As brightness increases, the space of our color perception shrinks, as these contours at increasing levels of brightness reveal.

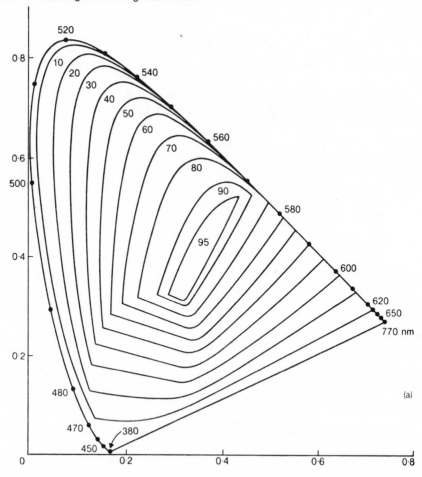

To complete this new exploration of structured color space, we must look at the "vertical" axis, thus far omitted. If we carry out the same investigation at increasing levels of light, we find that the same diagram by no means repeats itself, but rather, new contours develop, delineating a shrinking "tongue" of visibility. Color space contracts as light levels increase, and our sensitivity to color saturates (fig. 15). We see that at the highest levels, perception converges to a single, undifferentiated yellow-white. It is this entire three-dimensional structure which constitutes the full expanse of color space. Its remarkable contoured form tells us that there is no place in color space—no room in our heads—for a very bright blue, or red. As brightness increases, the idea of hue retreats.

Color vision in cosmic space

We, our planet, our star, and now we must add, our conscious psyches, are among the possibilities realized in cosmic space. Is there any way in which we can relate this study of the space of the consciousness of color to the review we made earlier of cosmic space? Much that we said there had to do with the flux and interchange of photons; the content of the cosmos consists to a large extent of radiation, in a general radiance which we noted carried infinitely detailed, transient signatures of the myriad entities and processes of the cosmos, from its first moments forward. We on earth are bathed in this radiation, to which our eyes are tuned to respond. Evidently, what our eyes have been shaped by evolution to intercept is not photons directly from our star—upon which it is not safe for us to gaze—but the reradiations arising from the absorption of the solar radiation and its reemission as reflection from organic molecules whose complex structures stamp the solar spectrum with elaborate absorption patterns. These are the signatures, implicitly colorful, of earth, chlorophyll, rock, sky, water, sand, and flesh, hair, eyes.

I have said "implicitly colorful," for all the intricate modulations they bear are the keys to color ready for consciousness. What mediates, first, is the quantum mechanical structure we must especially prize, that of the protein structure retinal fitted to the rhodopsin molecule (fig. 16). One photon can flip the configuration of retinal in its relation to the rhodopsin of a "cone" cell in the retina and initiate an electrical impulse, ultimately to go to the visual cortex. This is the foundation of sight, but not yet of color. Three types of cone cells bear correspondingly distinct protein molecules, selective photon absorbers, or resonant molecular filters permitting selective passage respectively to the red, green, and blue regions of the solar spectrum. It is the differential response of the retinal switches to these three protein filters that keys our eyes to the cosmos. Each hue represents a certain ratio of responses of the three filters, or three types of cone cells. These are the physical ground

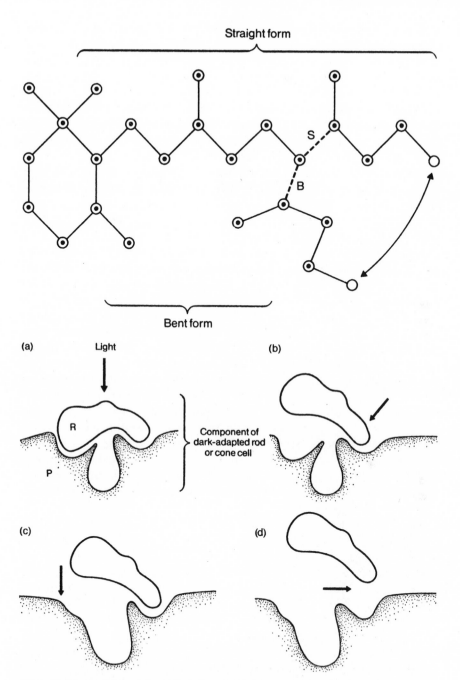

Figure 16. The rhodopsin molecule (top), the photon detector which is the basis of our power of sight. Vision is initiated when one segment of the molecule absorbs energy and straightens about the flexible bond at S. The interaction of rhodopsin with its protein base (bottom). The straightened molecule separates by stages from the base, culminating at (d) in the initiation of an electrical signal, going ultimately to the visual cortex.

of the three "primary" elements of color vision. The "pure hues" of the spectrum are in fact compound, each a ratio of primaries—and, curiously, never do we see the pure light of a primary itself. That is the origin of the fact that the primaries in figure 14 are not colors at all! It is the *ratio* of primaries which gives rise to all of the "pure" colors. Maxwell had rightly inferred that the ground of his triangle would lie in a threefold set of sense organs, and he understood well that pure colors were ratios of the primaries. His data did not, however, make clear that the primaries would lie nowhere within visual space.

It has been thought a great mystery that consciousness should arise from the "physical" world. It is true that we lack, still, a systematic theory of the interface between consciousness and the cosmos it dwells in and belongs to. But I believe we can see in this instance of color space, embedded in cosmic space, that the fit is propitious. We have two pieces of the puzzle, ready to mate. The radiation which bathes us on earth is signed with the quantum mechanical structures of the molecules of which earth and its creatures, including ourselves, consist. It is this radiation that consciousness must read. But as we have seen, the immediate ground of visual consciousness is a corresponding quantum mechanical structure, the retinal switch sensitive at the photon level and the selective, absorption filters in which it is embedded, set to feel out the structure of the photon spectra. The visual cortex, responding to these ratios in that set of responses, is the house of consciousness. All we have to do is to become systematic and write the equations that express the projection of the one system on the other. Then we can compute the capture of the neural process by consciousness. It used to be thought that consciousness, as subjective, was a realm closed to measurement and objective science. We see now, under the tutelage of a scientist whose work derives from Newton's and who experimented quantitatively with color consciousness far more than a century ago, that we need not hesitate.

Consciousness belongs to the cosmos, which is throughout implicitly colorful. We have seen how the structure of the cosmos has been read in the colors of the spectra, everywhere being emitted, absorbed, and passed on. More generally, our sensory organs and our brains know how to fetch consciousness out of the cosmic radiance, which is everywhere meaningful and everywhere speaks of the unity of that space in which it, like ourselves, is founded. We are speaking of processes that mark the interface between two spaces, between the psyche and the inclusive cosmos, from which ultimately we draw the unity of our own being. Evidently, understanding of the relationship of these spaces lies at the foundation of understanding ourselves. We have only to see how this crucial interface occurs. Our terms sound very different, but finally the question seems to be the same: we are still on the track of Parmenides' enigma, of the relation of the Many and the One.

IV. The space of all spaces

We live and move, it seems, in many spaces: each of them, with its own dimensionality, provides scope for one or another aspect of our being. Our investigation of color space suggests the variety these spaces may assume. Some, such as tone space, are realms of conscious experience analogous to color space; like the latter, they bear the dual aspect of, on the one hand, domains of consciousness, and on the other, a physical substrate which in some way supports and correlates with—whether causing or caused by—our mental experience. Thus there was a threefold structure which we recognized as first physical optics, the realm of light waves and lenses; then the physiology of vision, with its retinal chemistry and neural processing; and finally the conscious phenomena of color itself.

With sound, it is the same: a threefold space of sound waves, the physiology of the auditory system, and riding on all this, the experience of sound itself. If we refer specifically to tone, as the ground of music, we would narrow the reference and sharpen the experience: the octave, the diatonic intervals, and the structure of phrase and song constitute a space in their own right.

We might suggest that something similar occurs in the matter of style: that the art of a period, a school, or an artist is a space of its own—the blank canvas is a tabula rasa analogous to the empty boxes of our opening experiments, superficially "empty" but in fact loaded with the exacting gamut of possibilities which constitute the palette and art of Cézanne or van Gogh. [50] We speak of the limited or restricted art forms which are bound by tradition or primitive in their resources, "flat" lands, surely, of the arts and imagination. Dimensionality plays a decisive role in the richer spaces of the arts; everything we can rightly call a "space" must have a corresponding dimensionality which measures in some way the scope of its possibilities. As we move, however, into spaces which are made by human art rather than those given by nature, their subtle dimensions, which must be the ultimate principles of the art, become more difficult to discern. With that suggestion, however, we must leave this topic, turning back in closing to spaces given by nature, to identify if we can those which underlie and perhaps unify the others.

One such embracing space is that of the genetic code, for in the text of the DNA, that "book of life" to which so much attention is currently being given as we learn now not only to read but to manage it, and even to write into it, is housed the vast panorama of life-forms on earth. This is genetic space, the domain of all possibilities for life as we know or can imagine it; its dimensionality must enumerate the elemental principles of life, the underlying ways in which life-forms may vary and develop. In its physical form, it might seem extremely limited—

the double-coiled helix as a kind of linear matrix, topologically of some special interest but hardly rich in complexity; and the terms of the code itself, almost insultingly stupid with its mere four letters coding for an alphabet of amino acids, shaped always to the DNA as cast to template. Nevertheless, we know from Euclid, with his five brief postulates, how difficult it is to judge the potential abundance, the copiousness of a world *in potentia!* And it is exactly in this case of the seed that Aristotle best illustrates the mystery of what he calls the *nature,* the principle of motion of a thing which moves itself: as the acorn bears in itself the urge and the wisdom to yield the mature oak.

The DNA, which in its physical aspect is that coiled domain of nucleic acid, is at the same time the fount of all life, the *idea* of each life-form, even each developing stage of each life-form, and not just, in our case, the *human* but the individual: the idea of you, or me. In that genetic space inheres in the mode of possibility the prospect of all the desires, all the love or despair, all the skills, the very color space and tone space, which yield our unfolding lives. The DNA is a space which bears love and mind. It bears, as well, all the life-forms of our earth's biosphere. [51] It is a space which, with the present scientific commitment to the immense Human Genome Project, we are determined to learn to read. But how shall we read it? Can we fathom its dimensionality? Conventional physics and chemistry, even in their quantum-mechanical forms, can provide only a few clues: to follow such clues, we must be prepared to shed preconceptions about "science" and its methods and draw new lessons from the relations among the three levels of color space. As the experience of color inheres in the physics of light and the physiology of the retina, so love and wisdom inhere in the structures of the DNA. This intricately configured space of the genetic code must be the carrier and the immediate home of the ideas of Plato and the archetypes of Jung.

Within this space, one of the most impressive structures to emerge is the brain—lesser brains of all levels of complexity, and ultimately the brains of the higher mammals, and the human cortex. [52] Since the cortex is in some way adequate to the very idea of space, and the contemplation of spaces of all kinds lies within its folds, it must be possible to find a place for every space, and the cortex must be at one level the "space of all spaces." It is turning back upon itself now, to formulate the story of its own origins and thus to see itself in the unfolding of the genetic code from which it emerged.

This is a story told twice, both over the long times of the evolution of the animal nervous system and in the life span of each person, through the developmental formation and maturation of each individual brain. As speculation about spaces grows more complicated, we recognize that the cortical space houses visual space, including the color space we have examined, and that here arises—shall we say, "dwells"?—that consciousness whose delicately balanced mathematical structure Maxwell has led us to examine. It is within the folded topology of the cortex, a geometry which is at the same time exacting in its precision yet virtually bereft of straight lines, that these conscious spaces—sound, sight, touch, love, and fear—link to construct that inclusive space which is the totality and unity of our conscious being, the self, conscious of its own identity and continuity. For these distinct spaces evidently do not simply *add;* they map onto one another, so that a sound belongs to a place we can see, music maps onto dance, love maps onto a beloved face, regret onto a memory of a place or a single syllable of a lost voice.

If we say, then, that the self is the containing, inclusive space which weaves together all these conscious experiences, as the intricacies of the body in its neural, muscular, sensory, hormonal aspects weave the supporting physics and chemistry, the self is by no means the sum of these spaces, nor is it the aggregated system, however interwoven and linked. Always, each space, and then above all the inclusive space, is a unity before it is a sum. That is the crux of the matter: however it joins and includes, and however it empowers the vividness and life of the individual thing or experience and the individual place or moment, space does so only by virtue of being single and a whole, first. Space is always a whole before it yields the parts which fill it, and that whole bears promise of the parts which come to fill it. The measure of that promise, as such, is the dimensionality of the space.

Parmenides' wisdom is not only to confront the apparent contradiction that being lies both in the One and in the Many, but to embrace the antilogy, most powerful in the negative assertion: Being is not One, and it is also not Many. Parmenides speaks in antilogy, because our minds and our speech cannot simply join these two, yet each *is* only by virtue of the other. That is the mystery of space. Each of our moments is, only because the Self is. Each experience of color is, only because color space is. Each Self is, only because the Human is, while the Human is, only because all life is, in the bosom of genetic space.

This is a litany which it begins to seem easy, as a formula, to repeat. But the difficulty at the root of the concept of space, perhaps the key to our understanding of the meaning of freedom itself, is to find the relation in practice between part and whole. This means the relation between the autonomy of the individual and the ground of the individual in the social, the human, or the divine. In terms of a given act, it is a question of the sheer freedom and primacy of the immediate move—the stroke of the brush, the step in the dance, the phrase in the symphony—and the containing whole, the composition, the social act, the course of history.

Abbott's satire, solved, becomes earnest advice in all of this, which we may call the matter of spaces. The Flatlanders fear the Third Dimension, and their suppression comes not from the limitation entailed in their two dimensions so much as in their failure, through trepidation, to come to grips with dimensionality itself. They are marginally aware of Space—aware enough only to pass laws forbidding discussions of it. They take their own two-dimensionality as occasion for contriving traps: they confine themselves, their habits, and their minds in their little space, far more than the littleness of the space requires. Indeed, the funny thing about the Flatlanders is not that they live in two dimensions, but that they don't use the two dimensions at their command. By social fiat, their dimensionality is far less than their whole two-ness comprehends. [53]

What is the lesson in this, for us who likewise live in little spaces, in briefest times? We need the fourth dimension, not so much in order to book virtual excursions into it—though we will now want to do that—as to use a new understanding of higher dimensionalities as a means to comprehend what it means to live in a space at all. We need to be able to look back on ourselves, as astronauts have come to look upon the earth, in order to see our individuality not as pettiness, isolation, or vanity but as an expression of the power of the whole to bear fully upon the individual.

If we live among, and by virtue of, so many interweaving spaces, is there one primary space which is the ground and source of them all? This would, if we could find it, be the ground as well of our own being; it would be that which ultimately answers the question of the meaning of our lives. This primary and inclusive space, if we could find it, we would call the "cosmos." The atomism of Democritus and Lucretius essentially experiments with the thought of a world which is not a cosmos—there is no inclusive whole, all happens atomically, which means by chance; there is no answer to the question of meaning, questions of direction have no significance. [54] There is no containing or empowering space: in its stead there is only void, and things scattered meaninglessly in it.

Physicists, astronomers, and their like today are telling us a very different story, though they may not concern themselves to help us make the appropriate distinctions. [55] As I have sketched in an earlier article in *The Great Ideas Today*, the designers of our modern particle accelerators in their aspirations for ever-higher levels of energy are at the same time unfolding ever-deeper levels of the being of what they call "particles." Underlying these supposedly "material" atoms are symmetries from which they derive by the logic of the mathematics of groups. Behind each rank of Many lies, at a higher level of energy, a prior One. Ultimately, behind all the particles, theory points toward a "Supersymmetry" in which all apparent particles are one in kind. [56]

At the same time, other evidence has established as settled fact the expansion of the universe at a rate which can be measured to such an extent that extrapolation backward is possible, to a time when, again, "all things were together." This would be a moment, some 15 billion years ago, at which the expansion began. With an assumed indifference to sensibilities, this beginning of the expansion has been universally designated in the literature as the "Big Bang." Without questioning that it had the dynamic appearance of an unimaginable explosion, it is possible to insist on a more appropriate term. For if "all things" were indeed together, here is the origin of all that we are, care about—our love. We were there, before we took the forms in which we know ourselves now. Mind was there, love was there, for this was the origin of *all things*.

Principles of cooling with the ongoing expansion permit extrapolation back, thermodynamically, to the unimaginable temperatures and energies of this origin point. This is an excursion to immense energies, exactly paralleling that in the particle accelerators, and again theory points to the Supersymmetry. That is, the particles were not separate in kind at the beginning, just as they are thought to be one in kind at the least sizes and the highest energies to which our particle colliders are pointing now. The beginning in time, and the underlying foundation at the present moment, exhibit high symmetry, the One from which unfold the levels of Manyness. This is a domain of mind and love, far more than it is one of sheer calculation and formulaic law. Let us therefore give it a new, appropriate name. I suggest, by contrast with the *cataclysm* with which some think the world is doomed to end, its upward counterpart, the *anaclysm*—so far as I can determine, a word not yet employed by others and therefore available for our use. We will do better, then, to think of the beginning—the *anaclysm*—as less like a mechanical event and much more like a work of mind and passion, a vast opening chord, rather than an "explosion." As a symphony may be thought of as unfolding from its opening bars, so the cosmos unfolds in the manner of an ongoing act of mind, working out the symmetries latent in the first statement.

The importance of this concept for our present concern with space is that the unity, the One which is of the essence of the idea of space, is as well the One at the foundation of the particles of our present era, and the One which is the wholeness of that opening chord, the *anaclysm*. It is not that the past is simply remembered: the present processes of the universe, including the operations of our own bodies, minds, and passions, are unfoldings from the first unity: an image often suggested is that of the transition of phases in the freezing of ice from water. We are the Many emerged from that One and, more importantly, *implicit* in that One.

Here is evidence that we are indeed members of a cosmos: that there is a One at the foundation, in time and in principle, of our startling individuality—grounds to seek coherence and meaning in the course of one passing life. This One, the principle of the cosmos, is not in a remote place—"in space," as we say, or at a remote time. It is at the foundation of all Being and all present existence—each thing that is, is one, by virtue of it. We are, it seems, at this moment dwellers in a cosmos, the source of unity and being of ourselves, the source of meaning in our lives. This is the containing Space, from which—here on this speck of a planet attached to a grain of a star, one of hundreds of millions like it, constantly being born and dying throughout the universe—we draw our lives. "Space" is not somewhere else; it is we who are now star-dwellers, "somewhere" in the vast reaches of cosmic space. But that is not so much a terrifying geographic and temporal fact as an intellectual insight. The inclusive space is cosmic, unifying and supporting, the source and ultimate terminus of Mind, of our thoughts, hopes, and loves. It is the medium in which we grow, relate to one another, and thrive.

Newton could contrive to say only that space is the "sensorium" of God, meaning that all actions and coherence have their immediate source in and by virtue of it, and their ultimate meaning in God. Newton's formulation may today seem awkward and perhaps primitive, but each of us must, it would seem, seek out ways to incorporate into personal comprehension the imminent presence of cosmic space, as the origin, support, and ultimate meaning of our thoughts, loves, and lives. Those lesser spaces through and by means of which we maneuver from hour to hour, day to day, are themselves, if they are anything, offsprings of this containing cosmic space. Here is the One of Parmenides, and at the same time the possibility and last refuge of the Many.

---

1. The two sides of the relation between the One and the Many are figured in the dialogue in the persons of Parmenides and Zeno (*GBWW* I: 7, 486–511; II: 6, 486–511).

2. David Bohm has posed this question for our time, with an eye first to its foundations in quantum mechanics, but with regard to its largest significance as well, in *Wholeness and the Implicate Order* (London: Ark Paperbacks, 1980).

3. Thus, electoral campaigns are mapped out in "political spaces," theorists of music speak of "tone space," and users of statistics plot points in "data spaces." Physicists and engineers trace trajectories in terms of momentum and position in "phase space," and generalized coordinates may be used to describe systems in "configuration space" (*GIT* 1986, 251, 355). We will turn to a discussion of "color space" later in this essay.

4. David Hilbert and Stephan Cohn-Vossen, *Geometry and the Imagination* (New York: Chelsea Publishing Co., 1956), p. 52. Note the overall discussion of the concept of *space* in the *Syntopicon* (*GBWW* I: 3, 811–25; II: 2, 642–55).

5. The range and interest of the concept of "possibility" is suggested by Scott Buchanan in *Possibility* (London: Kegan Paul, Trench, Trubner & Co., Ltd., 1927).

6. The Greek word *kosmos* seems to begin with the notion of *order* and then to progress through *good order* and *ornament* to culminate in meaning the *universe*.

7. Aristotle's persuasive argument against the existence of space is found in his *Physics* (*GBWW* I: 8, 293; II: 7, 293).

8. *GIT* 1988, 171 (in an essay on "The New Pythagoreans"), and *GIT* 1992, 113 (in an essay on Newton).

9. In *Timaeus,* the world is assembled within something called *chora*, which, though regularly translated as "space," is rather a teeming receptacle (*GBWW* I: 7, 456, 458; II: 6, 456, 458). On the other hand, the *kenon*, or void, against which Aristotle argues in the passage cited in note 7, lacks any metric or order—elements essential to modern "space," which must support mathematically defined fields and strictly ordered motions.

This formless void is wrested into Latin as the *inane* of Lucretius, in which bodies can do no more than wander, swerve, and fall (*GBWW* I: 12, 16; II: 11, 17).

10. It was Postulate I that allowed you to draw the line of step 2, and Proposition 11 of Book I, itself of course utilizing the postulates, which permitted step 4. Step 6 takes us to Book XI, the book of "solid" figures, in which Proposition 12 empowers the construction (*GBWW* I: 11, 2, 8, 310; II: 10, 2, 8, 310).

11. Proposition 13, Book XI, explicitly disproves this possibility—as if Euclid had worried about—and was concerned to exorcise—the possibility of a fourth dimension!

12. For example, Henry Parker Manning, *Geometry of Four Dimensions* (New York: Dover Publications, 1956), may serve as our Euclid for four dimensions. An excellent study of four-dimensional geometry is Thomas F. Banchoff, *Beyond the Third Dimension* (New York: Scientific American Library, 1990).

13. H. S. M. Coxeter, M. Emmer, Roger Penrose, and M. L. Teubner, *M. C. Escher: Art and Science* (Amsterdam: North Holland, 1986). Later in this essay, in conjunction with figure 8, we will break out of this confinement to three dimensions.

14. Latin *posse*, "to be able," which yields *potens*, "powerful." The corresponding Greek term, which appears in Aristotle's definition of motion as "the actualization of the possible as possible," is *dynamis*, which gives us *dynamic* and, interestingly, *dynamite* (Aristotle's *Physics* [*GBWW* I: 8, 278; II: 7, 278]).

15. Euclid's term *aitema* suggests something asked of the reader, by way of agreement.

16. The Thirteenth Book of the *Elements* concludes with this truly remarkable seal upon his work:

I say next that *no other figure, besides the said five figures, can be constructed which is contained by equilateral and equiangular figures equal to one another* (*GBWW* I: 11, 395; II: 10, 395);

i.e., no further *regular* figure is possible.

17. Nicholas Lobachevski, *Geometrical Researches on the Theory of Parallels* (La Salle, Ill.: Open Court Publishing Co., 1914). For an introduction to Lobachevskian, or "hyperbolic" geometry, *see* Richard Courant and Herbert Robbins, *What Is Mathematics?* (London: Oxford University Press, 1941), pp. 218ff. A systematic text is Harold Eichholtz Wolfe, *Introduction to Non-Euclidean Geometry* (New York: Holt, Rinehart and Winston, 1945).

18. *See* Euclid's Fifth Postulate (*GBWW* I: 11, 2; II: 10, 2). Lobachevsky had only to cancel this postulate to yield, to his own surprise, a new world.

19. With yet another switch of postulates, Experiment 3(a) would fail—in Riemannian space, not even one parallel can be drawn, for all lines through the outside point intersect the original line; their behavior is that of great circles on the surface of the earth (Courant and Robbins, op. cit., p. 224).

20. The sum of the angles of a triangle is not a constant as in Euclid but is less than 180° and is a function of the size of the triangle. The triangle whose angle-sum is 0° is the biggest triangle in the world.

21. Lobachevsky's world is strange in many ways. For example, because of such relations as that of note 20, length is *absolute:* determination of one parameter fixes the shapes of all things in the world.

22. So Euclid seems to assume when he says, by way of definition, that "A *straight line* is a line which lies evenly with the points on itself." What is he doing but squinting along his line, like any good carpenter? (*GBWW* I: 11, 1; II: 10, 1).

23. Henri Poincaré, *Science and Hypothesis* (New York: Dover Publications, Inc., 1952), p. 69.

24. The geometrization of mechanics is discussed in various contexts in a variety of modern texts. E. Atlee Jackson, *Perspectives of Nonlinear Dynamics* (Cambridge: Cambridge University Press, 1989); Edward J. Beltrami, *Mathematics for Dynamic Modeling* (Boston: Academic Press, 1987).

25. Victor Zuckerkandl, *Man the Musician* (Princeton, N.J.: Princeton University Press, 1973), p. 45.

26. Edwin A. Abbott, *Flatland: A Romance of Many Dimensions* (New York: Dover Publications, 1952).

27. A nice example is found in Piero della Francesca's "Flagellation." Marilyn Lavin

has worked out quite exactly the point of entrance of a mystic light from another dimension, falling upon the figure of Christ (*Piero della Francesca: The Flagellation* [Chicago: University of Chicago Press, 1972], p. 48).

28. There seems a suggestion here of fractional dimensionality, as employed in our contemporary fractal theory, where it is suggested that a line in a plane surface may occupy more or less of the plane (Leo P. Kadanoff, "Chaos: A View of Complexity in the Physical Sciences," in *GIT* 1986, 86).

29. Is the name after all suggestive of "*Eng*"-land, where "*eng*" in German means "narrow"?

30. Figure 8 is generated by means of an imaging system of the author's, termed Paraspective™. It is so named because it invokes new principles of vision, appropriate to four dimensions and distinct from "perspective," which is appropriate to three. The figure is produced by placing the viewer's eye at a definite position and attitude in four-dimensional space and looking directly at the four-dimensional object—in this case, the tribar. The Paraspective™ system for thus converting the computer into a virtual optical instrument for seeing the fourth dimension is covered by a patent application.

31. Thus:

> . . . geometrical principles are always apodeictic, that is, united with the consciousness of their necessity, as: "Space has only three dimensions" (*GBWW* I: 42, 25; II: 39, 25).

32. The options are: one parallel (Euclid); unlimited parallels (Lobachevsky); no parallels (Riemann). *See* Wolfe, op. cit., pp. 173–74.

33. The Paraspective™ method used to produce figure 8, implemented in a computer, is an example of such a technology.

34. Responding, like Descartes, to objections to the first edition, Square points out (through an intermediary editor) that:

> . . . writing as a Historian, he has identified himself (perhaps too closely) with the views generally adopted by Flatland, and (as he has been informed) even by Spaceland, Historians; in whose pages (until very recent times) the destinies of Women and of the masses of mankind have seldom been deemed worthy of mention and never of careful consideration (Abbott, op cit., ix).

Is it out of order to compare the "Objections" and "Reply by the Author" accompanying Descartes's *Meditations* (*GBWW* I: 31, 104–15; II: 28, 330–41)?

35. "They anticipated with delight the confusion that would ensue" (Abbott, op cit., p. 30). Their wicked humor is very close to the quiet deviltry of Abbott himself.

36. Ibid., p. 11.

37. We may note that in the restricted environment of Lineland, sound and hearing go a long way toward substituting for the missing spatial dimension (ibid., p. 45).

38. Plato's seemingly Flatland-like organizing principles are developed in Books II–V of *The Republic* (*GBWW* I: 7, 310–73; II: 6, 310–73).

39. James Clerk Maxwell, "On the Theory of Compound Colours, and the Relation of the Colours of the Spectrum" (1860), in W. D. Niven, ed., *The Scientific Papers of James Clerk Maxwell* (New York: Dover Publications, 1965), pp. 410ff. I have written on Maxwell in this series; *see GIT* 1986, 219–67; Maxwell's treatise *Matter and Motion* was reprinted in that same volume (*GIT* 1986, 349–418).

40. Maxwell, "On the Theory of Compound Colours," p. 411.

41. Descartes in the *Geometry* establishes a systematic correlation between number and space, or between arithmetic and geometry. It is this correspondence which opens the way to the method we call "graphing," by which functional relations among numbers can be grasped as geometric patterns by the eye and the mind (Descartes, *Geometry* [*GBWW* I: 31, 295–353; II: 28, 523–81]).

42. I reviewed the discussion of conscious states as objects of science in an earlier article (*GIT* 1991, 168). The question of the experimental probing of consciousness is discussed in a recent article by Francis Crick and Christof Koch, "The Problem of Consciousness," *Scientific American* 267, no. 3 (September 1992): 152.

43. A. H. Munsell, *A Color Notation* (Baltimore, Md.: Munsell Color Co., Inc., 1947).

44. Maxwell describes the top ("or teetotum") in an "Account of Experiments on the Perception of Colour" (1857), in Niven, ed., op. cit., p. 263.

45. Newton's experiments with the prism, described in the *Optics,* stand as a paradigm of the processes of analysis and synthesis (*GBWW* I: 34, 375–544; II: 32, 375–544). Compare the experimental analyses of the sun's light which follow the early proclamation "The Sun's light consists of rays differing in reflexibility . . ." (Proposition 3; *GBWW* I: 34, 404; II: 32, 404), with the closing proposition "By mixing coloured lights, to compound a beam of light of the same colour and nature with a beam of the Sun's direct light . . ." (*GBWW* I: 34, 453; II: 32, 453).

46. Maxwell, "On the Theory of Compound Colours," opp. p. 444, figure 1 (the original color box) and figure 8 (a shortened form).

47. Maxwell, op. cit., p. 426.

48. Lewis Campbell and William Garnett, *The Life of James Clerk Maxwell,* 2nd ed. (London: Macmillan and Co., 1884), p. 233.

49. Hazel Rossotti, *Colour: Why the World Isn't Grey* (Princeton, N.J.: Princeton University Press, 1985), pp. 155ff.

50. The question of space in art, and the distinct "spaces" corresponding to distinct schools and artists, is beautifully discussed by Erwin Panofsky in the introductory chapter of *Early Netherlandish Painting* (New York: Harper & Row, 1971), i, pp. 1ff.

51. When one contemplates the virtually unimaginable numbers, and the altogether ordinary character of our particular star, the sun, with its scatter of planets, it seems no more than common sense to conclude that our biosphere must be merely one of a great many seeded throughout a universe which is full of life. Others, of course, need not be very much like our own. Thus, there are some 100 billion other stars (read: "suns") in our own galaxy, and more than a million galaxies in the universe (James S. Trefil, *The Moment of Creation* [New York: Charles Scribner's Sons, 1983], p. 8; Gareth Wynn-Williams, *The Fullness of Space* [Cambridge: Cambridge University Press, 1992], p. 2).

52. We should perhaps not too readily identify the "brain" with the cortex. I pointed in an earlier article to the sense in which the brain, with its essential hormonal modulatory system, may be thought of as belonging to the whole body (*GIT* 1991, 150, and references there).

53. As pointed out earlier, they seem to enter here, by way of social tuning, upon the nonintegral dimensionalities of "fractal space" (note 28 above). Interestingly, on the other hand, Square in his mental exuberance presses dimensionality to the suggestion of a space of infinite dimensions, now known as "Hilbert space," and regularly used by mathematicians and physicists.

54. Lucretius confronts directly and courageously "this terror and darkness of mind" (*GBWW* I: 12, 2; II: 11, 3). In response, he offers law, including the law of his own poetics, but no light. The same chill, and similar courage, are to be met in Jacques Monod, our modern Lucretius:

> The ancient covenant is in pieces; man knows at last that he is alone in the universe's unfeeling immensity, out of which he emerged only by chance. His destiny is nowhere spelled out, nor is his duty. . . .

As Lucretius proposes his poetic, Monod speaks of "the kingdom of ideas" (Jacques Monod, *Chance and Necessity* [New York: Vintage Books, 1971], p. 180).

55. Works of Trefil and Wynn-Williams were referred to in note 51. Two books which have especially guided public thinking on this question are Steven Weinberg, *The First Three Minutes* (New York: Bantam Books, 1979), and Stephen Hawking, *A Brief History of Time* (New York: Bantam Books, 1988). They have recently been joined by Leon M. Lederman, *The God Particle* (Boston: Houghton Mifflin, 1993).

56. A sense of these symmetries is suggested by the figures in an earlier article (*GIT* 1988, 180–200). "Supersymmetry" is identified by Trefil, op. cit., pp. 200ff.; *see* Hawking on the "grand unified theory," which he says is "not all that grand" as it does not yet include gravity; true unification would come with a putative "complete unified theory" (Hawking, op. cit., pp. 74, 166).

Latin-American Literature Today
Part Two: Beyond the "Boom"

René de Costa

René de Costa is a professor of Romance literatures and humanities at the University of Chicago and former director of its Center for Latin American Studies. His principal area of research and publication concerns the painting and poetry of the early twentieth-century avant-garde in France, Spain, and Latin America. Professor de Costa is best known in the United States for two books in English: *The Poetry of Pablo Neruda* (Harvard, 1979) and *Vicente Huidobro: The Careers of a Poet* (Oxford, 1984). He has also organized exhibitions in Madrid, Paris, and Chicago on the interrelationship of literature and the plastic arts in the work of Juan Gris (1985) and Vicente Huidobro (1987) and the visual poetry of Nicanor Parra and Joan Brossa (1992).

This essay is the second part of a discussion of contemporary Latin-American literature by Professor de Costa to appear in *The Great Ideas Today*. The first part was published last year.

L ast year, in the first part of this essay, we discussed what has come to be called the "boom" in Latin-American literature, its sudden emergence on the international scene in the 1960s, and the work of the pioneers who made it possible: Jorge Luis Borges, Pablo Neruda, Octavio Paz, Nicanor Parra, and Jorge Amado. This year we shall turn our attention to their successors, the writers of the "boom" itself and its aftermath: Carlos Fuentes, Julio Cortázar, Gabriel García Márquez, Mario Vargas Llosa, Isabel Allende, Clarice Lispector, and Rosario Castellanos. Back in the 1950s, at exactly the same point in time that Brazil's Jorge Amado attained international stature with the publication of *Gabriela, Clove and Cinnamon* (1958),* an epic novel of sex and sentiment, power and politics in the changing social milieu of his country, Mexico's Fuentes brought out *Where the Air Is Clear,* an equally ambitious retelling of the saga of his people.

Fuentes

"I am Mexican by will and imagination," [1] is how Carlos Fuentes has characterized himself, for he was born (1928) not in Mexico but in Panama City. While still an infant, his father (who was a career diplomat) was transferred to the Mexican embassy in Washington. Fuentes's early schooling was in the United States and later in Chile—with classmates José Donoso and Jorge Edwards, who would also develop into outstanding novelists in their own right—so he did not really come to know his own country until he was sixteen. But even then it was on a part-time basis: six months in Mexico City and six months in Buenos Aires, where his father was newly stationed. Yet more global hopscotching would have him alternating his university training in law between

---

*When referring to works which have already been translated into English, I will first give the English-language title, followed however by the date of first publication in the original language. Conversely, works which have yet to be translated into English—or whose titles have been radically altered—will be cited with their original titles, followed by a literal translation into English. Since translations are always approximations, and since this essay is based on a reading of the originals, I have sometimes found it necessary to retranslate certain passages. A complete bibliographic description of all works mentioned, both in the original language and translation, is provided in the endnotes.

Geneva and Mexico. It is perhaps for this reason that Fuentes's novels, which are intensely, indeed viscerally, Mexican, are equally universal and accessible to readers outside Mexico.

All writers have a certain set of assumptions about their readers, about what will be understood. Fuentes is somewhat different in that he writes about Mexico both for Mexicans *and* for the world. His very first novel, *Where the Air Is Clear,* a lengthy kaleidoscopic vision of mid-twentieth-century Mexico City, hailed as "the book of the year," [2] when it was first published in 1958, was translated into English just two years later. With a minimal plot and a multifarious range of characters—from taxi drivers, streetwalkers, and wetbacks to the upper echelons of the power elite, and an assortment of middle-class winners and losers in between—what then set this novel apart in Mexico (and in Latin America) was its urban setting. This is a novel of the metropolis.

It has been said that Fuentes did for Mexico City what John Dos Passos had done for New York with *Manhattan Transfer.* [3] And, like Dos Passos, Fuentes used the collage technique and the camera-eye: an artful montage of voices and vignettes, of close-ups and fadeaways ranging from the staid prerevolutionary Mexico of Porfirio Díaz to the savage entrepreneurial capitalism of the mid-1950s. All this is drawn together by a single, singular, and ubiquitous personage, minor character and occasional narrator, Ixca Cienfuegos, whose composite name, part Indian and part Hispanic, links the events of the present to Mexico's indigenous past. This is a novel of place.

Whereas Latin-American literature before had reveled in the exotica of its geography, the jungles and the highlands, the backlands and the great plains, with larger-than-life folkloric characters and caricatures, Fuentes's novel was down-to-earth, to the pavement, with the sights and smells of the city from its posh cocktail circuit to its low-life cantinas. The novel was both unusual and familiar—unusual, because Latin America's urban environment had no literary tradition to speak of, and familiar because metropolitan Mexico was as urbane as Buenos Aires, New York, or Paris. Yet, there was an exotic difference: its indigenous substratum, its past which is repeated in the present.

The title, *Where the Air Is Clear,* is both an ironic commentary on the acid rain that makes this industrial capital one of the most smog-ridden cities of our time, and an allusion to the conquest of Mexico by Hernán Cortés, who upon arriving at Tenochtitlán was reportedly greeted by the Aztec prince with these words: "Traveler, you have arrived at the region where the air is clear." [4] Cortés was not the first stranger to arrive, nor were the Aztecs. The site of present-day Mexico City in the fertile valley of central Mexico is the oldest metropolitan center of the Western Hemisphere; it was conquered by the Aztecs from the Toltecs, who in turn had taken it from the Olmecs, and had been coveted

Carlos Fuentes

and captured by countless other peoples before them. In this view of place, Cortés and the Spaniards are but one more arrival in a cyclic succession of conquerors that continues to the present. The bourgeois positivism which brought power and prosperity to a new ruling class under the technocratic regime of Díaz at the turn of the century was a continuation of this historical cycle. And, too, the latest oligarchy, the children of the Mexican Revolution of 1910, the ragtag descendants of the militia of Emiliano Zapata and Pancho Villa, Plutarco Elías Calles and Venustiano Carranza, are the new power elite, the most recent conquerors of this region "where the air is clear."

One of the novel's principal characters, Pimpinela de Ovando, a sleekly beautiful but impoverished aristocrat, reflects:

> I remember my grandmother said that just as the Porfirian aristocracy
> was horror-struck when Villa and Zapata marched into Mexico City,
> so she and the old families were horror-struck when Díaz marched in a
> century ago. . . , who will the aristocrats of the Revolution see marching
> in and be horrified by tomorrow? Mexico will always be Mexico. [5]

This central theme—"Mexico will always be Mexico"—is fleshed out by Ixca Cienfuegos. Scanning the cityscape through the tinted glass of a modern high-rise office building, he has a visionary view of its multi-layered history in a series of flashbacks from today to the yesterdays of the Revolution, of the doomed Empire of Maximilian and Carlotta, of independence from Spain, of the conquest by Cortés.

This historical underpinning serves as backdrop to the main thrust of the novel, which is contemporary, mid-twentieth-century Mexico, where the latest arrivals are the strawhatted Americans telling "stories about Kansas City to other elderly gringos who tell stories about Peoria." (40) Switching between major and minor scenes, Fuentes always lets his characters speak for themselves. We see what they see, and in this way we enter into the world of the novel as one enters into the life of the city, bombarded by impressions, snippets of conversations, glimpses into the life stories of the characters. The technique is narrative collage, and the effect is not unlike that attained by the great Mexican mural-ists (Rivera, Orozco, and Siqueiros), a vast and sweeping panorama of Mexico's past and its present.

History, the imaginative retelling of history, is one of Fuentes's principal concerns. Even in his essays, such as "From Quetzalcóatl to Pepsicóatl," [6] there is the same thematic interplay of change and per-manence. At this writing he has published over a dozen novels, always trying out new narrative techniques. In the brief and masterful *Aura* (1962) he experimented with the narrative "you," using the second-person singular to tell the story of a young history professor's discovery of his double in the persona of a nineteenth-century caudillo, creating a hypnotic effect on the reader. In this way we become the professor and experience the horror, what Freud called the *unheimlich* [sinisterness] of this realization:

> In the third photograph you see both Aura and the old gentleman,
> but this time they're dressed in outdoor clothes, sitting on a bench in
> a garden. The photograph has become a little blurred: Aura doesn't
> look as young as she did in the other picture, but it's she, it's he, it's . . .
> you. You stare and stare at the photographs, then hold them up to the
> skylight. You cover General Llorente's beard with your finger, and
> imagine him with black hair, and you only discover yourself: blurred,
> lost, forgotten, but you, you, you. [7]

In *Christopher Unborn* (1987), the story of Columbus—the before and after of discovery—is jocosely told from the womb; *The Old Gringo* (1985)—made into a motion picture with Jane Fonda and Gregory Peck—tells the story of American newspaperman Ambrose Bierce, who vanished in Mexico in the early days of the Revolution; and Fuentes's latest novel, *The Campaign* (1991), deals with the revolution for inde-pendence from Spain.

Although his fame rests on his novels, Fuentes is a no less accomplished playwright and literary critic. In a sense the Benjamin, the youngest of the New Novelists, he was the first to discern and describe the phenomenon with a book on *La nueva novela hispanoamericana* (The New Spanish American Novel, 1969), as well as the first to recognize that this cycle too was coming to completion a generation later with a moving essay on Julio Cortázar in the *New York Times Book Review* when the Argentine writer died in 1984:

> He is the first figure of the so-called Latin American boom to go. But for us he meant something more. . . . Julio Cortázar and Octavio Paz, both born in 1914, were the heads of my own generation. For those of us born around 1929, Cortázar and Paz, the two most alert esthetic minds of this Latin American generation, gave a sense to our modernity and allowed us to believe a bit longer in the adventure of the new, when everything seemed to say that novelty was no longer possible because progress was no longer meaningful. Both Cortázar and Paz spoke of something more than novelty or progress—they spoke of the radically new and joyful nature of every instant, of the body, the memory and imagination of men and women. [8]

That the "boom" was a generational phenomenon is quite clear from the perspective of today. Donoso, who was a classmate of Fuentes in his Chilean years, and became part of it only after the publication in 1970 of his fourth novel, *The Obscene Bird of Night*, has narrated an amusing account of its—and his—progress in *The Boom in Spanish American Literature: A Personal History.* [9] These writers all knew and admired one another, and at times, because of the vicissitudes of politics and economics, they even lived and wrote in the same places: Barcelona, Paris, Mexico City. In a spirit of convivial cooperation they read one another's manuscripts, introduced one another to publishers and literary agents, and reviewed and promoted one another's books.

Cortázar

Back in his own time, Julio Cortázar represented a changing of the guard from the previous generation. He got started in fiction with a helping hand from Borges, who published his first short story, "House Taken Over," in *Anales de Buenos Aires* (1946), with illustrations by his sister Norah Borges. Trained in language and literature, Cortázar began his career as a professor and translator. But, born as he was in Brussels, to Argentine parents, he learned French as a child, and when speaking Spanish, even in his mature years, was never quite able to eradicate the characteristic guttural "r." In 1951 he took up residence in Paris as a translator for UNESCO, becoming a French citizen in 1981.

His narrative prose, written in the Argentine variety of oral Spanish, reflects this dual cultural background, alternating in locale between Buenos Aires and Paris. He published three collections of short stories [10] and a novel, *The Winners* (1960), before becoming an international celebrity with the publication of *Hopscotch* in 1963.

This hefty novel, and the critical attention it received, was instrumental in consolidating the "boom." A "Table of Instructions" for the reader suggests two possible approaches to its 153 chapters: a conventional, linear reading of chapters 1–56 for the lazy reader, or a "hopscotch" sequence for the more adventurous, beginning with chapter 73 and continuing with chapters 1, 2, 116, 3, 84, 4, 71, and so on. *Hopscotch* is thus two novels, and presumably more should a reader care to create his own order. Portraying a Cortázar-like macho figure, Hector Oliveira, an Argentine adrift in Paris, and his girlfriend, La Maga, whom he first abandons and then tries to find again in Buenos Aires and Montevideo, it delighted the critics for its "open" quality, permitting no end of scholarly lucubrations. The novel continues to charm all readers because it is a perpetual source of surprise, peopled with a fascinating array of characters and extraordinary, indeed outlandish, events—such as a piano concert given in Paris by one Berthe Trépat. On this occasion, when Oliveira, seeking refuge from the rain, enters the dilapidated concert hall, there are only some twenty people present. The old, fat pianist plays so clumsily that one by one they all end up leaving. Oliveira, out of curiosity and compassion, stays on and ends up walking her home in the rain, soothing her with polite comments on the merits of her performance—way above the cultural level of the audience—which she of course believes. When he learns that she has no place to stay, he kindly offers to help her find a hotel and she promptly slaps him.

It is this sort of vignette, open to diverse interpretations—the pianist is insulted at what she interprets to be a bold proposition, or perhaps a polite rejection—which is Cortázar's forte. After the success of *Hopscotch,* there was a revival of interest in his shorter pieces, which had before passed largely unnoticed. Not surprisingly, there is now an established consensus that Cortázar, while an innovative and accomplished novelist, is a real master of the short story, rivaled only by Borges. It took time for readers, reading habits, and the critical establishment to catch up with both of them. With "House Taken Over," Cortázar is within everyone's reach.

This story, included in *Blow-Up,* [11] relates in a flat, matter-of-fact tone the daily routine of an elderly brother and sister who are living out their final days in the family's ancestral home. Their placid existence of eating and sleeping, cleaning and cooking, is suddenly interrupted when the brother notices a strange noise in one of the back rooms. He bolts the door shut and tells his sister what he has done:

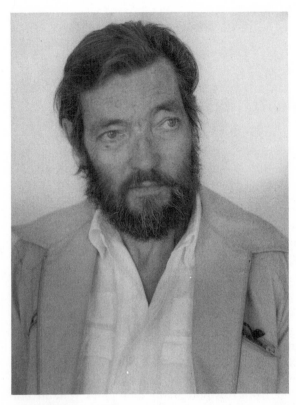

Julio Cortázar

> —I had to shut the door to the passage. They've taken over the
>   back part.
> She let her knitting fall and looked at me with her tired, serious eyes.
> —You're sure.
> I nodded.
> —In that case—she said, picking up her needles again—we'll have
>   to live on this side.

In the ensuing days, more and more rooms of the house are bolted shut until finally the sister realizes that "They've taken over our section." Before it is "too late" they decide to abandon the house, and in a touching humanitarian gesture lock it up and throw the keys away, lest some poor thief or vagabond decide to enter. The story, Cortázar's first, is now a classic, having spawned countless erudite interpretations, the most arcane of which is a book in which the text of the story is imprinted over the architectural plans of the house, graphically showing its progressively being "taken over." [12]

This ludic element, the idea of life and literature as a game, is basic to Cortázar's worldview. In an interview, realizing that his short stories have outboxed his novels, he said: "The novel wins by points, while the short story must win by a knockout." [13] And Cortázar has produced one knockout after another while continually refining the rules of the game.

In "Axolotl," [14] the story begins simply enough, with a man going to visit the aquarium at the Paris zoo. There he becomes captivated by a case housing pinkish salamanders from Mexico, or axolotls. Fascinated by their amphibious nature, by their delicate fingerlike feet with minutely human nails, he goes back day after day, until at one point, his face pressed against the glass of the aquarium, there is a shift in perspective:

> . . . my face came close to the glass again, I saw my mouth, the lips compressed with the effort of understanding the axolotls. I was an axolotl and now I knew instantly that no understanding was possible. He was outside the aquarium, his thinking was outside the tank. Recognizing him, being him myself, I was an axolotl and in my world.

Cortázar has deftly displaced the narrative focus, shifting us from the outside of the aquarium to the inside, from the real to the marvelous. The narrator is, or has become, an axolotl. Almost all of his stories use this same technique, moving us in just a few pages from normal everyday experience into the realm of the fantastic.

In "The Health of the Sick," [15] an entire family conspires to conceal from their infirm mother the accidental death of her favorite son, Alejandro. To protect her from this potentially fatal news, they invent a story that he was called away to Brazil on business and establish a correspondence, with the aid of friends in that country who send letters to the mother, ostensibly from Alejandro. When Alejandro continually postpones his return home, the mother suspects something is fishy, especially since the letters are always typed. After several years of this, the mother finally passes away, and all are relieved, until three days after the funeral one of Alejandro's letters from Brazil arrives:

> Rosa opened it and began reading without a second thought, and when she raised her eyes because they were suddenly blinded with tears, she realized that while she was reading, she had been thinking about how she was going to break the news to Alejandro that Mama was dead.

The family had been playing the game for so long that they no longer remembered it as such, but thought of it as part of their lives; the game had become reality.

A similar notion of games, of life as a ludic adventure, is the structuring principle behind "Manuscript Found in a Pocket." [16] Riding the Paris subway, with its elaborate maze of stops and connections, the solitary individual who is the narrator amuses himself flirting with female passengers, looking at their reflection in the window glass. If a woman notices him and looks back, he will then follow her—but only if she transfers or exits according to his preconceived plan. Although he has many times established eye contact, and even coincided in predicting the first stop or transfer on several occasions, he has never been lucky enough to correctly predict the entire trajectory. Taken by an especially attractive young woman, who gets off at the predicted station, and who seems to be transferring to the right line but then suddenly decides to exit, he breaks the rules and follows her up to the street. He nervously asks her to have a drink with him and she accepts; they continue to see one another and fall in love. But there is something wrong: the rules have been broken. They decide to try again. She dutifully takes a leave from her job so as to be able to ride the subway full-time in the hope that they will again meet and everything will turn out right. The story's title, "Manuscript Found in a Pocket," implies that things did not work out.

In another story ("Throat of a Black Kitten" [17]), again involving the Paris subway where people are crammed against one another, a man and woman's gloved fingers touch while their owners are grasping the handrail. As the car lurches, they touch again, giving rise to an absurd conversation in which the man and woman both refer to the independence of their hands and how these things cannot really be controlled. They end up in bed together at her place. At a certain point the lights go out, and the woman cannot control her hands to strike a match. In the darkness, her "uncontrollable" hand grasps the man's crotch in a vicelike grip, and a struggle ensues. The man breaks loose and runs outside, naked. He calls to her from the street, asking for his clothes, until the police come to take him away as a demented trouble-maker.

Cortázar's stories always involve the reader intellectually, obliging us to make the leap from the plausible to the fantastic, creating in the process a special kind of reality, one that is both familiar and strange, one in which the fantastic coexists with the real—indeed seems to be its logical corollary. A writer of the next generation, García Márquez, goes about things in exactly the opposite way, making the patently preposterous seem perfectly plausible, as in the artwork of his compatriot, the Colombian painter Fernando Botero—outlandishly huge, overblown renderings of familiar everyday figures.

García Márquez

In his acceptance speech for the Nobel Prize in 1982, Gabriel García Márquez began with a reference to Antonio Pigafetta, the Florentine navigator who accompanied Magellan on the first circumnavigation of the globe. This man of the Renaissance, says García Márquez, set down:

"Gabriel García Márquez . . . [makes] the patently preposterous seem perfectly plausible, as in the artwork of his compatriot, the Colombian painter Fernando Botero—outlandishly huge, overblown renderings of familiar everyday figures." "The Presidential Family," oil painting by Fernando Botero, 1967.

A rigorous chronicle, which nonetheless reads like a flight of the imagination. He reported how he had seen pigs with their stomachs up on their back. . . . He wrote of having seen a strange animal with the head and ears of a mule, the body of a camel, feet like a deer and a neck like a horse. [18]

A llama, of course. García Márquez goes on to recount other exotic things of Latin America—El Dorado, the Fountain of Youth, Mexico's nineteenth-century General Santana who had his amputated leg buried in a solemn state funeral, a theosophical Central American caudillo who relied on the swing of a pendulum to determine whether or not his food was poisoned and "who one day ordered all the street lamps of his country to be shrouded in red paper in order to combat an epidemic of scarlet fever," [19] Allende in the presidential palace, battling with a machine gun against the Chilean army and air force, the ongoing civil war in El Salvador which since 1979 was statistically turning out one new exile every twenty minutes—and concludes:

It is perhaps this colossal reality of Latin America, and not just its literary expression, which this year has won the attention of the Swedish Academy of Letters. Not a paper reality, but one that lives with us and determines each instant of our uncountable daily deaths, and which feeds a fountain of insatiable creativity, overflowing with misery and beauty, of which this nostalgic wandering Colombian is but one more statistic singled out by fate.

Poets and beggars, musicians and prophets, warriors and thieves, all we creatures of that outrageous reality have had to ask very little of the imagination, because the greater challenge for us has been the lack of conventional resources to render our everyday life believable. This, my friends, is the node of our solitude. [20]

It was with *One Hundred Years of Solitude,* published in Buenos Aires in 1967, that this forty-year-old "nostalgic wandering Colombian" was suddenly thrust into the limelight. He had not got off to an easy start. Born into a poor family in the rural outpost of Aracataca—a lowland Caribbean town whose streets are still unpaved—he first made his living as a journalist, writing columns for the local and then the national news-papers. It was in this way that he learned how to make the extraordinary seem real—so real, in fact, that one hair-raising account, a fourteen-installment *Story of a Shipwrecked Sailor* who managed to survive ten days adrift in the shark-infested Caribbean, earned him exile when it was first published in *El Espectador,* a leading Bogotá newspaper, in 1955. The story revealed the Colombian navy's complicity in a smuggling scheme. Republished in 1970, it too went on to become a best-seller.

García Márquez claims that he does not invent things but simply tells them as they are. The now legendary town of Macondo, the setting

Gabriel García Márquez

for several of his novels in the mode of Faulkner's Yoknapatawpha County, is much like García Márquez's hometown of Aracataca. Many of the exploits of one of its principal protagonists, the infamous Colonel Aureliano Buendía, who "organized thirty-two armed uprisings and lost them all," [21] he had heard from the mouth of his grandfather, Colonel Márquez. The ageless Ursula is modeled on his grandmother, the implacable Petra on an aunt with the same name. In a university symposium in Lima, back in 1967, when asked by Vargas Llosa why several generations of characters in *One Hundred Years of Solitude* all bear the same name (Aureliano Buendía), García Márquez, puzzled at first by the question, suddenly responded: "Is there anybody in this room who is not named after his father?" [22]

Writing about writing in a 1979 essay titled "The Fantastic, and Artistic Creation in Latin America," he insists that the principal problem facing the writer is the lack of words to make the continent's incredible reality seem somehow credible, "since what is real here always outdistances imagination." [23] By way of example he relates his first encounter with an axolotl, not in a Paris zoo but in a shop in a small town in Mexico. He, like Cortázar, was fascinated by its humanoid qualities, "but there was something else that impressed me more than the animal itself, it was the handwritten sign that was tacked up on the door: 'Axolotl Sirup For Sale'." [24]

One of his early novels, *No One Writes to the Colonel* (1961), is situated in Macondo, magical locus of *One Hundred Years of Solitude,* and may profitably be read as an introduction to that marvelous world, so real and yet so strange. Its protagonist, an unnamed colonel, who fought with Aureliano Buendía and who for the past fifty-seven years—"since the end of the last civil war" [25]—has been anxiously going to the Post Office every day in the expectation that one day his pension check will arrive. Organized in seven short unnumbered chapters, the novella is set in contemporary (1950s) Colombia, a country living in a state of siege, with censorship, curfews, and *la violencia* [26] under the real-life dictatorship of General Rojas Pinilla. All this however is merely back-drop for the personal story of the colonel, who lives on a day-to-day basis, nobly overcoming poverty and adversity as time passes him by. It is even touchingly funny, as when the colonel, in his daily pilgrimage to the Post Office, one day sees for the first time an airmail envelope and asks what it is. His friend, the town doctor, diligently tries to explain the workings of an airplane and the marvels of air travel, how planes can fly above the clouds, defying the weather, carrying people and mail between distant cities in a matter of hours, overnight to Europe. The colonel is perplexed by all this, until suddenly he makes the connection: "it must be like a [flying] carpet." (21) The "real" can only be appre-hended with the aid of myth.

The town's reality is accordingly topsy-turvy. People set their clocks by the sounding of curfew; so many chimes of the church bells indicate the moral rating of the new movie in town; the systematic political killings are so much a part of ordinary life that when there is a death from natural causes, the whole town gets dressed up in Sunday finery to bury the corpse. So much time has passed though, that the colonel needs to dig out his moth-eaten wedding suit to attend the funeral. Surprised by all this activity, the mayor dutifully comes out on the balcony of City Hall, striking a Mussolini-like power pose in bathrobe and slippers while the dead man's mother is "shooing the flies away from the coffin with a plaited palm fan." (8)

The extraordinary—here comic and pathetic, the "sorry smile" of black humor—is extrapolated to the level of magic realism in *One Hundred Years of Solitude.* That book begins in something like biblical time with the mythical founding of Macondo and moves at breakneck speed right up to the present day, all compressed in a family history, the one-hundred-year saga of the Buendías. Time is treated elliptically, with the past, present, and future all looping together, as in the novel's opening paragraph:

> Many years later, as he faced the firing squad, Colonel Aureliano Buendía was to remember that distant afternoon when his father took him to discover ice. At that time Macondo was a village of twenty adobe houses, built on the bank of a river of clear water that ran along a bed of polished stones, which were white and enormous, like prehistoric eggs. The world was so recent that many things lacked names. . . . (11)

The story of Macondo is the story of mankind laid over the grid of Colombian history, with its conquest and exploration, its succession of civil wars, its cycles of boom and bust, its contemporary political violence. All this and more is narrated in a tone of perfect naturalness, as though the extraordinary were an everyday occurrence and everything happens for the first time. Thus, when one of the characters, the town's founding father, José Arcadio Buendía, one day announces that "the earth is round, like an orange," (14) the revolutionary discovery is domesticated, with his wife getting angry at him for his "gypsy ideas":

> José Arcadio Buendía, impassive, did not let himself be frightened by the desperation of his wife . . . , he gathered the men of the village in his little room, and he demonstrated to them, with theories that none of them could understand, the possibility of returning to where one had set out by consistently sailing east. (14)

A messenger is sent out to register another of his inventions; blazing new trails through the wilderness,

> [He] crossed the mountains, got lost in measureless swamps, forded stormy rivers, and was on the point of perishing under the lash of despair, plague and wild beasts until he found a route that joined the one used by the mules that carried the mail. (13)

This tone, melding the clichés of objective historical narrative with the formulaic hyperbole of adventure fiction is what captivates the reader, making the marvelous seem both real and familiar. What could be farther from reality than the episode of Remedios the Beauty, who is one day blown away as she is hanging sheets out on the line? Logic would have the sheets blow away; lexical substitution allows us to envision Remedios "waving good-bye in the midst of the flapping sheets that rose up with her." (223) Another person is murdered in his swimming pool by assassins who creep up on him through the "openings in the tiles." (345–46) Sheets do blow away and tiles do have separations between them. These are the elements of fact which permit the marvelous to go unchallenged. To make things even more plausible, García Márquez adds "authenticating" detail: the murder took place, "one September morning, after having coffee in the kitchen"; (345) the witness to Remedios's ascension, "burning with envy, finally accepted the miracle, and for a long time she kept on praying to God to send her back her sheets." (223)

As the story progresses and the family divides and multiplies, we pass through various stages of history until we realize that time is not passing but is rather "turning in a circle." (310) Everything is foretold in the parchment papers being deciphered by the last of the family line, Aureliano Babilonia, who on the last MS page will read of his own death on the very last page of the novel we are reading:

> Before reaching the final line, however, he had already understood
> that he would never leave that room, for it was foreseen that the city of
> mirrors (or mirages) would be wiped out by the wind and exiled from
> the memory of men at the precise moment when Aureliano Babilonia
> would finish deciphering the parchments and that everything written
> on them was unrepeatable since time immemorial and forever more,
> because races condemned to one hundred years of solitude did not have
> a second opportunity on earth. (383)

García Márquez went on to other even more ambitious projects: the comically political *Autumn of the Patriarch* (1975), a long novel with shifting points of view which gives us a composite portrait of the archetypal Latin-American dictator; a short first-person novel in the voice of the aging, exiled Simón Bolívar plotting his return to power; and several collections of short fiction, the most successful of which was *Innocent Eréndira* (1978), containing the "Sad and Incredible Story" of a young girl forced into prostitution by her heartless grandmother. Yet it was only when he returned to the narrative style of the Macondo cycle, in *Love in the Time of Cholera,* telling a story about several generations of lovers and friends in a turn-of-the-century Caribbean city much like Cartagena, that García Márquez once again enjoyed the mass readership and the rave reviews of *One Hundred Years of Solitude.* With that novel, García Márquez had created a personal style, a unique way of making the reality of Latin America come to life on the printed page, a voice so singular that it could not be duplicated—not even by García Márquez himself—until Isabel Allende came along and with the aid of allusion adapted it to tell the story of her country, the larger-than-life saga of democratic Chile's fall into the dictatorship of Pinochet. But before turning to Allende, whose *House of the Spirits* was first published in 1982, it is appropriate to respect chronology and turn our attention to Vargas Llosa, an extraordinarily talented Peruvian, who gained international acclaim while still in his twenties with the publication of *The Time of the Hero* in 1962.

Vargas Llosa

Like Fuentes, Mario Vargas Llosa seemed destined for success. Handsome, well-educated, and articulate, he has written brilliant scholarly works on Flaubert (*The Perpetual Orgy: Flaubert and Madame Bovary,* 1975) and García Márquez (*Historia de un deicidio* [The History of a Deicide], 1971); short stories, essays, and plays; and over a dozen very different novels, each of which employs and creates a new narrative subject and technique. As if this were not enough to keep him busy, he recently tried his hand at politics, setting up his own political party in Peru and declaring himself a candidate for the presidency in the 1989 elections. That was his first and only failure. Through a series of surprise turns of event worthy of one of his own novels, his initial popularity was rapidly eclipsed by a hitherto unknown evangelistic candidate of Japanese immigrant origins, now President Alberto Fujimori. As García Márquez once said, it is difficult "to make our everyday reality believable." [27]

His first novel, *The Time of the Hero* (1962), was perhaps too believable: a gripping tale of scandal, corruption, and murder in mid-twentieth-century Peru. Set in a real-life military academy, the prestigious Leoncio Prado—where Vargas Llosa himself was once a student, having been interned there by his father, who caught the aspiring young writer in the "sissy" activity of scribbling verses—the novel moves back and forth in time, the before and after of the theft of some exam questions and the death of a cadet who turned informer. Although the subject matter seems simple—a Peruvian version of Musil's *Young Törless* (1906), the trials and tribulations of growing up in a boarding school—Vargas Llosa's indirect way of writing about it moves beyond cause-and-effect realism, involving the reader as witness, detective, and voyeur of violent conformist and nonconformist behavior in a broad cross section of society. Officers and cadets, adults and adolescents, their families and friends, from various socioeconomic levels and distinct provenances of Peru, are all brought together, or rather thrust together in the common enterprise of acculturation: teaching and learning how to "behave like men" in an authoritarian *machista* social order.

The novel begins in the barracks with a midnight roll of the dice which obliges the losing cadet to break into the teacher's office and copy down the exam questions for the "gang." The loser, Cava, under group pressure has no choice but to carry out his assigned mission. He does so but inadvertently breaks a windowpane, which prompts an investigation. Manly solidarity prevails among the cadets as all are confined to barracks and subjected to grueling punishment by the authorities, until the weakest, nicknamed "the Slave," breaks down and squeals. Later, in a rifle drill, he is shot in the back of the head. Is it an accident, or murder? The reader does not know because Vargas Llosa has structured the novel like a cinematic montage of narrative sequences, monologues, and flashbacks. Just who is telling or remembering what is never quite clear until the very end, when all the pieces of the puzzle come together. What keeps the reader interested is not so

Mario Vargas Llosa

much the desire to find out *what* happened, but why and how. To this end, a dazzling array of personages and plot lines diverge and intersect, driving the reader forward by the sheer impetus of events.

Unlike the fragmented narrative structures of the French *nouveau roman*—which was then in vogue, and where the story line is almost completely suppressed (and the reader is often bored)—Vargas Llosa uses fragmentation to enhance reader participation as each bit of new information suggests a slightly different version of events. The common denominator—despite the much touted military code of manliness—is cowardly betrayal by the youths and callous cover-up by the adults. At the novel's end, things return to normal, with the cadets—now marked by this experience—graduating and going on to their respective careers in military and civilian life, with the good name of the academy being protected, and with the sole dissident, Lieutenant Gamboa, a young teacher who took the military code of honor too seriously, being transferred out of the comfort of the academy to a remote post in the frigid Andean highlands. The lesson is clear that this is all part of growing up, what it means "to be a man" in contemporary society: to accept lies, deceit, and corruption as a normal part of the system, and if not, to be banished.

The novel, which could not be published in Vargas Llosa's native Peru, appeared in Spain, in the New Narrative series then being promoted by a Barcelona publisher, Seix Barral. The rave reviews it received in Spain and in Latin America catapulted the unknown twenty-six-year old onto the crest of the "boom." When the first copies arrived in Lima, they were summarily requisitioned by the military and burned in a public ceremony in the central patio of the Leoncio Prado military academy. Ironically true to Vargas Llosa's implied message, social forces proved to be more powerful than the individual, or at least local institutions, and this ludicrous auto-da-fé ultimately blazed the novel's way to best-seller status around the world. It was translated into English by Grove Press in 1966.

By that time, Vargas Llosa had already published his second novel, again with Seix Barral in Barcelona, *The Green House,* a scandalous story about a provincial house of ill-repute in northern Peru. While investigating the scenario for that novel, the writer became aware of a strange phenomenon that was taking place in the jungle backlands of Peru, where the discovery of reportedly vast oil reserves was bringing in all sorts of new settlers, mostly carpetbagging opportunists. This sort of rapid development increased the need for public services: roads, utilities—and police protection. All that, in turn, was accompanied by a logarithmic increase in violence against the indigenous population, whose young women were being sexually abused by the very soldiers who had been brought in to preserve law and order. Every problem begs a solution. The official response to this one was the subject of Vargas Llosa's *Captain Pantoja and the Special Service* (1978), a hilariously ribald novel written during the supposedly enlightened 1968–80 leftist military dictatorship.

Historically, the military in Peru has been an important institution. During colonial times, Lima, "The City of Kings," was the urbane capital of Spain's richest viceroyalty. Unlike Mexico City, an inland capital built on the Aztec ruins of Tenochtitlán, Lima was a new city founded on the coast, an ethnically Spanish center of power that ruled the indigenous population of the Andean highlands. During the wars of independence, Lima was the center of Spanish defense and the last garrison to fall. As a result, the new republic inherited a bloated, conservatively oriented officer class which has dominated Peruvian politics to this day, intervening often and at will in its self-imposed mandate to "restore order."

In *Captain Pantoja,* Vargas Llosa devastatingly parodies the military way of thinking with a skillful deployment of new high-powered narrative techniques. A variety of narrative devices, ranging from pseudo documents (letters, news reports, radio broadcasts, military communiqués, and behavioral surveys) to telescoping dialogues, creates a literary collage. As with *The Time of the Hero,* the reader is again engaged as a kind of witness—although now to an escalating succession of increasingly bizarre events as the "logical" solution to a problem spins out of control. A broad and bawdy humor draws us on into the highly complex narrative structure and keeps us turning the pages.

By telescoping fragments of speech enunciated at different times and places into a compositive narrative present, Vargas Llosa involves the reader as an observer of the action. In the opening chapter of the novel, for example, we seemingly witness firsthand the magnitude of the problem confronted by the authorities, along with its cause and effects, as Captain Pantaleón Pantoja, a model officer who has come up through the ranks, is being informed of his special assignment by his superiors:

> "O.K., let's take the bull by the horns," General Victoria seals his lips with a finger. "This business demands the utmost secrecy. I'm talking about the mission that's going to be entrusted to you, Captain. All right, let the cat out of the bag, Tiger."
>
> "In brief, the troops in the jungle are screwing the local women," [General] Tiger Collazos takes a breath, blinks and coughs. "There are rapes all over the place and the courts can't handle them all. The entire Amazon District is up in arms."
>
> "They bombard us daily with dispatches and accusations," General Victoria is plucking at his beard. "And protest committees arrive from even the most out-of-the-way little towns."
>
> "Your soldiers are dishonoring our women," Mayor Paiva Runhuí squeezes his hat and loses his voice. "Just a few months ago they molested my dear sister-in-law and last week they almost raped my own wife."
>
> "No, not my soldiers—the country's soldiers," General Victoria is making pacifying gestures. "Calm down, calm down, Mr. Mayor. The Army sincerely regrets your sister-in-law's misfortune and will do what it can to compensate her."
>
> "And do they call rape a 'misfortune' nowadays?" Father Beltrán gets rattled. "Because that's what it was: rape." . . .
>
> "They surprised my wife right in the church," the carpenter Adriano Lharque is sitting stiffly on the edge of his chair. "Not the cathedral, but the church of Santo Cristo de Bagazán, sir."
>
> "That's how it is, dear listeners," bellows Sinchi. "Neither fear of God nor respect for His sacred house nor the noble gray hairs of that dignified matron, who has already given two generations to Loreto, were able to restrain those sacrilegious, those lustful men." [28]

These same voices, those of the generals, the army chaplain, the radio announcer, the townspeople, and numerous others telescope into one another at different points throughout the novel, eventually becoming so familiar to the reader by their speech patterns that they no longer need identifying tags. The accumulative effect of this multilayered collage is comical, despite the gravity of what is being said and done. This is the art of black comedy, of the modern-day grotesque, producing what Pirandello called "il sentimento del contrario," a smile which is immediately followed by remorse and shame, for the reality of what is being parodied is indeed shameful.

Alternating with these voices, there are parodic versions of other familiar forms of discourse such as the military communiqués in which Captain Pantoja receives orders and reports back on his progress in training and recruiting a professional female brigade, the Special Service Corps, which travels by land, air, and sea to "service" the needs of the men. Captain Pantoja scientifically determines these needs with the aid of primitive Kinsey-type behavioral surveys—written questionnaires—and (why not?) his own empirical stopwatch calculations of his time to orgasm with his wife. As the story progresses, a veritable empire of prostitution is created, popularly dubbed "Pantiland." Demand increases and complications ensue in the form of interservice rivalries; the straitlaced Air Force wants no part of it, while the lusty Navy wants more. Eventually even the townspeople wish to be included, as in this letter of grievance from one of the initially protesting rural mayors, Paiva Runhuí:

> We consider it an offensive privilege that the Special Service belongs
> exclusively to the army barracks and the naval bases. . . . We demand
> that senior citizens with military service from these neglected Amazonian
> towns have the right to utilize that Service and at the same reduced rates
> as the soldiers. (107)

Success brings failure, and after a series of scandals, complicated in part by the emergence of an evangelistic preacher, the novel ends with the Service being disbanded and Captain Pantoja, like Lieutenant Gamboa of *The Time of the Hero,* being reassigned to the *puna,* the cold windswept plains of the Andean mountains. The whole matter is closed with typical establishment smugness, an "informed source" news report denying the military affiliation of the Special Service:

> [It] being only a civilian, commercial enterprise that has had incidental
> and merely tolerated, but never supported or officialized, relations with
> the Army. With this in mind, the same source added, an investigation
> of the said Special Service that the Army general staff should have
> ordered will be conducted with the purpose of discovering its origin,
> composition, functions and benefits in order to determine the legality,
> and if appropriate, its liabilities and pertinent sanctions. (217)

The novel reads like a dossier, with the diverse documents suddenly springing to life by means of the telescoping dialogues.

It is very easy for a successful writer to fall into the trap of a kind of formula fiction, satisfying reader demand and expectations with a new novel, new characters and a new plot, written in the proven style of the old. Not so with Vargas Llosa. Each of his many novels, which now number over a dozen, employs a new and different writing technique. To tell the real-life story of himself as a young adult—his many failed beginnings as a fledgling writer in Peru, his idyllic love, elopement, and marriage at nineteen to an older divorced woman, who just happened to be his aunt—he resorted to the model of a soap opera in *Aunt Julia and the Scriptwriter* (1977). In alternate autobiographical chapters, a wizened first-person voice recalls the saga of a young "Marito Vargas" and his enthrallment to the older Julia. The sentimental tone of melodrama is established in the very first words of the first chapter:

> In those long-ago days, I was very young and lived with my grandparents in a villa with white walls in the Calle Ocharán, in Miraflores. I was studying at the University of San Marcos, law, as I remember, resigned to earning myself a living later on by practicing a liberal profession, although deep down what I really wanted was to become a writer someday. I had a job with a pompous-sounding title, a modest salary, duties as a plagiarist, and flexible working hours: News Director of Radio Panamericana. It consisted of cutting out interesting news items that appeared in the daily papers and rewriting them slightly so that they could be read on the air during the newscasts. [29]

This yarn of "long-ago" is systematically interrupted by the even-numbered chapters, which are scripts for the serials being aired by the radio station, with cliff-hanging endings, as for example that of chapter two, where a young man discovers on his wedding day that his wife is several months pregnant by her brother:

> Would Red Antúnez desert his reckless, foolhardy spouse that very night? Might he have done so already? Or would he say nothing, and giving proof of what might be either exceptional nobility or exceptional stupidity, stay with that deceitful girl whom he had so persistently pursued? Would there be a great public scandal, or would a chaste veil of dissimulation and pride trampled underfoot forever hide this tragedy of San Isidro? (39)

At novel's end, in chapter twenty, after the young "Marito" and his Aunt Julia have successfully eloped, the two kinds of writing come closer together, although never quite converging—unlike the movie adaptation where the eloping couple turn on the car radio and find themselves to be a part of the serial. [30] Instead of the expected soap script, we are offered a kind of epilogue to the previous chapter, an update to what happened after the marriage. The autobiographical narrator reveals himself to be a successful novelist. After eight years of marriage, he and Aunt Julia divorced; and the writer is now remarried, this time to his cousin, with the result that Aunt Olga and Uncle Lucho

71

"had gone from being my wife's sister and brother-in-law to being my parents-in-law." (373)

Obviously Vargas Llosa did not have to go far to find literary materials with an air of the marvelous, he simply had to work out diverse ways to make believable the complex realities of the world around him. For this reason, in his approach to fictionalizing fact, each of his novels has required a different narrative technique. His life is his literature. One version of his quixotic incursion into political life has already been told by his campaign manager, his son by his second wife. Someday soon, perhaps, Vargas Llosa will tell his own version; one day he may even fulfill his ambition to be president of Peru.

The exceptional variety of innovative narrative procedures developed by the writers of the "boom" has made things difficult for those who followed, especially for those who, to use Harold Bloom's concept, suffered from an "anxiety of influence." There are many failed experiments in the more recent literature of Latin America, and this is not the place to chronicle them; but there are many successes as well. One extraordinarily successful writer, Isabel Allende, a niece of the late President Salvador Allende of Chile, simply decided to pick up where García Márquez had left off and write just like him.

Allende

Like García Márquez, Isabel Allende began her writing career as a journalist. Although born in Lima (in 1942, to a Chilean family), she was raised in Santiago. Shortly after graduating from high school, she began writing for *Paula,* a local magazine of fashion and the arts, eventually becoming its general editor. Like many Chileans of her generation, her life and career were altered by exile following the brutal military coup of General Augusto Pinochet in September 1973. In her own words:

> . . . after the military coup in Chile, when I had to leave my country, I couldn't work as a journalist, and for many years I remained in silence. I had no possibility of writing, or trying to communicate anything. So I did all sorts of odd jobs until 1981, when I sat down to write a letter to my grandfather. And that's the letter that became *The House of the Spirits.* [31]

That novel, published in Barcelona in 1982, became an instant international best-seller, the first by a woman to attain "boom" status. This was achieved despite an almost uniformly cold critical reception, partly because she was a forty-year-old unknown, but mostly because her novel seemed to many "a shameless cloning from *One Hundred Years of Solitude.*" [32] The critics' caviling had little effect on the reading public, whose escalating demand pushed the novel through seven printings in

Isabel Allende

less than a year. Much the same happened in 1985, when Knopf brought out an English translation. The hardcover edition went through three printings in less than a month, before going into paperback as a Bantam book in 1986. Its sales by now are in the millions. Allende has gone on to write three more novels and a collection of short stories, all of which enjoy a mass readership.

Exactly fifteen years separated *One Hundred Years of Solitude* from *The House of the Spirits,* the span of a generation. Older readers, who witnessed the "boom" from the outset, were put off at first by the García Márquez-like beginning of Allende's novel:

> Barrabás came to us by sea, the child Clara wrote in her delicate
> calligraphy. She was already in the habit of writing down important
> matters, and afterward, when she was mute, she also recorded trivialities,
> never suspecting that fifty years later I would use her notebooks to

reclaim the past and overcome terrors of my own. Barrabás arrived
on a Holy Thursday. He was in a despicable cage, caked with his
own excrement and urine, and had the lost look of a hapless, utterly
defenseless prisoner; but the regal carriage of his head and the size
of his frame bespoke the legendary giant he would become. It was a
bland, autumnal day that gave no hint of the events the child would
record. . . . [33]

Younger readers experiencing this kind of premonitory storytelling
for the first time were enthralled by its matter-of-fact description of
the patently fantastic and intrigued by the embedded portent of even
greater things to come. Both sets of readers were right. *The House of
the Spirits* is a kind of Chilean version of *One Hundred Years of Solitude*,
elevating to mythic proportions the story of a single family: four generations of Truebas, whose lives personify that of twentieth-century Chile
in its elliptical passage from feudal capitalism to liberal democracy,
from democratic socialism to primitive authoritarianism. And Allende
does make use of the fablelike narrative style of García Márquez—not
to make the marvelous seem real, but the reverse.

But this is not the only narrative style she employs. Interspersed
throughout the novel there is the first-person narration of Esteban
Trueba, a self-made man, the patriarch and progenitor of the family,
who tells his own highly personal version of events, elevating himself
to heroic stature through the collective voice of others. Penniless at
the story's outset in the 1920s, and enamored at first sight of Rosa
the Beautiful, he resolves to win her hand and goes off to the mines
in search of gold. The very day that he strikes pay dirt, he receives a
telegram informing him of Rosa's death:

> I traveled more than thirty hours without stopping to eat, not even
> noticing my thirst, and I managed to reach the del Valle home before
> the funeral. *They say* that I arrived covered with dust, without a hat,
> filthy and bearded, thirsty and furious, shouting for my bride. Little
> Clara, who at the time was just a skinny child, came out to meet me
> when I stepped into the courtyard, took me by the hand, and drew me
> silently toward the dining room. There was Rosa in the folds of the
> white satin lining of her white coffin, still intact three days after she had
> died, and a thousand times more beautiful than I remembered her, for
> in death Rosa had been subtly transformed into the mermaid she had
> always been in secret.
> "Damn her! She slipped through my hands!" *they say* I shouted, falling
> to my knees beside her. . . . (33–34)   [emphasis mine]

He marries the little sister Clara and founds the clan. Later, as an aging
conservative senator in the late 1960s:

> Everyone recognized him on the street. People made up jokes and
> anecdotes about him that were the talk of the town. *It was said* that

when he had his heart attack the day his son took off his clothes before
the gates of Congress, the President of the Republic called him to
his office to offer him the post of Ambassador to Switzerland, a job
appropriate to his age that would allow him to recover his health. *They
said* that Senator Trueba replied by slamming his fist down on the
presidential desk, knocking down the flag and the bust of the Founding
Father. (308) [emphasis mine]

This is the formulaic device of epic, where the narrator buttresses his
version of events through a consensual condensation of what others
have said.

Imbedded in the text are other formulaic devices, codes of meaning that condition our reading. In the previously cited example, the
narrative assertions that Rosa was "a thousand times more beautiful
in death," having been "transformed into the mermaid she had always
been" do not read as mere hyperbole because they have been legit-
imated by an anticipatory code from the rhetoric of sainthood: "still
intact three days after she had died." Similarly, Esteban Trueba's lordly
abuse of power, capriciously raping practically every young peasant
woman who catches his eye, is socially "justified" through a literary
allusion to the *Serranillas*, late medieval ballads of bawdiness in which
the knight-errant on encountering a beautiful shepherdess "beds her
down in the river." García Lorca used this same device in his *Romancero
gitano* [Gypsy Ballads, 1928]: "Y que yo me la llevé al río / creyendo
que era mozuela, pero tenía marido" [I took her to the river / believing that she was unwed, but she had a husband]. In *The House of the
Spirits,* when Esteban Trueba comes across his first fifteen-year-old in
the fields, he reacts instinctively:

He trotted up until he was right beside her. She heard him, but she
continued walking without looking up, following the ancestral custom
of all the women of her kind who bow their heads before the
male. . . . He threw his arm around her waist, swept her up with an
animal-like grunt, and placed her before him in the saddle. The girl
did not resist. He kicked his heels in the stirrups and they took off at a
gallop in the direction of the river. (57)

By alluding to literature, to the ready-made formulae of literary classics—to the *Don Juan* of Zorrilla, to the *Conde Lucanor,* to *Lazarillo de
Tormes,* to Cortázar, Neruda, and Vargas Llosa, among many others—
Allende does much more than simply "clone" from one García Márquez;
she creates a subtly complex new narrative structure whose power of
persuasion is generated by the literary tradition from which it is drawn.

The novel is a network of allusion, sometimes direct, but often indirect, as when Esteban's tomboy daughter enters womanhood. After her
first menstruation, at age fourteen, she is prohibited from playing with
her childhood companion, Pedro Tercero, the ranch hand's son. Not

understanding this seemingly arbitrary prohibition, she misses Pedro, and waking up in a cold sweat, instinctively gets dressed and goes out into the night:

> The delicate rain of the night had soaked the earth and trees, and her clothing felt slightly damp, her shoes cold. She inhaled the perfume of the drenched earth, the rotten leaves and the humus, which awakened an unknown pleasure in all her senses.
>
> Blanca arrived at the river and found her childhood friend sitting at the spot where they had met so many times. (145)

No further description is necessary. The reader, conditioned by literature, almost intuitively knows what will happen, and what in fact does happen: the children become lovers. Their impossible love—she the daughter of the patriarch, he the son of a peasant—is of course patterned on yet another literary model and serves as one of the driving elements in this novel of social, political, and sexual conflict in twentieth-century Chile. Although Chile is never mentioned, it is the recent history of this country which forms the chronological frame of the novel and is its real subject: the fall into dictatorship. Its most famous historical figures, Salvador Allende, Pablo Neruda, and General Pinochet, lend the reality of their lives and careers to the reality of the novel, appearing simply as the Candidate, the Poet, and the Dictator.

This is also a woman's novel, a novel by a woman, and offers a different perspective on the role of women in the world. In traditional Latin-American fiction, women are rarely protagonists, and when they are, their chief role seems to be that of Eve, the femme fatale. Allende's novel turns the system around, ridiculing the patriarch and showing us another kind of power, the power of being female. The novel is peopled by strong female characters, women who are in step with their times, and often one step ahead of them, four generations of strong-willed individuals: Nívea, Clara, Blanca, and Alba. The similarity of their names—all synonymous with white—is like the sameness of the male nomenclature in García Márquez's novel, but significantly different. Each is distinctly of her time; all are artists and feminists. Nívea embroiders and is a pioneer suffragette; her daughter Clara weaves and asserts herself over Esteban simply by ignoring his macho mandates; Clara's daughter Blanca does ceramics and when pregnant by Pedro decides to be an unmarried mother rather than submit to being someone's wife; her daughter Alba—our contemporary—is sexually liberated and becomes a revolutionary and a writer, the unifying "overvoice" of the novel. Each of these women in her own way creatively modifies the parameters of feminine conduct for her time. Their collective story, penned by Alba during the repressive regime of the Dictator, an anachronistic patriarch, is the story of human rights in the twentieth century.

Lispector

The career of Brazil's Clarice Lispector could almost be a character outline for one of the women in Allende's novels. Patiently writing fiction since the 1940s, living in the shadow of her husband's career as a diplomat, her recognition was slow in coming. Today she is considered to be a major Latin-American writer, *the* major writer of twentieth-century Brazil.

Brazil, like the United States, is an immigrant country populated by people from all over the globe. Lispector was born in Ukraine in 1925, a few months before her parents emigrated. Her writing is intensely introspective, reflecting back on itself, on the problems of writing about the insignificant people who are the subjects of her fiction: frowsy housewives, dumpy adolescents, illiterate maids, ordinary office workers, a failed writer. . . . Her short stories can be compared to those of Joyce for their use of the epiphany, culminating in a magic moment of revelation. "The Daydreams of a Drunk Woman," the opening story of *Family Ties* (1960), begins and ends before a mirror. At the outset, a woman is leisurely combing her hair, musing over her good life: married, with grown children, a vacation house—tomorrow she will "straighten up." The ironic trajectory of her self-satisfied reverie permits us to see that she is ordinary and vulgar, lazy and procrastinating, she knows that "she had really been born for greater things." [34] A few pages later, at the story's end, she sees herself differently, exploding "in a sudden outburst of affection; 'you slut,' she cried out, laughing." (36) Lispector's use of language is fascinating and truly unique. Her sentences seem to be pointing in two directions, saying contradictory things at the same time. The reader is obliged to read between the words, getting inside the character, between the author and the text.

Another story, "Preciousness," details the tribulations of an adolescent:

> She was fifteen years old and she was not pretty. But inside her
> thinness existed the almost majestic vastness in which she stirred, as in
> a meditation. And within the mist there was something precious. Which
> did not extend itself, did not compromise itself nor contaminate itself.
> Which was intense like a jewel. Herself. (102)

Getting up in the morning, preparing to go to school, this anonymous heroine plans a day whose principal objective is to "avoid having anyone look at her." (103) When the bus arrives, she gets on:

> . . . serious as a missionary, because of the workers on the bus who
> "might say something to her." Those men who were no longer just
> boys. But she was also afraid of boys, and afraid of the youngest ones
> too. Afraid they would "say something to her," would look her up
> and down. (103)

CLARICE LISPECTOR

The Foreign Legion

TRANSLATED BY GIOVANNI PONTIERO

On the way home from school, walking toward her house, the click-clack of her shoes is mingled with the click-clack of others walking behind her. She self-consciously begins to walk faster, then breaks out into a run for safety, finally fainting as she feels (imagines?) hands pawing her. When she comes to, she goes home white as a sheet and stuns her parents by demanding a new pair of shoes—big girl's shoes, hers make noise, they "attract too much attention." The story ends with an epiphany: "And she got her new shoes." (113)

This technique of Lispector's, placing us inside the minds of ordinary people, creates a spellbinding tension in the reader, impelling us to read on and in between the lines. In *The Hour of the Star* (1977), a novella which is probably her masterwork, the narrator is a man, "alias Clarice Lispector," [35] a professional writer who confesses that he is unable to finish the book, to give the right shape to the story because it is so insignificant, and "none the less real." (8) The ostensible subject is a homely waif, a semiliterate slip of a girl who has emigrated to São Paolo from the impoverished backlands of northeastern Brazil. The city is full of people like her—no talent, no education, no prospect for a future. The other subject is the author himself, "alias Clarice Lispector," who makes all kinds of false narrative starts, going on for page after page about how to get a grasp on this nothingness of the story to be told. The title page is like a table of contents, an outline of authorial frustration, whose thirteen entries read like chapter headings and cries of desperation by the author, one Rodrigo S.M.—with the penned-in signature of Clarice Lispector following the fourth.

All this serves to generate interest in what is seemingly insignificant and yet is so important: what is usually just a statistic, so many homeless, so many jobless, so many frustrated lives. The Gabriela of Amado is a superwoman, this slip of a girl is nothing. She has an underpaid job in a typing pool, which she is in danger of losing because she can't spell. At the butcher shop she meets her male counterpart, an illiterate tough from the northeast who ran away to São Paolo after killing someone in a knife fight. Both are inarticulate; a date consists of sitting silently together on a park bench, because it's free. He would like to be bullfighter; she would like to be movie star. The novella is full of such losers.

One day, after treating herself to a cup of hot chocolate, Macabéa becomes ill. Through an act of willpower she prevents herself from vomiting so as "not to squander that delicious chocolate." (66) On the advice of an office mate, she goes to see a doctor "who didn't charge much":

> The doctor, who was corpulent and given to perspiring, suffered from a nervous tic that caused him to purse his lips at regular intervals. As a result, he looked like a pouting infant about to burst into tears.
>
> This doctor had no ambition whatsoever. He saw medicine simply as a means of earning a living. It had nothing to do with dedication or concern for the sick. He was negligent and found the squalor of his patients utterly distasteful. He resented having to deal with the poor whom he saw as the rejects of that privileged society from which he himself had been excluded. It had not escaped him that he was out of touch with the latest trends in medicine and new clinical methods, but he had all the training he was likely to need for treating the lower orders. His dream was to earn enough money to do exactly what he pleased: nothing. (67)

He gives her an X ray and tells her that she is in the early stages of pulmonary tuberculosis. She doesn't understand the words and doesn't know if this is good or bad: "But being ever so polite she simply said: 'Many thanks'." (68) There is humor here: the doctor is a caricature, the girl's response is absurd. But the humor is pathetic, and in this way we are able to empathize with the plight of this helpless creature, this statistic whom Clarice Lispector brings to life.

The novella ends with the girl's death after a visit to a fortune-teller. She is told that she will have an encounter with a handsome blond foreigner. In a daze of ecstasy on leaving the salon, she steps into the street and is run over by a handsome blond foreigner. The narrator is in despair:

> Macabéa has murdered me.
> She is finally free of herself and of me. Do not be frightened. Death is instantaneous and passes in a flash. I know, for I have just died with the girl. Forgive my dying. It was unavoidable. If you have kissed the wall, you can accept anything. But suddenly I make one last gesture of rebellion and start to howl: the slaughter of doves! To live is a luxury.
> Suddenly it's all over.
> Macabéa is dead. The bells were ringing without making any sound. I now understand this story. She is the imminence in those bells, pealing so softly. The greatness of every human being. (85)

In this novella, which is an intriguing tour de force, Clarice Lispector has accomplished the impossible: she has given life to an anonymous statistic, she has used literature to create reality out of what was formerly "nothing."

In a very real and important sense, writing by Latin-American women today has expanded the horizons of literature. Allende artfully deconstructed the monolithic patriarchal system; Lispector put us inside the minds and bodies of the hitherto invisible "little women"; Rosario Castellanos, our last author in this essay, rounds out the revolution, showing us the other side of what it means to be "different" in a man's world.

Castellanos

In *Mujer que sabe latín . . .* (A Woman Who Knows Latin . . . , 1973),* there is a telling essay on Clarice Lispector deriding the establishment critics who simplistically insist on pigeonholing her with Virginia Woolf: another feminist, "a common outlook, the same tools of the trade." [36] Castellanos could have said much the same about the establishment's slow reception of her own work as she blazed beyond feminism, breaking important new literary ground in her poetry, novels, and plays.

Born into a rural landholding family in southern Mexico in 1925, she was expected to find fulfillment in being a housewife. She dutifully tried that for a time—even with a palatial "room of her own"—and then moved out to become a more complete person, a writer and a

---

*The title is the first part of a popular saying in Spanish: "Mujer que sabe latín, no halla marido ni tiene buen fin." (A woman who knows Latin won't get a husband or come to a good end.)

diplomat. When she died, in 1974, she was her country's ambassador
to Israel. With unintended irony she was buried in a state funeral in
Mexico's Pantheon of Illustrious Men, the first woman to be interred
there. She was also first in many other things, especially poetry, creating
a new literary space, rewriting masculine discourse, literally turning it
on its head.

In a poem titled "Interview" she self-confidently cuts a male journalist down to size:

> The reporter asks, with the shrewdness
> his profession has taught him:
> "Why, to what purpose do you write?"
>
> "Well, sir, it's obvious. Because someone
> (when I was a small girl)
> said that persons like myself do not exist.
> Because their bodies cast no shadow,
> because they register no weight on the scale,
> because their names are to be forgotten . . .
>
> "I write because one day (I was an adolescent)
> I looked in the mirror and no one was there.
> Can you imagine? A void. And those
> around me gushed importance . . .
>
> "Would you care to see my mausoleum?
> How do you like that corpse? It's merely
> an innocuous friendship.
> And that one's a sympathy that didn't jell
> and over there, a fetus. Just a fetus.
>
> "Don't ask more. Its classification?
> On the card it says: love, happiness,
> whatever. What's the difference.
> It was never viable. A fetus kept
> in alcohol. That is, a poem
> from the book you'll one day praise." [37]

The parenthetical asides, the colloquial language, and the rhetorical
questions give the text the air of a real interview. The illogicalities
of the rambling discourse, however ("How do you like that corpse?"),
make us read it with a special kind of attention, the attention reserved
for a poem. Yet, prosaic locutions like "over there," "whatever," "just
a fetus" whet our curiosity and add impact to the jarringly assertive
closure: "A fetus kept / in alcohol. That is, a poem / from the book
you'll one day praise."

Confident of her worth, Castellanos does not write to please, but
rather to jolt us into rethinking our assumptions about men and women.

Rosario Castellanos

Some poems are directed to men, some to women, and most to *all of us* united in our common humanness. "Act of Humility" transforms a much lauded feminine "trait" into something without virtue, jolting women into thinking about what they have allowed themselves to become. It is a deceptively simple poem in two short strophes: the first, a run-on accumulation of observations; the second, a single meandering sentence, artfully broken in several lines with ellipses at just the right places to set the reader up for the claim that women are just a bunch of cows:

> Long ago I was amazed
> at how easy it was to be nothing more than a cow.
> Ruminating was sufficient then, and the yearly issue of a new calf.
> Or observing without surprise the structure
> of the world and its phantoms.
> Or letting oneself get fat, and tamely
> moving with the rest toward the slaughter.
>
> Really, it is quite easy. But if
> we consider the matter with equanimity
> neither is it exactly heroic
> to be that which . . . after all . . . we are. (161)

A master of ellipsis, of the power of a pause, and of making the reader fill in the silence, saying the unsaid (or the unsayable), Castellanos often uses the avant-garde device of a blank space or a break in the line to extend the thrust of the lyric voice, amplifying in the process the radius of her reach, making a so-called woman's poem into a meaningful read for all of us.

By way of example, the following brief text, "Elegy," starts off faithful to its title as a familiar lament to a lost love. Suddenly, though, after only one line there is a break, a spatial pause, and the style of discourse shifts to read like an aside, a private reverie directed to no one in particular—and for this reason it ultimately touches us all, coming to us, sotto voce, as an intensely private soliloquy in which we are outside the poem, in the situation of voyeur, looking in on the death of desire:

> I was never so like a stone as when I was at your side.
>
> I who dreamt I was a cloud, or water,
> a breeze on a leaf,
> fire of a thousand lambent tongues,
> *I only knew how to lie there,*
> to weigh heavily, which is what a stone
> knows how to do
> around a drowning man's neck. (133)
>
> [emphasis mine]

Poetry, of course, is always most effective in its original language; translation usually loses or obscures some meaning. In this case, the original Spanish of the central line ("I only knew how to lie there") reads succinctly, "sólo supe yacer": the verb *yacer* having a double meaning, to "lie" in death, or to "lie" in carnal contact. This everyday verb, with its dual meaning, literal and biblical, is the trigger term which explodes "Elegy" into an epitaph.

Castellanos, like her immediate predecessor, the Chilean "antipoet" Parra, knew the power of everyday speech and exploited it to the utmost, imitating the voices of others, the ready-made modes of discourse of people from different educational levels and different walks of life. In "Kinsey Report," a long poem with several different speakers, she uses the format of the scientific survey to give voice to a married woman ("I always submit, out of obedience"), a single woman ("and I don't even charge"), a divorced woman ("I take a fling from time to time"), an abnegated recluse ("I wake up wet"), a lesbian ("my girlfriend and I understand each other well"), and the classic "señorita" patiently saving herself for Prince Charming:

> If he drinks too much
> I'll straighten him out.
> If he turns out to be a woman chaser
> well, I'll keep myself so attractive,
> so attentive to his desires, so splendid a housewife,
> such a prolific mother
> and superb cook

> that he'll be faithful in recognition
> of my merits, among which the greatest is patience. . .
>
> No, I haven't had a boyfriend. None,
> as yet. Tomorrow. (150–57)

Another hallowed "virtue" bites the dust, for we all anticipate that the patience of this last heroine will not bring her happiness. Castellanos's poetry is not prescriptive, but descriptive. She does not intervene to offer her opinions or conclusions; it is we who extrapolate; it is we (men and women) who see that the present order of things needs to be changed.

Literature does not change reality, it makes it comprehensible. The reality of Latin America in the last half of the twentieth century has moved from the fantastic to the real, a real which is neither marvelous nor magic, but mundane. Mexico or Montevideo in the 1990s is not much different from Paris or Peoria. Latin-American literature is now an integral part of world literature.

Postscript

There is one more aspect of Latin-American literature today which cannot be ignored: the writing in both English and Spanish, and sometimes even "Spanglish" or "Anglol," by authors with a Latin-American cultural background—those who are called, and call themselves, Chicanos, Latinos, Hispanics. This is another body of literature, not exactly within the scope of this essay. However, in recent years one of these writers has emerged with such force and brilliance that it seems imperative to take note of her here: Sandra Cisneros, a Chicana from Chicago, who writes in a multitude of voices from the barrio, at times with a childlike innocence, at times with a street-smart bravado, always, however, with a feel for language that somehow makes the local seem universal. Her first book of stories, *House on Mango Street* (1988), now adapted to the stage in Chicago by Amy Ludwig for Chameleon Productions, is in the voice of a young girl who is growing up "perilously fast"; [38] her latest book, *Woman Hollering Creek* (1991), is a chorus of grown women on the other side of innocence. In the title story there is an echo of García Márquez, or Isabel Allende, the kind of nonstop prose that in a single sentence transports the reader into the magic world of fiction:

> The day Don Serafín gave Juan Pedro Martínez Sánchez permission
> to take Cleófilas Enriqueta DeLeón Hernández as his bride, across her
> father's threshold, over several miles of dirt road and several miles of
> paved, over one border and beyond to a town *en el otro lado*—on the

other side—already did he divine the morning his daughter would raise her hand over her eyes, look south, and dream of returning to the chores that never ended, six good-for-nothing brothers, and one old man's complaints. [39]

This is the kind of writing that comes out of the oral tradition, by someone who knows how to tell a story, making it seem both magic and real—and believable. And that is what literature is all about. Latin-American literature today—from North and South America—has entered the mainstream.

1. *Myself with Others* (New York: Noonday, 1990), p. 4.

2. Emmanuel Carballo, "El año de la novela," *Novedades* (Mexico City), Dec. 28, 1958.

3. Daniel de Guzmán, *Carlos Fuentes* (New York: Twayne, 1972), p. 95.

4. Alfonso Reyes, "Visión de Anáhuac" (1915), collected in his *Obras completas* (Mexico: Fondo de Cultura, 1955), vol. 2, pp. 13–34.

5. *Where the Air Is Clear* (New York: Obolensky, 1960); I cite from the most recent Farrar Strauss printing (1990), p. 127, and henceforth will indicate page numbers parenthetically in the text.

6. *Tiempo mexicano* (Mexico: Joaquín Mortiz, 1971), pp. 17–42.

7. *Aura* (New York: Farrar, 1965), p. 70.

8. "Julio Cortázar, 1914–1984: The Simón Bolívar of the Latin American Novel," *New York Times Book Review* (March 4, 1984), p. 10.

9. First published in Spanish in 1972, it was brought out in English by Columbia University Press in 1977.

10. *Bestiario* (1951), *Final del juego* (1956), and *Las armas secretas* (1959); a selection of stories from these volumes were translated and published under the title *End of the Game and Other Stories* (New York, Random House, 1963); now retitled *Blow-Up and Other Stories* (New York: Pantheon, 1985).

11. Pages 10–16 (originally in *Bestiario*); *see* previous note.

12. Juan Fresán, *Casa tomada: traducción al diseño gráfico* (Buenos Aires: Minotauro, 1969).

13. Evelyn Picón Garfield, *Julio Cortázar* (New York: Ungar, 1975), p. 35.

14. In *Blow-Up*, pp. 3–9.

15. In *All Fires the Fire and Other Stories* (New York: Pantheon, 1973), pp. 30–48.

16. First published in *Octaedro* (1974); available in English in *We Love Glenda So Much* (New York: Vintage, 1984), pp. 249–63.

17. In *We Love Glenda. . .* , pp. 405–21.

18. "La soledad de América Latina," in *Diálogo sobre la novela latinoamericana* (Lima: Perú Andino, 1988), p. 13.

19. Ibid., p. 14.

20. Ibid., p. 15.

21. *One Hundred Years of Solitude* (New York: Harper, 1970); I quote from the first Avon printing (1971), p. 104 (pagination unchanged in subsequent printings), and henceforth will indicate page numbers parenthetically in the text.

22. "Diálogo entre Gabriel García Márquez y Mario Vargas Llosa," in *Diálogo sobre la novela latinoamericana*, p. 30.

23. "Fantasía y creación artística en América Latina y el Caribe," *Texto Crítico* (Xalapa), V, 14 (July–September 1979), p. 4.

24. "Fantasía y creación artística . . . ," p. 7.

25. *No One Writes to the Colonel and Other Stories* (New York: Harper, 1968), p. 3; henceforth page numbers will be indicated parenthetically in the text.

26. A term used to describe a seemingly interminable period of political assassinations unleashed with the *bogotazo* of 1948, when Jorge Eliécer Gaitán, a populist candidate for the presidency, was gunned down on the streets of Bogotá, the nation's capital.

27. "La soledad de América Latina," p. 15.

28. *Pantaleón y las visitadoras* (Barcelona: Seix Barral, 1973); translated into English as *Captain Pantoja and the Special Service* (New York: Grove, 1966); I quote from the more recent Harper (1978) edition, pp. 4–5. Henceforth, references to this edition will be indicated parenthetically in the text.

29. *La tía Julia y el escribidor* (Barcelona: Seix Barral, 1977); translated into English as *Aunt Julia and the Scriptwriter* (New York: Farrar, 1982). I quote from the first Avon edition (1983), p. 3 (pagination unchanged in subsequent printings), and henceforth will indicate page numbers parenthetically in the text.

30. Directed by Jon Amiel, with the title of *Tune in Tomorrow* (Cinecom Entertainment, 1990).

31. Jean W. Ross, "Interview," *Contemporary Authors* (Detroit: Gale, 1990), vol. 130, p. 7.

32. Enrique Fernández, "Send in the Clone," *Village Voice* (New York), June 4, 1985, p. 51.

33. *La casa de los espíritus* (Barcelona: Plaza & Janés, 1982); translated into English as *The House of the Spirits* (New York: Knopf, 1985). I quote from the more recent Bantam paperback (1986), p. 1, and henceforth will indicate page references to this edition parenthetically in the text.

34. *Laços de família* (São Paolo: Editôra do Autor, 1960), translated into English as *Family Ties* (Austin: University of Texas, 1972), p. 32; other page references to this edition will be indicated parenthetically.

35. *A Hora da Estrela* (Rio de Janeiro: José Olympio, 1977), translated into English as *The Hour of the Star* (Manchester: Carcanet, 1986), p. 7; further citations will be indicated parenthetically in the text.

36. "Clarice Lispector, la memoria ancestral," *Mujer que sabe latín* . . . (Mexico: SepSetenta, 1973), pp. 127–32.

37. *Meditation on the Threshold* (Tempe, Ariz.: Bilingual Press, 1988), p. 141; all further references to this bilingual selection of poems from *Meditación en el umbral* (Mexico: Fondo de Cultura, 1985) will be parenthetically indicated in the text.

38. *New York Times Book Review*, May 26, 1991.

39. *Woman Hollering Creek* (New York: Random House, 1991), p. 43.

Egonomics:
The Economics of Personal Conflict

Jon Elster

Jon Elster (b. 1940) is a Norwegian who in various writings has made substantial contributions to contemporary logic, economics, and political theory from the perspective of a social scientist. Rejecting traditional philo-sophical and political thought, he believes that "there are no societies, only individuals who interact with each other," and he has devoted much of his time to expounding what is called the theory of rational choice, by which is meant the self-interested motives that lead human beings to act as they do, often contradictorily and to their general disadvantage. He is not given to large formulations but writes in a minimalist style, setting forth small, carefully framed problems, often in terms of Game Theory, to illustrate human com-plexities, which he thinks so significant as to show that we have, each of us, multiple selves.

Among his many books are *Making Sense of Marx* (1985), *The Cement of Society* (1989), and *Local Justice* (1992). Now preparing a work of Tocqueville, Mr. Elster divides his time between Oslo, where he has an aca-demic appointment, and the University of Chicago, where he is the Ryerson Distinguished Service Professor of Political Science and Philosophy.

I. Introduction

The term *egonomics* was coined by Thomas Schelling in 1978 to denote the economic analysis of motivational conflicts within the person and the management ("self-management") of such conflicts. [1] In this essay I use the term in a somewhat wider sense, which can be brought out by drawing a contrast with standard economic theory. [2] In that theory, the economic agents are assumed to be rational, unitary actors, endowed with self-interested and unchanging preferences. An economic agent is "nothing but" a clothes hanger for his preferences or, if you will, his utility function. Egonomics, by contrast, explores the possibility that agents may be irrational, non-selfish, and non-unitary, and that their preferences may be subject to systematic forms of change.

Most of egonomics rests on the idea, which may be taken literally or mainly as a metaphor, of multiple selves. [3] We can distinguish between three varieties of this idea: successive selves, alternating selves, and divided selves. When people are young, they have different preferences from those they have when they are old—including different ideas about what to do when they get old. [4] This is an instance of a conflict between successive selves. Conflict between alternating selves is illustrated by the person who makes a resolve each morning to go to bed early and then in the evening feels wide awake and decides to stay up late. [5] Conflict within a divided self may be illustrated by the opposition between *homo economicus* and *homo sociologicus*—between the part of the person who feels the pull of material self-interest and the part who is under the sway of social norms.

However, egonomics also allows for the possibility that one self may be privileged compared to the others and act strategically to impose some unity on the unruly community. The idea of *self-control* involves control by one self of another self or selves. To the idea of *division* within the self we must add that of a *hierarchy*. To use Freud's metaphor, one part of the self (the ego) may be compared to the rider and another part (the id) to the horse. Although the horse may sometimes throw the rider from the saddle, it is incapable of trying to train or force the rider to act in accordance with its interests. To extend the metaphor, a third part of the self (the superego) may be seen as an incubus imposed

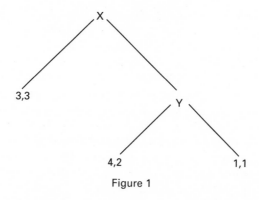

Figure 1

on the ego and weighing it down with its demands. Later, we shall see how George Ainslie's work has made it possible to state these insights in a non-metaphoric way.

These are issues that have been the concern of philosophers, moralists, novelists, and psychologists for a long time. As we shall see, they preoccupied Aristotle, Saint Paul, Augustine, Montaigne, Pascal, Descartes, Leibniz, Samuel Johnson, Hume, Austen, Stendhal, Tocqueville, Hans Christian Andersen, Marx, and Freud, among many others. They are certainly not the exclusive domain of a new discipline, "egonomics." The distinguishing feature of that discipline is simply that it approaches them with a new set of analytic tools, derived from economic theory. More generally, and more modestly, egonomics could be defined as an approach to these issues which is "inspired by" the economic way of thinking. The ideas of scarcity, choice, maximization, planning, trade-offs, externalities, bargaining, and collective action can, at least occasionally, suggest new insights into questions that have racked the best minds for centuries or millennia.

The proof of this particular pudding must, of course, be in the eating. In this Introduction I shall only offer one sample: why people may benefit from having fewer or worse options rather than more or better ones. Schelling, once again, pioneered this idea as it applies to the interaction of different agents. [6] His insight can be stated in terms of a game between two players, X and Y (fig. 1).

In this game, X moves first. He can either terminate the game by moving left, in which case both get a reward of 3, or move right, in which case Y has the next move. In that case, Y can ensure 2 for herself and 4 for X if she moves left, whereas both get 1 if she moves right. Clearly, if Y is rational, she will move left. Similarly, if X is rational and knows that he can count on Y's rationality, he will move right. Note, however, that the outcome (4,2) is not what Y would most prefer. She would rather that X move left to the outcome (3,3). One way in which Y can achieve this goal is to *eliminate the option of going left at the second stage* or to reduce her payoff at that stage from 2 to 0. In that case, X will know that the outcome of going right will be (1,1). To avoid that outcome, he will rationally go left. In other words, Y obtains her best outcome by eliminating one of her options or by reducing the amount she would get by choosing that option.

More concretely, suppose that X and Y are opposing armies. X's first move corresponds to the choice between opening negotiations and attacking. If X chooses to attack, Y then has the choice between retreating and fighting. Because a war would be so destructive, it would then be in Y's interest to retreat. However, the commander of Y may use the classical stratagem of burning his bridges or his ships, thereby making retreat physically impossible and, as a consequence, bringing X to the negotiation table.

Individuals can also engage in such behavior with respect to themselves. The classical example is provided by Ulysses and the Sirens [7] involving a strategic relationship between an early and a later Ulyssean self. The early self, predicting that the later self if left to its own devices will succumb to the song of the Sirens, acts strategically to make that surrender physically impossible by making the men tie him to the mast and put wax in their own ears. On reflection, such behavior is very common. If I am afraid of my tendency to drink too much, I may limit my purchase to a small bottle. If I am afraid I will do something stupid at the office party, I may stay away. If I want to quit smoking, I can announce my intention publicly in a way that will ensure a great loss of prestige if I fail. In Stendhal's novel *Lucien Leuwen,* Madame de Chasteller provides herself with a chaperone to protect herself against the temptation of giving in to Lucien.

Two more complicated examples may be taken from treatment for mental illness or drug addiction. The Norwegian "Law of Psychic Health Protection" has the unique feature that a person may voluntarily seek irreversible admission to a mental hospital. To be precise, the medical director may lay down the condition for admission that the patient shall not be permitted to leave within three weeks of the admission date, even should he desire to do so. Even more drastically, "In a cocaine addiction center in Denver, patients are offered an opportunity to submit to extortion. They may write a self-incriminating letter, preferably a letter confessing their drug addiction, deposit the letter with the clinic, and submit to a randomized schedule of laboratory tests. If the laboratory finds evidence of cocaine use, the clinic sends the letter to the addressee." [8] If the addressee is suitably chosen, the patient's knowledge that reception of the letter will damage him substantially may deter him from backsliding.

Christmas savings clubs provide a further example. [9] For many years, such clubs paid no interest. Members deposited money each week but could only withdraw the money on December 1. We may explain the existence of these institutions by saying that they allowed members to pay a premium to protect themselves against their future lack of willpower. But one can also get the *bank* to pay the premium. Many banks allow for higher interest on accounts that can only be drawn upon once a year, more frequent withdrawals being penalized. A person who was afraid that he might not stick to his New Year's resolution to save could use this device to protect himself and gain the higher interest as a bonus. In this case premature withdrawal is not made impossible, as in the Christmas club, only more costly than it would otherwise have been. However, the general principle is similar.

Let me also mention two proposals—not implemented so far to my knowledge—along similar lines. We know that many people are afraid of going to the dentist. They make appointments, only to break them a day or two before they are due. To overcome this tendency, they might authorize their dentist to bill them thrice the normal fee for a canceled appointment. It is also well known that many people who buy one-year subscriptions to health centers stop going after the first couple of weeks. The problem might be overcome if a center, instead of charging $1,000 a year, charged $4,000 and then paid the clients $50 for each week they turned up. [10]

Weakness of will and self-control are perhaps the core issues of ego-nomics in its development so far. I shall have more to say about them below. But as the remainder of this essay will show, there are many other phenomena of intrapersonal conflict, manipulation, and change. I shall proceed as follows. Section II offers a succinct statement of the standard theory of rational choice. In the following sections, exceptions to and deviations from the standard model are noted. Section III provides a more general discussion of weakness of will, including but not limited to the special case of inability to delay gratification. Section IV discusses the phenomenon of "excess of will" and other self-defeating applications of instrumental rationality. Section V applies some principles of egonomics to the processes of preference formation and belief formation. Section VI discusses the mysterious ability of the mind to derive pleasure (and pain) from its own operations, through memory, anticipation and imagination. Section VII considers some of the intricate relationships among rationality, social norms, and emotions. In Section VIII, finally, I discuss all these mechanisms from the perspective of the agent who knows that he is subject to them and wants to exploit them, eliminate them, or limit the damage they can do to him. This implies a theory of self-control as a form of *imperfect rationality*—a theory of how one can rationally cope with one's known tendency to behave irrationally. It also implies a theory of *character planning*—a theory about how to change one's preferences so as to get the best out of life. Finally, it implies a theory of *life planning*—a theory of how to make choices in the present so as to take full account of their future consequences.

II. The theory of rational choice

The theory of rational choice is first and foremost a normative or prescriptive theory. It tells people how to choose and to act in order to achieve their aims as well as possible. It offers also, but only secondarily, an explanatory account of human behavior. In this perspective, the hypothesis is that one can explain how people act by assuming that they follow the prescriptions of the normative theory. In the following, I adopt the latter perspective.

The basic structure of rational-choice explanation of behavior is set out in figure 2. It involves three distinct conditions. First, for an action to be rational, it has to be the best means of satisfying the desires of the agent, given his beliefs. In itself, this is a very weak requirement. If I want to kill a person and I believe that the best way of doing so is to make a doll representing him and stick a pin through it, then according to this weak definition I act rationally if I make the doll and pierce it with a pin. We would hardly be satisfied with this conclusion, however, not because the homicidal desire is irrational (it may be immoral, but that is another matter), but because the beliefs are transparently ill-founded.

Second, therefore, we need to stipulate that the beliefs themselves are rational, in the sense of being grounded in the information that is available to the agent. These may be beliefs about factual matters or about general lawlike connections. In particular, they will include beliefs about the *opportunities* available to the agent. In fact, rational-choice theory is often stated in terms of desires and opportunities rather than desires and beliefs. In that "reduced" version, the theory says that a rational agent chooses the most-preferred element in his opportunity set. In some simple choice situations, this formulation is adequate. In general, however, we need to take account of the fact that the full set of objective opportunities available to the agent may not be known to him. Today, for instance, governments do not really know whether it is possible to develop commercially viable fusion power. Or, to take

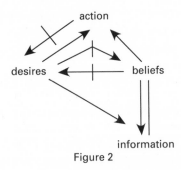

Figure 2

a more mundane example, an automobilist arriving in an unknown city without a map will not know the full set of paths that will take him through it.

In such cases, the agent must use whatever information he has, to form some belief or subjective estimate of the alternatives. The fact that it is subjective does not in itself detract from its rationality. On the contrary, *the concept of rationality as here defined is subjective through and through.* To be rational does not mean that one is invariably successful in realizing one's aims: it means only that one has no reason, after the fact, to think that one should have acted differently. Nor does a rational belief have to be true: it must only be well grounded in the available information. Beliefs are rational if they are formed by procedures that in the long run tend to produce more true beliefs than any alternative procedure, but on any particular occasion the belief thus formed may not correspond to the facts. This being said, belief formation *is* vulnerable to distorting influences of various kinds. Some of these are more in the nature of mistakes, as when we get sums wrong in arithmetic. Others, however, belong to the category of *motivated irrationality,* as when the adding-up errors made by a salesman systematically (although non-intentionally) work out to his favor. [11] In Section V I shall have more to say about such mechanisms.

However, a belief is not made rational simply by being well grounded in the available information. If the automobilist is in a hurry, he should perhaps buy a map to acquire more information about the feasible paths. The third condition for rational behavior, therefore, is that the agent should acquire an optimal amount of information or, more accurately, invest an optimal amount of time, energy, and money in gathering such information. Clearly, it will often be irrational not to invest any time in collecting information. If one is buying a house or a car, one should compare several options and investigate each of them in some depth. Equally clearly, there are occasions when there is a danger of gathering too much information. If a doctor makes too many tests before deciding on treatment, the patient may die under his hands. A general who insists on accurate information about the enemy's movement before attacking can easily be taken by surprise. In war, it may be more rational to follow Napoleon's advice: "On s'engage, et puis on voit." In between these extremes, there exists an optimal level of search, a "golden mean." (Whether this optimum can be known is another matter, to which I shall return.)

As depicted in figure 2, there are several factors which determine the amount of information that a rational agent will gather. The agent's beliefs about the expected costs and expected value of gathering the information will obviously matter. His desires—i.e., how important the decision is to him—will also enter into the calculus. Indirectly, therefore, the desires of the agents will enter into the process of belief formation. However, the blocked arrow from desires to beliefs in figure 2 is intended to indicate that a direct influence, as in wishful thinking, is inadmissible. (The other blocked arrows will be explained in Section V.)

Let me repeat that the arrows in figure 2 have a dual interpretation. On the one hand, they have the normative import of an optimality relation. On the other hand, they stand for causal relations. Thus an agent is rational if his desires and beliefs cause him to adopt the course of behavior that will best promote his desires, given his beliefs; and similarly for the other arrows. It follows that there are two ways in which the theory may fail: by *indeterminacy* or by *irrationality*. On the one hand, the theory may fail to define a uniquely defined action, belief, or amount of information. There might be several optima, or none. On the other hand, the agents might fail to conform to the prescriptions of the theory. In this essay, I focus on problems of irrationality. In Section IV, however, I shall also discuss some issues related to indeterminacy.

From inspection of figure 2 it is clear that the desires stand in a privileged position, as the unmoved mover of rational choice. This corresponds to a long-standing tradition in philosophy. As Hume said, "Reason is, and ought only to be the slave of the passions. . . ." [12] If one were to talk about rational desires, or about conditions under which a given desire might be said to be rational or irrational, one would elevate reason into a judge rather than a slave. As indicated by the blocked arrow from desires to beliefs in figure 2, passion should not be allowed to set itself up as an arbitrary tyrant. Even a slave needs some independence to serve his master well; beliefs born of passion serve passion badly. [13]

Another succinct expression of the supremacy of desires is the proverbial expression, "De gustibus non est disputandum." [14] One cannot argue about preferences. Any desire, or taste, is as good as any other. Some like vanilla, others like chocolate, and there's an end to it. In Section V I offer some objections to this view. Here I shall just mention one conundrum. Economists have introduced the terms *time preference* and *time discounting* for the fact that people value their welfare or utility differently according to the time at which it is experienced. Typically, the present and near future count for more than the distant future. Although part of the difference can be explained by the fact that we know that we shall die, but not when, empirical studies find that people discount the future much more heavily than can be justified on the basis of mortality tables. In fact, the reckless behavior of many young people suggests that they care less about the future than older people do, contrary to what the argument from mortality would imply. The young often act as if they were to die tomorrow and are intent on enjoying life while they can, whereas older people act as if they would live forever.

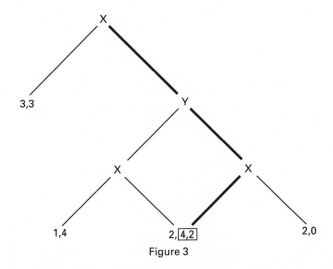

Figure 3

Most mainstream economists would hesitate to say that time preferences are irrational. For them, such preferences are nothing more
than a taste: some like the present, others like the future, and there's
an end to it. If high discounting of the future leads to self-destructive
behavior such as addiction, that only goes to show that addiction can
be rational. [15] However, I believe that it goes against intuition to
exempt time preferences from rationality assessment. Total, reckless
disregard of the future can lead to a miserable life and early death.
It seems perverse to claim that this attitude is as rational as a more
prudent outlook that also takes account of long-term effects of present
behavior. There is no *reason* for attaching more weight to one part
of one's life than to another, whereas there is a reason for giving
them equal weight, viz., that in this way one's life as a whole will be
better.

The exposition of rational-choice theory summarized in figure 2 is
incomplete on one point that deserves further discussion. As far as that
earlier discussion went, it could have been an analysis of the behavior
of Robinson Crusoe on his island before the arrival of Friday. However,
many important choices turn crucially on the presence of other agents
and on the anticipation of their choices. In the framework of figure 2,
strategic considerations enter at the point of belief formation. Before
he can act, an agent often has to form a belief about what other agents
are likely to do, knowing that they, too, make up their minds on the
basis of what they think he is likely to do. Figure 1 provides a simple
example. Here, X has to anticipate what Y will do before making up
his mind. However, Y has no occasion to worry about what X will do.
Figure 3 provides a more complex example, in which each party must
take account of what the other will do.

In this game X, counting on Y's rationality *and* counting on Y's counting on X's rationality, will begin by going right. At the next node in the game, Y will also go right, counting on X to go left in the final move. The outcome, therefore, will be (4,2). The reasoning behind these statements is as follows. From Y's perspective, she knows that if she goes left X will go right, leaving Y with 1. If she goes right, X will go left, leaving Y with 2. She will, therefore, go right. X knows, therefore, that if he goes right in his first move, Y will make a move that enables him to get 4, whereas he would only get 3 by going left in his first move. He will, consequently, move right. (As before, Y could induce him to go left if she could somehow reduce her reward from 2 to 0.) To reach his belief about what Y will do at the second stage, X needs the information that Y is rational *and* that she believes him to be rational. To reach her belief about what X will do at the last stage, Y only needs the information that X is rational. Note, therefore, that if Y has that information, but X does not have the information that she has it, he will not be able to form a rational belief about what she will do. The situation will be one of indeterminacy.

The analysis of belief formation in strategic interactions is usually referred to as *game theory*. Games with successive moves, such as those depicted in figures 1 and 3, are analyzed by moving from the last stages of the game up to the first stage. Games with simultaneous and independent moves require a different kind of analysis. A brief discussion follows.

Let us limit ourselves, merely for convenience, to two-person games. Each player has a set of possible choices, or strategies, at his disposal. When both players have chosen a strategy, both will receive a reward or payoff as a function of their choices. The task of game theory is to define the decisions that rational players will make under such circumstances. Because the moves are independent, the players cannot write a contract to realize a particular outcome. They have to reach an implicit agreement, by tacit convergence rather than explicit coordination. This problem of mutual adaptation, first recognized at the end of the seventeenth century, was for long thought to be unsolvable. It was believed to give rise to an infinite regress, "I think that he thinks that I think that he thinks . . ." that could never find any stable resting point.

The Gordian knot was cut, or the regress short-circuited, in work done by Ernst Zermelo, Émile Borel, and John von Neumann in the early years of this century. They introduced the notion of a game-theoretic *equilibrium,* a set of strategies that are optimal against each other. For the case of two-person games, we can illustrate the idea with two duopolists who have to decide how much to produce independently of each other. Given two such choices, demand will determine the price and, therefore, the profit of each producer. An equilibrium pair of choices has the property that neither duopolist would want to change his decision, given the decision of the other. Diagrammatically, this can be represented as in figure 4.

It stands to reason that if one duopolist increases his production, thus lowering the price, the other maximizes his profit by producing less. (This is equivalent to the perhaps more intuitive idea that when the price goes up, they will maximize profits by producing more.) The best-response curves will look, therefore, as in figure 4. The equilibrium is where the two curves cross: this pair of quantities are best responses to each other. This outcome is the *solution* to the game, that is, the focal point for tacit convergence. Because these quantities are optimal against each other, neither duopolist has an incentive to deviate from it. It is clear that this mutual optimality is a necessary condition for an outcome to be a solution. We shall see in a moment, however, that it is not a sufficient condition.

The duopoly game has two important features. First, there is only one equilibrium point. Second, neither player has a dominant strategy, that is, a strategy that is the optimal response to any strategy that the other player might choose. Figure 5 describes four well-known games that lack one or the other of these features.

In each game there are two players, X and Y. Each player has the choice between two strategies. In three of the games, these are called C and D, for "Cooperation" and "Defection." For each pair of strategy choices each player receives a reward or payoff, with the reward to X indicated as the first number and the reward of Y as the second. The circled outcomes are equilibria of the games, corresponding to pairs of strategies that are optimal against each other.

The Prisoner's Dilemma is the best-known of all strategic games. A huge literature has grown up around it, in the two-person version given here or in the more general *n*-person version discussed later. It

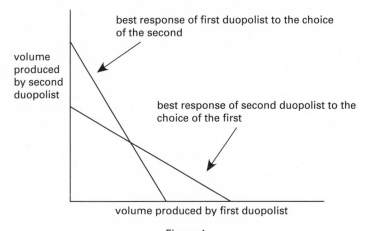

Figure 4

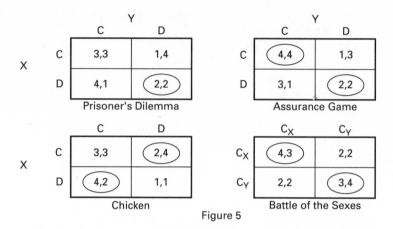

Figure 5

got its name from the following anecdote. Two prisoners are arrested, suspected of a crime, and put in separate cells. The police give the following instructions to each of them: "If you testify against your friend and he remains silent, you'll go free and he'll get ten years of prison. If both of you testify against one another, you'll get five years each. If both of you remain silent, you'll get one year each." Clearly, it is better for both if both choose the cooperative strategy and remain silent than if both defect and testify. Yet for each prisoner it is better to testify, regardless of what the other does. Defection, in other words, is a dominant strategy. Rational individuals acting independently of each other cannot attain the obviously desirable outcome of mutual cooperation. This is the case in trade union formation, cartel formation, pollution and littering, voting, and innumerable other situations. Some egonomical applications are considered in the next section.

The Assurance Game offers a more benign dilemma. Although mutual defection is an equilibrium point of the game, so is mutual cooperation. And as the latter is better for both parties, we will expect it to become the focal point for tacit convergence. This conclusion presupposes that the payoff matrix is common knowledge, that is, known by both players, known by both to be known by both, ad infinitum. Suppose, namely, that one player wrongly believes that the preferences of the other player are as in the Prisoner's Dilemma. Expecting the other to defect, he will choose to defect in his turn. Tax evasion may offer an example. Suppose that all taxpayers have Assurance Game preferences: they would like to pay their fair share of taxes, but only if others do so as well. Uncertainty about the preferences of other taxpayers may then lead them to defect.

The game of Chicken got its name from a deadly ritual of American juvenile culture: two car drivers are on a head-on collision course, and the first to swerve is "Chicken." This game, too, has two equilibria, in each of which one driver swerves and the other remains on course. Unlike the Assurance Game, however, the game of Chicken offers no clue as to which equilibrium will be chosen as rational players. The game, in fact, has no solution. The players will not be able to form rational beliefs about each other. Perhaps both will play safe and swerve—but this outcome is not an equilibrium. If one driver expects the other to swerve, he will do the opposite. Brinkmanship in war is the classical example of such behavior.

The Battle of the Sexes is named after the following sex-stereotyped anecdote. Suppose that a husband and a wife want to spend an evening together. His preferences are for going to a boxing match (C_X), hers are for going to the ballet (C_Y). They have a common interest in being together rather than apart, but opposed interests with regard to what they shall do in common. As in the game of Chicken, there are two equilibria; and as in that game, the situation offers no cue as to which of them will be the focal point of tacit convergence.

This thumbnail survey of strategic games was intended to bring out three points. First, individually rational behavior can be collectively disastrous. Second, a player's ability to form an accurate belief about what the other player will do depends on his information about the situation, and in particular on his information about the preferences and the information of the other player. Third, even with full information rational belief formation may be impossible: some games are inherently indeterminate. For the purposes of egonomical analysis, the first and the third point are the most important. As we shall see, something like the Prisoner's Dilemma can arise within the person as well as across persons (Section III). Also, indeterminacy of belief may trigger psychological mechanisms that go beyond rational choice (Section IV).

III. Weakness of will and time discounting

The archetypal interpersonal conflict is that expressed by Saint Paul: "For I do not do the good I want, but the evil I do not want is what I do" (Romans 7:19). It is reflected, too, in Augustine's famous prayer: "Give me chastity and continency, only not yet" (*GBWW* I: 18, 57; II: 16, 72). Aristotle referred to this phenomenon as incontinence or weakness of will (*akrasia*) (*GBWW* I: 9, 395–403; II: 8, 395–403). It must be distinguished both from inconstancy (change of will or desire) and from inconsistency (self-contradictory or self-defeating desires). As Aristotle noted, Socrates said that "no one . . . acts against what he judges best—people act so only by reason of ignorance" (*GBWW* I: 9, 395; II: 8, 395). Partly rejecting and partly accepting this view, Aristotle offered his own explanation by appealing to "the possibility of having knowledge in a sense and yet not having it, as in the instance of a man asleep, mad, or drunk. But now this is just the condition of men under the influence of passions; for outbursts of anger and sexual appetites and some other such passions, it is evident, actually alter our bodily condition, and in some men even produce fits of madness. It is plain, then, that incontinent people must be said to be in a similar condition to men asleep, mad, or drunk" (*GBWW* I: 9, 397; II: 8, 397).

But it is not clear that this explanation is adequate. When I fail to do the exercises I have prescribed for myself or to save for my old age, there is no need to suppose that I am under the sway of a passion that induces a temporary forgetfulness of what is best for me. I know full well that I ought to make the effort, and yet my will fails. Exactly how this happens remains a puzzle. [16] We can describe the phenomenon in general terms, and offer a somewhat more precise characterization of some particular cases, but the causal mechanism eludes us.

Weakness of will can be defined in terms of five conditions:

1. I have a desire to do x.
2. I have a desire to do y.
3. I believe that x and y are incompatible.
4. I believe that, all things considered, I should do x.
5. I do y.

In the best-studied case, which I consider in some detail below, x corresponds to a long-term goal and y to some short-term desire. I desire to avoid both the long-term pain of having bad teeth and the short-term pain of going to the dentist. I know I cannot avoid both. I believe I should go to the dentist, and I do in fact make an appointment with him. But the day before my appointment I call him up to cancel. Weakness of will could also arise in the opposite case, in which y corresponds to a long-term goal and x to some short-term desire. Suppose I do regular exercises to keep in shape. On a particular occasion, my limbs are so stiff that the exercises are quite painful. All things considered, I believe it would be best for me if I gave myself a break and skipped my exercises just for once. After all, one day does not make much of a difference. However, the very thought of breaking my promise to myself makes me feel so guilty that I decide to do my exercises after all. I shall return to this phenomenon in the concluding section. In another set of cases, x and y might be acts that promote, respectively, the welfare of others and my own welfare. I may form a resolution to visit an aging relative and put it off until it is too late. Conversely, even if less typically, x might be the act that promotes my own welfare and y the act that promotes the welfare of others. Many women, for instance, have been socialized into thinking that their welfare takes second place to that of their family members. As above, feelings of guilt may prevent them from giving themselves a break.

Let us now consider the first case—the incontinent choice of a short-term pleasure over a long-term benefit—in more detail. Earlier, I said that for mainstream economists the relation between present and future pleasures is like that between vanilla and chocolate ice cream: a matter of taste. I did not intend to say that the taste has to be an exclusive one, so that somebody who prefers vanilla will never have chocolate. Rather, people may like both kinds of ice cream and trade them off against each other. To bring out the point more clearly, I shall switch from the chocolate-vanilla example to a choice that involves meat and potatoes.

We assume that people have preferences with regard to different combinations or pairs of meat and potatoes. Sometimes, they will be indifferent between two such pairs, e.g., between one that has a lot of meat and little potatoes and one that has a lot of potatoes and little meat. The curve labeled X in figure 6 is called an indifference curve because the agent is indifferent among all the pairs that lie on this curve. The curve labeled Y is another such indifference curve. The agent prefers any pair on Y to any pair on X, but is indifferent among all pairs on a given curve. The shape of the curves expresses the *trade-off* between meat and potatoes. When the agent has only a little meat, as in point A, a small loss of meat must be compensated by a large increase in potatoes to make him as well off as he was before. When he already has a lot of meat, as in point B, the same loss of meat can be offset by a smaller increase in potatoes.

Similarly, the fact that an agent prefers the present over the future does not imply that he does not care about the future at all, only that there is a trade-off between how much he gets and how soon he gets it.

A trade-off of this kind is expressed in figure 7. At time 1, the agent knows that at time 3 he shall receive a reward worth 10. With regard to any earlier moment such as time 2, we can ask him to specify the amount he would need to receive at time 2 in order to be indifferent *at*

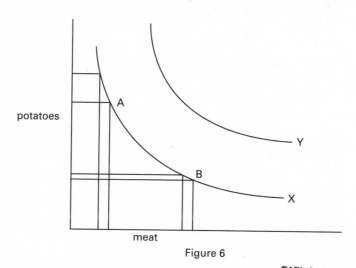

Figure 6

time 1 between getting that amount at time 2 and getting 10 at time 3. Figure 7 indicates that from the perspective of time 1, he is indifferent between getting 4 at time 2 and getting 10 at time 3. Moreover, at time 1 he is also indifferent between getting 2 at time 1 and getting 10 at time 3. The *present value* of that future reward is 2.

Let us now consider an agent faced with a choice between a smaller, earlier reward and a larger, delayed reward.

At time 1, a reward of 6 is made available to the agent. He can either take it or wait until time 2 to get a reward of 10. The time preferences as shown in figure 8 immediately tell us that he will take the smaller reward rather than wait for the larger one. At time 1, the present value of the larger reward is about 3, much less than the smaller reward. Moreover, at any time before time 1, the present value of the earlier smaller reward is larger than that of the delayed, larger reward. If we

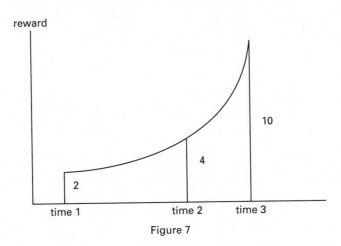

Figure 7

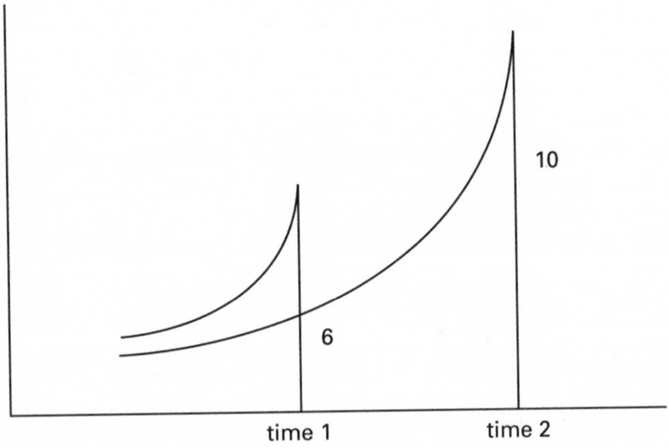

Figure 8

ask the agent, well ahead of time 1, what he will do at time 1, he will answer that he intends to take the earlier reward. And when the time to choose arrives, he will in fact do what he said he would. This is *not* an instance of weakness of will, because there is no conflict between what the agent intends to do and what he in fact does.

The shape of the time preference curve in figure 7 reflects an assumption that people discount the future *coherently*, in the following sense. Consider three moments: time 1, time 2, and time 3. At time 1, the agent is indifferent between getting a given reward at time 3 and getting two-fifths that reward at time 2. At time 2, a time-coherent agent will also be indifferent between getting two-fifths the reward at time 2 and the full reward at time 3. In other words, the *relative* evaluation of the rewards offered at times 2 and 3 is not affected by the time at which the evaluation is made, although the absolute evaluation is. If the relative evaluation was time-dependent, the agent might not be able to stick to his decisions. He might think, at time 1, that at time 2 he will be indifferent between the two options, and yet at time 2 find himself to prefer the earlier, smaller reward. More to the point, at time 1 he may prefer the larger reward to the smaller reward, and yet find that his preferences are reversed at time 2.

Such preference reversal can be interpreted as weakness of will. It seems reasonable to assume that the preferences that the agent forms well ahead of the time of choice reflect his well-considered judgment. At the time he makes his appointment with the dentist, he fully believes that avoiding the long-term pains of toothache is more important than avoiding the short-term pain of the dentist's drill. However, as the latter pain becomes imminent, his evaluation of the two options is reversed. Acting against his own better judgment, he cancels the appointment.

This predicament is expressed in figure 9, showing time preference curves that cross each other at time 0 before the early reward becomes available. Prior to that time, e.g., at time t*, the agent believes that he ought to take the greater, delayed reward. However, as the time of choice approaches, the earlier, smaller reward becomes preferred. The agent, we typically say, yields to temptation.

In many cases, this is indeed an accurate description. I may have decided not to order sweets at the restaurant, but when the dessert trolley comes around, I simply cannot help myself. Many cases of weakness of will are like this—but not all. As mentioned above, failures to exercise or to save are not due to the presence of an overwhelming temptation. Rather, they occur because *the structure of subjective time is warped,* in the way described in figure 9. Although recognized by R. H. Strotz as early as 1955, the phenomenon of incoherent time references did not receive much attention until Ainslie observed that it can be derived from a more general law of behavior, the so-called matching law formulated by Richard J. Herrnstein. [17] Ainslie has also marshaled impressive empirical evidence which suggests that such time preferences are the rule rather than the exception.

It is important to note that preference reversal can occur without any change in the agent: it illustrates incontinence rather than inconstancy. As we move from left to right in figure 9, the agent remains the same. The only change occurs in the environment. To bring the point home, consider the following parable. A young man inherits five million dollars. He decides that he will use half of the inheritance to go on a big spending spree in the first year, and then live off the interest for the rest of his life. However, at the beginning of the second year, he decides to use half of what remains, one and a quarter million, to go on a somewhat smaller spree, and then live off the remaining one and a quarter for the rest of his life. At the beginning of the third year, he changes his mind once again, in favor of a moderate spree and a smaller annuity; and so on. In this story the agent does not change at all; at the beginning of each year, he is guided by the same, albeit incoherent, time preferences: to spend half of his fortune in that year and then divide the other half evenly over the rest of his life.

In the preceding we have tacitly presupposed that the agent faces a single choice between an early, small reward and a delayed, larger reward. Some cases are indeed like this. Someone who postpones going to the dentist with an aching tooth knows that he is exposing himself to greater pain later on. But many cases have a more complicated structure. First, the delayed reward often takes the form of many small increments in welfare rather than a single big gain. The exercises I do on any given day have a slight, virtually imperceptible impact on my health on all later days. However, the sum total of all these small gains is typically larger than the welfare foregone by doing the exercises. Second, many of these choice situations occur over and over again. The

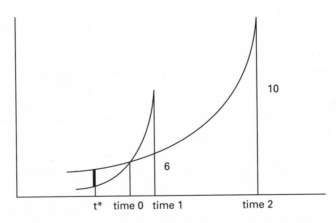

Figure 9

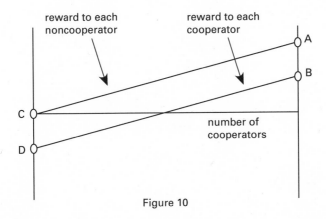

Figure 10

choice whether to do my exercises or to stay in bed is one I face every morning. Every day that I go shopping I have to fight my desire to buy a pint of butter pecan ice cream, knowing that if I buy it I shall not be able to resist consuming it.

Such cases present an intrapersonal analogue to the Prisoner's Dilemma, where the game is played not among different individuals but among the successive "selves" of one person. [18] To motivate this idea, let me first explain how the two-person Prisoner's Dilemma explained in Section II can be generalized to an arbitrary number of persons. [19]

We assume, as before, that each individual has a choice between co-operating and defecting (i.e., not cooperating). We assume, moreover, that the rewards of cooperators and noncooperators depend on the number of cooperators, as indicated in figure 10. The act of voting, doing one's civic duty, can serve as an example. The more people who vote, the greater the legitimacy and stability of the democratic system—a fact from which both voters and nonvoters benefit. However, the net benefit of voters is smaller than that of nonvoters because they incur the costs of voting. The key point is that the incremental stability of

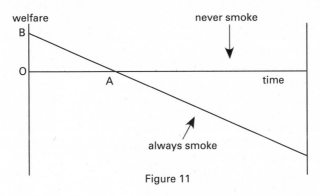

Figure 11

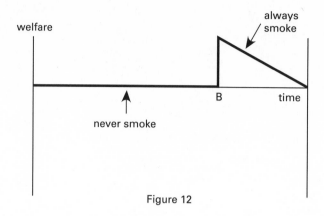

Figure 12

democracy caused by a single voter is very small, and certainly not enough to offset the costs to him of voting, that is, the trouble and sometimes the expense involved in going to the polls. However, the sum of all the small benefits he creates for other citizens exceeds the cost to him of voting. *It is better for all if all vote, but better for each not to vote.* The points A, B, C, D correspond to the four outcomes in the two-person Prisoner's Dilemma: unilateral noncooperation, universal cooperation, universal noncooperation, and unilateral cooperation. In addition, there are a number of intermediate possibilities.

We can apply similar reasoning to construct an intrapersonal Prisoner's Dilemma. Consider, for instance, the habit of smoking. Using the metaphor of successive selves, we can say that each smoking self imposes a small harm on each of its successor selves. As before, the sum total of these small harms exceeds the momentary benefits, such as relaxation, from smoking. And as before, the harm, if any, that the current self imposes on itself by smoking is less than the momentary benefit. Hence, we might conclude, in terms of the pleasure-pain calculus it is better for all selves if all selves abstain from smoking, but better for each to smoke.

However, a moment's reflection shows that these statements are somewhat inaccurate. The analogy between the interpersonal and the intrapersonal case is not, in fact, exact. Because of the asymmetry of time, earlier selves cannot be harmed by the actions undertaken by later selves. As indicated in figure 11, it is better for the earlier selves if all selves smoke than if all abstain. To be precise, smoking is better than abstaining up to the time A, at which the cumulative damage from past smoking equals the current benefit from smoking. It is better for *the person* if he never smokes than if he always smokes: the area of the triangle over the horizontal line is smaller than that of the triangle below the line. And yet at any given moment smoking may look preferable.

This line of argument suggests that one ought to start smoking (or stop exercising, or whatever) toward the end of life. The optimal time profile of abstaining and smoking would seem to be as indicated by the thickly drawn line in figure 12. The conclusion is somewhat undermined by the following two considerations. First, although we know that we shall die, we usually do not know the exact date. Second, our life span is itself affected by our smoking behavior. Yet even taking these facts into account, egonomics does suggest that it makes sense to be somewhat less hard on oneself in one's old age. Certainly, there is no point anymore in saving, except for one's children. However, as we shall see in the final section, habits of abstention may be as hard to kick as addictions.

Above I asserted that it is better for the person if all selves abstain than if all selves smoke, but better for each self to smoke. The second half of that statement assumes that each self is interested only in its own pleasures, and not in those of its successors. In other words, the present value of future pleasures is zero. The similar assumption in the interpersonal case is that each individual cares only about his own welfare and not at all about that of others. In both cases, the Prisoner's Dilemma will be "solved"—that is, the cooperative behavior will be elicited—if each self or agent counts the welfare of others on a par with his own. In the interpersonal case, this would be a utilitarian motivation: to maximize the sum total of welfare or happiness in society. In the intrapersonal case, the motivation would be a prudential one: to maximize the agent's total welfare over time.

In most actual cases, agents behave neither in a totally shortsighted and selfish manner nor in a totally prudential and utilitarian manner. People attach some importance to the future, but less than they attach to the present. They care somewhat about others, but less than they care about themselves. Whether the Dilemma will be solved in such cases depends on a number of factors. Clearly, it matters *how much* they care about others, and how much others care about their cooperation. Also, the tendency to cooperate or to behave prudentially depends on the cost of cooperating, as measured for instance by the distance between the two lines in figure 10 or the distance OB in figure 11. Finally, cooperation and prudence may depend on one's ability to overcome problems of weakness of will.

IV. Excess of will and hyperrationality

The phenomenon of "excess of will"—a phrase taken from Leslie H. Farber—is not exactly the opposite of weakness of will. [20] It does not denote an excessive amount of willpower but rather the misguided and self-defeating attempt to achieve by the will what cannot be achieved at will. Paradigmatic cases include intentional attempts to overcome insomnia, sexual impotence, or stuttering by sheer will. Consider insomnia, for instance. The following stages seem to correspond to a common pattern. First, one tries to will an empty mind, to blot out all preoccupying thoughts. The attempt, of course, is contradictory and doomed to fail, since it requires a concentration of mind that is incompatible with the absence of concentration one is trying to bring about. Second, upon understanding that this is not going to work, one tries to induce a state of pseudo-resignation to insomnia. One acts, that is, as if one were persuaded that sleep is going to elude one, by taking up a book, having a snack or a drink, etc. But at the back of one's mind there is always the idea that one can cheat insomnia by ignoring it, and that the cheerful indifference to sleep will make sleep come at last. Next, real resignation sets in, based on a real, not a sham, conviction that the night will be long and bleak. And then, finally and mercifully, sleep comes. For veteran insomniacs, who know the game inside out, the last stage never arrives. They know too well the benefits of resignation to be able to attain it.

Sleep belongs to the class of *states that are essentially by-products*. [21] Although such states may *come about* as the by-product of intentional action, they cannot be *brought about* as the main, intended goal of such action. Or, rather, they cannot be brought about by will in the direct, immediate sense in which one may raise one's arm at will. Indirect strategies are often possible. For instance, I can will sleep at two removes, by taking a sleeping pill. I return to such stratagems in the concluding section. Here, I shall focus on the "naive" attitude, which precludes (and precedes) the use of such sophisticated remedies.

Impotence and stuttering are largely similar to insomnia. The reason why they cannot be overcome at will is due to the phenomenon of *interference*. The very act of trying interferes with the state one tries to achieve. Attempts to achieve spontaneity and forgetfulness stumble over themselves in the same way, which is why the injunctions "Be spontaneous" or "Please forget what I told you" are unlikely to succeed.

Another class of cases includes such states as self-respect and self-esteem. Every year, millions of books are sold which hold out the prospect of raising one's self-esteem by sheer bootstrapping. By telling oneself "I am OK," or using similar incantations, one is supposed to achieve the self-confidence to go out and achieve things which will justify that confidence. Although I do not know of any studies of the long-term effects of such books, I strongly believe that in most cases they are insignificant or even harmful. The technique amounts, in fact, to putting the cart before the horse. Self-esteem can only arise as a by-product of activities undertaken for other motives than that of raising one's self-esteem. Hence, for instance, work relief programs initiated for the sole purpose of maintaining the morale of the work force are unlikely to succeed in that aim. [22]

A similar analysis applies to beliefs. Often, holding a certain belief may be instrumentally useful, independently of its truth value. Thus it has been argued that "protective self-deception" can be a cure for addiction: if the individual can convince himself—or pay others to convince him—that the dangers of addiction are even greater than they in fact are, he is more likely to get off the hook. [23] Or consider a famous argument of Pascal's: If there is a God the belief that there is a God will be extremely useful, and if there is no God the belief will cause me little harm; conversely, lack of faith will have extremely bad consequences in the first case and matter relatively little in the second. [24] However, it goes against the canons of reasoning to believe in a proposition simply because of the useful consequences that will flow from believing in it. [25] The justification of a belief must be sought upstream rather than downstream, in the reasons for holding the belief rather than in the effects of holding it. Even someone persuaded by Pascal's argument might find himself unable to muster the requisite belief. Pascal's solution to this dilemma is discussed in the final section.

Self-fulfilling beliefs might appear to be a special case. Thus we may view *trust* as the decision to believe that another will behave decently and honestly, hoping that this very belief will induce that behavior. Montaigne argued, however, that such calculated trust will fail to achieve its objective: "It is an excellent way to win the heart and mind of another man to go and trust him, putting yourself in his power— provided it be done freely, quite unconstrained by necessity, and on condition that the trust we bring is clear and pure, and that at least our brow is not weighed down by hesitation." [26] The paradox is that only noninstrumental trust will bring the instrumental benefits one is hoping for. In theory, one might be able to fake genuine trust and derive the corresponding benefits. In practice, faking tends to be shown up by the brow "weighed down by hesitation." As research on lying has shown, people have little control over the facial expressions that betray falseness or insincerity. [27]

The thrust of these arguments and examples is that there is a need to circumscribe the boundaries of reason. In fact, *the first task of a theory of rational choice must be to inquire into its own limitations.* There are mental states that simply are not attainable as the direct outcome of rational decision making. As Farber puts it, "I can will knowledge, but not wisdom; going to bed, but not sleeping; eating, but not hunger; meekness, but not humility; scrupulosity, but not virtue; self-assertion or bravado, but not courage; lust, but not love; commiseration, but not sympathy; congratulations, but not admiration; religiosity, but not faith; reading, but not understanding." [28] In fact, even utility—happiness or welfare—has the tantalizing property of eluding the mind that reaches out for it. As Donald Davidson observes, "Moralists from Aristotle to Mill have pointed out that trying to be happy is unlikely to produce happiness." [29] I am not claiming that this observation undermines the economist's sacrosanct notion that people strive to maximize utility, but it ought to make us question the tacit assumption that they generally succeed in doing so. [30]

The refusal to respect the limits of reason is a specific type of irrationality that we may refer to as *hyperrationality.* The by-product fallacies are but one species of this genus. Another species derives from the need of human beings to have decisive reasons for each and every choice they make. To be in a state of indeterminacy is so painful that people want to avoid it if they can. To do so, they often adopt the hyperrational strategy of gathering more information than is rationally warranted. Consider again the driver who is about to drive through a town he has never visited before. When entering the town, he has a choice between driving left or right, with no signs to guide him. He can either choose one road at random or stop to buy a map. The latter course will enable him to make a rational decision, in the sense of a decision that he can defend by an appeal to reasons. But it may not be rational to take that course, if it takes more time to buy the map and figure out the fastest road than he can expect to save by doing so.

This may not seem like a very important problem. But there are other cases in which the need to have reasons for everything can lead one seriously astray. Samuel Johnson was concerned with this issue, as is evident from these excerpts from Boswell's *Life:*

> Life is not long, and too much of it must not pass in idle deliberation how it shall be spent; deliberation, which those who begin it by prudence, and continue with subtilty, must, after long expence of thought, conclude by chance. To prefer one future mode of life to another, upon just reasons, requires faculties which it has not pleased our Creator to give us (*GBWW* I: 44, 149; II: 41, 149).
>
> We talked of the education of children; and I asked him what he thought was best to teach them first. JOHNSON. "Sir, it is no matter what you teach them first, any more than what leg you shall put into your breeches first. Sir, you may stand disputing which is best to put in first, but in the mean time your breech is bare. Sir, while you are considering which of two things you should teach your child first, another boy has learnt them both" (*GBWW* I: 44, 128; II: 41, 128).
>
> "He did not approve of late marriages, observing that more was lost in point of time, than compensated for by any possible advantages. Even ill assorted marriages were preferable to cheerless celibacy" (*GBWW* I: 44, 182; II: 41, 182).

The first passage argues that in some decisions, such as the choice of a career, there is no right answer to be found: one might just as well flip a coin at the outset as to engage in a lengthy process of deliberation which, in the end, will do no better. The other passages argue that even when there is a right answer, the time we spend on finding it may be excessive, compared to the expected gains. Again, we might just as well flip a coin, or take the first opportunity that presents itself. A rational decision-making procedure must take account of the fact that *cost-benefit analysis itself is costly.* When people fail to draw the proper implications of this fact, it need not simply be an oversight. It can also happen because they are, as it were, *addicted to reason.*

Professionals often face problems of this sort. Consider a doctor who has to decide on the treatment of a severely wounded patient. On the one hand, he knows that the more time he can spend on determining the diagnosis, the better his chances to save the life of the patient, other things being equal. On the other hand, he knows that other things are not equal, because every minute spent on diagnosis increases the risk of the patient dying on him. Military officers and businessmen regularly find themselves in similar predicaments. In these lines of work, success comes to those who can resist the Sirens of reason, and recognize that sometimes what matters is to reach some decision, almost *any* decision, rather than the mythical best decision. [31] As Montaigne said, "As for military exploits, anyone can see that Fortune plays a major part in them; even in our very reflections and deliberations there certainly has to be an element of chance and good luck mingled in with them; all that our wisdom can do does not amount to much: *the more acute and lively she is the more frailty she finds within herself and the more she distrusts herself.*" [32]

The legal system invites hyperrationality. It is a general principle of the law that the legal process should not be constrained by costs. Prosecutors, litigants, and defendants should be allowed to present their case, bring witnesses, and appeal decisions unconstrained by the costs to society of doing so. In the long run and in the general case, the practice can probably be justified by its social benefits. In some cases, however, it may have perverse and undesirable effects. The example I have in mind is that of child custody litigation. [33] Under the current law in most Western countries, the allocation of custody is guided by "the best interest of the child." The legal implementation of this principle is that the court should decide whether the father or the mother is better suited to have the main responsibility for bringing up the child. The determination can be very time-consuming. Because of scheduling problems and successive appeals, it can take as much as two years before a final decision is reached. In the meantime, the child undergoes a great deal of suffering. In fact, in a large class of divorces, in which both parents are perfectly capable of raising the child, the cost to the child of the custody litigation is larger than the cost of ending up with the "wrong" parent. Where that is so, the process of determining what is in the best interest of the child is against the best interest of the child. [34] Children, in fact, would probably be better served by a simple, mechanical principle, such as return to the maternal presumption rule or even the flip of a coin. In the words of some prominent writers on the topic, "Simplicity is the ultimate sophistication in deciding a child's placement"; echoing a phrase by Descartes, "The greatest subtlety lies in not applying any subtlety"; or Pascal's dictum, "Nothing is so much in conformity with reason as this disavowal of reason." [35]

V. Some mechanisms of preference and belief formation

In the "standard model" of rational choice set out in Section II, the desires or preferences of the agent are usually taken as given and constant. Their explanation is usually relegated to other disciplines, such as biology, psychology, or sociology. The beliefs of the agent are not similarly taken as a given but assumed to be optimal responses to the agent's information, which is further supposed to be the result of an optimal search process. In this section I explore some other approaches.

Recall from Section II that in the "reduced" form of rational-choice theory, action is the joint outcome of desires and opportunities. The following two propositions are implicit in the theory. First, the desires are given independently of the opportunities. This condition is reflected in the blocked arrow from beliefs to desires in figure 2. (Recall here that the beliefs include beliefs about the opportunities.) Second, the desires are independent of the action. This condition is reflected in the blocked arrow from action to desires in figure 2. The blocking of these arrows expresses the idea that such influences are normatively undesirable. However, as we shall see, they may be quite widespread in actual behavior.

A classic example of preferences being shaped by the available opportunities (or, more accurately, by the agent's belief about the opportunities) is the fable of the fox and the sour grapes. [36] Upon finding the grapes were out of his reach, the fox decided that they were not really very attractive. Innumerable examples of this mechanism can be found in everyday life. If I do not get the promotion I coveted, I rationalize defeat by telling myself that the top job involves so much stress that it is not worth having anyway. If a woman turns down my proposal of marriage, it may not take long before I find reasons for disliking her. In the late nineteenth century, many Chinese intellectuals responded to Western superiority by asserting that the high-technology path was an option that China had faced and rejected centuries before. [37] People living under conditions of Communist totalitarianism often managed to persuade themselves that unemployment was worse than massive inefficiency, that drug abuse was worse than rampant alcoholism, and that the only freedom offered by capitalist societies was the freedom for rich and poor alike to sleep under the bridges.

Underlying such "adaptive preferences" is the mechanism of "cognitive dissonance reduction" described by Leon Festinger. [38] Cognitive dissonance is the tension or uneasiness that arises when two or more elements of our conscious mind are at odds with one another, for instance when we strongly desire an object that we also believe we cannot get, or when we have made a decision while harboring the suspicion that another choice might have been superior. In such cases, there is a tendency to adjust one of the elements to get it in line with the other and reduce the dissonance. This mechanism operates unconsciously, "behind our back" as it were, and can be detected only by its results. As we shall see in the final section, it must be sharply distinguished from the conscious character planning advocated by Buddhist or Stoic philosophers.

The claim, made above, that preferences can be shaped by the decision might appear more obscure. How can the desires, which precede the action in the causal sequence, be shaped by the latter? Taken literally, the idea is indeed meaningless. However, there is evidence for some closely related mechanisms. Assume that relative to the agent's initial preference, the two top-ranked options appear almost equally good. If the agent chose one without a change of preference, he might constantly be torn about whether he had made the right choice, especially if the decision was an important or irreversible one. To reduce the dissonance this state would entail, he can then do one of the following. On the one hand, he can adjust his preferences before making the choice, so as to make one of the options appear clearly superior to the other. [39] On the other hand, he can go ahead and make the choice and then, after the fact, readjust his preferences so as to feel more confident in the decision he just made. [40] In a one-shot decision, such adjustments make little difference to what would have happened in any case. It makes the agent feel more at peace with himself, without any detrimental side effects. However, the choice-induced preferences might also come into play on later occasions, when the decisions might differ from what they would otherwise have been. In fact, an agent might be led to choose alternatives that he would have decisively rejected if guided by his initial preferences. The tale by Hans Christian Andersen discussed below illustrates this possibility in a closely related case.

Clearly, these mechanisms are related to the phenomenon of hyperrationality discussed in Section IV. The common feature is a *need for certainty* which may, to some extent, be seen as a sign of irrationality and immaturity. Conversely, it has been said that "the ability to tolerate ignorance [is] an essential characteristic of the scientific attitude." [41] The need for certainty takes different expressions in the two cases. Whereas the preferences of the hyperrational agent remain unaffected, he goes to irrational lengths in gathering information about the alternatives. The agent described in the previous paragraph is not irrational in the same clear-cut sense. However, if the choice-induced preference change makes him steadily worse off in a material sense, as in the Andersen tale, we might question his rationality. Also, the very fact of being the plaything of psychic forces that operate outside the agent's conscious control might seem hard to square with the intuitive notion of what it means to be rational.

It is less clear that the victim of the "sour grapes" syndrome is irrational. By adapting to the inevitable, he is not made worse off materially, and he would seem to be made better off psychologically. However, we may raise a couple of questions. First, the close analogy between adaptive preference formation and wishful thinking (*see* below), and the clear irrationality of the latter, might suggest that the former, too, is a sign of irrationality. Second, there may be a tendency for people to "overadapt" to circumstances in a way that involves nontrivial costs. Suppose my rival at the office gets the promotion that I coveted. Although my first reaction is to denigrate the job I failed to get, my second may be to denigrate the rival who got it. The self-poisoning of the mind that can occur on these occasions is very different from the peaceful resignation to the inevitable that characterizes more conscious and deliberate forms of adaptation.

The converse of the sour grapes syndrome we might call "counter-adaptive preference formation," as in the proverb "The grass is always greener on the other side of the fence." We need to distinguish three different phenomena: people can align their preferences with what they do not have, with what they cannot have, and with what they are not supposed to have. The first is the sheer desire for novelty, as distinct from conservatism or preference for the status quo. Some examples are offered below. The second is the tendency to desire objects that are not merely absent or forbidden, but strictly unattainable, as if the fox were to develop a craving for grapes simply because he could not have them. Children are often attracted to other children's toys, only to lose all interest when they get the same toy for themselves. The third corresponds to the proverb "Forbidden fruit tastes best," as distinct from a preference for legitimate options. The attraction of extramarital relationships often owes a great deal to this mechanism. Conversely, it has often been argued that liberalizing divorce laws will increase rather than decrease the stability of marriages. Montaigne wrote that "We thought we were tying our marriage-knots more tightly by removing all means of undoing them; but the tighter we pulled the knot of constraint the looser and slacker became the knot of our will and affection. In Rome, on the contrary, what made marriages honoured and secured for so long was freedom to break them at will." [42]

Sometimes, conservatism and the desire for novelty can operate simultaneously. I know from my own profession—no doubt similar phenomena occur elsewhere—that upon receiving an offer from another university, academics are often torn and indecisive. On the one hand, they believe that their intermittent inclination to take up the offer and move elsewhere could be due to an irrational preference for novelty. On the other hand, they fear that their intermittent reluctance to accept the offer may be due to an equally irrational fear of novelty. I believe that sometimes both beliefs are in fact warranted. What happens in such cases is that the agent's preferences over the states become inextricably intertwined with preferences over the change from one state to another. The agent may truly be said not to know his own mind—perhaps because there is nothing for him to know!

Hans Christian Andersen's story "What Father Does Is Always Right" illustrates the pure preference for novelty. In this tale a farmer goes to the market in the morning to sell or exchange his horse. First, he meets a man with a cow, which he likes so much that he exchanges it for the horse. In successive transactions, the cow is then exchanged for a sheep, the sheep for a goose, the goose for a hen, and the hen, finally, for a sack of rotten apples. The farmer's road to ruin is paved with apparent stepwise improvements.

Egonomics can model this story in the following way. [43] Consider a person who at successive times is asked to choose between two consumption bundles, each containing varying quantities of two different goods. Assume, moreover, that his preferences change in a way that corresponds to a strong desire for novelty, so that he will always accept a change from the bundle (a_1, a_2) to another bundle (b_1, b_2) if $a_1 < a_2$ and $a_1 < b_1$. In words, he will always accept a change that gives him more of the good of which he currently has less. If, for instance, we consider the sequence $(1/4, 3/4), (1/2, 1/4), (1/6, 1/2), (1/3, 1/6) \ldots$, we can see that at any stage he will prefer the next bundle over the one currently in his possession, and yet the sequence converges toward zero. The agent, to use a fanciful expression, is improving himself to death.

Let us now turn to some mechanisms of belief formation, using as our point of departure the blocked arrow from desires to beliefs in figure 2. Although proscribed by rationality, the phenomenon of wishful thinking is of course massively widespread. It can be seen as a form of maximization, with two special features. First, the agent is merely seeking the short-term pleasure of believing that he will get what he wants rather than the long-term satisfaction of actually getting it. Second, the process is one of unconscious adjustment and adaptation rather than one of conscious choice. As I said above, we cannot choose our beliefs, and even if we could we would not choose beliefs simply for the immediate gratification they can offer.

Wishful thinking has much in common with adaptive preference formation. They are both triggered by a phenomenon of cognitive dissonance: I wish that x were the case, but I believe that x is not the case. In this predicament the mature or rational reaction is to try to make x

the case or, failing that, to accept that I have to live with my frustrated desire. The Serenity Prayer of Alcoholics Anonymous sums it up: "God grant me the serenity to accept the things I cannot change, courage to change the things I can, and the wisdom to know the difference." Alternatively, we may cope by ceasing to wish for x or by adopting the belief, in the face of the evidence, that x is in fact the case. When all the signs indicate that I will be denied promotion, I may either tell myself that the job I sought is not worth having or persuade myself that I will get it. When the woman I court rejects me, I may interpret her refusal as a conventional ploy—or find some character flaw in her that offers me a modicum of peace of mind. In fact, as in Mr. Collins's proposal to Elizabeth Bennet in *Pride and Prejudice,* the refusal itself may be seen as indicating a stubborn character that would not be conducive to a happy marriage. Whereas some nineteenth-century Chinese faced with the challenge from the West reacted by downplaying the value of technical achievements, others engaged in wishful thinking by arguing that it was possible to adopt Western technology without sacrificing the Chinese essence—to have industrialization without modernization. [44]

A puzzling and ill-understood problem concerns the relation between wishful thinking and self-deception. The latter notion implies that the self is divided: one part of the agent knows the truth, and another part denies it. The former does not have this implication. When people spontaneously attach excessive weights to the evidence that favors the belief they would like to be true, there is no reason to assume that they have already carried out a more accurate assessment which then has to be denied. Wishful thinking is irrational but not paradoxical. Self-deception, by contrast, is often thought to embody a paradox. [45] It is not a mere compartmentalization of belief but an active, intentional, motivated process. It is difficult to understand how this process takes place—and equally hard to deny that it sometimes does. In fact, to say that one is never subject to self-deception could be an instance of that very phenomenon.

To see the paradox more clearly, let us take a Freudian perspective and view self-deception as involving a relationship between the conscious and the unconscious self. The unconscious self believes something to be the case, and the conscious self does not. There are then two possibilities. Either the agent of deception is the unconscious, which somehow refrains from bringing the forbidden thought to the attention of the unconscious. But why would the unconscious do that? As usually conceived, it cares about nothing but the immediate gratification of the organism. Or the agent is located in the conscious self, which actively denies or represses the forbidden thought. But to repress a thought you must first have it—and then you cannot repress it. The state of not-thinking-about-something or not-believing-that-something-is-the-case is essentially a by-product, as explained in the previous section.

Needless to say, there are innumerable other mechanisms of preference formation and belief formation in addition to those surveyed here. I have focused on this particular set of mechanisms because they are related to the economic idea of maximization. Cognitive dissonance reduction, whether it takes the form of changing the agent's desires or his beliefs, is a tension-minimizing or peace-maximizing mechanism, at least with respect to the short run. However, as we have seen, the adjustment of desires or beliefs to reduce dissonance can also have undesirable side effects or long-term consequences. The desire of the conscious self to maximize long-term, overall welfare is constantly undermined by the tendency of the unconscious to seek immediate gratification. Rationality involves the ability to use indirect strategies, of the type "one step backward, two steps forward." An agent who will accept a change if and only if it brings immediate improvement will often do badly in the long run. Andersen's farmer offers one illustration of this general proposition. The myopic pleasure-seeking of the unconscious mind offers another.

Nevertheless, these phenomena do at least exhibit a degenerate form of rationality. The phenomena of counteradaptive preferences and of congenital pessimism—the tendency to believe that the world is *not* as one would like it to be—are more puzzling. These mechanisms seem to generate dissonance rather than reduce it. They do not even provide short-term gratification, let alone serve any long-term purpose. Perhaps we can explain their operation by assuming a short circuit in "the wirings of the pleasure machine," to use Amos Tversky's felicitous phrase. But there might also be a deeper explanation. The congenital pessimist is not simply one who errs systematically on one side: he often seems to derive a perverse pleasure from his gloomy predictions. Frustrated desires, too, might have their own rewards, perhaps by encouraging the delicious feeling of righteous indignation at those who are deemed responsible for their frustration. People become trapped in certain sources of pleasure which, in the long run, have mainly destructive effects.

VI. Memory, anticipation, imagination [46]

The mind has a curious ability to generate pleasure and pain from its own operations, independently of interaction with the external world. Reliving past experiences in memory, savoring future experiences in anticipation, and daydreaming about possible experiences are, for some people most of the time and for most people some of the time, more important sources of pleasure and happiness than their current lives. Conversely, people can be made miserable by painful memories, dread of the future, and thoughts about what they could have done but did

not. Writers have discussed these sources of pleasure and pain, sometimes coming to opposite conclusions. Against Tennyson's " 'Tis better
to have loved and lost than never to have loved at all," we may set
Donne's " 'Tis better to be foul than to have been fair." Psychologists
and, more recently, economists have tried to consider such phenomena
in a more systematic way. This section is an attempt to summarize some
of their findings and hypotheses.

In egonomics, any event is subject to a kind of triple counting. It
can affect our welfare first through anticipation, then through direct
experience, and finally through memory. To understand the interaction between these sources of welfare, we may model the relation of
the present self to earlier and later selves on the relation between one
individual and another. We all know from experience that the great
fortune of a friend can solicit both a feeling of joy and a pang of envy.
Hume provided a classical analysis of this phenomenon:

> In general we may observe, that in all kinds of comparison an object
> makes us always receive from another, to which it is compar'd, a
> sensation contrary to what arises from itself in its direct and immediate
> survey. A small object makes a greater one appear still greater. A
> great object makes a little one appear less. Deformity of itself produces
> uneasiness, but makes us receive new pleasure by its contrast with a
> beautiful object, whose beauty is augmented by it; as on the other hand,
> beauty, which of itself produces pleasure, makes us receive a new pain
> by contrast with any thing ugly, whose deformity it augments. The case,
> therefore, must be the same with happiness and misery. The direct
> survey of another's pleasure naturally gives us pleasure, and therefore
> produces pain when compar'd with our own. His pain, consider'd in
> itself, is painful to us, but augments the idea of our own happiness, and
> gives us pleasure. [47]

In what must be one of the first instances of egonomical argument—
extending reasoning from the interpersonal case to the intrapersonal
case—Hume then goes on to observe that an agent's memory of his
past experiences has a similarly dual effect on his current welfare:

> Nor will it appear strange, that we may feel a reverst sensation from
> the happiness and misery of others; since we find the same comparison
> may give us a kind of malice against ourselves, and make us rejoice for
> our pains, and grieve for our pleasures. Thus the prospect of past pain
> is agreeable, when we are satisfy'd with our present condition; as on
> the other hand our past pleasures give us uneasiness, when we enjoy
> nothing at present equal to them. The comparison being the same, as
> when we reflect on the sentiments of others, must be attended with the
> same effects. [48]

For an example, suppose I have just had a meal at a superlatively
good French restaurant. The impact of that meal on my welfare at

later times can be decomposed into two mechanisms, which we may refer to as *the consumption effect* and *the contrast effect*. On the one hand, the memory of a good meal is a good memory, which I can carry with me for the indefinite future: this is the consumption effect. On the other hand, the effect of that wonderful meal will tend to reduce my enjoyment of meals served at more ordinary French restaurants: this is the contrast effect. In one sense, I am better off for having had that meal; in another sense, I am worse off. The net effect can be either negative or positive. [49]

A similar dual effect arises in the case of anticipation. On the one hand, there is a consumption effect, manifested in the phenomena of *savoring* and *dread:* good or bad feelings in the present caused by anticipation of good or bad events in the future. [50] On the other hand, there is a contrast effect, as the present may compare more or less favorably with the future. Anticipation of future happiness may make one more keenly aware of the mediocrity of the present; imagine for instance a prisoner in his cell thinking about life after his release. [51] Again, the net effect of these two opposing mechanisms could be negative as well as positive. Because the future, unlike the past, is to some extent under our control, the future-oriented consumption and contrast effects can also affect behavior. Suppose we can look forward to a pleasant event in the future. If the contrast effect dominates the consumption effect, we would want to speed it up as much as possible. Conversely, if the pleasure from savoring is greater than the pain induced by the contrast with the present, we may want to postpone the enjoyment for as long as possible. Similarly, a person who dreads very much going to the dentist may want to move the visit up as much as possible, to get it over and done with.

In the earlier discussions about going to the dentist, I assumed that fear of the pain would rather have the opposite effect—that of inducing the person to postpone or cancel his visit. There are in fact two opposing forces at work here. Suppose a person has the choice between going to the dentist earlier or later. By postponing the visit, he can reduce the present (discounted) costs of the future pain. However, he will also extend the period during which he will suffer the dread of having to go the dentist. Hence, the present cost of that dread will be increased. If the person discounts the future heavily, whereas he is not much subject to dread, he will postpone the visit. If he tends to feel a lot of anticipatory anguish, whereas he discounts the future at a low rate, he will choose the earlier date. But even if he discounts the future very heavily, he might still choose the earlier date, viz., if his dread pulls him even more strongly in the opposite direction.

The extent to which a person discounts the future cannot, therefore, be read off directly from his behavior. The preference for a larger delayed reward over an earlier small reward may be due to the pleasures of savoring rather than to a strong willpower. The fact that some children prefer to have the best part of the meal at the beginning, whereas others want to have it at the end, can be explained without assuming any differences in the rate of time discounting. Conversely, as we have just seen, the decision to have a painful experience sooner rather than later can be due to strong feelings of dread in the present rather than to a low rate of time discounting.

Imagination—daydreaming, wistful thought experiments, and the like—is subject to similar laws. The consumption effect in daydreaming is similar to that of memory: dreaming about a good experience is itself a good experience. Similarly, compulsive imagery about unpleasant experiences is inherently unpleasant. We also find the contrast effect: returning from a daydream to reality, we are more keenly struck by the drabness and mediocrity of the latter. Again, the net effect of such escapism can be either negative or positive. However, imagination also offers a special feature that is absent from both memory and anticipation. In our daydreams, we can offer ourselves anything and do anything. We can imagine gaining a million dollars, and then, mentally running out of money, increase it to ten million or—why not?—a billion. Paradoxically, this very lack of constraints reduces the value of daydreaming. It suffers, in Ainslie's wonderful phrase, from a *shortage of scarcity*. [52] To enhance the value of daydreaming we have to impose some rules on it, for instance by limiting ourselves to events that have an element of plausibility. [53] The novelist's craft is subject to rules of this kind, for instance by limiting the role of coincidences, excluding sudden changes of character, and the like.

However, once again this may cut both ways: the more plausible and well-constructed our daydream, the more painful the return to reality. In *The Old Regime and the French Revolution,* Tocqueville argued, for instance, that "patiently endured so long as it seemed beyond redress, a grievance comes to appear intolerable once the possibility of removing it crosses men's minds." [54] In other writings he suggested the very opposite idea: the possibility of improvement may serve as a safety valve and make people content with their miserable lot: "In a country where it is not impossible that a poor man may come to the highest offices of the State, it is much easier to continue excluding the poor from any share of control over government, than in those countries where all hope of rising to a higher rank is denied them. The idea of the imaginary grandeur to which he may one day be called, places itself continually between the poor man and the contemplation of his real miseries." [55] Here, Tocqueville emphasizes the consumption effect of the imaginary improvement, rather than the contrast effect. In actual cases, both mechanisms can be expected to operate.

Consider once again the contrast effect in memory. Sometimes, a memorable experience exercises its deflating effect on later experiences for a very long time. A widow who remarries may find that her new marriage is permanently spoiled by the memory of her first husband, although she would have been happy enough with the second had he been the first. Conversely, a marriage may gain in happiness if it exceeds the expectations set by a previous marriage. Here, present happiness is affected by the distant past, which serves as a permanent anchor or reference point. However, the contrast effect does not inherently depend on *change*, because present happiness can also be affected by using future or imaginary states as reference points. Some women, perhaps, are dissatisfied with their first husbands because they fail to live up to the ideals they have absorbed from novels or movies; others might find a surplus of joy when their similarly induced fears prove to be false.

There exists another mechanism, however, by which present happiness is essentially dependent on change from the worse toward the better. Leibniz described it when, arguing against Locke, he wrote that "je trouve que l'inquiétude est essentielle à la félicité des créatures, laquelle ne consiste jamais dans une parfaite possession qui les rendrait insensibles et comme stupides, mais dans un progrès continuel et non interrompu à des plus grands biens." [I find that uneasiness is essential to the happiness of created beings, which never consists in complete possession—this makes them insensible and, as it were, stupid—but in continuous and uninterrupted progess toward the greatest good.] [56]

More recently, this insight was elaborated in one of the key works of egonomics, *The Joyless Economy* by Tibor Scitovsky. Using a distinction between comfort and pleasure, which corresponds to Leibniz's distinction between possession and progression, Scitovsky writes as follows:

> If the pleasing changes in arousal are changes from a level associated with discomfort toward the level associated with comfort, then it logically follows that pleasure will always accompany the relief of discomfort and will seem the more intense the greater the discomfort that is being relieved. It also follows that for the level of arousal to move towards its optimum, it must first be at a non-optimal level. In familiar terms, discomfort must precede pleasure. . . . An illuminating proposition follows from [this] rule: too much comfort may preclude pleasure. That proposition may contribute to an explanation of the widespread dissatisfaction with our standard of living. [57]

According to this argument, the source of pleasure is not simply that the present is superior to the past, but that it is superior to the immediate past. For an example, consider the pleasures of downhill skiing. The thrill that is sought does not derive mainly from the speed but from the change of speed, that is, the acceleration. Slowing down, while not pleasurable in itself, is a condition for the pleasure of speeding up. Similarly, fasting may be a condition for the pleasures of eating, just as holding a steady job may be a condition for enjoying a holiday.

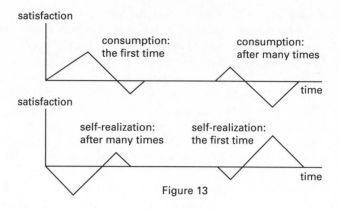

Figure 13

A more general version of this argument is the "opponent-process" theory proposed by Richard L. Solomon. [58] He claims that as a rule, the cessation of a positive experience tends to generate a negative one and vice versa. Thus, upon being told that she does not have the breast cancer she feared, a woman does not return to her normal emotional state but instead experiences intense euphoria. Conversely, interruption of a pleasurable sexual experience creates in most people an acute irritation, and it takes some time before they can return to an emotionally neutral state. Moreover, as we shall see in a moment, repetition of these processes has a very definite temporal pattern. Solomon claims that these mechanisms are very generally observed. Although the empirical evidence may not fully support him, the ideas are suggestive and valuable. In particular, I believe they can illuminate the distinction between two life-styles, that of passive consumption and that of active self-realization.

As depicted in the upper half of figure 13, pleasurable consumption episodes are followed by pains of withdrawal. This effect is most obvious in drug consumption but is to some extent present in other forms of consumption too. When we walk out of the movie theater or come to the end of the book, we often feel empty and mildly depressed. With repeated consumption episodes, the positive component tends to become less important, whereas the withdrawal pains loom larger. The activity is then supported mainly by fear of the withdrawal symptoms rather than by the positive satisfaction it generates. Compulsive readers, TV-viewers, or gamblers, for instance, seem to be afraid of being alone with themselves. As Pascal said about the gambler, they need a *divertissement*. [59] Even when the pattern of increasing withdrawal pains is not found, that of decreasing satisfaction, due to satiation, is very widely observed.

Self-realization through the work of the hand or the mind has a very different pattern. A vivid description, drawn no doubt from his own experience, was offered by Marx:

It seems quite far from [Adam] Smith's mind that the individual, "in his normal state of health, strength, activity, skill, facility," also needs a normal portion of work, and of the suspension of tranquillity. Certainly, labor obtains its measure from the outside, through the aim to be attained and the obstacles to be overcome in attaining it. But Smith has no inkling whatever that this overcoming of obstacles is in itself a liberating activity. . . . [Labor] becomes attractive work, the individual's self-realization, which in no way means that it becomes mere fun, mere amusement, as Fourier, with grisette-like naïvété, conceives it. Really free working, e.g. composing, is at the same time precisely the most damned seriousness, the most intense exertion. [60]

The lower half of figure 13 is an attempt to flesh out this insight, viz., that work, at its best, is neither mere drudgery nor mere fun. Initially, each episode of creative activity is quite painful. Moreover, in the earlier episodes the painful component dominates over the pleasurable one. Both observations confirm the German proverb, "Aller Anfang ist schwer." [All beginning is difficult.] The first time we attempt to design a dress, sail a vessel, play the piano, or write a scientific article is usually a painful experience. Although we may feel some pleasure upon completing the task, it may not be sufficient to make the episode as a whole worthwhile. Even later, after practice, starting up is difficult. However, the initial pains gradually decrease over time, whereas the subsequent satisfaction increases.

The time patterns of consumption and self-realization enter into the explanation of why the latter is comparatively rare, at least in our societies. Self-realization requires some ability to defer gratification. Individuals who discount the future very heavily will, therefore, prefer to engage in consumption, in which the reward comes first whereas the pains only appear later. Some implications of these facts are further discussed in the final section.

VII. Rationality, social norms, and emotions

The theory of rational choice set out in Section II embodies an important ideal for behavior. Generally speaking, people want to be rational and are dismayed when they find out that they are not. In practice, however, the ideal is regularly violated, and people may even take some pride in violating it. Two important sources of such irrational behavior are *social norms* and *emotions*. Social norms are capable of making people act against their interest. Emotions are capable of making people act against their self-interest *and* against social norms. At the same time, there are very close connections between emotions and social norms, in that emotions serve as the ultimate enforcer of social norms and conventions.

123

To see the difference between rational behavior and behavior guided by social norms, we may begin by noting that the former is essentially instrumental and forward-oriented. [61] Rational-choice theory tells people how to behave if they want to achieve some future goal or end. The imperatives of rationality are conditional on future states to be realized. Social norms, by contrast, are imperatives that are either unconditional or, if conditional, not forward-oriented. Simple unconditional norms are injunctions such as "Do not eat human flesh!" or "Do not marry your sibling!" Conditional social norms include the injunction to help those who helped you in the past, and to hurt those who hurt you in the past. A more complicated norm is that embodied in "everyday Kantianism": one should do x rather than y if it would be better for all if all did x than if all did y. A person who throws litter in the street instead of looking for a wastebasket will often be censored by a question that reflects this norm: "What if everybody did that?"

For such norms to be *social*, two conditions have to be fulfilled. First, they have to be shared with other people in the society—either in society as a whole or in some smaller community or group. Second, they have to be enforced in part by the sanctions of other people. These sanctions can range from raised eyebrows to serious forms of social ostracism, such as refusing to trade with the norm-violator or to offer him one's daughter in marriage. However, even material punishment or deprivation serves mainly as a vehicle for the emotions that norm-violations generate in the observer: anger, indignation, disgust, and contempt. Being a target of these emotions gives rise to the intensely unpleasant emotion of shame. The main enforcer of social norms, in fact, is the anticipation of the feeling of shame that violation of the norm would entail. The feeling usually involves the anticipated presence of other observers, but not invariably. For instance, one may feel ashamed of failing to experience the appropriate emotions—grief and joy, respectively—at the funeral of a close relative or at one's own wedding. Although others are not in a position to observe the absence of these emotions, there may still be a feeling of shame.

Implicit in what I have just said is that there are two sorts of connections between emotions and social norms. On the one hand, emotions sustain and support social norms, by the correlated emotions of indignation in the observer and shame in the agent. On the other hand, there are social norms that regulate which emotions are appropriate and inappropriate to feel on a given occasion. In addition, there are social norms that regulate which emotions are appropriate or inappropriate to *express* on a given occasion. As Paul Ekman observes, "At funerals, one can note almost a 'pecking order' of grief expressions based on the rights to mourn. A man's secretary cannot look sadder than his wife unless she intends to state something quite different about the true nature of their relationship." [62]

Social norms regulate large areas of social life, as a few examples will show. The most prominent are rules of etiquette, dress, language, etc. These norms have a paradoxical feature: on the one hand, the behavior they regulate is intrinsically unimportant, but on the other hand, we only need to read Proust's account of life in the upper French nobility to see that for some individuals they may come to dominate all other matters. At the other extreme are norms with consequences for life and death, such as norms of revenge in societies that are based on the vendetta or blood feud. [63] Many matters of intermediate importance are also governed by social norms. There are norms that prohibit what used to be called "behavior contrary to nature," such as cannibalism, incest, homosexuality, and sodomy. At the workplace there is a strong norm, "Neither a chiseler nor a rate-buster be," which regulates the work effort that workers put in. There are many norms that regulate the proper and improper use of money, such as the norm that it would be socially inappropriate to walk up to someone at the front of a bus queue and ask to buy that person's place. There are norms that enjoin people to choose the cooperative strategy in Prisoner's Dilemma situations, such as the norm of everyday Kantianism cited above, as well as a "norm of fairness" that tells people to do their share of cooperation if others do so as well. Finally we may cite norms of fair distribution, ranging from the norm of equality to norms that link the share of individuals to their need, contribution, or desert.

Behavior according to social norms is, as I said, irrational in the sense that it is not oriented toward outcomes. Because the norms are not sensitive to the consequences of action, they may induce behavior that is very much against the interest of the agent. Norms of revenge may dictate behavior that will predictably lead to the agent's own death. At a more trivial level, if I am late for an important meeting, it would surely be rational to ask the person at the front of the bus queue to sell his place to me. If he accepts, we are both better off; if he refuses, neither is worse off; and yet the norm prevents me from asking and him from accepting.

However, on some occasions the lack of regard for consequences can have good consequences. Consider again the game in figure 1 above. Assume that player Y is a prominent mafioso, well known, as are all mafiosi, for never making empty threats. Once a threat has been uttered, their code of honor forces them to carry it out, at any cost or risk to themselves. Under these circumstances, Y can credibly threaten to move right if X moves right, and in that way force X to go left. This is not to say that "it is rational to be irrational," only that a known propensity to behave irrationally can on occasion have favorable consequences for the agent. [64] Note, however, that the argument presupposes that X *is* guided by instrumental rationality. If he, too, subscribes to a norm of honor that tells him never to give in to threats, he will go right and both agents will be worse off than if both had been rational. As we have supposed that the norms are shared with others, this case will in fact be the typical one. Hence mafiosi probably do better in Brooklyn, where they can exploit the rational behavior of most others, than in Sicily.

Above I discussed emotions as regulators of, and regulated by, social norms. But there also exist spontaneous emotions that do not owe their existence to social norms. Anger, joy, sadness, grief, love, hate, jealousy, and envy, to name but a few, are universal reactions to universally occurring situations. Although there may be norms that tell me to feel joy at the day of my wedding or grief at a funeral, these emotions usually occur on occasions that are not subject to any such regulation. The emotions have a number of characteristic features. [65] They typically go together with physiological or psychological *arousal,* ranging from intense to very mild (as in the case of the aesthetic emotions). Each emotion usually has well-defined outward signs, in bodily posture, tone of voice, or facial expression. Moreover, it usually has associated with it certain action tendencies: to hit in anger, to destroy in envy, to flee in fear, to hide in shame, to dance in joy, and so on. Unlike mere feelings, such as nausea and vertigo, an emotion has an *object:* it is about something. As first noted by Hume, the object of an emotion must be distinguished from its *cause.* [66] When I am angry at my spouse, the cause of my anger may be a scolding from my boss at the job.

The emotions are, as I said, capable of overriding both self-interest and social norms. The agent who is under the sway of passion is often deaf and blind to consequences, including both his direct material interest and the sanctions that others might impose on him as a norm-violator. Consider first vengeance, undertaken in hot blood. In modern Western societies, where the predominant norm is that of turning the other cheek rather than retaliating in kind, revenge will often be the object of social disapproval. Moreover, revenge tends to be pointless and wasteful if viewed in purely instrumental terms. For another example, consider romantic love. Stendhal observes in *De l'amour* [On Love] that whereas conventional love always manages to align itself with one's personal interest, the true sign of passionate love is that it is capable of making one act against one's interest. [67] He also notes that a true sign of passionate love is that it makes the lover behave in ridiculous ways, contrary, that is, to social norms. [68] Consider finally envy. [69] The person who yields to this murky passion will rarely be approved by others, nor will he serve his own interest well.

As in the case of social norms, the emotions may occasionally serve the interests of the agent. [70] An angry person may get his way where a more rational individual would have to make a concession. There is no reason, however, to expect that a person will in general benefit from having an irascible temper. He may benefit on each interaction

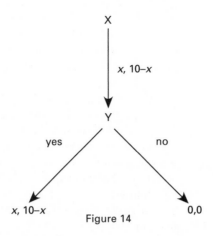

Figure 14

with others, but as people shy away from him there will be fewer such interactions.

We should not think of these three motivations—instrumental rationality, social norms, and emotions—as regulating different kinds of behavior. Rather, any single piece of behavior may simultaneously be affected by all of these motivations. It will be the task—as yet almost unexplored—of egonomics to articulate this interaction. A suggestive example may be taken from the experimental study of "ultimatum bargaining." [71]

In this game (fig. 14), the two players have to divide $10 between themselves by the following procedure. First, X proposes a division: $x to himself, and $(10−x) to player Y. Next, Y can either accept the proposal, in which case the proposed division is carried out, or reject it, in which case neither gets anything. We may assume that divisions have to be in entire dollars, excluding fractions of a dollar.

Under these conditions it is clear that if both players are rational and self-interested, know each other to be so, and so on, X will make a proposal of (9,1), which will be accepted by Y. However, the experimental results are very different. Instead of offering the "rational minimum" of $1 to Y, player X typically takes $6 or $7 for himself, leaving $3 or $4 for Y. Moreover, if X makes a proposal that leaves Y with only $2 or $3, it is typically rejected. We may explain the behavior of Y by assuming that he is under the sway of a norm of equality, or that he feels indignation at being taken advantage of. The behavior of X may be explained either by assuming that he is motivated by a form of moderate altruism, or that he anticipates that player Y might turn him down if offered too little.

My concern here is with the behavior of Y. If he had been motivated only by his rational self-interest, he would accept all offers equal to or greater than $1 for himself. If he had been motivated only by the norm of equality, or moved only by his aversion to being taken advantage of, he would reject all offers that give him less than $5. What we observe is neither of these "pure" outcomes, but an intermediate state of affairs that seems to owe something both to instrumental and to noninstrumental considerations. In this case, we may think of "rationality" and social norms (or emotions) as constituting a parallelogram of forces, with the observed behavior as the resultant. In other cases, interest might act as a constraint on the norm: I may follow the norm of doing my civic duty to vote, but not if it rains very heavily and my car has broken down. In still other cases, the norms may act as a constraint on self-interest: the classical idea of market behavior assumes that economic agents, although ruthlessly competitive, are constrained by honesty and truthfulness. The point is that there is a need to understand the mechanisms by which the different motivations we have discussed in this section interact, at the level of the individual, to generate behavior.

VIII. Conclusion: Egonomics and self-control

Up to this point this article has been a study in "positive" egonomics, with a focus on the explanation of behavior. As in economics more generally, we can also adopt a normative perspective and ask what egonomics can teach us about how to live our lives as well as possible. Here, issues of self-control and self-management come to the forefront. In addition, egonomics suggests that certain life-styles are more rewarding and gratifying than others.

The question of self-control was already addressed in the introductory section. There, I discussed how people can overcome their weakness of will by committing themselves ahead of time to certain courses of action, either by making other alternatives physically impossible or by making them excessively costly. However, egonomics tells us that we must also take account of the cost of self-control. Assume that the agent is at time t* in figure 9 above and contemplates taking an action that will make him prefer the later, delayed reward at all times up to time 1. At time t*, the benefit of self-control is the difference in the present values of the two rewards, indicated by the distance (drawn in heavy line) between the two curves at that time. The costs of self-control are the value at t* of whatever sacrifices the agent has to make between t* and time 1 to ensure that he will make the right choice at time 1. Clearly, a rational agent will not precommit himself to the later reward if the costs of self-control exceed the benefit. For instance, Christmas savings clubs that pay no interest on deposits might cease to become attractive if the ordinary bank rates go up. A person might hesitate to commit himself irreversibly to hospital treatment if there is a risk that urgent family or business matters would come up in the meantime.

Precommitment involves action upon the external world. Ainslie has discussed another strategy of self-control, which only requires mental rearrangement of the costs and benefits of the various courses of action. [72] Suppose I am debating whether to do my exercises, and I tell myself "I'll skip them just once—that can't matter." However, I may then remind myself that "tomorrow will be just like today—if I skip them today, won't I also do so tomorrow?" By this argument I am raising the stakes—failure to do my exercises today will predict failure in the future as well, by a kind of intrapersonal domino effect. Consequently, as Ainslie shows by a formal argument, the chances of sticking to my resolution are raised. Specifically, he shows that the effect of "bunching" the choices in this way is to shorten the time interval between the crossover point and time 1 in figure 9. The argument is both puzzling and convincing. Although reputation effects are very important in dealing with other people, [73] it is more puzzling that they can also be useful in dealing with oneself. Yet I believe that most readers will agree that reasoning of this kind is very important as a barrier to backsliding and procrastination. Sometimes, people manage to cooperate in the interpersonal Prisoner's Dilemma by asking themselves the Kantian question, "If not me, who?" [74] Similarly, they may achieve self-control in the intrapersonal Dilemma by asking, "If not now, when?"

However, this kind of self-control may also involve costs. Here, the risk is that by bunching all future choices together I create an excessively rigid system of rules, which may destroy all spontaneity and turn me into the kind of Victorian personality whose first principle is that "every gain on the wrong side undoes the effect of many conquests on the right." [75] The fear of creating an unhappy precedent will force me to stick to the rule even on occasions when there are good reasons for violating it. My guilt may make me follow the rule even when I believe that I should give myself a break. Hence we observe an apparent paradox: self-control as a form of weakness of will. However, in the Freudian perspective of id, ego, and superego, there is no paradox here. The ego is, as it were, fighting a two-front war: against the excessive impulsiveness of the id, and against the excessively compulsive measures that the superego deploys to control those impulses. Weakness of will may take the form of losing out to one or the other of these enemies.

Excess of will, or willing what cannot be willed, may be seen as a misplaced exercise in self-command. However, insight into the by-product fallacy may lead to the use of more sophisticated strategies. In Buddhism, for instance, the goal is the elimination of will. [76] Clearly, this is not something that can be achieved at will. However, one can proceed gradually, using the will to eliminate the will, and taking care that at each stage enough will is left to reach the next stage. At the end, no desires will be left, not even the desire to be devoid of all desire.

The argument depends on the existence of a series of actions which converge toward the state of no-will. It will not work if the process converges to a positive amount of willpower, or if the time of convergence to zero exceeds the duration of a human life. Similarly, when planning for spontaneity, might there come a point when one is too spontaneous to carry on with the plan, and yet not spontaneous enough for the plan to have been fulfilled? The common difficulty underlying these problems may be called *the hammock problem,* after the following experience. Gently rocking myself to sleep in a hammock, I found that just when sleep was coming, my body became so relaxed that I could no longer sustain the rhythmic motion that led me to sleep, and so I woke up and had to start all over again.

Above, we noted that Pascal's wager argument might be met with the objection that it is impossible to adopt religious faith at will. However, Pascal had foreseen this problem. He recommends to the would-be believer to imitate the sincere believers: "Suivez la manière par où ils ont commencé: c'est en faisant tout comme s'ils croyaient, en prenant de l'eau bénite, en faisant dire des messes, etc. Naturellement même cela vous fait croire et vous abêtira." [77] [Follow the way by which they began; by acting as if they believed, taking the holy water, having masses said, etc. Even this will naturally make you believe, and deaden your acuteness (*GBWW* I: 33, 216; II: 30, 216).] Pascal, in other words, encourages us to reverse the usual causal sequence. Instead of viewing religious acts as following from the faith, one may adopt the behavior in order to induce the belief. Moreover, the rituals of Catholicism will stupefy us, so that we will forget that a purely instrumental calculation was at the origin of the faith. To be successful, the process of inducing belief must include a *self-erasing* element.

Above, I dismissed the adaptation of preferences to circumstances as a sign of immaturity or even irrationality. In doing so, I explicitly had in mind a process of unconscious alignment rather than the deliberate and conscious adjustment advocated by the Stoics or Spinoza. For someone living in poverty, or in times of trouble and difficulty, it makes a lot of sense to down-scale aspirations and expectations, to learn to be content with little, and not worry about what one cannot have anyway. The task is difficult and may require considerable application. Under some circumstances, it may not be worth the trouble. It makes little sense, for instance, to spend one's life learning not to be afraid of death. Once again, egonomics does not simply point to the need for and the possibility of self-control and self-management: it also makes us ask whether the benefits are likely to exceed the costs.

The main difference between the two forms of adaptation is that the person who is subject to the "sour grapes" syndrome tends to downgrade what he cannot have and perhaps, as we saw, those who do have what he cannot have, whereas the Stoic tends to upgrade what he has. If I fail to get the promotion I coveted, I need not tell myself and others that it was not worth having anyway. Instead, I can decide to make a virtue out of necessity, to enjoy the greater amounts of leisure that go with the lower ranking position, and to cultivate simpler tastes that are within my income. Serenity on the one hand, self-poisoning of the mind on the other: the contrast could not be greater.

Stoicism, Buddhism, and other forms of conscious character planning need not take the form of resignation to the inevitable. One may set out to desire little and be content with little simply because one believes that is the road to happiness, even if one could easily obtain the where-withal to satisfy more ambitious desires. Now, a claim of this sort might appear dubious. If someone is passed over for a promotion, we might not believe him if he said that he could easily have been promoted had he wished, but that he preferred the simpler life at a lower rank. Instead, we might suspect him to be a victim of the sour grapes syndrome. Montaigne tells an amusing story to this effect: "When Thales condemned preoccupations with thrift and money-making he was accused of sour grapes like the fox. It pleased him, for fun, to make a revealing experiment; for this purpose he debased his knowledge in the service of profit and gain, setting up a business which in one year brought in as much wealth as the most experienced in the trade were hard put to match in a lifetime." [78]

The interplay of memory, anticipation, and experience discussed in Section VI also suggests ways in which people might improve their lives by choosing wisely. Consider first deliberate exploitation of the contrast effect. For instance, people might do well to shy away from isolated memorable experiences that will devalue all subsequent items of the same kind. "If the best can come only rarely, it is better not to include it in the range of experiences at all." [79] Conversely, people might deliberately seek out unpleasant experiences to make even ordinary ones appear in a glowing light. "The ideal lower end-point might be a strong electric shock, unbearable but quickly over. The shock would have to be readministered occasionally, whenever it dropped from the context or whenever its memory ceased to be dreadful." [80] Although the latter option would not have many takers, I believe the former has some appeal.

Consider next the exploitation of the endowment effect for hedonic purposes. People certainly do seem to invest in memories. Phrases like "we'll remember this for the rest of our lives" ease the massive expenditures associated with huge weddings and expensive cruises and actually help the participants to enjoy them rather than to focus on their shrunken savings. However, the reasoning is suspiciously circular: if people did not enjoy these events in the present, there would not be any good memories later, but the reason they are enjoyed in the present is that one is already savoring the memory. In fact, deliberate memory creation may often be out of reach. Many of the good things in life are characterized by surprise, spontaneity, serendipity, and lack of planning. Hence the idea of novelty seeking for the purpose of memory creation borders on the paradoxical or self-defeating, as in the "Be spontaneous!" paradox. To act in the present for the sake of future memory streams could easily undermine the spontaneity and value of the immediate experience and devalue the stream of memories flowing from it. Reliving old loves can be wonderful, but memory investment by itself hardly justifies engaging in a love affair. People who go on vacation constantly on the lookout for the opportunity to take photographs that will remind them later of what a wonderful time they had may not have much of a wonderful time. To the extent that good memories are essentially by-products of activities undertaken for quite different ends, planning is self-defeating: it becomes part of the problem rather than of the solution. However, some activities do lend themselves well to deliberate memory creation: if two pleasant restaurant dinners are valued equally with one spectacular dinner, one should choose the latter for the sake of the good memories.

Scitovsky's distinction between comfort and pleasure has clear implications for behavior. By having one's meals at regular intervals, the pleasure from eating is much enhanced. Some people prefer Chicago's dramatically changing seasons to the monotony of the Californian climate. And there is the story of the man who had a thirst he would not sell for ten dollars, and of the man who hit himself with a hammer on the head because it felt so good when he stopped. Also, there is evidence that people choose to have wage profiles that increase yearly rather than flat or declining profiles of equal (discounted or undiscounted) value. [81] I suspect that some would even choose an increasing profile over a flat profile with a *larger* value. If this phenomenon was actually observed, it might be seen as expressing the irrational desire for novelty discussed in Section V. However, it might also be seen as an entirely rational response to the desire to seek pleasure rather than comfort. We probably need to draw a distinction between pathological novelty seekers and the rest of us. The former should be encouraged to limit their search for change and pleasure, whereas most of us should probably be encouraged to cultivate pleasure as a source of happiness.

The distinction between consumption and self-realization also has implications for choice of life-style. If an individual who opts for consumption can afford to diversify his activities so that he never reaches the later stages of satiation and withdrawal pains, his life may be happy enough. People with fewer resources will probably be better off opting for self-realization. In that case, diversity ought to be shunned. Rather than being a jack-of-all-trades, one should aim at being master of one.

Many of the activities that recommend themselves from an egonomical point of view have a common feature: they require the ability to delay gratification. To invest in memory creation one may have to forego current consumption. To seek pleasure rather than comfort, one first must create a state of discomfort. To exploit the contrast effect, one may have to forego good experiences and seek out some bad ones. To stop from embarking on the slippery slope to ruin, Andersen's farmer would have to look further than the choice at hand and anticipate how that choice might influence later decisions. Hence problems of time discounting and weakness of will come to the forefront. This is an important reason why the problems of weakness of will and self-control are at the core of egonomics, and a recurrent theme of the present essay.

---

1. Thomas C. Schelling, "Egonomics, or the Art of Self-Management," *American Economic Review: Papers and Proceedings* 68 (1978): 290–94. *See also* chaps. 3 and 4 of Schelling's *Choice and Consequence* (Cambridge, Mass.: Harvard University Press, 1984), and his "Self-Command: A New Discipline," in George Loewenstein and Jon Elster, eds., *Choice over Time* (New York: The Russell Sage Foundation, 1992), pp. 167–76.

2. *See*, notably, Gary Stanley Becker, *The Economic Approach to Human Behavior* (University of Chicago Press, 1976).

3. For a number of approaches to this idea *see* Jon Elster, ed., *The Multiple Self* (Cambridge University Press, 1986).

4. For discussions of this case, *see*, notably, Derek Parfit, *Reasons and Persons* (Oxford University Press, 1984).

5. George Ainslie, *Picoeconomics* (Cambridge University Press, 1992), pp. 90–91, 158–62.

6. Thomas C. Schelling, *The Strategy of Conflict* (Cambridge Mass.: Harvard University Press, 1960), chap. 2.

7. Jon Elster, *Ulysses and the Sirens*, rev. ed. (Cambridge University Press, 1984).

8. Schelling, "Self-Command," p. 167.

9. Richard H. Thaler and Hersh M. Shefrin, "An Economic Theory of Self-Control," *Journal of Political Economy* 89 (1981): 392–406.

10. The idea is due to Richard Thaler (personal communication).

11. David Francis Pears, *Motivated Irrationality* (Oxford University Press, 1984).

12. David Hume, *A Treatise of Human Nature,* ed. L. A. Selby-Bigge (Oxford University Press, 1960), p. 415.

13. This is a central theme in a book that has inspired many of the ideas in the present essay, Paul Veyne, *Le pain et le cirque* (Paris: Éditions du Seuil, 1976).

14. George Joseph Stigler and Gary S. Becker, "De Gustibus Non Est Disputandum," *American Economic Review* 67 (1977): 76–90.

15. Gary S. Becker and Kevin M. Murphy, "A Theory of Rational Addiction," *Journal of Political Economy* 96 (1988): 675–700.

16. The seminal modern discussion is that of Donald Davidson, "How Is Weakness of the Will Possible?" reprinted as chap. 2 in his *Essays on Actions and Events* (Oxford University Press, 1980).

17. R. H. Strotz, "Myopia and Inconsistency in Dynamic Utility Maximization," *Review of Economic Studies* 23 (1955–56): 165–80; Ainslie, *Picoeconomics*, chap. 3.

18. Jon Elster, "Weakness of Will and the Free-Rider Problem," *Economics and Philosophy* 1 (1985): 231–65.

19. Thomas C. Schelling, *Micromotives and Macrobehavior* (New York: Norton, 1978), chap. 7.

20. Leslie H. Farber, *Lying, Despair, Jealousy, Envy, Sex, Suicide, Drugs and the Good Life* (New York: Basic Books, Inc., 1976).

21. Jon Elster, *Sour Grapes* (Cambridge University Press, 1983), chap. 2.

22. Jonathan R. Kesselman, "Work Relief Programs in the Great Depression," in John L. Palmer, ed., *Creating Jobs: Public Employment Programs and Wage Subsidies* (Washington, D.C.: Brookings Institution, 1978), pp. 153–99.

23. Gordon C. Winston, "Addiction and Backsliding: A Theory of Compulsive Consumption," *Journal of Economic Behavior and Organization* 1 (1980): 295–324.

24. Pascal, *Les Pensées,* ed. Léon Brunschvicg (Paris: Éditions Garnier Frères, 1961), no. 233 (cf. *GBWW* I: 33, 213–16; II: 30, 213–16).

25. Bernard Williams, "Deciding to Believe," in his *Problems of the Self* (Cambridge University Press, 1973), pp. 136–51.

26. Montaigne, *Les Essais,* trans. M. A. Screech (Oxford University Press, 1992), I.24 (cf. *GBWW* I: 25, 54; II: 23, 108).

27. Paul Ekman, *Telling Lies,* rev. ed. (New York: Norton, 1991).

28. Farber, op. cit., p. 7. Actually, Farber is wrong on one point: one cannot will lust (*see* the chapter on "Fiascoes" in Stendhal's *De l'amour* [Paris: Gallimard, 1980]).

29. Donald Davidson, *Essays on Actions and Events,* p. 70.

30. *See,* notably, Tibor Scitovsky, *The Joyless Economy,* rev. ed. (Oxford University Press, 1992).

31. I am *not* claiming that in such cases the best decision is to flip a coin or to take the first opportunity that comes to mind. The doctor should certainly pause for a few moments to take stock of the patient's condition. And, in one of Johnson's examples, one ought not to propose to the first woman one meets after coming of age. Rather, my claim is that there is no optimal amount of time to be spent on search and deliberation, only lower and upper bounds, which may be close to each other or far away from each other. Hyperrationality involves a tendency to go beyond the upper bound; the tendency to fall short of the lower bound may involve different kinds of irrationality.

32. *Les Essais* I.24; italics added (cf. *GBWW* I: 25, 53; II: 23, 107).

33. Jon Elster, *Solomonic Judgements* (Cambridge University Press, 1989), chap. 3.

34. In *Solomonic Judgements* I argue that the child custody process illustrates both the principle underlying the first quotation from Boswell's *Life of Johnson* and the principle underlying the other two cited passages. There may not be any right answer to the question of which parent is the more fit for custody; and if there is one, the costs of finding it may be greater than the gains.

35. Joseph Goldstein, Anna Freud, and Albert J. Solnit, *Beyond the Best Interests of the Child,* 2nd ed. (New York: Free Press, 1979), p. 116; Descartes, Letter to Princess Elisabeth of Bohemia, January 1646, in Adam and Tannery, eds., *Oeuvres Complètes* (Paris: Vrin, 1897–1910), vol. 4, p. 357; Pascal, *Les Pensées,* no. 272 (cf. *GBWW* I: 33, 222; II: 30, 222).

36. Elster, *Sour Grapes,* chap. 3.

37. Joseph Richmond Levenson, *Confucian China and Its Modern Fate,* vols. 1–3 (Berkeley and Los Angeles: University of California Press, 1968), vol. 1, pp. 69ff.

38. Leon Festinger, *A Theory of Cognitive Dissonance* (Stanford University Press, 1957).

39. Roger Shepard, "On Subjectively Optimum Selection among Multiattribute Alternatives," in M. W. Shelley and G. L. Bryan, eds., *Human Judgment and Optimality* (New York: Wiley, 1968), pp. 257–80.

40. Jack W. Brehm, "Postdecision Changes in the Desirability of Alternatives," *Journal of Abnormal and Social Psychology* 52 (1956): 384–89; Paul Veyne, *Le pain et le cirque,* p. 708.

41. Keith Thomas, *Religion and the Decline of Magic* (Harmondsworth, England: Penguin, 1973), p. 790; *see also* Otto Neurath, "Die verrirten des Cartesius und das Auxiliarmotiv: Zur Psychologie des Entschlusses" (1913), translated in Otto Neurath, *Philosophical Papers 1913–1946* (Dordrecht, Holland: D. Reidel Pub. Co., 1983), pp. 1–12.

42. *Les Essais* II.15 (cf. *GBWW* I: 25, 299; II: 23, 399).

43. Carl Christian von Weizsäcker, "Notes on Endogenous Change of Tastes," *Journal of Economic Theory* 3 (1971): 345–72.

44. Levenson, *Confucian China and Its Modern Fate,* vol. 1, pp. 65ff.

45. *See* Pears, *Motivated Irrationality.*

46. The argument in this section draws heavily on Jon Elster and George Loewenstein, "Utility from Memory and Anticipation," in Loewenstein and Elster, eds., *Choice over Time,* pp. 213–34.

47. *A Treatise of Human Nature,* pp. 375–76.

48. Ibid.

49. Amos Tversky and Dale Griffin, "Endowment and Contrast in Judgments of Well-

Being," in Richard J. Zeckhauser, ed., *Strategy and Choice* (Cambridge, Mass.: MIT Press, 1991), pp. 297–318.

50. George Loewenstein, "Anticipation and the Valuation of Delayed Consumption," *Economic Journal* 97 (1987): 667–84.

51. Conversely, although much more rarely, the thought of future suffering may enhance the value of the present.

52. Ainslie, *Picoeconomics*, p. 258.

53. Daniel Kahneman and Amos Tversky, "The Simulation Effect," in Kahneman, Paul Slovic, and Tversky, eds., *Judgment under Uncertainty* (Cambridge University Press, 1982), pp. 201–8.

54. Tocqueville, *The Old Regime and the French Revolution* (New York: Anchor Books, 1955), p. 177.

55. Tocqueville, "Political and Social Condition of France," *Westminster Review* (April–July 1836): 150.

56. Gottfried W. Leibniz, *Nouveaux essais sur l'entendement humain*, chap. 20, §36, in Leibniz, *Philosophische Schriften*, ed. Tibor Gerhard (Leipzig, Germany, 1875–90), vol. 5, p. 175.

57. Scitovsky, *The Joyless Economy*, p. 62.

58. Richard L. Solomon, "The Opponent-Process Theory of Acquired Motivation: The Costs of Pleasure and the Benefits of Pain," *American Psychologist* 35 (1980): 691–712.

59. On gambling, *see* Pascal, *Les Pensées*, no. 139 (*GBWW* I: 33, 196–99; II: 30, 196–99); on reading, Victor Nell, *Lost in a Book: The Psychology of Reading for Pleasure* (New Haven: Yale University Press, 1988), p. 227.

60. Marx, *Grundrisse* (Harmondsworth, England: Penguin, 1973), p. 611.

61. Jon Elster, *The Cement of Society* (Cambridge University Press, 1989), chap. 3.

62. Paul Ekman, "Biological and Cultural Contributions to Body and Facial Movements in the Expression of Emotions," in Amélie O. Rorty, ed., *Explaining Emotions* (Berkeley and Los Angeles: University of California Press, 1980), pp. 73–102, at p. 88.

63. Jon Elster, "Norms of Revenge," *Ethics* 100 (1990): 862–85.

64. Robert H. Frank, *Passions within Reason* (New York: Norton, 1988).

65. Nico H. Frijda, *The Emotions* (Cambridge University Press, 1986).

66. *A Treatise of Human Nature*, p. 277.

67. *De l'amour*, chap. 1.

68. Ibid., chap. 5.

69. Jon Elster, "Envy in Social Life," in Richard J. Zeckhauser, ed., *Strategy and Choice*, pp. 49–82.

70. Jack Hirshleifer, "On the Emotions as Guarantors of Threats and Promises," in John Dupré, ed., *The Latest on the Best* (Cambridge, Mass.: MIT Press, 1987), pp. 307–26.

71. Werner Guth, Rolf Schmittberger, and Bernd Schwarze, "An Experimental Analysis of Ultimatum Bargaining," *Journal of Economic Behavior and Organization* 3 (1982): 367–88.

72. Ainslie, *Picoeconomics*, chap. 5.

73. Robert Wilson, "Reputations in Games and Markets," in Alvin E. Roth, ed., *Game-Theoretic Models of Bargaining* (Cambridge University Press, 1985), pp. 27–62.

74. George Quattrone and Amos Tversky, "Self-Deception and the Voter's Illusion," in Jon Elster, ed., *The Multiple Self*, pp. 35–58.

75. Alexander Bain, cited in Ainslie, *Picoeconomics*, p. 144.

76. S.-C. Kolm, "The Buddhist Theory of 'No-Self'," in Jon Elster, ed., *The Multiple Self*, pp. 233–66.

77. *Les Pensées*, no. 233 (*GBWW* I: 33, 216; II: 30, 216).

78. *Les Essais* I.25 (cf. *GBWW* I: 25, 57; II: 23, 111).

79. Allen Parducci, "The Relativism of Absolute Judgments," *Scientific American*, December 1968, pp. 84–90, at p. 90.

80. Allen Parducci, "Value Judgments: Toward a Relational Theory of Happiness," in J. Richard Eiser, ed., *Attitudinal Judgment* (New York: Springer-Verlag, 1984), pp. 3–21, at p. 16.

81. Robert H. Frank, "Frames of Reference and the Intertemporal Wage Profile," in Loewenstein and Elster, eds., *Choice over Time*, pp. 371–82.

Reconsiderations of Great Books and Ideas

Infinity and Controversy

Otto Bird

Otto Bird was executive editor of *The Great Ideas Today* from 1964 to 1970 and its consulting editor from 1970 until 1988. He makes frequent suggestions as to articles and reprints, reads faithfully and comments upon each year's manuscripts, and since 1981 has contributed pieces of his own to "Reconsiderations of Great Books and Ideas."

Mr. Bird's connection with the *Great Books of the Western World* set goes back to his three years as associate editor of *The Syntopicon,* beginning in 1947. Trained as a philosopher with particular interest in logic and medieval thought, he became subsequently a member of the faculty at the University of Notre Dame, where he founded and directed the general program of liberal studies from 1950 to 1963, and where he was university professor from 1970 until his retirement in 1976.

In addition to essays and reviews, Mr. Bird has written *Syllogistic Logic and Its Extensions* (1964), *The Idea of Justice* (1967), and *Cultures in Conflict: An Essay in the Philosophy of the Humanities* (1976). He was also a major contributor to the *Propædia,* or *Outline of Knowledge,* of the fifteenth edition of the *Encyclopædia Britannica.* In 1991 Mr. Bird published his autobiography, *Seeking a Center: My Life as a "Great Bookie."*

In thinking about infinity, "let us remember," Galileo wrote, that we are dealing with matters "which transcend our finite understanding. . . . In spite of this, men cannot refrain from discussing them, even though it must be done in a roundabout way" (*GBWW* I: 28, 142; II: 26, 142). Galileo wrote these words in the first day's discussion of the *Two New Sciences*, which was published in 1638. He knew from his knowledge of Aristotle that the infinite had been a subject of controversy among the ancient Greek thinkers. Were he alive on earth today he would find that the controversy is still going on.

The most recent occurrence of it has come with the appearance of a book on the infinite by the philosopher A. W. Moore, who reaches the conclusion that the infinite contains more problems of greater interest than mathematics is capable of handling. The mathematician Roger Penrose, on reviewing the book, claims that the philosopher has failed to make good his case and recommends that consideration of the infinite should be left in the care of mathematics, as though this is the place where it properly belongs.

That is the controversy this essay proposes to investigate. It will begin with consideration of the case stated by the philosophers, then look to that of the mathematicians and, after a brief analysis of the position of the moralists, confront the controversy itself and attempt to judge which side has made the stronger case.

The philosophers

Aristotle provides a good beginning for consideration of the way that philosophers think about the infinite. He develops a considerable theory of the infinite and, more importantly, takes a position that has continued to represent a basis for thinking about the infinite.

In his *Physics* Aristotle distinguishes five different senses in which the term "infinite" is used. It may be said of

(1) What is incapable of being gone through, because it is not in its nature to be gone through (the sense in which the voice is "invisible").

(2) What admits of being gone through, the process however having no termination, or (3) what scarcely admits of being gone through.

(4) What naturally admits of being gone through, but is not actually gone through or does not actually reach an end.

Further, everything that is infinite may be so in respect of addition or division or both. (*GBWW* I: 8, 281–82; II: 7, 281–82)

The example of the invisible applies to the first three senses of "infinite." A thing may be invisible because it does not belong to the kind of things that are visible, such as the voice which is an audible, not a visible. Or, second, a thing may be visible by nature and yet be poorly or scarcely seen because of obscureness or distance. Third, a thing may be a visible and yet not be actually seen because of complete darkness. Likewise, the infinite may be so because it is not the kind of thing that can be gone through; it is a non-traversable. It can also be said of what is traversable, yet is not traversed either because of its difficulty or because we are incapable of accomplishing it. The most proper sense of "infinite" is the final one, that of the infinite by addition as numbers and by division as magnitudes.

Besides distinguishing the various ways in which the term is used, Aristotle also notes that belief in the existence of the infinite has arisen mainly from five considerations:

(1) From the nature of time—for it is infinite.

(2) From the division of magnitudes—for the mathematicians also use the notion of the infinite.

(3) If coming to be and passing away do not give out, it is only because that from which things come to be is infinite.

(4) Because the limited always finds its limit in something, so that there must be *no* limit, if everything is *always* limited by something different from itself.

(5) Most of all, a reason which is peculiarly appropriate and presents the difficulty that is felt by everybody—not only number but also mathematical magnitudes and what is outside the heaven are supposed to be infinite because they never give out in our *thought*.

The last fact (that what is outside is infinite) leads people to suppose that body also is infinite, and that there is an infinite number of worlds. (*GBWW* I: 8, 281; II: 7, 281)

Since the focus of our concern here is the relation between the philosophical and mathematical theory of the infinite, it is significant that this early example of thinking about it is not primarily concerned with the mathematical infinite. Of the five senses of the term that Aristotle gives only one is mathematical. The other four appeal to the notion of traversing: what cannot be driven through or across (*dielthein*) or that lacks a way through (*diexodon*). Mathematics does not enter until the fifth sense with the reference to addition and division.

The texts just cited occur in the *Physics,* where Aristotle is analyzing physical phenomena. Hence in seeking reasons for belief in the existence of the infinite, he finds, not unexpectedly, that physical and not mathematical reasons predominate: never-ending time, the ceaseless coming to be and passing away of things, the physical limitation of one thing by another. He also lists two others, one of which is explicitly mathematical, namely, the division of magnitude. The final one he considers the most significant: the infinite is believed to exist because certain things never give out in thought (*me hypoleipein*), such as number, magnitude, and what is outside the heaven. Aristotle may have placed greatest emphasis upon this last reason because of his conviction regarding the relation between thought and existence. Thus he asserts:

> To rely on mere thinking is absurd, for then the excess or defect is not in the thing but in the thought. One might think that one of us is bigger than he is and magnify him *ad infinitum.* But it does not follow that he is bigger than the size we are, just because some one thinks he is, but only because he *is* the size he is. (*GBWW* I: 8, 286; II: 7, 286)

Writing as a physicist or natural philosopher, Aristotle declares the problem regarding the infinite is to investigate whether there is a sensible magnitude which is infinite and, if so, in what way it is infinite. Although he held that the space of the world or universe is finite, he did maintain that both time and motion are infinite. Hence his theory of the infinite can best be determined by seeing how he considered time and motion to be infinite. Here is his argument for thinking that such is the case:

> Now since time cannot exist and is unthinkable apart from the moment, and the moment is a kind of middle-point, uniting as it does in itself both a beginning and an end, a beginning of future time and an end of past time, it follows that there must always be time: for the extremity of the last period of time that we take must be found in some moment, since time contains no point of contact for us except the moment. Therefore, since the moment is both a beginning and an end, there must always be time on both sides of it. But if this is true of time, it is evident that it must also be true of motion, time being a kind of affection of motion. (*GBWW* I: 8, 335; II: 7, 335)

Time, however, is only one of the ways in which infinity manifests itself. Another and a different way appears in the division of magnitudes. Time and the generations of mankind are infinite in the sense that "one thing is always being taken after another, and each thing that is taken is always finite, but always different." Thus this day and the present generation have come to be after the passing away of the preceding ones and will themselves give way to their followers. Only the present finite day is actually. There are infinitely many days and generations, according to Aristotle, both behind and ahead of the present one, but they exist only potentially, as capable of coming to be or of having been (*GBWW* I: 8, 284; II: 7, 284).

The infinite by division of a spatial magnitude is different in that the finite section taken away by dividing remains and does not pass away. The infinite lies in the capacity of the divided line to be continually divided as long as the division pursues a constant ratio. Thus potentially a finite line can be bisected and half of it bisected again, etc., etc., so as to pursue $1/2$, $1/4$, . . . The infinite by addition of numbers proceeds in the opposite direction: given a number, one can always obtain another larger number by addition. In any given case one will have a finite number, but potentially the process could be continued without end (*GBWW* I: 8, 284; II: 7, 284).

By this analysis Aristotle claims that he has explained how the infinite both is and is not: it is not as an actual existing entity; yet it is as a potentiality. The infinite is accordingly defined as that which is "such that we can always take a part outside what has been already taken." It is thus contrasted as a part with that which is complete and whole—the whole being "that of which nothing is outside," so as not to be lacking what it ought to have, "as a whole man or a whole box" (*GBWW* I: 8, 285; II: 7, 285).

It is significant that Aristotle thinks of the infinite in terms of whole and part. For the modern mathematics of the infinite does the same, as will be seen, only to reach a radically different conclusion.

Aristotle was not the only thinker in antiquity to be interested in the infinite. Lucretius was another, and in his poem *On the Nature of Things* he celebrates the teaching of the ancient Atomists, especially Epicurus. About the universe and space he writes:

> The universe is limitless, unbounded
> In any of its areas; otherwise
> It would have to have an end somewhere, but no—
> Nothing, it seems, can possibly have an end
> Without there being something out beyond it.
>
> (*GBWW* I: 12, 13; II: 11, 13)

To confirm his claim Lucretius asks us to suppose that there is a limit to the void or space and then imagine one running to the farthest rim and throwing a javelin outward. "Will it keep on going / Full force, or do you think something can stop it?" (*GBWW* I: 12, 13; II: 11, 13). Faced with this dilemma, he holds that you have to admit that "a final boundary line / Is nowhere in existence" (ibid.).

However, this example collapses three terms and identifies them, as though what is unbounded is unlimited and therefore infinite. But a contrary example shows that is not necessarily the case. Imagine a sphere of finite radius: It is limited by the finite size of its radius without thereby being bounded by anything else.

Both time and motion are also infinite according to Lucretius:

> Out of the infinite come the particles [the atoms]
> Speeding above, below, in endless dance.
> By nature space is deep and space is boundless,
> So that bright shafts of lightning could not cross it,
> Given eternal time, nor could they lessen
> The area before their onward course.
> There is too much space, all here and there, around them,
> No limit to that infinite domain.
>
> (*GBWW* I: 12, 13; II: 11, 14)

Like space and time the number of entities in the universe is also infinite:

> And nature will not have it that the sum
> Of things set any limits for themselves,
> Forcing matter to be limited
> By void, and void be limited by matter.
> This alternation, this recurrence, makes
> The total limitless. . . .
> > Matter and space,
> I say again, are equally infinite.
>
> (*GBWW* I: 12, 13; II: 11, 14)

Jumping twenty centuries down to the present, we find Einstein declaring that "the theory of expanding space, together with the empirical data of astronomy, permit no decision to be reached about the finite or infinite character of (three-dimensional) space." He wrote this in 1916 in the monograph entitled *Relativity: The Special and the General Theory: A Popular Exposition* (*GBWW* II: 56, 235). The situation still remains the same. Neither theory nor observation can determine conclusively one way or the other whether space is infinite.

Kant on infinity

Kant takes the same position but holds it for different reasons. He claims that there are what he calls three antinomies, each of which raises a problem about the infinite in relation to the world: whether it is infinite in space, in time, or in parts. About none of these, Kant maintains, can a definite answer be established, since equally good reasons can be given both for and against, thus resulting in a contradiction and constituting what he calls an antinomy.

Time is considered together with space in the first antinomy, expressed as follows: "The world has no beginning, and no limits in space, but is, in relation both to time and space, infinite" (*GBWW* I: 42, 135; II: 39, 135). On the supposition that the world is infinitely old, then up to the present moment "an eternity must have elapsed, and therewith passed away an infinite series of successive conditions or states of things in the world." But an infinite cannot be completed by traversing it. "It follows that an infinite series already elapsed is impossible and that, consequently, a beginning of the world is a necessary condition of its existence" (ibid.). So too for space. If infinitely extended in space, "the world must be an infinite given total of coexistent things." But to think such a totality we must be able to enumerate all its parts and look upon it as completed: "that is to say, an infinite time must be regarded as having elapsed in the enumeration of all co-existing things; which is impossible. . . . The world is consequently, as regards extension in space, *not infinite,* but enclosed in limits" (ibid.). With regard to both time and space the world is finite.

However, Kant claims it can also be proved that the world is infinite in both respects. Suppose it is finite and had a beginning in time, "it follows that there must have been a time in which the world did not exist, that is, a void time. But in a void time the origination of a thing is impossible; because no part of any such time contains a distinctive condition of being, in preference to that of non-being (whether the supposed thing originate of itself, or by means of some other cause)." But the world exists now and is therefore, "in relation to past time, infinite" (ibid.). So too with regard to space. If it is finite, the world "must exist in a void space, which is not limited" and hence there must be a relation of things not only *in space* but also *to space.* But for the world as an absolute whole there is no correlate to which the world can be related: "this relation of the world to a void space is merely a relation to *no object.*" Consequently, this limitation or finiteness is nothing, and "the world, as regards space, is not limited, that is, it is infinite" (ibid.).

According to Kant's arguments, it cannot be concluded that the time and space of the world is either finite or infinite, since each can be both proved and disproved. In both cases it is worth noting that the infinite in question is that of greatness or the infinite of addition, and it is rejected as actual on the ground that it cannot be traversed so as to be taken as a whole.

Such an antinomy Kant calls "a natural and unavoidable illusion" in that reason is arguing apart from any reference to sense-experience; so "pure reason," as he uses the term (*GBWW* I: 42, 133; II: 39, 133). The first antinomy errs in claiming to take the world as a whole, which is impossible since that cannot be given in sense-experience.

However, Kant does not forbid all thinking about the infinite. He declares that the infinite can serve as a rule for reason in thinking: "a principle for the enlargement and extension of experience as far as is possible . . . [that] forbids us to consider any empirical limits as absolute." Asked to produce a straight line *ad infinitum,* we "must not cease to produce it" (*GBWW* I: 42, 158; II: 39, 158).

Still to be considered is the question whether the world is infinite by division. This is the subject of Kant's second antinomy of pure reason. As he phrases it, the question amounts to asking whether or not every composite substance consists of simple parts, i.e., parts that are indivisible. As before, Kant finds arguments both pro and con. In both cases the argument is indirect by assuming the opposite and showing that it leads to contradiction.

First, that the world cannot be infinitely divisible but consists of simple parts: suppose that it in fact can be so divided. A composite thing has parts that together make the composition. Upon imagining a division of it, some part must remain, since there has to be something more than just composition, namely, something of which the composite thing is made up. But we have supposed that division can go on without reaching a simple. In that case there would be nothing, which is absurd. The opposite then must be true, namely, "that the substantial composite in the world consists of simple parts" (*GBWW* I: 42, 137; II: 39, 137).

Second, proof that it is infinitely divisible: suppose that it is not but consists of simples that are indivisible. The composition of a composite thing occurs in space, and "the space, occupied by that which is composite, must consist of the same number of parts as is contained in the composite. But space does not consist of simple parts, but of spaces." Any simple part (if there were any) would then also have its accompanying space and would not be simple but composite. "It follows that the simple must be a substantial composite, which is self-contradictory." The opposite then must be true, namely, that there are no simples that are indivisible, but the world is infinitely divisible (*GBWW* I: 42, 137; II: 39, 137).

Given the two contradictory proofs, we must conclude that whether or not the world is infinitely divisible is a question that cannot be decided. Like the questions regarding the finitude or infinitude of space and time, it poses what Kant calls a "transcendental illusion" that results from attempting to decide questions that transcend sense-experience (*GBWW* I: 42, 157; II: 39, 157).

Here it deserves noting that for Kant as for Aristotle the importance of infinity lies in questions about the world and is not restricted to mathematics. Like Aristotle, Kant also considers the infinite as what cannot be traversed and thus claims that "an infinite aggregate of actual things cannot be considered as a given whole" (*GBWW* I: 42, 135; II: 39, 135).

Aquinas

Aquinas, writing as a theologian, is primarily interested in infinity as an attribute of the all-perfect God. For this reason he has to go beyond Aristotle's discussion of the subject. He needs to show that there is a way in which the infinite can denote an attribute of perfection as distinct from the way in which it signifies an imperfection. By appealing to the difference between matter and form, he notes that we obtain two distinct ways of understanding the infinite. A thing is called infinite because it is not finite, he writes; it is not finished or terminated. But there are two different respects in which a thing is finished and made definite. A block of marble in the hands of a sculptor is so much unworked or unformed matter that is potential, and capable of being formed into a particular statue. As such, with respect to the form that it is capable of receiving from the sculptor, it is incomplete or imperfect. Materially considered as so much potentiality, the infinite denotes an imperfection, an incompleteness. However, when the sculptor works the marble into a bust of Aristotle, he gives to the matter a form and so finishes it and brings it to completion as a work of sculpture. Hence, formally considered, the infinite can denote a perfection.

With regard to both finite and infinite, there are these two distinct ways of considering. Thus Aquinas writes:

> Matter indeed is made finite by form, because matter, before it receives its form, is in potency to many forms, but on receiving a form, it is terminated by that one. Again, form is made finite by matter, because form, considered in itself, is common to many, but when received in matter, the form is determined to this one particular thing. Now matter is perfected by the form by which it is made finite; therefore infinite as attributed to matter, has the nature of something imperfect, for it is as it were formless matter. On the other hand form is not made perfect by matter, but rather its fulness is contracted by matter; and hence the infinite, viewed on the part of the form not determined by matter, has the nature of something perfect. (*GBWW* I: 19, 31; II: 17, 31)

The infinity that is attributed to God is the infinity of the second kind, one of perfection. As immaterial, God is not limited or restricted by matter since His being "is not a being received in anything, but He is His own subsistent being." God is not restricted to but one specific kind of being, as are all particular existents.

While investigating the way in which God is infinite, Aquinas also considers whether an actual infinite can exist either in magnitude or multitude. This is a question that gains in significance with the development of the modern mathematics of the infinite.

He denies that there is any actually existing infinite material body, since any body is terminated by its surface and as existing in matter is terminated by that matter. Nor is there any actually existing infinite magnitude, since space is infinite only potentially as capable of being endlessly divided or extended. But it is the argument against an actually existing infinite multitude that is of greatest interest in light of the mathematics of the infinite which posits such an infinite, as we will see. On this subject Aquinas writes that it

> is impossible, since every kind of multitude must belong to a species of multitude. Now the species of multitude are to be reckoned by the species of numbers. But no species of number is infinite; for every number is multitude measured by one. Hence it is impossible for there to be an actually infinite multitude, either absolute or accidental. Likewise multitude in nature [*in rerum natura existens*] is created, and everything created is comprehended under some clear intention of the Creator [*certa intentione creantis*], for no agent acts aimlessly [*in vanum agens aliquod operatur*]. Hence [*necesse est*] everything created must be comprehended in a certain number. Therefore it is impossible for an actually infinite multitude to exist, even accidentally. (*GBWW* I: 19, 34; II: 17, 34)

But more on this text when we come to consider Georg Cantor's theory of the infinite, since Cantor held these two arguments the strongest against an actual infinity of numbers.

On the question regarding the infinity of time, i.e., of the eternity of the world, Aquinas agrees with Kant that no rationally conclusive argument can be given either for or against it. Yet unlike Kant he claims that we know from the revelation of God contained in the book of Genesis that the world had a beginning in time:

> But that God is the Creator of the world; hence that the world began, is an article of faith, for we say, "I believe in one God," etc. [in the Nicene Creed]. And again . . . that Moses prophesied of the past, saying, *In the beginning God created heaven and earth,* in which words the newness of the world is conveyed. Therefore the newness of the world is known only by revelation; and therefore it cannot be proved demonstratively. (*GBWW* I: 19, 253; II: 17, 253)

The mathematicians

Galileo remarked, as already noted, that thinkers cannot refrain from discussing the infinite. He also then proceeded to provide evidence of that fact. He did so in a way that comes close to the way in which modern mathematics deals with the infinite. As has been true since the infinite first came to be discussed, the question arises whether it is thinkable at all. If thinking about it results in contradictions, it would seem that the infinite is not a subject that can be thought about consistently. That the subject does land in contradictions happened to the thought of the ancient thinkers, as shown in Zeno's paradoxes about motion. Galileo provides another example in the sphere of numbers by exposing an oddity about the relation between square numbers and their roots, as follows:

> A squared number is one which results from the multiplication of another number by itself; thus 4, 9, etc., are squared numbers which come from multiplying 2, 3, etc., by themselves. . . . Just as the products are called squares so the factors are called sides or roots; while on the other hand those numbers which do not consist of two equal factors are not squares. Therefore if I assert that all numbers, including both squares and non-squares, are more than the squares alone, I shall speak the truth, shall I not? (*GBWW* I: 28, 144; II: 26, 144)

That is conclusion No. 1.

Suppose now we should inquire how many square numbers there are:

> One might reply truly that there are as many as the corresponding number of roots, since every square has its own root and every root its own square, while no square has more than one root and no root more than one square. . . . But if I inquire how many roots there are, it cannot be denied that there are as many as there are numbers because every number is a root of some square.

Hence our conclusion No. 2:

> We must say that there are as many squares as there are numbers because they are just as numerous as their roots, and all numbers are roots. (Ibid.)

This conclusion is exhibited more clearly once we begin to write down the integers and their squares:

1	2	3	4	5	6	7	8	9	10 . . .
1	4	9	16	25	36	49	64	81	100 . . .

According to conclusion No. 1, there are more numbers than squares. Not only this, Galileo points out, "but the proportionate number of squares diminishes as we pass to larger numbers." Thus among the first 100 numbers, as we have just seen, there are only 10 squares:

> that is, the squares constitute 1/10 part of all the numbers; up to 10,000, we find only 1/100 part to be squares; and up to a million only 1/1000 part; on the other hand in an infinite number, if one could conceive of such a thing, he would be forced to admit that there are as many squares as there are numbers all taken together. (Ibid.)

According to conclusion No. 1, there are more numbers than there are square numbers. But conclusion No. 2 declares that there are just as many squares as numbers, a flat contradiction. What then can be said about the thinkability of the infinite? Galileo concludes thus:

> So far as I see we can only infer that the totality of all numbers is infinite, that the number of squares is infinite, and that the number of their roots is infinite; neither is the number of squares less than the totality of all numbers, nor the latter greater than the former; and finally the attributes "equal," "greater," and "less," are not applicable to infinite, but only to finite, quantities. (Ibid.)

Perhaps the most significant item in this conclusion, judged in relation to more recent developments, is that Galileo is comfortable in thinking about the "totality of all numbers," i.e., in thinking of the totality as a whole, even though an infinite one.

The next significant step in the development of the controversy came with the invention of the calculus by Newton and Leibniz. That was at first conceived of as the introduction of a new kind of number, the "infinitesimal," which as the word itself indicates involves reference to infinity. Recourse to an infinitesimal came about from the attempt to calculate the velocity of a moving body at an instant whose distance from its starting point x, which is a function, i.e., depends upon the time it has been moving, $f(t)$, a problem in which Galileo had been interested. Solution was obtained by imagining the measurement of the speed over an infinitely small time interval, the infinitesimal dt. Calculation with dt revealed that it has strange features. Added to a natural number it functions as zero and can be ignored. Yet it is not zero when division is involved where it can function as the denominator of a function, which zero cannot be. Thus the infinitesimal seemed both to be and not to be the same as zero. Such strangeness led the philosopher Bishop Berkeley in 1734 to write an essay entitled "The Analyste; or A Discourse Addressed to an Infidel Mathematician," which carried the long subtitle:

> Wherein it is examined whether the object, principles, and inferences of the modern Analysis are more distinctly conceived, or more evidently deduced, than religious Mysteries and points of Faith.

Since Berkeley's day the understanding of the calculus has eliminated the infinitesimal and any reference to it. In its place the idea of a limit has been substituted, an operational process which enables one to approach as closely as one wants without ever supposing an actual infinitesimal being reached. Although this notion was not worked out and rigorously applied in the calculus until the nineteenth century, Newton had already thought of it. He wrote that there was no need to introduce infinitely small quantities, since they could be thought of as "limits to which the ratios of quantities vanishing without limit always approach, to which they may come up more closely than by any given difference but beyond which they can never go" (quoted in Moore, 65).

Georg Cantor

The mathematics of the infinite that prevails today is largely the work of Georg Cantor (1845–1918). He was the founder of set theory and in developing it introduced a new kind of numbers which he called "transfinite numbers." The investigation of these numbers now provides the basis of the mathematical account of infinity.

Cantor defined a set as "any collection into a whole M of definite and separate objects m of our intuition or our thought. These objects are called the 'elements' of M" (Cantor, 85). In other words, a set is a many that can be thought of as a one. Thus its elements are prior, and there is no restriction whatsoever on what kind they are, whether the same or different. Yet a set cannot be a member of itself, as we will see.

In his analysis of infinite sets, i.e., of sets containing infinitely many objects, Cantor met Galileo's observations, as it were, head-on. Instead of the square numbers and the non-squares with which Galileo worked, let us take the natural numbers or the positive whole numbers with which we count and which provide the foundation for all the other kinds of numbers. Within the set of natural numbers 1, 2, 3, . . . , which comprise one set, we can distinguish two subsets, one of the even numbers (those divisible by 2) and the other of the odd numbers (not so divisible). So considered, it would appear that the set of all natural numbers is greater than the set of even numbers, since two sets are greater than one. However, we find that there are just as many even numbers as there are natural numbers, since every one of the even numbers has a place within the order of natural numbers, as we have seen in the example of square numbers.

It should be noted that in this comparison between the natural numbers and even numbers, two different criteria have been appealed to: (1) that of subsets contained within a set, and (2) the correlation of the elements of one set with those of another set. By the first criterion the set of even numbers is less than that of the natural numbers as a part is less than a whole. By the second criterion, correlating the elements of the two sets we find that the two sets are equal or of the same size. The different results come about because by the first criterion we are dealing with finite numbers, comparing two subsets with the one set containing both, whereas by the second criterion of correlation we are considering an infinite many.

The difference between these two considerations provided Cantor with the basis for differentiating the infinite from the finite: A finite set is such that it is equivalent to none of its parts. But an infinite set is such that it has parts which are equivalent to it (Cantor, 108). In an infinite set, a subset of it is equal to the whole set, so that a part is as great as a whole, whereas in a finite set this is not so, for there a whole is greater than a part.

So far, we have not denied Galileo's claim that the terms "greater," "less," and "equal" do not function in the same way when applied to both finite and infinite considerations. However, this does not mean that such terms of comparison have entirely no use as applied to the infinite. This, Cantor proceeded to show when he claimed that one infinite set could be proved to be greater than another. In so doing, he asserted that he had discovered a new kind of number, which he named "transfinite," and of which he wrote:

> The transfinite numbers themselves are in a certain sense *new irrationals*.
> . . . One can absolutely assert: the transfinite numbers *stand or fall* with
> the finite irrational numbers; they are alike in their most intrinsic nature;
> for the former like these latter (numbers) are definite, delineated forms
> or modifications of the actual infinite. (Dauben, 128)

In fact, both irrational and transfinite numbers were discovered in the same way: by considering a diagonal.

The irrationals were discovered by the ancient Pythagorean mathematicians. They were used to working with the natural numbers 1, 2, 3, . . . and also with rational numbers, such as fractions expressed as the ratio of two natural numbers, $1/2$, $2/3$, $3/4$. . . . Believing that they could find such numbers wherever they looked, they even went so far as to claim that all things are made of numbers, by which they meant finite parts or elements. Then they stumbled upon a fact—to their horror, it is said—that could not be expressed by either a natural or a rational number. Yet it was a simple and common occurrence in geometry, since it was no more than the diagonal of a square. Given a square each of whose sides is taken to equal 1, its diagonal does not equal a length that can be expressed as a ratio of two natural numbers. By the Pythagorean theorem of triangles, the square on the diagonal equals the sum of the squares on the other two sides or $d^2 = 1^2 + 1^2$ or 2^2, which is to say that $d = \sqrt{2}$, and since this is not a rational number it came to be called an irrational. Today it is common to express the value of $\sqrt{2}$ as the unending decimal 1.4142 . . . . Rationals too can be expressed as unending decimals. Thus $1/3 = 0.3333$ . . . , $1/2 = 0.5000$ . . . , etc. In fact, a rational number can be distinguished from an irrational one by its capability of being expressed as a repeating decimal expression, whereas an irrational cannot.

We thus have distinguished three kinds of numbers: natural, rational, and irrational. Together these came to be called "real numbers," since it was held that they suffice to measure the real world. Even the irrational are needed for this: as $\sqrt{2}$ measures the diagonal of a square and pi (π) the ratio of the circumference to the diameter of a circle.

Cantor in investigating infinite numbers discovered that the rational numbers, which include the natural numbers as a subset (since, e.g., $2 = 2/1$) are themselves denumerable. They can be correlated one-to-one with the natural numbers and so both are equivalent or have the same size. However, when he looked at the real numbers he found, to his surprise, that they are not denumerable.

His proof of this assertion consists in constructing a square out of the real numbers so as to make possible a consideration of its diagonal. Since every real number can be expressed decimally, we will construct the square with them and correlate each one with a natural number. As an example, we will use the four real numbers already mentioned and attend only to their decimal parts. Thus $\sqrt{2}$ will be taken as $\sqrt{2} - 1 = 0.4142$ . . . . We then obtain the beginning of a square of real numbers that could be enlarged indefinitely in which we draw the diagonal thus:

1st number	0 .	3	3	3	3	. . .	$(\frac{1}{3})$
2nd number	0 .	1	4	1	5	. . .	(pi)
3rd number	0 .	4	1	4	2	. . .	$(\sqrt{2})$
4th number	0 .	5	0	0	0	. . .	$(\frac{1}{2})$

We now proceed to write out a new number obtained by moving along the diagonal and choosing at each row and column a number different from the one that is there. Thus at the 1st number we write 4 instead of 3; at the 2nd 3 instead of 4; at the 3rd 3 instead of 4; and at the 4th 3 instead of 0. And thus obtain the number 0.4333.

We note at once that it has a distinctive property: it is a new number, different from any in our little square. Furthermore, we can always do this, however far we extend the square. But we are assuming that the real numbers have been correlated with *all* the natural numbers. Hence by following the diagonal procedure we will always be able to find a new and different number from any in the square. If then the natural numbers have been exhausted, which is our assumption, the resulting new number does not correspond to any natural number. We have used up all the natural counting numbers. This new real number must then lie outside and beyond the natural numbers. In short, the real numbers are non-denumerable, and we have discovered an infinity greater than the denumerable infinite of the natural and rational numbers. We have two different infinite sets and they are not of the same size, one being greater than the other. Counter then to Galileo's assertion, Cantor could claim that even infinites can be compared, relative to size, as greater, equal, or less.

Cantor went on to show how to obtain still other transfinite numbers, how to operate with them, even how to measure them. The resulting set theory has come to serve as a unifying principle for much of mathematics. It also underlies the "new math" that was introduced into the schools more than a generation ago.

With the transfinites Cantor not only introduced a new kind of numbers. He also invented a new notation for them. Since the letters of the Greek and Latin alphabets already had many uses in mathematics, he proposed to designate the transfinite numbers by the first Hebrew letter aleph ($\aleph$) with subscripts. Thus aleph-zero or aleph-null ($\aleph_0$) designates the cardinal transfinite number for the denumerable set of all natural numbers and all sets equivalent to it, just as the cardinal natural number 3 designates all sets of triples. Aleph-one is the next largest transfinite. Cantor held that it designated the totality of the real numbers and hence represented the number corresponding to the continuum and for this reason is often written as c. However, Cantor was unable to prove that c is the next largest transfinite after aleph-zero.

However, for our purposes there is no need to go further into the mathematics of set theory. It is the controversy over the infinite that is the focus of our interest.

Cantor, unlike many mathematicians, was much concerned with the objections that philosophers and theologians made against the actual infinite. He knew the theological speculation about the infinity of God and found in it confirmation of his own theory of the transfinites. Hence he engaged in much correspondence with neo-scholastic Catholic theologians on the subject and succeeded in persuading some of them that his theory did not conflict with Catholic doctrine (Dauben, 144–46).

Cantor held that the two strongest arguments against his position were those of Aquinas against the existence of an actually infinite multitude, which we have discussed previously. Where Aquinas writes of a "multitude," Cantor would understand a set, but he refused to admit the first claim that there is no infinite number to measure an actual infinite, since any number is specified by a one. Against this, Cantor could claim that he had shown another way of determining the elements of a set, not by reaching a number specified by a one, but by correlating the elements with all the natural numbers that taken together constitute a set. Hence he had a number, namely, aleph-zero, and Aquinas's argument was overcome.

The second objection is more strictly theological in that it is based on the providential direction of God, claiming that any creature is created with a definite intention, since otherwise it would be acting in vain. But if it is definite, then it is finite, not infinite. Hence among creatures there is no actual infinite as an actual multitude. Aquinas admitted that in the case of time and motion there might be an infinite. But he maintained that neither of these could be an actual infinite, as a whole given all at once, since either would be infinite only successively (*GBWW* I: 19, 33; II: 17, 33). Cantor was a religious man and may well have believed that the Creator has a definite intention for every creature. But he could also claim that the success of his transfinite set theory provided evidence that the actual infinite serves a definite purpose.

Of greater significance than meeting such objections is Cantor's effort to distinguish his transfinites from the infinity of God. To achieve this he noted:

> The actual infinite arises in three contexts: *first* when it is realized in the most complete form, in a fully independent other-worldly being, *in Deo*, where I call it the Absolute Infinite or simply Absolute; *second* when it occurs in the contingent, created world; *third* when the mind grasps it *in abstracto* as a mathematical magnitude, number, or order type. I wish to make a sharp contrast between the Absolute and what I call the Transfinite, that is the actual infinities of the last two sorts, which are clearly limited, subject to further increase, and thus related to the finite. (Rucker, 10)

Here the crucial distinction, as Cantor emphasizes, is that which separates the first infinite from the other two: the absolute God whose infinity differs from all others. However, with regard to basically different kinds of sets Cantor draws another distinction that bears significantly upon the problem of the infinite:

> If we start from the notion of a definite multiplicity . . . (a system, a totality) of things, it is necessary, as I discovered, to distinguish two kinds of multiplicities (by this I always mean *definite* multiplicities).
>
> For a multiplicity can be such that the assumption that *all* of its elements "are together" leads to a contradiction, so that it is impossible to conceive of the multiplicity as a unity, as "one finished thing." Such multiplicities I call *absolutely infinite* or *inconsistent multiplicities*. . . .
>
> If on the other hand the totality of the elements of a multiplicity can be thought of without contradiction as "being together," so that they can be gathered together into "*one* thing," I call it a *consistent multiplicity* or a "set." (*Sourcebook*, 114)*

The transfinites are thus to be sharply distinguished from two other infinities: from the infinite God as the "*Infinitum aeternum increatum*" on the one hand, and from multiplicities that are inconsistent, which mathematicians now call "classes" rather than sets. The infinite that is Cantor's concern he expressly calls the "*Infinitum creatum sive Transfinitum*" (Dauben, 145).

What is it about some collections or multiplicities that makes them inconsistent? Perhaps the simplest way of exhibiting that inconsistency is to ask: How large is the collection of all transfinite numbers? Should not it also be a number? Yes and no. On the one hand, that number should be larger than all the others, since it is the count of them. Yet, on the other hand, it should also include itself as one of the transfinite num-

---

*Sourcebook: From Frege to Gödel: A Source Book in Mathematical Logic, 1879–1931, ed. Jean van Heijenoort (Cambridge, Mass.: Harvard University Press, 1967).

bers. Faced with this inconsistency or contradiction, Cantor declared that such a collection was too big to be counted and hence not a set.

This argument shows that no set can be a member of itself; the set of all natural numbers is not a member of itself. This fact is the basis for the most famous version of the contradiction known as Russell's paradox. Bertrand Russell formulated this in terms of classes by asking whether the class of all classes is a member of itself. It both is and is not. As a class it should be a member, while if it is not, then it does not include all classes. Russell discovered this contradiction in the work of the great German logician Gottlob Frege, and not in that of Cantor. Cantor was not bothered by the paradox; since he had already noted it and dismissed it, he did not count it as a set at all but named it for what it is, an inconsistent multiplicity.

The first reactions to Cantor's theory were divided. Such eminent logicians as Frege and Russell welcomed the transfinite numbers, as did the mathematician Richard Dedekind. But others no less eminent were strongly opposed. This was especially true of Cantor's former professor at the University of Berlin, Leopold Kronecker, whose authority was such that he could prevent publication of Cantor's early papers as well as thwart his professional advancement. Kronecker maintained that mathematics should be restricted to finite operations upon the integers, and hence he vigorously rejected the transfinites as so much nonsense. For him "God made the natural numbers, all else was the work of man."

Poincaré, the great French mathematician, rejected Cantor's theory as "a perverse pathological illness." Bergson, the leading French philosopher of the time, dismissed the claim that the continuum had been reduced to numbers as the same mistake that scientists make in treating time as a series of points. Time like motion is continuous. Along that continuum "we can imagine possible stoppages," or points along the way. "But with these positions, even with an infinite number of them, we shall never make movement" or time or the continuum (*GBWW* II: 55, 80).

The American mathematical philosopher C. S. Peirce held that Cantor had failed to prove the infinity of the real numbers as a complete set and that at most it existed as only a potential, not an actual, infinite, since no matter how many real numbers one might obtain there would always be more in the waiting. Peirce thus reiterates Aristotle's analysis of the infinite by admitting a potential infinite, but denying an actual one.

The moralists

There remains still another issue that arises in the discussion of the infinite. This concerns the way in which man relates to the infinite, especially in desire and knowledge. Philosophers have maintained that, morally considered, this relation may be bad as well as good.

One thing commonly identified as an infinite evil is the love of money, which indeed Saint Paul castigates as the "root of all evils" (1 Timothy 6:10). Aristotle explains the rootedness:

> The origin of this disposition in men is that they are intent upon living only, and not upon living well; and, as their desires are unlimited, they also desire that the means of gratifying them should be without limit. (*GBWW* I: 9, 452; II: 8, 452)

In a comment upon this fact about human nature Aquinas explains that it is based upon the power of the soul that contains the desire for sensible goods, which he calls "concupiscence":

> Because concupiscence of the end is always infinite, since the end is desired for its own sake, for instance, health, and thus greater health is more desired, and so on to infinity; just as, if a white thing of itself dilates the sight, that which is more white dilates still more. . . . Consequently those who place their end in riches have an infinite concupiscence of riches. . . . The same applies to the concupiscence of any other things. (*GBWW* I: 19, 752; II: 17, 752)

Since the desire for the end as an end in itself is infinite, the desire is evil when it is directed to a false end, i.e., to an object or objects incapable of satisfying and fulfilling the human desire for happiness.

The cause of the infinite character of a desire for the end Aquinas attributes to the power of the intellect "in so far as it can consider a thing infinitely, as appears in the addition of numbers and lines" (ibid.). Interest in the mathematical infinite of itself provides evidence of human concern with the infinite.

However, the strongest evidence of this lies in the desire for the last end that is happiness:

> For happiness is the perfect good, which, quiets the appetite altogether since it would not be the last end if something yet remained to be desired. Now the object of the will, that is, of man's appetite, is the universal good, just as the object of the intellect is the universal true. Hence it is evident that nothing can quiet man's will except the universal good. This is to be found not in any creature, but in God alone. (*GBWW* I: 19, 622; II: 17, 622)

But since God is infinite, the desire for happiness as the last end is nothing less than the desire for the infinite.

For Kant too the infinite is a matter of human concern. He claims that immortality, along with freedom and God, constitute the basic principles of the moral life. But for this life to achieve its end, a "*progress in infinitum*" is practically necessary:

Now, this endless progress is only possible on the supposition of an *endless* duration of the *existence* and personality of the same rational being (which is called the *immortality of the soul*). (*GBWW* I: 42, 344; II: 39, 344)

Thus, evidence of still another source of the desire for an infinite is found in that for the immortality of an endless future.

This belief has a very long history. Expression of it can be found in Homer's *Iliad,* where the Trojan heroes, Sarpedon and Glaucon, speculate during a lull in the battle why it is that they are honored as though they were immortal. Sarpedon declares:

Man, supposing you and I, escaping this battle, would be able to live
on forever, ageless, immortal, so neither would I myself go on fighting
in the foremost nor would I urge you into the fighting where men win
glory. But now, seeing that the spirits of death stand close about us
in their thousands, no man can turn aside nor escape them, let us go
on and win glory for ourselves, or yield it to others. (*GBWW* I: 4, 85;
II: 3, 145)

Hence glory won in battle provides a kind of immortality in the ongoing memories of humankind.

According to Plato, the desire for immortality reaches far beyond that for military glory. It lies at the root of love and permeates all of human life. For "love is of the immortal . . . the mortal nature is seeking as far as is possible to be everlasting and immortal." In the body it seeks to perpetuate itself through generation and "the love which all men have of their offspring; for that universal love and interest is for the sake of immortality." But the soul too desires to beget. Its offspring are the result of wisdom and virtue such as are found in the works of poets, legislators, and statesmen, and of scientists and philosophers. All, from the love and desire for beauty, aspire to the "contemplation of beauty absolute," so as to "become the friend of God and be immortal." (*GBWW* I: 7, 165–67; II: 6, 165–67)

Even Marcus Aurelius, who believed there was nothing for a person after death, could not avoid expressing his regret at such a condition, thereby implicitly betraying a desire for immortality:

How can it be that the gods after having arranged all things well
and benevolently for mankind, have overlooked this alone, that some
men and very good men, and men who, as we may say, have had most
communion with the divinity, and through pious acts and religious
observances have been most intimate with the divinity, when they
have once died should never exist again, but should be completely
extinguished? (*GBWW* I: 12, 307–9; II: 11, 291)

The opposite situation is to be found in the Gospels. There Jesus is presented as the one who possesses the power to grant eternal life (John

17:2). A dramatic example of the desire for immortality is provided by the story of the rich young man who sought out Jesus to ask him: "Good master, what good thing shall I do that I may have eternal life?" But he then left in sorrow on being told that he should divest himself of his riches (Matthew 19:16–22).

Karl Barth, the Swiss German Lutheran philosopher of the twentieth century, claims that the desire for infinity is rooted in the very nature of man:

> He may be told a thousand times that in order to reach infinity he has only to keep walking along finite paths—and this he certainly does. . . .
> But a thousand times, in spite of all the guidance and instruction he has received, he fails for one reason or another to find satisfaction in the path of finitude. What he finds is related to what he seeks as $1 : \infty$; and this is an intolerable state of affairs to him, for he cannot believe that $1 = \infty$. (*GBWW* II: 55, 507)

Knowledge and the desire for it reveal another opening onto the infinite. Mathematicians, as we have seen, have devoted much thought to it and have become convinced that they have overcome it. Yet one can still ask why mathematicians and philosophers have been so much attracted to the infinite.

Plato provides one of the answers to this question. He finds it in the relation of the intellect to truth. Appealing as he frequently does to the example of mathematics, he has Socrates discuss the activity and purpose of geometry. Socrates claims that "knowledge is the real object of the whole science." But what kind of knowledge? He answers: "The knowledge at which geometry aims is knowledge of the eternal, and not of aught perishing and transient" (*GBWW* I: 7, 394; II: 6, 394). Such a claim rests on the apparently evident characteristic of a true mathematical theorem, such as the Pythagorean theorem about triangles. Of a right-angled Euclidean triangle it has always been true, is now true, and always will be true that the square on the hypotenuse equals the sum of the squares on the other two sides; hence that truth is eternal. Plato holds that all pure or abstract mathematics achieves the same end. But mathematics leads on to the study of philosophy, and this aims eventually at the "most pure being—that which is concerned with the invariable, the immortal, and the true" (*GBWW* I: 7, 423; II: 6, 423). To know a truth that is eternal is, however, to reach what is without beginning or end, and so infinite.

Aristotle is no less certain than Plato that the highest knowledge aims at eternal truth. In the account of scientific method in the *Posterior Analytics* he declares that the strongest demonstration must have both premises and conclusions that are eternal. Hence of things that are perishable there can be no strictly scientific demonstration (*GBWW* I: 8, 104; II: 7, 104).

Cantor holds much the same position. He could claim that his theory of the transfinites had established a truth about infinity and, even more than that, it led on to a still greater one in a better understanding of the infinity of God (Dauben, 146).

There is still another way in which knowledge of the truth bears upon infinity: namely, that the search for it is unending, and no matter how far it may go, there will always remain more to seek. According to Pascal, "all sciences are infinite in the extent of their researches" (*GBWW* I: 33, 182; II: 30, 182).

A proof of this in the field of mathematics was produced in 1931, raising consternation among both mathematicians and philosophers. It was the article by Kurt Gödel entitled in its English translation from the German, "On formally undecidable propositions of *Principia mathematica* and related systems." The work referred to is that by Whitehead and Russell in which they endeavored to show that all of mathematics could be derived from a few logical axioms and rules of inference as a base. Ever since Euclid had demonstrated how the mathematics of his time could be organized in an axiomatic system, this method had come to be the best and preferred one for showing how a great many truths can be proven and related together in one overall system. The aim was completeness in the sense that every well-formed proposition in mathematics could be proved or refuted. To test this result some procedure must exist by which the question can be decided for any proposition capable of being expressed in the system. Gödel set out to find such a procedure for *PM,* and he succeeded in formulating a proposition that was undecidable in the system: one that could be neither proved nor refuted.

Gödel obtained this proposition—a nightmare for a mathematician or a logician—by arithmetizing the system of *PM.* He showed how it is possible to translate all its formulas, its primitive elements as well as its theorems, into finite sequences of the natural numbers. He thus produced an isomorphic double in the field of arithmetic of anything expressed in the notation of *PM,* of which he then could make an arithmetical analysis. He next employed the diagonal method such as Cantor used for the real numbers and obtained a new formula $F(v)$ "such that $F(v)$ interpreted according to the meaning of the terms in *PM* says: v is a provable formula." He could then "construct an undecidable proposition in the system *PM* that is a proposition A for which neither A nor *not-A* is provable" (*Sourcebook,* 597). This conclusion demonstrated that the axiomatic system of *PM,* far from being complete for all of mathematics, was not even so for the domain of arithmetic. Furthermore, the method of demonstration would also hold for any other axiomatic base that might be chosen.

What further does the Gödel theorem show that bears upon the infinite? A single text from Gödel suffices for an answer: "The human mind is incapable of formulating . . . all its mathematical intuitions. . . . This fact may be called the 'incompletability' of mathematics" (Moore, 172). But if incomplete, then unending or infinite. It is not just that in mathematics not everything can be proved. Since proof in mathematics is convertible with truth, there always remain further truths to seek.

Controversy

Interest in the infinite and puzzlement have existed for a very long time: in fact, during the whole of our intellectual history. However, only with the rise of the theory of the transfinite over the last century has sharp controversy developed over how best to account for it. In it, mathematicians are opposed to philosophers.

The most strident staking of position has come from the side of mathematics. The article on infinity in the *Encyclopedia of Philosophy,* addressing the question of what it means to say something is infinite, claims:

> It is a striking fact that until the work of Bolzano and Cantor a clear and satisfactory answer had not been provided . . . and what is clear [in the earlier work] is from a modern point of view wrong (vol. 4, pp. 183–84).

More recently the controversy has arisen over a book by a philosopher on the infinite and a review of it by a mathematician. The disagreement has been sharp and is especially significant in that the basic issue has been identified as that of describing or defining the infinite. Roger Penrose, the mathematician and author of a book on the mind and computers entitled *The Emperor's New Clothes,* maintains that set theory provides the best account of infinity and finds himself disconcerted at being unable "to appreciate many of the issues that seem greatly to trouble so many philosophers" (Penrose, 1155, col. 1). A. W. Moore, the philosopher, scoffs at the idea that the infinite is completely caught in identifying it by the property "enjoyed by any set whose members can be paired off with the members of one of its proper subsets—as though *this* were the last word on everything that exercised Aristotle, Kant, Hegel, and the rest" (Moore, 198).

The mathematical theory of the infinite, as we have seen, rests at bottom on the idea of numbers, and of these the natural or counting numbers are taken as the paradigm of all the others. They provide the means of identifying the various infinites and the essential principle of the diagonal procedure used by both Cantor and Gödel. Yet even our little survey of the philosophers on the subject bears out Moore's contention that their concern has gone far beyond numbers: to questions regarding the infinite in time, space, the universe, God, and the desires of humankind for wealth, happiness, immortality, and knowledge. None of these subjects is clarified or explained by the mathematical definition of an infinite set. This is true even of Gödel's theory of incompleteness, for although the proof depends upon numbers, it carries the implication that the search for truth can never be complete.

There are also two respects in which Cantor's analysis of the infinite goes beyond the transfinite. Cantor himself admitted as much, especially in his correspondence with theologians. As we have seen, he sharply distinguished the Absolute Infinity of God from both the infinite in the world and the transfinite numbers. Both of the latter he stated are "clearly limited, subject to further increase, and thus related to the finite" (Rucker, 10). Mathematical analysis also breaks down when it reaches inconsistent multiplicities, as Cantor called them. Examples of such are the totality of everything thinkable and, more famously, the totality of all sets. Since the latter results in contradiction, even though it may involve an infinity, it does not qualify as a set. Penrose admits that "there seems to be no clear-cut rule for deciding when a class is sufficiently respectable to qualify as a set," but he does not see it as anything to worry about (*loc. cit.*). Moore, however, refuses to admit such an evasion. "Although distinguishing between collections of different kinds in this sort of way can have a perfectly legitimate rationale," he writes, "especially in formal contexts, it is surely a mistake to think that it enables us to escape this particular paradox" of the Set of all Sets (Moore, 150).

What then can be said about this controversy itself? Are philosophers and mathematicians discussing the same subject when they argue about the infinite? Although there are marked differences in what they have to say about it, it cannot be denied that in certain respects they mean the same thing. They are not referring to two entirely different things that are called by the same name of "infinite." Both agree that in one respect this is something that goes on endlessly, that one cannot traverse or get through it, and that one can continue counting by the natural numbers without reaching a greatest one. But disagreement occurs as soon as it is asked whether, granting this much, is it still possible to grasp that thing as a one and a whole. Philosophers for the most part deny that it can be, in such a sense as to constitute an actual infinite. Those whose thought on the matter we have discussed bear this out. To them many more could be added, such as Locke, Berkeley, Hume and the empiricists, and Wittgenstein. Against them mathematicians and mathematical philosophers such as Russell maintain that the infinite *can* be grasped as one whole and cite, as evidence, transfinite set theory. Their infinite is jealously guarded. Of it the mathematician David Hilbert declared, "No one shall be able to drive us from the paradise that Cantor created for us" (*Sourcebook*, 376).

The crux of the disagreement concerns the distinction between the potential and actual infinite. Philosophers have no trouble in admitting a potential infinite. A line is capable of being endlessly divided and numbers of being continually increased. But even in this sense the infinite is limited to thought. It is not a potential that can become actual, as one who is capable of walking may arise and actually walk. Aristotle says, "the infinite does not exist potentially in the sense that it will ever actually have separate existence; it exists potentially only for knowledge" (*GBWW* I: 8, 574; II: 7, 574). Actually any part of a potential infinite, say of a divided line or a given number, is always finite. And for Aristotle, as was emphasized earlier, the possibility of conception in thought is no guarantee whatever of existence in fact or actuality.

But for Cantor this is not at all the case. For him the existence, at least of mathematical objects, is assured if they can be thought of in themselves and of being related to other objects without any inconsistency. As soon as these conditions are satisfied, Cantor wrote, such objects "can and must be regarded as existent and real in mathematics" (Dauben, 128–29). In short, he claimed, as with the infinities of set theory, thought itself suffices to prove actual existence.

Neither Aristotle, Aquinas, nor Kant accept such a proof as conclusive. They hold that more than thought or reason is required to justify actual existence. In this respect many mathematicians like Penrose and Gödel expressly side with Plato's support of the world of ideas against the Aristotelian grounding in the actual world of fact.

However, as Aristotle declared after expressing his criticism, "our account does not rob the mathematicians of their science, by disproving the actual existence of the infinite" (*GBWW* I: 8, 286; II: 7, 286).

References

Aquinas, Saint Thomas. *The Summa Theologica*. Translated by Father Laurence Shapcote, revised by Daniel J. Sullivan.

Aristotle. *The Works*. The Oxford Translation. Edited by W. D. Ross.

Barth, Karl. *The Word of God and the Word of Man*. Translated by Douglas Horton.

Cantor, Georg. *Contributions to the Founding of the Theory of Transfinite Numbers*. Translated by Philip E. B. Jourdain. La Salle, Illinois: The Open Court Publishing Co., 1941.

Dauben, Joseph Warren. *Georg Cantor: His Mathematics and Philosophy of the Infinite*. Princeton, New Jersey: Princeton University Press, 1990.

Einstein, Albert. *Relativity: The Special and General Theory*. Translated by Robert W. Lawson.

The Encyclopedia of Philosophy. Edited by Paul Edwards. New York: The Macmillan Company & the Free Press, 1967.

Galilei, Galileo. *Concerning the Two New Sciences.* Translated by Henry Crew and Alfonso de Salvio.

Gödel, Kurt. *On formally undecidable propositions of* Principia mathematica *and related systems,* in *Sourcebook.*

Hilbert, David. *On the Infinite,* in *Sourcebook.*

Homer. *The Iliad.* Translated by Richard Lattimore.

Kant, Immanuel. *The Critique of Pure Reason.* Translated by J. M. D. Meiklejohn.

Lucretius. *The Way Things Are.* Translated by Rolfe Humphries.

Marcus Aurelius. *The Meditations.* Translated by George Long.

Moore, A. W. *The Infinite.* London and New York: Routledge, 1990.

Pascal, Blaise. *Pensées.* Translated by W. F. Trotter.

Penrose, Roger. "Things beyond Saying," in *Times Literary Supplement,* Oct. 26–Nov. 1, 1990.

Plato. *The Dialogues.* Translated by Benjamin Jowett.

Rucker, Rudy. *Infinity and the Mind: The Science and Philosophy of the Infinite.* New York: Bantam Books, 1983.

"Notes from Yon Exaltations Caught"
Church Singing and the Fathers

Bruce Venable

Bruce Venable was born in Portland, Oregon, where he was educated in public and parochial schools. He attended St. Mary's College of California, from which he received a B.A. (philosophy), and in 1976 he got a doctorate in classics at the University of Washington, Seattle. His professional career has been spent at St. John's College, Santa Fe, New Mexico, where he has been a tutor—the only rank conferred by the faculty there—since 1973.

He has written essays on Plotinus, whose *Six Enneads* appear in the *Great Books of the Western World* (I: 17, 1–360; II: 11, 301–678), and on a certain Saint Symeon, of whom he has published a discussion in *Orthodox Outlook* (U.K.) 6, no. 1 (1989). His chief interest, however, is in liturgical music. He often leads choral groups at St. John's and enjoys choir singing himself at the Russian Cathedral in London. His other interests are cycling and hiking, gardening, and concertgoing. A previous article by him on music as a liberal art appeared in *The Great Ideas Today* 1991.

N o one can fail to be impressed by the tenacity with which religion maintains, even in our own times, its alliance with music. Not only do churches and synagogues preserve music regarded as properly religious, little subject to prevailing musical fashions, and therefore seldom heard elsewhere, but music itself seems to be regarded as uniquely appropriate to religious ceremonial. Social history, however, makes clear that every aspect of life was at one time accompanied by its proper music: weddings and funerals, work of all sorts, planting and harvest, games, social dancing, meals, and drinking. Modern religion retains this archaic character amid other modern institutions that are no longer so accompanied. Anthropologists declare that archaic societies regarded all such common activities as in some broader sense religious, as affirmations of the inherited social order, taught to the ancestors by the gods and preserved as a manifestation of their favor. The disappearance of the other characteristic social musics follows the loss of the sacred character of the social life they once accompanied, leaving behind a truncated form of religion as the only properly religious activity.

One would like to know whether there is a deep connection between music and religious ceremonial, or whether the continued attachment of religion to music is only another sign of that social conservatism which is detectable in other aspects of modern religious life.

The witness of social history allows us to infer rather that music is both originally and intrinsically sacred, an inference confirmed by the mythology of all peoples. Further, indirect confirmation may be seen in the contemporary survival of half-numinous patriotic music, and in the incongruous solemnity of the classical music concert. Attendance at the latter is almost obligatory for certain classes of people, of whom moreover the greatest public propriety is required: they may not eat or drink, talk, laugh, or flirt during the performance, which, however, they are not expected particularly to understand but only vaguely to appreciate. Even comic operas are by preference given in the original foreign languages so that the audience will not be tempted to giggle at the jokes and so disrupt the uncomprehending, pious decorum. No comparable intensity of ritual is demanded at an exhibition of painting or sculpture. And it is only classical music that makes such demands of its audience, for genuinely popular music has lost any sense of occasion or even performance, having become a part of the circumambient urban noise. The classical concert alone asserts itself as a cultural ceremony in which those with any pretension to refinement reaffirm their devout allegiance to the art that in the Western world has always had the loftiest intellectual and spiritual aspirations. This atavism of the classical music concert may perhaps explain as well the notorious reluctance of audiences to accept anything perceived as innovation.

Christians seem from the beginning to have been particularly devoted to music and remain so today; the various modern churches seem more doggedly faithful to their own musical traditions than to almost anything else, congregations being more conservative about style and repertory than concertgoers even. The Fathers of the early Church were loud in their praise of singing. Saint Ambrose, the friend and teacher of the blessed Augustine, is typical: "A psalm is a blessing upon the people, the common voice of all, a profession of faith in song, devotion full of authority, the joy of freedom, happiness spoken aloud, the resonance of bliss." [1] But beyond all praise of earthly music is the picture of music as the very form of heavenly beatitude: the redeemed will sing round the throne of the Almighty just as the angels do now.

This essay will try to explain the extraordinary importance of music for Christianity. After a survey of the ancient evidence for Christian attitudes toward music, it will seek a deeper understanding of these attitudes in the philosophical background of the Christian church fathers and will conclude with a sketch of the new philosophy of created being to which the Fathers were led and which is embodied in the liturgy of the Church. The contents of the essay therefore become increasingly conjectural and speculative as it proceeds.

Pagan antecedents

The history of Christian music is problematic from the beginning, partly because of a lack of precise evidence for the early period and partly because of a recurrent conflict of ideals, present at all periods and visible even today. The problem, or at least a characteristic vagueness, begins with the Last Supper, where we know that the apostles sang a "hymn" that may or may not have been the "Hallel" psalms that concluded what may, or again may not, have been a Passover seder. [2] The epistles of Saint Paul imply a generally favorable attitude to singing in church and are thought by some to contain quotations from primitive hymns. Other early accounts of Christian liturgy often refer to the singing of psalms or hymns but do not tell us what they actually were.

Much more frequent in early Christian literature are thunderous denunciations of pagan music, to whose inherently sacred or ritual nature they thereby attest. [3] The music of pagan society was itself pagan

"The Last Supper," fresco by Andrea del Castagno (1421?–57). "... the Last Supper, where we know that the apostles sang a 'hymn' that may or may not have been the 'Hallel' psalms that concluded what may, or may not, have been a Passover seder."

and as such to be rejected by Christians as pernicious. [4] The Fathers of the Church included in their utter detestation not only the music that accompanied idolatrous cults and sacrifices but also the music of weddings, funerals, dances, banquets, and the theater. The Fathers invariably describe this music as coarse and lascivious, an implicit offense to their extreme sexual delicacy, and almost invariably as instrumental music, naming—and with hideous loathing—the lyre and harp, the flutes, recorders, drums, and castanets. Christian music was by contrast always only singing, sober and chaste. Unfortunately, we can only imagine what any of this music was, since pagan music survives in fragments that give us little idea of how they sounded in performance, while Christian music seems not to have been written down at all until much later. We too might be repelled by the overt texts and shrill timbres of pagan music and drawn toward piety by the grave or glad psalmody of the early Church, we cannot tell. [5]

It is clear even so that the revulsion of the Fathers was not rustic, possibly Semitic, incomprehension of a sophisticated Hellenic music, because it was precisely the highly educated Saint Clement of Alexandria and the philosophical apologist Saint Justin Martyr who first expanded themselves in prophetic warnings of the poison lurking in pagan music, while much later, in the fourth century, the battle was waged most implacably by the Attic eloquence of Saint Basil and Saint John Chrysostom. All these authors wished to reconcile Christianity with classical secular culture and allied themselves therefore with its long tradition of specifically philosophical puritanism.

For Plato and Xenophon the absence of a flute girl at a drinking party was already a sign that the occasion was a respectable one at which the rational pleasures of conversation and disputation were to be enjoyed, eschewing pleasures more dubious. In his more ambitious flights, of course, Plato envisaged a reform by which Greek music would be purged of all wanton or enervating modes, retaining only the severe, more bracing, Dorian. He also objected to new-fangled instruments capable of chromatic modulations that violated the integrity of the traditional melodies. There were puritanical cranks among the Romans as well, not only the censorious [Marcus Porcius] Cato, who despised all things Greek as effeminate (for the innovations deplored by Plato had flourished nonetheless), but also the more moderate Livy, who regretted that such Eastern luxuries as chamber music during dinner had corrupted primitive Republican simplicity. Juvenal the satirist at least pretended to find such Oriental refinements distasteful and demoralizing.

One does not usually think of Epicureans as puritanical, and of course they had a dreadful reputation for bad behavior among adherents of other philosophical schools and the general public; but they were puritans all the same, mistrusting not only sex but culture as well. "Flee from culture, and I mean all of it, my dear boy, as you set sail in your little boat," wrote Epicurus to a beloved disciple, for whom he wrote a detailed scientific treatise of celestial and meteorological phenomena, urging him at the close to remember these arguments at all times and so escape from mythology. No wonder that Epicureans had a reputation for vulgarity. [6]

Philosophers continued to incline toward puritanism during the Imperial period. Stoics like Seneca, Marcus Aurelius, Lucan, and Persius give the impression that they lived amid lurid scenes of riot and dissipation, from which they struggled to keep themselves unsoiled. This upper-class Stoicism influenced Clement of Alexandria, as it had earlier Philo Judaeus, to condemn the battery of loud instruments played at symposia, inciting drunkenness and indecency, as well as the harsh instruments of war that stir up wrath and aggression. (The mention of this once-prevalent Christian pacificism suffices to show that the puritanism of the early Church sought to govern all human passions, not only the sexual.) The Neoplatonic and Neopythagorean movement, which was everything there was of the most chic from the third century on, contributed to the fashionable puritanism of the intelligentsia. Even the horrible Julian the Apostate learned from this pagan esotericism to be a puritan. His teacher of oratory at Antioch, the pagan Libanius, was not quite so austere as his fellow citizen Saint John Chrysostom, but *almost*.

The severity of these patristic denunciations of instrumental music, becoming only more strident and sarcastic as time went on, is the more remarkable in the face of the abundant biblical testimony to the elaborate musical liturgy of the Temple, which had long ceased to exist in Jerusalem, but whose trumpets and harps, timbrels and psalteries, tabrets and loud cymbals, continued to resound in the Psalms.

The Fathers were divided in their approach to this obvious difficulty. Some interpreted the musical instruments allegorically, as indicating different parts of the soul, perhaps, or different virtues, or different stages of the spiritual life. These were the Fathers of the Alexandrian tradition, who adopted a like attitude toward all Scripture, not just the awkward bits: they sought an inner, spiritual or mystical, meaning in the events narrated in the Bible as history. The Antiochene school of exegesis, which attributed a greater importance to the letter of Scripture, admitted that these instruments were actually used in the Temple, but as a divine concession to the spiritual naiveté of the people, corrupted perhaps by their long sojourn among the carnal-minded Egyptians. Moses led the people from the gross materialism of idolatry toward spiritual worship of the invisible God by means of a liturgy purified of images, but still richly sensuous. No one can fail to notice that it was Aaron, who actually fashioned the golden calf, who became the first high priest. One is not to suppose that the Lord God enjoyed the sound of the Temple music, any more than that He desired the savor of incense and burnt offerings, but that He accepted the innocent intentions of His still-childish people. That the people were supposed eventually able to see through the liturgy is suggested by the beautiful words of Solomon at the dedication of the Temple; he never mentions ritual or sacrifice at all but returns again and again to the theme of private prayer and supplication to God. [7]

The Antiochene and Alexandrine approaches are nonetheless complementary because they share the conviction that Christian worship is to be spiritual. Everyone quoted John's Gospel: "But the hour cometh, and now is, when the true worshippers shall worship the Father in spirit and truth; for the Father seeketh such to worship Him. God is a Spirit; and they that worship Him must worship Him in spirit and truth." [8]

Here again the pagan philosophical tradition was relevant, for it was a commonplace that silent worship is alone worthy of the God who transcends not only matter but speech. Thus Porphyry, the disciple of Plotinus: "Neither speech expressed in sound is appropriate to Him, nor even inner speech, so long as it is polluted by any passion of the soul; rather we worship Him through mere silence and pure thoughts. Only when we are joined and likened to Him can we offer our own being-lifted-up as a holy sacrifice to God, at once a song to Him and our own salvation. In a passionless state of soul and in contemplation of God this sacrifice is brought to perfection." [9] Plotinus himself wrote: "Let us call upon God, not in spoken words, but stretching ourselves out with our soul into prayer to Him, able in this way to pray alone to Him who is alone" [GBWW I: 17, 211; II: 11, 521]. [10] Much is here implied that this essay will try to unfold, but already we sense the idea of prayer as a gesture in which the whole person lifts itself up as a purified oblation to its creator.

This exalted idea was taught as well by Philo, who, although a Jew, had his posterity almost entirely in Christendom. The whole visible world, he said, is not adequate to thank and honor God its creator, but hymns of praise lifted by the sounding and singing of the invisible intellect are alone worthy of being offered to Him. [11] And Philo was the one who introduced the search for spiritual meanings into biblical interpretation.

It is vital not to misunderstand here. When we hear the word "spiritual," we are liable to take it as one of the two contrasting areas into which the critique of Descartes divided it: either as the mental, logical, or conceptual, or else as a delicate emotional susceptibility to thoughts about the divine. The Fathers of the Church, however, as yet ignorant of the achievements of Descartes, taught that the practical goal of the Christian life was to reduce this dualism of thought and feeling to the original integrity of human nature, a free cooperation of intuitive knowledge and instinct. "Spirit" was their name for this unity.

The Fathers were rather extraordinarily fond of musical metaphors of spiritual unity. They used them to express the original coherence of all created order—the unity, that is, of the created form and the divine creative intention—a harmony of outside and inside into which no discord has yet entered. They used musical metaphors to describe the recovered equipoise of a virtuous personality as well as the sweetness of a social life imbued with charity. Such musical metaphors were part of the common stock of antiquity, deriving from the Pythagorean and Platonic sense that cosmic order, personal virtue, and human community result from inner harmony rather than obedience to external laws. The patristic penchant for metaphors is a symptom of their gradual rapprochement with classical liberal education, of which music had long been a part, both as theory and as a practical vehicle to civilize the young. Metaphors had already been adopted by Philo; the idea that the order of the universe is music even though it is inaudible, and that the praise of the intellect is a hymn even if it is unspoken, is a great favorite with him. [12] But in order to understand how the Fathers thought through these metaphors it is essential to return to their origins in pagan philosophy and their subsequent place in the system of pagan education, which the Fathers eventually and in part reluctantly accepted. The reconciliation of primitive Christianity with Hellenic learning is a long story, but a part at least should be told here for the sake of the light it casts on the philosophical background of the Fathers and in particular on the high role attributed there to music. [13]

Pagan education

It may seem surprising, especially to those educated in the parochial schools of modern America, that the Christian Church did not from the beginning claim the right and duty to set up schools in which primary education could be integrated with the teaching of catechism and Christian morality. There existed in early centuries the same kind of mutual suspicion and contempt between Christians and pagan society that led the Roman Catholic bishops assembled at the Third Plenary Council of Baltimore in 1886 to decree the "absolute necessity and obligation" that every parish in America establish primary and secondary schools and the corresponding obligation that parents send their children to them. The relative isolation of Roman Catholic culture that resulted was regarded as confirming the incompatibility of Catholic and secular ideals. [14] The early Church had moreover the example of the Jewish schools that were established everywhere in the diaspora for the exclusive study of Hebrew, Bible, and Mishna.

Christian children of early times were in fact sent to pagan schools, where they learned their letters by copying out lists of pagan gods and heroes and memorizing maxims from Homer or Virgil that were not always edifying to a young Christian conscience. Extremists did not fail to denounce this collusion with false religion and morality. The world still rings with the cry of Tertullian: "What has Athens to do with Jerusalem?" The failure of the rigorists to keep the rival cities apart was due in part to an evident practical need: even Tertullian had to admit that Christian children had to learn how to read, and here was pagan society well equipped with primary schools. The failure to establish independent schools cannot be attributed to the cultural lethargy of the majority of Christians who were content, then as now, to coexist with paganism. They seemed quite aware that Hellenism contained in its various rival philosophies several coherent alternatives to Christianity, and they could not have been unaware of the hostility and scorn of even their less well-educated and philosophically committed neighbors. The official persecutions as well, although intermittent, could be savage.

The deeper reason for ancient Christian collaboration with pagan education was the belief that Christianity was not only faith and cult, but culture as well, a formation of the entire human person. "Thou shalt love the Lord thy God in thy whole heart and in thy whole being and in thy whole mind." Christianity made a claim upon the whole of human life, not only upon belief and behavior. Human life was to form a newly integrated whole in Christ, just as Christ in His incarnation assumed a whole human person. Christians could not then be content, like Stoic sages, to hand over large areas of human life into the power of the enemy. Nothing could be abandoned to fate, because all was to be redeemed and reunited. Salvation includes restoration in Christ of the original perfection of human nature as granted to Adam and Eve in Paradise. The affirmation of the power and goodness of nature contained in Hellenism could not as such offend Christians. Hence they did not, as did Jews after the destruction of the Temple, turn their backs upon secular wisdom and establish schools where nothing was taught but the sacred texts. That the rabbinical schools were able amid the greatest of adversities to preserve the soul and kernel of Judaism was a miracle of devotion, tenacity, and courage, but the self-absorption required to preserve it meant that the world would not be redeemed by Judaism after all. In the Alexandria of the Ptolemies, the home of Philo, Judaism opened its doors to converts and translated the Bible into Greek for the whole world to read. After the exile from Palestine the rabbis regretted this openness and kept a day of mourning to lament that Torah had ever been divulged in the language of the gentiles. [15] Philo, the first Jewish religious philosopher, was for many centuries to be the last.

All this was different in Christianity. Partly in response to an external history that gradually became more favorable, but more deeply out of a native impulse, a Christian philosophy began to be born, as one day, when the times might permit, there would be born a Christian politics and a Christian civil law, as Christianity undertook the arduous task, not of defining its own path through the world and out of it again, but of redeeming the world itself, or, better said, of fulfilling the promise of redemption inherent in the world since its creation.

Desiring thus a redeemed intellectual life and finding in the pagan schools an adequate vehicle of intellectual culture, Christians continued to send their children to them, not of course without dreadful warnings against contamination by paganism. Even after the triumph of the Church, however, the school curriculum did not shed its pagan garments, so that children continued to copy out lists of heathen deities and the insidious maxims of the poets. In the Byzantine world, indeed, secular education remained much what it had always been, while theology as such was taught by monks and bishops. The situation in the Latin West developed quite differently because of the early disintegration of civil society and urban life. There the monasteries assumed the precious burden of classical education.

That an underlying caution about Hellenism persisted even in the serene Byzantine East, however, is evidenced by the fact that the emperor Justinian, rigorist and authoritarian and an aspiring theologian to boot, finally closed the university of Athens, which had remained unrepentantly pagan, in 529—the same year in which Saint Benedict founded the abbey of Monte Cassino.

Higher education, that in particular conveyed by Athens, concerns this study nearly, because it was only there that music exerted its claim to be a part of wisdom, or at least an essential preparation for wisdom, in its role as one-quarter of the quadrivium among the liberal arts. Our accepted vision of these arts conceals from our devout gaze much of the real conflict of ideals in ancient education. [16]

The full scheme appeared only in outline in pagan primary education. Children were taught to read, write, and spell, and to appreciate and memorize ancient poetry—mostly Homer and the gnomic poets, later the tragedians. They also learned arithmetic and singing, and how to play the flute and the lyre. They were often trained as choruses to take part in civic religious ceremonies. Much of their time was occupied with gymnastics, games, and sports.

The subjects of the quadrivium, although not the name, are first mentioned as a group by Plato's Protagoras, who mentions "calculation, astronomy, geometry, and music" as "arts" to which the poorer sorts of sophists—with a glance toward Hippias—"drag back" their unwilling pupils, instead of leading them onward to the proper adult citizen's study of how prudently to manage one's own affairs and those of one's city. The expression "drag back" suggests that these arts were in Protagoras' view only grammar school subjects [cf. GBWW I: 7, 43; II: 6, 43].

In *The Republic* [*GBWW* I: 7, 295–441; II: 6, 295–441], however, Socrates introduces them as "theoretical" studies, branches of higher learning that prepare for philosophical *theoria* by accustoming the soul to immaterial objects of knowledge and so providing a kind of dream vision of reality. Their function is cathartic and propaedeutic: "to facilitate the conversion of the soul itself from becoming to truth and being" [cf. *GBWW* I: 7, 393; II: 6, 393]. "In these studies a certain organ of each person's soul is purified and rekindled after having been corrupted and blinded by other studies" [cf. *GBWW* I: 7, 394; II: 6, 394]. They are to be taught in a definite order and pursued in a particular manner, avoiding both practical applications as well as any suggestion of their autonomy.

Arithmetic is given the rather odd name "the study of the one," because it begins with the puzzles and paradoxes concerning the unit and refers back to them all the problems of number and magnitude [*GBWW* I: 7, 393; II: 6, 393]. Arithmetic is followed by geometry, which is called "(a) knowledge of the eternal" [*GBWW* I: 7, 394; II: 6, 394]. Plane geometry is followed by the study of solids, even though this science has scarcely been invented as yet. (The significance of inserting stereometry is underlined by the fact that the speakers in the dialogue are about to go straight on to astronomy when Socrates calls attention to the omission at 528a.) The addition of stereometry makes astronomy already the fourth study [*GBWW* I: 7, 395; II: 6, 395]. Astronomy is to present abstract problems of bodies in motion, leaving to one side the actual celestial phenomena [*GBWW* I: 7, 396; II: 6, 396]. As always, it is the principles that are important. Music is brought in as a study akin to astronomy, as the Pythagoreans are said to affirm. [17] Here again the attunement of audible concords is set aside in favor of discovering what numbers are inherently concordant (although this would seem to make it more akin to arithmetic, even though numbers do not move.) Finally, the student is to grasp the "community and kinship" of all these studies [*GBWW* I: 7, 396–97; II: 6, 396–97].

But "quadrivial" studies are in fact only the "prelude" to the "song of dialectic," because they do not "lay hold of being itself" but only "dream about being" [*GBWW* I: 7, 396–97; II: 6, 396–97]. They should thus not properly be called sciences (*epistêmai*) but only understanding (*diánoia*), that is, functions of discursive thought, reserving science as the proper name of dialectic, the knowledge of being itself [*GBWW* I: 7, 398; II: 6, 398].

Glaucon, Socrates' interlocutor in this part of the discussion, had already been led to recognize that the objects of the dianoetic arts are in fact images of the proper objects of intellect (*nous*), the *eídê* or forms, even though the objects of *diánoia* are intelligible (*noêtá*) if they are considered in conjunction with their eidetic principles [*GBWW* I: 7, 387; II: 6, 387]. (This last bit must seem very obscure here, but I shall return to it at an opportune moment, at which its importance will make it at least seem clearer.)

That mathematical objects are the images of the real objects of dialectic explains why they appear in inverted order as the student moves from arithmetic to astronomy and music, beginning with the ineffable unit and culminating in the harmoniously ordered whole. Dialectic, as knowledge not of images but of reality, would proceed from the harmoniously ordered All to the ineffable One. But this inverted mirroring of the real world in the mathematical world is only adumbrated in *The Republic*. Whether Plato ever taught it explicitly is a subject of much debate among the learned. [18]

I have protracted this exposition in order to bring out two points that determined the spiritual direction of ancient higher education: (1) that the mathematical arts, including music, are preparatory to theology and (2) that they have a purifying effect on the soul, because through them the soul comes to resemble the immaterial objects of its contemplation. [19] The quadrivium ever thereafter had a spiritual purpose.

The quadrivium is implied also by the *Timaeus*. The soul of the world, which is unquestionably an astronomical entity, containing and controlling the motions of the Same and the Other, that is, the celestial equator and the ecliptic, is ordered through a nexus of ratios carefully arranged to include arithmetical, geometric, and harmonic proportions. The technicalities are hard to understand, but the image of the universe as a musical structure was perennially attractive in antiquity and long beyond and provided a constant stimulus to studying the quadrivium. [20]

The quadrivium was finally exalted to the rank of a mystical initiation in the *Epinomis*, which, whether it was written by Plato himself or one of his immediate disciples, drew from the astronomical doctrine of the *Timaeus*, already instinct with devotional feelings, a veritable astral religion in which the stars and planets would be worshiped in a new international cult, without, however, being identified with the Olympian gods whose names they bear. [21]

The central liturgy of this new religion would naturally be contemplation of the nocturnal sky. But in order to be rightly adored, the heavens must first be rightly perceived as a system of regular motions. Thus in the *Epinomis* a sequence of four quadrivial studies prepares the soul for astronomy, which is not only observation and science but worship as well. The preparatory studies are arranged, as already in *The Republic*, in order of increasing dimensions: arithmetic, geometry, stereometry, with music somehow interconnecting the complex of heavenly bodies. To one who pursues these studies with his eye on unity, "one inherent bond" of the celestial revolutions will become apparent. [22] Such a theorist reduces his multiple perceptions to one and becomes himself in the process a unity out of a manifold. Again, contemplation assimilates the beholder to the beheld. In the next life the celestial theorist will enjoy a single fate: to be happy, wise, and blessed all at once. The quadrivium thus leads to beatitude in a twofold movement: mathematics is identified with philosophy (because the objects of the mathematical sciences are the highest objects of knowledge), while wisdom is identified with astral piety.

Although this doctrine does not seem to everyone to be very good Platonism, it is nonetheless the answer to a problem raised in the *Laws* about the teaching of astronomy [*GBWW* I: 7, 729–30; II: 6, 729–30]. The Athenian stranger objects to the use of the word *planets,* because it means "wanderers," while the planets themselves, being divine, cannot simply wander about the sky but must move in a rational pattern. The "one inherent bond" of the *Epinomis* passage would link all the apparently irregular celestial motions into a single "system of number and composition of harmony," [23] showing that even the so-called planets do not really wander. Here then is the origin of that epochal endeavor to "save the appearances" to which ancient astronomy devoted itself. [24] The harmonious system of the sidereal motions is offered by the *Epinomis* as the final object of human contemplation (where *The Republic* had offered the system of the Ideas unified by the Good). But contemplation of the heavens cannot unify the soul, as contemplation ought to do, assimilating the soul to the object it beholds, unless the heavens themselves are seen as a single object of contemplation. The quadrivial studies of the *Epinomis* have therefore a properly religious function: to reveal to educated vision the divine heavens as a unified being that can unify and so divinize the soul that beholds them.

Aristotle refers favorably to this astral religion at the end of Book XII of the *Metaphysics* [*GBWW* I: 8, 604–5; II: 7, 604–5], giving us a clue thereby to much of the argument that precedes: why, for example, the unmoved mover, having been a thing in the neuter gender, suddenly becomes masculine and is called "God" [*GBWW* I: 8, 603; II: 7, 603]. Aristotle wrote, probably in earlier life, a now-lost dialogue *About philosophy,* from which sufficient quotations in ancient writers survive to inform us that it propagated a similar astral gospel and that it was very widely read in antiquity, by Cicero, Seneca, Plutarch, Philo, Clement of Alexandria, Lactantius, Synesius, all the philosophers, of course— the authors, whoever they were, of the Hermetic Corpus—and perhaps also the authors of *Proverbs* and the *Wisdom of Solomon.* [25] This work of Aristotle, together with the *Timaeus* and *Epinomis,* was the source of that Stoicizing cosmic piety that became the personal religion of the educated and half-educated classes until the end of antiquity, and which resurfaced in certain learned quarters throughout the Middle Ages and the Renaissance and is currently flourishing anew. [26]

The "one inherent bond" of the *Epinomis* could be interpreted as the living soul of the universe, an all-pervading fiery spirit, the inner logos of cosmic processes, the unchanging providence of intramundane deities, or the omnipresent wisdom of the God of the Bible. The power of mathematical studies to excite a triumphant vision or a flitting glimpse of this universal harmony shed a mystical glamour over the quadrivium that has never entirely faded. Already in *The Republic* the labor of quadrivial education is described as leading up toward the light, "as some people are said to have ascended out of Hades into the company of the gods" [*GBWW* I: 7, 391; II: 6, 391].

Despite the enduring popularity of astral religion, the specifically Platonic attempt to introduce the astral version of the quadrivium into higher education was from the beginning opposed by a reaction in favor of an education based on the study of the poets. The conservatives had a broad basis of support in society because the strenuous studies recommended by the Platonists could be seen as incompatible either with aristocratic *désinvolture* [casualness] or with golden democratic mediocrity. Plato's contemporary Isocrates was the first exponent of this antiscientific humanism that gradually prevailed against quadrivial studies, even in their more ordinary form (and which vanquished philosophical education again in the Renaissance, when Rabelais and Montaigne led the attack on the popular front, followed, at a safe distance, by the Jesuits). The trivium came into vogue as a tripartite advanced literary study that taught the aspiring gentleman and public man how to think clearly, write elegantly, and speak persuasively. The new higher literary studies, with oratory as their crown, were apt preparation not only for political life but also for the profession of law, which assumed new importance under the universal Roman imperium. Because, however, a philosophical veneer was still regarded as a desirable sign of one's intellectual refinement, even in circles least susceptible to mystical glamour, handbooks of the philosophers' opinions and collections of useful quotations were produced to supply authors with the requisite ornaments.

Meanwhile philosophy and its ancillary quadrivial studies became an extreme educational option, almost a cult: one "entered into philosophy" as one was later to "enter the religious life." A philosopher of the imperial period could be told at a glance by his old-fashioned dress and his unfashionable beard. He dedicated himself to philosophy as others might profess a new religion. He might even have been converted to philosophy by the interior monitions of gracious divine presence. Proclus was so converted by Athena, who guided and protected him throughout life even as she had done for Heracles, leading him through labors and trials to immortality. [27] Proclus even recorded his gratitude in a hymn. But when he was first turned toward philosophy he was completely deficient in the mathematics required for entrance into the Academy, his early training having been purely literary and legal (he had even studied Latin), so that he had to set himself to learn mathematics and Aristotelian logic from the beginning. [28]

The emergence of Christian music

How the Fathers fit as individuals into this variegated context is a bit difficult to specify. I am certain that there exist fat volumes entitled *The Secular Education of the Church Fathers,* but I have not found and read them. Nor are the Fathers themselves very forthcoming about their lives at school (hence the length of this digression), and they are unusually coy when it comes to philosophy. Although their surface attitude is generally hostile, they were compelled nonetheless to study and ponder pagan books. The early apologists such as Saint Justin Martyr and Athenagoras needed to explain Christianity in terms intelligible to the educated classes they hoped to convince. But theologians were indebted to philosophy for more than terminology when they constructed a system of Christian wisdom as profound and comprehensive as its pagan rivals. The pattern of attack and adaptation is masterfully described by Jaroslav Pelikan, who refers especially to the apologists, Clement of Alexandria and Origen, and, of all people, to Tertullian. [29]

Most of what we can discern of the education of the Fathers is of the literary sort, which anyone could infer from their evident oratorical skill. Saint Basil and Saint Gregory of Nazianzus spent years studying rhetoric in Athens. [30] For it is a fact that, however much the Fathers insist that the Gospel be proclaimed in language of primitive apostolic simplicity, they exercised in practice every artifice and adornment of oratory, including all the philosophical and devotional commonplaces of their era. [31] They did not need to go beyond the handbooks and florilegia to learn about celestial mathematics and the music of the spheres. To appreciate the deeper views that lay behind the rhetorical commonplaces, they would of course have had to study philosophy, which they could easily have done in Athens where the rival sects were all well represented, but this move across town seems to have been thought somewhat compromising because philosophy ultimately demanded a spiritual allegiance that rhetoric did not. The inner circle of a philosophical school was a kind of confraternity living a common life devoted to a shared ideal and practicing a private cult.

If we try to look in on this common life, so well hidden even in its own time, we may find the beginnings of an answer to a question that I have felt trembling at the edge of all this discussion, and which I must answer if I am ever to approach more nearly the attitude of the Fathers to church singing: what can be the relation of quadrivial music to the practical musical arts of composition and performance?

The obvious thing to say is that there never was, and by nature never could be, a connection between anything so concerned with the eternal as the ancient quadrivium and anything so subject to fashion and changing taste as practical music. [32] But I do not wish to say this obvious thing. We are curiously well informed about ancient practical music in

A decorative letter from a 13th-century Latin bible shows a group of monks singing from an antiphonary. This is a book which contains the choral selections of the Divine Office.

the sense that, although very little of the actual music has come down to us, we possess a simply enormous literature about it, comprising detailed and highly technical instructions about intervals, tetrachords, scales, modes, and tunings, as well as musical and poetic meters. The most famous Greek names are Aristoxenus, Ptolemy the astronomer, Philodemus, the pseudo-Plutarch, and Aristides Quintilianus, while Boethius, Cassiodorus, and Martianus Minneus Felix Capella passed much of the Greek theory, sometimes badly garbled, to the Latin Middle Ages and beyond them to us. [33] I find much of this technical literature absolutely stupefying, and the same goes for the even more enormous modern secondary literature, in which almost nothing said by one of the ancient authorities has not become the object of a magnificent scholarly controversy. But even I can see that this esoteric but practical learning situates itself firmly in the hallowed context of quadrivial music by means of the evidently obligatory prologue, the *laus musicae*, in which the author pulls out his handbook of apt quotations and examples in order to praise the divine origins and celestial pattern of music, recount the tale of Pythagoras discovering the perfect consonances, the exploits of the famous musicians of legend: Orpheus taming wild beasts and

Amphion and Zethus building the walls of Thebes with their lyres, Arion with his dolphin, the song of the Sirens, and the rest. They dilate upon the sober, uplifting effect of the good old music and deplore the languor and moral collapse produced by the horrid new music, just as is done today. All the commonplaces and rhetorical flourishes retained their place in musical literature, because it never ceased to be relevant to attribute the goodness and nobility of good and ennobling music to its remaining faithful, during whatever vicissitudes of fashion, to its natural, therefore eternal and invincible, principles of consonance. People try to affirm the same things nowadays, only they do not have the Platonic metaphysics to back them up.

The Neoplatonists, for whom cosmic music was not a pretty idea but a philosophy of being, heard practical music as emerging or emanating from its transcendent cause as an echo or sympathetic vibration. The musically ordered cosmos creates, as an audible image of itself, the human art of music in the same way that the Good, according to *The Republic,* generates the sun as its offspring, image, and extension of its ordering power in the visible world. Human music is not the lifeless and powerless image of cosmic music but rather its extension into sound and movement. Conversely, through the power of earthly music the inept and graceless among men are brought back into sympathy with cosmic harmony and attain from this readjustment a humanly possible immortality [*GBWW* I: 7, 455, 476; II: 6, 455, 476]. The power of this sympathy operates in both directions, leading outward and leading back upward again. Human music is first of all an *exegesis,* a leading out into sound, of the unheard celestial music, a commentary and interpretation of it. This exegetic power is why music belongs in the quadrivium, as a science of objective nature: discovery, contemplation, and participation. As an objective science music has an eternal object, which does not, however, repose aloft in marmoreal abstraction from human beings but generates audible music and so exerts an anagogic power to lift human life up into the celestial music that theoretical music contemplates. Theoretical music is thus the turning point between these two balanced motions.

This understanding of music explains what it was doing in the quadrivium at all. At first sight its inclusion is puzzling, because, in contrast with the endless development of number and shape, those elements of music that are susceptible of a strictly mathematical treatment are after all rather few: the perfect consonances, those aspects of rhythm expressible as meter, and those aspects of form expressible as symmetry. These are the essence of all musical art indeed, but the doctrine of them may be expounded in a short treatise. The so-called harmonic ratios, which play an important role in the world-model of the *Timaeus,* are properly speaking a part of arithmetic and do not require a whole fourth quadrivial art for themselves. Yet we see everywhere in the tradition that music is the last and highest of the quadrivial arts—because so far as I can see human music embodies those partly ineffable aspects of order which the universe itself was felt to possess in an eminent sense, and which the objective study of the universe could not possibly fail to include: not only consistency, regularity, and intelligibility, but the sweetness, the grace, the persuasive and therapeutic power of these. Music was included in the quadrivium precisely so that the universe itself could be represented as a musical structure, as living form pervading and moving all things, a form celebrated by theoretical music and manifested in practical music.

The Neoplatonists felt strongly this complementarity of musical theory and practice as a sign of their commitment not only to contemplate the universe but to belong to it, not only to venerate the musical substance of the universe but to share it. Nicomachus, for example, makes the revealing remark that no one will be able to penetrate his abstruse arithmetical theology who is not exercised in musical theory and in the playing of musical instruments. [34] We find in the fictional lives of Pythagoras written by Porphyry and Iamblichus that the Pythagorean communities sang and played instruments every day as a part of their common life, a canonical daily liturgy that corresponds to the monastic prayer of the hours. Porphyry quotes the prayers to be said upon rising in the morning and before retiring at night. We possess also a small collection of hymns by Proclus that formed, I am certain, a part of the liturgy of his own Neoplatonic confraternity. The life of Proclus by his disciple Marinus contains several clues, among them a reference to the prayer said to the rising moon. Music was also a part of their spiritual discipline and therapy: songs in different modes calmed the distraught, assuaged the anxious, and aroused the indolent. [35] The fictional Pythagoreans and the actual Neoplatonists (if I am right in thinking that these lives of Pythagoras were a means of advertising the attractions of life in a kind of Neoplatonic monastery) would have had then to absorb the technical lore of modes and tunings in order to compose and perform their own music. Their use of music as devotion and medicine tends to obliterate the distinction between a theoretical (or liberal) and a fine art of music. Our own use of "theoretical" misleads us with its implied distinction of pure and practical reason.

Greek *theoria*, however, was not analysis abstracted from experience but contemplation, which is, again, not dreamy musing, but rapt attention and a striving for conformity with what one beholds. *Theoria* can be simply contrasted neither with perception nor with practice, because the elements of theoretical music are themselves already music. *Theoria* is thus both the origin and the goal of musical art, because the soul that is healed by music contemplates its perceptible beauty more intently and is so brought more nearly into contact with its divine archetypes of consonances and order. Liturgical *theoria* is moreover an experience created and shared with others and bears fruit in a strengthened common life. The term *applied art* alters its usual meaning in accordance with the inversion of values typical of Platonism: rather than implying the degradation of theoretical music bent down to mundane instruments and human voices, it names the anagogic art by which the mundane turns itself back upon the heavenly as it applies its heart unto wisdom. As always, it is not Platonic to distinguish too nicely between intellectual and moral virtue. [36]

Vocal vs. instrumental music

This Neoplatonic ontology (we shall have another dose of it later) provides the philosophical context in which the patristic understanding of music took shape. When the Fathers were trying to reconcile the instrumental music of the Temple with their own exclusively vocal music, they sought either to allegorize the instruments, Alexandrian fashion, as parts or functions of the soul that are meant to act in concert, or to emphasize, Antiochene fashion, the gradual uplifting of the people's religious perception through the sensuous appeal of concerted music. The allegorical view comes round to the moral view because both suggest that Christian vocal music likewise induces to piety, but at a more interior level of psychic or spiritual integration, which the older rites prepared and prefigured. Christian worship employs only song because singing is a more spiritual action than playing an instrument: that is, singing is more a unity of body and soul and of thought and feeling and therefore a more intense *theoria*. The discussion here of the Fathers will hint at the pagan background and will eventually be seen to take an authentic Neoplatonic direction.

One of the Fathers who was most explicit about the higher spirituality of singing was Niceta, bishop of Remesiana, now Bela Palanka in Serbia, who wrote in Latin about the beginning of the fifth century. He is believed to have written the Te Deum, one of the most beloved of Christian hymns during all ages. "The parts of the old law that were carnal," he says, "are all rejected by the new law: for example, circumcision, animal sacrifice, the dietary laws, trumpets, harps, cymbals, and drums. These instruments are now understood as parts of the human body and give out a more articulate resonance." Singing affects us more deeply than instrumental music because "a psalm penetrates to the soul as it gives pleasure. The hardness that the old law's severity was unable to twist out of the human heart, the sweetness of song has simply excluded."

It is clear, by the way, that Niceta assumed everyone would join in the singing, because he advised those who do not sing well not to remain silent and so deprive themselves of the benefit of singing but to try to blend in softly with the others. [37] The music of a divine service should be conceived and planned as a whole in which a tasteful sequence of psalms, prayers, and lessons give the same kind of pleasure as a succession of contrasting and complementary dishes in a banquet. I do not know too much more about this amiable bishop, but it may be relevant that he is the first author to use the expression "the communion of saints" as an article of the Creed.

Many people assert that explicit ecclesiastical legislation from the earliest times forbade the playing of musical instruments in church. Orthodox Christians, whose practice still excludes them, pride themselves on yet another example of their unbroken fidelity to apostolic customs. Even the *New Grove Dictionary of Music and Musicians* asserts that such an explicit prohibition is contained in something called "Canon 74 of St. Basil." But if one's diligence succeeds in unearthing this mysterious document, one discovers that it only prohibits a reader, one who chants the biblical lessons at the liturgy, from learning to play the guitar and threatens him with excommunication unless he desists. [38] This so-called canon (it has nothing to do with Saint Basil's authentic writings) belongs with some other so-called canons, none of great age or authority, that forbid those who practice dubious professions from seeking baptism. Among those excluded are actors, dancers, fencing masters, charioteers, gladiators, wrestlers, athletes (for all public games were civic liturgies offered to the pagan gods), and all instrumental musicians. [39]

The very idea of instrumental music was so abhorrent that no one seems ever to have thought it necessary to forbid its use in church. A recent scholar has said: "A careful reading of all the patristic criticism of instruments will not reveal a single passage which condemns the use of instruments in church." [40] The first person to protest against the innovation of their use seems to have been Erasmus, about 1500. Before this time, it is not clear that in the West even the organ was used to accompany church singing. The music of the early church, in any case, was such that instrumental accompaniment was always irrelevant.

Many people likewise assert that the early church inherited its music from synagogue singing, just as the structures of Christian worship were inherited from the liturgical forms of the synagogue. Many incautious deductions have been drawn from these paired assumptions. Even so meticulous a scholar as Dom Gregory Dix refers in a most influential book to the custom of singing psalms between the biblical lessons, which is indeed a very widespread Christian practice, as "a custom which must have been familiar to our Lord and His Apostles, since it was universal in the synagogue of their day." [41] But again, not only do we not possess this music of the early synagogue, there is in fact not the slightest evidence that psalms were sung in the synagogue at all, at least not before the eighth century. [42] What we find, for example, in the two New Testament descriptions of synagogue service, Jesus at Nazareth and Paul at Antioch, is Scripture reading followed by commentary and nothing else. [43] It is usually assumed that the Scripture reading had already, as it does now, the musical form of a cantilation, determined by the syntax of the text, but there is again no evidence for this practice until much later.

Researches in this century have revealed quite striking similarities between certain allegedly primitive Christian melodies, such as the Gregorian chant for the Lamentations of Jeremiah during Holy Week, and some used now in the synagogues of culturally isolated places like Yemen, but believed to have been preserved from ancient times. Some regard the parallels as proof that the early church borrowed such melodies from the contemporary synagogue, while others are content to remain unpersuaded. Derivation from a common near-Eastern milieu at an uncertain period is perhaps a more prudent inference than direct borrowing, especially as we do not know what was the role of music in the synagogue service during the time of the development of the Christian liturgy. Mutual borrowing is certainly not out of the question. [44] But it is in any case significant that the music of the synagogue, as distinct from the lost music of the Temple, has traditionally been exclusively vocal.

Why this unanimity of church and synagogue? The minimum view is that both are religions that cherish a revealed scripture whose words only the human voice can articulate. The minimum and perhaps exclusive function of any sacred music would be to render these words audible in the liturgical assemblies, distinct, and emphatic.

Certain of the Fathers can be marshaled in defense of a function so limited. Jerome advises a monk that when he sings alone in his hermitage *dulcedo vocis* is not required but only *mentis affectus*, not sweetness of tone but sincerity of heart. [45] Again, commenting on the famous "psalms, hymns, and spiritual songs" passage of the Epistle to the Ephesians, Jerome warns everyone to sing only in such a way that not the voice of the singer but the words of Christ give us pleasure. [46] The blessed Augustine, another musical puritan, in an extended reflection on his own response to church singing, recalls the view of Saint Athanasius that psalmody should more resemble recitation than song. [47] Augustine was troubled, as puritans will be, that he was more affected by the artistic beauty of the singing than by the truth of the words sung and was tempted to find here a separation of outer matter from inner meaning. His concern was shared by ecclesiastical legislators who sought from time to time to restrain the too luxurious growth of liturgical song. Among many synodal decrees I quote that of the little-known Council of Clovesho, which offered this perennially relevant advice: "Let priests not croon after the fashion of secular poets nor by their dramatic declamation obscure the meaning of the sacred words, but let them rather utter distinctly a simple, reverent melody according to the custom of the Church." [48] One would love to know what extravagances provoked this rather satirical rebuke, but of course we do not.

Warfare between musical Roundheads and Cavaliers was renewed at intervals, especially perhaps when some musical or theological revolution was in simultaneous progress. A sudden outburst of hostilities in the twelfth century came in response to the invention of polyphony, and another prolonged campaign in the sixteenth century followed the rise of Protestantism. The terms of battle were always the same, although the actual music allegedly quarreled over changed continuously. Thus William Prynne's violent denunciation in 1633 of "effeminate, delicate, lust-provoking Musicke" adapts a lurid description of the evils of polyphonic church music from the *Speculum charitatis* of Saint Aelred of Rievaulx, written in 1160, without any apparent awareness that the object of the Saint's indignation was entirely different. Anglican defenders of polyphony often availed themselves of the venerable patristic tradition of *musica speculativa;* a good example is Richard Hooker, in whose defense all the traditional conceits and pious legends reappear. [49]

Still, no one seems to have thought that there should be no church singing whatsoever. Nothing analogous to iconoclasm, the rejection of all pictorial imagery, has ever so ravaged the Church as to banish all musical art. Even the solitary ascetics of the Egyptian desert rendered their endless psalmody as some kind of audible song. Saint John Chrysostom, who could be suspicious about these things, thought that it was lovely: "They stand singing hymns with much symphony and gracefully moving melody; neither harp nor flutes nor any other musical instrument gives out such a sound as one may hear when these holy ones sing in deepest tranquillity and solitude." [50] The unlettered Egyptian monks were more down-to-earth than impressionable Greek bishops: singing, they said, was a good way to restore an inner calm disturbed by manual labor in the hot sun or by unwelcome company. [51] The redoubtable Abba Pambo warned his disciples that the newfangled poetical and melodic forms that were finding their way, despite Athanasius, into the liturgy of Alexandria were an obstacle to the contrite remembrance of one's sins that was the perpetual occupation of a true monk. [52] Evagrius Ponticus, the first theorist of desert spirituality and a keen student of the heart, was a bit more positive. He observed that continuous psalmody quiets the passions of anger and intemperance, the ungenerous enemies of friendship. [53] He even enigmatically declared psalmody to be "the image of the wisdom that shows itself in many ways." [54] The darkness of this utterance may reflect Evagrius' pre-monastic existence as a learned Greek.

The diffused influence of this tradition is, however, to be discerned in the story widely propagated by the church historian Socrates, writing in the early fifth century, that antiphonal psalmody, in which two choirs answer one another across the church, was introduced into this world by Saint Ignatius of Antioch, who had a vision of the angels in heaven praising the Holy Trinity in alternating chorus and so taught his people to imitate on earth the celestial liturgy. [55] Saint Dionysius the Areopagite develops at large this idea that worship is transmitted from the highest rank of angels, where the Seraphim dance around God, singing with never silent lips the triple hymn first heard by Isaiah, "Holy, holy, holy, Lord of Sabaoth: all creation is full of Thy glory." The Seraphim reveal the beauty of this hymn to the lower ranks of angels, who otherwise do not hear it, whence it is revealed to inspired prophets and saints. [56] The hymns of the church reflect the hymns of the angels and so bring human souls into harmony with the ritual of the world to come, concord with the divine, with ourselves, and with one another. [57] The best-loved moment in the Byzantine liturgy today is still the "Cherubic Hymn": "We who in a mystery represent the Cherubim and sing the thrice-holy hymn to the life-giving Trinity, let us lay aside all the cares of this life." We shall see more later about this feeling of the Orthodox faithful that their liturgical life is permeated by archetypes.

Christians therefore must sing in order to join their artless hymns to the cries of the Seraphim on high, the floods clapping their hands, the hills making merry together, day speaking to day and night unto night imparting knowledge, with the morning stars singing together and the sons of God shouting for joy, all creation telling the glory of God.

Music as meaning

The biblical concert of praise reinforced the unheard Pythagorean harmony of number and measure to produce the patristic acclamation of the universe as articulate music resounding the mercy and majesty of the Creator. The philosophical origin of the metaphor shows that it is not decorative but ontological. The metaphor of being as music goes beyond the static textbook-Platonic language of image and imitation. When Saint Dionysius desires to show the power of his symbolic theology, that the ineffable divine power descends to us through images and reflections of itself and that we rise again through those images to the divine, he abruptly employs a metaphor of sound and echo: "For matter, because it possesses its authentic existence from That which is truly beautiful, contains throughout its entire ordered array certain echoes of the intelligible splendor, through which one may be lifted up again toward the immaterial archetypes." [58] Not a few echoes here and there, a few clues hidden like amulets in the rocks, a few faint traces in the mud, not one thin, remnant beam of light piercing the fetid gloom of our earthly prison, but the entire uninjured divine work everywhere

A 14th-century French manuscript illumination shows Mass being celebrated (top) and an assembly of nuns and monks proceeding through a convent's cloister (bottom). The nuns (bottom, left) are holding hymnals.

announcing its victorious presence. If the language of imitation suggests a static disposition of similar forms, the language of sound and echo suggests an interplay of mutual responses and sympathetic vibrations. If music is the original substance and condition of the universe, it is not a dead system inertly subject to law but a figured canticle responding part to part, our own little part to the whole, and the whole freely emerging from the parts. Thus Saint Gregory of Nyssa: "The feeling together and breathing together of all things toward one another, arranged in sequent order and variety, is the primal, archetypal, and true music." [59]

Gregory often combines this Stoicizing idea, learned from Philo and Clement of Alexandria, of creation as a harmonious coincidence of opposites, with the idea of God the creator elevated above all oppositions, a more properly Neoplatonic idea that gives a new sense to the Stoic cosmology, which tends to identify, more closely than some find comfortable, God and His creation. [60] Gregory offers a genuinely new Christian ontology that, in brief, interprets created being as dynamic participation in divine being. We care about this new ontology because of the new importance that it gives to human freedom, formerly a source of discord, but now disclosed as a moment in the eternal unfolding of the cosmic symphony. Christians give back their whole lives, attuned but not amalgamated through charity, as a polyphonic hymn "from a living psaltery, a harp with a soul of many strings." [61] I shall return later to the anthropology implied by the experience of the human person as a living instrument of the divine praise.

This focus on music as action, as the specifically human share in a universal re-creative action, depends, as an intellectual view, upon retaining music as a quadrivial art. The fidelity of the Fathers to the Platonic-Pythagorean tradition saved them from the semantic muddle in which music has found itself since the end of the Renaissance, when music was effectively removed from the company of the mathematical arts to be studied as a part of rhetoric. [62] The devotion of the Fathers as preachers to the art of rhetoric might easily have tempted them in this direction. Although the move might also seem justified by the inseparability of sacred music and words, it brings them in fact into an irreconcilable conflict that plays into the hands of puritanism, because, when music and language are considered as parallel, the question of "meaning" is immediately imposed upon music in the same way as it naturally arises in language. If music is seen as having "meaning" in the same sense as language, puritans will insist that this unwelcome excess of musical meaning be reduced by restricting church music to the simplest possible melodies, a reduction that will surely restrict as well the pleasure that is mysteriously associated with music.

Let me say at once that I find the term *meaning* more portentous than critically useful in leading us to any firm analogy between the "meanings" of music and language. The phrase *language of music* is of course frequently used, but anyone who attempts to give precise sense to the vocabulary, morphology, grammar, and stylistics of music will soon abandon the project in despair. People are impelled, I believe, to this quixotic attempt by the observation that a musical composition and a composition in words such as a poem both have a premeditated structure, but this does not seem to have led anyone to a persuasive demonstration of an analogy of these structures. [63]

I shall try to show the kind of difficulties the Fathers avoided by keeping music in the quadrivium. When they insist that we ought to "mean" the words we sing in church (their usual interpretation of Saint Paul's phrase "singing in your hearts unto God" [64]), one might suppose that the melody is meant to "express" the text, making one wonder what this new expression might be. Certain people will be instantly suspicious if "expression," however heartfelt, is supposed to add "new meaning" to the words, as if they were somehow deficient in significance. Puritans will of course suspect that human emotions are being smuggled in. One tends to assume that no one would want even a prose recitation of the sacred text to be an "expressionless" monotone, but this assumption may be neither old nor universal. Some people, like the blessed Augustine, believed that any "style" imposes upon the text a human individuality that ought rather be extinguished or absorbed into it. Even these astringent critics did not deny that the heart must be lifted up with the voice into song; simply speaking a sacred text was not done in the ancient world. Almost anyone would have gone as far as flexible phrase-structured intonations, with more or less florid punctuations and cadences, such as the modern Greek formulae for announcing the Gospel, something both graceful and ornate but completely guided by the grammar of the text, not an independent, purely musical form.

A purely musical form would seem to introduce a purely musical meaning, which one would again wish to compare with the textual meaning to see if they conflict, or would even wish to ask what their agreement could mean, if they are admitted from the beginning to be meanings of two different orders. Conflict and agreement of meaning would hence be equally problematic.

That music and text can conflict somehow anyone would admit who finds at least some music inappropriate for liturgical use, although not otherwise objectionable as music. Everyone, surely, dislikes some music now used in churches or synagogues, simply because it seems somehow unsuitable, whether it is too long or too loud, too difficult and so requiring a too obviously professional virtuosity, too reminiscent of a context felt as alien to religion, or in some other way inimical to piety. The adjectives *sentimental, vulgar, cheap,* and *flashy* are of course always available to the critic of church music. Whatever one's taste, however, as soon as one allows music a meaning or expressivity comparable but different from those of plain words, one must anticipate that these may be incompatible. Nor would it be easy for us now to abandon the notion of the nonverbal "meaning" of music, given that being able to recognize and respond to it is for us the first sign of any musical sophistication. Church music becomes a problem, not only for the puritan but for the pious, if any such independent musical meaning is perceived as in unlawful competition with the meaning of the sacred text.

The theoretical side of this conflict did not arise for the Fathers because they had accepted music as a human enjoyment of the natural order and not an arbitrary invention that could compete with nature. Hence came their fondness for the nonbiblical micro/macrocosm idea, a sign of their lasting truce with classical education. It is not so much that a human individual shares the external form as that humanity shares the animating energy of the world created by the invisible God, of whose elusive beauty it is the visible image.

The Fathers had also the biblical doctrine of human creation in God's image. They began, as early as the second century, to develop the rather sparse biblical references into an anthropology of God-likeness that would remain their point of meeting with pagan anthropology. [65]

Image is another one of those words, like *spirit*, that we no longer understand as did the Fathers. We think of a painted or photographic likeness: the image externally resembles the original but differs entirely in substance and has no necessary spatial relation to it. The Fathers always remembered the description of Christ as "the image of the invisible God," [66] to which none of what we usually notice applies: Christ cannot externally resemble the invisible Father, but the two are one in substance and action. The Fathers were more inclined therefore to consider not a painted image but the image in a mirror as the point of analogy. The apparition suspended in a mirror is the presence there of the original, united with the original by an unbroken stream of light. When the Fathers speculated about the divine image, wondering where it was found, whether in the intellect or the free will, or in the simplicity or immortality of the soul, they were in any case unable to see it as a possession or prerogative of human nature contained and content within itself (nothing at all like Kantian moral autonomy). The divine image is an uninterrupted contact or openness or receptivity to God. If the likeness grows tarnished, darkened, or obscured, it is never weakened or distorted. The human person is itself a form of the divine presence, its heart bathed in uncreated light.

Nothing, consequently, neither Stoical puritanism, nor Platonic dualism, nor ascetic self-denial, tempted the Fathers finally to choose between nature and the divine. The goal of the Christian life was rather to restore their right relationship and so to reawaken in the created image its inherent harmony, justice, and vigor, opening it to a limitless participation in the infinite divine life. [67]

The effects of music

Music represented the boundless vitality of original creation and had, moreover, a unique power to revive it in us. Music embodied the unity of thought and feeling that prepares and prefigures the unity of the spirit that transcends both moral order and private emotion. Music was hence a proper part of the ascetic discipline that renders the entire human person the medium of unity in the spirit. Thus arose the Fathers' belief that the human person, body and soul, is, like the universe, a musical structure only awaiting its perfection as a living instrument of the divine praise. "The person who is likened to God is beautiful, not beautified: for his is the true beauty and that is God." [68]

The Fathers could not then be so misled even by their own puritanism that they welcomed the anti-Pythagorean Aristoxenus, who argued that sensation and not mathematics determined the musical consonances, or Philodemus, who concluded that music had no rational moral significance at all but provided only sensuous enjoyment: only language can gratify the rational desire for meaning, while music may be let run riot with the passions.

The Fathers accepted instead the classical explanation of why music affects human character, while other objects of perception do not. "Why is it," Aristotle asked, "that rhythms and melodies, although they are mere sounds, resemble moral characters, while tastes and colors do not? Is it not because sounds are motions just as human actions are? The active force of sounds forms a moral character or disposition, while other sensations do not." [69]

The ordered motions of music enter into the body to induce ordered inner motions that produce in turn the emotions of pleasure, as the soul shares the agreeably natural motions of the body, stimulated by art. If we find too materialistic this continuity of motion and emotion, or nature and art, it only proves that we are more ambivalent about the body than were the ancients, even the puritanical church fathers.

This classical understanding permitted the blessed Augustine to overcome (almost) his reservations about church singing: "All the affects of our spirit have, answering to their diversity, proper modes in sound and singing, which arouse them by a hidden kinship. . . . Thus I realize anew the great utility of singing with liquid tone and gracious melody, and so fluctuate between the peril of pleasure and the sensation of restored spiritual health." [70]

The restoration of spiritual health effected by ritual music is explained in certain of the later Neoplatonic writers, when that tradition had discarded its earlier indifference to cult. Although Neoplatonism and Christianity were officially hostile to one another, they had many affinities all the same, and I have already mentioned that the Fathers were often reading Neoplatonic books on the sly. I have chosen to present Hermeias of Atarneus as my chief source here, because, as one of the less gifted writers, he transmits the teaching of his illustrious masters in a more assimilable form. The gorgeous version of these doctrines, bristling with technical subtleties, found in the *Elements of Theology* of Proclus, could not have been so easily absorbed and adapted, as I believe it was, by Christian tradition.

In his commentary on Plato's *Phaedrus* Hermeias expounds the four kinds of divine madness or enthusiasm: musical, ritual, prophetic, and erotic, of which only the first two concern us here. [71]

Although "enthusiasm" often meant only "excitement," especially that produced by the more frenzied sorts of music, Hermeias wants us to be aware of its literal meaning "to be in God" (ἐν Θεῷ εἶναι). Enthusiasm implies an immanence the reverse of that implied by "inspiration," which suggests that the spirit descends into the artist, rather than that the artist ascends into the spirit. Hermeias makes great use of the idea that the enthusiastic soul is taken up into the god that moves it.

Hermeias inquires what parts of the soul are affected by enthusiasm and so reminds us of the ordinary teaching that distinguishes between sensations and thoughts and again, among thoughts, between discursive thinking (*diánoia*) and immediate apprehension (*nous*).

Above these cognitive activities there is, he says, a point or pinnacle of unity within the soul, its peak or apex, an image of vestige of God, the One which surpasses all beings. By this point the soul is suspended from the One and through this point the soul is united with the One: contact is unbroken but usually unconscious. Although hidden and indeed unable to manifest itself directly, the apex, "the One of the soul," is not isolated within the soul nor merely a presence there but is the very unity *of* the soul, which unifies the diverse cognitive and emotional powers of the soul and of the body as well. When the apex comes to life within God through enthusiasm, the experience pervades the soul and reaches the body. This is a common Neoplatonic idea, originating in Plotinus and frequently mentioned by Proclus, but nowhere the object of an extended discussion. It is a mystical idea, with an obvious affinity with the patristic "image of God" idea, although any historical connection remains elusive, partly because something about it seems to have made the Fathers exceedingly uncomfortable. [72]

We may learn, Hermeias continues, the truth of this doctrine of enthusiasm by considering how the soul comes to exist. He proceeds to what seems at first an excessively esoteric doctrine of the soul's relative self-creation, but the event will, I believe, justify the patience of the reader. Part of the difficulty is that I have not been able to find convenient translations of some technical terms that must nevertheless be frequently repeated. [73]

The soul, although immortal and indestructible, has a dependent existence. The soul comes to exist, or, perhaps better said, comes into this present existence, "out of" its causes, the divine intellect and the gods themselves. (Another part of the difficulty, which I cannot do anything to diminish, is that Hermeias, as an orthodox pagan Neoplatonic theologian, employs both a monotheistic language of one divine creative intellect and a polytheistic language of many divine creators, leaving their reconciliation to a yet more esoteric discussion. [74]) The gods who cause the soul to exist are themselves unified around the One and give to the soul an image of the One, "the One of the soul," around which its diverse existence is unified. The divine intellect, whose existence is nothing but thinking, gives to the soul an intellectual existence.

Someone is bound to object that surely it would be much simpler to say that the divine intellect gives the soul an intellectual nature or gives it the power of thought. But Hermeias uses his odd language (which I am trying to represent in English) for several real reasons. First, he does not want to say that the soul has a power of thought, as if it merely *could* think if it chose to do so, but that it comes into life already thinking. Second, he avoids the language of "nature" because he does not want the soul to seem like a loose conglomerate, composite, or heap of different sorts of "natures" that might be thought merely to have come together and might exist separately. Third, he wishes to describe the soul as an existence, a diverse but concerted life already in progress. Finally, he wishes to emphasize that this ongoing existence is continuous with powers both higher and lower than the soul. Therefore, he says, the divine intellect causes the soul to exist, not by simply getting it into existence as something let fall from its hand, but by giving it a share of its own intellectual existence, its own continuous thinking. But "coming into existence" always implies a certain descent and a certain scattering of the concentrated power of the cause. Whereas the divine intellect is eternally thinking of everything knowable, it gives to the soul an image or reflection of its knowledge, namely, an occasional but unerring glimpse of the knowable, that moment of intuition that the Greeks called *nous*.

The two highest aspects of human existence, unity and intellectuality, derive from its causes, the gods and the divine intellect, and are its dependent existence. "Dependent" means that the soul remains in contact with its causes, while "existence" means that these aspects are truly its own life, not bits of divine essences merely placed within it. The latter supposition would parcel out the divine being among the many souls and not provide a basis for any "enthusiastic" union of souls with the divine or with one another.

But the soul also comes into existence out of itself. It has its own power of discursive thinking, by which it joins up sensations into experiences and goes on to form judgments and conclusions. It generates this intellectual life out of its own material, so to speak, and thus fills itself with content and perfects itself as an intellectual existence that can reach up to and so receive a pure intuition from the divine intellect, an intermittent but genuine act of the soul, not a mere event within it or a pure gift for which it had in no way prepared itself. There is no break between the dependent and independent existence of the soul.

Hermeias wishes to avoid the notion that the soul is an empty receptacle of experiences for which its capacity would be determined by the limitations of its nature. Such a soul would have a nature in common with other souls, to which sensations and experiences would be merely added and so remain external to its real being. Hermeias does not speak of a nature at all but rather of a created existence, created by the gods from above and by itself from below. The existence that the soul creates for itself out of its experiences is therefore as much essential existence, as much its real being, as the existence created by the gods—as much essential, that is, to a complete existence, comprising both depth and height. The soul does not merely accumulate experiences within the fixed boundaries of its given nature, nor is it merely these accumulated experiences. Rather the soul generates itself out of its experiences as a living and growing form whose real being is its becoming. Hermeias thus rejects the distinction between being and having: between experiences that the soul merely has and a real being that the soul merely is and which is inaccessible to experience.

All this while Hermeias has allegedly been explaining something about enthusiasm. He has in fact been trying to bridge the gap we might feel between the artistic and the ecstatic moments in our experience of music, between the laborious preparation, the learning of doctrine and the mastery of craft, and the transient but transcendent glory of insight, of invention, or a perfect performance. But we pay for the ecstasy when we confess that it is a step outside our existence into a realm where we have neither claim nor control, a region of supernatural grace without connection and therefore in competition with the ordinary world. Unable to sustain these moments of ecstasy, to support them from below at all, we are tempted, then resigned, to leave them as isolated experiences, valuable no doubt but external to our selves, moments in which we are possessed but from which we possess nothing.

Hermeias aims to reclaim enthusiasm by restoring the arts as true performances, acts by which the soul forms its existence, gives itself shape and coherence, concentrates its innate vigor, elevates itself by thought and labor toward the experiences that seem indeed to surpass its efforts and intentions but which, because they were impossible without that effort and relentless stretching-out-toward, are not only divine gifts but human achievements.

When Hermeias reaffirms the Pythagorean practice of musical therapy, that music joins and settles the scattered powers of the soul, drawing them into renewed harmony, he intends no metaphor but ontology. The power of music creates (or, from the point of view of

A German woodcut showing a medieval choir, 1479. The choir is singing Gregorian chant. Originally called plainsong or plainchant, this monophonic form of music developed during the earliest centuries of Christianity to accompany the Mass and canonical hours.

the human ideal, re-creates) proper connection among the shattered fragments of the soul, renewing their wholeness and strength. Because music comes from the senses through the feelings into consciousness and flows back again into emotion and movement, it unites (or, again, reunites) mind, soul, and body in a single, manifold act. As music integrates the soul it rescues the body from awkward, habitual, or automatic movements. [75] Music's role in the moral education of both children and adults is thus essential, because no other art has this re-creative virtue. Musical enthusiasm pervades and illumines the soul and brings to the body grace and free movement. Hermeias, indeed, includes music in redemption, because it brings the human complex into such an intensity of inner consociation that it feels reawakening its unbroken but unnoticed point of contact with the One.

To follow Hermeias further into the Neoplatonic mythology of human origins and eschatological hopes cannot be my concern here, but only to recall his conviction that the present feeble, flitting, discontinuous life is not the authentic human condition. Neither, however, is happiness a lost paradise whose gates are evermore closed to us, but a power of self-creation that still gives out intimations of its unaltered presence within us. We acknowledge this presence living in music as the desire and demand of the soul to become form only through incessant formation but never to rest content with its own performances.

Hermeias refers to an act by which the intellect surpasses discursive thinking and grasps its object "by simple thrusts and touchings." For Neoplatonism, as already for Aristotle, this act of direct contact discloses that the intellect and its objects belong together, are not outside one another nor foreign to one another. Such an experience attains knowledge without abstraction, without simplifying its object by an intervening concept. The object is seized concretely as present awareness, occupying and giving its form to the entire field of inner vision.

Most people, but for music, would know nothing of such an act or might suppose it only a kind of mystical transport granted to privileged but passive souls. They would not know that it is an achievement of the intellect, its self-creation and self-transcendence.

We make with music, however, such a transparently intelligible contact: we think just what we hear and do not abstract from it a derived content, a poetical paraphrase of its "meaning." The experience is of the intellect because we think just what we hear and are not magically entranced or enchanted by it. The contact is moreover entirely intelligible because music, as a work of premeditated art, contains no moment, however unanticipated by us, of which we cannot give an account: how it emerged and what were its consequences, how it might have been different and not wrong, and why it is right exactly as it is. In music even the unique and unrepeatable is intelligible for us, showing that it is understood through itself alone in the very place of its occurrence and not by reference to any extracted categories. Contemplation in the Greek sense of *theoria* occurs here: an act of sustained attention, calm but alert, to any object that gives itself to be known without intercession. Only mathematics has a comparable transparency but lacks, except to true mathematical theorists, the same sensuous immediacy. Music is that plenitude of pure existence in which the opposition of perception and understanding (which can also be stated as the opposition of matter and form) is overcome.

The problem of meaning can now be resolved. Music, because it lacks the opposition of matter and form, has no content but its actual shape in time, a pure, immediate, and concrete existence. Any analogy with the meaning of language is therefore superfluous. Speech has actual meaning, despite the systematic rationality of grammar, only with reference to other real things held in common by its speakers, the world of events and objects, even as language shapes our perception and use of that common world. Music does not lead down these vanishing perspectives. A piece of music, although founded upon acoustic laws that are a part of the objective order, is nonetheless not a thing existing among other common objects, still less is it an indirect reference to these objects, but is a self-creating existence: it generates itself through art and is therefore an integral whole and not a mere gesture or reflex, offering itself as an experience available to everyone.

Music as performance

At this point I abandon any pretense of explaining Hermeias and begin to interpret the Neoplatonic theorems in the direction of the properly Christian experience of music, guided largely by my own experience of the liturgy of the Orthodox Church, but not without constant reference to the concert hall as well.

The single art of music comprises both the constructive discipline of composition and the expressive discipline of performance, which are related as potency to act, because only performance fulfills the composition. In our present situation, however, composers and performers are commonly not the same persons and, one regrets to observe, a certain jealousy and rivalry between them has tended to split up the neatly Aristotelian existence of the art into two only externally related arts. In former times composers were more likely to write music for their own use, either as Mozart appeared as a soloist in his own piano concertos, as Palestrina or Bach or any church musician wrote music for their own choirs to sing, or as Handel wrote operas and oratorios for himself to produce on the stage.

Several causes have combined to aggravate the mere fact of the more common modern separation of the two roles. The first, in order of sheer horribleness, was the titanism of the artistic personality. Composers became, not quite so early as Renaissance painters, heroic figures wrestling, like the demiurge in the *Timaeus,* to impose a beautiful order upon a reluctant or recalcitrant matter, itself formless. (Such heroism is meaningless without the modern image of a passive or neutral nature to which positive values are added by art.) The second cause was the image of the composer as revolutionary, smashing tired academic traditions and subverting the old-fashioned habits of performers. (Beethoven remains the most enduring image of the lonely, crabby genius, contending with his times and with the elements.) The third was the rise of the equally heroic performer, whether it was the poetic dreamer, the seductive enchanter, the technical wizard, the hierophant or visionary, initiating the audience into mysteries hidden from all but him, the performer who confesses his innermost feelings, the martyr to art who suffers in our presence, straining and striving—the maniac, the fussbudget, and the superstar. A fourth cause is the preponderance on our concert programs and therefore in the education of musicians of music so old that performers have lost living contact with it and seize the opportunity to create it anew. All these causes conspire to diminish the sense of responsibility linking the performer to his text.

The pity of this situation is that it consigns feeling to someone's private possession, usually the performer's by default (because the composers we really like are all dead), as something he adds to the text out of his delicate soul, rather than as anything belonging to the text, which is seen as something inert, waiting to be brought to life. But feeling, in any sense, is not separate from perceiving and is simply what arises when we grasp or comprehend (by which I certainly do not mean analyze) our perceptions. In the act of performance is found therefore the primary emotional content of music, a content that seems otherwise so undefinable.

The center of this emotional content is what one might hesitate to call "sincerity," but for which I can find no word less inadequate. ("Authenticity" is recommended by its etymology but is now clearly impossible.) Sincerity may be defined negatively by the absence of those egoistic distractions caricatured in the previous paragraph; defined positively, it is the humblest attention to the text, that sets its skill and knowledge below the text, waiting to be at its service, seeking nothing, but quietly alert to the moment when the text opens itself, unwraps itself, penetrates and occupies the one who has waited to be filled. Attention is concentration, but not the kind of concentration that, like a muscular contraction, awaits its moment to spring upon its object, seize and extract its meaning, and so reveal its own power of interpretation. Sincerity is the undistracted effort to allow a deliberated musical structure to come to life in time, to remove the obstacles, both in the performer and in any possible audience, to its giving the formless flow of time a deliberate musical form. If we insist that this effort requires imagination of the performer, it must be imagination in the Aristotelian sense: the capacity to receive impressions and hence the ability to empty ourselves of premature content so as to receive those impressions without distortion or prejudice.

An effort so selfless cannot be counterfeited: the simulations of it are too grotesquely mechanical. If a performer says to himself: "Chopin is the poet of the keyboard, the essence of his art is free rhythm," but then goes on to impose his own pitiless system of *rubati*, of coy rhythmical gestures and jerks, we will wish that he had paid more attention to the subtleties of the text and spared us his spurious originality. Another sort of performer is so involved in bringing out the details of each individual passage that the whole is broken up into discontinuous pianistic "moments" and loses any coherence (or drama: I would not have what I am saying reduced to a preference for "classical" over "romantic" interpreters). Others sweep across such meticulous nuances in search of some overarching and overwhelming effect.

The sincere performer faithfully transmits not only the text itself, as this has shown itself to his patient contemplation, but also his particular effort to realize it on this occasion, without any hint of repetition or method, of tricks or mannerisms found on a previous occasion. The hearers experience through empathy the inflections, the nuances of insight, the invention of the performer, the adjustments, the travail, the sacrifices even, that make this performance come alive with emotion, here united with the free intellectual articulation of the performance. This unity is already an evidence of the spiritual in the patristic sense. When music neglects the spirit and consents to be an emotional gesture, of nervous excitement or rage or despair or artistic vanity, it ceases to be music at all and apes a prelinguistic stage of sign language, pointing at the emotions but not containing them. The proper musical emotion is compact and concentric with performance, a double realization of the composition as produced and heard, shared but not divided among performer and listeners.

Participation is therefore essential to music, because music has no being detached from performance or at least from its need to be performed. This need distinguishes its mode of being from that of a painting, which is realized once by the painter and then endures through time, inviting but not requiring participation. (There is more about painting further on.) Music is in this way more akin to architecture, which, although it can be viewed as an autonomous arrangement of forms in space, like music printed on a page, is essentially, not accidentally, intended to be lived in, is meant to realize its static being as the form of the existence of its inhabitants lived out through time. Music, like architecture, is essentially ceremonial and essentially sacred. [76] Everything is sacred that affirms that an indivisible divine being is present in a human moment in response to the human effort to make itself a vehicle of the divine power. The secular is merely a divine being that has lost consciousness of itself and so fancies itself independent of the divine whole of being.

Music resembles architecture also in that it gives the listener a sensation of surrounding space, a sensation that I hesitate to call unquestionable only because it has been so often doubted by psychologists of perception. It is not only that "high" and "low" are applied to tone (for this might be a metaphor for "intense" and "relaxed"); nor that "volume" is attributed to sound; nor even that we are able to determine the direction from which sounds approach us (for there is nothing specific to music in this perception). I mean rather that music creates a space around the listener, excited and filled with activity, detached from its source in the voice or instrument that produces the sound, activity impressing itself immaterially upon us from every side. Such a space is not equipped with a uniform Newtonian geometry, homogeneous and unaltered by its contents, but is more like four-dimensional Minkowski space, whose metrics are uniquely determined by the proper time of the music itself, a time which in turn is no equable flowing but the variable rhythmic shape of the actual performance. Thus space flows along with time and is no longer the inactive receptacle of temporal events.

Space as actualized by music is not an aggregate of places laid next to one another in a uniform geometric grid but a flexible texture of mutual evocations and responses, not a succession of indifferent moments but a form in motion, a system of tendencies toward being. An unaccompanied melody, especially one which, like a Gregorian chant, does not imply an underlying harmonic basis, already extends itself as such a transition of states of excitement, while in true polyphony the lines of tension are laid across and over one another in a ductile pattern that may, to use more visual metaphors not altogether inaptly, be transparent or grow dense and overcrowded as our ability to perceive the coordinated trajectories is strained. The individual melodies are not simple paths through a neutral tonal space; each melody is rather a surface or field contoured and textured by its energy at every moment. Here again music is seen to manifest the cosmic sympathy as envisaged by Saint Gregory of Nyssa.

The space activated by the presence of music resembles in general the space concept of ancient physics: a finite shape whose points, unlike those of a uniform void, have each a definite tendency to motion, whether up or down in sublunary space, or round and round in the heavens. Each tendency implies interaction of bodies, because space is completely filled with bodies in contact. Their motion actualizes the kinetic value of each point of space and brings into play the overall rhythmic space of the cosmos. Space is therefore not an empty schema but a universal dynamic event.

The stylistic observations made earlier about different approaches to performance here return to their ontological origins in the Pythagorean view that music represents to us inner qualities of the natural world. The emotional qualities of music are therefore not added from without to the sound as symbolized in the score but are the dynamic structure of the music itself as realized in a sensitive performance. Nor is the performer expressing himself, bringing himself into view, or even expressing the musical text. Rather, he is revealing space and time pervaded in its musical structure by an immaterial power. Music does not so much express the exclusively inner world of the psyche as it reveals an aspect of the external world that is kin to the psyche: that freedom too is nature. [77]

The freedom of nature includes freedom from empty, automatic, or mechanical repetition. Nature does not produce endless copies of its archetypes. The Neoplatonic view is that the endless variations of the concrete individual unroll in time the infinite, inherent richness of the archetype, a richness too concentrated in its source to be expressed by anything less than an infinite time. Knowledge of the individuals is therefore knowledge of the archetype itself and cannot be disregarded as some less-than-knowledge of mere accidents. This is at last that promised moment ([The Republic: GBWW I: 7, 387; II: 6, 387]; cf. page 174) which explains what Socrates means by claiming that dianoetic knowledge of the images would become eidetic knowledge of the principles or archetypes if images and archetypes were seen in conjunction.

The constant demand of a musical composition, consequently, to be re-presented means that it never rests in a fixed noetic position with the listener but instead carries on a relentless struggle, not only against being reduced to its written form, but against all past performances as well. Music refuses the idea of a definitive performance that would render the composition a comprehended perfection fixed in memory. Indeed, music never yields itself as a finished meaning at all but retains within itself, undiminished, its strangeness and novelty, an unfailing source of communion among performers and listeners.

That being, as eternally self-creating, is inexhaustible as a central theorem of Neoplatonic metaphysics. The divine fullness of being is identified with a multiplicity of intelligible forms. This actual multiplicity of forms does not segment or delimit, does not parcel out, an originally limitless, formless divine being, a fullness of being paradoxically empty of actual content. The actual existence of things rather discloses the essential formedness of being itself. Nor does real being lurk somewhere inconceivably behind the world we can perceive. [78] Real being is the divine creative being incessantly realized as the actual fullness of the created world. Instinct with divine originating energy, the universe is a *life* that can only attain form in an incessant becoming, by means of the mutual struggle and discharge of forces held in a complex state of equilibrium. From this is derived the interplay of tension and relaxation that characterizes so much of Western music.

Harmony and liturgy

Pythagorean musicology, so improbably (it seemed) adopted by the church fathers and given by them the currency it retains even now in the Western tradition, so far from reducing the essence of music to something monumental and abstract, remote from performance and perception, is in fact the origin of those ideas about music as dynamic form and ordered motion that have occupied so much of this essay. "Harmony comes into being in every way out of contraries," said the early Pythagorean Philolaus, "for harmony is the union of multifarious things and the agreement of things that think differently." [79]

That musical tones are inherently ordered is of course the heart of the Pythagorean musicology, for the Pythagoreans discovered that the string lengths of the octave have the exact ratio of one to two, a fact that could never have been predicted and therefore can never be sufficiently wondered at and admired. Philolaus proposes that this numerical relation of tones is nonetheless dynamic. Not only does the octave hold together the opposition of the high and the low, but the octave is also composed of two unequal consonances generated out of itself, namely, the fifth and the fourth, expressed by the numerical ratios 2:3 and 3:4. The fifth and fourth have not only unequal ratios but different dynamic qualities and yet derive from the octave and coalesce in it again.

Renaissance theorists in this Pythagorean tradition like Gafurius spoke of music as "discordia concors," forming its harmony from contrary aspects. If we think instead of the overtone series, we are irresistibly led to feel that the overtones emerge and arise out of the fundamental in an effortless but directed motion upward. Whether we hear in the overtone series octaves, fourths and fifths, major triads, or the entire diatonic order, or an eventual chromatic scale, or even microtones, we feel them in any case dynamically related to their origin and to one another. Even the mere matter of music is already music, already ordered motion. The octave itself is not static but has the same function in music as the circle in ancient astronomy: a progressive motion that returns eternally to its beginning.

The astronomer Ptolemy, in the third book of his theory of harmony, works out an almost unbelievably detailed double analogy among the structures of music (intervals, tetrachords, modes, tunings, and modulations), the human soul (its parts, faculties, virtues, and activities), and the motions of the heavens and planets. He states the leading principle of these analogies as follows: "In general, each thing naturally ordered shares in a certain *logos* both in its motions and its underlying matter;

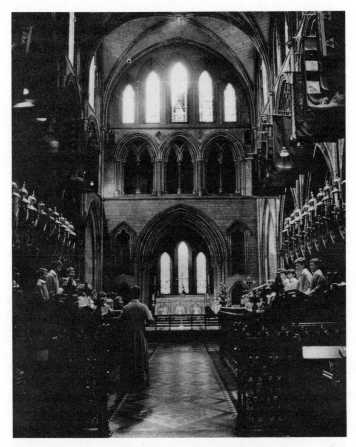

A present-day boy's choir at St. Patrick's Church in Dublin, Ireland.
"Music, like architecture, is essentially ceremonial and essentially sacred . . . it gives the listener a sensation of surrounding space."

this logos, in those things that can keep it intact, becomes in them generation and growth and perfection and everything that is attributed to the better part of things. If the logos is deprived of its native power, all things tend toward the worse." [80] The divine power enters into all things—sounds, souls, and the heavens—and becomes in them their ordered life and motion.

Church singing is the practice of this ontology in the service of the divine mysteries of the Christian church, mysteries that transcend but subsume the world of nature, not ignoring or negating it but fulfilling its unity with the universal divine life. At the beginning of the Divine Liturgy (the Eucharist or Holy Communion) of the Orthodox Church, the doors of the sanctuary are opened, the deacon bids the people stand up, the priest lifts above his head the Gospel-book, and says, while making the sign of the cross with the book: "Blessed is the Kingdom of the

203

Father and of the Son and of the Holy Ghost, now and ever and unto ages of ages." The Liturgy is the real presence on earth of the heavenly kingdom, not a memorial of an ancient divine condescension or a ritual reenactment of it as if Christ were sacrificed anew, nor a symbol of any transformation of the soul, but complete divine reality: the presence of the eternal in time and as time, in space as space. The attitude of the Orthodox faithful to the church building itself demonstrates their worship of this presence.

Consider only the icons, whose predominance in the devotional life of Orthodox people is a source of such wonderment (and even scandal) to other Christians. Icons are just paintings of religious subjects, one might suppose, but the clergy offer them incense and bow to them, while the people prostrate themselves, kiss them, light candles, and stand absorbed in contemplative conversation with them. There is a natural basis for this relationship. Colors themselves have emotional potencies, [81] and, when organized into the created space of a painting (not necessarily by the technique of perspective), the space offers itself to the observer, even in an art gallery, drawing him into itself and entering into him, opening a space within him as it occupies his entire field of attention, even as he bends his entire attention upon the painting. Here already is communion, an interpenetration of activities, almost an exchange of essences, as the spatial is infused with feeling and feeling is spatialized.

This invitation to communion is the essence of all sacred art, transcending but subsuming the nature of all art. The figures of the saints and angels painted on the walls of a Byzantine church are not decoration for the building but are living participants in the Divine Liturgy, not pictures but presences. When the interior surfaces of the church are covered with their solemn and joyous figures, vivid against an unvarying gold, it is as if the corporeal thickness of the walls vanishes and a perspective opens up on all sides into the endless kingdom that envelops space and time.

The Orthodox faithful are wont to feel this spatial presence of eternity is an astonishingly literal way. Thus Procopius exclaimed about Justinian's new church of the Holy Wisdom in Constantinople: "You would say that the space is not illuminated by the sun from outside, but that the radiance grows from within, such is the abundance of light poured about the sanctuary." [82]

But the piety of the people does not surpass the liturgical texts in expressing the essentially divine reality of the liturgical action, for the liturgy is more a divine action than a form of words. Just before the doors of the sanctuary are opened, the deacon says: "Now it is time for the Lord to act." The priest prays during the singing of the Trisagion, the hymn of the seraphs that Isaiah and Saint Ignatius heard: "Thou hast counted us worthy to stand at this present time before the glory of Thy holy altar," and again, during the Cherubic Hymn: "For it is Thou who offerest and art offered, Thou who receivest and art Thyself received, O Christ our God." At the Great Entrance it is Christ Himself who enters to consummate the sacrifice. The liturgy is the representation in this moment and place of the one sacrifice of Christ, who offers Himself on the heavenly altar eternally to the Father and in the Holy Ghost. As co-celebrants and communicants in time of the one offering of Christ, the faithful share in an event within the eternal life of the Holy Trinity. By identifying themselves with this one oblation of Christ, the people who came as individuals bring themselves and are brought into unity as the Church.

The people offer themselves together and so come together as free but nonestranged persons. Just before the singing of the Creed, the deacon proclaims: "Let us love one another, that with one mind we may confess," and the people conclude: "The Father, Son, and Holy Ghost, consubstantial, undivided Trinity." In former times, the people exchanged the kiss of peace at this point, a custom known to Saint John Chrysostom, who comments: "In the mysteries we kiss one another, that we though many may be one." [83] In the liturgy is realized, through the living presence of Christ who in His incarnation assumed not an individual soul and body, but human nature entire, the essential relatedness of human persons, sundered by error and sin.

Music itself, as understood by the Pythagorean/Neoplatonic tradition adopted by the Fathers, clearly means just all this experience, but surely one would want to know what actual music could not be unworthy to accompany an event so august, or rather, what actual music would be its embodiment in sound? The musics of the Orthodox churches have seldom utterly abandoned the ideal but are not likely to be familiar to most of my readers, so I shall try instead to describe the appropriateness of the parallel phenomenon in the Western tradition.

The body of Gregorian chant possesses all that the patristic ideal requires. In the light of the entire preceding discussion, I shall define this quality as "self-createdness." Chant is formally contained within its own musical resources in such a way that the melodies from the simplest to the most elaborate form a continuum of inner development. One feels no discontinuity, no stylistic break calling attention to itself, between the barest recitation tones sung by all together and the most ornate solo chants. The single system of modes and melodic germs create out of themselves an inexhaustible richness and variety of actual melodies able to express any mood or affect. If at first it seems austere and penitential, one has only to attend more intently to hear poise and tranquillity, but also radiance, rising fervor, and exaltation, descending again perhaps into sorrowful recollection of sin, humility, and grief, closing on a note of grateful confidence. Everything that the Fathers wished from singing is here. Nor is there any sense of restriction, of technical limitations, of possibilities refused; every feeling is present, just as it is, in purely human dimensions, without exaggeration, embellishment, or dissembling, without appeal to its uniqueness or privacy, all is open and shared with all.

For those who learn and sing this music daily, their artistic empathy with performers is transformed into sympathy with one another, the first flower of divine charity, even as artistic sincerity becomes devotion. The sacred words are quietly present, borne aloft by the supple melody into prayer. The melodic flow of the divine service expands and contracts, even as the Fathers saw the world forming itself out of the infinite ocean of the divine love. [84]

What could one contrast with this as conspicuously unfaithful to the patristic ideal? Many well-known things of course: one might attempt to deride the lovely and splendid church music of Haydn, Mozart, Beethoven, and Schubert that makes the liturgy seem a pompous festive ceremonial performed by officials on the people's behalf, denying them their own act of self-creation as God's elect. But it might be more profitable, in this narrow space, to consider a notable landmark of musical art, until quite recently almost unknown, but now frequently enough performed and recorded to be a point of reference: the Mass of Guillaume de Machaut. Recall only the first "Kyrie," just one page of the score. It is an intricate miracle of construction: almost every note is set in place and motion by one of several interlocking formal patterns: the *cantus firmus,* a Gregorian melody divided into two-measure sections, a fixed sequence of note values in many voices, imitations and contrary motions, cross-rhythms, exchanges, and hockets, the complex whole exquisitely controlled and coordinated. "Sounds like one of your favorite descriptions of the Pythagorean worldview," I think you might say. Indeed I cannot say "no" to this music myself, nor banish it from the church for which it was made to the concert hall. But I am, like the blessed Augustine, troubled by doubt. Its exquisite formal finish yields a suavity and panache, a sweetness, something overt, something of display, a kind of self-satisfied artistic completeness that is contrary to the movement of prayer. No single-voiced chant, however extended in length or range, no matter how many notes are set to a single syllable, gives me a comparable unease. I think I shall have to leave it there, but I do wonder what the Fathers would have thought.

In his commentary on the Psalms, which are, after all, not the textbook but the hymnbook of the church, the blessed Augustine explains the word *jubilus,* a wordless song (something comparable to the long final wordless melisma of a Gregorian *alleluia*): "A *jubilus* is a sound signifying that the heart is giving birth to something that it cannot say. To whom then is this jubilation proper but the ineffable God? For God is beyond speech and cannot be named. If you cannot speak, but ought not to remain silent, what can you do but jubilate? Your heart rejoices without words because the immense breadth of its joys cannot endure the bounds of syllables." [85]

1. *In psalmum primum ennarratio, Patrologia latina* 14: 924d (hereafter cited as *PL*). Saint Ambrose is more famous for saying "He who sings prays three times," but unfortunately no one seems to know just where he said this.

2. Matthew 26:30.

3. A useful collection of texts, carefully chosen, well translated, and briefly annotated, is *Music in Early Christian Literature*, ed. James McKinnon (Cambridge: Cambridge University Press, 1987).

4. Christians were not the only ones to be so suspicious. A fondness for Greek song was among the questionable activities of the brilliant but heterodox rabbi Elisha ben Avuyah: *Babylonian Talmud* tractate Hagigah 15b and *Encyclopaedia Judaica* 6:668–70.

5. The inseparable association of instrumental music with every aspect of pagan life is documented with innumerable citations of the ancient writers (in the original languages) and with beautiful illustrations by Johannes Quasten, *Music and Worship in Pagan and Christian Antiquity* (Washington, D.C.: National Association of Pastoral Musicians, 1983). The Fathers never ceased forbidding Christians to play instruments or even to listen to them, although repeated condemnations of a forbidden practice tend to suggest that it was continuing anyhow.

The surviving fragments of ancient music are collected by Egert Pöhlmann, *Denkmäler altgriechischer Musick* (Nürnberg: Hans Carl Verlag, 1970). He includes the one example of a Christian hymn written down in the pagan notation, the famous Oxyrhynchus fragment; the melody does not seem to most scholars at all to resemble any of the surviving pagan music: cf. A. W. J. Holleman, "The Oxyrhynchus Papyrus 1786 and the Relationship between Ancient Greek and Early Christian Music," *Vigiliae Christianae* 26 (1972), 1–17.

Recording Christian music in the old notation does not seem to have occurred to anyone else; indeed, Isidore of Seville (ca. 560–636), usually a rather well-informed author, seems unaware that it is even possible to preserve music in writing: "nisi enim ab homine memoriâ teneantur soni, pereunt, quia scribi non possunt." ["For unless sounds are retained in human memory, they perish, because they are not able to be written down."] *Etymologicarum* III.15.2. Manuscripts containing Christian chants accompanied by a musical notation that we can begin to decipher do not appear before the ninth or tenth century. The vexatious details are explained by Egon Wellesz, *A History of Byzantine Music and Hymnography* (Oxford: Clarendon Press, 1961), and by Willi Apel, *Gregorian Chant* (Bloomington: Indiana University Press, 1958).

6. The quotation is fragment B 33 in Cyril Bailey's standard edition *Epicurus: The Extant Remains* (Oxford: Clarendon Press, 1926), wherein also is contained the treatise "To Pythocles."

Nietzsche was another puritanical reformer who decried the moral and intellectual irresponsibility of accepting unexamined the cultural values embodied in art and feared especially the debilitating effect of modern music: *Menschliches, Allzumenschliches* [Human, All Too Human] II. Vorrede 3.

7. 1 Kings 8.

8. John 4:23–24.

9. *De abstinentia* II.34; this passage, with another in which a similar view is attributed to Apollonius of Tyana, is quoted by Eusebius in his much-read apologetic work, the *Demonstration of the Gospel*, written in the early fourth century.

10. *Ennead* V.1.6, 9–12 (*GBWW* I: 17, 211, 213–14; II: 11, 521, 523–24).

11. *De Plantatione* 126.

12. *De Somniis* I.33–37.

13. The best introduction to the subject is H. I. Marrou, *A History of Education in Antiquity* (New York: Sheed and Ward, 1956), part three, chapters ix and x. His account gives access to the sources to which I shall here only allude.

14. The old *Catholic Encyclopedia* (New York: Encyclopedia Press, 1913) reveals these attitudes with startling clarity in its remarks at the beginning of the article "Schools" and later on in the same article under the heading "Principles embodied in the parochial schools" (vol. XIII, 554–56 and 561).

15. *Babylonian Talmud,* gloss to Negillat Ta'anith, 50.

16. Marrou, op. cit., brings these out very well.

17. *GBWW* I: 7, 396; II: 6, 396. Porphyry claims that the quadrivium was already taught as such by the Pythagoreans and quotes the beginning of the *About arithmetic* of Archytas to prove it (cf. Ingemar Düring, *Porphyrios Kommentar zur Harmonienlehre des Klaudios Ptolemaios* [Göteborg: Elanders Boktryckeri Aktiebolag, 1932], 56). Not everyone believes that Porphyry was reading a genuine pre-Platonic Pythagorean work, however. To Nicomachus is due the neat scheme that divides quantity into continuous and divisible (that is, magnitude and multitude) and subdivides each into unmoved and moved and assigns one quadrivial art to each of the four subdivisions. Through Boethius this scheme was transmitted to the Latin Middle Ages.

18. No one has expounded the properly dialectic import of this dianoetic propaedeutic more perspicuously than Eva Brann in her essay "The Music of the *Republic,*" published in *Agon* I (1967), but now more accessible in *The St. John's Review* XXXIX, vol. I, 1 (1989–90), 1–103, esp. 78–91.

19. *Republic* (*GBWW* I: 7, 382, 386; II: 6, 382, 386); *Theaetetus* (*GBWW* I: 7, 530; II: 6, 530); *Timaeus* (*GBWW* I: 7, 476; II: 6, 476). The theorem that knowledge transforms the knower after the likeness of the known (or realizes their inherent likeness) is ancient in Greek thought and explains the mystical air that surrounds the experience of knowledge for Greeks. A. J. Festugière explains the background and its Platonic development in his *Contemplation et vie contemplative selon Platon* (Paris: J. Vrin, 1967), esp. 334–57. It is the foundation of Aristotle's analysis of perception and knowledge (*de anima* [*GBWW* I: 8, 657–58, 662; II: 7, 657–58, 662]). From both sources it flowed into Neoplatonism where it attained an unparalleled expansion. Two characteristic passages are Plotinus I.6.9,29–34 and Proclus *in Timaeum* I.212,12–27. It entered also into the thought of Saint Paul: cf. 2 Corinthians 3:17–18. Consult also Werner Jaeger, "The Greek Ideas of Immortality," *Harvard Theological Review* 52 (1959), 135–47, esp. 144–47. Byzantine spirituality is in its devotion to this theorem completely and utterly Greek.

20. *Timaeus* (*GBWW* I: 7, 449; II: 6, 449). The commentary of F. M. Cornford is indispensable: *Plato's Cosmology* (New York: The Liberal Arts Press, 1957), 66–93.

21. The authenticity of this dialogue has been endlessly disputed. Diogenes Laertius (II.37) said that it was added by Philip of Opus, one of the Platonic inner circle, as an appendix to the *Laws* (*GBWW* I: 7, 640–784; II: 6, 640–784); its function would have been to explain the astronomical theology that was to be the hidden wisdom of the nocturnal council of the law-governed but non-philosophical city. Proclus too denied that the dialogue was written by Plato (*in rem publicam* II.134). Paul Friedländer, however, found it difficult to believe that none of it at all was written by Plato himself: *Plato* (Princeton, N.J.: Princeton University Press, 1969), III.560, n.28. A. J. Festugière was at least sometimes inclined to believe it authentic: *La Révélation d'Hermès Trismégiste* (Paris: Gabalda, 1949), II.158, n.1.

22. *Epinomis* 991e–992a.

23. *Epinomis* 991e2.

24. For the expression "saving the appearances," cf. Proclus, *Hypotyposis* 5.10, and Simplicius, *in de caelo* 292b.

25. Cf. Proverbs 8:22–31 and Wisdom 7:21–8:18.

26. The great scholar of this universal Hellenistic cosmic religion is A. J. Festugière, the entire second volume of whose *La Révélation d'Hermès Trismégiste,* entitled *Le dieu cosmique,* lays open to view its origins, ramifications, and significance.

27. Eva Brann, op. cit., brings out very well the analogy of Heracles and Socrates. Athena's invisible assistance to the hero during his labors is movingly depicted in the metopes of the temple of Zeus at Olympia. Her role in the life of Proclus is sympathetically discussed by A. J. Festugière, "Proclus et la réligion traditionelle," *Études de philosophie grecque* (Paris: J. Vrin, 1971), III.575–84. On "conversion to philosophy," consult H. I. Marrou, *Saint Augustin et la fin de la culture antique* (Paris: Bibliothèque des Écoles françaises d'Athènes et de Rome, 1958), 161–73, and A. D. Nock, *Conversion, the Old and New in Religion from Alexander the Great to Augustine of Hippo* (Oxford: Clarendon Press, 1933), 164–86.

28. Marinus, *Vita Procli* 8–9.

29. *The Christian Tradition: A History of the Development of Doctrine* (Chicago: University of Chicago Press, 1971), I.27–55.

30. H. I. Marrou, *A History of Education in Antiquity,* 279.

31. The disparity between the theory and practice of the Fathers is discussed by Eduard Norden, *Die antike Kunstprosa* (Leipzig: Teubner, 1896), II.529–73. There is no point in being satirical about patristic eloquence: the truth is impotent if it cannot persuade.

32. Thus Philip Merlan in the chapter "The Origin of the Quadrivium" in his *From Platonism to Neoplatonism* (The Hague: Martinus Nijhoff, 1968), 94.

33. The literature may now be found in excellent translations, well fortified with notes, in *Greek Musical Writings, Volume 1: The Musician and His Art; Volume 2: Harmonic and Acoustic Theory,* ed. Andrew Barker (Cambridge: Cambridge University Press, 1984 and 1990). The careful article by R. P. Winnington-Ingram in the *New Grove Dictionary of Music and Musicians* (VII, 659–72) provides a succinct and reasonable introduction.

34. Photius, *Biblioteca,* cod. 187.

35. Porphyry, *vita Pythagorae* 11 and 40 (Leipzig: Teubner, 1886); Iamblichus, *de vita pythagorica* 15 and 25–26 (Stuttgart: Teubner, 1975).

36. The Greek idea of *theoria* reached its widest expansion in Plotinus' treatise thereon: III.8. Aristotle makes a revealing observation about the teaching of drawing to the young. Many suppose that it is to make them knowledgeable about art and less likely to be deceived in their purchases when they grow up. But he maintains that it makes one "theoretical about the beauty of bodies," that is, to have a good eye: *Politica* 1338a40–b2 (*GBWW* I: 9, 543; II: 8, 543).

37. Sermon "de utilitate hymnorum," ed. C. H. Turner, *Journal of Theological Studies* (Oxford), 24 (1922–23), 225–52; the quoted passages are from sections ix, v, and xiv.

38. Grove 4:368 does not give a reference, but the text may be found, translated from the surviving Arabic translation, in W. Riedel, *Die Kirchenrechtsquellen des Patriarchats Alexandrien* (Leipzig, 1900), 267. Because this book is not easy to find, I give Riedel's version: "Wenn ein Anagnost die Guitare schlagen lernt, soll er gelehrt werden, es zu beichten(?). Kehrt er dann nicht wieder dazu zürück, so soll seine Strafe sieben Wochen betragen. Will er dabei bleiben, soll er abgesetzt und aus der Kirche ausgeschlossen werden."

39. Thus the *Apostolic Constitutions* VIII.32.9, ed. F. X. Funk, 534. But this work is in fact a literary composition of about 380, does not emanate from any church council or synod, and possesses no apostolic authority whatever, although it no doubt represents attitudes and practices at the time and place of its composition.

40. James McKinnon, "The Meaning of the Patristic Polemic Against Musical Instruments," *Current Musicology* (1965), 71.

41. *The Shape of the Liturgy* (Westminster [U.K.]: Dacre Press, 1945), 39.

42. James McKinnon, "The Exclusion of Musical Instruments from the Synagogue," *Proceedings of the Royal Musical Association* 106 (1979–80), 77–87; J. A. Smith, "The Ancient Synagogue, the Early Church, and Singing," *Music and Letters* 65 (1984), 1–16.

43. Luke 4:16–22 and Acts 13:13–42.

44. Abraham Idelsohn, "Parallelen zwischen gregorianischen und hebraisch-orientalischen Gesangsweisen," *Zeitschrift für Musikwissenschaft* 9/10 (1922), 515–24. The interdependence of synagogue and church liturgy during the first millennium is discussed, with copious citations of texts and melodies, by Eric Werner, *The Sacred Bridge* (London and New York: Columbia University Press, 1959).

45. *Epistle* 125.15, *PL* 22: 1081.

46. *PL* 26: 528–29; the text is Ephesians 5:19.

47. *Confessions* (*GBWW* I: 18, 83; II: 16, 105–6): "modico flexu vocis."

48. This council was held in 747. The text may be found in *Councils and Ecclesiastical Documents Relating to Great Britain and Ireland,* edited after Spelman and Wilkins by A. W. Haddan and William Stubbs (Oxford: Clarendon Press, 1871), III.366: "Ut presbyteri saecularium poetarum modo in ecclesia non garriant, ne tragico sono sacrorum verborum compositionem ac distinctionem corrumpant vel confundant, sed simplicem sanctamque melodiam secundum morem Ecclesiae sectentur." The odd thing about Clovesho itself is that, although at least seven councils were held there in the eighth and ninth centuries, no one now seems to know where it was. The historical context of the utterly memorable synod of 747 can be learned from Margaret Deanesly, *The Pre-Conquest Church in England* (London: Adam and Charles Black, 1961), 220–23.

49. *Of the Laws of Ecclesiastical Polity* (1597), V.38–39. A pleasant account of the highly

eventful Tudor and Jacobean situation may be found in John Hollander, *The Untuning of the Sky* (Princeton, N.J.: Princeton University Press, 1961), chapter V.

A notable event in more recent times was the famous "Motu proprio" issued by Pope Pius X in 1903. It must have been very important for him, because it was practically the first thing he did after his election, even before his wide-ranging attacks on other forms of "modernism." He decreed that Gregorian chant was the proper music of the Roman Church and after it the unaccompanied polyphony of the sixteenth century; modern works were not forbidden, but anything of a theatrical or meretricious nature was to be suppressed. No instruments other than the organ could be used without special permission from the bishop, and even its role was to be secondary and modest. Boys and not women were to sing the soprano parts, and solo singing was discouraged. Commissions were to be appointed in every diocese to watch over all these things, and seminarians were to be instructed in the true principles of church music.

At about this same time the Russian church abandoned its strict censorship of church music (among other now-popular pieces, it had forbidden the liturgical use of Tchaikovsky's *Divine Liturgy* op. 41); the lifting of the censorship was followed by a period of unprecedented creativity by many composers, including Rachmaninoff; the composers of the "Moscow School" may be said to have solved at last the problem of how to harmonize the ancient Russian chants so as to preserve their linear melodic integrity and at the same time satisfy a religious public that had become addicted to the richness of Western harmony. Aleksandr Kastalsky, Pavel Chesnokov, Nikolaj Kompanyeysky, and Johannes von Gardner are the greatest names to which, now, new names will be added.

50. *In epistolum primum ad Timotheum*, homilia 4:14, *Patrologia graeca* (hereafter cited as *PG*), 62: 576.

51. *Apophthegmata patrum*, Johannes Curtes 35, *PG* 65: 216.

52. Quasten, *op cit*, 94–95 and 117 n.206.

53. *Praktikos* 15; *On prayer* 83. These works have been translated, somewhat too freely, by John Eudes Bamberger OCSO, (Kalamazoo, Mich.: Cistercian Publications, 1981).

54. *On prayer* 85.

55. *Historia ecclesiastica* VI.8, *PG* 67: 692.

56. *De coelesti hierarchia* VII.4 and XIII.4, *PG* 3: 210d–212d and 304b–308b.

57. *De ecclesiastica hierarchia* III.5, *PG* 3: 432a–b. This most interesting writer, who claims to be the disciple of Saint Paul mentioned in Acts 17:34, is manifestly nothing of the kind but rather an adherent of the last phase of Neoplatonism who wrote, probably in Syria, at the beginning of the sixth century.

58. *De coelesti hierarchia* II.4, *PG* 3: 144b.

59. *In inscriptiones psalmorum*, *PG* 44: 441c. Saint Gregory begins the long passage of which this sentence is the climax with an account of the micro/macrocosm idea, which he says he heard about "from one of the wise," a typical example of patristic reserve about philosophical sources. His philosophical inclinations have remained less concealed than usual because of the industry of a number of modern scholars. The places where he mentions Greek philosophers by name, usually unfavorably, are collected by Harold F. Cherniss, *The Platonism of Gregory of Nyssa* (Berkeley: University of California Publications in Classical Philology 11, 1930), 1–12; Cherniss sought to prove that Gregory was not so much expressing Christianity in philosophical language as expressing philosophy in Christian language and therefore using Christian doctrine as a justification for becoming a Platonist. The upshot of this argument is that Gregory is not a Father of the Church at all but some kind of Origenizing heretic. The case for an utterly Orthodox Gregory is made by Jean Daniélou, *Platonism et théologie mystique: doctrine spirituelle de Saint Gregoire de Nysse* (Paris: Aubier, 1944). A less inflammatory claim is that Gregory wished to justify Christianity from philosophical principles, a justification that might transcend both reason and faith and establish unique claims for theology. Moderate but sympathetic accounts of Gregory's activities are: Brooks Otis, "Cappadocian Thought as a Coherent System," *Dumbarton Oaks Papers* 12 (1958), 95–124, and Werner Jaeger, *Early Christianity and Greek Paideia* (Cambridge, Mass.: Belknap Press of Harvard University Press, 1961).

60. Cf. *in Ecclesiasten* VII, *PG* 44: 724d; *de hominis opificio* I, *PG* 44: 129b–d and XIII, *PG* 44: 165a; cf. Plotinus IV.4.23–41.

61. Eusebius, *in psalmum* 91:4, *PG* 23: 1172–73. Similar musical imagery is especially audible in the devotional poetry of seventeenth-century England: George Herbert ("The Temper," "Repentance," "Deniall," "Easter," among many others), Henry Vaughan

("The Morning-watch," "Church-Service"), Thomas Traherne ("On Christmas Day," "Bells"), John Donne ("Hymne to God, my God, in my sicknesse"), and, very abundantly and learnedly, John Milton, who only goes to show that even a Puritan can be interested in *musica speculativa*.

A full-dress treatment of the imagery is Leo Spitzer, *Classical and Christian Ideas of World Harmony: Prolegomena to an Interpretation of the Word "Stimmung,"* ed. (carelessly, it is true) Anna Granville Hatcher (Baltimore: Johns Hopkins University Press, 1963).

62. May I call the reader's attention to my discussion of this interesting historical moment in *GIT* 1991.

It is also interesting to notice how logic has tended in modern times to migrate into the quadrivium, so as to be studied in connection with mathematics.

63. Out of a vast and perplexing literature I mention two articles on my side of the question: George P. Springer, "Language and Music: Parallels and Divergencies," *For Roman Jakobson* (The Hague: Mouton and Company, 1956), 504–13; Robert A. Hall, "La struttura della musica et del linguaggio," *Nuova Rivista musical italiana* 7 (1973), 206–25.

Something compels me to mention as well the intrepid attempt by Deryck Cooke to establish melodic intervals and harmonies as a precise language of the emotions: *The Language of Music* (London and New York: Oxford University Press, 1959). Who can fail to be interested in a book that remarks that "only those who still believe strongly in the concept of happiness cling to the major third" (page 54)?

64. Ephesians 5:19.

65. The biblical passages are Genesis 1:26–31 and 2:7; Psalms 8:5–7; Wisdom 2:23; John 1:9 and 17:21–23; 1 Corinthians 15:47–49; 2 Corinthians 3:18. Saint Irenaeus of Lyon was the first to get to work on it, but almost everyone had some thoughts about it.

66. Colossians 1:15.

67. That eternal blessedness will be an endless progress into the divine mystery (rather than, for example, an unchanging vision of the divine essence) is the center of the spirituality of Saint Gregory of Nyssa, especially elaborated in *The Life of Moses* and the *Commentary on the Song of Songs*. An excellent study is that of Jean Daniélou, "The Dove and the Darkness in Ancient Byzantine Mysticism," in *Man and Transformation* (New York: Pantheon Books, 1964), 270–96. He brings out very forcefully the dynamic and transfiguring character of *theoria* in Byzantine spirituality.

68. Clement of Alexandria, *Paedogogus* III.1. The entire passage is redolent of musical imagery.

69. *Problemata* 19, 920a.

70. *See* note 47.

71. *Hermiae Alexandrini in Platonis Phaedrum Scholia,* ed. P. Couvreur (Paris: E. Bouillon, 1901), 84–93; the Platonic text is *Phaedrus* (*GBWW* I: 7, 123–24; II: 6, 123–24), from which one can see that Hermeias has replaced the "poetic" madness of the text with "music," which in the ancient sense included poetry, of course, but Hermeias offers no explanation.

72. I hardly know how to guide the reader in this dark matter that has always escaped my grasp, nor do I think the reader is likely to consult the dense but probing treatment of Werner Beierwaltes that is nonetheless the best known to me: *Proklos: Grundzüge seiner Metaphysik* (Frankfurt am Main: Vittorio Klostermann, 1979), 367–82. Less abstruse but in his own way elusive are the various works of Jean Trouillard, especially "La monadologie de Proclus," *Revue Philosophique de Louvain* 57 (1959), 309–20. In English I know only J. M. Rist, "Mysticism and Transcendence in Later Neoplatonism," *Hermes* 92 (1964), 213–25.

73. The *Elements of Theology* of Proclus is in fact systematically arranged by the degree of self-constitution possessed by each order of beings; the final section is devoted to souls (propositions 184–211), of which propositions 191, 195, 197, 206, and 211 are those closest to the exposition of Hermeias, although I ought to warn the curious that it is not a book easy to consult piecemeal. The revised text, translation, and commentary of E. R. Dodds (Oxford: Clarendon Press, 1963) is essential.

74. Propositions 113–65 of the *Elements of Theology* expound the role of the pagan gods in Neoplatonic metaphysics.

75. A discussion of sacred dance could evidently have found a place here but did not because (1) being even more ephemeral an art than music, it has left even fewer traces from antiquity, and (2) it has not had a large role in Christian worship except in Ethiopia.

76. The genial aphorism that architecture is "frozen music" is often attributed to Schlegel, but I have been unable to locate the source. Goethe attributed the expression "petrified music" to himself, *Conversations with Eckermann* (March 23, 1829). He used the suggestion memorably in *Faust, Part Two,* act one, scene "Rittersaal," near the end, lines 6443–50. One might also recall Valéry's "Le cantique des colonnes."

The analogy of the two arts was standard in the Middle Ages and still alive in the Renaissance. Recall the architect Alberti's warning to his colleague Matteo de' Pasti, during the erection of the church of San Francesco at Rimini, that if he arbitrarily altered the proportions of the pilasters, "Si discorda tutta quella music," "All that music will get out of tune." Cf. Rudolf Wittkower, *Architectural Principles in the Age of Humanism* (London: Warburg Institute, 1949), 103.

77. The influence of Victor Zuckerkandl on these last four paragraphs cannot be concealed: *Sound and Symbol: Music and the External World* (Princeton, N.J.: Princeton University Press Bollingen series, 1956). But Zuckerkandl was not so interested in freedom.

78. Certain turns of phrase in these last two sentences (including an English version of the German word *Gestalthaftigkeit*) suggest that memories of Heidegger have crept in here, but I cannot trace their exact source.

79. Philolaus is quoted by the Neopythagorean Nicomachus of Gerasa, *Introduction to Arithmetic* II.19.

80. III.4: *Die Harmonienlehre des Klaudios Ptolemaios,* herausgegeben von Ingemar Düring (Göteborg: Elanders Boktryckeri Aktiebolag, 1930), 95, 11–16.

81. Wladimir Kandinsky has some memorable pages on the emotional qualities of colors in his *On the Spiritual in Art* (New York: Solomon R. Guggenheim Foundation, 1946), but some people find them fanciful.

82. *De aedeficiis* I.i.30.

83. *In Ioannem homilia* 79, *PG* 59: 426.

84. The explanatory notes added by Dom Joseph Gajard, OSB, to the older series of recordings of chants sung by the monks of Solesmes have seemed to some rather precious and even sentimental, even as some find the Solesmes style itself rather too mannered, but they preserve nonetheless the impressions that the chants can make upon a sensitive musician who sings them every day of his life.

85. *Ennaratio in psalmum* 32:3, *PL* 36: 283.

PART THREE

Special Features

The Ambiguity of Nationalism

Maurice Cranston

Maurice Cranston has taught political science at the London School of Economics, where he occupies the chair formerly held by Michael Oakshott, for the past thirty years. He is the author of the standard biography of John Locke and numerous works of political theory, notably on the subjects of liberty and human rights. He has contributed on several occasions to *The Great Ideas Today* and is currently at work on the final volume of a three-part biography of Jean-Jacques Rousseau, which is based on many years' research on original manuscripts. In this biography he develops the argument first put forward in *GIT* 1985 and *GIT* 1986 that Rousseau must be understood both as a rationalist and a romantic, and one who, holding up a mirror to himself, rediscovered the nature of man as a political animal. Professor Cranston has also published translations of *The Social Contract* and *A Discourse of Inequality* (cf. *GBWW* I: 38, 321–66, 387–439; II: 35, 321–66, 387–439), both for Penguin Books.

With the decline of communism, nationalism has become the most powerful, if not the dominant, ideology of our time. We might have expected this even if Mikhail Gorbachev had not predicted that it would happen and warned us that it would bring about the dissolution of the Soviet Union and widespread civil war. Communism has always had a paradoxical attitude toward nationalism. On the one hand, it encouraged those nationalist movements, in Asia and Africa, which resisted Western European imperialism. On the other hand, it suppressed nationalisms in Europe that opposed its own designs. After Lenin's successful revolution of 1917, the Communist government perpetuated the imperialist structure of the old Russian Empire, and after World War II, Stalin extended the dominance of the Soviet Empire over the whole of Eastern Europe, using both force and cunning against any manifestation of nationalism in those territories. This contradiction in Soviet policy was justified in the language of Marxist theory by an appeal to the boldly simple argument that while "progressive" nationalism, which opposed capitalist regimes, is good, "reactionary" nationalism, which opposed Communist regimes, is bad. [1]

We should perhaps hesitate to condemn the absurdity of this argument, for there is something profoundly ambiguous in most people's attitude, if only in the assertion that my nationalism is good, and yours is bad. Those who claim autonomy for their own group are quick to deny it to their neighbors, as we observe in the exchanges between Protestants and Catholics in Ulster, Serbs and Croats in Bosnia, Armenians and Azeris in Nagorno-Karabakh, Muslims and Hindus in Kashmir, and between several other such communities.

Nationalism as an ideology is no more than an extreme form of a belief which has attained almost universal assent in the twentieth century. It was well expressed by J. S. Mill at a time when it was not so widely held: "Where the sentiment of nationality," he wrote in 1861, "exists in any force, there is a *prima facie* case for uniting all the members of the nationality under the same government, and a government to themselves apart. This is merely saying that the question of government ought to be decided by the governed." [2] At about the same time Tocqueville wrote, "The interests of the human race are better served by giving every man a particular fatherland than by trying to inflame his passions for the whole of humanity." [3]

These propositions seem clear enough, but problems arise when it comes to applying them in practical politics. Mill himself developed his argument in a manner which looks almost as paradoxical as Lenin's; he supported national self-government in Ireland but not in India, for the United States but not for the Confederate States of America, for Belgium but not for Flanders. Of course, Mill could have answered any critics by saying that circumstances alter cases, but he was not, in fact, much criticized. The right of nationalities to autonomy as he expressed it became a standard part of liberal, democratic, progressive, enlightened political theory as a general if not an absolute right; the case for their independence was, after all, only a *prima facie* case.

It was later claimed by Woodrow Wilson as the "right to self-determination" and incorporated in the Fourteen Points which were accepted by both victors and vanquished in the peace of 1918. Wilson sometimes spoke as if he were giving voice to an eternal truth, and yet the whole idea of a nation possessing the right to rule itself is a distinctly modern one. The ancient and medieval worlds would not have understood it. Our distant ancestors had not even the language in which to think about it. The word *nation* as we use it did not exist. The Romans had *natio,* which they employed to designate communities larger than families, smaller than tribes. Medieval French universities spoke of groupings of foreign students as *nations,* naming as the nations of "Picardie," for example, or "Normandie" those students from different zones of Europe which had only the loosest connections, if any, with the provinces known as Picardie and Normandie.

Modern historians sometimes refer to the Senate and People of Rome—the SPQR (Senatus Populusque Romanus)—as the Roman *nation,* but the Romans neither used their word *natio* in that way nor possessed what Mill called "the sentiment of nationality"; they had only the sentiment—together with the institution—of citizenship. Before modern times, people did not think of themselves as forming nations. Professor Carlton J. H. Hayes, of Columbia University, whose book on *The Historical Evolution of Modern Nationalism* of 1931 remains a key work on the subject, suggests [4] that human beings originally lived in tribes—that is, small homogeneous communities based on kinship—and afterward in empires—that is, large, heterogeneous groupings based on conquest. Nations came very much later in human history.

Early formulations

The word *nation* entered the language of politics only in the seventeenth- and eighteenth-century Age of Reason, although those who used it intended it to designate something which dated from an earlier point in time. Voltaire, for example, said that the French nation was the creation of the French kings. [5] In medieval feudal times, on his analysis, "France" was a mere geographic expression—an area of Europe divided into duchies, principalities, and counties over which the French king was simply the first peer of a realm that only nominally incorporated warring Gascons, Normans, Angevins, Bretons, and the rest under one dynastic banner. According to Voltaire, it was the historic achievement of successive French kings to end the anarchy and knit together all these different communities into one *patrie*, royal subjects united by common allegiance and taught to feel a common identity, thus acquiring a consciousness of being French—much the same sentiment that Mill referred to. The Kingdom of France was seen by Voltaire as being transformed from the territory subject to the French crown into the society of people brought together under that crown; in making a civil society the kings had made a nation.

Voltaire was a royalist, and we must distinguish his conception of the nation, as a royalist conception, from others which emerged in the eighteenth century. One of the reasons why there are different sorts of nationalism—among which we may feel entitled to separate the good from the bad—is that there are different ideas as to what constitutes a nation. In Voltaire's time there was more than one school of thought: those who defined the nation, as he did, as a political entity and those who understood it in other ways. The first group includes the leading political philosophers of the Enlightenment—Locke, Montesquieu, and Rousseau; [6] among the others was Adam Smith, who saw the nation as an economic unit, while Giambattista Vico, Edmund Burke, and Johann Gottfried von Herder [7] depicted the nation as a product of culture and history.

Among exponents of the conception of the nation as a political entity there are at least as many republicans as there are royalists. While the royalists define the nation as the kingdom, or the community of the king's subjects, the republicans define it as the community of citizens: for both, the nation is the people, organized under a system of law and sovereignty. [8]

In Voltaire's lifetime—and his long life extended from the high noon of Louis XIV's absolutism to the eve of the French Revolution—most French people felt, as he did, that their nation was the French Kingdom, and their patriotism was a sentiment devoted to king and country. There were very few republics in eighteenth-century Europe; those which did exist—Venice, Geneva, Lucca, Genoa—were city-states, and a city, being too small to constitute a kingdom, was felt at the same time to be too small to constitute a nation. Nevertheless, the idea of the nation played a central role in the arguments for republican government which were developed in the Enlightenment—nowhere to greater purpose than in the New World. [9] In republican theory the central act of the foundation of the state is either the transfer of sovereignty from the king to the people or the institution of popular sovereignty by an original social contract. In either form this founding act entails the transformation of people into *a* people, a series of persons becoming a pledged group, at once imposing law upon itself collectively and accepting severally the commitment to obey.

The republican conception of the nation is thus no less political than the royalist; both see the nation as the people united in a sovereign community, as members of a state, the only difference being that whereas sovereignty is conferred by the royalists on a monarch, the republican people keeps sovereignty in its own hands. In both cases, the nation is the creature of will: the will of the king's subjects or the will of the republic's citizens.

The word *nation* makes a significant appearance in the title of one of the great books of the Enlightenment—Adam Smith's *The Wealth of Nations* (GBWW I: 39; II: 36). This book, which Smith took ten years to write and which he published in 1776 at age fifty-four, is a pioneering work of what was then the fairly new science of economics. Smith looked upon the nation as an economic unit, and his political economy was based on the model of domestic economy, the nation being seen by him as a household writ large. Although Smith was a proud Scotsman, having very little contact throughout his life with things English, he did not have Scotland in mind when he used the word *nation* but economic units such as that which the United Kingdom of Scotland, England, and Ireland constituted. Smith's theory did not call for the existence of what Mill spoke of as a "sentiment of nationality," since it was a purely rationalist construction. Smith argued that if every member of the national society pursues his own personal economic advantage, an "invisible hand" could be relied on to transform the enterprise for the public, or national, advantage. He rejected the mercantilist conception of a rich nation as one which retained within its borders as much gold and silver as possible and argued that the richest nation is one which either produces or can command from others the greatest quantity of consumable goods. Although Smith made much of sympathy and altruism in his moral theory, his economic theory relied wholly on self-interest as a motive for human action. Such an approach was in accord with the cosmopolitan spirit of the Enlightenment. Feelings of solidarity with one's fellowmen, for Adam Smith—as for Diderot and most of the French Encyclopédistes—were thought to be as desirable as feelings of solidarity with the whole human race, rather than with one's fellow Scotsmen or Frenchmen. Shared material interest could be relied on to bind one to one's immediate neighbors.

Dissatisfaction with this rationalist image of economic man, a creature at once selfish and humanitarian, marks a breech between the Enlightenment and its romantic critics, beginning with Rousseau. [10] For while Diderot and Rousseau both spoke of the existence of a "general will" within each individual's breast, Diderot believed it was put there by Nature to prompt individuals to act for the general good of the whole of humanity, whereas Rousseau claimed that a "general will" could only be developed in a particular civil society and only be directed toward the general goal of that civil society—or nation—of which the individual was a member.

Rousseau's argument did much to inspire the development of yet another conception which emerged in the thinking of the eighteenth century, namely, that of the nation as the creation of culture and history rather than of will. Vico, Burke, and Herder do not deny that a nation is composed of people who choose to live together; they visualize such people as united not by obedience to a certain dynasty or by the pledge of a "social contract," [11] but by the circumstance of sharing the same language, the same religious beliefs and observances, the same traditions, customs, habits, mores, and manners. All these cultural factors put together unite people into social groupings, and it is these groupings, on this theory, which constitute nations or nationalities. It was not asserted that such groupings should necessarily be awarded political autonomy: but Herder, at least, urged the members of the group to become more conscious of their cultural identity as nations. Herder, being a German, wanted to make the Germans develop a sense of their "Germanness," to cultivate in themselves Mill's "sentiment of nationality," which in the eighteenth century they seemed not to have. The political division of Germany into some three hundred separate states was not what worried Herder; what he protested was the extent to which German taste was dictated by foreign fashions, German art dominated by foreign models, the German language itself scorned by the German scholars who wrote in Latin and by German aristocrats who spoke French. [12]

The eighteenth century

These two concepts of the nation—as a political entity on the one hand and as a cultural entity on the other—inform the two distinct forms of nationalism that emerged in the eighteenth century. Political nationalism came to assume particular importance in the unfolding of the two great political events of that century, the American Revolution and the French Revolution. Thomas Jefferson, in his wording of the American Declaration of Independence, points to the moment in history when "one people" are impelled by necessity "to dissolve the political bands which have connected them with another." He speaks, it will be noticed, of "a people" and not "a nation"; indeed, in the language of Jefferson's politics it was only as a result of their secession from British rule that the American people became a nation—the inhabitants of thirteen colonies by a declared act of will ceased to be part of the imperial community and, by assuming a new identity, gave birth to a nation. Individuals who dissented from this new "social contract" and wished to remain part of the imperial structure of loyalties had perforce to withdraw (in practice to Canada). Of course, the new nation was not so unequivocally "one" as Jefferson's wording suggests, for the constitution which emerged from the Revolution was a federal structure incorporating an equivocal concept of the state—the state denoting, in one sense, the autonomous commonwealth which each of the thirteen colonies instituted, and at the same time, the federal republic which incorporated them all. Jefferson was happy to proclaim two loyalties—to Virginia and to America; but a double political loyalty did not prove easy for everyone: the unity of the United States had to be reestablished by Lincoln and his army less than a century later. [13]

The American Revolution had a powerful influence on the French Revolution, especially after 1793, when the French revolutionists forsook the enterprise of establishing a liberal monarchy on the English model, which had formerly seemed the most enlightened one in the world, as proclaimed by Voltaire, and set up a republic with a population five times as large as the United States. There emerged what Professor Hayes calls "Jacobin nationalism," [14] proclaiming not only "the sovereignty of the nation" but the right of the actual citizenry to participate in the government of their republic. "Democratic nationalism" might be a better name for this, for already in the United States there were moves toward that enlargement of the suffrage which were to culminate in the Jacksonian reforms. Logically, some measure of democracy might seem to be entailed by the republican idea of a nation ruling itself, for if the people is to be sovereign, it is arguable that it should do what monarchs do when they are sovereign, namely, enact the laws and make the policy decisions which the people act upon.

The nationalism of the French Revolution stopped short of anything like full democracy, but it did make much of being popular and plebiscitary and evoking mass enthusiasm, and this characteristic continued beyond the Jacobean phase into the Napoleonic era of the Revolution. At the same time, French revolutionary nationalism developed another characteristic, later known as chauvinism: the belief among its adherents that the French nation could do no wrong. [15] Napoleon's own attitude toward nationalism was hardly less ambiguous than Lenin's. On the one hand, he encouraged the Hungarians and the Poles to be political nationalists—to resist the imperial claims of Austria and Russia over their territories; on the other hand, he called on the Hungarians and Poles to bend their wills to the greater purposes of France and submit to the one Empire that was destined to lead the human race toward liberty, equality, and fraternity. Napoleon preached nationalism as he practiced imperialism.

By doing so he provoked what proved to be the most aggressive manifestation of nineteenth-century European nationalism: German nationalism. [16] The founding philosopher of this movement was Johann Gottlieb Fichte, who combined political nationalism with cultural nationalism and added certain distinctive features to both. He argued first, with Herder, that the German-speaking people of Europe constituted a nation by virtue of their linguistic and related forms of identity, and he went beyond Herder to demand that this people ought to be united politically in one German state. Fichte backed up this proposal by claiming that the Germans were not only a culturally distinct people but a culturally and indeed morally superior people, thus echoing the chauvinistic claims that had been made for the French by the French Napoleonic nationalists.

At the period of Fichte's lifetime, a good claim could be made for German cultural superiority. Whereas in the early seventeenth century the Germans were still backward and rudely cultivated, by the end of the eighteenth century they could boast of having in Kant the greatest philosopher, in Goethe the greatest poet, and all the greatest musicians of the Western world; moreover, they were rapidly developing the best universities and the best scientific laboratories. The humiliation of defeat by Napoleon's armies only added to the impetus for Germans to vindicate their claim to consideration and respect; Fichte suggested they could do so only by establishing a German national state that could match the dimensions and the power of Napoleon's French Empire. In making this demand Fichte had the support of virtually all the younger German writers of his time—Novalis, Heinrich von Kleist, and Friedrich Hölderlin among them, giving it an aesthetic as well as a moral dimension.

After Napoleon's defeat of the Prussian armies in 1806, Fichte published his *Addresses to the German Nation*, [17] calling on that "nation" to transform itself into a state. In doing so he depicted the purpose of such a state as the realization of Germany's true place in the world, which was that of an instrument for the moral regeneration of all mankind. In short, Fichte took over from Napoleon the claim to a universal as well as a national mission. A German state, Fichte wrote, would serve as a model for other peoples, for it was the destiny of Germany to educate humanity and lead it upward and onward: "It is you Germans," he told his readers, "who possess most clearly the germ of human perfectibility and to whom belongs the first place in the development of mankind. . . . There is no escape. If you sink, mankind will sink with you."

Such extravagant language expresses the spirit of a Romantic age, but Fichte provided German nationalism with something more than mere rhetoric. He gave German nationalism a new concept of freedom. The political nationalism of the eighteenth century, whether royalist or republican, Voltairean or Jeffersonian, had asserted the right of the individual at the same time as the freedom of the nation. German nationalism, under the inspiration of Fichte, merged the freedom of the individual in the freedom of the nation, or rather submerged it, so that the individual was offered freedom only as an integral part of the greater whole, the organic state. Whereas the Americans and the French proclaimed declarations of the rights of man, the German nationalists proclaimed declarations of the rights of the people, or *Volk*.

The nineteenth century

In the course of the nineteenth century there emerged another concept of the nation, defining it no longer as a political, economic, or cultural group but as a race. This concept was to have unfortunate consequences: [18] it claimed to be more scientific than those concepts of the nation which rested on such vague criteria as religion, language, culture, or the *Volksgeist*. By dividing mankind into races which could be distinguished by color, skull shape, facial structure, and other empirical traits, theorists such as Gobineau in France, James Hunt in England, and Otto Ammon in Germany proceeded to argue that racial groups could be shown scientifically not only to be distinct but to possess different degrees of merit. The belief that some races were superior to others went together with the evolutionary, Darwinian attitudes of the later Victorian age, which succeeded the romantic notions of the earlier period. The harmful effects of this development became evident as criteria for exclusion supplemented the criteria for inclusion which the cultural nationalists had emphasized. [19] Racial nationalism proved almost more eager to determine who was out than who was in. For example, the conception of the German nation or the French nation as a race promptly served to isolate the Jews from the national community. In language and general culture, the Jews were indistinguishable from other Germans or Frenchmen, and their religion no more excluded them than dissent excluded Protestants from multi-confessional German states or from *La France laïque*. But on the basis of racial criteria, the Jews were said to be essentially different, with the result that a minority which had been persecuted in medieval times because of its religious singularity came to be persecuted anew on grounds of supposed racial singularity. [20]

At the same time as the racial theorists stigmatized some groups as inferior, they nourished fantasies about the superiority of others. By pointing to fairly obvious physical characteristics, and classifying large groups of human beings as Mongoloid, Negroid, and so forth, these theorists fortified the political ambitions of white people—classified "scientifically" as Caucasoid—to dominate the members of colored groups and the pretensions of Nordic or Teutonic groups to attempt mastery over Slavs and Latins. Thinking in terms of race thus bred "racism" to such an extent that the word *race* can no longer be used dispassionately. The words *ethnic* and *ethnicity* are generally preferred today. *Ethnic* comes from the Greek word *ethnos,* and while it is hardly more precise than the Italian word *razza* from which *race* derives, it is at least free from overtones of emotion and prejudice and an inheritance of pseudoscience.

An ethnic group is not a political group, although it may coincide with one. It is a social group defined by certain physical and genetically inherited characteristics. Ethnic nationalism, such as African nationalism, builds its concept of the nation around the ethnic group, which can be perceived, so to speak, from the outside—recognized in the case of African nationalism in the blackness of the skin of its members, no longer allowed to be a badge of inferiority but rather of distinctiveness and beauty.

This ethnic concept of the nation stands in marked contrast to that put forward by Ernest Renan in 1882 in his famous lecture: "What Is a Nation?" Renan claimed that a nation was a civil association which lived in the inwardness of its members. A nation, he argued, could not be explained in terms of shared language, for language did not unite the English-speaking or the Spanish-speaking peoples of the world; it could not be explained in terms of shared religion, since Christianity did not unite the peoples of Europe, nor explained in terms of race, since blood did not unite the Teutonic tribes. The factors which held together the members of a civil association, said Renan, were shared feelings, shared loyalties, shared memories, experiences, and expectations. Above all it was the agreement of hearts beating in unison: "To have done great things together and have the will to do more are the essential conditions for people to be *a* people. A nation is a plebiscite renewed every day." [21]

Renan was writing in the 1880s, and his work was largely animated by a desire to consolidate the attachment of the French people to a French state—the Third Republic—which failed to command anything like universal adherence among its citizens. [22] In a hundred years the French state had passed through a series of revolutions—with republican, imperial, conservative-royalist, liberal-royalist, republican, imperial, and then republican constitutions following one another in swift succession. If the same spirit was to inhabit so many different bodies, it would need to be very alive to its identity and vitality. Renan provided a mystical concept of the nation which was intended to be impervious to political and constitutional upheavals in the French state. He was not the only one to have that aim. Joan of Arc was perhaps the first to expound the vision, and as late as 1940 Charles de Gaulle invoked it when he declared: *"La France, c'est moi,"* despite the fact that the legal government of France was established at Vichy and that most Frenchmen considered de Gaulle to be a traitor. De Gaulle's France was a "platonic ideal" of the French nation that existed above and beyond defeated and dishonored "empirical" France, which acknowledged Marshal Henri-Philippe Pétain as its head.

Given that modern thought has produced a variety of answers to Renan's question "What is a nation?" we could not expect to find a single form of nationalism; at best we may hope to distinguish some family resemblances between the several forms of nationalist ideology and some explanation for those differences. Some of those differences can be readily connected to the character of particular societies in which the ideology has taken root. Nationalism in Germany, for example, has always attracted particular attention from historians because of the far-reaching changes it provoked. In view of the political structure of the German-speaking world at the time that Fichte wrote his *Addresses to the German Nation,* its program was radical indeed: for the creation of a single German state in 1806 could only be accomplished after the abolition of almost three hundred existing states, imperial in Austria, royal in Bavaria and Prussia, princely, ducal, or episcopal elsewhere. In the event, Austria was powerful enough to thwart the Fichtean enterprise until Prussia became strong enough to realize it and institute a German state by the enlargement of the Prussian kingdom.

Liberal nationalism

The nationalism which emerged in Germany in the early nineteenth century was not peculiar to Germany. A similar fusion of political nationalism with cultural nationalism was developed by the Italians, another set of people more or less united by their language and general culture, but divided politically into a series of separate states, some royal, some ducal, some republican, some papal, some subject to foreign rule. The leading Italian nationalists—Giuseppe Mazzini, Alessandro Manzoni, Giuseppe Garibaldi—saw their purposes as twofold: first the elimination of cultural differences in the Italian-speaking world, which were rather more marked than those in the German-speaking world, and then the unification of the Italian peninsula and islands into a single civil society. The Italian nationalists were somewhat more modest than the Germans in their claims for the superiority of Italian culture, decidedly more individualistic, not to say anarchic, in their conceptions of freedom, and rather more fervent in their hatred of alien domination than devout in their reverence for any form of national Italian state.

The Italian nationalist movement also attracted more support and sympathy from other countries than did German nationalism, doubtlessly because adherence to the ideals of the Rights of Man as well as the rights of the nation kept it within the liberal tradition. Italian nationalism is one example of what Professor Hayes calls "liberal nationalism," [23] and which he associates with the teaching of Jeremy Bentham (cf. *GIT* 1993, pp. 334–63). Bentham was one of the first philosophers to give the notion of International Law concrete content, setting out a scheme of world order in which peace was secured by an arrangement of sovereign nations living contentedly side by side like a necklace of pearls without a string to unite them. Imperial domination of one state by another would, according to the principles of Bentham's nationalism, be wholly eliminated, liberty would be equally assured for the individual and the nation, and unimpeded commerce between independent states would breed mutual prosperity and trust.

Bentham himself tried to further this type of liberal nationalism by helping the Greeks in their efforts to liberate themselves from the Turkish Empire, a struggle in which his friend Lord Byron died what was regarded as a hero's death. In these two personalities, liberal nationalism can be seen to have received the blessing of both utilitarianism and romanticism. [24] It also recruited the support of more prosaic if more powerful political figures such as François Guizot, prime minister of Louis-Philippe's France, and William Ewart Gladstone, prime minister of Victorian England, before being transmitted in the liberal inheritance to Woodrow Wilson in America.

To the extent that liberal nationalism came to be absorbed in the ideologies of governing political parties, it became hedged in with certain qualifications. Liberal nationalism welcomed the rebellion of the South American colonies against the imperial rule of Spain and Portugal; [25] but few liberal parties, still less the liberal governments of Great Britain, France, and Holland, favored the secession of their own colonies in Africa or Asia, on the grounds that the inhabitants of those colonies were not "ripe," as had been the colonists of the United States, Brazil, Argentina, or Peru, for independence. John Stuart Mill, whose profession was that of official in the India House in London, explained that the aim of British policy in India was, essentially, to train the Indian people for self-government by providing the example of disinterested British bureaucrats ruling the Indians, like the Guardians in Plato's Republic.

Liberal nationalism was perhaps the most widespread form of nationalism in nineteenth-century Europe. In countries which already enjoyed political independence it took the form of cultural nationalism, calling upon artists to cultivate the national character of their art and to resist cosmopolitan or foreign influences. This was the main thrust of nationalism in Russia, where Aleksandr Pushkin became a model for future Russian poets when in 1820 he turned away from European literary models in *Ruslan and Lyudmila* to construct a new style of verse on the basis of old Russian folk literature. His masterpiece *Yevgeny Onegin* is a novel in verse which takes the whole of Russian life as its province; and Pushkin, though he died in a duel at the age of thirty-seven, established a tradition of literature, perpetuated by Mikhail Lermontov, Tolstoy, Ivan Turgenev, and Chekhov, that was wholly directed toward the articulation of Russian experience and the exploration of Russian inwardness. Russian musicians were no less nationalistic: Mikhail Glinka made a deliberate break with the cosmopolitan ideas he had learned as a student in Italy and sought inspiration in Russian folk music; Aleksandr Borodin, Modest Mussorgsky, and Nikolay Rimsky-Korsakov demonstrated their "Russianness" and commitment to a national music by turning their backs on the conservatories and the westernized professors. Russia already had a state; cultural nationalism sought to give it a soul.

If nationalism in Russia was mainly cultural, in Poland it was primarily political. [26] Poland did badly in the carve-up of Europe at the Congress of Vienna in 1815, and worse as both the Russian and Prussian rulers proceeded to rob the Poles of what little freedom remained to them. Nationalism in these circumstances looked to artists and poets to give voice to national protest and resistance. The Poles had no need, as had the Germans and the Italians, to conceive a nation. Poland as a kingdom had a long history, and the program of its nationalists was a simple one: to restore that which had been abolished by alien conquerors, to recover a lost autonomy. The Polish insurrections of 1830, 1846, and 1863 were all suppressed, but they kept alive the "consciousness of nationality," while the poetry of Adam Mickiewicz and the music of Chopin reminded the world of the continuing existence of Poland as a cultural nation, despite its absence from the political map of Europe.

Scandinavia's situation was more complicated. In Sweden and Denmark nationalism was cultural nationalism: both those kingdoms enjoyed undisputed political autonomy; for thinkers and artists who were self-consciously "national" in their outlook, the task was to bring to light what was distinctively Swedish or Danish in their heritage and, like their contemporaries in Russia, to produce a new "national" art. In Norway and Iceland nationalism was as political as it was cultural: and this difference reflected the fact that neither Norway nor Iceland was an independent state in the nineteenth century. Norway was under Swedish rule, Iceland under Danish, and moreover in the case of Norway, Swedish political control was coupled with Danish cultural hegemony. The Norwegian poet Henrik Arnold Wergeland published in 1830 an epic entitled *Creation, Humanity, and Messiah,* which served in effect as a manifesto of national liberation. Its impact was reinforced by the publication in the following years of large collections of Norwegian folktales by Peter Christen Asbjørnsen and of Norwegian ballads by Magnus Brostrup Landstad. The aim of all these publications was to assert Norway's claim to be something more than a Scandinavian province, and the movement realized its aim in 1905 when an independent Norwegian kingdom was finally reestablished with the consent of Sweden. In Iceland, the poets were effective allies of the nationalist leader Jón Sigurdsson and, by enlarging Iceland's cultural heritage, furthered its claim to political autonomy, although it was only during World War II that Iceland became a fully independent state.

In Spain and Great Britain nationalism posed more complex problems. The Spanish had never in the Iberian Peninsula, nor had the English in the British Isles, been able to establish the kind of unified political and cultural nation which the French kings had, as Voltaire proudly observed, created in France. The Spanish and English kings had instead established empires, far-flung around the world, and as diverse in culture, language, religion, and life-styles as it is possible to imagine. As part of these grand enterprises, the Spanish consolidated the five kingdoms of the peninsula into one, while the English united their kingdom with that of Scotland by agreement and incorporated the defunct kingdoms of Ireland and Wales by force.

Neither the Spanish nor the English succeeded in creating among the inhabitants of those regions a universal sentiment of nationality. While the energies of both realms were directed to the enlargement of empire overseas, this lack of unity at home was largely ignored. Scotsmen in the nineteenth century, under such influences as that of Sir Walter Scott, asserted their membership in a Scottish nation, without denying their allegiance to the king and Parliament they shared with the English. We see little evidence of what might be called "English nationalism"; and British nationalism is barely indistinguishable from British imperialism. Benjamin Disraeli in politics and Rudyard Kipling in literature are the British equivalents of the flag-waving French nationalists; and both sought to exalt the British Empire rather than the British nation.

Welsh nationalism—a cultural movement in its origins, defending the old Welsh language against the spread of English—was not especially vocal until the twentieth century, but Irish nationalism has a longer history, and Irish resistance represented for centuries the main obstacle to the English ambition of uniting the British Isles under a single crown and government. [27] Christianity took earlier and deeper roots in Ireland than in Britain, and a rich tradition of art and scholarship originated in the Irish monasteries in the sixth and seventh centuries, while the inhabitants of the larger island were more concerned with warfare. The arrival of the Anglo-Norman King Henry II in Ireland in 1171 marked the beginning of an English occupation of the country, and this ended only in 1922 with the establishment of the Irish Free State in the southern counties, while it continues to this day in the northern counties. Although the Irish nobility was largely Anglicized, or lost its lands to English intruders, the ordinary Irish people never came to regard the English as anything other than an occupying power;

the English exploited Ireland economically, and their efforts to impose the Protestant religion by force only provoked a more bitter and determined hostility. Irish nationalism in the nineteenth century was directed toward achieving what was called "Home Rule," and the British Liberal Party, when it obtained a majority in the House of Commons, promised to concede it. Opposition from the Conservative Party and the House of Lords delayed this process, abetted by a unionist movement of Protestants in Northern Ireland, an articulate minority which had no wish to be ruled by the Catholic majority. The Catholics and Protestants in Ireland were in fact so alien to each other that they came to constitute, in one sense of the word, two nations.

The great misfortune of the British Isles is that those two face each other today in unconcealed hostility in the province of Northern Ireland, the Protestants declaring themselves to be British and waving the Union Jack, the Catholics declaring themselves to be Irish and waving the tricolor of the Dublin republic. In the united Ireland to which the Victorian Liberals proposed to grant Home Rule, the Protestants would have been a militant minority; in the Province of Northern Ireland, which the treaty of 1922 kept as part of the United Kingdom, the Catholics are a militant minority. Protestants and Catholics do not live in different parts of the country as Greeks and Turks live in different parts of Cyprus; they are intermingled, so that partition in Ireland has not served to keep old enemies apart; and democracy, insofar as it has turned out to be the rule of the more numerous Protestants of Northern Ireland over the alienated Catholic minority, is democracy without consensus and therefore a very imperfect democracy, plagued by terrorism.

Nationalism has also generated terrorism in the Iberian Peninsula. Again it is the terrorism of minorities. Since the unity and independence of the Spanish Kingdom had been long established, the aims of Spanish nationalism were cultural rather than political in the nineteenth century. Its character was not dissimilar to the cultural nationalism of Russia, namely, to proclaim the "Spanishness" of Spanish culture, and to repudiate the cosmopolitan, neoclassical, French and Italian influences which had been powerful in Spain in the eighteenth century. The most important writers who emerged in Spain after the French Revolution—Espronceda y Delgado, Rivas, and Zorrilla—set out deliberately to recover the distinctively Spanish qualities which had shaped Spanish literature through several centuries of its existence. They looked back to the earliest love poems which the troubadours carried from Spain into Provence, to the *pastourelles* of Galicia, the picaresque tales of Castille, to Catalonian romances of chivalry, to Cervantes, and to Pedro Calderón and *El Cid*.

The problem which Spanish nationalism encountered was that in stimulating the recovery of past cultural achievements it generated a revival of the old provincial loyalties, especially in Catalonia and the Basque regions, where there was a certain separate cultural identity. Nationalism thus produced in Spain what was in a way a mirror image of itself, as well as its antithesis—separatism. [28]

"Separatism" is usually a pejorative word. It is Madrid's word for what Basques would call "nationalism"; it is London's word for what Scotsmen would call "nationalism." As we have noted, cultural nationalism need not be separatist. Sir Walter Scott proclaimed the cultural identity of the Scottish nation, but he did not advocate political separation of Scotland from the United Kingdom. Pierre Trudeau proclaimed the cultural identity of Quebec, while resisting secession from Canada. Similar attitudes have been assumed by champions of cultural nationalism in such places as Brittany, Wales, Flanders, and the Alto Adige.

Often cultural nationalism stops short of political nationalism or "separatism" for practical reasons: the Swiss canton of the Grisons has its own language and folklore, but it could not well sustain itself economically or militarily today as the independent political unit it once was. [29] However, in the modern age ideological visions and passions often prevail over calculations of costs and benefits.

Most political societies in history, whether empires, kingdoms, or republics, have been what we should now call "multicultural"; and they have usually worked tolerably well. The Austrian Empire commanded the loyalty of its diverse subjects for many generations, primarily, perhaps, because it protected them from Turkish invaders, but also because it provided a reasonably efficient system for the administration and enforcement of law. The rule of law is the first essential of any government, and from the point of view of the humble individual— "destined," as Burke put it, "to walk the obscure path of laborious life"—it does not greatly matter so long as law prevails that the sovereign who imposes that law is a member of a different religious, cultural, or ethnic group from himself.

Governments in the past have very rarely been democratic, and if you are ruled by a royal family or an aristocracy, you can hardly expect them, if you are a simple ordinary person, to have much in common with yourself, or even to wish they did, so long as they are just, benign, and capable rulers. It is when democratization is introduced that the differences begin to matter. For democratic government means in practice the rule of the majority, and if you are a member of a permanent minority in your country, you risk finding yourself outvoted and overruled and even perhaps persecuted by your neighbors. The enthronement of the majority thus brings about the crystallization of the fears and anxieties of minorities. To the extent that the twentieth century has produced the triumph of democracy, of the principle of majority rule, it has also provoked the drama of minority resistance and in many cases the solidification of minorities as alienated groups.

With the decline of empires, minorities within minorities have, like boxes within boxes, taken shape and challenged the redistribution of power. We have seen how demands for "Home Rule" for the Irish were followed by demands for freedom in Ireland for Protestant Ulster, and when that cry was heeded, by cries for freedom in Protestant Ulster for the Catholic minority. The collapse of Communist imperialism in Eastern Europe has generated a similar pattern of nationalisms within nationalisms as communities within communities have become vocal after years of imposed silence.

Many people take pleasure in the idea of a multicultural society. One of the reasons why Voltaire admired the England of George I was that different communities lived peaceably together. "In London," he wrote, "the Jew, the Moslem and the Christian do business together as if they were of the same religion, and they give the name of 'infidel' only to those who go bankrupt." [30] Again, as a royalist, Voltaire attributed this easy coexistence of different communities to the fact that all the inhabitants experienced the same impartial rule of an exalted monarch. In a republic, where every citizen shared in the sovereignty, Voltaire feared that such communities would need to be more uniform. And indeed in the United States, where democracy progressed, the system of the cultural "melting pot" became a favored instrument of public policy. Immigrants who arrived from all sorts of different language zones and ethnic groups were turned into Americans by being taught the national language, English, and by acquiring the national life-style which characterized the all-American family. Professor Gordon Wood of Brown University in a recent book [31] argues that the American settlers, in ending their political allegiance to the English Crown, cast off their patriarchal domestic and social traditions and cultivated the morals and manners appropriate to republican citizens, and that this American version of the republican family was the model which all who later sought a new life in the New World found themselves expected to adopt and, for the most part, did adopt. In this way cultural uniformity, of the sort that Tocqueville observed and analyzed in 1835, replaced in the republican United States the multicultural variety which prevailed under the monarchy of the British Empire. While he criticized it gently, Tocqueville suggested that this cultural uniformity was one of the secrets of the success of democracy in America. It promoted mutual understanding. Tocqueville would probably have regarded current proposals for multicultural education in American schools, for bilingualism in public institutions, and other such changes as inimical to democratic harmony. Biculturalism in Canada has clearly been politically divisive; multiculturalism in America could easily provoke even greater fission.

The twentieth century

Nationalism of one kind helped propel the states of Europe to war in 1914. This was the chauvinist form of nationalism that was expressed in the German desire to prove itself the mightiest power in Europe, in the French desire to reverse the humiliation of defeat in 1870 by a victory in arms over Germany, and in the British desire to outshine all rivals in colonial expansion. Nationalism of another kind—that which asserts the right of peoples to self-determination—enjoyed certain success with the victory of the Allied armies in 1918. But it was a limited success, partly because the concrete interests of the victorious powers were given priority over the demands of abstract principles, and second because of the genuine difficulty of finding an answer to Renan's question: "What is a nation?"

Interest and principles combined in dictating the carve-up of the defeated German, Austrian, and Turkish empires: but the shape of the several pieces into which they were carved was less readily determined. The different groups—cultural, linguistic, religious, or ethnic—were not located in clearly definable areas around which political borders could easily be drawn. But once these borders were settled after 1918, nations in the sense of nation-states were founded; old kingdoms were revived, new kingdoms invented, republics instituted. After World War II most of these nation-states were kept in being in the peace settlement of 1945, either by Communist *diktat* or by the mute assent of war-weary populations.

The collapse of communism in the 1980s produced an upsurge of nationalism. One of the first results of Gorbachev's policy of *glasnost* was fighting between the peoples of two of the Soviet republics—Christian Armenia and Muslim Azerbaijan. With both ethnic and religious differences coming into play, the situation was an explosive one. There was also the historical factor of Armenia's past experience of genocide. Every Armenian child since 1915 has been brought up with the memory of the Armenian holocaust in that year at the hands of the Ottoman Turks. In the Armenian mind, the Azeris of Azerbaijan have always been associated with that massacre—which is not entirely fair, for the Azeris are not Turks but they are Muslims, and Armenians have always been afraid of them. The presence of the Red Army under the Soviet Union allayed those fears but did not extinguish them.

The Armenians of the Soviet Union do not all live in the republic of Armenia, and the first focus of conflict was Nagorno-Karabakh, an enclave of 4,400 square kilometers wholly within Azerbaijan. The population of the enclave was 188,000 in that year, 76 percent Christian Armenians, the rest Muslim Azeris. The demand of the Christian majority for the union of Nagorno-Karabakh with the Republic of Armenia prompted sporadic fighting with Azeris which became more intense when the Red Army withdrew in 1991. Diplomatic efforts by Iran and the UN to mediate had only a partial success against a background of increasing nationalist fervor on both sides and the inevitable mutual recriminations which a resort to violence breeds.

Marx's partner, Engels, spoke of the Russian Empire in 1866 as "the detainer of an immense amount of stolen property, which would have to be disgorged in the day of reckoning." [32] Stalin postponed the day of reckoning by devising in 1936 a constitution for the Soviet Union that gave it a spuriously federal appearance; on paper the existence of independent republics was recognized, while in reality the policies of those republics were dictated by the Communist party leadership in Moscow. However, by bringing the formal structures of independent republics into being, Stalin's constitution gave the Russian nationalist Boris Yeltsin the means to challenge the central authority of Gorbachev and demolish the Soviet Union, in effect to transform bogus independence into real independence.

Yeltsin's achievement would have been more straightforward if the Russian republic had been more unified, but the Russian republic is itself a federation of so-called republics. Although 80 percent of the 147 million population is of ethnic Russians, the federation contains no less than 100 other ethnic groups. A few of these number 5,000 or less and make no claim for political autonomy, but several have called for the devolution of power from Moscow to local authorities. Some ethnic groups, such as the Chechens of the Caucasus and the Tatars of Tatarstan—a "republic" of 3.7 million on the Volga—have already proclaimed themselves nations and voted for independence. The Chechens, like the Armenians, are united by memories of past sufferings. They were put together with the Ingush by Stalin in one of the bogus "republics" he created in 1936 and then deported en bloc after the war to Central Asia as punishment for alleged collaboration with the German invaders. Khrushchev allowed the Chechens to return to the Caucasus in 1957, but their hostility to Russian rule remained intense. [33] In some of the new states which have emerged with the dissolution of the Soviet Union, Russian ethnic groups are themselves minorities. Moldavia is a conspicuous example of this. When the Moldavian Soviet Republic, with a majority of ethnic Romanians, declared its independence as "Moldova" from the U.S.S.R. in September 1991, with the aim of ultimate union of Romania, the ethnic Russian minority proclaimed its independence in a self-styled Dnestr Republic. This rebellion was significant enough to prompt the Romanians to decide against immediate union; the regime of Bucharest, already embarrassed by a discontented Hungarian minority, was reluctant to incorporate further zones of conflict.

Romania, like France, has now a significant ultranationalist political party, the *Romania Mare,* which proposes, along the lines of Jean-Marie

Le Pen's *Front National* in France, that ethnic minorities should be deported. [34] Only a few such minorities have expectations of finding a home elsewhere. The Jews, welcomed in Israel, are an exception to the rule, as are the ethnic Germans, to whom the constitution of the Bundesrepublik promises resettlement. In 1990, half of Romania's 200,000 ethnic Germans left the poverty-stricken ex-Communist state for the bright lights of Chancellor Kohl's Germany, and despite subsequent appeals from both the Bonn and Bucharest governments for this well-educated minority to stay, the emigration has continued.

However, for all its problems with minorities, Romania has a sound prospect of survival as a nation-state, which is not the case in some of the other states created after World War I. Clearly Yugoslavia was no less destined than was the Soviet Union to disintegrate once the dominion of communism was removed. One has only to glance at the profile of Sarajevo, for example, with its crowded skyline of Muslim minarets, Catholic spires, and Orthodox domes to be impressed by the evidence of its multiculturalism, and to understand its tragic fate, once nationalist passions were unleashed. The demographic map is no less striking: for although the boundaries of Serbia, Croatia, Montenegro, Macedonia, Slovenia, and Bosnia-Hercegovina were sharply drawn on the old Yugoslav map, important enclaves of Serbs within Croatia and of Croats and Serbs within Muslim Bosnia, and smaller minorities in other sections of old Yugoslavia, make up a mosaic which thwarted the efforts of Lord Owen and Cyrus Vance to produce an acceptable geographic basis for a "federal" solution to the civil war.

There was perhaps never any strong and universal "sentiment of nationality" in Yugoslavia. The state was clobbered together under a king by the Allies in 1918 and kept together by Tito and the Communist party when the Crown was abolished; there was hardly any free expression of political opinion under either regime, and passions were left to smolder below the surface.

Czechoslovakia seemed for some years to be a more successful creation of the 1918 peace. If the Sudeten German minority was perhaps a less willing element, the Czechs and Slovaks appeared happy enough to unite as a bicultural republic, even to become "Czechoslovaks," acquiring a sense of Czechoslovak nationality. The Czechoslovak state resembled in several respects that which developed as a result of the union of Scotland with England in 1706. Among the Slovaks, as among the Scots, there was a certain awareness that for a poorer contractant, there are solid material advantages to be derived from marriage to a richer partner. However, in Slovakia the movement which called itself "nationalist," and was called by the Czechs "separatist," was more willing than the Scots to pay the price of total secession. The unity of Czechoslovakia was therefore doomed, once the opportunity for secession arose.

The seige of Bosnian Sarajevo by the Serbs, a grim chapter in the disintegration of Yugoslavia since the collapse of communism, has been cruel. (Left and opposite page) "Sniper Alley," the only road by which food-filled warehouses at the airport could be reached by relief trucks, was made impassable by Serbian gunfire from the hills above.

Prisoners (right) wait in one of Serbia's notorious detention camps. Two men (below) cook a meal among the ruins of Sarajevo. Grieving women and children (opposite page) crowd into whatever transportation is available as they flee the violence in Bosnia.

In Romania the Hungarian minority joined hands with the Romanian majority in the 1980s in resisting the Soviet Union and communism—the bicultural city of Timișoara being the starting point of the rebellion against Nicolae Ceaușescu. But the Hungarian population of Romania seems always to have retained a deep sense of belonging to the Hungarian cultural nation as distinct from the Romanian, and the existence of an autonomous Hungary as a neighboring state has kept alive the hope among many Hungarian-speaking inhabitants of Transylvania that their region might one day be detached from Romania and united with Hungary. The only problem is that, once again, no clear boundary can be drawn between the Hungarian-speaking and Romanian-speaking areas of Transylvania: it is a biethnic, bilingual, bicultural—or some would say, a binational—province.

The Hungarians of Transylvania are not the only minorities with a kindred state nearby to which they attach part of their loyalty and to which they look for protection. Majorities are often nervous of such minorities, and because they are nervous become hostile toward them. Ever since Turkey sent its army in 1974 into Cyprus to detach Turkish-speaking zones from the Greek-speaking state, other mixed societies have feared more such "big brother" interventions. In Bulgaria, the million-strong Turkish minority has long experienced an uneasy toleration: in 1985, Todor Zhivkov's government introduced a cultural assimilation program which prompted some 300,000 Turks to emigrate. As a result, the Turkish political leaders in Bulgaria tried, after the end of communism, to broaden the ethnic base of their organization and set up the Movement for Rights and Freedoms seeking support from all the minorities in Bulgaria. Such a move away from ethnic politics, has, however, been fairly unrepresentative of general European trends. Even in France, the successful growth of Le Pen's *Front National* must be seen as a manifestation more of ethnic than of ideological politics, for when electors who vote for him are asked why they do so, most explain that they do not share his fascistic ideas but support his policy of repatriating Muslim immigrants.

The nationalism of the *Front National* is of a fairly unusual kind in the present age: a racist nationalism which exceeds in its virulence that of the Conservative party in South Africa. If thousands of voters in France support its candidates in election, it seems to be because they see the growing number of Muslim immigrants as competitors for scarce jobs, scarce housing, and scarce welfare benefits; and such Frenchmen further dislike the Muslims because they refuse to assimilate culturally (in the ways that Portuguese or Jewish and other immigrants to France have done) but rather proclaim their differences by wearing distinctive clothes, praying ostentatiously to Allah in the public streets, and otherwise offending the standards of propriety and decorum so dear to the hearts of the conservative French bourgeoisie and working classes.

A certain type of French nationalism thus finds itself face to face with more than one type of Muslim nationalism. At the time of the Algerian War in the 1950s there was a fairly clear confrontation between French imperialist nationalism, eager to keep the Algerian colony as part of the French national state, and the Algerian nationalism of the Front de Libération Nationale, determined to set up an independent Algerian state ruled by its Arab majority. Since that time there has developed a more complex ideological confrontation; beyond Algerian nationalism, there is now an Arab nationalism, based on the premise that all the Arab peoples inhabiting areas stretching from the Middle East to Morocco constitute a nation; and beyond that again, there is Islamic nationalism, based on the belief that all adherents of the Muslim faith, including besides the Arabs the inhabitants of Indonesia, Pakistan, Bangladesh, Iran, and Turkey, constitute together a single Islamic nation. The civil conflict which has simmered in Algeria since 1991 is essentially between adherents of two rival nationalisms—the old Algerian nationalism which dates from the war against France, and is dedicated to the sovereignty of the Algerian state, and the newer Islamic nationalism which seeks to merge the population of Algeria into the wider community of Muslim believers subject to the law of the Koran. There is, however, a certain lack of coherence in the ideology of both the Arab nationalists and the Islamic nationalists. They talk of an Arab nation and an Islamic nation as something political, not merely cultural, but have no design for a pan-Arab or pan-Islamic state.

Beyond Europe

African nationalism is a sub-Saharan phenomenon, ethnic in character, and dedicated to a simple aim: Africa for the Africans. [35] In practical terms, this means that African nationalism is more concerned to reject alien rule—and in particular, rule by Europeans—than to elaborate any image of "an African nation." Léopold Senghor of Senegal and others once made much of what they called *négritude*, [36] attaching a mystical value to the "blackness" of black Africans, which may, in the case of Senghor and other French-educated Africans, be seen as echoing the vision of Renan and the mystical nationalists of the Third Republic (1871–1940) in France.

Before the intrusions of European empires into Africa, the African peoples lived in tribes, and sometimes also, as in Egypt, Ethiopia, and Zululand, in kingdoms. It could perhaps be said of one or two of these kingdoms, as Voltaire said of France, that they became nations. However, the political map of Africa had by the end of the nineteenth century been settled between European conquerors, and when independent African states came into being in the 1960s, their boundaries were not those of ancient kingdoms but those of the former colonies. If the departure of the European rule was universally welcomed—at least by African nationalists and their sympathizers—a sentiment of nationality did not always manifest itself among the inhabitants of liberated colonies. In Nigeria, for example, some communities tried to set up an independent state in Biafra; the people of Mali succeeded in breaking away from Senegal. The leading tribes of Southern Rhodesia, when it became Zimbabwe, did not readily merge into a single civil association. Throwing off European tutelage, Africans found they had little choice but to live together in groupings dictated by the past European presence. In such circumstances, it is understandable that a "sentiment of Africanness," or *négritude*, might be stronger than a sentiment of being Nigerian or Tanzanian or Zambian or *Zairien*.

Asian nationalisms are the product of a different history. Both China and Japan established empires which were ethnically homogeneous, their people united in religion, culture, and traditions, in marked contrast to the Western empires, which were almost by definition multicultural. The Chinese emperors were no less successful than the French kings in fusing their subjects into *a* people. In Japan, an island empire that was shut off from the outside world for hundreds of years, and never before 1945 subject to foreign conquest, the national religion of Shintoism combined with history to produce a society of people acutely conscious of its identity and its distinctiveness from all others. Where European incursions into China led to the formation of a defensive nationalist movement which refused to accept Chinese inferiority, Japanese success in the war of 1905 against Russia stimulated an aggressive nationalist movement which sought to assert Japanese superiority. In neither case was there any doubt about what the nation was and who belonged to it.

On the Indian subcontinent and in Southeast Asia, where the inhabitants of both the mainland and the islands formed a mosaic of ethnic groups and linguistic communities even more diverse one from another than those of Europe, the awakening of a national consciousness was almost inevitably a signal for war, not only against alien imperial intruders but against neighbors. Nothing that could be called "Asian nationalism" on the lines of "African nationalism" has emerged to seal the inhabitants of Asian countries in bonds of fellow feeling. There is no sense of Asian ethnicity to match Senghor's *négritude*. What we have witnessed in Asia are forms of nationalism which provide new motives for hatred in areas where overpopulation and natural penury diminish people's sense of human solidarity. Religious differences generate even more conflict in Asia than they do in Europe: the Christians of East Timor and the Hindus of Bali have often been treated as enemies instead of fellow citizens by the Muslim majority in Indonesia, while the condition of near civil war which has prevailed for years in Sri Lanka between Sinhalese and Tamils is fueled by mistrust between Buddhists and Hindus. Religious differences dictated the separation of the old Indian Empire of the British Raj into Pakistan (predominantly Muslim) and India (predominantly Hindu) and still make a unified state of Kashmir impractical.

The great Indian poet and philosopher Rabindranath Tagore was always a stern critic of nationalism, which he saw as a European ideology, foreign to the traditions of India and the East. He observed that the Indians had no word for *nation* and argued that the only "self-government" worth having was the individual's mastery of the self. [37] Tagore connected nationalism with the spirit which had driven the peoples of Europe into the fratricidal strife of World War I. He criticized Mahatma Gandhi for adopting European political ideas on the one hand, while opposing European rule and European modernization on the other. There can be no disputing that Gandhi learned his policies as a law student in England and as a civil rights activist in South Africa: it could be said of his nationalism, as Lord Acton said of Mazzini's, that it was born of exile. [38] Gandhi tried to take back to India the Western progressive idea of the sovereign nation-state without all the other Western progressive ideas of industrial and military development. In this aim he failed, notwithstanding his success in persuading the British in 1947 to relinquish their imperial rule, for virtually every other Indian nationalist leader, including Jawaharlal Nehru, the country's first prime minister, favored modernization, industrialization, and development as economic necessities for a twentieth-century state that wished to defend its boundaries, feed its inhabitants, and educate its children.

In Europe, many nationalists of an earlier time were romantics, yearning nostalgically for an earlier age when a simpler culture was seen as having held people of all classes together in shared experiences and common values. Herder collecting German folklore, Walter Scott publishing old Scottish ballads, Eamon de Valera trying to revive Gaelic as the national language of Ireland, were all backward-looking in this way; but the more recent nationalists of Asia and Africa have almost invariably been modernizers, animated not simply by what Kenneth Minogue has called "a collective grievance against a foreign oppressor," [39] but by a desire to secure for their peoples the material advantages of the Western standard of living. The most prominent leaders of Asian and African nationalism—Nehru, Kwame Nkrumah, Léopold Senghor, Jomo Kenyatta, Patrice Lumumba, Milton Obote, Julius Nyerere—have been, like Gandhi, Western-educated and, unlike Gandhi, converted to the Western progressive ethos, even while often rejecting the capitalist economic system which historically made Western progress possible.

Problems and issues

Critics of nationalism, such as Lord Acton and Tagore, have often been idealists of another kind, with a religious belief in the universal brotherhood of man; this they see as imperiled by the separation of human beings into nations, which easily turn from docile herds into warring packs; they see also, in the cult of the nation, the loss of the sovereignty of the individual person over his or her own soul as it is merged in the sovereignty of the group over the group.

Lord Acton argued that the best state was the one which enabled several nationalities to live in freedom under the same system of law. "If," he wrote in his essay on nationality, "we take the establishment of liberty for the realization of moral duties to be the end of civil society, we must conclude that those states are most perfect which . . . include various distinct nationalities without oppressing them. . . . A state which is incompetent to satisfy different races condemns itself." [40]

Lord Acton was anxious to clarify the distinction between a "sentiment of nationality" and patriotism. The sentiment of nationality was a mere sociological phenomenon; people might have it or they might not. The question was one of fact. But patriotism, he emphasized, belonged to the sphere of morality. Patriotism was a disposition to respect, to love, and to make sacrifices for one's country. One's country was nothing so vague as a nation; it was one's *patrie,* or homeland, the state, whether royal or republican, to which one owed one's allegiance, the political society for which one should be willing to bear arms and if need be to die.

Writing in 1862, Lord Acton dissented from the opinion of many of his fellow liberals that national freedom was necessary to individual freedom: "The co-existence of several nations under the same State is a test, as well as the best security of its freedom," he wrote. "It is also one of the chief instruments of civilization." [41]

Lord Acton praised the Austrian and British empires for holding diverse peoples together in the bond of peace. He agreed with Tagore in regarding nationalism as an ideology calculated to cause war. And undoubtedly certain nationalist writers of the nineteenth century exalted war. Even Hegel, who preached the union of opposites embracing all contradictions, argued that war was a necessary element in the process of struggle by which the idea of freedom realized itself in history. If men did not fight, he suggested, they would stagnate. Nietzsche, who rejected almost everything else in Hegel's philosophy, agreed. War for the superior man, or *Übermensch,* was proof of his superiority. For Nietzsche, who regarded the love of peace as a mark of the "slave mentality" of Christianity, war was an activity which "hallows every cause." Numerous other writers argued that the experience of fighting together sharpens people's feeling of belonging together, and hence their "sentiment of nationality."

What can be seen as national wars, as distinct from dynastic wars, date from about the middle of the eighteenth century. The War of the Austrian Succession between 1740 and 1748 was still a war to determine which royal family should sit on a European throne, but the Seven Years War of 1756–63 was already a war for national aggrandizement and also the first truly global conflict. [42] Unfortunately, national wars proved to be increasingly bloody. Dynastic wars were fought between professional armies according to rules of chivalry which kept the casualties within limits. When Napoleon took over the command of Revolutionary France he put every man into uniform, tore up the rules of chivalry, and sent millions of soldiers to their death. Nationalism, coming into history in the age of revolutions, had to fight Napoleon's sort of war.

Philosophers of peace have been almost uniformly agreed that lasting tranquillity could not be established in the world unless the demands of nationalism were limited—unless, that is to say, some authority superior to the nation-state was generally recognized. In medieval Christendom, the Catholic church enjoyed that universal authority; it could not prevent Christian princes from going to war with one another, but it secured obedience to certain laws of warfare and so mitigated the suffering war caused. After the Reformation destroyed the unity of the church, philosophers sought other means to limit and regulate warfare. Virtually all the means they proposed entailed setting up a supranational institution to which each nation-state should yield some measure of sovereignty.

Ideas of this kind were already expounded in the seventeenth century by the Duc de Sully and William Penn, among others, but they achieved more urgency in the eighteenth century with the development of the modern nation-state and modern warfare. The Abbé de Saint-Pierre published a *Project for Perpetual Peace* in 1713 and Kant his celebrated essay *On Perpetual Peace* in 1796: both envisaged the formation of world authorities with schemes which were acted upon only in the twentieth century by the creation of the League of Nations and the United Nations.

Unfortunately there was a contradiction between the program of nationalism and the program of world union, for the one entailed the recognition of total national sovereignty and the other the sacrifice of at least some measure of national sovereignty. In the short history of the League of Nations, this contradiction proved ruinous. Even the United Nations has more often proved itself a forum for the assertion of national rights to autonomy than of the original goal of world unity. For example, the United Nations Covenant on Civil and Political Rights, which was adopted in 1966, registered in its first article the basic dogma of twentieth-century nationalism, namely, that "all peoples have the right of self-determination."

It may be protested that this assertion is not distinctive of twentieth-century nationalism; already it can be found in that central document of Jacobinism, the Declaration of Rights of 1795, where it is declared that "Each people is independent and sovereign, whatever the number of individuals who compose it and the extent of the territory it occupies. This sovereignty is inalienable." [43] No such assertion of "each people's" rights had occurred in the original French Declaration of the Rights of Man in 1789; and even the German liberal Declaration of Rights of 1848, which proclaimed the rights of the German *Volk* to freedom and autonomy, did not extend that right to any and every people "whatever the number of individuals who compose it and the extent of the territory it occupies."

Nineteenth-century liberal nationalism was insistent that a nation must be constituted of a people numerous enough to sustain their independence. The concept of the nation as a viable economic unit was central to such thinking. For a nineteenth-century state to sustain itself as an economic unit it would have to have achieved a certain measure of industrialization, and this in turn required the participation of a sizable population: an industrial ministate could not exist. Rousseau himself realized this when he warned the Corsicans that they could only enjoy independence as a small island if they maintained a purely rural economy, resisting modernization. Modernization, industrialization, and commercial progress could only be experienced in larger economic units, and this is why nineteenth-century liberals, who all disagreed with Rousseau on the subject of progress, wanted full-size nation-states,

states on the scale of a kingdom, not states on the scale of a city or a canton or small island.

The great Italian nationalist Mazzini, for example, never approved of Irish nationalism because he did not believe that Ireland was populous enough to sustain an independent national economy. J. S. Mill, who disagreed with Mazzini, thought the only way to rebut Mazzini's argument was to show that Ireland *was* populous enough to sustain an economy separate from that of the United Kingdom. Although classical economics and the liberal political movements which invoked its principles favored free trade on an international scale, the participants in this scheme of things had to be nations in a thoroughly modern progressive sense, not anachronistic hangovers from a past age such as San Marino or Liechtenstein or Monaco, which, in any case, only endured under the protection of full-size neighbors—Italian, Swiss, and French, respectively, in those three instances.

Walter Bagehot once wrote that "nation-making" was the chief activity of nineteenth-century political evolution. [44] The greater part of that "nation-making" was constructive—putting together numerous smaller states into the greater nation-states of Germany and Italy. "Nation-making" in the other direction, dismantling large empires into smaller nation-states, was a minor feature of the enterprise. Mazzini was by no means alone among the nationalists of his time in thinking that several political units in Europe were simply not big enough to qualify as nations. In the *Dictionnaire politique,* published in Paris in 1842, it is suggested that there is something "ridiculous" in classifying Portugal and Belgium as nations, because they are patently too small. [45]

The influential German economist Friedrich List, writing in 1885, gives a particularly emphatic warning against regarding smaller groups of people as nations:

"A large population, and an extensive territory endowed with manifold national resources, are essential requirements of the normal nationality. . . . A nation restricted in the number of its population and in territory, especially if it has a separate language, can only possess a crippled literature, crippled institutions for promoting art and science. A small State can never bring to complete perfection within its territory the various branches of production." [46]

It is worth remembering that List was greatly influenced by the ideas of Alexander Hamilton, which he studied during his stay in the United States in the 1820s; [47] and policies known as "federalist" in America reappear as "nationalist" in List's theories, economic arguments being the basis of pleas for the creation of large states—*Grossstaatenbildung* as it came to be known in Germany. Even Mill, the champion of moderately small nations such as Ireland, could not tolerate the idea of there being nation-states any smaller than Ireland. "Nobody," he wrote, "can suppose that it is not more beneficial to a Breton, or a

Basque of French Navarre, to be brought into the current of the ideas and feeling of a highly civilised and cultivated people—to be a member of the French nationality, admitted on equal terms to all the privileges of French citizenship, sharing the advantages of French protection, and the dignity and prestige of French power—than to sulk on his own rocks, the half-savage relic of past times, revolving in his own little mental orbit, without participation or interest in the general movement of the world." [48]

From these words it is clear that what Mill called the *prima facie* case for national self-determination did not apply to those communities which were, in his terms, too backward. In practice this meant that he considered as "good nationalism" that of communities such as Italy, large enough to sustain a modern progressive state, and as "bad nationalism" that of communities such as Brittany, with no such potentialities. Many such small communities have indeed accepted that the loss of independence is the price that must be paid for progress. The history of Switzerland over the past few hundred years has been one of step-by-step surrender of autonomy from the cantons to the federal government at Bern; [49] and the gradual disappearance of the oldest Alpine language, Romansh. [50] But at least the government at Bern cannot be accused of forcing the people to give up their traditional language, as General Francisco Franco attempted in Spain to suppress the use of Catalan and the Basque language.

Bagehot's claim that "nation-making" was the chief evolutionary enterprise of nineteenth-century politics might be countered by the suggestion that "empire-building" was a still more conspicuous activity of the age. Even Belgium and Portugal responded to the scorn of those who considered them "ridiculously" small by building—or, in the case of Portugal, consolidating—colonial empires, to ensure that their dimensions as an economic unit were handsomely extensive, however limited their territory in Europe. This economic preoccupation with size meant that liberals such as Mill and Acton were, as we have noted, in favor of imperial systems.

Liberal opinion in the nineteenth century had thus more than one motive for resisting the kind of nationalism which was directed toward the breaking up of empires into fragments. When they favored such policies it was where they were directed against empires considered retrogressive, notably the Spanish Empire and the Ottoman Empire. The creation of Mexico, Bolivia, Peru, Argentina, Paraguay, and the rest of the Latin-American nations through the dismemberment of the Spanish domains in the New World was as warmly welcomed by liberals in Europe as it was by liberals in the United States. The liberation of Greece from the Turkish rule was a cause especially dear to liberal hearts because the Greeks were glamorized as the descendants of Pericles and Aristotle, the heirs of ancient freedom, and cherished as fellow

Christians, while the Ottoman Empire was despised as an instrument of Muslim tyranny and Levantine corruption. The pleasure nineteenth-century liberals took in observing the vast expanse of the South American continent divided into a dozen nation-states and their enthusiasm for the efforts of Greeks to secede from the Ottoman Empire did not mean that those liberals wished to see the whole southeastern quarter of Europe divided into nation-states. "Balkanization" was their pejorative word for this process. Much as they detested the Ottoman Empire, they did not wish to see it disintegrate into ministates incapable of autonomy; apart from the exceptional case of Greece, they wished only to see the Ottoman domains transferred to other and more progressive empires, the Russian, British, French, and especially the Austrian. [51]

Toward the end of the nineteenth century, however, European liberal nationalism ended its alliance with imperialism. The belief that a people must be large enough to constitute an economic unit ceased to dominate nationalist thinking. The establishment of a united Italy in the 1860s, and a united Germany in the 1870s, satisfied what might be called the constructionist program of nationalism: and thereafter the deconstructionist program—taking empires to pieces—came to the forefront. Moreover, in the scramble for African colonies, sheer militaristic aggrandizement took over from the more progressive purposes of earlier colonization. The Boer War at the turn of the century, when British conservative imperialists tried to crush the independence of the Afrikaner settlers in the Transvaal, prompted British liberals to reject imperialism and support the claims of the Afrikaners to be a "nation," small as that nation was.

The influence of American liberalism was also significant. For beside the Hamiltonian tradition which informed List's *Grossstaatenbildung,* there was also the Jeffersonian tradition in American political thought, favoring the small political unit, decentralization, and the right of a people to decide for itself when the time was ripe for its independence. Woodrow Wilson, a professor of political science before he became president of Princeton and then president of the United States, was the key figure in this restatement of liberal nationalism. When he expressed his policy in the word *self-determination,* he revived and conferred moral authority on the old Jacobin claim that "each people is independent and sovereign." Lord Acton's belief that the loose dominion of the Austrian Empire favored freedom in Europe was rejected as absurd; Mill's claim that British rule in India was simply educating the Indians for self-government was dismissed as erroneous. Twentieth-century liberal nationalism, with Wilson as its first great champion, was squarely anti-imperialist, no longer terrified of "Balkanization" or *Kleinstaaterei.*

The Treaty of Versailles of 1919 in which Wilson was in a position to set the goals—if not in a position to enforce adherence to them—brought to light the inherent problems of self-determination. The Ottoman and Austrian empires were dissolved, and the German Empire diminished so that the map of Europe could be redrawn. Certain nationalist demands were satisfied, but since most of the new states which emerged were, as we have seen, just as multiethnic, multilingual, and multicultural as the empires that had been broken up, it meant that at least as many nationalists were dissatisfied as were satisfied with the outcome. [52] With two unabashed imperialists, Stalin and Churchill, calling the shots in the peace settlement at Yalta after World War II, there was little hope for any European nationalist achieving further satisfaction until the collapse of communism in the late 1980s.

Nationalist activity after 1945 being concentrated on the decolonization of Africa and Asia has restored the concept of the nation as an economic unit to the head of the agenda. Countries such as Nigeria, Indonesia, Kenya, or Senegal could not be considered ethnic, linguistic, religious, or cultural units, for their inhabitants were richly diversified. What united them was the experience of having been governed for a century or so by the same European power. Since that European power was seen as the adversary of their claim to nationhood, it was paradoxical to see in it the only begetter of their nationhood. Why should the people of Nigeria remain together if they had done so in the past only for the pleasure of the government in London? The obvious answer was that by staying together they could enjoy the advantages of a modern economic unit.

The social anthropologist Ernest Gellner argues that nationalism is significant for the Third World because the nation-state is a crucial element in a process of change leading from traditional society to modern society. Modern society, he suggests, centers on industrialization. [53] Traditional society is highly structured; every man knows his place in it, because that place hardly ever changes. But without change there is no progress. Aristotle said that moral development requires a village for it to happen at all, and something larger than a village to achieve its full potentialities. Gellner carries the argument further, suggesting that modern man needs to be literate and technically competent, and therefore needs the resources of a fair-size nation-state. Gellner does not claim that the illiterate colonial masses themselves understand this, but rather that the native elites who develop in the colonial society discern it. In effect, they see the advantage of retaining the boundaries established by the colonial power as a political unit with the right economic dimensions to develop into a nation on the Western model. "Nationalism," Gellner writes, "is not the awakening of nations to self-consciousness: it invents nations where they do not exist." [54] Elsewhere he suggests, "Men do not in general become nationalists from sentiment or sentimentality, atavistic or not, well-based or myth-founded: they become nationalists through genuine, objective, practical necessity, however obscurely recognised." [55]

Gellner may be correct; from the point of view of a Third World country, the transformation of a colony into a nation-state may be the objectively necessary step toward modernity. In Europe itself, economists since 1945 have increasingly argued that the nation-state is no longer, for a society already developed, a progressive economic unit. The European Economic Community, culminating in the creation of a single European market in 1993, has in effect superseded the nation-state as the framework within which Western European economic activity operates. Politically it is a halfway house between the Europe of independent sovereign states and a federal Europe, or, rather, a compromise between the two, for many adherents of the European Economic Community insist that it is *not* leading the Western European states toward federal union, and that it will never entail a sacrifice of national sovereignty beyond the modest degree already accepted by the twelve member states under the Treaty of Rome.

Perhaps "modest" is not a word that would be accepted by those opposed to membership of the EEC in the states concerned. They would claim that while allowing Brussels to dictate the size of eggs that may legally be sold, for example, or the amount of lead permitted in paint, are relatively trivial matters, the acceptance of community law as superior to national law in the definition of crime, for example, is a radical derogation of national autonomy. In this context, nationalism has acquired a new lease on life in several EEC states as a movement of resistance to what is seen as Eurofederalism. This new nationalism is not based on economic arguments but on traditionalist or conservative sentiment which has revealed itself not only in Denmark, a small country eager to preserve its identity, but also in France and England, countries more accustomed to bestowing laws on other peoples than to having laws bestowed on them. And yet despite these reservations, the general trend in Western Europe in recent years has been to break down first the economic and then the political barriers between nations; and it may well be that the institution of a free-trade zone of the United States, Canada, and Mexico will be the start of a similar process in North America. As the nation-state in the form with which we are familiar has existed only since the waning of the Middle Ages, there is no reason to believe that it will last indefinitely; the nation-state is modern, but as we have seen in the fields of art and culture, the modern has already begun to yield to the postmodern.

---

1. Marx always spoke contemptuously of nationalism as "a *petit-bourgeois* ideology," but Lenin encouraged it to the extent that it was a force against "imperialism." In his book *Imperialism, the Highest Stage of Capitalism* of 1916, Lenin put forward the view that empire-building was motivated by the capitalist search for markets and for cheap war materials. This was not based on Marx's analysis but on that of an English economist, J. A. Hobson, whose book *Imperialism* of 1902 was directed against British repression of the Boers in South Africa.

2. J. S. Mill, *Considerations on Representative Government* (London: Longmans Green, 1888), p. 120 (*GBWW* I: 43, 425; II: 40, 425). In the same essay Mill writes, "it is in general a necessary condition of free institutions that the boundaries of governments should coincide in the main with those of nationalities" (op. cit., p. 122; *GBWW* I: 43, 426; II: 40, 426).

3. Cited in Boyd C. Shafer, *Faces of Nationalism* (New York: Harcourt Brace Jovanovich, 1972), p. 343.

4. Carlton J. H. Hayes, *The Historical Evolution of Modern Nationalism* (New York: Richard Smith, 1931), p. 1. For an updated version of Hayes's history, written from a somewhat different perspective, *see* Anthony D. Smith, *Theories of Nationalism* (London: Duckworth, 1971).

5. *See* Voltaire, *The Age of Louis XIV*, ed. and trans. J. H. Brumfit (New York: Oxford Voltaire Foundation, 1965).

6. *See* Maurice Cranston, *Philosophers and Pamphleteers, Political Theorists of the Enlightenment* (New York: Oxford University Press, 1986).

7. *See* Hans Reiss, *The Political Thought of the German Romantics* (Oxford: Blackwell, 1955).

8. During the French Revolution the Abbé Sieyès asked, "What is a nation?" and answered, "A body of associates living under one common law and represented by the same legislature." Quoted by Elie Kedourie, *Nationalism* (London: Hutchinson, 1960), p. 15.

9. J. G. A. Pocock argues in *The Machiavellian Moment* (Princeton, N.J.: Princeton University Press, 1975) that the republican tradition was even more important than the philosophy of Locke in shaping American ideas of liberty in the eighteenth century.

10. Rousseau was one of the most eloquent champions of the idea that the nation should be the object of one's love. He contrasted the vigorous national spirit of the ancient Spartans with the stark cosmopolitanism of his own world, "There are today no longer Frenchmen, Germans, Spaniards, even Englishmen; there are only Europeans." Advising the Poles on their future government, Rousseau wrote: "It is the test of education to give each human being a national form, and to direct his opinions and tastes so that he will be a patriot by inclination, by passion, and by necessity. On first opening his eyes, a child must see his country, and until he dies, must see nothing else" (*Political Writings*, ed. C. E. Vaughan [Cambridge: Cambridge University Press, 1915], vol. 2, p. 437).

11. Edmund Burke in a famous passage wrote: "Society is indeed a contract, but it is not a partnership in things . . . of a temporary and perishable nature. It is a partnership in all science, a partnership in all art, a partnership in every virtue and in all perfection. . . . As the ends of such a partnership cannot be obtained in many generations, it becomes a partnership between . . . those who are living, those who are dead and those who are yet to be born" (*Reflections on the Revolution in France*, ed. C. C. O'Brien [New York: Penguin-Viking, 1968], pp. 194–95).

12. Herder looked on language as "the external and visible badge of those differences which distinguish one nation from another" (Kedourie, op. cit., p. 64).

13. Abraham Lincoln in his later and most eloquent speeches discarded the word *union* for the word *nation* in referring to the United States. Commemorating the dead at Gettysburg, he declared his high "resolve" that "this nation, under God, shall have a new birth of freedom."

14. Hayes, op. cit., p. 45.

15. The word *chauvinism* derives from the name of Nicolas Chauvin, an enthusiastic soldier in the service of Napoleon, who proclaimed the superiority of his country in all things, military and civil, and expressed the greatest scorn for others.

16. Among the many books on this subject the following are notable: Hans Kohn, *The Idea of Nationalism* (New York: Macmillan, 1944), and *Prelude to Nation-States* (Princeton, N.J.: Van Nostrand, 1967); Eugene N. Anderson, *Nationalism and the Cultural Crisis in Prussia* (New York: Farrar and Rinehart, 1939); F. M. Barnard, *Herder's Social and Political Thought* (Oxford: Clarendon Press, 1965); Louis Snyder, *The Meaning of Nationalism* (New Brunswick, N.J.: Rutgers University Press, 1954); Friedrich Meinecke, *Cosmopolitanism and the Nation State*, trans. Robert B. Kimber (Princeton, N.J.: Princeton University Press, 1970).

17. Translated by R. F. Jones and G. H. Turnbull (Chicago: Open Court, 1922).

18. For a powerful exposition of those consequences, *see* Jacques Barzun, *Race, A Study in Modern Superstition* (New York: Harper & Brothers, 1937; rev. ed. 1965).

19. ". . . the text simply was that nations would not be governed by foreigners," John Emerich Edward Dalberg-Acton, Lord Acton, *Essays on Freedom and Power,* ed. Gertrude Himmelfarb (Glencoe, Ill., 1948), p. 180.

20. Darwinian theories of social selection were put to the service of anti-Semitism in Ernest Haeckel's *Welträtsel* (1899), Étienne Drumont's *La France juive* (1866), and Houston Stewart Chamberlain's *Die Grundlagen des XIX Jahrhunderts* (1903). Richard Wagner in *Judentum in der Musik* (1850) had already used racial arguments to depict the Jew as the eternal enemy of the Aryan. "Racialist thinkers," writes Kenneth Minogue, "have hovered like vultures around the laboratory of anthropological inquiry, snatching here the corpse of a dead theory, there a raw lump of the living flesh" (*Nationalism* [New York: Basic Books, 1960], p. 157).

21. Renan's theory may be seen as a variant of Rousseau's conception of the nation as a creation of will, but his concern was mainly with the factors which shape people's will, and unlike the economists, he singled out the spiritual and altruistic feelings as determinants of volition.

22. Renan was also writing in the aftermath of the defeat of France by the Prussian army in the 1870–71 war. He suggested that the "regeneration of Germany" prompted by Fichte and others after Napoleon's defeat of Prussia in 1806 afforded a model for the moral regeneration of France.

23. Hayes, op. cit., p. 135.

24. *See* Frederick Rosen, *Bentham, Byron and Greece* (New York: Oxford University Press, 1992).

25. The experience of the thirteen British Colonies in severing their links with the home country and creating a republic in North America was the obvious inspiration for the activities of the nationalists of Latin America in the early nineteenth century. *See* Gerhard Masur, *Nationalism in Latin America* (New York: Macmillan, 1966) and Leopoldo Zea, *The Latin-American Mind* (Norman, Okla.: University of Oklahoma Press, 1963).

26. Russian nationalism, however, was not purely cultural. Even Pushkin, the model poet, was an eager supporter of Russian imperialism against Polish nationalism.

27. Minogue, op. cit., p. 25.

28. Shafer, op. cit., refers several times to "the Basque nation," an entity which Spanish nationalists claim has no existence. It was the policy of General Franco's "Nationalist" regime to repress the use of the Basque (and Catalan) language and other cultural manifestations in order to prevent the development of a "sentiment of nationality" in those areas. Franco's Nationalist revolution was a movement of the political right, which represented a conservative reaction against the cosmopolitan socialistic and anticlerical tendencies of the Spanish "Republicans," as well as their policy of devolving power to regions.

29. Benjamin R. Barber, in *The Death of Communal Freedom* (Princeton, N.J.: Princeton University Press, 1974), laments the loss of Swiss cantonal independence to the Swiss federal union, on the grounds that "strong democracy" is possible only in small-scale political units. This is a modern restatement of Rousseau's argument in *The Social Contract.*

30. Voltaire, *Oeuvres complètes*, ed. L. Moland (Paris, 1877–85), vol. XXII, pp. 99–100.

31. Gordon S. Wood, *The Radicalism of the American Revolution* (New York: A. A. Knopf, 1992).

32. Cited in Tony Barber, *The Independent on Sunday* (London), April 19, 1992, p. 12.

33. *See* Stephen R. Bowers, *Ethnic Politics in Eastern Europe* (London: Research Institute for Study of Conflict, 1992), p. 10.

34. The *Romania Mare* party even proclaims the ideas of "national socialism," Bowers, op. cit., p. 13.

35. Colin Legum, *Pan-Africanism* (London: Pall Mall Press, 1962), p. 36.

36. For an explanation of this concept, *see* Abiole Irele, "*Négritude* or Black Cultural Nationalism" in *Journal of Modern African Studies*, vol. 3, no. 3 (1965).

37. Rabindranath Tagore, "The Call of Truth," *Modern Review*, vol. 30, no. 4, pp. 429–33.

38. "Exile is the nursery of nationality." Cited in Minogue, op. cit., p. 135.

39. Minogue, op. cit., p. 104.

40. Cited in Kedourie, op. cit., p. 133. Lord Acton (1834–1902) was unusual among British Victorian parliamentarians in being both a Liberal and a Roman Catholic. Educated in Germany, he concluded from his observations of the nationalist movement in

that country that concentration on freedom for the public collectivity was inimical to freedom for the private citizen. He had a prophetic vision of nationalism developing into totalitarianism, as happened in the twentieth century under Mussolini in Italy and Hitler in Germany. *See* Gertrude Himmelfarb, *Lord Acton: A Study in Conscience and Politics* (London: Routledge and Paul, 1952).

41. Lord Acton, op. cit., p. 185.

42. John Bowle, *A History of Europe* (London: Jonathan Cape, 1979), p. 467.

43. Cited in Louis Jaume, *Le Discours jacobin* (Paris: Fayard, 1989), p. 407. In the mouths of the Jacobins—the left-wing followers of Maximilien de Robespierre during the French Revolution—these words were empty rhetoric. The Jacobins seized power in 1793 by a coup d'état and imposed a centralized government, controlled by a "Committee of Public Safety." This committee sent out representatives into every corner of France to purge the population and the army and to spread terror by arrests and persecutions. They were not the last ideologues in history to impose dictatorship in the name of popular sovereignty.

44. *Physics and Politics* (Boston: Beacon Press, 1956), chap. 16: "Nation-making" (*GIT* 1968, 441–68). Walter Bagehot (1826–77) attempted to apply the Darwinian theory of evolution through a struggle for existence to political history. He presents the nation-state as the latest stage of evolutionary development and the best guarantee of continued orderly progress.

45. *See* E. J. Hobsbawm, *Nations and Nationalism* (New York: Cambridge University Press, 1990), p. 30.

46. *The National System of Political Economy* (London: J. B. Lippincott and Co., 1885), p. 175.

47. Friedrich List took part in the national economic debates in America during his time in the United States and published an account of them in his *Outline of American Political Economy* (Philadelphia, 1827). Hobsbawm writes: "[List] clearly formulated a characteristic of the 'liberal' concept of the nation which is usually taken for granted. It has to be of sufficient size to form a viable unit of development. If it fell below this threshold it had no historic justification" (op. cit., p. 30). *See also* W. Notz, "List in America," *American Economic Review* XVI (1926), pp. 249–65.

48. *Considerations on Representative Government* (London: Longmans Green, 1888), p. 122 (*GBWW* I: 43, 426; II: 40, 426).

49. In Switzerland, as in America, a civil war took place before the country could be permanently sealed together as a unified political nation. This was the "*Sonderbund*" War of the 1840s—the *Sonderbund* being a sessionist confederation of Catholic cantons (Lucerne, Uri, Schwyz, Unterwalden, Zug, Fribourg, and Valais) set up in breach of the pact of federation. A federal army under General Dufour took the field against the rebels and the war ended within a month. A revised constitution increased the powers of the federal, as opposed to the cantonal, authorities.

50. The fourth language in most official Swiss publications today is not Romansh but English.

51. Albert Sorel wrote: "When Turkey leaves the sickbed for the grave, Austria will take its place" (cited in Bowle, op. cit., p. 583).

52. Mazzini drew up a map of a future Europe of nations. It contained only twelve states and federations. The Wilson formula at Versailles produced twenty-six states: the creation of the Irish Free State in 1921 brought the number to twenty-seven. The aspirants to nationhood in Europe have been subsequently calculated to be forty-nine (Hobsbawm, op. cit., p. 32).

53. Ernest Gellner, *Thought and Change* (London: Weidenfeld and Nicolson, 1964); and *Nations and Nationalism* (New York: Oxford University Press, 1983).

54. Gellner, *Thought and Change*, p. 168.

55. Ibid., p. 160. In *Nations and Nationalism* (pp. 48–49) Gellner writes: "Nations as a God-given way of classifying men, an inherent . . . political destiny, are a myth; nationalism, which sometimes takes pre-existing cultures and turns them into nations, and often obliterates pre-existing cultures: *that* is a reality."

An Introduction to North American Indian Thought

George Anastaplo

George Anastaplo and his wife, Sara Prince Anastaplo.

George Anastaplo has prepared for *The Great Ideas Today* a half-dozen introductions to systems of non-European thought: Confucian (1984), Hindu (1985), Mesopotamian (1986), Islamic (1989), Buddhist (1992), and North American Indian (1993).

Mr. Anastaplo is a professor of law at Loyola University of Chicago and lecturer in liberal arts at the University of Chicago. Among his books are *The Constitutionalist: Notes on the First Amendment* (1971), *Human Being and Citizen: Essays on Virtue, Freedom, and the Common Good* (1975), *The Artist as Thinker: From Shakespeare to Joyce* (1983), *The Constitution of 1787: A Commentary* (1989), and *The American Moralist: On Law, Ethics, and Government* (1992). He recently has been honored by the publication in his name of a two-volume work, *Law and Philosophy: The Practice of Theory* (1992). The sixty-three contributors to this collection include Sara Prince Anastaplo, who is also a contributor to the article on Greece in the *Encyclopædia Britannica*.

Speak of me as I am. Nothing extenuate,
Nor set down aught in malice. Then must you speak
Of one that loved not wisely but too well;
     . . . of one whose hand,
Like the base Judean, threw a pearl away
Richer than all his tribe. . . .

                          (*Othello*) [1]

I

It can be saddening to review collections of North American Indian myths, legends, and stories, even though there is much in that legacy which can be a source of wonder and delight. [2] What is saddening is that human beings as imaginative and as interesting as these native American peoples should have, for so long and so vigorously, been treated as mere savages. They were, therefore, systematically beaten into submission wherever they were not simply exterminated. [3]

It is sobering to recognize how rich and varied an Indian heritage there has been "out there," much of which is now mangled. Even so, a remarkable array of tales is still available to us, with many inventive and good-natured episodes on display. But however considerable the material that has survived, in some form or other, much more has evidently been lost.

Europeans on this continent have always had a curious way of dealing with the Indians they encountered. On the one hand, Indians could routinely be regarded as dangerous barbarians who were virtually impossible to civilize. On the other hand, Indian names and Indian heroes could eventually be shown respect, so much so that ordinary people can now be proud of the Indian blood they might have in their veins. Indian names *are* all around us: Massachusetts, Ohio, Michigan, Illinois, Chicago, Wisconsin, Iowa, the Mississippi, and Seattle. Yet the best of what the Indians had to offer is but dimly perceived by most of us.

Alexis de Tocqueville and scholars influenced by him have noticed the somewhat aristocratic character of Indian life, a way of life that usually preferred hunting and war to agriculture and commerce. But this approach to the Indians, however sympathetic it is in some respects, neglects the richness of their life, something which I attempt to suggest on this occasion. The Indians generally appeared at their most formidable, if not at their worst, as strangers and enemies; they appeared more and more civilized and worthy of respect as one got to know them, at least until disease and demoralization wrecked their way of life.

The peoples I refer to as North American Indians, whatever the proper names for them should be, were scattered across what we now know as the contiguous forty-eight states of the American Union. There is far too much intriguing material for me to exhaust my subject in this article. Much of what I say will have to disregard critical differences between the many Indian tribes.

II

A sampling from a dozen stories should serve to illustrate the surprising things that the Indians have had to offer the human race. In most cases it is probably impossible to determine how far back these things go—but it does seem that some Indian stories, occasionally in several versions, have origins long before the coming of the Europeans. A marvelous, sometimes a dark, imagination is evident here, as in the uses made by the Indians of European stories.

The Snohomish (in the Northwest) say that people were not pleased with the way the Creator had made the world:

> The sky was so low that the tall people bumped their heads against it. Sometimes people would do what was forbidden by climbing up high in the trees and, learning their own words, enter the Sky World.
>
> Finally the wise men of all the different tribes had a meeting to see what they could do about lifting the sky. They agreed that the people should get together and try to push it up higher.
>
> "We can do it," a wise man of the council said, "if we all push at the same time. We will need all the people and all the animals and all the birds when we push." . . . Everyone made poles from the giant fir trees to use in pushing against the sky. [4]

They pushed all together again and again until they managed to get the sky up to where it has been ever since. [5]

The Nez Percé say that "before there were any people in the world, the different animals and trees lived and moved about and talked together just like human beings. The pine trees had the secret of fire and guarded it jealously, so that no matter how cold it was, they alone could warm themselves. [6] But Beaver managed to steal a live coal:

> The pines immediately raised a hue and cry and started after him. Whenever he was hard pressed, Beaver darted from side to side to

dodge his pursuers, and when he had a good start, he kept a straight course. The Grande Ronde River [in Idaho] preserves the direction Beaver took in his flight, and this is why it is tortuous in some parts of its course and straight in others.

After running for a long time, the pines grew tired. So most of them halted in a body on the river banks, where they remain in great numbers to this day, forming a growth so dense that hunters can hardly get through. A few pines kept chasing Beaver, but they finally gave out one after another, and they remain scattered at intervals along the banks of the river in the places where they stopped. [7]

A story from Northern California reports that at one time early in the life of the earth, "It did not thunder or lightning, since there were no trees to be struck." [8]

An Acoma story says that in the beginning two female human beings were born underground. They eventually made their way to the earth's surface and its light, taking with them two baskets they had found "full of presents: seeds of all kinds, and little images of many animals." [9] This was the means used by the Creator of the world to supply the earth with living things. Eventually one of the sisters took dirt from her basket in order to give life to many gods. "And so everything was as it should be." [10]

A Modoc account of the origins of life on earth includes this report:

The [Chief of the Sky Spirits] broke off the small end of his giant [walking] stick and threw the pieces into the rivers. The longer pieces turned into beaver and otter; the smaller pieces became fish. When the leaves dropped from the trees, he picked them up, blew upon them, and so made the birds. [11]

Notice what this and like accounts assume about the common elements shared by all living things.

The Papago tell what happened when the Creator was saddened by his recognition of the inevitable deterioration of things:

One day the Creator was resting, sitting, watching some children at play in a village. The children laughed and sang, yet as he watched them, the Creator's heart was sad. He was thinking: "These children will grow old. Their skin will become wrinkled. Their hair will turn gray. Their teeth will fall out. The young hunter's arm will fail. These lovely young girls will grow ugly and fat. The playful puppies will become blind, mangy dogs. And those wonderful flowers—yellow and blue, red and purple—will fade. The leaves from the trees will fall and dry up. Already they are turning yellow." Thus the Creator grew sadder and sadder. It was in the fall, and the thought of the coming winter, with its cold and lack of game and green things, made his heart heavy. [12]

The stage is now set for some benevolent experimentation:

255

Yet it was still warm, and the sun was shining. The Creator watched the play of sunlight and shadow on the ground, the yellow leaves being carried here and there by the wind. He saw the blueness of the sky, the whiteness of some cornmeal ground by the women. Suddenly he smiled. "All those colors, they ought to be preserved. I'll make something to gladden my heart, something for these children to look at and enjoy."

The Creator took out his bag and started gathering things: a spot of sunlight, a handful of blue from the sky, the whiteness of the cornmeal, the shadow of playing children, the blackness of a beautiful girl's hair, the yellow of the falling leaves, the green of the pine needles, the red, purple, and orange of the flowers around him. All these he put into his bag. As an afterthought, he put the songs of the birds in, too.

Then he walked over to the grassy spot where the children were playing. "Children, little children, this is for you," and he gave them his bag. "Open it; there's something nice inside," he told them.

The children opened the bag, and at once hundreds and hundreds of colored butterflies flew out, dancing around the children's heads, settling on their hair, fluttering up again to sip from this or that flower. And the children, enchanted, said that they had never seen anything so beautiful. [13]

This charming account continues with an awareness of the limitations of this Creator:

The butterflies began to sing, and the children listened smiling.

But then a songbird came flying, settling on the Creator's shoulder, scolding him, saying: "It's not right to give our songs to these new, pretty things. You told us when you made us that every bird would have his own song. And now you've passed them all around. Isn't it enough that you gave your new playthings the colors of the rainbow?"

"You're right," said the Creator. "I made one song for each bird, and I shouldn't have taken what belongs to you."

So the Creator took the songs away from the butterflies, and that's why they are silent. "They're beautiful even so!" he said. [14]

This "correction" in the creative endeavor testifies to something seen again and again in Indian stories: the trial-and-error approach that even the most exalted personages have to rely upon. The Europeans who dealt so vigorously, if not even harshly, with the Indians they confronted in the New World had an infallible divinity to model themselves upon. These Europeans probably could not imagine how imaginative their primitive enemies were—and how their divinities could be reasoned with and even corrected. A Flathead story, which may have its counterparts in other parts of the world, goes like this:

Coyote was talking one day when he met Old Woman. She greeted him and asked where he was headed.

"Just roaming around," said Coyote.

"You better stop going that way, or you'll meet a giant who kills everybody."

"Oh, giants don't frighten me," said Coyote (who had never met one). "I always kill them. I'll fight this one too, and make an end of him."

"He's bigger and closer than you think," said Old Woman.

"I don't care," said Coyote, deciding that a giant would be about as big as a bull moose and calculating that he could kill one easily.

So Coyote said good-bye to Old Woman and went ahead, whistling a tune. On his way he saw a large fallen branch that looked like a club. Picking it up, he said to himself, "I'll hit the giant over the head with this. It's big enough and heavy enough to kill him." He walked on and came to a huge cave right in the middle of the path. Whistling merrily, he went in.

Suddenly Coyote met a woman who was crawling along on the ground. "What's the matter?" he asked.

"I'm starving," she said, "and too weak to walk. What are you doing with that stick?"

"I'm going to kill the giant with it," said Coyote, and he asked if she knew where he was hiding.

Feeble as she was, the woman laughed. "You're already in the giant's belly."

"How can I be in his belly?" asked Coyote. "I haven't even met him."

"You probably thought it was a cave when you walked into his mouth," the woman said, and sighed. "It's easy to walk in, but nobody ever walks out. This giant is so big you can't take him in with your eyes. His belly fills a whole valley." [15]

Coyote must improvise, which improvisation extends not only to feeding his fellow prisoners by carving fat off the walls of the "cave" they are in but also to contriving a mode of killing the giant that would permit them all to escape. The darker side of the often childlike Indian imagination becomes more evident here.

A Penobscot tale from Maine, on the origin of corn and tobacco, goes like this:

A famine came upon the people and the streams and lakes dried up. No one knew what to do to make it different. At length a maid of great beauty appeared and one of the young men married her. But she soon became sad and retiring and spent much time in a secret place. Her husband followed her one day and discovered that she went to the forest and met a snake, her lover. He was sad, but he did not accuse her; he loved her so much he did not wish to hurt her feelings. He followed her, however, and she wept when she was discovered. Clinging to her ankle was a long green blade of a plant resembling grass. She then declared that she had a mission to perform and that he must promise to follow her instructions; if so, he would obtain a blessing that would comfort his mind in sorrow and nourish his body in want, and bless the people in time to come. She told him to kill her with a stone axe, and to drag

"A remarkable array of [Indian] tales is still available to us, with many inventive and good-natured episodes on display." Andrew Johnson, a storyteller from the Northern Shoshone tribe, uses hand gestures as symbols paralleling the spoken words.

her body seven times among the stumps of a clearing in the forest until the flesh was stripped from the bones, and finally to bury the bones in the center of the clearing. He was told to return to his wigwam and wait seven days before going again to the spot. During this period she promised to visit him in a dream and instruct him what to do afterward. He obeyed her. In his dream she told him that she was the mother of corn and tobacco and gave him instructions how to prepare these plants to be eaten and smoked. After seven days he went to the clearing and found the corn plant rising above the ground and the leaves of the tobacco plant coming forth. When the corn had borne fruit and the silk of the corn ear had turned yellow he recognized in it the resemblance to his dead wife. Thus originated the cultivation of corn and tobacco. These plants have nourished the bodies of the Indians ever since and comforted their minds in trouble. [16]

We are likely to be troubled by the willingness of the loving husband to kill his wife and then shred her body as he had been directed by her to do. Was this made easier for the tribe to accept because she had been discovered in a compromising relation? This reminds us that most of the stories have moral presuppositions upon which they draw, although another version of this story from the same tribe has no hint of misconduct on the woman's part. [17] A much more benign version of the same story is told by the Osage, which has the stately elk so moved by joy on one occasion that he rolled over and over upon the earth: "[A]ll his loose hairs clung to the soil. The hairs grew, and from them sprang beans, corn, potatoes, and wild turnips, and then all the grasses and trees." [18]

A Tlingit story records the fate of a giant who loved to kill human beings, eat their flesh, and drink their blood. A man kills the giant when he discovers that the giant's heart is in his left heel.

> Yet the giant still spoke. "Though I'm dead, though you killed me, I'm going to keep on eating you and all the other humans in the world forever!"
>
> "That's what you think!" said the man. "I'm about to make sure that you never eat anyone again." He cut the giant's body into pieces and burned each one in the fire. Then he took the ashes and threw them into the air for the winds to scatter.
>
> Instantly each of the particles turned into a mosquito. The cloud of ashes became a cloud of mosquitoes, and from their midst the man heard the giant's voice laughing, saying: "Yes, I'll eat you people until the end of time."
>
> And as the monster spoke, the man felt a sting, and a mosquito started sucking his blood, and then many mosquitoes stung him, and he began to scratch himself. [19]

Are we to understand, by the way, that the "dead" giant required the deceived man's cooperation in order to be transformed into the ubiquitous mosquitoes?

Transformations of a different kind are reported in an Iroquois story about Raweno, the Everything-Maker, when he was busy creating various animals. He was working on Rabbit, and Rabbit was saying: "I want nice long legs and long ears like a deer, and sharp fangs and claws like a panther." "I do them up the way they want to be; I give them what they ask for," said Raweno. He was working on Rabbit's hind legs, making them long the way Rabbit had asked all his legs to be. It was at this moment that Raweno became angry at the yet unformed Owl for pestering him and for refusing to shut his eyes while Raweno worked on Rabbit:

> [Raweno] grabbed Owl, pulling him down from his branch, stuffing his head deep into his body, shaking him until his eyes grew big with fright, pulling at his ears until they were sticking up at both sides of his head.
>
> "There," said Raweno, "that'll teach you. Now you won't be able to crane your neck to watch things you shouldn't watch. Now you have big ears to listen when someone tells you what not to do. Now you have big

eyes—but not so big that you can watch me, because you'll be awake
only at night, and I work by day. And your feathers won't be red like
cardinal's, but gray like this"—and Raweno rubbed Owl all over with
mud—"as punishment for your disobedience." So Owl flew off, pouting:
"Whoo, whoo, whoo."

Then Raweno turned back to finish Rabbit, but Rabbit had been so
terrified by Raweno's anger, even though it was not directed at him,
that he ran off half done. As a consequence, only Rabbit's hind legs
are long, and he has to hop about instead of walking and running.
Also, because he took fright then, Rabbit has remained afraid of most
everything, and he never got the claws and fangs he asked for in order
to defend himself. Had he not run away then, Rabbit would have been
an altogether different animal.

As for Owl, he remained as Raweno had shaped him in anger—
with big eyes, a short neck, and ears sticking up on the side of his head.
On top of everything, he has to sleep during the day and come out
only at night. [20]

We may well wonder what it means to say that both Rabbit and Owl existed or could make requests before they were formed as we know them.

A Wintu tale indicates how grotesque American Indian tales could
become. A young woman, out where she was not supposed to be, had
a finger stuck by a splinter while cutting maple bark. She sucked the
blood and spat it out. The story continues:

Then more blood came, and though she sucked and sucked, she could
not stop the flow. Meanwhile the sun began to set. She kept on sucking
until early evening, unable to help herself. Suddenly she happened to
swallow blood and smelled the fat. It tasted sweet. So she ate her little
finger, and then ate her whole hand. Then she devoured both her
hands. Then she ate her leg, ate both her legs. Then she ate up her
whole body. Then her head alone was left. [21]

But the head rolled along, consuming everything it encountered—until
it fell into a river, where a riffle pike jumped up and swallowed it. [22]

A Blackfoot story tells about the fateful decision of another woman.
Old Man created the woman and the child. After he gave them the
power of speech the woman and Old Man had this encounter:

At once the woman asked: "What is that state we are in, walking,
moving, breathing, eating?"

"That is life," said Old Man. "Before, you were just lumps of mud.
Now, you live."

"When we were lumps of mud, were we alive then?" asked the
woman.

"No," said Old Man, "you were not alive."

"What do you call the state we were in then?" asked the woman.

"It is called death," answered Old Man. "When you are not alive,
then you are dead."

"Will we be alive always?" asked the woman. "Will we go on living forever, or shall we be dead again at some time?"

Old Man pondered. He said: "I didn't think about that at all. Let's decide it right now. Here's a buffalo chip. If it floats, then people will die and come back to life four days later."

"No," said the woman. "This buffalo chip will dissolve in the water. I'll throw in this stone. If it floats, we'll live forever and there will be no death. If it sinks, then we'll die." The woman didn't know anything yet, because she had been walking on earth for just a few hours. She didn't know about stones and water, so she threw the stone into the river and it sank.

"You made a choice there," said Old Man. "Now nothing can be done about it. Now people will die." [23]

It should be immediately added that women are not usually considered the principal or original source of human afflictions in the Indian stories. Rather, women are often looked to by the community for wisdom and guidance. What women do, we can be told, is as great as what warriors do. [24] And, we are shown, women can sacrifice themselves for their loved ones and the community, as one Multnomah maiden did when her people were threatened by an epidemic. Her body was found at the foot of the cliff from which she had thrown herself in compliance with a prophecy. She took "the moon coming up over the trees across the river" as a token that her self-sacrifice was called for. We complete this sampling of North American Indian materials with the conclusion of that story:

Then her father prayed to the Great Spirit, "Show us some token that my daughter's spirit has been welcomed into the land of the spirits."

Almost at once they heard the sound of water above. All the people looked up to the cliff. A stream of water, silvery white, was coming over the edge of the rock. It broke into floating mist and then fell at their feet. The stream continued to float down in a high and beautiful waterfall.

For many summers the white water has dropped from the cliff into the pool below. Sometimes in winter the spirit of the brave and beautiful maiden comes back to see the waterfall. Dressed in white, she stands among the trees at one side of Multnomah Falls. There she looks upon the place where she made her great sacrifice and thus saved her lover and her people from death. [25]

She, unlike the woman who acted in ignorance about the properties of stones in water, can be said to have known what she was doing. She, like her father after her, had asked for a token ratifying her sacrifice. It is instructive to notice that the ratification in each case was nothing extraordinary: the moon coming up over the trees in her case, the waterfall in his case.

III

I will be commenting on various elements in the sampling of a dozen stories I have just provided. Dozens upon dozens of equally intriguing stories could have been chosen. One frequently used element in Indian tales is clever improvisation, as may be seen in the way that Coyote adapted himself to having wandered into the stomach of the giant. Improvisation as a way of life may be seen in the figure of the Trickster, whether he be a divinity, a human being, or an animal.

Here is how a leading American anthropologist has described the worldwide Trickster figure:

> Few myths have so wide a distribution as the one, known by the name of *The Trickster*. . . . For few can we so confidently assert that they belong to the oldest expressions of mankind. Few other myths have persisted with their fundamental content unchanged. The Trickster myth is found in clearly recognizable form among the simplest aboriginal tribes and among the complex. We encounter it among the ancient Greeks, the Chinese, the Japanese and in the Semitic world. Many of the Trickster's traits were perpetuated in the figure of the mediaeval jester, and have survived right up to the present day in the Punch-and-Judy plays and in the clown. Although repeatedly combined with other myths and frequently drastically reorganized and reinterpreted, its basic plot seems always to have succeeded in reasserting itself.
>
> Manifestly we are here in the presence of a figure and a theme or themes which have had a special and permanent appeal and an unusual attraction for mankind from the very beginnings of civilization. In what must be regarded as its earliest and most archaic form, as found among the North American Indians, Trickster is at one and the same time creator and destroyer, giver and negator, he who dupes others and who is always duped himself. He wills nothing consciously. At all times he is constrained to behave as he does from impulses over which he has no control. He knows neither good nor evil yet he is responsible for both. He possesses no values, moral or social, is at the mercy of his passions and appetites, yet through his actions all values come into being. But not only he, so our myth tells us, possesses these traits. So, likewise, do the other figures of the plot connected with him: the animals, the various supernatural beings and monsters, and man. [26]

The curious adventures of which Trickster is capable may be seen in this episode from the Winnebago Trickster Cycle:

> Soon [the buffalo] sank in the mire and Trickster was immediately upon him with his knife and killed him. Then he dragged him over to the cluster of wood and skinned him. Throughout all these operations he used his right arm only.
>
> In the midst of these operations suddenly his left arm grabbed the buffalo. "Give that back to me, it is mine! Stop that or I will use my knife on you!" So spoke the right arm. "I will cut you to pieces, that

is what I will do to you," continued the right arm. Thereupon the left arm released its hold. But, shortly after, the left arm again grabbed hold of the right arm. This time it grabbed hold of his wrist just at the moment that the right arm had commenced to skin the buffalo. Again and again this was repeated. In this manner did Trickster make both his arms quarrel. That quarrel soon turned into a vicious fight and the left arm was badly cut up. "Oh, oh! Why did I do this? Why have I done this? I have made myself suffer!" The left arm was indeed bleeding profusely. [27]

It is significant, perhaps, that the Trickster is "possibly the most important single figure in North American Indian lore," its "pre-eminent figure in all his bewildering yet wonderful complexity." [28] Supernatural spirits seem to enjoy a good laugh. [29] The complicated intellectual activity seen in the Trickster testifies further to the liveliness of the Indian imagination. The tales can be quite sophisticated, with a high level of verbal skills, anything but crude emanations from the morose savages the Indians are sometimes taken to be. [30]

It is also significant, perhaps, that there is among the American Indians no national story, no major intertribal accounts of a great adventure or an authoritative theology or moral doctrine. Thus, there is nothing comparable to what Homer and Hesiod could do among the Greeks or Confucius among the Chinese. With hundreds of languages spoken by the various indigenous peoples of what is now the United States, there may have been no nation from which "national" poets or sages could emerge. [31]

Why, then, should the Trickster have mattered as much as he evidently did among the Indians? (Although women can play tricks, the Trickster is, I believe, almost always, if not always, a male.) Odysseus can be described by Homer as a man of many wiles, but is there not much more to him than those wiles? Cronus and Prometheus can be several times referred to as tricksters by Hesiod (in his *Theogony*), but they can be handled by Zeus, who is also much more than a trickster. The modern Greeks have a trickster hero in Karaghiozis, the shadow-play character, but they also make much, even more, of Alexander the Great, the commander who could be reluctant to "steal a victory." Moreover, whatever the Indian fascination with the Trickster, much is made in Indian stories both of keeping one's promises and of the perfidy of the white man.

To make as much of the Trickster as the Indians do—much more than is made of him among other peoples perhaps—may reflect a special view of the universe, a view which relies more upon will and less upon understanding than we are accustomed to. It relies more upon magic than upon science in accounting for what happens among human beings. This may have had something to do with the inability of Indians, by and large, to adjust usefully to technological challenges.

Among figures of Indian mythology, none is more important than
the Trickster, who has different names in different tribes. Variously
depicted as an animal, a monster, or a man, he is the creator and
destroyer of his people, a god of sorts who is neither good nor evil,
having only appetites and passions—the life force itself in all its
dark complexity. This sculpture by Bill Reid shows him as Raven,
venerated by the Haida Indians in British Columbia, standing on
a clamshell that holds creatures he is about to transform into
the first Haida.

Thus, one must notice, in considering the place of the Trickster in Indian stories, not only what the Trickster provides but also, and perhaps more important, what he takes the place of or excludes. The primacy of the Trickster in Indian lore, including as it does what can only be called divine shenanigans, is to suggest an intimate combination of the high and the low, perhaps even the denial of a difference in principle between the high and the low, at the very least an indifference to the distinction.

IV

What we would consider low may be seen in the bawdiness frequently found in Indian stories. But we should notice that the English-language oral tradition has not been without its robust bawdiness at times. The Indian oral corpus, or what is left of it, happens to have been recorded at a time when people generally were more open than they have been until recently in speaking about sexual matters.

The Indians do seem to have been life-enjoying peoples, even though their ways of life often left them on the brink of annihilation from famine or disease. But their enjoyment could sometimes turn around grim-sounding themes. For example, stories of grinding teeth where men would least want women to have them are found everywhere in the New World. There are Asian and European equivalents, but they are not as vivid as here. [32]

At times, Indian stories seem cruder than those we are used to seeing in print; sometimes they can be terrible in their implications. The terrible, if not even the ugly, may be seen, for example, in an incestuous exploitation of a horrified sister by her persistent brother, which accounts for the relation of the pursuing male moon and the fleeing female sun in the heavens. [33]

But *comic* sexuality may be much more prevalent, as in a story about keeping the Devil in the Inferno which could well have gone back to Boccaccio. [34] A discussion of the merits of reclaiming stolen wives— a question debated in the white man's literature, too, as with Helen of Troy—is instructive, particularly when it is pointed out what kind of wife is thought by others to be worth stealing. [35]

However questionable some of the bawdiness in the Indian stories may seem, the dominant impression there can be of the childlike, the naive, and the innocent, quite unlike the sleazy sophistication to which we have had to become accustomed. The healthiness of Indian sexuality may be seen in the announcement recorded by one narrator upon the discovery of sexual pleasure: "It's too good to be properly described." This would be a good motto for our time, discouraging the desperate efforts at depiction of sexuality encountered all around us. [36]

V

Sexuality is not as critical among the Indians as it has often been among Europeans in accounting for the origins of things. For the Indians, it often seems, a single creation or a single series of events does not suffice to explain the complexity of the world or the existence of evil. [37] It is several times indicated that thinking and naming made things appear. [38]

Much is made of water in various Indian accounts of the beginning, perhaps reflecting thereby either the memory of a gigantic flood or some collective awareness of, say, experience in the womb or both. The earth is sometimes said to have been made of mud brought up by some animal from deep beneath the water. [39] The heavenly bodies, and especially constellations, can be repeatedly explained (as in some ancient Greek legends) in terms of the consequences of earthly episodes. [40]

The ways in which human beings are said to have originated are many. Often, depending on the tribe and the circumstances, human beings are traced back to particular animals. (Totems or taboos can result from these associations.) Even stranger for us are the stories, such as we have seen, which have crops dependent on human bones or on the shredding of "human" flesh. [41] In various ways, that is, the affinity between earth, vegetation, and man is indicated.

Also strange for us are those Indian stories which have the Creator, rather than a surrogate, sacrificing himself for the good of mankind. Thus, one creator has himself killed so that people will not want to live forever, with the bad consequences of immortality. [42]

It can be difficult to read the Indian stories with the discipline and imagination they probably require. They tend to be terse and subtle; much was evidently left to the audience; much is taken for granted, especially since it was usually an audience accustomed to elaborating upon the tales it heard. [43] Various of the stories I have retold here had moral lessons to teach, or at least moral presuppositions on which they depended and which they reinforced.

There is evident again and again in the Indian stories a lively concern for the sacred, the beautiful (including the erotic), the healthy, and the common good.

VI

The common good depends, in practice, on an awareness of limits set by nature, if not also on goals suggested by nature. Whatever the Indian understanding of nature, which I will soon say something about, a kind of natural law or a respect for something like natural right can be seen at work among the Indians. This is evident in the lessons taught by the stories they told, as well as in the way their communities were organized.

They knew, for example, how various animals, birds, and insects conduct themselves and what various plants do and are good for. They sensed what can and cannot be. We notice that they put the more outlandish stories in the long-distant past. It is prudent in these matters to assume that most peoples, or at least the intelligent storytellers they instinctively depend on, have a minimum of common sense.

It is often said that the Indians lived "close to nature." [44] Even though one may wonder how close to nature a people can be who do not really know what nature is, it is probably true that nature asserts herself even when she is not recognized as such or understood. This can be reassuring: we can expect that long-established peoples have managed to work out sensible ways of life, however difficult a tradition-bound people may find it to adjust quickly when they confront an abrupt and massive change in circumstances.

The sensibleness of the Indians may be seen in the ways they generally organized their lives, treasured certain things, and talked about how they should conduct themselves. They were for centuries a better-ordered people than Europeans originally imagined them to be. The self-interest of Europeans often made it difficult for them to see clearly those aboriginal peoples who seemed to stand in the way of what the Europeans took to be salutary economic and political developments.

The sensibleness of the Indian way may be seen in a Caddo creation story in which a woman is told by a voice how to plant and harvest corn. The voice, which is never heard again, concludes, "Now you have everything you need. Now you can live. Now you will have children and form a new generation. If you, woman, should plant corn, and something other than corn comes up, then know that the world will come to its end." [45] We can see here an awareness of what we call the natural process, just as the author of the Hebrew Bible (with no word for *nature* available to him either) exhibits such an awareness in reporting that animals and plants appear according to their own kind.

VII

John Collier, a former United States Commissioner of Indian Affairs, was moved to say this about the Indians in 1947:

> They had what the world has lost. They have it now.
>
> What the world has lost, the world must have again, lest it die.
>
> Not many years are left to have or have not, to recapture the lost ingredient. . . .

268

What, in our human world, is this power to live? It is the ancient, lost reverence and passion for human personality, joined with the ancient, lost reverence and passion for the earth and its web of life.

This indivisible reverence and passion is what the American Indians almost universally had; and representative groups of them have it still.

They had and have this power for living which our modern world has lost—as world-view and self-view, as tradition and institution, as practical philosophy dominating their societies and as an art supreme among all the arts. [46]

The Indian "reverence and passion for the earth and its web of life" that Mr. Collier described can lead people to speak of Indians as very close to nature, as open to and respectful of nature. But the Indian perspective, important though it may be, is more that of the outdoorsman than that of the naturalist. For better or for worse, it is not the scientific approach, which (so far as we know) is ultimately Greek in origin. The Indians can remind us here of the Egyptians and the Babylonians with their vast quantities of observations about the heavens, observations that the scientifically minded Greeks were evidently able to put to a more theoretical use than had been done by those who compiled them.

Our study of Indian thought permits us better to appreciate what nature and the systematic study of nature mean. Science, we can again see, is a Greek way of talking about nature. By and large, the Indians were far more interested in a practical grasp of things than in a theoretical understanding of the world. In fact, we must wonder, is it possible to have genuine theoretical interests if one does not know what *nature* is? The Indians, it seems, were more attuned to art than to science and were more interested in evocative stories than in any systematic understanding of things. Did they "believe in" their stories about why the animals, including human beings, and the earth and heavens are the way they are? If they had alternative explanations which they took seriously, they do not show up in the anthologies I have seen of materials collected from them over the past five centuries.

What is implied by that nature which the Indians do not seem to have spoken of? *Nature* means, among other things, that there need be no beginning or end to the movements and combinations of matter and their consequences. For example, death is shown in various Indian stories to have been invented or chosen rather than being intrinsic to things. [47] Much the same may be seen with respect to the origins of, or any living being's access to, the sun, light, and fire, all of which can be said to depend on animal or other decisions and efforts. On the other hand, a reliance upon nature, or *not* looking to particular events as decisive, implies the conquest of time, the depreciation of history.

The Indian approach, I have suggested, means that the way things look, their attributes, the way they are and act, are all keyed to events, or acts of will, not to something innate in things. This applies, I have

The grave dignity of Indian faces: Vincent Ponzo, head of the Bannock tribe (Wyoming) in traditional dress (above). On the facing page, an old woman at an All Indian Idaho Expo (top); a Chumash of Southern California (bottom); a dancer at the Plains Indian Powwow, a ceremonial and social gathering marked by dancing and feasts (right).

also suggested, not only to human beings and other living things, but also to features of the land, sea, and sky. Even the earth can be spoken of as having once been a human being. [48] It is taken for granted in many Indian stories that human beings were once much closer to the animals than they are now.

The colors and shapes of animals, their behavior (for example, how the Coyote runs), the ways trees and other vegetation are, and what the terrain is like—all of these can be traced back to particular humanlike events. Once, indeed, not only the animals and trees could feel and talk but even rocks. [49] For example, it could matter to a large rock whether it had a blanket to cover it, so much so that it could go rolling after Coyote when he took back the blanket which he had previously bestowed upon the rock. [50]

A Tewa tale suggests the collaboration between human beings and other living things in dealing with what we would call natural forces. It is an account of how Tiny Flower and his wife White Corn were rescued by birds when they fled from the "personage with great pow-

ers, whose duty it was to make rain, thunder, and clouds every day," a great personage who had stolen White Corn for his mate. [51] He had been killed by the couple but he was able to come back to life and to pursue them:

> It was not long before the sky darkened and thunder and lightning began to play all around White Corn and Tiny Flower as they ran.
>
> When they passed the river with red water, rain had caught up with them. By the time they reached Yunque, it was falling faster and faster. Tiny Flower urged White Corn to keep running, for they were just a mile away from home.
>
> The Rio Grande was the next river they crossed, and hail began to fall. All kinds of birds were circling above them, but they kept running. They had only a few hundred yards to go when the hail became so heavy that they could not move.
>
> Tiny Flower and White Corn lay on the ground, and all the birds that had been following—crows, eagles, hawks, owls, sparrows, and more— swooped down and protected the man and woman with their spread wings. The birds that were on top of this great canopy were struck by hail and became spotted, while the ones underneath, like the crows, kept their solid colors. When the rain and hail stopped, Tiny Flower promised the birds that in the next four days he would bring them four deer to eat. [52]

All this is not to deny that the Indians knew—perhaps far better than most Europeans knew—how some things were and acted in nature. But their understanding of things was still fundamentally different. This is reflected in the central importance of transformations in their scheme of things: there are repeated shiftings from one thing to another, shiftings back and forth, reflecting the underlying connections between things that they insist upon, the ultimate oneness of things. [53] In the Bible, transformations of this kind (such as water into wine) are rare— and they can be designated as miracles.

The significance of sometimes bizarre shiftings among species in Indian stories suggests that there is no fixed nature, *nor* any Darwinian notion of evolution or adaptation. We have already noticed Indian stories in which there is no natural basis of, or cause for, death. The cause of the eventual end of the world can be put in terms of Beaver steadily gnawing at the center pole that holds up everything, gnawing faster when he is angry. [54] The shiftings go even further, as may be seen in the movements back and forth between life and death. One consequence of this is the critical place for ghosts and spirits in Indian stories. A human being can be married to someone who turns out to be a snake or a grizzly bear or an eagle or a ghost. Yet it can be said, in recognition of the fundamental difference between life and death, that the dead live in darkness and that it is far better to be alive. [55]

To describe and account for things as the Indians tended to do is, I have suggested, not to recognize the primacy of the rational, at least as Europeans understand the rational. [56] I have further suggested that the Indians may not truly have seen things as they are, however familiar they were with them. Thus, we have stories in which the Morning Star and the Evening Star are regarded as different, with their mating producing the first human being. [57]

How much, then, *did* the Indians know about nature as nature? Their limitations here may be seen in the attribution of speech and hence reason to all living things at one time or another. Their view of nature reminds us that the observation of facts and a lively imagination cannot suffice for understanding. [58] One consequence of the emphasis upon choice and history that I have described is that chance becomes critical, with a "personalization" of much of what one observes. History, or rather memory, was more important for the Indians (as for the Jews) than for European Christians. But the European emphasis upon reason, especially in the service of a certain kind of religious faith, could also mean that a concern with the baleful effects of witchcraft could be far more important for the Europeans than for the Indians. [59]

That is, the age of reason could produce epidemics of monsters to which the Indian psyche may have developed an immunity.

VIII

We must consider further, if only briefly, the significance of the Indians' lack of access either to nature or to a substantial substitute for it, as among the ancient Chinese and Hindus or as among the ancient Israelites. The Indians rely upon magic and formulas in place of a wisdom keyed to nature, however much of a sound moral sense there is in much of what they believe. Their ritualistic approach to things may be seen in their almost obsessive emphasis upon the number *four*. This number seems to be intimately related to the four cardinal directions, directions which work with the movement from the rising to the setting of the sun. (This may reflect the importance of physical mobility for most Indians.) It is in keeping with the emphasis upon *willing* rather than upon *discovering* that the four directions can be said to have been *made*, not found. [60] The four directions can also be accounted for by the way that four monsters once happened to fall. [61]

To question the ultimate wisdom of the Indians' approach to things is not to question their nobility. Indeed, there is often some tension, as is evident in the Greek tragedies, between the noble and the wise. Was it not the noble strain in the Indians that Tocqueville could identify as aristocratic and that could contribute, when suppressed, to their demoralization? Self-esteem very much matters in these situations, and repeated defeats can be devastating to the spirited soul. Wisdom, on the other hand, permits sensibleness and compromises—that is to say, prudence.

The American statesman could have said of the Indians in North America in the eighteenth and nineteenth centuries what the Roman statesman could say of the tribes in Britain more than a millennium earlier: "Our greatest advantage in coping with tribes so powerful is that they do not act in concert. Seldom is it that two or three states meet together to ward off a common danger. Thus, while they fight singly, all are conquered." [62]

I have suggested that an enduring prudence probably depends on an overall grasp of things grounded in an awareness (whether or not articulated) of nature. The Indian tales we have, which are often like either war stories or accounts of athletic contests among us today, tend to close off inquiries rather than to suggest questions. An underlying problem here, which is difficult to address properly, is what the appropriate use by the human race has been since 1492 of the vast resources of the Western Hemisphere. It was, and still is, difficult to be both fair and persuasive in dealing with this problem.

IX

The most dramatic characteristic of the Indian way of life may have been its interest in war and hunting, interests related to the somewhat aristocratic tenor of that way of life. Various warlike activities, such as horse-stealing forays, were evidently regarded by the Indians as fit diversions for their young men. No doubt there were considerable differences among tribes, with some of them adept in subsistence farming, but there were fundamental similarities as well, especially when Indians were compared to Europeans. It proved difficult for Europeans to accommodate themselves to the Indian way of thinking and of acting. One striking similarity among the Indians is that there is relatively little discussion in their surviving materials about forms of government or about political decisions, except perhaps in connection with devising tactics for war or the hunt.

The typical European response to the Indians in the seventeenth and eighteenth centuries is reflected in the way they are described in the Declaration of Independence of 1776, where one of the grievances against the king of Great Britain is the following:

> He has excited domestic insurrections amongst us, and has
> endeavored to bring on the inhabitants of our frontiers, the merciless
> Indian savages, whose known rule of warfare is an undistinguished
> destruction of all ages, sexes, and conditions.

Chief Joseph of the Nez Percé in 1877 led his tribe toward Canada
when their Oregon lands were appropriated. Forced to surrender
after a brilliant retreat, he spoke with resignation for his people:
"From where the Sun now stands, I will fight no more forever."

The critical places where the Indians were encountered in those days,
we can see here, were "our frontiers," for it was there that the Europeans were constantly pressing to enlarge their holdings.

What particularly colored the European perception of the Indians
was their appetite for the scalps of the enemy, an appetite that could
also indulge itself in the torture of prisoners. [63] It is true that Chief
Joseph's Nez Percé warriors, in their late nineteenth-century battles
with the United States Army, never took scalps. [64] But did not this
condemn by implication most of the other Indian tribes?

One Indian story after another takes it for granted that scalping is
perfectly proper. Why did it matter as much to them as it did? This
is not to deny that far worse things were done to the Indians, and for
much longer, by the Europeans than the Indians were ever *able* to do
to the Europeans who found scalping so abhorrent. Scalping did seem
the thing for young men to do: they would set out on an expedition to

slaughter unknown men and to collect scalps of alien peoples as tokens of their courage and prowess in war. [65] In one story, the heroes can be depicted as laboring under a tremendous burden of scalps while they continue to look for "the scalp of all scalps" with which to cap their exploits. [66] It is almost as an afterthought that they can be instructed that they should stop killing innocent people. [67]

The importance of displaying one's prowess may be seen in the curious Indian institution of the *coup,* the mere touching of an enemy in battle, even while killing is going on all around. This is related to the respect shown by Indians for the courage of enemies, even of those whom they felt obliged to torture to death. Their sense of honor did not preclude recourse to deception, as may be seen in the respect shown for the cunning of various tricksters. [68] Still, the Indians were easily deceived by Europeans, while they themselves got an undeserved reputation for treachery. [69]

It should also be noticed that conflicts between Indian tribes were rarely wars of extermination. Fighting could be seen almost as sport to which warriors could be urged by their women. The argument could even be made that a diversity of language was good in that it permitted men to fight, something that permits proper fulfillment of the male. Besides, without war there would develop such ills as an excess of population. [70]

But whatever the failings of the Indians in this respect, we have noticed that the depredations of the Europeans could be far worse. This is testified to by the mostly futile injunction laid down in the Northwest Ordinance of 1787, where it is said,

> The utmost good faith shall always be observed towards the Indians;
> their lands and property shall never be taken from them without their
> consent; and in their property, rights and liberty, they never shall be
> invaded or disturbed, unless in just and lawful wars authorized by
> Congress; but laws founded in justice and humanity shall from time
> to time be made, for preventing wrongs being done to them; and for
> preserving peace and friendship with them.

It may well be, as we shall see, that the principles of the Europeans were in critical respects superior to those of the Indians. But, by and large, the Indians were probably more conscientious in living up to their principles than the Europeans were in living up to theirs.

X

Indian principles, we have noticed, make much of fighting. They would fit more easily into the world of Homer's *Iliad* than into the world either of Homer's *Odyssey* or of Hesiod's *Works and Days.* Many of the tribes could despise, as Chief Joseph did, "the white half-men who scratch in the ground." [71] Yet does not agriculture serve as the basis of civilization as we know it?

Indian principles also taught that those who misbehave are apt to suffer. Youngsters could hear the moral, "You see, because you wanted nothing for yourself, everything has come to you." [72] It is also taught that the good are entitled to use deception in crippling and otherwise restraining the wicked. [73]

We have also noticed the importance for the Indians of the sacrifice of oneself for the community. One's tribe could be considered the favored people of the Creator. The original names of many of the tribes mean, in their respective languages, "*the* people" or "the real people." Each tribe considered itself to have a sacred trust, with appropriate spirits to look after it.

Individuality, as we know it, was discouraged. The young man, upon maturing, might be left alone for days at a time on a vision quest. This was done in order to permit his soul to commune with the spirits of his people, to learn what he had in him, and to dedicate himself properly to the common purpose. It was not designed to develop traits of independence and personal initiative, which do not seem to have been valued. Neither the principles nor the experiences of the Indians supported the opinion of Europeans, especially the Europeans on this continent, that an enlightened self-interest could be depended on to promote the common good. Nor did the Indians see the common good as much as the Europeans did in terms of an ever-rising standard of living.

However much the Indians made of subordination of oneself to the communal interest, tribes did find it difficult to unite properly in dealing with common threats. [74] This was a problem that was independent of the presence of the Europeans: the Indians north of the Rio Grande had had thousands of years to develop before 1492. These North American Indians can be seen as having by then, if left to themselves, probably taken their intellectual and social development as far as their principles and aspirations called for and permitted. We are obliged to wonder, in a way perhaps that they did not, what the truly human life consists of.

XI

There is not, among the Indians north of the Rio Grande, the same evident sense of a high civilization that may be seen in, say, ancient China or ancient India. The American Indian perception of civilization is closer to that of Huck Finn, who eventually "light[s] out for the Territory ahead of the rest" in order to escape civilization, having "been there before" and not finding it to his liking. [75]

Indian adaptations to what the Europeans have had to offer have been mixed. The horse was quickly taken on and put to good use, the gun to perhaps less good use, and alcohol to disastrous use. Technology and agriculture have, by and large, not been in the spirit of the Indian way of life. [76]

The most important thing the Europeans could have offered the Indians was philosophy—and hence a truly informed awareness of what is fully human. This is related to ethics, or a thoughtful morality, but it is not limited to that. One consequence of the philosophical approach, which of course most Europeans neglected then as they do now, is that it obliges one to question the importance of "one's own." Philosophy, in however diluted a form, makes itself felt among many people in the West through Christianity. Christianity itself builds somewhat on Platonic thought, or the life of the mind. Since the life of the mind as we know it has never been critical to the Indian way of life, it may help to explain why the Indians as a people have not been particularly interested in Christianity. It did not help, of course, that many of the "Christians" that the Indians first encountered, and suffered from, were self-serving hypocrites. Even so, I suspect that the emphasis upon the Great Spirit one now finds in Indian stories has been shaped in part by the influence of Christianity. Islam, with its more militant tones and its greater reliance upon a pre-Koranic poetic tradition, might have done better in some ways than Christianity among North American Indians in the sixteenth and seventeenth centuries.

And so we must face up to the challenge implicit in much that I have noticed: is not the European way of life ultimately preferable to the typical Indian way of life? One cannot assess the Indian way properly, or its response to the European alternative, until one addresses this question squarely, even if it cannot be readily answered. Did the Indians fail to recognize as superior the things that make one more fully human? Have the Indians failed to appreciate the best of the Europeans at least as much as the Europeans have failed to appreciate the best of the Indians? There may be mutual failures here: the fault may be greater among the Europeans, but the damage may be greater among the Indians.

Much of what we have just now been considering can be seen to address the question of why Aristotle believed that the *polis,* rather than either a nomadic tribe or a small village, on the one hand, or a massive city or an empire, on the other, is the natural habitat for the human being.

XII

We must wonder, of course, how much we can truly grasp of what the Indian life was like before it was corrupted by extensive contact with the Europeans. Of the Indian materials we now have, how much has been filtered through European eyes and consciousness? Would it not be natural for the somewhat Europeanized Indians themselves to repudiate elements of their heritage that now look dubious? And have some of the more potent stories been diluted, especially those that rely upon an audience of a certain character and experience? With such questions the workings and significance of an oral tradition can be investigated.

Then there is the simple problem of adequate translations of what the Indians used to say, especially since many of the Indian languages are themselves either extinct or at risk even among Indians. The very names now given to tribes, and perhaps even the term *tribe,* can be challenged as themselves distortions. The word *Indian* itself depended of course on a European misconception of how far west Christopher Columbus had gotten when he finally reached land. There may be a happy accident here, however, in that the name *Indian* did happen to anticipate what is now generally taken to be the case, that the North American Indians came here more than twenty thousand years ago from Asia.

We may well wonder what traces there are in Indian languages, customs, and stories of their distant Asian connections. These should be further studied, not least for what they can suggest about the way of life that preceded the now-dominant Chinese and Hindu ways of life on the Asian mainland. Also, we can perhaps learn thereby what might have happened in various parts of Europe and the Middle East before the rise of civilization in Egypt and Greece. We can at least see the stuff out of which later, more sophisticated, stories and cosmologies developed, even as we recognize that something truly mysterious happened when human beings first became aware not only of nature but (perhaps even more significant) of their awareness of that awareness, an awareness which includes the recognition that nature has her salutary effects even on those who are but dimly aware of her.

XIII

I bring this account to a close by speaking briefly about the future of the Indians in the United States. We owe a debt to the anthropologists who have done so much to help salvage the materials that we have of what would otherwise almost certainly and even more rapidly have been a vanishing Indian heritage. These anthropologists, some of whom are themselves Indians, have been vigilant in their efforts to counteract to some extent the depredations visited upon the North American Indians by all too many politicians in the service of thoughtless and self-serving non-Indian constituents.

Chief Seattle of the Puget Sound tribes is commemorated by a sculpture
in the city that bears the name given to it by settlers to whom he remained
loyal during the Indian uprising of the 1850s. He is also buried in Seattle.

Anthropologists and politicians alike are both in need of correction
here. The politicians have generally failed to appreciate the merits of
the Indians; the anthropologists have generally failed to appreciate their
defects. The former erred on the side of realism, the latter erred on
the side of brotherhood. Still, however defective the Indian grasp of the
world, it can be superior to what many among us today stand for who
go in for consumerism and for a mindless addiction to our conventional
"leisure-time activities." [77]

It is appropriate to notice, considering our own concerns these days,
that the Indians of old may have something vital to contribute to the
environmental movement. We all, Indians and non-Indians alike, can
learn from what the Indians once somehow knew. They had access to
the real treasures of North America, not just the gold, fur, and agricultural products that the Europeans yearned for. It is remarkable what
a rich trove of stories there are still all around us among the Indians,
stories that Europeans by and large have been unaware of for centuries.
Rich as that treasure trove may be, however, it is obvious that few of
our forebears would have come over here to learn what the Indians
had to teach. Still, it may be that the Indians can be fully seen for the
first time, by Indians as well as by non-Indians, only because of the
inquiring spirit nourished by the philosophical mode that the European
way of life both permits and encourages. [78]

The Indian can help us become more intimate with the land, as well as with the earliest manifestations of humanity on this planet. One Brule Sioux story observes that the white man needs to have "earth wisdom, making him listen to what the trees and grass tell him." [79] A proper study of Indians can help non-Indians see themselves better, including the African-Americans who have had their complex heritage shattered even more than that of the American Indians.

The last sentiments here come from Indians. First, there is a talk (evidently a non-Indian rendering in poetic terms of a talk) to the governor of Washington Territory in 1854 by the great Dwamish chief, Seattle. It is an eloquent talk in which we should be able to hear various of the elements of Indian thought that I have attempted to sketch in this account. We should be able to hear as well the pious accents of ancient Sparta, Troy, and Rome, especially in the following excerpt:

> To us the ashes of our ancestors are sacred and their resting place is hallowed ground. You wander far from the graves of your ancestors and seemingly without regret. . . .
>
> Your dead cease to love you and the land of their nativity as soon as they pass the portals of the tomb and wander way beyond the stars. They are soon forgotten and never return. Our dead never forget the beautiful world that gave them being. [80]

Finally, there is a fragment from a Dakota poet, an Indian who echoes here a timeless teaching by Socrates:

> You cannot harm me,
> you cannot harm
> one who has dreamed a dream like mine [81]

---

1. William Shakespeare, *Othello,* act 5, sc. 2, lines 342–48 (cf. *GBWW* I: 27, 243; II: 25, 243). "Judean" has been said to refer to an infidel or disbeliever—perhaps to Herod, who slew Marianne in a fit of jealousy, or to Judas Iscariot, the betrayer of Jesus. Some editors prefer "Indian" to "Judean." *See* David M. Bevington, *The Complete Works of Shakespeare* (Glenview, Ill.: Scott, Foresman and Co., 1980), p. 1167.

See, for other articles in this series of introductions to non-European thought, note 31 below. An article on African thought should complete the series. *See,* on law, civilization, and African-American circumstances, George Anastaplo, *Human Being and Citizen: Essays on Virtue, Freedom, and the Common Good* (Chicago: Swallow Press, 1975), p. 175.

2. In this article I deal primarily with the Indian tribes north of the Rio Grande and South of the Arctic, emphasizing aspects of North American Indian thought that I do not find in most accounts. South of the Rio Grande the remarkable social institutions among the Aztecs, Incas, and Mayas were critically compromised by their systematic reliance upon human sacrifice.

3. The "Indian count" in 1990 was 1,516,540 (for thirty-nine states and the District of Columbia). *See* Dirk Johnson, "Census Finds Many Claiming New Identity: Indian," *New York Times*, March 5, 1991, p. A10. "Over a million Indians occupied the area covered today by the forty-eight states, but [their] physical and cultural variation were many" (William T. Hagan, *American Indians* [Chicago: University of Chicago Press, 1979], p. 2). The populations south of the Rio Grande were much larger, with perhaps twenty-five million Indians in the whole of the Western Hemisphere. See *Encyclopædia Britannica*, 15th ed., s.v. "American Indians."

See, for an instructive discussion from a Tocquevillian (and hence somewhat prudential) perspective of the policies of the government of the United States toward the Indians, Ralph Lerner, *The Thinking Revolutionary: Principle and Practice in the New Republic* (Ithaca, N.Y.: Cornell University Press, 1987), pp. 139f., 174f.

4. Richard Erdoes and Alfonso Ortiz, eds., *American Indian Myths and Legends* (New York: Pantheon Books, 1984), p. 96. The "liberating" effect of "learning their own words" can remind us both of the story of the eating of the forbidden fruit in the Garden of Eden and of the story of the building of the Tower of Babel. *See* Anastaplo, "On Trial: Explorations," 22 *Loyola University of Chicago Law Journal* 765 (1991): 767–84; the text at note 38 below. Also instructive here is the cooperation assumed between "all the people and all the animals and all the birds."

5. Erdoes and Ortiz, p. 96. It is *said* in the story that the word for *Lift together (Ya-hoh)* is the same in all the Indian languages. *See also* the Papago account of the career of Montezuma and the consequent raising of the sun so as to produce winters (ibid., pp. 487–89). The Cherokee tribe, on the other hand, tell about first having had to bring the sun down closer to the earth for light and heat and then having had to raise it "to the height of four men" to make the sun bearable. In the process the crawfish had its flesh turned red, making it inedible (ibid., pp. 105–7).

6. Ibid., p. 343.

7. Ibid. Why did the pine trees hoard fire as they did? Partly to protect themselves from forest fires?

8. Ibid., p. 108.

9. Ibid., p. 98.

10. Ibid., p. 105. An editorial note here adds, "The Hopis tell this as the tale of Bahana, the lost White Brother, replacing the sisters with brothers throughout. This version from Acoma shows Spanish influence in the mention of 'sin,' a concept unknown on this continent until after Columbus; the role of the snake in tempting Nao-tsiti [in the Acoma version] may also be colored by knowledge of the Bible." *See* Anastaplo, "Rome, Piety, and Law: Explorations," 38 *Loyola University of New Orleans Law Review*, Part 8 (1993). *See also* the passage quoted in the text at note 16 below.

To say that "everything was as it should be" suggests an intuition (ancient or more recent?) about the nature of nature. *See* sections VI and VII.

11. Erdoes and Ortiz, pp. 85–86. *See also* the passage quoted in the text at note 13 below.

12. Ibid., pp. 407–8.

13. Ibid., p. 408. *See also* the passage quoted in the text at note 11 above.

14. Ibid. Is not natural right implied in the birds' argument, invoking as they do the justice of respecting contractual undertakings?

15. Erdoes and Ortiz, p. 223. It is not indicated how the giant digests anyone who may be alive inside his stomach.

16. Frederick W. Turner III, *The Portable North American Indian Reader* (New York: Penguin Books, 1974), pp. 25–26. Did the killing of the wife with an axe and the shredding of her body suggest that her husband was not really a loving, but rather a furious, spouse? Is there here a sublimated form of cannibalism as well? Compare Genesis 3:20 (on Eve as "the mother of all living"). *See also* note 10 above, the passage quoted in the text at note 25 below, and the text at note 41 below.

17. *See* Erdoes and Ortiz, pp. 12–13.

18. Ibid., p. 119. *See*, for a grimmer version of this kind of story, accounting for the development of medicine, Turner, pp. 28–29.

19. Erdoes and Ortiz, pp. 192–93. We can be reminded here of the vulnerability of Achilles because of *his* heel.

20. Erdoes and Ortiz, pp. 398–99. Consider how, in this and other Indian stories, the accounting for various parts of a body compares with modern evolutionary accounts. *See* the text at note 54 below. *See also* note 58 below. *See*, on tricks played with eyeballs and why Veeho ends up with mismatched eyeballs, ibid., pp. 379–81.

Will seems to be critical in understanding the whole in the Indian accounts. *See* the text at note 48 below, and the text at note 60 below.

21. Erdoes and Ortiz, p. 210.

22. Ibid. *See*, on the chase of a severed head, ibid., pp. 230–34. *See also* the text at note 50 below.

23. Ibid., p. 470. The nature of stones and of water is drawn upon here. Should we be reminded again of Eve and her fateful choice? *See*, for another version of this story, Turner, p. 160. Variations are probably inevitable when an oral tradition is relied upon. (This may be seen as well in the Greek stories, as with respect to the career of Helen of Troy. *See*, on how Helen's abduction should have been regarded, the text at note 35 below.) How death began is a question frequently addressed in Indian stories. *See* the text at note 47 below.

24. *See* Erdoes and Ortiz, p. 50.

25. Ibid., p. 308. *See also* the passage quoted in the text at note 16 above, and the passage quoted in the text at note 41 below.

26. Paul Radin, *The Trickster: A Study in American Indian Mythology* (New York: Bell Publishing Co., 1956), p. ix. Do the Indians, by having retained archaic forms of stories that had long been superseded on the Asian mainland, permit us to investigate both the power and the limitations of primitive thought? *See*, e.g., note 41 below. *See*, on tricksters, Plutarch, *Life of Numa Pompilius*, XV, 3–4 (*GBWW* I: 14, 57; II: 13, 57).

27. Radin, p. 8. *See also* the text at note 39 below.

28. Turner, pp. 30, 106.

29. *See* William K. Powers, *Beyond the Vision: Essays on American Indian Culture* (Norman, Okla.: University of Oklahoma Press, 1987), p. 12.

30. *See*, e.g., Karl Kroeber, ed., *Traditional Literatures of the American Indian* (Lincoln, Neb.: University of Nebraska Press, 1981), pp. 12–13.

31. *See* ibid., p. 45. *See also* note 3 above. *See*, for my introductions to various forms of non-European thought, the following articles: "An Introduction to Confucian Thought" (*GIT* 1984, 124–70); "An Introduction to Hindu Thought: The *Bhagavad Gītā*" (*GIT* 1985, 258–85); "An Introduction to Mesopotamian Thought: The *Gilgamesh* Epic" (*GIT* 1986, 288–313); "An Introduction to Islamic Thought: The Koran (*GIT* 1989, 234–82); "An Introduction to Buddhist Thought" (*GIT* 1992, 218–47). *See also* note 1 above.

32. *See* Alice Marriott and Carol K. Rachlin, *Plains Indians Mythology* (New York: New American Library, 1975), pp. 15, 18–19. *See also* Erdoes and Ortiz, pp. 284–85, 363; Turner, p. 128.

33. *See* Erdoes and Ortiz, pp. 160–62. Consider, also, Herodotus, *The History*, I, 199 (*GBWW* I: 6, 45; II: 5, 45); Anastaplo, "Rome, Piety, and Law," Part 9, Prologue and Epilogue (on Apollo and Daphne).

34. *See* Erdoes and Ortiz, p. 358; Boccaccio, *The Decameron*, III, 10. *See*, for a grimmer story adapted perhaps from European sources, Erdoes and Ortiz, pp. 315f.

35. *See* Erdoes and Ortiz, p. 93. *See also* Herodotus, *The History*, I, 1–4 (*GBWW* I: 6, 1–2; II: 5, 1–2); Homer, *Iliad*, Book I (*GBWW* I: 4, 3–9; II: 3, 1–12); the text at note 51 below; and note 23 above.

36. *See* Erdoes and Ortiz, p. 45. *See also* Anastaplo, *The Constitutionalist: Notes on the First Amendment* (Dallas, Texas: Southern Methodist University Press, 1971), p. 548, n. 126. It is reported, about the discovery of sexual pleasure, that its original discoverers did not have to encourage others: "When [they] got back to the camp, they found nobody there. All the male creatures and the women beings had already paired off and gone someplace, each pair to their own spot. They didn't need to be told about this

new thing; they had already found out" (Erdoes and Ortiz, p. 45). The private character of "this new thing" is taken for granted. *See*, on that freedom of expression which can be subversive of a healthy privacy, Anastaplo, *Amendments to the Constitution of the United States: A Commentary* (Baltimore, Md.: Johns Hopkins University Press, forthcoming), Lecture No. 5, Section IV. *See*, on obscenity, Anastaplo, *Human Being and Citizen*, p. 117.

37. *See* Turner, pp. 36f.

38. *See*, e.g., Erdoes and Ortiz, p. 111. *See also* Genesis 2:18–24, 3:20; Anastaplo, *The Artist as Thinker: From Shakespeare to Joyce* (Chicago: Swallow Press, 1983), pp. 357–62; note 4 above.

39. *See*, e.g., Marriott and Rachlin, pp. 30f. *See also* the text at note 10 above.

40. *See*, e.g., Erdoes and Ortiz, pp. 96–97, 174–75, 205–9, 296–97. *See also* note 53 below.

41. *See*, e.g., ibid., pp. 12–13; the passage quoted in the text at note 16 above. Compare the Binding of Isaac and the Sacrifice of Jesus. *See* Anastaplo, "On Trial," pp. 854–73, 882–919. Consider also the sowing of the dragon's teeth to produce the ancestors of the Thebans in Greece. *See* note 26 above.

42. *See* Erdoes and Ortiz, pp. 78f.

43. *See*, on the reading of the Confucian *Analects*, note 31 above. Consider how *we* fill out, with the help of our personal experiences and our imagination, radio accounts of basketball, baseball, or football plays. *See*, on the improvisations and interpretations by storytellers, Kroeber, pp. 49–56.

44. *See*, e.g., Erdoes and Ortiz, p. 128.

45. Ibid., p. 122.

46. John Collier, *The Indians of the Americas* (New York: W.W. Norton & Co., 1947), pp. 15–16. *See*, on Commissioner Collier's policies, Hagan, pp. 155–61.

47. *See*, e.g., Erdoes and Ortiz, pp. 79–80. Consider also the stories about the roles of Coyote and others in bringing death into the world. *See*, e.g., Kroeber, pp. 26–34. *See* as well the text at note 23 above, and the text at note 54 below.

48. *See* Erdoes and Ortiz, p. 14. Consider the Greek *Gaea* and our *Mother Earth*.

49. *See*, e.g., ibid., pp. 85–87. Thus, a Pueblo woman can say, "We were here before the rocks were hard."

50. *See* ibid., p. 337. *See also* the passage quoted in the text at note 21 above. Consider the care with which the Japanese select rocks for their gardens.

51. *See* Erdoes and Ortiz, p. 285. *See also* the text at note 35 above.

52. Ibid., pp. 289–90. *See*, on why human babies take a year or so to walk, ibid., p. 151.

53. "My imagination brings me to speak of forms changing into new bodies" (Ovid, *Metamorphoses*, I. 1–2). *See also* Montesquieu, *The Spirit of Laws*, Book 28, epigraph (*GBWW* I: 38, 230–62; II: 35, 230–62); the text at note 40 above. Compare the text at note 45 above.

54. *See* Erdoes and Ortiz, p. 484.

55. *See* ibid., p. 442. One can be reminded of Achilles' complaints to Odysseus in Hades. *See* Homer, *Odyssey*, Book XI (*GBWW* I: 4, 243–49; II: 3, 406–18).

56. One side effect may be the rareness of madness (as we usually know it) in the Indian stories we have. Compare, e.g., Erdoes and Ortiz, p. 434. What is to be made of the deadly recourse to alcohol for which Indians became notorious? *See*, on madness, Anastaplo, *The Artist as Thinker*, pp. v, 338–39.

57. *See* Marriott and Rachlin, pp. 16–19. How did the Greeks, or perhaps the Egyptians or Babylonians before them, learn that the Morning Star and the Evening Star were the same?

The Indians (with the possible exceptions, among those north of the Rio Grande, of some tribes in the American Southwest) are also confused about the relation between the length of the year and the periods of the moon, evidently not appreciating that the year is not keyed primarily to the movements of the moon. *See* Erdoes and Ortiz, p. 13.

58. Observation alone can tempt one to say, for example, that since bears can walk like people they must be the ancestors of human beings. *See* Marriott and Rachlin, pp. 43f. *See also* note 20 above.

59. *See*, on the European witch-hunting craze, Anastaplo, "Church and State: Explorations," 19 *Loyola University of Chicago Law Journal* 61 (1987): 65–86. Some early

Christian observers of the native peoples in North America did tend to see them as "perfect children of the Devil" (Increase Mather, *A Brief History of the War with the Indians in New-England* [1676], in Richard Slotkin and James K. Folsom, eds., *So Dreadfull a Judgment: Puritan Responses to King Philip's War 1676–1677* [Middletown, Conn.: Wesleyan University Press, 1978], p. 116). *See,* on the Indians as believers in ghosts and witches, Samuel Cole Williams, ed., *Adair's History of the American Indians* (New York: Promontory Press, 1930), pp. 38–39. *See,* on the Indians as devil-worshipers, Roy Harvey Pearce, "The 'Ruines of Mankind': The Indian Mind and the Puritan Mind," *Journal of the History of Ideas,* vol. 13 (1952): 200.

60. *See* Erdoes and Ortiz, pp. 77f. *See also* note 20 above.

61. *See* ibid., p. 121. *See also,* on the directions, ibid., pp. 38–39, 50, 59. Four winds can be spoken of as related to the four directions, with the winds dependent on the moods, or will, of Ga-oh. *See* ibid., pp. 40, 42.

62. Tacitus, *Life of Agricola,* sec. 12 (*GGB* 6, 280). *See* the text at note 74 below. A critical difference, in the long run, may have been that Agricola and his successors provided a liberal education for the sons of the British chiefs that the Romans conquered. *See* ibid., sec. 21. Compare Hagan, p. 11; *The Annals of America,* vol. 1, pp. 497–98 (Benjamin Franklin on the futility of educating the Indians).

63. *See,* on the refinements of scalping and torture (and not only by Indians), *Adair's History,* pp. 158, 318, 415–19, 454, 460. *See also* Hagan, pp. 8, 15, 17, 22, 36, 106, 119; Slotkin and Folsom, pp. 90, 107, 115–17, 213, 218, 318, 326, 332; note 69 below. Compare Plutarch, *Life of Lycurgus,* XXII, 5 (*GBWW* I: 14, 44; II: 13, 44).

64. *See* Robert Penn Warren, *Chief Joseph of the Nez Percé Who Called Themselves the Nimipu "The Real People"* (New York: Random House, 1983), pp. 17, 54–55.

65. *See* Turner, pp. 51f.

66. Ibid., pp. 52–53.

67. *See* ibid., pp. 53–54.

68. Consider, on the multitribal story of why the tails of prairie dogs are short, Marriott and Rachlin, pp. 75f. The prairie dogs did learn to post guards thereafter. *See also* ibid., pp. 57f. *See,* on the Trickster, section II, above.

69. On the other hand, James Fenimore Cooper could conclude chapter 30 of *The Last of the Mohicans* with an invocation of "the inviolable laws of Indian hospitality." He could also describe, as at the beginning of chapter 33 of this novel, "evidence of the ruthless results which attend Indian vengeance." *See* note 63 above. *See,* on the variety of experiences of Europeans held captive by Indians, Annette Kolodny, "Among the Indians: The Uses of Captivity," *New York Times Book Review,* Jan. 31, 1993, p. 1. Particularly instructive is Mary Rowlandson's famous account of her captivity, during which she suffered the extreme privations of her captors while being treated with more courtesy than had been expected by her. *See* Slotkin and Folsom, pp. 301f. An instructive introduction to Cooper's work is provided in Catherine H. Zuckert, *Natural Right and the American Imagination: Political Philosophy in Novel Form* (Savage, Md.: Rowman and Littlefield Publishers, 1990).

70. *See* Erdoes and Ortiz, pp. 92–94.

71. Warren, *Chief Joseph,* p. 51.

72. Marriott and Rachlin, p. 55.

73. *See* Erdoes and Ortiz, pp. 77f. We can be reminded here both of the relation between Jacob and Esau and of the counsel of Machiavelli.

74. *See* the passage quoted in the text at note 62 above. The limitations of the Indians were such that they could neither understand the best nor anticipate the worst of what the Europeans had to offer.

75. *See* Mark Twain, *Adventures of Huckleberry Finn,* final paragraph (*GBWW* II: 48, 395). It should be remembered, however, that the deadliest villain in Twain's *Adventures of Tom Sawyer* is Injun Joe.

76. Hopeful reports on the Indians' receptivity to an agricultural way of life were a regular feature of President Jefferson's annual messages to Congress. When Indian tribes did attempt to settle down to an agricultural way of life they were not well received by Europeans eager for their lands. *See,* e.g., Hagan, pp. 68–69, 73–81, 88–91, 130.

See, for the opinion in some circles that the Indians were really descended from the ancient Jews, *Adair's History,* pp. xxviii–xxx, 16f., 143–44, 153f. Did not this kind of opinion influence the development of Mormon doctrines in the nineteenth century?

77. One of the more heartening things I have heard about the American Indians today is that they have almost no interest in television. That may turn out to be their secret weapon if they are to have the kind of resurgence that should benefit both them and the non-Indians in this country. *See*, on the abolition of broadcast television, Anastaplo, *The American Moralist: On Law, Ethics, and Government* (Athens, Ohio: Ohio University Press, 1992), pp. 245–74.

78. *See*, for the virtues and limitations of the Indians' aristocratic way of life, Zuckert, pp. 20f. "Like many a chief before and after him, Pontiac had found the individualism of the Indian an unsurmountable obstacle [in organizing them]" (Hagan, p. 26). *See also* ibid., pp. 56 (Tecumseh as "a man with a breadth of vision rare among Indians"), 61, 90.

79. *See* Erdoes and Ortiz, p. 495.

80. Turner, pp. 251–53. *See*, on death and dying, Anastaplo, *Human Being and Citizen*, pp. 214–21. *See also* note 10 above.

81. Turner, p. 239. *See*, on Socrates and the city, Anastaplo, *Human Being and Citizen*, pp. 8–29, 203–13.

The Jeffersonian City

Peter D. Paul

Peter D. Paul is a practicing architect and planner and is senior partner of The Paul Partnership, New York. He has a graduate degree in urban design from City College, New York, and undergraduate degrees from Johns Hopkins University and the Maryland Institute of Fine Arts, with additional studies at the Massachusetts Institute of Technology.

He worked with the National Commission on Urban Growth Policy during the Johnson administration, when he wrote an introductory essay for the Commission Report and articles about urban development for the now-defunct *City Magazine*.

Since that time, his papers and presentations on the history of urban development have concentrated on changes over time in places as diverse as Richmond, Miami, and Albuquerque; industrial cities in New England such as Fitchburg and Worcester; and Athens, Greece. Another area of concentration has been the relationship between formal and vernacular housing forms in cities. He also held, at Long Island University, an exhibit of axonometric drawings tracing the evolution of the American state capitol in relationship to the American corporation. Still another exhibit, presented at the University of New Mexico, described the relationship between Anglo-American, Hispanic, and twentieth-century rationalist traditions of city building.

An exploration of the roots of American cities must lead back to Thomas Jefferson, who more than anyone else of his generation affected the shape of the United States today. His ideas about the form of a democratic state were the basis for organizing the continent with independent states and settling it with small farms and towns—and with cities as well. This essay begins with Jefferson's role in planning and building Richmond as the capital for an independent State of Virginia, as he considers the nature of the democratic state in *Notes on the State of Virginia* [hereafter referred to as *Notes*] during the 1780s. During the 1790s these ideas about Virginia were extended to the settlement of the United States as a whole and the establishment of the federal capital at Washington. In 1803, as president, he expanded the boundaries of the United States with the Louisiana Purchase and said that New Orleans would become the greatest city the world has ever seen.

With Jeffersonian democracy, Americans could create a new form of city, different from both the traditional European cities of the past and the new kinds of industrial cities then developing in Europe. The American Revolution rejected the forms of political organization that produced the cities of Europe.

The traditional European city was organized around the authority of church or royalty, with industrial craftsmen settled in tight neighborhoods dominated by craft guilds. To Jefferson, the future strength of the United States would be a result of developing the agricultural potential of its vast interior. It was not an island forced to trade for prosperity like its former colonial master and therefore to industrialize to make articles of trade. New American towns and cities would serve the needs of independent farmers. Agrarians would develop and control their own cities.

If the Jeffersonian city was conceived as a direction for a democratic society, the American industrial city was not. Alexander Hamilton was pursuing a national strategy of industrial development when his Society for Useful Manufactures began developing Paterson, New Jersey, at the end of the eighteenth century. This industrial city about fifteen miles west of New York used the falls of the Passaic River to power its mills. Hamilton mobilized the capital to build an industrial city by developing a site that offered power and transportation.

288

The American industrial city was in direct opposition to Jefferson's strategy of national development through agriculture. Industrialization dominated nineteenth-century city building. After being established as agricultural towns, the fastest growing cities on the midwestern frontier were products of industrialization. Although industrialization was a more advanced form of economic organization, the motives for city building represented by the Richmond and the Paterson models continued to coexist. Industrial capital assured immediate growth for the cities it favored. Now, however, industrial capital, which was mobile at the beginning of urbanization, has become even more liberated from particular places. By the end of the twentieth century, the outflow of capital in quest of higher returns has left many older nineteenth-century industrial cities stranded. Their dominant industries have closed or moved out, leaving people and places behind that are no longer useful.

The Jeffersonian city, like any traditional agrarian settlement, is rooted in a specific geographic place. Its form is a slow accumulation of the work of generations of people who built it. At the same time, it is open-ended and always unfinished. In the early planning and building of Richmond and Washington, location and plan follow this pattern. The evolution of the Jeffersonian city begins when Richmond becomes the postrevolutionary capital of Virginia, then the largest American state. Jefferson was writing *Notes* during this period, from about 1780 to 1785.

Jefferson's *Notes on Virginia*

The written expression of Jefferson's concepts for reshaping the country to realize the promises of the Declaration of Independence starts with his "Queries" in the *Notes*, begun in 1780 while he was governor of Virginia. [1] The only book Jefferson wrote, it is an extended personal inquiry into the nature of the new democratic state, written at a time when no one knew the future course of the new democracy, or Jefferson's future role in giving it shape.

On the surface, *Notes* is a completed questionnaire. The French consul, François Marbois, interested in considering opportunities of trade with the United States, gave the set of Queries to a Joseph Jones, a Virginia delegate to the Constitutional Convention in Philadelphia. Jones forwarded the questionnaire to the governor to complete. [2] To Jefferson, these questions provided a form for examining not only what the state was, but what it might become when independence secured the opportunity for self-realization. The Queries discuss the role of agriculture, commerce, and cities, as well as government and laws, in the development of the state.

The responses to these queries suggest the rationale for Jefferson's new cultural landscape of democracy. After establishing Richmond as independent Virginia's new capital, he applied the same principles to a seat of government for the new federation of states in the new federal city of Washington, whose initial planning and building he directed. The same outlook is reflected in the plan for settling the wilderness territories as autonomous states, and then, by acquiring the Louisiana Territory from France, defining the United States as a continental power.

Jefferson's political instincts were brilliant, and his views were more than personal ones. He displayed a genius for identifying and articulating the hopes of many of his generation. James Madison and James Monroe were his closest confidants from the time the three worked together to move independent Virginia's new capital city to Richmond. Jefferson's voice gave strong direction to the country's latent energy, turning ideas into institutions and creating new forms for democracy on the landscape.

The structure which Jefferson used in the Declaration of Independence in 1776 shows his way of connecting thought with action. The Declaration consists of:

1. a statement of principles,
2. a bill of complaints against the crown,
3. resulting action of the colonies in declaring independence.

In the Declaration of Independence, Jefferson tells how colonial status, which restrained the states' initiatives to address unsatisfactory conditions, justified the act of declaring independence.

In a comparable way Jefferson's comprehensive and harsh critique of the state's prerevolutionary condition in *Notes* justifies the acts that will change it. We may paraphrase some of these critical views of how the state had developed under colonial conditions as Jefferson sees it. He contends that Virginia, and indeed all of North America, is a land with abundant natural features and resources, but:

1. The agricultural pattern is misdirected; it is destroying the land and enslaving the people
2. There is no adequate system of trade routes serving most of the state and forming a structure of internal commerce
3. The social system based on slavery is destructive to master and slave, and inherently unstable
4. There is no system of public education to improve the skills of the people
5. There are no cities and towns worthy of the name to serve as centers of trade, culture, and government
6. The manufactures are rudimentary and of poor quality
7. There are only a few good buildings in the state, and the people persist in building poor and temporary structures.

As long as the colonial forms of power remained, simply eliminating the control of the king did not constitute a democratic revolution. When Jefferson asks what fundamental changes are needed in the form of the American state, it is a geographic question as much as a political one. Virginia becomes a model for the future form of the democratic society, something he could not find in eighteenth-century Europe, whose towns and cities were under the dominance of monarchies and their established churches. Thus, the democratic experiment of state building is perceived as an exploration of the unknown, without any guide except reason.

Notes provides a complex set of careful observations as the background for pending actions that are the logical sequel to the Declaration of Independence. This became Jefferson's civic program. In the fifty years between the time he wrote the Declaration of Independence and his death in 1826, he devoted himself to forming the future geography of the United States. As he continued to examine the country, expanding the breadth of outlook shown in *Notes,* his ideas affected the division of the land between farms and towns, the kind of towns and cities that came into being, the creation of universities and libraries, and the locations and forms of the seats of state and local government.

Problems are stated without identifying a matching course of action to solve them. Because there are no democratic models, the form of a "solution" may be unknown. It may be inappropriate, Jefferson thinks, to impose a solution on a democratic society, and even if this were accepted, the country has no money to realize it. Consider the section about Virginia's cities (Query XII):

> . . . we have no towns of any consequence. Williamsburgh, which,
> till the year 1780, was the seat of our government, never contained
> above 1800 inhabitants; and Norfolk, the most populous town we ever
> had, contained but 6000. . . . There are other places, at which . . . the
> laws have said there shall be towns; but Nature has said there shall
> not. . . . [3]

Although Jefferson identifies Virginia's need for a commercial center that will encourage domestic commerce, he does not say what to do to create one. Jefferson does not tell us here that he has already moved the capital city to the best site in the state to build the missing commercial center. In 1781 Richmond's future was not assured. In part, Jefferson is explaining how he and his colleagues want to rearrange the commercial as well as the political geography of Virginia. We will explore the context of *Notes* shortly.

The small farmers of the state need commercial cities located where rivers will transport their products for processing and shipping. The locations for such cities cannot be imposed on the landscape by the will of a monarch or even a legislature. Jefferson identifies the geographic "circumstances" by which states and cities will prosper in the new democratic society.

This appreciation of the American landscape in *Notes* is more than a personal digression on Jefferson's part. He articulates a fundamental theme in American culture, perhaps the first influential statement of an American outlook that kept tracts of wilderness as national parks for the people, acting as a balance between nature and cities.

> The passage of the Patowmac through the Blue ridge is perhaps one of the most stupendous scenes in nature. You stand on a very high point of land. On your right comes up the Shenandoah, having ranged along the foot of the mountain an hundred miles to seek a vent. On your left approaches the Patowmac, in quest of a passage also. In the moment of their junction they rush together against the mountain, rend it asunder, and pass off to the sea. [4]

We recall that the *Journals* of Lewis and Clark, whose expedition to find the headwaters of the Missouri was commissioned by Jefferson, are modeled after *Notes* in their careful daily observations of what their authors found, recording the harshness of the landscape and its extremes of temperature, rain, and aridity. Lewis and Clark note the utility of the land and the customs of its people, but they also describe the unfamiliar beauty of its vast plains. [5] That aspect of the exploration is at the root of what became the public will to preserve a part of the natural landscape for future generations.

The form of *Notes* shows a close observation of nature; scientific inquiry replaces adulation of the deity. But *Notes* is more than facts; Jefferson's reflections evoke a vision of the new democratic society emerging in an endless wilderness. Nature, geography, even gardens become an integral part of the Jeffersonian city.

For the next four decades, Jefferson's actions and letters enlarged the reflections in *Notes*. Jefferson's queries were unending; he marked the pages of the published manuscript with changes. It was his intention to produce a revised edition, but he never did; *Notes* remained a perpetual working draft. [6]

The beginning of Richmond

Notes was not intended as a philosophical discourse. Read in isolation it seems merely descriptive. However, it was written by a man who had just led a successful political effort to move his state's center of political power inland, after 170 years at tidewater, by relocating the capital to Richmond. His later positions of influence and power allowed Jefferson to apply his Queries about Virginia to the entire country. Today, *Notes* must be read in the context of his public actions. In addition, Jefferson's sketches and public buildings, which were largely disregarded during the nineteenth century, [7] can be seen today as another way he expressed ideas about the form of democratic institutions evolving on the American landscape.

With the support of the up-country legislators, Jefferson had introduced a bill in 1776 to move the capital from Williamsburg to Richmond, but it was not until 1779, under threat of siege by the British, that the measure passed. When the move occurred in 1780, Richmond was a small town of about 700 people at the falls of the James River.

Tidewater delegates intended the move to be temporary. They assumed that once hostilities were over, the government would return to Williamsburg, the seat of colonial government. Few people lived there full time; they came from the plantations when the legislature was in session. Jefferson estimated a maximum of 1,800 full-time residents, but 1,000 is more likely. [8] Many of the permanent residents were servants and tradespeople to the Governor's Palace, the Assembly Building, and the Anglican Church. The College of William and Mary, located at Williamsburg and run by the Church of England, was Virginia's college. As the capital of Tidewater culture, Williamsburg reflected and furthered the views of the plantation aristocracy. Both were economically dependent on trade with London.

Tidewater Virginia's numerous rivers carried much of Virginia's trade directly to London, bypassing even the port city of Norfolk. [9] As governor in 1780, Jefferson began to develop *Notes*. He saw that the state's agricultural economy, based on tobacco as a cash crop, meant continued dependence on foreign trade. Jefferson's statistics tell us that exports of tobacco have twice the value of all grains exported, [10] even though production and trade are declining as a result of the war. Thus, even if the Revolution assures political independence, the state is still tied to England economically. In addition, Jefferson deplores the social effects of the tobacco culture as a foundation for democracy and recommends that the state's agriculture turn instead to the wheat culture of the inland counties:

> [Tobacco] is a culture productive of infinite wretchedness. Those
> employed in it are in a continued state of exertion beyond the powers
> of nature to support. Little food of any kind is raised by them; so that
> the men and animals on these farms are badly fed, and the earth is
> rapidly impoverished. The cultivation of wheat is the reverse in every
> circumstance. Besides clothing the earth with herbage, and preserving
> its fertility, it feeds the laborer plentifully, requires from them only a
> moderate toil, except in the season of harvest, raises great numbers of
> animals for food and service and diffuses plenty and happiness among
> the whole. We find it easier to make an hundred bushels [about 5,500
> pounds] of wheat than a thousand weight of tobacco, and they are worth
> more when made. [11]

Jefferson rejects the argument of European economists that a nation must develop its manufactures to employ the surplus population from the plantations. He notes that the quality of domestic production is adequate for staple goods but that for refined manufactures Americans should continue to turn to the workshops of Europe, rather than improve the quality of their native industries. [12] Wealth associated with the export trade continued to accumulate in ports such as Philadelphia, Boston, and New York. Norfolk was Virginia's port, and Jefferson acknowledges that it will remain the port for overseas trade. But he rejects a future based on manufactures that concentrate the state's people in Norfolk or in new industrial cities near the Tidewater region. Instead, the new state will be reorganized so that it has not only a port but also a commercial capital city to encourage domestic development through inland trade. "We never had an interior trade of any importance," [13] Jefferson says. The capital at Richmond will support the needs and interests of the small farmers, who will be the backbone of the new democratic society. Following the state's longest river, inland trade from interior farms will flow to the head of navigation at Richmond.

In 1780 Jefferson himself laid out an ambitious plan for the capital city of Richmond, which shows clearly that *he* did not intend the move to be temporary. His city plan shows a grid of streets on a two-mile-long axis; the 1733 church and the old town were to the east of the Shockoe valley; the capitol and the new town were to the west. [14] Jefferson selected the best site for the capitol buildings at the center of a high escarpment called Shockoe Hill, where the capitol would sit like an acropolis above the commercial city, the harbor, and the falls. In the six-block area that was set aside as the capitol square, Jefferson planned to build a group of structures to house the departments of state government, as well as a market. The capitol square also became the city's first park. No North American city had projected a plan of such scale before. The plan of Philadelphia, which was then the largest city in the United States, extended for only a mile between the Delaware and the Schuylkill rivers.

The grid plan of Philadelphia was the apparent precedent for the Richmond plan. It was a plan repeated for towns between Lancaster and Charlotte, North Carolina. This area was settled by independent farmers in a stream of inland migration that passed through the interior of Virginia. In addition, Jefferson knew and liked Philadelphia, apparently finding it even more handsome than London. [15] However, he had more fundamental reasons for using the grid.

> To Jefferson and others of the classical persuasion, the methodical and orderly qualities of the grid were compatible with their philosophic view of the world—a compatibility that had also argued for Greek acceptance of grid planning in the colonial towns of the sixth century B.C. [16]

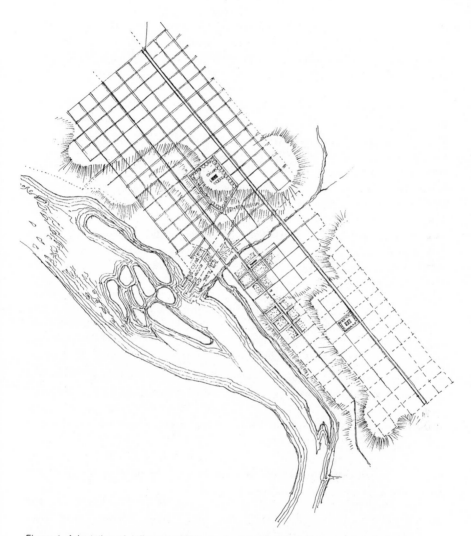

Figure 1. Adaptation of Jefferson's 1780 plan for the extension of the village of Richmond to serve as Virginia's capital. (On the theory that many readers will scan the illustrations and captions before reading the article, the figures parallel the article providing a synopsis of it. Since Jefferson's drawings best express many of the ideas in the article, the drawings must be considered direct quotations from Jefferson. See also the section "Figures," beginning on page 323, for expanded descriptions of the illustrations.)

The grid plan had the advantage of being open-ended for future growth, as well as following a domestic precedent. It is not rigidly maintained. While the grid pervades Jefferson's organization of space at all scales, he interrupts it to emphasize and preserve some of the particularities of nature. In the Richmond plan the escarpments, notably the capitol square, are selected as points of natural emphasis, and the symbolism of the acropolis is an integral part of his concept of the city.

Later developments

At the same time that he started writing *Notes,* Jefferson began drawing plans for a capitol building and governor's house. [17] He was apparently so busy thinking about the future of the state and its capital that he underestimated the threat of attack from the approaching British. They caught an unusual southeast wind to sail up the James and burn the town. [18]

Jefferson decided to retire forever from public life in 1781 under the shadow of an inquiry by the House of Delegates for his unsuccessful defense of Richmond. [19] He outlined his reasons in a letter to Monroe and concludes:

> However . . . I may think public service and private misery inseparably linked together, I have not the vanity to count myself among those whom the state would think worth oppressing with perpetual service. I have received a sufficient memento to the contrary. [20]

Jefferson resigned as governor of Virginia in 1781 and, during a long period of retreat and reflection, he developed the Queries in *Notes* as a commentary on American conditions. The text explores the questions that were to occupy his public career in the quarter century from his appointment as ambassador to France in 1784 until his retirement from the presidency in 1809—a period when he was the person most active in setting up institutions and physical patterns of a new country to realize the concepts of democratic rule.

His wife's illness, which led to her death in the middle of 1782, destroyed Jefferson's plans to assume the peaceful life of a private citizen at Monticello and led to a severe despondency. He retreated to Shadwell, his country lodge about fifty miles south of Monticello, where his reflections found their way into continuing development of *Notes.*

The discussion in the *Notes* of rivers and commerce, of cities and agriculture, develops a rationale for the location of settlements to support an independent agricultural economy utilizing the surfeit of empty land in the United States. Commerce in surplus grain must follow the rivers to places where it can be processed and marketed. These places must provide the farmers with the equipment and products that they need for agriculture. At the head of navigation of the state's longest river system, the falls can be used to grind wheat into flour and power basic industries so the agricultural economy can be established. In a democracy, the farmers and people from country towns who rely on this settlement can best protect their interests by chartering and directing its institutions through a government which they control. The city at the falls will be the capital of the state.

Jefferson is developing a new concept of what the democratic state should become when it turns its back on the Old World and, burning its dependence on the ships of trade, breaks the economic bonds that tied the American states to England. In this conception, the United States must not imitate either the forms of the old European city of established craft guilds or the industrial city that was succeeding it. He thought of them as products of an old social order, which did not apply here. Jefferson's well-known rejection of the great cities of Europe in *Notes* (Query XIX) is even more emphatic in rejecting industry as a basis for building the American state.

> Corruption of morals . . . is the mark set on those, who . . . for their subsistence, depend for it on the casualties and caprice of customers. Dependence begets subservience and venality, suffocates the germ of virtue, and prepares fit tools for the designs of ambition. . . . *While we have land to labour then* [author's emphasis], let us never wish to see our citizens occupied at a work-bench. . . . The mobs of great cities add just so much to the support of pure government, as sores do to the strength of the human body. It is the manners and spirit of a people which preserve a republic in vigour. [21]

Moreover, wheat culture, which will be the basis for the future growth of the state, is carried out by small farmers, not by a plantation economy. Wheat feeds both the people who raise it and those who live in the towns nearby. Surplus grain is a valuable commodity for trade. The prosperity of Philadelphia was based on the grain produced in the small farms of the Great Valley west of the city. The same fertile valley extended southwest from Pennsylvania through Virginia and into the Carolinas. Its farmers were not the original English settlers who held the Tidewater plantations, but Germans, Scots, and Irish who came later. [22] Jefferson was turning to the small farmers of the wheat and grain culture as a productive force on which to build his agrarian federation.

After Jefferson returned to public life as ambassador to France in 1784, he remained committed to the development of Richmond. Madison and Monroe, his closest confidants, remained active in the political life of the state, each serving as governor. The Tidewater delegates regularly advanced the argument for returning the seat of government to Williamsburg, which had the public buildings to accommodate the

Scale 1 square = 1'   Virginia Capitol: End elevation – Study

Figures 2, 3, and 4. Drawings by Jefferson for the Virginia Capitol show the front of the building (above) and the first-floor plan (opposite, bottom). Jefferson had French architect Charles-Louis Clérisseau prepare a plaster model of the building (opposite, top).

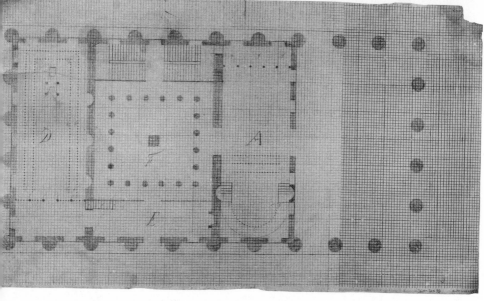

delegates. The town of Richmond and its inland supporters responded by undertaking the construction of a suitable capitol building to accommodate the functions of government. Jefferson, in correspondence with Madison, submitted his own design for the Virginia Capitol, [23] and through Madison's intercession, the foundations already in place were altered and Jefferson's design constructed.

Jefferson's Virginia capitol design was based on a classical temple, using the Maison-Carrée at Nîmes, France, as its model. The temple portico of Jefferson's capitol building re-created the image of a classical Greek city dominated by an acropolis. Nineteenth-century views of Richmond present that image clearly, and once built, it attracted imitators. It was the first modern use of a classical temple form for a public building, and it anticipated the Greek Revival as an architectural style by a generation. Jefferson's concept of the new Anglo-American city placed the symbol of democratic government above everything else. [24]

Both the rationale for locating Virginia's capital city and its plan were repeated when South Carolina planned its new capital city of Columbia in 1786 and North Carolina planned its new capital city of Raleigh in 1792. Columbia was located between South Carolina's coastal plantations and the small upland farms settled in the Great Valley. The action, taken in a time of crisis, was intended to hold the conflicting cultures of the state together by placing the seat of common government between them. After selecting an unsettled site at the falls of the state's longest river, a commission of citizens planned the new city in 1786. [25] Columbia applied the same grid approach as Richmond, but to a site two miles square. Boulevards 150 feet wide intersected at the center, where a block was set aside for the capitol building itself. The town was subdivided into half-acre lots located in a grid of ten blocks to the mile. Proceeds from the sale of lots raised the money for construction of the capitol building itself. (North Carolina followed the same rationale and the same pattern in 1792 by acquiring a capital site near the center of the state at Raleigh. The 400-acre site was divided into one-acre lots, which were sold to construct a capitol building.)

Columbia, which introduced the section-line boulevards and mile-square supergrid, expanded the organizing concepts that Jefferson had used at Richmond. This pattern, which relates city blocks to the section-line subdivision of the states, was characteristically repeated in practically all towns and cities throughout the western territories. [26] The Jeffersonian city starts as a neutral framework of streets and lots. Its citizens create the institutions which follow, placing them within the framework of property lines. A block may be filled with tenements or livery stables, with a school or a library, with mansions or the city hall. Whatever happens depends on decisions made by future citizens.

Columbia became South Carolina's capital city in reality when Governor Charles Pinckney, a Jeffersonian Democrat, convened the first legislature in the nearly completed capitol building in 1790. Columbia was the first new capital city to realize one of the central institutions in Jefferson's program. In order to have educated people to run state government, the 1801 legislature authorized the first state-*supported* university. Opened in 1805 a few blocks from the capitol, [27] South Carolina College was the modest beginning of the state university system characteristic of autonomous U.S. states.

The District of Columbia

In 1790, with Richmond and Columbia as working models, the United States Congress authorized the creation of a new federal capital city which would become the seat of government in 1800. Building a new federal city between the northern and southern states was part of an arrangement to compensate the agrarian southern states for the costs of Hamilton's plan to have the federal government pay the debt the states had incurred to fight the War of Independence. [28] Jefferson was able to propose the new capital plan to benefit the agrarian states because he knew exactly what he wanted to do and how he could do it. The location of Washington was also opportune for western settlement. In *Notes* Jefferson had identified the location at the falls of the Potomac as the terminal of the best and shortest trade route to the Midwest and the interior of the country that lay beyond. [29] *Notes* provided the rationale for the future location of Washington. President George Washington, whose home was nearby, readily accepted it, as Jefferson knew he would.

The process for building the federal city followed the tested pattern of Columbia, but on a larger scale. The federal government acquired a largely unsettled site ten miles on each side from the states of Maryland and Virginia and planned to finance construction of the public buildings through the sale of lots, as Columbia had done.

Jefferson drew his own plan for the federal city, [30] following the same concepts as the Richmond plan. Jefferson's plan for Washington defines and builds only the public buildings which the government can afford—the Capitol and president's house—and places them on the most prominent physical locations. He proposes large public gardens along the river. The rest of the plan remains a neutral grid on which future generations of citizens can build a commercial city with new institutions which the founders could not fully envision—and certainly could not afford.

To provide a plan for the federal city, President Washington turned to Pierre-Charles L'Enfant, who was considered the best-trained engineer and architect in the United States. It was L'Enfant's plan, with its grand classical vistas and avenues, that was at first adopted, not

Jefferson's. L'Enfant and Jefferson agreed on the location of principal buildings, but the French planner dismissed Jefferson's simple grid concept as the naive work of an amateur. Soon, however, President Washington found he was unable to deal with L'Enfant's demands for the funds and authority to realize his plan. The president then assigned the job of building the federal city to his secretary of state, Mr. Jefferson, who dismissed L'Enfant. [31]

The Richmond experience led Jefferson to push forward with the construction of the public buildings; if the federal city was not ready to operate in 1800, the Philadelphia and New York industrialists would certainly seek to retain the capital. Jefferson initiated competitions for the design of the public buildings of Washington and entered his own design anonymously into the competition for the president's house. [32] James Hoban, an Irish immigrant, who apparently designed the capitol building in Columbia, won that competition. Jefferson's competition rules provided that the designs should avoid colonial precedents and should rely on current interpretations of classical sources. Andrea Palladio provided the common source for the very different entries by Hoban and Jefferson. Hoban stayed in Washington to construct public buildings as well.

By 1800, the president's house was ready for use. Except for modifications to its porticoes, it has remained substantially as first designed. Only the Senate wing of the Capitol had been built at that time, however, and it was not yet heated. The Capitol remained unfinished or in the process of modification or enlargement until 1865, when the present dome, which appears daily on television as the symbol of the legislative branch, was completed. It is much closer in profile to a Jefferson sketch done at the time of the competition than anything proposed or built before the 1850s. However, the dome is an integral part of the Capitol expansion designed by Thomas Ustick Walter of Philadelphia and selected by President Millard Fillmore in 1852.

The experience of trying to construct Washington showed that, whatever Jefferson's intentions, the United States did not have the trained people needed to build the new cities. While in Paris, Jefferson had enlisted the French architect Charles-Louis Clérisseau to prepare the drawings and plaster model needed to build the Virginia Capitol. He had studied examples of new French architecture, in which Claude-Nicolas Ledoux and others were experimenting with ways to use simplified classical building forms for new types of institutions. [33] Jefferson had the most extensive architectural library in the United States and lent L'Enfant plans of European cities for reference while he prepared his Washington plan.

After the Washington experience, Jefferson turned his attention to improving the technical skills of the country. Fortunately, Hoban had arrived in Washington just weeks before the competition deadline, with

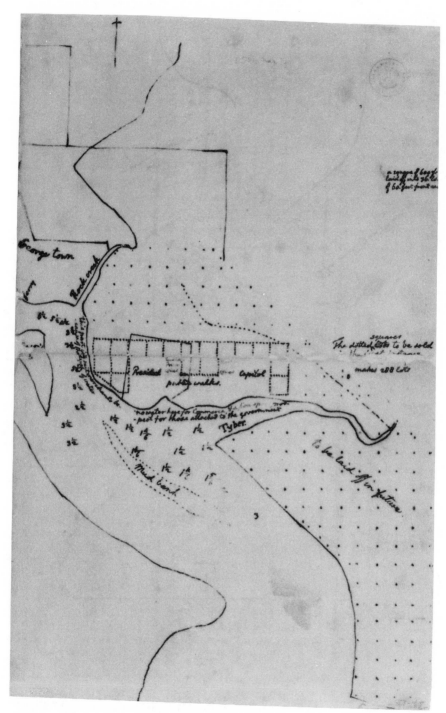

Figure 5. In 1791 Jefferson created this plan for Washington.

letters of introduction from Charleston, to manage the building of the president's house. He spent the rest of his career in Washington handling construction of as many of the government buildings as he could. In 1803, as president, Jefferson appointed English-born Benjamin Henry Latrobe as surveyor of public buildings, to complete the Capitol. He also accepted the American-born Robert Mills, who at twenty-one had won the competition to design the first building for South Carolina College, as an architectural apprentice and protégé. They realized the elements that make the modern city work. For example, Latrobe designed waterworks and bank buildings for Philadelphia. He also trained a generation of talented students. Mills, usually remembered as the designer of the Washington Monument, planned the South Carolina Railroad, the longest in the world when completed in the 1830s; his state asylum in Columbia was a new kind of institution; he pioneered fireproof construction and initiated a classical tradition for public buildings with his Treasury Building for Andrew Jackson's administration. [34] Thus, an improvement in the technology and skills needed to build new American cities was a direct result of Jefferson's actions.

Turning to the West

A way of providing for orderly settlement of the western territories had to be faced while Washington, D.C., was under way. The concept of creating new, autonomous states, equal in status and power to the established states, was revolutionary:

> As the author of a series of land ordinances, Jefferson organized the spatial and political geometry of the national territory. Upon the diverse contours of a vast and growing public domain, the ordinances and the Land Act of 1796 imposed a rectangular survey system. In the country west of the Alleghenies, government surveys formed the basis of land division, the guide for laying out of roads and streets, even the pattern for aligning fences, plantings, and houses. Later, utilities and transport lines would conform to the grid that now covers three-quarters of the continental United States. The chief module of this rectilinear pattern was the 640-acre, or one-mile-by-one-mile, section. [35]

Jefferson's 1784 plan for the settlement of the Northwest Territory [36] shows the unorganized region between the Alleghenies and the Mississippi divided into ten states by east-west divisions along every two degrees of parallel beginning at forty-five degrees (northern boundary of New York State), and a north-south division at eighty-six degrees west. In the absence of detailed knowledge of topography, precise geometric boundaries allowed orderly settlement with a minimum of territorial disputes.

The plan proposed states of 20,000–30,000 square miles—much larger than the New England states (e.g., New Hampshire contains about 10,000 square miles) but not as large as Virginia. Virginia set a precedent by ceding control of its territories west of the Alleghenies for autonomous new states with democratic governments. Under the 1784 plan, a new territory could be admitted as a state when its population equaled that of the least populous of the original states. As other states followed Virginia's lead by giving up their western lands, each secured a port west of the Alleghenies, where rivers flowed to the Mississippi. Although some meridian lines proposed in Jefferson's division, such as the southern boundary of Tennessee at thirty-five degrees, were followed, Congress rejected the specific state designations in favor of establishing more natural boundaries later when the territories were better known. However, the states west of the Mississippi followed the kind of abstract boundaries that Jefferson proposed. The results were the rectangles of Colorado and Wyoming, and three-degree slices that define the Great Plains states west of the Missouri River's north-south course. States were divided into 160-acre farms following the section-line grid. Initially, no towns or cities were planned within these abstract boundary lines; that was left to the will of the people when they settled, and to the natural circumstances of the geography they would discover.

Vermont, the first new state (admitted in 1792), was a 10,000-square-mile area separated from New York. Its main port was at Burlington along the Lake Champlain trade route between the Hudson and the St. Lawrence. The capital was located at Montpelier near the head of the Winooski, the longest river flowing entirely within the state. With the university located at Burlington, and industry in small cities outside of the port and capital, Vermont demonstrated the model of the new American state at the northern frontier.

Other states which followed in rapid succession were larger than Vermont but still sparsely populated. Illinois alone was big enough to swallow all of England, the former colonial master, with space remaining for Chicago and its suburbs.

In 1803 Jefferson negotiated the purchase of the Louisiana Territory from France. It contained the remaining watershed of the Mississippi River, doubling the area of the United States. Although the Constitution gave him no right to do so, and $15,000,000 required for the purchase was neither available nor authorized, geography and fears of foreign competition were the driving factors in Jefferson's determination to acquire these western lands. Clearly, at the time, there were not enough people to fill such vast amounts of space, nor enough skills or capital to build cities there.

Jefferson applied the same concept of the free flow of commerce to the mouth of the river to his view of the Florida Territory, which Monroe later acquired. [37] It was the urgency to people the continent with an Anglo-American culture that drove the later concept of Manifest Destiny as the country pushed its territories to the Pacific by 1850.

In 1804 Jefferson wrote to the governor at New Orleans, which the United States had just acquired as a part of the Louisiana Purchase:

> The position of New Orleans certainly entitles it to be the greatest city the world has ever seen. There is no spot on the globe to which the produce of so great an extent of fertile country must necessarily come. It is three times the greater than that on the Eastern side of the Alleghany which is to be divided among all the seaports of the Atlantic states. [38]

The letter reveals many aspects of Jefferson's view of cities. The "greatest city the world has ever seen" will be at the mouth of the continent's greatest river, handling and shipping the surplus of millions of farms, on some of the richest farmland in the world. Who needed industry?

President Jefferson's mind is already busy planning the city. The letter summarizes the idea of the open city organized around its gardens with basic geometry as its form.

> [To prevent the spread of disease, we] should decide at once that our cities should be thin-built . . . in building cities in the U.S. we should take the chequer board for our plan, leaving the white squares open and unbuilt for ever, and planted with trees. [39]

The checkerboard arrangement was later used in the original plan for at least two western cities. In Jeffersonville, Indiana, the original squares were soon subdivided and built over. However, in Jackson, Mississippi, the plan was partly realized. Some of Jackson's open squares remain and some are used for public buildings, while others have been built over. The rationale of health and safety, which Jefferson uses to justify the New Orleans plan, and the scientific rationale for the openness for the plan at Columbia, remain part of the legal framework for city building today.

The pattern and rationale for the characteristic grid form of "thin-built" U.S. towns and cities was established around the beginning of the nineteenth century with a clear program of democratic intentions. It is evident in the equal and repetitive division of land, whether in the arrangement of farms or in the regular street grid of cities. These city plans are intentionally without artistry and carry no assurances of ultimate success. Gradually, over many generations, the institutions which give form and meaning to the city may rise up from an open framework of property divisions in those places which the circumstance of nature and commerce favor. As at Richmond and Charlottesville, architectural forms will be the symbols of these democratic institutions.

Jefferson simply outlined forms and concepts and left examples for democratic settlement patterns in autonomous states and in the com-

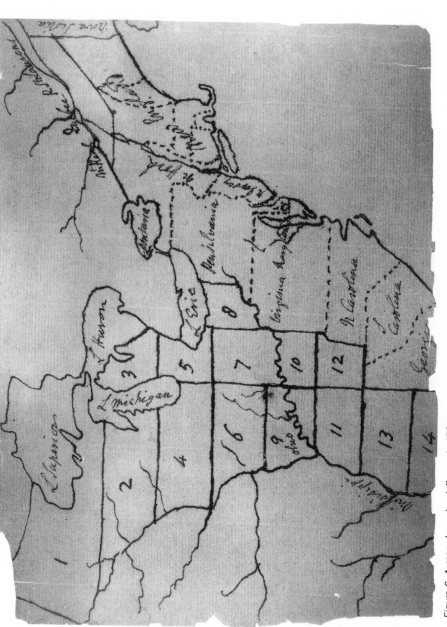

Figure 6. A map drawn by Jefferson in 1784 shows his proposal for dividing into states an area that includes the Northwest Territory. The actual Northwest Ordinance of 1787 specified not less than three or more than five territories.

mercial cities which their future citizens would build. He intentionally rejected the pattern of traditional European cities, built around the institutions of church and monarchy, and started a new direction for cities based on the stated principles of democracy. It is the autonomous states with their towns and cities that turn the millions of independent farms into a working democracy.

Jefferson developed concepts for democratic cities. What happened to them?

Notes from the 1990s

At the beginning of this essay, I used Jefferson's late-eighteenth-century agrarian intentions for founding Richmond and Hamilton's industrial goals for founding Paterson to illustrate opposing directions for the future. Although the United States became an industrial power by the beginning of the twentieth century, the agrarian viewpoint persisted in a continuing tradition of cities in small states whose development was never dominated by industry. This tradition is opposite to that of the industrial city, as Jefferson himself realized and everybody now writing about nineteenth-century history is quick to note.

Jefferson presented a lucid concept of settlement for an agrarian society and, recognizing the dangers of dominance by industrialization, established a federal system of autonomous states to protect it. As a result, agrarian cities and states have continued to coexist with industrialization in the United States, in ways that are quite different from England. As the United States became an industrial power during the nineteenth century, agricultural regions benefited by exchanging food products with industrial cities for things like steel, locomotives, and automobiles.

By the end of the nineteenth century, the big cities in the United States were industrial cities. Although towns and cities based on agriculture generally developed first along the frontier, it was industry that accelerated the growth of cities through the first three decades of the twentieth century. [40] Beginning in the Northeast, industrialization flourished on the agricultural frontier as the original Northwest Territory became the industrial heartland of the Midwest. Industrial capital, which produced economies more dynamic than their agricultural origins, encouraged these cities to expand their technological specialties during a period of booming growth. Thus, in Ohio, Youngstown became a major steel-producing center, Akron became the "rubber capital of the world," and Toledo provided the world with a "glass" capital. These industrial economies were based on technological and industrial leadership for products that could be shipped all over the country and the world. Even their critical raw products came from world trade. Youngstown was no more affected by a lack of local iron ore than Akron was by the inability of Ohio's climate to support rubber plantations.

Industrialization changed both the organization of cities and the relationship between the city and its agricultural region in ways that fundamentally opposed Jefferson's concepts of western settlement. Oscar Handlin's historic overview [41] identifies a failure of imagination occurring in the process of industrialization after the 1920s. Today that turning point can be seen in the plight of many declining industrial cities, which have never recovered from their waning fortunes.

The twentieth-century response was new technologies. After the discovery in 1901 of the Spindletop oil field in East Texas, the amount of petroleum available in the United States grew exponentially; that made the automobile industry feasible, and together they created a whole new industrial landscape. Mobilization for World War II, and the cold war that followed, created and sustained new territories for industrial processes with their hierarchical organizations and built a new generation of cities, especially in California and the Sunbelt.

However, when the people of industrial Paterson were no longer asked to manufacture locomotives, they were not able to get jobs making cars, unless they were willing to move to Detroit. Aircraft and missile manufacturing jobs were in California. New England textile mills, where the Industrial Revolution had started in the United States, began closing during the 1920s to move south. Often nothing took their place. After World War II, many older industrial cities, which had grown so vigorously a half-century earlier, began to decline in population. Initially this decline was explained by the movement of people and industries to the suburbs, but with each successive census, many older industrial cities, even with their suburbs, were seen to be growing much more slowly than the country as a whole. By the time of the 1990 census, an ever-increasing number of metropolitan areas were declining in population [42] and could no longer anticipate the traditional American outlook of prosperity through growth.

The values expressed by industrial capitalism may be compared to those of a society based on hunting and gathering, whose nomadic settlements are not permanently fixed in the landscape because the people must be ready to move on, searching for jobs in new areas of industrial growth.

Although the infusion of capital led to the spectacular growth of industrial cities in the past, later twentieth-century experience shows that they often stagnate or decline when capital goes hunting for new ways to gather profits from faster growing regions. In contrast to societies based on hunting and gathering, the resources and settlements of agrarian societies are fixed in place. Agricultural cities and regions in the United States have persisted and grown without going through the

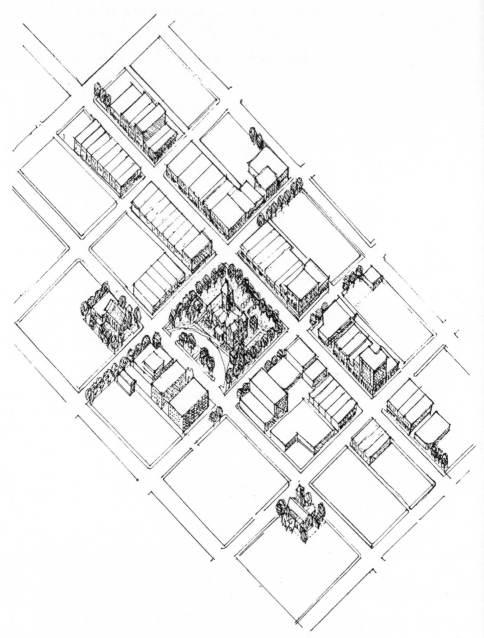

Figure 7. A contemporary sketch of Marshalltown, Iowa, a typical small city center.

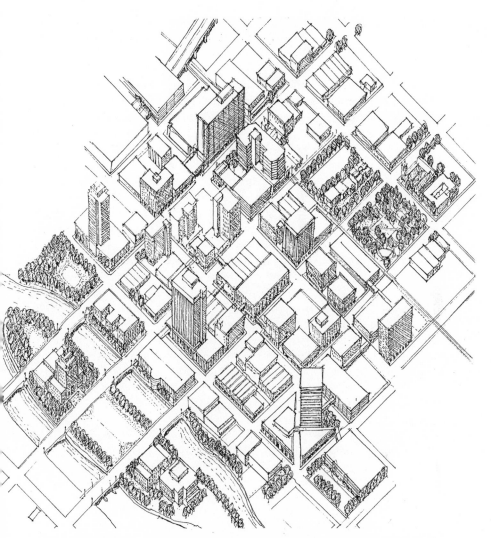

Figure 8. Cedar Rapids, Iowa, many times larger than Marshalltown, has developed along a river.

kind of industrial evolution once considered essential to the evolution of cities. While the Jeffersonian tradition has quietly persisted, it has also evolved in scale and technology.

Today the country has 250 million people instead of the 3 million to 5 million of Jefferson's time. At the time that Jefferson developed his view of the American state, Virginia, the largest one, had about a half-million people, the same as Vermont or Wyoming today. The original State of Virginia, which Jefferson describes, was later subdivided into the two additional states of Kentucky and West Virginia. Following Jefferson's original strategy, Richmond received the agricultural products and basic commodities of the countryside; its commerce and basic processing supported farmers, mechanics, and merchants. The nineteenth-century wheat trade flowing from small farmers in the Great Valley made Richmond the state's commercial capital. Power from the falls turned the wheat into flour. From the port below the falls, the surplus wheat was shipped abroad as an article of trade. By the 1840s, wheat flour shipped from Richmond became the largest staple of trade between the United States and South America. [43] The city processed lumber, coal, and iron brought there by the canal—and (unfortunately, from Jefferson's point of view) tobacco.

Jefferson continued to influence the building of Richmond; he brought such leading American architects of his time as Latrobe and Mills to Richmond to design its public buildings. [44] Its industrial growth did not disturb Jefferson. By the early decades of the nineteenth century, political conditions had changed his views on industry from those he expressed in *Notes:*

> You tell me I am quoted by those who wish to continue our dependence on England for manufactures. There was a time when I might have been so quoted with more candor, but within the thirty years which have since elapsed, how are circumstances changed! . . . Shall we make our comforts, or go without them at the will of a foreign nation? . . . experience has taught me that manufactures are now as necessary to our independence as to our comfort; . . . [how] will our *surplus* labor be then most beneficially employed in the culture of the earth, or in the fabrication of art? We have time yet for consideration, before that question will press upon us; and the maxim to be applied will depend on the circumstances which shall then exist; for in so complicated a science as political economy, no one axiom can be laid down as wise and expedient for all times and circumstances. . . . [45]

The urban aspects of Jefferson's settlement strategy worked as he intended—and far better than anyone who saw Jefferson as opposed to cities expected. During the early nineteenth century, Richmond's Gallego Mill superseded the mills of Philadelphia as the largest in the United States, and it remained the largest American mill until the

Washburn Mills in Minneapolis, at the head of the Mississippi, were built during the 1870s. [46] Today Jefferson's Richmond is Virginia's center of government and commerce and, through the banks concentrated there, has become the state's center of financial power. But it remains a city of modest size by today's standards.

The very term *culture*, which Jefferson uses, is derived from a root meaning cultivation of the soil. [47] During the nineteenth century the wheat culture, on which Jefferson's settlement strategy was based, moved west. Small farms producing wheat, and mills that turned it into flour, built a succession of new cities with the spread of western settlement. Rochester, a milling center where the Erie Canal crossed the falls of the Genesee, called itself the "Flour City," [48] but it was soon superseded by newer cities surrounded by even vaster fields of grain. By the end of the nineteenth century, the production of the old Northwest and the new territories overshadowed that of Virginia. By that time, grain production far exceeded anything imaginable at the beginning of the nineteenth century.

Independent mechanics in small towns and cities made life easier and more productive for independent farmers. For example, a midwestern blacksmith named John Deere invented a steel plow that made it easier to turn the soil; that started the evolution of machinery that soon affected every aspect of agricultural production. Farmers were quick to adopt machinery and techniques that helped them to produce even more on the rich level prairies of the new territories, where conditions were optimal for mechanizing grain production.

The settlement pattern of the new territories encouraged not only towns but small commercial cities of moderate size as centers of the various states. Conceptually, the land was organized into six-mile-square townships; this provided schools and churches at a time when travel distance was based on walking and wagons. Township organization set up a small village pattern. Normally twelve to twenty-five townships were organized into a county, which had a principal town as county seat and trade center. In wheat-producing areas small villages at grain elevators along the railroad had to be a maximum distance of eight miles from the farm to allow a farmer's wagon to unload and return in a day. [49]

By the 1990s, with a day's journey measured in hundreds of miles, these agricultural villages and small towns were declining because people traveled to the regional city, and while industrial cities declined, many agricultural cities of this kind gained in population. They contained not only the markets but the services needed for modern agriculture. Urban historians such as Handlin have recommended that cities be studied as parts of their region [50] and that the particularities of individual cities be studied in depth. One of the best studies of the evolution of a Plains city in its agricultural region is Lawrence Graves's four-volume

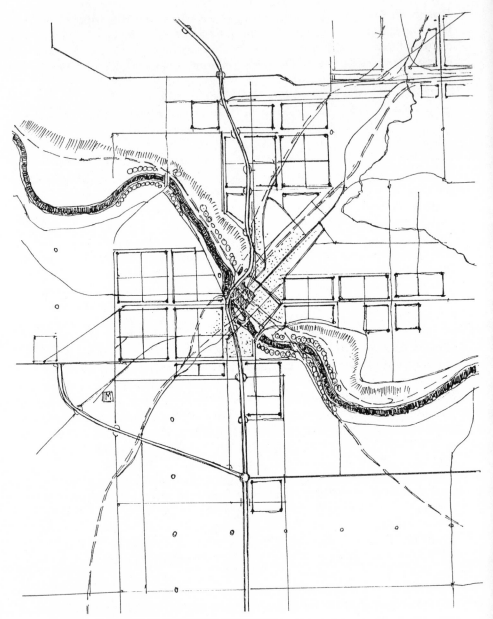

Figure 9. The expansion of Cedar Rapids, Iowa.

History of Lubbock. [51] An insignificant town in 1920, Lubbock, Texas, in 1990 was an agrarian city of 180,000 people; it was larger than any of New England's industrial cities outside of Boston. J. B. Jackson, the cultural geographer noted for his observations about the meanings of the landscape, says of the new American city:

> almost all up-to-date American cities west of the Mississippi are variations on a basic prototype, and that prototype is Lubbock, Texas. . . . There is a new kind of city evolving in America . . . and on a small scale Lubbock tells us what those new cities look like. [52]

As a state capital, Lincoln, Nebraska, is an even clearer paradigm of the Jeffersonian city for the purposes of this essay.

Although these agrarian cities are of modest size, they are often larger and more varied than industrial cities. Their economy is not dominated by a single employer or industry, and they may not have any major industrial employers. Instead, the largest employer is often the state government, and perhaps a state university, followed in order by the city and county governments, some hospitals, the telephone company, and finally a branch of an electronics maker or outside food-processing industry. There are also many smaller firms oriented to the specialized needs of the region's farms. In the history of Lubbock, Graves shows how the sometimes ingenious technology of High Plains mechanized cotton farms was developed locally with the help of the state university, when the problems were too specialized to interest large industries elsewhere. [53]

A Jeffersonian city such as Lincoln is often the capital of a less populous state, but an agrarian city like Lubbock is still the center of a 20,000-square-mile region, larger in area than many states. The political skills of the city promote the interests of the region to the state and federal governments. In contrast to the industrial city, the agrarian economy depends on the products of the earth around it and is largely controlled by power remaining within the region. It will often be the seat of a major state university, or at least an educational center. It will be an inland city, probably located on a river, and will have a much closer relationship to its natural surroundings than large cities or industrial cities. It will be "lightly built" and will probably have an open-ended grid plan tied into the supergrid of surrounding farms that have been converted to urban land as the city expanded. It will have fewer extremes of wealth and poverty than industrial or great cities, and a lower percentage of its people will live in suburbs. It will be a center for local rather than national capital. It will have an airport which connects the region to the rest of the country. Since the state charters corporations and institutions to serve its needs, its locally based banks and insurance companies are among its larger employers.

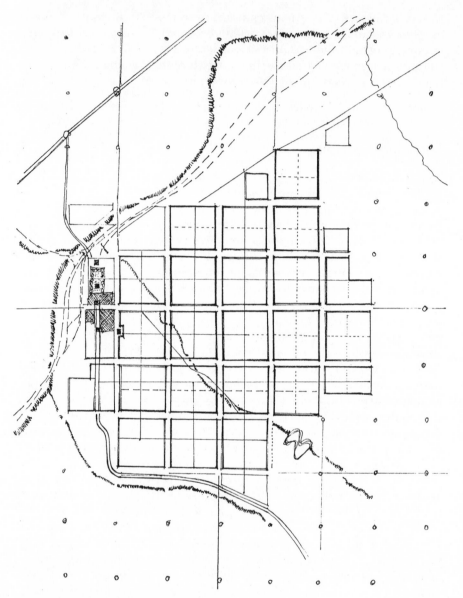

Figure 10. Lincoln, Nebraska—"a paradigm of the Jeffersonian city."

Cold war priorities are now past. The petroleum economy of the oil patch, which began with a surplus of oil, is now declining, with lower production and dwindling reserves. Jefferson's agrarian outlook prevails in times of peace when the energies of a secure and independent people can build their autonomous states. Whether the people live on farms or in cities, their settlements are places rooted in the earth.

A period of major investment in American city building came to an end with the 1980s. An experiment in economic determinism moved capital more freely than ever before to the fastest growing parts of the country, looking for the highest returns. The economic result was uncontrolled overbuilding, as real estate markets collapsed in all parts of the country. The concept of the city as a by-product of economic forces controlled entirely by the market failed. It needs to be replaced by more viable concepts for stabilizing and improving our cities.

The essay has shown that certain American city patterns are a direct product of the intentions of Jeffersonian democracy. I have rejected the earlier twentieth-century view that equates urbanization with industrialization as part of the inevitable progress of cities, because it does not fit the demographic facts of the 1990s. By examining the pluralistic origins, outlooks, purposes, and results found in the variety of American cities, we can resume the unfinished task of improving the United States as an urban society during the next millennium.

Conclusion

I want to conclude where Jefferson did—first with his comment on a continuing national attitude, and then by suggesting the culminating achievement of his life as an example.

> A country whose buildings are of wood, can never increase in its improvements to any considerable degree. Their duration is highly estimated at 50 years. Every half century then our country becomes a tabula rasa, whereon we have to set out anew, as in the first moment of seating it. Whereas when buildings are of durable materials, every new edifice is an actual and permanent acquisition to the state, adding to its value as well as to its ornament. [54]

Jefferson's abstract concept for settling the new territories with a pattern of equal farms evolved in time to a pattern of cities based on the specific geography of place and the actions of the people of each state.

An autonomous state creates institutions, which are the foundation of the city. It begins with the instruments of government—capitol, courthouse, and town hall. Once the settlement is secure and thriving, the state charters other institutions—operating departments of the state, universities, medical centers, banks, insurance companies, and other corporations. The institutions of the state congregate in the centers of cities where they originated, to grow and change as needed over the generations to come.

When he planned Richmond, Jefferson knew that its institutions must develop gradually. Each generation would conceive and build new institutions and replace some of the earlier ones. Strong institutions tend to encourage new ones that are mutually supportive. The most dynamic institutions either dominate a portion of the central area of the city or move to the perimeter in order to expand.

The Virginia Capitol in Richmond was Jefferson's first venture into public architecture. It was his first effort to translate abstract concepts of a democratic society into a concrete element of a democratic city. When he wrote to Madison asking about the building, he appealed to

the comfort of laying out the public money for something honourable,
the satisfaction of seeing an object and proof of national good taste, and
the regret and mortification of erecting a monument to our barbarism.
. . . You see I am an enthusiast on the subject of the arts. . . . it's object
is to improve the taste of my countrymen, to increase their reputation,
to reconcile to them the respect of the world and procure them
it's praise. [55]

Although the building was completed according to his intentions as the Virginians understood them, it was not until the twentieth century, when the capitol expanded, that the portico was rebuilt to follow the model which Clérisseau had prepared under Jefferson's direction.

That tradition of enlarging and improving the symbol of government continued. Capitols in the new territories symbolized the growing maturity of each state. In Nebraska, for example, a ferry company built the first territorial capitol building in Omaha in 1855, at no cost to the state, in order to keep the business of the capital city at its landing on the banks of the Missouri River. When Nebraska became a state in 1869, the citizens moved the capital to a tiny village, which they renamed Lincoln. The first capitol building in Lincoln was so poorly constructed that it had to be replaced within twenty years. The capitol continued to evolve as a symbol of the state on its site at the center of the city until 1932, when the present landmark building, distinctive and unique to Nebraska, was completed. [56] Around successive buildings housing the capital as a landmark and institutional symbol at its center, a city on the Plains grew in a tradition that Jefferson began with his actions in Richmond.

The continuing evolution at Lincoln is a paradigm of the search for permanence, stability, and sense of place in an American city. In the traditional view, improvement of the city is a goal worth pursuing for its own sake—not as a rest stop on a highroad to riches. While

Figure 11. The evolution of the Nebraska Capitol in Lincoln. (Bottom to top) the original capitol, built in 1869; its replacement, constructed in 1889; and the present structure, completed in 1932.

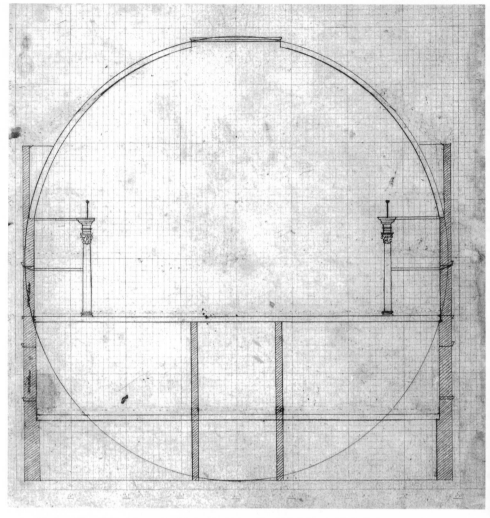

Figures 12 and 13. Jefferson's plan for the University of Virginia rotunda includes a cross section of the building (above) and the front elevation (opposite).

recognizing the straitened circumstances of his time, Jefferson is clearly showing that cities improved in lasting ways will be a continuing source of pride for their people.

Traditionally, places with a culture of abundance have employed the energies of their people in internal improvements. Many American universities can be examined as physical models for working and living places, for their relationship of built to natural environment, and as dynamic models which balance permanence and change.

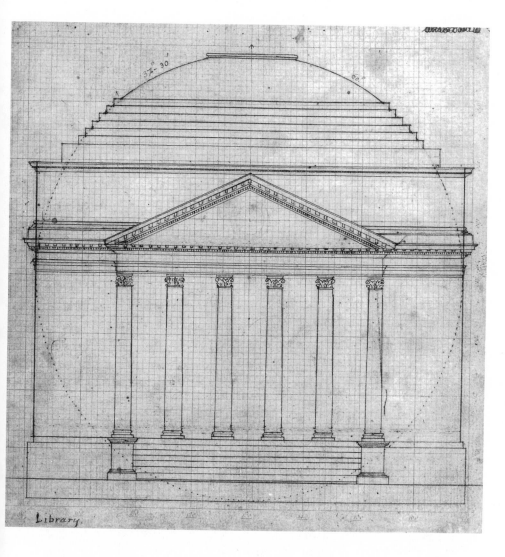

Library.

Jefferson asked to be remembered in his epitaph for the Declaration of Independence, the Virginia Statute of Religious Freedom, and the University of Virginia. He not only organized the university and set up its programs, he designed and supervised the construction of the campus, as a community, laboring for years over details of its buildings and gardens. The University of Virginia campus, now beautifully restored and maintained, provides a more direct vision of Jefferson's realized hopes for the public realm than anything he wrote.

The culminating work of his career is a physical paradigm for the civilized community in the American landscape.

321

Figure 14. Jefferson's bird's-eye view of the University of Virginia. Looking to the west, the outer rows of buildings, labeled A through F, are dormitories and student dining halls. The ten buildings of the inner rows are pavilions and dormitories. The pavilions contained classrooms on the ground floor and living space for professors on the second floor. The rotunda, not yet built, would stand to the right at the head of the lawn that lies between the inner rows of buildings.

Author's note

Why reexamine Jefferson's views on American cities? I began with the traditional view that Jefferson was opposed to cities but kept encountering facts that did not fit that view. Away from the Northeast, the effect of Jefferson's hand on the landscape loomed larger than I expected. This essay was a chance to reexamine all of Jefferson's views on cities.

When I worked on the question of urban policy with the National Commission on Urban Growth Policy in the 1960s, my outlook toward urban history relied strongly on the work of the Harvard–MIT Joint Center for Urban Studies and was affected by the methods of the social sciences and their critique of history. The question of urbanization of sparsely settled western states introduced me to some of the literature and outlooks used in the preparation of this article. The work of the commission was a casualty of the Vietnam priorities and the urban riots of 1968, but I continued to follow demographic and physical changes, not explained by industry, oil, or military bases, by focusing on Lubbock and Albuquerque.

Approaching urban history by looking in depth at representative cities is the result of approaches recommended by Handlin and Philip M. Hauser, among others. A detailed survey of cultural resources in Newark in the late 1970s left a particularly strong impression of the difficulties that befell a once great industrial city in the twentieth century. That survey also generated a greater reliance on visual materials, especially the use of bird's-eye views that John Reps has championed as a way of recording urban phenomena. As a result, I have been developing a technique for using three-dimensional maps to record changes over time.

The Richmond piece of this puzzle is the accidental result of a daughter's decision to go to college in an unfamiliar city. I had seen references about Jefferson's early association with the capitol in Richmond but was able to fit them into a coherent view only after repeated visits, which allowed me to explore and to record how the city had started and how and why it had changed. It was there that I encountered Jefferson's ghost walking the capitol square at twilight.

Figures

Figures 1–6. The Jeffersonian City-State

When we examine Jefferson's 1780 plan for the extension of the village of Richmond to serve as Virginia's capital (fig. 1), we find that it not only realizes the planning principles he would suggest in 1791 for Washington but is the direct model and antecedent for the cities of the western expansion.

Note the use of grid paper, which was characteristic of Jefferson's drawings, in his later drawings for the Virginia Capitol (figs. 2 and 4). That building was Jefferson's first venture into public architecture, and the first modern use of the classical Greek temple form in a modern public building. It anticipates the widespread use of Greek Revival architecture in the United States beginning in the 1820s for public, commercial, and residential buildings.

In his Washington Plan (fig. 5), Jefferson identifies the location of the Capitol and the president's house in the general locations where they were placed and shows public gardens and walks along the river. He identifies a grid of blocks for immediate development but reserves land, indicated by the grid of dots filling the plain below the escarpment, for future expansion. The plan was rejected by L'Enfant as "naive" and was not followed.

The plan for the division of the Northwest Territory (fig. 6) shows a still larger scale of Jefferson's political geography. All three of these public scales are unified in public intent and formally, by the use of the grid, oriented to cardinal directions.

Figures 7–8. The Jeffersonian City Center

A typical small present-day city of 25,000 (fig. 7) in what were the new territories that Jefferson acquired west of the Mississippi, has developed around the center of government at the courthouse square, here with its five blocks of commercial activity most evident. But it also has the public educational system and even the library and galleries that Jefferson advocated. In place of a dominant church, there are a number of smaller ones, and fraternal and civic organizations as well. All of these institutions, that came after the town was founded, find their own place in the ubiquitous undifferentiated grid of streets. They expand, move, and even fade with the changes of each generation.

A city many times larger, shown in figure 8, built in a splendid setting along a river, appears at first glance to be the "Paris of the Plains" with its public civic buildings on the island instead of the Gothic cathedral of Paris's Île de la Cité. But the U.S. city avoids the grandeur of the boulevards of Paris, and even Washington, by intention. Beyond the island, there is the same grid of streets as the typical small city. There are more and larger institutions and commercial enterprises; there are distinctive buildings, a fine library and museums, and even public squares planted with gardens. There are skyscrapers, a distinctive American building form, even in this medium-sized city. The grid of streets changes very little, but the buildings and institutions within them have changed continuously as the city evolved from a town. Figure 7 and figure 8 both follow the same model and Jeffersonian precedents.

Figure 9. Expanding City (Cedar Rapids)

The western city expands outward incorporating farms whose boundaries follow the U.S. section-line grid. Main highways and commercial extensions following section lines are simply realizing a plan laid down before the original settlement. The form of the U.S. city is a result of the regular section-line grid meeting the specific natural courses of rivers and geographic features. This city has used the river to advantage to create a sense of place. In this diagram the mile-square sections developed for suburban use are shown solid on the natural landscape, with the sections still used for agriculture shown as a grid of points. The city center is the dark area at the center. The diagram intentionally parallels Jefferson's Washington sketch.

Figure 10. Logic of Expansion (Lincoln)

In the accompanying essay, Lincoln, Nebraska, is suggested as a paradigm of the Jeffersonian city. The capitol, university, and other institutions of the state are concentrated in Lincoln; it is also a center of finance and commerce, and a processing center for agricultural products. Using the same technique and scale as the expanding city diagram, Lincoln is shown expanding entirely to the east, almost entirely within the "city" limits. Lincoln's growth follows its own logic and models, which are different from the patterns for Great Cities.

Figure 11. Nebraska Capitol Evolution (Lincoln)

The Nebraska Capitol is Lincoln's greatest landmark, but the original capitol building completed hurriedly in 1869 was so badly built that the masonry started to crumble before it was finished. However, it was planned so that two wings could be added; once they were finished a new center portion was built. The state built the wings of the present capitol around the second one and then demolished it to complete the central tower. The evolution and refinement to a permanent landmark occurred entirely in the original capitol square at the intended center of Lincoln.

Figures 12–14. Jefferson's University of Virginia

In the Jeffersonian city, the landmark building is a symbol of the institution within the neutral grid of sections, streets, and property lines. The University of Virginia, which is the culminating work of Jefferson's life, is much more than a philosophical idea for a university; it is a brilliant physical model of a landmark building related to buildings and gardens to house a working community in a specific place. Note both the form of the rotunda, which accommodates the library, emerging from the graph paper in his drawing, and the way of seeing the ranges of dormitories and pavilions as a whole. Jefferson's vision is a highly structured and purposeful one, as his own drawings show.

The University of Virginia is intact and beautifully restored. The only way to experience it is to visit it.

---

1. This essay uses two editions of *Notes on the State of Virginia:* NSV, ed. William Peden (Chapel Hill: University of North Carolina Press, 1955); and NSV-2, ed. Merrill D. Peterson (New York: The Viking Press, 1975). The latter also includes letters referred to later.

2. NSV; Peden's introduction describes the origins of *Notes on the State of Virginia*, p. xii.

3. NSV, pp. 108–9.

4. NSV, Query III, Mountains, p. 19. Peden notes that this section was often quoted by early nineteenth-century editors who held the work as a whole in low esteem.

5. *History of the Expedition Under the Command of Lewis and Clark,* ed. Elliott Coues, 3 vols. (New York: Dover Publications, Inc., 1965); first printed by New York: F. P. Harper, 1893. This edition includes Jefferson's "Memoir of Meriwether Lewis," 18 August 1813.

6. NSV, editor's notes, Preface, p. v.

7. See *The Eye of Thomas Jefferson,* ed. Richard Guy Wilson (Charlottesville: University of Virginia Press, 1980). A descendant of Thomas Jefferson gathered his drawings during the late nineteenth century and deposited them in the Massachusetts Historical Society. The 530 drawings were cataloged and introduced by an essay by Fiske Kimball in 1915. While much of this book, which accompanied a bicentennial exhibit, shows the artistic influences on Jefferson, it also includes many of his sketches and describes his method of working on graph paper. The drawings, which show other aspects of Jefferson's way of thinking, were published more widely in the late 1970s.

8. NSV, Query XII, Counties and Towns, p. 108.

9. B. A. Brownell and David Goldfields, eds., *The City in Southern History: The Growth of Urban Civilization in the South* (Port Washington, N.Y., and London: National University Publications, Kennicat Press, 1977).

10. NSV, p. 167.

11. NSV, Query XX, Subjects of Commerce, pp. 166–68.

12. NSV, p. 169.

13. NSV, p. 164.

14. *See* R.P. Winthrop, *Architecture in Downtown Richmond* (Richmond, Va.: Junior Board of Historic Richmond Foundation, 1982), pp. 1–2. Other local sources consistently make the same reference, but an original drawing of the plan is not available. The Latrobe map of 1792 seems to be the earliest drawing of the city. Figure 1 is reconstructed from the description applied to the present street plan of Richmond, which is unchanged.

15. *See* Morton Gabriel and Lucia White, *The Intellectual Versus the City: From Thomas Jefferson to Frank Lloyd Wright* (Cambridge, Mass.: University of Harvard Press, 1962). Chapter 1 is a discussion of Jefferson, which covers his favorable attitude toward Philadelphia in relationship to European cities.

16. Lois A. Craig, ed., *The Federal Presence* (Cambridge, Mass.: MIT Press, 1978), p. 5.

17. Wilson, op. cit., pp. 226–29. Drawings in Jefferson's hand on graph paper showing a plan for the capitol building, which was largely realized five years later, and unrealized plans for a governor's mansion, are dated 1780–81 by this source.

18. Refer to a biography for the circumstances of the British invasion. Fawn McKay Brodie, *Thomas Jefferson: An Intimate History* (New York: Norton, 1974), ascribes the British occupation of Richmond to uncharacteristic east winds which allowed the ships to sail up the James River quickly and indicates the lack of money to arm the militia.

19. NSV also refers to the poor condition of Virginia's naval fleet, p. 91, Marine Force:

> Before the present invasion of this State by the British . . . we had three vessels of 16 guns, one of 14, five small gallies, and two or three armed boats. They were generally so badly manned as seldom to be in condition for service. Since the perfect possession of our rivers assumed by the enemy, I believe we are left with a single armed boat only.

20. NSV-2, Letter to Monroe, 20 May 1782, p. 365.

21. NSV, Query XIX, Manufactures, p. 165.

22. Jean Gottman, *Megalopolis, The Urbanized Northeastern Seaboard of the United States* (New York: The 20th Century Fund, 1961). *See* the chapter "Agriculture in the Northeast," which describes how William Penn's approach to agriculture promoted the prosperity of Philadelphia in the eighteenth century.

23. NSV-2, Letter to Madison from Paris, 20 September 1785, pp. 388–90. In Paris, Jefferson received a letter asking him to prepare plans for the capitol in Richmond. He did so using the Maison-Carrée, an ancient temple in Nîmes, as a model and with the help of the French architect Charles-Louis Clérisseau forwarded a plaster model—which the people would understand—to Richmond. In the meantime, construction had already started using a plan the commissioners had drawn. Jefferson urges Madison to persuade them to follow the model he is sending:

> But how is a taste in this beautiful art to be formed in our countrymen, unless we avail ourselves of every occasion when public buildings are to be erected, of presenting to them models for their study and imitation? Pray try if you can effect the stopping of this work.

The capitol was completed according to the commissioners' interpretation of Jefferson's plan; their mistakes were corrected in 1910, when the capitol was expanded and the central building restored according to Jefferson's original model.

24. The acropolis image is clearly shown by Latrobe's watercolor, which appears in Wilson, op. cit.; by Matthew Brady's photographs, which appear in *Architecture in Virginia* (published for the Virginia Museum by Walker & Co., New York, 1968); and by the description by Robert Mills quoted in Craig, op. cit., p. 25:

> I remember the impression it made on my mind when first I came in view of it coming from the South. It gave me an idea of the effect of those Greek temples which are the admiration of the world.

25. Helen Hennig, *The Founding of Columbia* (Columbia: University of South Carolina Press, 1940), chapter 1.

26. Craig, op. cit., p. 5, estimates that three-quarters of the continental U.S. is now covered by the section-line grid.

27. Ibid., and *WPA Guide to North Carolina*, reprinted by University of South Carolina Press, Columbia, 1988; originally printed by University of North Carolina Press, Chapel Hill, 1939. *See* pp. 149–51. The emphasis here is on state support for higher education. Georgia and North Carolina chartered state universities earlier, and the University of North Carolina was in operation a decade before, but it did not receive funds from the state until 1887.

28. *Life and Selected Writings of Thomas Jefferson*, edited and with introduction by Adrienne Koch and William Peden (New York: The Modern Library, 1944): "The Anas" 1818, p. 117, by Jefferson. Note that this volume contains another version of *Notes*, which because of significant editorial omissions is *not* recommended.

29. NSV, pp. 15–16. Jefferson argues that the Ohio and therefore western trade is 580 miles closer to the Potomac at Alexandria than it is to New York, is interrupted by only one portage, and is ice free.

30. Craig, op. cit. The plan for Washington in Jefferson's hand was published as part of the Federal Architecture Project during the 1970s, drawing on material in the federal archives during the 1970s; the sketch gives a clear indication of how Jefferson thought about cities. The book gives a good account of Jefferson's views on settlement. *See* introduction and pp. 23–33.

31. John W. Reps, *Town Planning in Frontier America* (Columbia: University of Missouri Press, 1980). *See* pp. 224–28. *See also* Daniel Reiff, *Washington Architecture 1791–1861* (Washington, D.C.: Commission on Fine Arts, 1971). *See* chapter 1, pp. 1–17, for discussion of Jefferson's role during L'Enfant's planning of Washington.

32. *See* discussion of the competitions in Reiff, op. cit., and in Wilson, op. cit., pp. 238–41. Although Jefferson entered the competition for the president's house, he fully accepted James Hoban's winning entry. It was built under Hoban's direction and remains as designed today, with the addition of projected porticoes by Latrobe.

33. *See* Wilson, op. cit., esp. pp. 167 et seq., for a discussion of French architectural thought during the time that Jefferson was in Paris. A generation of French émigré architects made an important contribution to U.S. architecture in the first two decades of the nineteenth century. J. J. Ramee's Union College Plan in Schenectady, which precedes the University of Virginia by five years, follows the same French model of a lawn with a central domed building looking into the distance along an open axis.

34. *See* Craig, op. cit., for references to Mills, pp. 56–62; Latrobe, pp. 34–39. A biography of Latrobe is available, and an older one of Mills by Gallagher. Mills' autobiography, however, is not entirely credible.

35. Craig, op. cit. pp. 4–5.

36. NSV-2, pp. 254–58, *Report of a Plan of Government for the Western Territory*, manuscript of a report of 1784 committee in Jefferson's handwriting. *See also* Craig, op. cit., p. 2, for reproduction of Jefferson's sketch for suggested division of territories into states. In the discussion of Jefferson's proposed subdivision of the Northwest Territory the question of how many people a democratic state could effectively accommodate is never addressed directly. Areas and populations discussed here are interpolated to show a measure of what existed during Jefferson's time. Certainly subdivision into smaller states was seen as a way to bring government closer to the people at a time when Vermont separated from New York, Kentucky from Virginia, and Maine from Massachusetts.

37. NSV-2, Letter to John Breckenridge, 12 July 1803, pp. 494–96. His view of territory is expressed in the letter, which says: ". . . we shall certainly obtain the Floridas, and all in good time."

38. NSV-2, Letter to Governor William C. C. Claiborne, 7 July 1804, p. 499.

39. NSV-2, Letter to Breckenridge, op. cit., also contains the checkerboard city recommendation.

40. Oscar Handlin, *The Historian and the City* (Cambridge: MIT Press, 1963). *See* Handlin's overview essay, "The Modern City as a Field of Historical Study," pp. 1–26.

41. Ibid.

42. U.S. Census 1990.

43. Paul S. Dulaney, *The Architecture of Historic Richmond*, 2nd ed. (Charlottesville: University of Virginia Press, 1976), pp. 8–9. Also Chicago Board of Trade, *Grains: Production, Processing, Marketing* (1992).

44. Dulaney, op cit., pp. 4–6, and subsequent entries, describe the Richmond work of these two architects so closely associated with Jefferson during his presidency.

45. NSV-2, Letter to Benjamin Austin, 9 January 1816, p. 549.

46. *Grains,* op. cit.

47. *American Heritage Dictionary* (1979), s.v. "culture," from Latin *colere, cultus:* to till, cultivate. Definitions include "1. The cultivation of the soil; tillage. . . . 6. A style of social and artistic expression peculiar to a society or class."

48. Blake McKelvey, *Rochester on the Genesee* (Syracuse, N.Y.: Syracuse University Press, 1973). This is a summary of McKelvey's four-volume history of Rochester, which is cited by Philip M. Hauser and others as one of the landmark works in urban history. McKelvey divides success phases of the city's development as "The Flour City" and "The Flower City."

49. John Hudson, *Plains Country Towns* (Minneapolis: University of Minnesota Press, 1985).

50. Handlin, op. cit., pp. 3–4, in which he notes that the relationship of the city with forces outside its limits is a necessary part of the study of any city, and p. 24, which notes that "The differences between city and countryside have been attenuated almost to the vanishing point."

51. Lawrence Graves, *A History of Lubbock,* Lubbock, Texas, in three volumes published 1959–61. Recommended in *The Study of Urbanization* by Charles Glaab, "The Historian and the American City: A Bibliographic Survey," pp. 53–80. A fourth volume was published in 1986 to update the history.

52. J. B. Jackson, "The Vernacular City," in *Center,* vol. 1 (Austin: University of Texas at Austin, Rizzoli Press, 1985), p. 25.

53. Graves, op. cit., chapter on South Plains agriculture.

54. NSV, Query XV, Colleges, Buildings, and Roads, p. 154.

55. NSV-2, Letter to Madison from Paris, 20 September 1785, p. 390.

56. Henry-Russell Hitchcock and William A. Seale, *Temples of Democracy* (New York: Harcourt Brace Jovanovich, 1976).

A Philosophical Problem to Be Solved

Mortimer J. Adler

Mortimer J. Adler received his Ph.D. from Columbia University in New York and taught at the University of Chicago for many years. Editor of *The Great Ideas Today,* he is also chairman of the Board of Editors of Encyclopædia Britannica, Inc., and editor in chief of the 1990 edition of *Great Books of the Western World.*

Dr. Adler is the director of the Institute for Philosophical Research, which was founded in 1952 for the study of ideas of Western thought. He is also an honorary trustee of the Aspen Institute for Humanistic Studies, where he teaches each summer.

The author of more than forty-five books, Dr. Adler has most recently completed *The Four Dimensions of Philosophy,* to be published in 1993. *A Second Look in the Rearview Mirror,* the sequel to his autobiography *Philosopher at Large* (1977), was published last year.

This short essay poses a philosophical problem that confronts us as recently as this century, in fact in the last half of this century. No author of great books in preceding centuries appears to have recognized it, although it arises in the context of views propounded in the fourth century B.C. by Aristotle and in the thirteenth century by Aquinas.

Let me begin my elucidation of the problem by stating the Aristotelian and Thomistic doctrine concerning the intellect. It asserts that the human intellect is an immaterial power of the human soul, in contrast to all the powers of sense, imagination, and memory that are embodied in the sensitive organs, together with the human brain.

Thus, for example, the eye and brain are the organs of vision. We see with them, and one cannot see without them. The action of these organs constitutes vision. But when we think intellectually, while we cannot think without action on the part of our brains, *we do not think with them*. The action of the brain may be a necessary, but it is not a sufficient cause of our intellectual performance. Thought involves the action of an immaterial power, the intellect, although this cannot operate by itself.*

That is the Aristotelian and Thomistic view of the matter. Of course, for materialists and all those who are optimistic about artificial intelligence machines, there is only an analytic distinction, not an existential one, between mind and brain. Materialists hold that every aspect of human thinking at the highest intellectual levels is explained by neurophysiological research—if not yet, then in the future. Eventually, if not now, knowledge of the brain's structure and its electrochemical action will be able to account for such activity.

Yet those who think that all human thought will ultimately be explained in purely physical terms must face a puzzle that has emerged only as recently as the last hundred years.

It is generally recognized that human beings differ in the degree of their power to think conceptually and intellectually. Einstein, as a theoretical physicist, had that power to a much higher degree than

---

*For a twentieth-century statement of this doctrine, *see* my book *Intellect: Mind Over Matter* (New York: Macmillan, 1990), especially chapters 4 and 5 where, I think, a conclusive argument for the immateriality of the intellect is advanced and where the failure of artificial intelligence to produce intellectual thinking is explained.

most human beings do. What is true of Einstein is true of other great mathematicians and theoretical physicists. But when, after Einstein's death, his brain was taken out of his head and examined, it was found to be no more in its gross weight than, and also no different in structure from, the brains of ordinary human beings. Comparisons of the brains of other so-called intellectual geniuses have shown the same lack of physical distinction. Hence the antimaterialist is justified in thinking that brains alone cannot account for high intellectual performance.

Even if the activity of the brain is necessary for such performance, some added cause must be posited to account for it; and according to Aristotle and Aquinas that must be an immaterial power of the human soul—the intellect.

This power, which is present in all human beings, must be greater in some human beings than in others. While all human beings are by nature equal—none being more or less human than another, all having the same species-specific powers—some have much more intellectual power than others. How is this possible?

Genetic research has discovered that high degrees of intellectuality run in families.* Gifted children are recognized in their early years; mathematical genius in particular, which reveals itself in the very young, suggests hereditary factors, a transmission by genes.

But the genes are material causes and, as such, can act to produce only material effects. If there is hereditary genius in the intellectual sphere, the genes cannot account for it, *if* intellectual power is immaterial. By the same token, if gifted children are genetically determined, their genetically determined endowment cannot be a superior degree of a purely immaterial power, the intellect. It does not even appear, as we have seen, that they have superior brains.

Aquinas sought for an explanation of the fact that some individuals can think intellectually better than others. In the first part of the *Summa Theologica*, in Article 7 of Question 85 (*GBWW* I: 19, 459–60; II: 17, 459–60), he explicitly asked whether one person can understand the same thing better than another person can. He answered this question affirmatively by saying that some men have bodies of better disposition, and their souls have, as a result, a greater power of understanding— that is, a higher degree of intellectual power. We see, he went on, that "those who have delicate flesh are of apt mind." This occurs in the powers of which the intellect has need in its operation. Those in which the sensitive, imaginative, and remembering powers are better disposed are also better disposed to understand.

In saying this, Aquinas did not think he was abandoning his view that, unlike the senses and the imagination, the intellect is an immate-

---

*See *Hereditary Genius* (London: Macmillan, 1869; reprinted in 1914) by Sir Francis Galton, who was a contemporary of Charles Darwin and shared his view concerning artificial breeding in domestic animals.

rial power of the human soul. Even though its operation may depend on such bodily powers as those of the senses and the imagination, such dependence is quite consistent with the thesis that the intellect is immaterial and cannot be reduced to the action of the brain. The brain is not the material organ of intellectual thought, as eye and brain are the physical organs of vision. There *is* no organ of intellectual thought, nor as far as we know can such thoughts be accounted for in purely physical terms.

I can now state the problem to which at present we have no solution. *What is the cause of superior intellectual power?* If the intellect is immaterial power, that superiority cannot be genetically caused. If superior intellectual gifts are found in very young children, their ability cannot be caused by special nurturing and training—that is, by human effort. If only an immaterial cause can produce an immaterial effect, an immaterial being such as God must be the cause of the intellectual superiority of a relatively few human beings. But that does not explain how the difference comes about in the natural order of things, where it appears to lie—where its transmittal is hereditary.

The question to be answered is, *what is transmitted when we speak of superior intellectual ability?* Is this a faculty that certain people have and others do not, or is it simply a greater degree of some power that all persons share? If we believe the first, what is it that we think we have identified? It was said of Richard Feynman, the most brilliant physicist of his time, that no one could understand how he arrived at his most startling insights, that the process was beyond comprehension even by the most capable minds. Hence the characterization of him as a genius, as being ultimately mysterious, inexplicable in his ability. The challenge we offer here is to solve that mystery, to explain that capacity as being either radically distinct, implying an ultimately different species, or simply a potential that every human being has, though only a few of us ever realize it.

Readers of *The Great Ideas Today* are invited to come up with a solution, a convincing explanation of this puzzle. We will print the response of the reader whose proposal best reveals an understanding of the relevant considerations set forth in our statement of the problem. In addition, this individual will be rewarded with the gift of a set of the second edition of *Great Books of the Western World*. Responses should be mailed to *The Great Ideas Today*, 101 East Ontario Street, Suite 300, Chicago, Illinois 60611. Entries, which should be typed, should be no longer than ten double-spaced pages and must be received by January 15, 1994. In the event that no entry is serious enough to deserve the prize, none will be printed, nor will the prize be awarded. The editors' decision is final. Employees of Encyclopædia Britannica, Inc., are not eligible.

PART FOUR

Additions to the Great Books Library

Bentham

John Stuart Mill

Editor's Introduction

Jeremy Bentham (1748–1832), who is the subject of the following essay by John Stuart Mill (for an account of whose life readers may consult *GBWW* I: 43; II: 40), is remembered as both a critic of legal institutions and a propounder of them; as an influential writer on economics; and above all as the chief exponent of the philosophy or system of belief known as Utilitarianism. This, as the term implies, holds the value of everything that concerns human beings to consist in its utility. But by utility Bentham meant, as he said, "that property in any object whereby it tends to produce pleasure, good or happiness, or to prevent the happening of mischief, pain, evil or unhappiness to the party whose interest is considered." Assuming as he did that all men wish to maximize their pleasure (which he took to be the same as their happiness) and minimize their pain, he held that the proper aim of human laws everywhere was "the greatest happiness of the greatest number," and as he believed that every rational man knows as a matter of course what his happiness is, or may be, Bentham thought it sufficient to provide him with statutes and institutions that would achieve it. Thus, much of his life was spent in devising legislation and even whole constitutions that were designed to this end—constitutions for, among others, the emergent South American republics, which gained their freedom in his day, and whose leaders consulted him as an authority on the drafting of new laws.

Bentham came to these ideas through his study of law at Oxford, in particular Blackstone's *Commentaries* (*GIT* 1989, 286–315), which he found defective in their acceptance of the legal system by which Englishmen were governed—in what he characterized as their "antipathy to reform." His first book, *A Fragment on Government* (1776), set forth his views on this subject. He addressed himself to it again, more generally, in *An Introduction to the Principles of Morals and Legislation* (1789). By then he had become famous, and his advice was sought by men in other countries besides his own on the codification of laws; in 1792 he was made a French citizen. His efforts as a lawmaker were not in the end very successful, however, being often absurdly detailed or otherwise impractical, and eventually he became contented with theoretical statements, many of them written for the *Westminster Review,* an influential periodical he founded in 1823. Among the reforms he recommended for Great Britain, which were regarded as far too radical in that day—which indeed have not all been instituted since—were annual elections, equal electoral districts, wide suffrage, and the secret ballot.

Mill (1806–73), whose father, James Mill, was Bentham's fervent disciple, may be said to have grown up on Utilitarianism, which was the directive of the famous (or infamous) education his father gave him (*see* the chapters from his *Autobiography* in *GGB* 6, 5–47, where he describes the mental breakdown to which this led). The younger Mill could hardly have been other than a Utilitarian in turn, as in fact he always was. He too regarded himself as a philosophical radical. "From the winter of 1821," he wrote, "when I first read Bentham, and especially from the commencement of the *Westminster Review,* I had truly what might be called an object in life; to be a reformer of the world. My conception of my own happiness was entirely identified with this object."

It was clear, however, or it became clear over time, that he accepted Bentham's doctrine only with grave reservation, the gist of which is set forth in the following essay. To expand somewhat on that, it may be said that Mill could not accept Bentham's belief that all men everywhere would have the same desires, that the same code of law would do for them all, and that nothing more was required than to show them what as rational beings they would recognize they needed. This might have been the case, Mill thought, at certain times in the past, when society had been stable and those without education had been content to accept the authority of others who had it. But it was not so in Bentham's time, or his. Society was then in transition, he believed, between one set of laws and institutions and another. In such an age, though the demand for reform might be loud, there was no way to realize it because men were not prepared to hear—because the noise of their own factionalism drowned out—the words that the wisest among them were saying. Mill thought this state of affairs reflected something more than a mere change of conditions. He thought conditions had moral and psychological consequences which made it impossible for men to accept reforms unless they were conceived in terms that met the sense they had of their particular needs, that were appropriate to the times in which they actually lived. Bentham was too abstract in his aims, Mill believed—ironically enough, since Bentham was nothing if not scornful of abstractions and held always that facts alone are necessary to the philosopher. Mill's own effort was to find the right terms of reform for his own age, and the right language in which to state them. It is a further irony that his words, or some of them, seem permanent to us, while Bentham's, taking permanence for granted, are for the most part only relics of the man and his time.

Bentham

There are two men, recently deceased, to whom their country is indebted not only for the greater part of the important ideas which have been thrown into circulation among its thinking men in their time, but for a revolution in its general modes of thought and investigation. These men, dissimilar in almost all else, agreed in being closet-students—secluded in a peculiar degree, by circumstances and character, from the business and intercourse of the world: and both were, through a large portion of their lives, regarded by those who took the lead in opinion (when they happened to hear of them) with feelings akin to contempt. But they were destined to renew a lesson given to mankind by every age, and always disregarded—to show that speculative philosophy, which to the superficial appears a thing so remote from the business of life and the outward interests of men, is in reality the thing on earth which most influences them, and in the long run overbears every other influence save those which it must itself obey. The writers of whom we speak have never been read by the multitude; except for the more slight of their works, their readers have been few: but they have been the teachers of the teachers; there is hardly to be found in England an individual of any importance in the world of mind, who (whatever opinions he may have afterward adopted) did not first learn to think from one of these two; and though their influences have but begun to diffuse themselves through these intermediate channels over society at large, there is already scarcely a publication of any consequence addressed to the educated classes, which, if these persons had not existed, would not have been different from what it is. These men are Jeremy Bentham and Samuel Taylor Coleridge—the two great seminal minds of England in their age.

No comparison is intended here between the minds or influences of these remarkable men: this were impossible unless there were first formed a complete judgment of each, considered apart. It is our intention to attempt, on the present occasion, an estimate of one of them; the only one, a complete edition of whose works is yet in progress, and who, in the classification which may be made of all writers into Progressive and Conservative, belongs to the same division with ourselves. For although they were far too great men to be correctly designated by either appellation exclusively, yet in the main, Bentham was a Progressive philosopher, Coleridge a Conservative one. The influence of the former has made itself felt chiefly on minds of the Progressive class; of the latter on those of the Conservative: and the two systems of concentric circles which the shock given by them is spreading over the ocean of mind have only just begun to meet and intersect. The writings of both contain severe lessons to their own side, on many of the errors and faults they are addicted to: but to Bentham it was given to discern more particularly those truths with which existing doctrines and institutions were at variance; to Coleridge, the neglected truths which lay *in* them.

A man of great knowledge of the world, and of the highest reputation for practical talent and sagacity among the official men of his time (himself no follower of Ben-

337

tham, nor of any partial or exclusive school whatever) once said to us, as the result of his observation, that to Bentham more than to any other source might be traced the questioning spirit, the disposition to demand the *why* of everything, which had gained so much ground and was producing such important consequences in these times. The more this assertion is examined, the more true it will be found. Bentham has been in this age and country the great questioner of things established. It is by the influence of the modes of thought with which his writings inoculated a considerable number of thinking men, that the yoke of authority has been broken, and innumerable opinions, formerly received on tradition as incontestable, are put upon their defense and required to give an account of themselves. Who, before Bentham (whatever controversies might exist on points of detail), dared to speak disrespectfully, in express terms, of the British Constitution, or the English Law? He did so; and his arguments and his example together encouraged others. We do not mean that his writings caused the Reform Bill, or that the Appropriation Clause owns him as its parent: the changes which have been made, and the greater changes which will be made, in our institutions, are not the work of philosophers, but of the interests and instincts of large portions of society recently grown into strength. But Bentham gave voice to those interests and instincts: until he spoke out, those who found our institutions unsuited to them did not dare to say so, did not dare consciously to think so; they had never heard the excellence of those institutions questioned by cultivated men, by men of acknowledged intellect; and it is not in the nature of uninstructed minds to resist the united authority of the instructed. Bentham broke the spell. It was not Bentham by his own writings; it was Bentham through the minds and pens which those writings fed—through the men in more direct contact with the world, into whom his spirit passed. If the superstition about

ancestorial wisdom has fallen into decay; if the public are grown familiar with the idea that their laws and institutions are in great part not the product of intellect and virtue, but of modern corruption grafted upon ancient barbarism; if the hardiest innovation is no longer scouted because it is an innovation—establishments no longer considered sacred because they are establishments—it will be found that those who have accustomed the public mind to these ideas have learned them from Bentham's school, and that the assault on ancient institutions has been, and is, carried on for the most part with his weapons. It matters not although these thinkers, or indeed thinkers of any descriptions, have been but scantily found among the persons prominently and ostensibly at the head of the Reform movement. All movements, except directly revolutionary ones, are headed, not by those who originate them, but by those who know best how to compromise between the old opinions and the new. The father of English innovation, both in doctrines and in institutions, is Bentham: he is the great *subversive*, or, in the language of continental philosophers, the great *critical* thinker of his age and country.

We consider this, however, to be not his highest title to fame. Were this all, he were only to be ranked among the lowest order of the potentates of mind—the negative, or destructive philosophers; those who can perceive what is false, but not what is true; who awaken the human mind to the inconsistencies and absurdities of time-sanctioned opinions and institutions but substitute nothing in the place of what they take away. We have no desire to undervalue the services of such persons: mankind has been deeply indebted to them; nor will there ever be a lack of work for them, in a world in which so many false things are believed, in which so many which have been true are believed long after they have ceased to be true. The qualities, however, which fit men for perceiving anomalies, without perceiving the truths which would

Jeremy Bentham

rectify them, are not among the rarest of endowments. Courage, verbal acuteness, command over the forms of argumentation, and a popular style will make, out of the shallowest man, with a sufficient lack of reverence, a considerable negative philosopher. Such men have never been wanting in periods of culture; and the period in which Bentham formed his early impressions was emphatically their reign, in proportion to its barrenness in the more noble products of the human mind. An age of formalism in the Church and corruption in the State, when the most valuable part of the meaning of traditional doctrines had faded from the minds even of those who retained from habit a mechanical belief in them, was the time to raise up all kinds of skeptical philosophy. Accordingly, France had Voltaire, and his school of negative thinkers, and England (or rather Scotland) had the profoundest negative thinker on record, David Hume: a man, the peculiarities of whose mind qualified him to detect failure of proof, and want of logical consistency, at a depth which French skeptics, with their comparatively feeble powers of analysis and abstraction, *stopped* far short of, and which German subtlety alone could thoroughly appreciate or hope to rival.

If Bentham had merely continued the work of Hume, he would scarcely have been heard of in philosophy; for he was far inferior to Hume in Hume's qualities and was in no respect fitted to excel as a metaphysician. We must not look for subtlety, or the power of recondite analysis, among his intellectual characteristics. In the former quality, few great thinkers have ever been so deficient; and to find the latter, in any considerable measure, in a mind acknowledging any kindred with his, we must have recourse to the late Mr. Mill— a man who united the great qualities of the metaphysicians of the eighteenth century with others of a different complexion, admirably qualifying him to complete and correct their work. Bentham had not these peculiar gifts; but he possessed others, not inferior, which were not possessed by any of his precursors; which have made him a source of light to a generation which has far outgrown their influence, and, as we called him, the chief subversive thinker of an age which has long lost all that they could subvert.

To speak of him first as a merely negative philosopher—as one who refutes illogical arguments, exposes sophistry, detects contradiction and absurdity; even in that capacity there was a wide field left vacant for him by Hume, and which he has occupied to an unprecedented extent; the field of practical abuses. This was Bentham's peculiar province: to this he was called by the whole bent of his disposition: to carry the warfare against absurdity into things practical. His was an essentially practical mind. It was by practical abuses that his mind was first turned to speculation—by the abuses of the profession which was chosen for him, that of the law. He has himself stated what particular abuse first gave that shock to his mind, the recoil of which has made the whole mountain of abuse totter; it was the custom of making the client pay for three attendances in the office of a Master in Chancery, when only one was given. The law, he found on examination, was full of such things. But were these discoveries of his? No; they were known to every lawyer who practiced, to every judge who sat on the bench, and neither before nor for long after did they cause any apparent uneasiness to the consciences of these learned persons, nor hinder them from asserting, whenever occasion offered, in books, in parliament, or on the bench, that the law was the perfection of reason. During so many generations, in each of which thousands of educated young men were successively placed in Bentham's position and with Bentham's opportunities, he

alone was found with sufficient moral sensibility and self-reliance to say to himself that these things, however profitable they might be, were frauds and that between them and himself there should be a gulf fixed. To this rare union of self-reliance and moral sensibility we are indebted for all that Bentham has done. Sent to Oxford by his father at the unusually early age of fifteen—required, on admission, to declare his belief in the Thirty-nine Articles—he felt it necessary to examine them; and the examination suggested scruples, which he sought to get removed but, instead of the satisfaction he expected, was told that it was not for boys like him to step up their judgment against the great men of the Church. After a struggle, he signed; but the impression that he had done an immoral act never left him; he considered himself to have committed a falsehood, and throughout life he never relaxed in his indignant denunciations of all laws which command such falsehoods, all institutions which attach rewards to them.

By thus carrying the war of criticism and refutation, the conflict with falsehood and absurdity, into the field of practical evils, Bentham, even if he had done nothing else, would have earned an important place in the history of intellect. He carried on the warfare without intermission. To this, not only many of his most piquant chapters, but some of the most finished of his entire works, are entirely devoted: the *Defence of Usury;* the *Book of Fallacies;* and the onslaught upon Blackstone, published anonymously under the title of *A Fragment on Government,* which, though a first production, and of a writer afterward so much ridiculed for his style, excited the highest admiration no less for its composition than for its thoughts and was attributed by turns to Lord Mansfield, to Lord Camden, and (by Dr. Johnson) to Dunning, one of the greatest masters of style among the lawyers of his day. These writings are altogether original; though of the negative school, they resemble nothing previously produced by negative philosophers; and would have sufficed to create for Bentham, among the subversive thinkers of modern Europe, a place peculiarly his own. But it is not these writings that constitute the real distinction between him and them. There was a deeper difference. It was that they were purely negative thinkers, he was positive; they only assailed error, he made it a point of conscience not to do so until he thought he could plant instead the corresponding truth. Their character was exclusively analytic, his was synthetic. They took for their starting point the received opinion on any subject, dug round it with their logical implements, pronounced its foundations defective, and condemned it: he began *de novo*, laid his own foundations deeply and firmly, built up his own structure, and bade mankind compare the two; it was when he had solved the problem himself, or thought he had done so, that he declared all other solutions to be erroneous. Hence, what they produced will not last; it must perish, much of it has already perished, with the errors which it exploded: what he did has its own value, by which it must outlast all errors to which it is opposed. Though we may reject, as we often must, his practical conclusions, yet his premises, the collections of facts and observations from which his conclusions were drawn, remain forever, a part of the materials of philosophy.

A place, therefore, must be assigned to Bentham among the masters of wisdom, the great teachers and permanent intellectual ornaments of the human race. He is among those who have enriched mankind with imperishable gifts; and although these do not transcend all other gifts, nor entitle him to those honours "above all Greek, above all Roman fame," which, by a natural reaction against the neglect and contempt of the ignorant, many of his admirers were once disposed to accumulate upon him, yet to refuse an admiring recognition of what he was, on account of what he was not, is a much worse error, and one which, pardon-able in the vulgar, is no longer permitted to any cultivated and instructed mind.

If we were asked to say, in the fewest possible words, what we conceive to be Bentham's place among these great intellectual benefactors of humanity; what he was, and what he was not; what kind of service he did and did not render to truth; we should say—he was not a great philosopher, but he was a great reformer in philosophy. He brought into philosophy something which it greatly needed, and for want of which it was at a stand. It was not his doctrines which did this, it was his mode of arriving at them. He introduced into morals and politics those habits of thought and modes of investigation which are essential to the idea of science; and the absence of which made those departments of inquiry, as physics had been before Bacon, a field of interminable discussion, leading to no result. It was not his opinions, in short, but his method that constituted the novelty and the value of what he did; a value beyond all price, even though we should reject the whole, as we unquestionably must a large part, of the opinions themselves.

Bentham's method may be shortly described as the method of detail; of treating wholes by separating them into their parts, abstractions by resolving them into Things, classes and generalities by distinguishing them into the individuals of which they are made up; and breaking every question into pieces before attempting to solve it. The precise amount of originality of this process, considered as a logical conception—its degree of connection with the methods of physical science, or with the previous labours of Bacon, Hobbes, or Locke—is not an essential consideration in this place. Whatever originality there was in the method—in the subjects he applied it to, and in the rigidity with which he adhered to it, there was the greatest. Hence his interminable classifications. Hence his elaborate demonstrations of the most acknowledged truths. That murder, incendiarism, robbery, are mischievous actions, he will not take for granted without proof; let the thing appear ever so self-evident, he will know the why and the how of it with the last degree of precision; he will distinguish all the different mischiefs of a crime, whether of the *first*, the *second,* or the *third* order, namely, 1. the evil to the sufferer, and to his personal connections; 2. the *danger* from example, and the *alarm* or painful feeling of insecurity; and 3. the discouragement to industry and useful pursuits arising from the *alarm,* and the trouble and resources which must be expended in warding off the *danger.* After this enumeration, he will prove from the laws of human feeling that even the first of these evils, the sufferings of the immediate victim, will on the average greatly outweigh the pleasure reaped by the offender; much more when all the other evils are taken into account. Unless this could be proved, he would account the infliction of punishment unwarrantable; and for taking the trouble to prove it formally, his defense is, "there are truths which it is necessary to prove, not for their own sakes, because they are acknowledged, but that an opening may be made for the reception of other truths which depend upon them. It is in this manner we provide for the reception of first principles, which, once received, prepare the way for admission of all other truths." To which may be added, that in this manner also we discipline the mind for practicing the same sort of dissection upon questions more complicated and of more doubtful issue.

It is a sound maxim, and one which all close thinkers have felt, but which no one before Bentham ever so consistently applied, that error lurks in generalities: that the human mind is not capable of embracing a complex whole, until it has surveyed and catalogued the parts of which that whole is made up; that abstractions are not realities *per se,* but an abridged mode of expressing facts, and that the only practical mode of dealing with them is to trace them back to the facts (whether of experi-

ence or of consciousness) of which they are the expression. Proceeding on this principle, Bentham makes short work with the ordinary modes of moral and political reasoning. These, it appeared to him, when hunted to their source, for the most part terminated in *phrases.* In politics, liberty, social order, constitution, law of nature, social compact, etc., were the catchwords: ethics had its analogous ones. Such were the arguments on which the gravest questions of morality and policy were made to turn; not reasons, but allusions to reasons; sacramental expressions, by which a summary appeal was made to some general sentiment of mankind, or to some maxim in familiar use, which might be true or not, but the limitations of which no one had ever critically examined. And this satisfied other people; but not Bentham. He required something more than opinion as a reason for opinion. Whenever he found a *phrase* used as an argument for or against anything, he insisted upon knowing what it meant; whether it appealed to any standard, or gave intimation of any matter of fact relevant to the question; and if he could not find that it did either, he treated it as an attempt on the part of the disputant to impose his own individual sentiment on other people, without giving them a reason for it; a "contrivance for avoiding the obligation of appealing to any external standard, and for prevailing upon the reader to accept of the author's sentiment and opinion as a reason, and that a sufficient one, for itself." Bentham shall speak for himself on this subject: the passage is from his first systematic work, *Introduction to the Principles of Morals and Legislation,* and we could scarcely quote anything more strongly exemplifying both the strength and weakness of his mode of philosophizing.

It is curious enough to observe the variety of inventions men have hit upon, and the variety of phrases they have brought forward, in order to conceal from the world, and, if pos-

sible, from themselves, this very general and therefore very pardonable self-sufficiency.

1. One man says, he has a thing made on purpose to tell him what is right and what is wrong; and that it is called a "moral sense": and then he goes to work at his ease, and says, such a thing is right, and such a thing is wrong—why? "Because my moral sense tells me it is."

2. Another man comes and alters the phrase: leaving out moral, and putting in common in the room of it. He then tells you that his common sense tells him what is right and wrong, as surely as the other's moral sense did: meaning by common sense a sense of some kind or other, which, he says, is possessed by all mankind: the sense of those whose sense is not the same as the author's being struck out as not worth taking. This contrivance does better than the other; for a moral sense being a new thing, a man may feel about him a good while without being able to find it out: but common sense is as old as the creation; and there is no man but would be ashamed to be thought not to have as much of it as his neighbours. It has another great advantage: by appearing to share power, it lessens envy; for when a man gets up upon this ground, in order to anathematise those who differ from him, it is not by a sic volo sic jubeo [I want it, I command it], but by a velitis jubeatis [you want it, you must command it].

3. Another man comes, and says, that as to a moral sense indeed, he cannot find that he has any such thing: that, however, he has an understanding, which will do quite as well. This understanding, he says, is the standard of right and wrong: it tells him so and so. All good and wise men understand as he does: if other men's understandings differ in any part from his so much the worse for them: it is a sure sign they are either defective or corrupt.

4. Another man says, that there is an eternal and immutable Rule of Right: that that rule of right dictates so and so: and then he begins giving you his sentiments upon anything that comes uppermost: and these sentiments (you are to take for granted) are so many branches of the eternal rule of right.

5. Another man, or perhaps the same man (it is no matter), says that there are certain practices conformable, and others repugnant, to the Fitness of Things; and then he tells you, at his leisure, what practices are conformable, and what repugnant: just as he happens to like a practice or dislike it.

6. A great multitude of people are continually talking of the Law of Nature; and then they go on giving you their sentiments about what is right and what is wrong: and these sentiments, you are to understand, are so many chapters and sections of the Law of Nature.

7. Instead of the phrase, Law of Nature, you have sometimes Law of Reason, Right Reason, Natural Justice, Natural Equity, Good Order. Any of them will do equally well. This latter is most used in politics. The three last are much more tolerable than the others, because they do not very explicitly claim to be anything more than phrases: they insist but feebly upon the being looked upon as so many positive standards of themselves, and seem content to be taken, upon occasion, for phrases expressive of the conformity of the thing in question to the proper standard, whatever that may be. On most occasions, however, it will be better to say utility: utility is clearer, as referring more explicitly to pain and pleasure.

8. We have one philosopher, who says, there is no harm in anything in the world but in telling a lie; and that if, for example, you were to murder your own father, this would only be a particular way of saying, he was not your father. Of course when this philosopher sees anything that he does not like, he says it is a particular way of telling a lie. It is saying, that the act ought to be done, or may be done, when, in truth, it ought not to be done.

9. The fairest and openest of them all is that sort of man who speaks out, and says, I am of the number of the Elect: now God himself takes care to inform the Elect what is right: and that with so good effect, and let them strive ever so, they cannot help not only knowing it but practising it. If therefore a man wants to know what is right and what is wrong, he has nothing to do but to come to me.

Few will contend that this is a perfectly fair representation of the *animus* of those who employ the various phrases so amusingly animadverted on; but that the phrases contain no argument, save what is grounded on the very feelings they are adduced to justify, is a truth which Bentham had the eminent merit of first pointing out.

It is the introduction into the philosophy of human conduct, of this method of detail—of this practice of never reasoning about wholes until they have been resolved into their parts, nor about abstractions until they have been translated into realities— that constitutes the originality of Bentham in philosophy and makes him the great reformer of the moral and political branch of it. To what he terms the "exhaustive method of classification," which is but one branch of this more general method, he himself ascribes everything original in the systematic and elaborate work from which we have quoted. The generalities of his philosophy itself have little or no novelty: to ascribe any to the doctrine that general utility is the foundation of morality would imply great ignorance of the history of philosophy, of general literature, and of Bentham's own writings. He derived the idea, as he says himself, from Helvetius; and it was the doctrine no less of the religious philosophers of that age, prior to Reid and Beattie. We never saw an abler defense of the doctrine of utility than in a book written in refutation of Shaftesbury, and now little read—Brown's *Essays on the Characteristics;* and in Johnson's celebrated review of Soame Jenyns, the same doctrine is set forth as that both of the author and the reviewer. In all ages of philosophy one of its schools has been utilitarian—not only from the time of Epicurus, but long before. It was by mere accident that this opinion became connected in Bentham with his peculiar method. The utilitarian philosophers antecedent to him had no more claims to the method than their antagonists. To refer, for instance, to the Epicurean philosophy, according to the most complete view

we have of the moral part of it, by the most accomplished scholar of antiquity, Cicero, we ask anyone who has read his philosophical writings, the *De finibus* for instance, where the arguments of the Epicureans do not, just as much as those of the Stoics or Platonists, consist of mere rhetorical appeals to common notions, to εἰκότα and σημεῖα [probabilities and signs] instead of τεκμήρια [proofs], notions picked up as it were casually, and when true at all, never so narrowly looked into as to ascertain in what sense and under what limitations they are true. The application of a real inductive philosophy to the problems of ethics is as unknown to the Epicurean moralists as to any of the other schools; they never take a question to pieces and join issue on a definite point. Bentham certainly did not learn his sifting and anatomizing method from them.

This method Bentham has finally installed in philosophy; has made it henceforth imperative on philosophers of all schools. By it he has formed the intellects of many thinkers, who either never adopted, or have abandoned, many of his peculiar opinions. He has taught the method to men of the most opposite schools to his; he has made them perceive that if they do not test their doctrines by the method of detail, their adversaries will. He has thus, it is not too much to say, for the first time introduced precision of thought into moral and political philosophy. Instead of taking up their opinions by intuition, or by ratiocination from premises adopted on a mere rough view, and couched in language so vague that it is impossible to say exactly whether they are true or false, philosophers are now forced to understand one another, to break down the generality of their propositions, and join a precise issue in every dispute. This is nothing less than a revolution in philosophy. Its effect is gradually becoming evident in the writings of English thinkers of every variety of opinion and will be felt more and more in proportion as Bentham's writings are diffused, and as the number of minds to whose formation they contribute is multiplied.

It will naturally be presumed that of the fruits of this great philosophical improvement some portion at least will have been reaped by its author. Armed with such a potent instrument, and wielding it with such singleness of aim; cultivating the field of practical philosophy with such unwearied and such consistent use of a method right in itself, and not adopted by his predecessors; it cannot be but that Bentham by his own inquiries must have accomplished something considerable. And so, it will be found, he has; something not only considerable, but extraordinary; though but little compared with what he has left undone, and far short of what his sanguine and almost boyish fancy made him flatter himself that he had accomplished. His peculiar method, admirably calculated to make clear thinkers, and sure ones to the extent of their materials, has not equal efficacy for making those materials complete. It is a security for accuracy, but not for comprehensiveness; or rather, it is a security for one sort of comprehensiveness, but not for another.

Bentham's method of laying out his subject is admirable as a preservative against one kind of narrow and partial views. He begins by placing before himself the whole of the field of inquiry to which the particular question belongs, and divides down until he arrives at the thing he is in search of; and thus by successively rejecting all which is not the thing, he gradually works out a definition of what it is. This, which he calls the exhaustive method, is as old as philosophy itself. Plato owes everything to it and does everything by it; and the use made of it by that great man in his Dialogues, Bacon, in one of those pregnant logical hints scattered through his writings, and so much neglected by most of his pretended followers, pronounces to be the nearest approach to a true inductive method in the ancient philosophy. Bentham was probably not aware that Plato had anticipated him

in the process to which he too declared that he owed everything. By the practice of it, his speculations are rendered eminently systematic and consistent; no question, with him, is ever an insulated one; he sees every subject in connection with all the other subjects with which in his view it is related, and from which it requires to be distinguished; and as all that he knows, in the least degree allied to the subject, has been marshaled in an orderly manner before him, he does not, like people who use a looser method, forget and overlook a thing on one occasion to remember it on another. Hence there is probably no philosopher of so wide a range in whom there are so few inconsistencies. If any of the truths which he did not see had come to be seen by him, he would have remembered it everywhere and at all times and would have adjusted his whole system to it. And this is another admirable quality which he has impressed upon the best of the minds trained in his habits of thought: when those minds open to admit new truths, they digest them as fast as they receive them.

But this system, excellent for keeping before the mind of the thinker all that he knows, does not make him know enough; it does not make a knowledge of some of the properties of a thing suffice for the whole of it, nor render a rooted habit of surveying a complex object (though ever so carefully) in only one of its aspects tantamount to the power of contemplating it in all. To give this last power, other qualities are required: whether Bentham possessed those other qualities we now have to see.

Bentham's mind, as we have already said, was eminently synthetical. He begins all his inquiries by supposing nothing to be known on the subject, and reconstructs all philosophy *ab initio*, without reference to the opinions of his predecessors. But to build either a philosophy or anything else, there must be materials. For the philosophy of matter, the materials are the properties of matter; for moral and political philosophy, the properties of man, and of man's position in the world. The knowledge which any inquirer possesses of these properties constitutes a limit beyond which, as a moralist or a political philosopher, whatever be his powers of mind, he cannot reach. Nobody's synthesis can be more complete than his analysis. If in his survey of human nature and life he has left any element out, then, wheresoever that element exerts any influence, his conclusions will fail, more or less, in their application. If he has left out many elements, and those very important, his labours may be highly valuable; he may have largely contributed to that body of partial truths which, when completed and corrected by one another, constitute practical truth; but the applicability of his system to practice in its own proper shape will be of an exceedingly limited range.

Human nature and human life are wide subjects, and whoever would embark in an enterprise requiring a thorough knowledge of them has need both of large stores of his own, and of all aids and appliances from elsewhere. His qualifications for success will be proportional to two things: the degree in which his own nature and circumstances furnish him with a correct and complete picture of man's nature and circumstances; and his capacity of deriving light from other minds.

Bentham failed in deriving light from other minds. His writings contain few traces of the accurate knowledge of any schools of thinking but his own; and many proofs of his entire conviction that they could teach him nothing worth knowing. For some of the most illustrious of previous thinkers, his contempt was unmeasured. In almost the only passage of the *Deontology* which, from its style, and from its having before appeared in print, may be known to be Bentham's, Socrates and Plato are spoken of in terms distressing to his greatest admirers; and the incapacity to appreciate such men is a fact perfectly in unison with the general habits of Bentham's mind. He

had a phrase, expressive of the view he took of all moral speculations to which his method had not been applied, or (which he considered as the same thing) not founded on a recognition of utility as the moral standard; this phrase was "vague generalities." Whatever presented itself to him in such a shape, he dismissed as unworthy of notice, or dwelt upon only to denounce as absurd. He did not heed, or rather the nature of his mind prevented it from occurring to him, that these generalities contained the whole unanalyzed experience of the human race.

Unless it can be asserted that mankind did not know anything until logicians taught it to them—that until the last hand has been put to a moral truth by giving it a metaphysically precise expression, all the previous rough-hewing which it has undergone by the common intellect at the suggestion of common wants and common experience is to go for nothing; it must be allowed that even the originality which can, and the courage which dares, think for itself is not a more necessary part of the philosophical character than a thoughtful regard for previous thinkers, and for the collective mind of the human race. What has been the opinion of mankind has been the opinion of persons of all tempers and dispositions, of all partialities and prepossessions, of all varieties in position, in education, in opportunities of observation and inquiry. No one inquirer is all this; every inquirer is either young or old, rich or poor, sickly or healthy, married or unmarried, meditative or active, a poet or a logician, an ancient or a modern, a man or a woman; and if a thinking person, has, in addition, the accidental peculiarities of his individual modes of thought. Every circumstance which gave a character to the life of a human being carries with it its peculiar biases; its peculiar facilities for perceiving some things, and for missing or forgetting others. But, from points of view different from his, different things are perceptible; and none are more likely to have seen what he does not see than those who do not see what he sees. The general opinion of mankind is the average of the conclusions of all minds, stripped indeed of their choicest and most recondite thoughts, but freed from their twists and partialities: a net result, in which everybody's particular point of view is represented, nobody's predominant. The collective mind does not penetrate below the surface, but it sees all the surface; which profound thinkers, even by reason of their profundity, often fail to do: their intenser view of a thing in some of its aspects diverting their attention from others.

The hardiest assertor, therefore, of the freedom of private judgment—the keenest detector of the errors of his predecessors, and of the inaccuracies of current modes of thought—is the very person who most needs to fortify the weak side of his own intellect, by study of the opinions of mankind in all ages and nations, and of the speculations of philosophers of the modes of thought most opposite to his own. It is there that he will find the experiences denied to himself—the remainder of the truth of which he sees but half—the truths, of which the errors he detects are commonly but the exaggerations. If, like Bentham, he brings with him an improved instrument of investigation, the greater is the probability that he will find ready prepared a rich abundance of rough ore, which was merely waiting for that instrument. A man of clear ideas errs grievously if he imagines that whatever is seen confusedly does not exist: it belongs to him, when he meets with such a thing, to dispel the mist, and fix the outlines of the vague form which is looming through it.

Bentham's contempt, then, of all other schools of thinkers; his determination to create a philosophy wholly out of the materials furnished by his own mind, and by minds like his own; was his first disqualification as a philosopher. His second was the incompleteness of his own mind as a representative of universal human nature.

In many of the most natural and strongest feelings of human nature he had no sympathy; from many of its graver experiences he was altogether cut off; and the faculty by which one mind understands a mind different from itself, and throws itself into the feelings of that other mind, was denied him by his deficiency of Imagination.

With Imagination in the popular sense, command of imagery and metaphorical expression, Bentham was, to a certain degree, endowed. For want, indeed, of poetical culture, the images with which his fancy supplied him were seldom beautiful, but they were quaint and humorous, or bold, forcible, and intense: passages might be quoted from him both of playful irony and of declamatory eloquence, seldom surpassed in the writings of philosophers. The Imagination which he had not was that to which the name is generally appropriated by the best writers of the present day; that which enables us, by a voluntary effort, to conceive the absent as if it were present, the imaginary as if it were real, and to clothe it in the feelings which, if it were indeed real, it would bring along with it. This is the power by which one human being enters into the mind and circumstances of another. This power constitutes the poet, insofar as he does anything but melodiously utter his own actual feelings. It constitutes the dramatist entirely. It is one of the constituents of the historian; by it we understand other times; by it Guizot interprets to us the middle ages; Nisard, in his beautiful Studies on the later Latin poets, places us in the Rome of the Caesars; Michelet disengages the distinctive characters of the different races and generations of mankind from the facts of their history. Without it nobody knows even his own nature, further than circumstances have actually tried it and called it out; nor the nature of his fellow creatures, beyond such generalizations as he may have been enabled to make from his observation of their outward conduct.

By these limits, accordingly, Bentham's

knowledge of human nature is bounded. It is wholly empirical; and the empiricism of one who has had little experience. He had neither internal experience nor external; the quiet, even tenor of his life, and his healthiness of mind, conspired to exclude him from both. He never knew prosperity and adversity, passion nor satiety: he never had even the experiences which sickness gives; he lived from childhood to the age of eighty-five in boyish health. He knew no dejection, no heaviness of heart. He never felt life a sore and a weary burthen. He was a boy to the last. Self-consciousness, that demon of the men of genius of our time, from Wordsworth to Byron, from Goethe to Chateaubriand, and to which this age owes so much both of its cheerful and its mournful wisdom, never was awakened in him. How much of human nature slumbered in him he knew not, neither can we know. He had never been made alive to the unseen influences which were acting on himself, nor consequently on his fellow creatures. Other ages and other nations were a blank to him for purposes of instruction. He measured them but by one standard; their knowledge of facts, and their capability to take correct views of utility and merge all other objects in it. His own lot was cast in a generation of the leanest and barrenest men whom England had yet produced, and he was an old man when a better race came in with the present century. He saw accordingly in man little but what the vulgarest eye can see; recognized no diversities of character but such as he who runs may read. Knowing so little of human feelings, he knew still less of the influences by which those feelings are formed: all the more subtle workings both of the mind upon itself, and of external things upon the mind, escaped him; and no one, probably, who, in a highly instructed age, ever attempted to give a rule to all human conduct, set out with a more limited conception either of the agencies by which human conduct *is,* or of those by which it *should* be, influenced.

This, then, is our idea of Bentham. He was a man both of remarkable endowments for philosophy, and of remarkable deficiencies for it: fitted, beyond almost any man, for drawing from his premises conclusions not only correct, but sufficiently precise and specific to be practical: but whose general conception of human nature and life furnished him with an unusually slender stock of premises. It is obvious what would be likely to be achieved by such a man; what a thinker, thus gifted and thus disqualified, could do in philosophy. He could, with close and accurate logic, hunt half-truths to their consequences and practical applications, on a scale both of greatness and of minuteness not previously exemplified; and this is the character which posterity will probably assign to Bentham.

We express our sincere and well-considered conviction when we say that there is hardly anything positive in Bentham's philosophy which is not true: that when his practical conclusions are erroneous, which in our opinion they are very often, it is not because the considerations which he urges are not rational and valid in themselves, but because some more important principle, which he did not perceive, supersedes those considerations and turns the scale. The bad part of his writings is his resolute denial of all that he does not see, of all truths but those which he recognizes. By that alone has he exercised any bad influence upon his age; by that he has, not created a school of deniers, for this is an ignorant prejudice, but put himself at the head of the school which exists always, though it does not always find a great man to give it the sanction of philosophy: thrown the mantle of intellect over the natural tendency of men in all ages to deny or disparage all feelings and mental states of which they have no consciousness in themselves.

The truths which are not Bentham's, which his philosophy takes no account of, are many and important; but his nonrecognition of them does not put them out of existence; they are still with us, and it is a comparatively easy task that is reserved for us, to harmonize those truths with his. To reject his half of the truth because he overlooked the other half, would be to fall into his error without having his excuse. For our own part, we have a large tolerance for one-eyed men, provided their one eye is a penetrating one: if they saw more, they probably would not see so keenly, nor so eagerly pursue one course of inquiry. Almost all rich veins of original and striking speculation have been opened by systematic half-thinkers: though whether these new thoughts drive out others as good, or are peacefully superadded to them, depends on whether these half-thinkers are or are not followed in the same track by complete thinkers. The field of man's nature and life cannot be too much worked, or in too many directions; until every clod is turned up the work is imperfect; no whole truth is possible but by combining the points of view of all the fractional truths, nor, therefore, until it has been fully seen what each fractional truth can do by itself.

What Bentham's fractional truths could do, there is no such good means of showing as by a review of his philosophy: and such a review, though inevitably a most brief and general one, it is now necessary to attempt.

The first question in regard to any man of speculation is, what is his theory of human life? In the minds of many philosophers, whatever theory they have of this sort is latent, and it would be a revelation to themselves to have it pointed out to them in their writings as others can see it, unconsciously molding everything to its own likeness. But Bentham always knew his own premises, and made his reader know them: it was not his custom to leave the theoretic grounds of his practical conclusions to conjecture. Few great thinkers have afforded the means of assigning with so much certainty the exact conception which they had formed of man and of man's life.

Man is conceived by Bentham as a being susceptible of pleasures and pains, and governed in all his conduct partly by the different modifications of self-interest, and the passions commonly classed as selfish, partly by sympathies, or occasionally antipathies, toward other beings. And here Bentham's conception of human nature stops. He does not exclude religion; the prospect of divine rewards and punishments he includes under the head of "self-regarding interest," and the devotional feeling under that of sympathy with God. But the whole of the impelling or restraining principles, whether of this or of another world, which he recognizes, are either self-love, or love or hatred toward other sentient beings. That there might be no doubt of what he thought on the subject, he has not left us to the general evidence of his writings, but has drawn out a "Table of the Springs of Action," an express enumeration and classification of human motives, with their various names, laudatory, vituperative, and neutral: and this table, to be found in Part I of his collected works, we recommend to the study of those who would understand his philosophy.

Man is never recognized by him as a being capable of pursuing spiritual perfection as an end; of desiring, for its own sake, the conformity of his own character to his standard of excellence, without hope of good or fear of evil from other source than his own inward consciousness. Even in the more limited form of Conscience, this great fact in human nature escapes him. Nothing is more curious than the absence of recognition in any of his writings of the existence of conscience, as a thing distinct from philanthropy, from affection for God or man, and from self-interest in this world or in the next. There is a studied abstinence from any of the phrases which, in the mouths of others, import the acknowledgment of such a fact. If we find the words "Conscience," "Principle," "Moral Rectitude," "Moral Duty" in his Table of the Springs of Action, it is among the synonyms of the "love of reputation"; with an intimation as to the two former phrases, that they are also sometimes synonymous with the *religious* motive, or the motive of *sympathy*. The feeling of moral approbation or disapprobation properly so called, either toward ourselves or our fellow creatures, he seems unaware of the existence of; and neither the word *self-respect,* nor the idea to which that word is appropriated, occurs even once, so far as our recollection serves us, in his whole writings.

Nor is it only the moral part of man's nature, in the strict sense of the term—the desire of perfection, or the feeling of an approving or of an accusing conscience—that he overlooks; he but faintly recognizes, as a fact in human nature, the pursuit of any other ideal end for its own sake. The sense of *honour,* and personal dignity—that feeling of personal exaltation and degradation which acts independently of other people's opinion, or even in defiance of it; the love of *beauty,* the passion of the artist; the love of *order,* of congruity, of consistency in all things, and conformity to their end; the love of *power,* not in the limited form of power over other human beings, but abstract power, the power of making our volitions effectual; the love of *action,* the thirst for movement and activity, a principle scarcely of less influence in human life than its opposite, the love of ease—None of these powerful constituents of human nature are thought worthy of a place among the "Springs of Action"; and though there is possibly no one of them of the existence of which an acknowledgment might not be found in some corner of Bentham's writings, no conclusions are ever founded on the acknowledgment. Man, that most complex being, is a very simple one in his eyes. Even under the head of *sympathy,* his recognition does not extend to the more complex forms of the feeling—the love of *loving,* the need of a sympathizing support, or of objects of admiration and reverence. If he thought at all of any of the deeper feelings of human

nature, it was but as idiosyncrasies of taste, with which the moralist no more than the legislator had any concern, further than to prohibit such as were mischievous among the actions to which they might chance to lead. To say either that man should, or that he should not, take pleasure in one thing, displeasure in another, appeared to him as much an act of despotism in the moralist as in the political ruler.

It would be most unjust to Bentham to surmise (as narrow-minded and passionate adversaries are apt in such cases to do) that this picture of human nature was copied from himself; that all those constituents of humanity which he rejected from his table of motives were wanting in his own breast. The unusual strength of his early feelings of virtue, was, as we have seen, the original cause of all his speculations; and a noble sense of morality, and especially of justice, guides and pervades them all. But having been early accustomed to keep before his mind's eye the happiness of mankind (or rather of the whole sentient world), as the only thing desirable in itself, or which rendered anything else desirable, he confounded all disinterested feelings which he found in himself, with the desire of general happiness: just as some religious writers, who loved virtue for its own sake as much perhaps as men could do, habitually confounded their love of virtue with their fear of hell. It would have required greater subtlety than Bentham possessed, to distinguish from each other feelings which, from long habit, always acted in the same direction; and his want of imagination prevented him from reading the distinction, where it is legible enough, in the hearts of others.

Accordingly, he has not been followed in this grand oversight by any of the able men who, from the extent of their intellectual obligations to him, have been regarded as his disciples. They may have followed him in his doctrine of utility, and in his rejection of a moral sense as the test of right and wrong: but while repudiating it as such, they have, with Hartley, acknowledged it as a fact in human nature; they have endeavoured to account for it, to assign its laws: nor are they justly chargeable either with undervaluing this part of our nature, or with any disposition to throw it into the background of their speculations. If any part of the influence of this cardinal error has extended itself to them, it is circuitously, and through the effect on their minds of other parts of Bentham's doctrines.

Sympathy, the only disinterested motive which Bentham recognized, he felt the inadequacy of, except in certain limited cases, as a security for virtuous action. Personal affection, he well knew, is as liable to operate to the injury of third parties, and requires as much to be kept under government, as any other feeling whatever: and general philanthropy, considered as a motive influencing mankind in general, he estimated at its true value when divorced from the feeling of duty—as the very weakest and most unsteady of all feelings. There remained, as a motive by which mankind are influenced, and by which they may be guided to their good, only personal interest. Accordingly, Bentham's idea of the world is that of a collection of persons pursuing each his separate interest or pleasure, and the prevention of whom from jostling one another more than is unavoidable may be attempted by hopes and fears derived from three sources—the law, religion, and public opinion. To these three powers, considered as binding human conduct, he gave the names of *sanctions:* the *political* sanction, operating by the rewards and penalties of the law; the *religious* sanction, by those expected from the Ruler of the Universe; and the *popular,* which he characteristically calls also the *moral* sanction operating through the pains and pleasures arising from the favour or disfavour of our fellow creatures.

Such is Bentham's theory of the world. And now, in a spirit neither of apology nor of censure, but of calm appreciation, we are to inquire how far this view of human nature and life will carry anyone—how much it will accomplish in morals, and how much in political and social philosophy: what it will do for the individual, and what for society.

It will do nothing for the conduct of the individual, beyond prescribing some of the more obvious dictates of worldly prudence, and outward probity and beneficence. There is no need to expatiate on the deficiencies of a system of ethics which does not pretend to aid individuals in the formation of their own character; which recognizes no such wish as that of self-culture, we may even say no such power, as existing in human nature; and if it did recognize, could furnish little assistance to that great duty, because it overlooks the existence of about half of the whole number of mental feelings which human beings are capable of, including all those of which the direct objects are states of their own mind.

Morality consists of two parts. One of these is self-education; the training, by the human being himself, of his affections and will. That department is a blank in Bentham's system. The other and coequal part, the regulation of his outward actions, must be altogether halting and imperfect without the first; for how can we judge in what manner many an action will affect even the worldly interests of ourselves or others, unless we take in, as part of the question, its influence on the regulation of our, or their, affections and desires? A moralist on Bentham's principles may get as far as this, that he ought not to slay, burn, or steal; but what will be his qualifications for regulating the nicer shades of human behaviour, or for laying down even the greater moralities as to those facts in human life which tend to influence the depths of the character quite independently of any influence on worldly circumstances—such, for instance, as the sexual relations, or those of family in general, or any other social and sympathetic connections of an intimate kind? The moralities of these questions depend essentially on considerations which Bentham never so much as took into the account; and when he happened to be in the right, it was always, and necessarily, on wrong or insufficient grounds.

It is fortunate for the world that Bentham's taste lay rather in the direction of jurisprudential than of properly ethical inquiry. Nothing expressly of the latter kind has been published under his name, except the *Deontology*—a book scarcely ever, in our experience, alluded to by any admirer of Bentham without deep regret that it ever saw the light. We did not expect from Bentham correct systematic views of ethics, or a sound treatment of any question the moralities of which require a profound knowledge of the human heart; but we did anticipate that the greater moral questions would have been boldly plunged into, and at least a searching criticism produced of the received opinions; we did not expect that the *petite morale* [insignificant questions of morality] almost alone would have been treated, and that with the most pedantic minuteness, and on the *quid pro quo* principles which regulate trade. The book has not even the value which would belong to an authentic exhibition of the legitimate consequences of an erroneous line of thought; for the style proves it to have been so entirely rewritten that it is impossible to tell how much or how little of it is Bentham's. The collected edition, now in progress, will not, it is said, include Bentham's religious writings; these, although we think most of them of exceedingly small value, are at least his, and the world has a right to whatever light they throw upon the constitution of his mind. But the omission of the *Deontology* would be an act of editorial discretion which we should deem entirely justifiable.

If Bentham's theory of life can do so little for the individual, what can it do for society?

It will enable a society which has attained a certain state of spiritual development, and the maintenance of which in that state is otherwise provided for, to prescribe the rules by which it may protect its material interests. It will do nothing (except sometimes as an instrument in the hands of a higher doctrine) for the spiritual interests of society; nor does it suffice of itself even for the material interests. That which alone causes any material interests to exist which alone enables any body of human beings to exist as a society, is national character: *that* it is, which causes one nation to succeed in what it attempts, another to fail; one nation to understand and aspire to elevated things, another to grovel in mean ones; which makes the greatness of one nation lasting and dooms another to early and rapid decay. The true teacher of the fitting social arrangements for England, France, or America is the one who can point out how the English, French, or American character can be improved, and how it has been made what it is. A philosophy of laws and institutions, not founded on a philosophy of national character, is an absurdity. But what could Bentham's opinion be worth on national character? How could he, whose mind contained so few and so poor types of individual character, rise to that higher generalization? All he can do is but to indicate means by which, in any given state of the national mind, the material interests of society can be protected; saving the question, of which others must judge, whether the use of those means would have, on the national character, any injurious influence.

We have arrived, then, at a sort of estimate of what a philosophy like Bentham's can do. It can teach the means of organizing and regulating the merely *business* part of the social arrangements. Whatever can be understood or whatever done without reference to moral influences, his philosophy is equal to; where those influences require to be taken into account, it is at fault. He committed the mistake of supposing that the business part of human affairs was the whole of them; all at least that the gislator and the moralist had to do with. Not that he disregarded moral influences when he perceived them; but his want of imagination, small experience of human feelings, and ignorance of the filiation and connection of feelings with one another made this rarely the case.

The business part is accordingly the only province of human affairs which Bentham has cultivated with any success; into which he has introduced any considerable number of comprehensive and luminous practical principles. That is the field of his greatness; and there he is indeed great. He has swept away the accumulated cobwebs of centuries—he has untied knots which the efforts of the ablest thinkers, age after age, had only drawn tighter; and it is no exaggeration to say of him that over a great part of the field he was the first to shed the light of reason.

We turn with pleasure from what Bentham could not do, to what he did. It is an ungracious task to call a great benefactor of mankind to account for not being a greater—to insist upon the errors of a man who has originated more new truths, has given to the world more sound practical lessons, than it ever received, except in a few glorious instances, from any other individual. The unpleasing part of our work is ended. We are now to show the greatness of the man; the grasp which his intellect took of the subjects with which it was fitted to deal; the giant's task which was before him, and the hero's courage and strength with which he achieved it. Nor let that which he did be deemed of small account because its province was limited: man has but the choice to go a little way in many paths, or a great way in only one. The field of Bentham's labours was like the space between two parallel lines; narrow to excess in one direction, in another it reached to infinity.

Bentham's speculations, as we are already aware, began with law; and in that department he accomplished his greatest triumphs. He found the philosophy of law a chaos, he left it a science: he found the practice of the law an Augean stable, he turned the river into it which is mining and sweeping away mound after mound of its rubbish.

Without joining in the exaggerated invectives against lawyers, which Bentham sometimes permitted to himself, or making one portion of society alone accountable for the fault of all, we may say that circumstances had made English lawyers in a peculiar degree liable to the reproach of Voltaire, who defines lawyers the "conservators of ancient barbarous usages." The basis of the English law was, and still is, the feudal system. That system, like all those which existed as custom before they were established as law, possessed a certain degree of suitableness to the wants of the society among whom it grew up—that is to say, of a tribe of rude soldiers, holding a conquered people in subjection, and dividing its spoils among themselves. Advancing civilization had, however, converted this armed encampment of barbarous warriors in the midst of enemies reduced to slavery into an industrious, commercial, rich, and free people. The laws which were suitable to the first of these states of society could have no manner of relation to the circumstances of the second; which could not even have come into existence unless something had been done to adapt those laws to it. But the adaption was not the result of thought and design; it arose not from any comprehensive consideration of the new state of society and its exigencies. What was done, was done by a struggle of centuries between the old barbarism and the new civilization; between the feudal aristocracy of conquerors, holding fast to the rude system they had established, and the conquered effecting their emancipation. The last was the growing power, but was never strong enough to break its bonds, though ever and anon some weak point gave way. Hence the law came to be like the costume of a full-grown man who had never put off the clothes made for him when he first went to school. Band after band had burst, and, as the rent widened, then, without removing anything except what might drop off of itself, the hole was darned, or patches of fresh law were brought from the nearest shop and stuck on. Hence all ages of English history have given one another rendezvous in English law; their several products may be seen all together, not interfused, but heaped one upon another, as many different ages of the earth may be read in some perpendicular section of its surface—the deposits of each successive period not substituted but superimposed on those of the preceding. And in the world of law no less than in the physical world, every commotion and conflict of the elements has left its mark behind in some break or irregularity of the strata: every struggle which ever rent the bosom of society is apparent in the disjointed condition of the part of the field of law which covers the spot: nay, the very traps and pitfalls which one contending party set for another are still standing, and the teeth not of hyenas only, but of foxes and all cunning animals, are imprinted on the curious remains found in these antediluvian caves.

In the English law, as in the Roman before it, the adaptations of barbarous laws to the growth of civilized society were made chiefly by stealth. They were generally made by the courts of justice, who could not help reading the new wants of mankind in the cases between man and man which came before them; but who, having no authority to make new laws for those new wants, were obliged to do the work covertly and evade the jealousy and opposition of an ignorant, prejudiced, and for the most part brutal and tyrannical legislature. Some of the most necessary of these improvements, such as the giving force of law to trusts, and the breaking up of entails, were effected in actual opposition to the strongly-declared will of Parliament, whose clumsy hands, no match for the astuteness of judges, could not, after

repeated trials, manage to make any law which the judges could not find a trick for rendering inoperative. The whole history of the contest about trusts may still be read in the works of a conveyance, as could the contest about entails, till the abolition of fine and recovery, by a bill of the present Attorney General; but dearly did the client pay for the cabinet of historical curiosities which he was obliged to purchase every time that he made a settlement of his estate. The result of this mode of improving social institutions was that whatever new things were done had to be done in consistency with old forms and names, and the laws were improved with much the same effect as if, in the improvement of agriculture, the plough could only have been introduced by making it look like a spade; or as if, when the primeval practice of ploughing by the horse's tail gave way to the innovation of harness, the tail, for form's sake, had still remained attached to the plough.

When the conflicts were over, and the mixed mass settled down into something like a fixed state, and that state a very profitable and therefore a very agreeable one to lawyers, they, following the natural tendency of the human mind, began to theorize upon it and, in obedience to necessity, had to digest it and give it a systematic form. It was from this thing of shreds and patches, in which the only part that approached to order or system was the early barbarous part, already more than half superseded, that English lawyers had to construct, by induction and abstraction, their philosophy of law; and without the logical habits and general intellectual cultivation which the lawyers of the Roman empire brought to a similar task. Bentham found the philosophy of law what English practicing lawyers had made it; a jumble, in which *real* and *personal* property, *law* and *equity, felony, praemunire, misprision,* and *misdemeanour,* words without a vestige of meaning when detached from the history of English institutions—mere tide-marks to point out the line which the sea and the shore, in their secular struggles, had adjusted as their mutual boundary—all passed for distinctions inherent in the nature of things; in which every absurdity, every lucrative abuse, had a reason found for it—a reason which only now and then even pretended to be drawn from expediency; most commonly a technical reason, one of mere form, derived from the old barbarous system. While the theory of the law was in this state, to describe what the practice of it was would require the pen of a Swift, or of Bentham himself. The whole progress of a suit at law seemed like a series of contrivances for lawyers' profit, in which the suitors were regarded as the prey; and if the poor were not the helpless victims of every Sir Giles Overreach who could pay the price, they might thank opinion and manners for it, not the law.

It may be fancied by some people that Bentham did an easy thing in merely calling all this absurd, and proving it to be so. But he began the contest a young man, and he had grown old before he had any followers. History will one day refuse to give credit to the intensity of the superstition which, till very lately, protected this mischievous mess from examination or doubt—passed off the charming representations of Blackstone for a just estimate of the English law, and proclaimed the shame of human reason to be the perfection of it. Glory to Bentham that he has dealt to this superstition its deathblow—that he has been the Hercules of this hydra, the Saint George of this pestilent dragon! The honour is all his—nothing but his peculiar qualities could have done it. There were wanted his indefatigable perseverance, his firm self-reliance, needing no support from other men's opinion; his intensely practical turn of mind, his synthetical habits—above all, his peculiar method. Metaphysicians, armed with vague generalities, had often tried their hands at the subject and left it no more advanced than they found it. Law is a matter of business; means and ends are the things to be considered in it, not abstractions: vagueness was not to be met by vagueness, but by definiteness and precision: details were not to be encountered with generalities, but with details. Nor could any progress be made, on such a subject, by merely showing that existing things were bad; it was necessary also to show how they might be made better. No great man whom we read of was qualified to do this thing except Bentham. He has done it, once and forever.

Into the particulars of what Bentham has done we cannot enter: many hundred pages would be required to give a tolerable abstract of it. To sum up our estimate under a few heads: First: he has expelled mysticism from the philosophy of law, and set the example of viewing laws in a practical light, as means to certain definite and precise ends. Second: he has cleared up the confusion and vagueness attaching to the idea of law in general, to the idea of a body of laws, and the various general ideas therein involved. Third: he demonstrated the necessity and practicability of *codification,* or the conversion of all law into a written and systematically arranged code: not like the Code Napoleon, a code without a single definition, requiring a constant reference to anterior precedent for the meaning of its technical terms; but one containing within itself all that is necessary for its own interpretation, together with a perpetual provision for its own emendation and improvement. He has shown of what parts such a code would consist; the relation of those parts to one another; and by his distinctions and classifications has done very much toward showing what should be, or might be, its nomenclature and arrangement. What he has left undone, he has made it comparatively easy for others to do. Fourth: he has taken a systematic view of the exigencies of society for which the civil code is intended to provide, and of the principles of human nature by which its provisions are to be tested: and this view, defective (as we have already inti-

mated) wherever spiritual interests require
to be taken into account, is excellent for
that large portion of the laws of any country which are designed for the protection
of material interests. Fifth: (to say nothing
of the subject of punishment, for which
something considerable had been done before) he found the philosophy of judicial
procedure, including that of judicial establishments and of evidence, in a more
wretched state than even any other part of
the philosophy of law; he carried it at once
almost to perfection. He left it with every
one of its principles established, and little
remaining to be done even in the suggestion of practical arrangements.

These assertions in behalf of Bentham
may be left, without fear for the result, in
the hands of those who are competent to
judge them. There are now, even in the
highest seats of justice, men to whom the
claims made for him will not appear extravagant. Principle after principle of those
propounded by him is moreover making
its way by infiltration into the understandings most shut against his influence, and
driving nonsense and prejudice from one
corner of them to another. The reform of
the laws of any country according to his
principles can only be gradual and may be
long ere it is accomplished; but the work
is in progress, and both parliament and
the judges are every year doing something,
and often something not inconsiderable,
toward the forwarding of it.

It seems proper here to take notice of
an accusation sometimes made both against
Bentham and against the principle of codification—as if they required one uniform
suit of ready-made laws for all times and
all states of society. The doctrine of codification, as the word imports, relates to the
form only of the laws, not their substance;
it does not concern itself with what the
laws should be but declares that whatever
they are, they ought to be systematically
arranged, and fixed down to a determinate
form of words. To the accusation, so far as
it affects Bentham, one of the essays in the

collection of his works (then for the first
time published in English) is a complete answer: that "On the Influence of Time and
Place in Matters of Legislation." It may
there be seen that the different exigencies
of different nations with respect to law occupied his attention as systematically as any
other portion of the wants which render
laws necessary: with the limitations, it is
true, which were set to all his speculations
by the imperfections of his theory of human nature. For, taking, as we have seen,
next to no account of national character
and the causes which form and maintain
it, he was precluded from considering, except to a very limited extent, the laws of
a country as an instrument of national culture: one of their most important aspects,
and in which they must of course vary according to the degree and kind of culture
already attained; as a tutor gives his pupil
different lessons according to the progress
already made in his education. The same
laws would not have suited our wild ancestors, accustomed to rude independence,
and a people of Asiatics bowed down by
military despotism: the slave needs to be
trained to govern himself, the savage to
submit to the government of others. The
same laws will not suit the English, who
distrust everything which emanates from
general principles, and the French, who
distrust whatever does not so emanate.
Very different institutions are needed to
train to the perfection of their nature, or
to constitute into a united nation and social
polity, an essentially *subjective* people like
the Germans and an essentially *objective*
people like those of Northern and Central
Italy; the one affectionate and dreamy, the
other passionate and worldly; the one trust-
ful and loyal, the other calculating and suspicious; the one not practical enough, the
other overmuch; the one wanting individuality, the other fellow-feeling, the one failing for want of exacting enough for itself,
the other for want of conceding enough
to others. Bentham was little accustomed
to look at institutions in their relation to

these topics. The effects of this oversight must of course be perceptible throughout his speculations, but we do not think the errors into which it led him very material in the greater part of civil and penal law: it is in the department of constitutional legislation that they were fundamental.

The Benthamic theory of government has made so much noise in the world of late years; it has held such a conspicuous place among Radical philosophies, and Radical modes of thinking have participated so much more largely than any others in its spirit, that many worthy persons imagine there is no other Radical philosophy extant. Leaving such people to discover their mistake as they may, we shall expend a few words in attempting to discriminate between the truth and error of this celebrated theory.

There are three great questions in government. First, to what authority is it for the good of the people that they should be subject? Second, how are they to be induced to obey that authority? The answers to these two questions vary indefinitely, according to the degree and kind of civilization and cultivation already attained by a people, and their peculiar aptitudes for receiving more. Comes next a third question, not liable to so much variation, namely, by what means are the abuses of this authority to be checked? This third question is the only one of the three to which Bentham seriously applies himself, and he gives it the only answer it admits of—Responsibility: responsibility to persons whose interest, whose obvious and recognizable interest, accords with the end in view—good government. This being granted, it is next to be asked, in what body of persons this identity of interest with good government, that is, with the interest of the whole community, is to be found? In nothing less, says Bentham, than the numerical majority: nor, say we, even in the numerical majority itself; of no portion of the community less than all, will the interest coincide, at all times and in all respects, with the in-

terest of all. But, since power given to all, by a representative government, is in fact given to a majority, we are obliged to fall back upon the first of our three questions, namely, under what authority is it for the good of the people that they be placed? And if to this the answer be, under that of a majority among themselves, Bentham's system cannot be questioned. This one assumption being made, his "Constitutional Code" is admirable. That extraordinary power which he possessed, of at once seizing comprehensive principles, and scheming out minute details, is brought into play with surpassing vigour in devising means for preventing rulers from escaping from the control of the majority; for enabling and inducing the majority to exercise that control unremittingly; and for providing them with servants of every desirable endowment, moral and intellectual, compatible with entire subservience to their will.

But *is* this fundamental doctrine of Bentham's political philosophy a universal truth? Is it, at all times and places, good for mankind to be under the absolute authority of the majority of themselves? We say the authority, not the political authority merely, because it is chimerical to suppose that whatever has absolute power over men's bodies will not arrogate it over their minds—will not seek to control (not perhaps by legal penalties, but by the persecutions of society) opinions and feelings which depart from its standard; will not attempt to shape the education of the young by its model, and to extinguish all books, all schools, all combinations of individuals for joint action upon society, which may be attempted for the purpose of keeping alive a spirit at variance with its own. Is it, we say, the proper condition of man, in all ages and nations, to be under the despotism of Public Opinion?

It is very conceivable that such a doctrine should find acceptance from some of the noblest spirits, in a time of reaction against the aristocratic governments of modern Europe; governments founded

357

on the entire sacrifice (except so far as prudence, and sometimes humane feeling interfere) of the community generally, to the self-interest and ease of a few. European reformers have been accustomed to see the numerical majority everywhere unjustly depressed, everywhere trampled upon, or at the best overlooked, by governments; nowhere possessing power enough to extort redress of their most positive grievances, provision for their mental culture, or even to prevent themselves from being taxed avowedly for the pecuniary profit of the ruling classes. To see these things, and to seek to put an end to them, by means (among other things) of giving more political power to the majority, constitutes Radicalism; and it is because so many in this age have felt this wish, and have felt that the realization of it was an object worthy of men's devoting their lives to it, that such a theory of government as Bentham's has found favour with them. But, though to pass from one form of bad government to another be the ordinary fate of mankind, philosophers ought not to make themselves parties to it, by sacrificing one portion of important truth to another.

The numerical majority of any society whatever must consist of persons all standing in the same social position, and having, in the main, the same pursuits, namely, unskilled manual labourers; and we mean no disparagement to them: whatever we say to their disadvantage, we say equally of a numerical majority of shopkeepers, or of squires. Where there is identity of position and pursuits, there also will be identity of partialities, passions, and prejudices; and to give to any one set of partialities, passions, and prejudices absolute power, without counterbalance from partialities, passions, and prejudices of a different sort, is the way to render the correction of any of those imperfections hopeless; to make one narrow, mean type of human nature universal and perpetual, and to crush every influence which tends to the further improvement of man's intellectual and moral

nature. There must, we know, be some paramount power in society; and that the majority should be that power is on the whole right, not as being just in itself, but as being less unjust than any other footing on which the matter can be placed. But it is necessary that the institutions of society should make provision for keeping up, in some form or other, as a corrective to partial views, and a shelter for freedom of thought and individuality of character, a perpetual and standing Opposition to the will of the majority. All countries which have long continued progressive, or been durably great, have been so because there has been an organized opposition to the ruling power, of whatever kind that power was: plebeians to patricians, clergy to kings, freethinkers to clergy, kings to barons, commons to king and aristocracy. Almost all the greatest men who ever lived have formed part of such an Opposition. Wherever some such quarrel has not been going on—wherever it has been terminated by the complete victory of one of the contending principles, and no new contest has taken the place of the old—society has either hardened into Chinese stationariness, or fallen into dissolution. A centre of resistance, round which all the moral and social elements which the ruling power views with disfavour may cluster themselves, and behind whose bulwarks they may find shelter from the attempts of that power to hunt them out of existence, is as necessary where the opinion of the majority is sovereign as where the ruling power is a hierarchy or an aristocracy. Where no such *point d'appui* [fulcrum] exists, there the human race will inevitably degenerate; and the question whether the United States, for instance, will in time sink into another China (also a most commercial and industrious nation), resolves itself, to us, into the question, whether such a centre of resistance will gradually evolve itself or not.

These things being considered, we cannot think that Bentham made the most useful employment which might have been made of his great powers, when, not content with enthroning the majority as sovereign, by means of universal suffrage without king or house of lords, he exhausted all the resources of ingenuity in devising means for riveting the yoke of public opinion closer and closer round the necks of all public functionaries, and excluding every possibility of the exercise of the slightest or most temporary influence either by a minority or by the functionary's own notions of right. Surely when any power has been made the strongest power, enough has been done for it; care is thenceforth wanted rather to prevent that strongest power from swallowing up all others. Wherever all the forces of society act in one single direction, the just claims of the individual human being are in extreme peril. The power of the majority is salutary so far as it is used defensively, not offensively—as its exertion is tempered by respect for the personality of the individual, and deference to superiority of cultivated intelligence. If Bentham had employed himself in pointing out the means by which institutions fundamentally democratic might be best adapted to the preservation and strengthening of those two sentiments, he would have done something more permanently valuable, and more worthy of his great intellect. Montesquieu, with the lights of the present age, would have done it; and we are possibly destined to receive this benefit from the Montesquieu of our own times, M. de Tocqueville.

Do we then consider Bentham's political speculations useless? Far from it. We consider them only one-sided. He has brought out into a strong light, has cleared from a thousand confusions and misconceptions, and pointed out with admirable skill the best means of promoting, one of the ideal qualities of a perfect government—identity of interest between the trustees and the community for whom they hold their power in trust. This quality is not attainable in its ideal perfection and must more-

over be striven for with a perpetual eye to all other requisites; but those other requisites must still more be striven for without losing sight of this: and when the slightest postponement is made of it to any other end, the sacrifice, often necessary, is never unattended with evil. Bentham has pointed out how complete this sacrifice is in modern European societies: how exclusively, partial and sinister interests are the ruling power there, with only such check as is imposed by public opinion—which being thus, in the existing order of things, perpetually apparent as a source of good, he was led by natural partiality to exaggerate its intrinsic excellence. This sinister interest of rulers Bentham hunted through all its disguises, and especially through those which hide it from the men themselves who are influenced by it. The greatest service rendered by him to the philosophy of universal human nature is, perhaps, his illustration of what he terms "interest-begotten prejudice"—the common tendency of man to make a duty and a virtue of following his self-interest. The idea, it is true, was far from being peculiarly Bentham's: the artifices by which we persuade ourselves that we are not yielding to our selfish inclinations when we are had attracted the notice of all moralists, and had been probed by religious writers to a depth as much below Bentham's as their knowledge of the profundities and windings of the human heart was superior to his. But it is selfish interest in the form of class-interest, and the class morality founded thereon, which Bentham has illustrated: the manner in which any set of persons who mix much together and have a common interest are apt to make that common interest their standard of virtue, and the social feelings of the members of the class are made to play into the hands of their selfish ones; whence the union so often exemplified in history, between the most heroic personal disinterestedness and the most odious class-selfishness. This was one of Bentham's leading ideas, and almost the only one by which he contributed to the elucidation of history: much of which, except so far as this explained it, must have been entirely inexplicable to him. The idea was given him by Helvetius, whose book, *De l'Esprit,* is one continued and most acute commentary on it; and, together with the other great idea of Helvetius, the influence of circumstances on character, it will make his name live by the side of Rousseau, when most of the other French metaphysicians of the eighteenth century will be extant as such only in literary history.

In the brief view which we have been able to give of Bentham's philosophy, it may surprise the reader that we have said so little about the first principle of it, with which his name is more identified than with anything else; the "principle of utility," or, as he afterward named it, "the greatest-happiness principle." It is a topic on which much were to be said, if there were room, or if it were in reality necessary for the just estimation of Bentham. On an occasion more suitable for a discussion of the metaphysics of morality, or on which the elucidations necessary to make an opinion on so abstract a subject intelligible could be conveniently given, we should be fully prepared to state what we think on this subject. At present we shall only say that while, under proper explanations, we entirely agree with Bentham in his principle, we do not hold with him that all right thinking on the details of morals depends on its express assertion. We think utility, or happiness, much too complex and indefinite an end to be sought except through the medium of various secondary ends, concerning which there may be, and often is, agreement among persons who differ in their ultimate standard; and about which there does in fact prevail a much greater unanimity among thinking persons than might be supposed from their diametrical divergence on the great questions of moral metaphysics. As mankind are much more nearly of one nature, than of one opinion about their own nature, they are more

easily brought to agree in their intermediate principles, *vera illa et media axiomata* [those true and intermediate axioms], a Bacon says, than in their first principles, and the attempt to make the bearings of actions upon the ultimate end more evident than they can be made by referring them to the intermediate ends, and to estimate their value by a direct reference to human happiness, generally terminates in attaching most importance, not to those effects which are really the greatest, but to those which can most easily be pointed to and individually identified. Those who adopt utility as a standard can seldom apply it truly except through the secondary principles; those who reject it generally do no more than erect those secondary principles into first principles. It is when two or more of the secondary principles conflict that a direct appeal to some first principle becomes necessary; and then commences the practical importance of the utilitarian controversy; which is, in other respects, a question of arrangement and logical subordination rather than of practice; important principally in a purely scientific point of view, for the sake of the systematic unity and coherency of ethical philosophy. It is probable, however, that to the principle of utility we owe all that Bentham did; that it was necessary to him to find a first principle which he could receive as self-evident, and to which he could attach all his other doctrines as logical consequences: that to him systematic unity was an indispensable condition of his confidence in his own intellect. And there is something further to be remarked. Whether happiness be or be not the end to which morality should be referred—that it be referred to an *end* of some sort, and not left in the dominion of vague feeling or inexplicable internal conviction, that it be made a matter of reason and calculation, and not merely of sentiment, is essential to the very idea of moral philosophy; is, in fact, what renders argument or discussion on moral questions possible. That the morality of actions depends on the consequences which they tend to produce, is the doctrine of rational persons of all schools; that the good or evil of those consequences is measured solely by pleasure or pain, is all of the doctrine of the school of utility, which is peculiar to it.

Insofar as Bentham's adoption of the principle of utility induced him to fix his attention upon the consequences of actions as the consideration determining their morality, so far he was indisputably in the right path: though to go far in it without wandering, there was needed a greater knowledge of the formation of character, and of the consequences of actions upon the agent's own frame of mind, than Bentham possessed. His want of power to estimate this class of consequences, together with his want of the degree of modest deference which, from those who have not competent experience of their own, is due to the experience of others on that part of the subject, greatly limit the value of his speculations on questions of practical ethics.

He is chargeable also with another error, which it would be improper to pass over, because nothing has tended more to place him in opposition to the common feelings of mankind, and to give to his philosophy that cold, mechanical, and ungenial air which characterizes the popular idea of a Benthamite. This error, or rather one-sidedness, belongs to him not as a utilitarian, but as a moralist by profession, and in common with almost all professed moralists, whether religious or philosophical: it is that of treating the *moral* view of actions and characters, which is unquestionably the first and most important mode of looking at them, as if it were the sole one: whereas it is only one of three, by all of which our sentiments toward the human being may be, ought to be, and without entirely crushing our own nature cannot but be, materially influenced. Every human action has three aspects: its *moral* aspect, or that of its *right* and *wrong;* its *aesthetic* aspect, or that of its *beauty;* its *sympathetic* aspect, or that of its *loveableness.*

The first addresses itself to our reason and conscience; the second to our imagination; the third to our human fellow-feeling. According to the first, we approve or disapprove; according to the second, we admire or despise; according to the third, we love, pity, or dislike. The morality of an action depends on its foreseeable consequences; its beauty, and its loveableness, or the reverse, depend on the qualities which it is evidence of. Thus, a lie is *wrong*, because its effect is to mislead, and because it tends to destroy the confidence of man in man; it is also *mean*, because it is cowardly—because it proceeds from not daring to face the consequences of telling the truth—or at best is evidence of want of that *power* to compass our ends by straightforward means, which is conceived as properly belonging to every person not deficient in energy or in understanding. The action of Brutus in sentencing his sons was *right,* because it was executing a law essential to the freedom of his country, against persons of whose guilt there was no doubt: it was *admirable*, because it evinced a rare degree of patriotism, courage, and self-control; but there was nothing *loveable* in it; it affords either no presumption in regard to loveable qualities, or a presumption of their deficiency. If one of the sons had engaged in the conspiracy from affection for the other, his action would have been loveable, though neither moral nor admirable. It is not possible for any sophistry to confound these three modes of viewing an action; but it is very possible to adhere to one of them exclusively, and lose sight of the rest. Sentimentality consists in setting the last two of the three above the first; the error of moralists in general, and of Bentham, is to sink the two latter entirely. This is preeminently the case with Bentham: he both wrote and felt as if the moral standard ought not only be paramount (which it ought), but to be alone; as if it ought to be the sole master of all our actions, and even of all our sentiments; as if either to admire or like, or despise or dislike a person for any action which neither does good nor harm, or which does not do a good or a harm proportioned to the sentiment entertained, were an injustice and a prejudice. He carried this so far, that there were certain phrases which, being expressive of what he considered to be this groundless liking or aversion, he could not bear to hear pronounced in his presence. Among these phrases were those of *good* and *bad taste*. He thought it an insolent piece of dogmatism in one person to praise or condemn another in a matter of taste: as if men's likings and dislikings, on things in themselves indifferent, were not full of the most important inferences as to every point of their character; as if a person's tastes did not show him to be wise or a fool, cultivated or ignorant, gentle or rough, sensitive or callous, generous or sordid, benevolent or selfish, conscientious or depraved.

Connected with the same topic are Bentham's peculiar opinions on poetry. Much more has been said than there is any foundation for, about his contempt for the pleasures of imagination, and for the fine arts. Music was throughout life his favourite amusement; painting, sculpture, and the other arts addressed to the eye, he was so far from holding in any contempt, that he occasionally recognizes them as means employable for important social ends; though his ignorance of the deeper springs of human character prevented him (as it prevents most Englishmen) from suspecting how profoundly such things enter into the moral nature of man, and into the education both of the individual and of the race. But toward poetry in the narrower sense, that which employs the language of words, he entertained no favour. Words, he thought, were perverted from their proper office when they were employed in uttering anything but precise logical truth. He says, somewhere in his works, that, "quantity of pleasure being equal, push-pin is as good as poetry"; but this is only a paradoxical way of stating what he would equally have said

of the things which he most valued and admired. Another aphorism is attributed to him, which is much more characteristic of his view of this subject: "All poetry is misrepresentation." Poetry, he thought, consisted essentially in exaggeration for effect: in proclaiming some one view of a thing very emphatically, and suppressing all the limitations and qualifications. This trait of character seems to us a curious example of what Mr. Carlyle strikingly calls "the completeness of limited man." Here is a philosopher who is happy within his narrow boundary as no man of indefinite range ever was; who flatters himself that he is so completely emancipated from the essential law of poor human intellect, by which it can only see one thing at a time well, that he can even turn round upon the imperfection and lay a solemn interdict upon it. Did Bentham really suppose that it is in poetry only that propositions cannot be exactly true, cannot contain in themselves all the limitations and qualifications with which they require to be taken when applied to practice? We have seen how far his own prose propositions are from realizing this Utopia: and even the attempt to approach it would be incompatible not with poetry merely, but with oratory, and popular writing of every kind. Bentham's charge is true to the fullest extent; all writing which undertakes to make men feel truths as well as see them, does take up one point at a time, does seek to impress that, to drive that home, to make it sink into and colour the whole mind of the reader or hearer. It is justified in doing so, if the portion of truth which it thus enforces be that which is called for by the occasion. All writing addressed to the feelings has a natural tendency to exaggeration; but Bentham should have remembered that in this, as in many things, we must aim at too much, to be assured of doing enough.

From the same principle in Bentham came the intricate and involved style, which makes his later writings books for the student only, not the general reader. It was from his perpetually aiming at impracticable precision. Nearly all his earlier, and many parts of his later writings, are models, as we have already observed, of light, playful, and popular style: a Benthamiana might be made of passages worthy of Addison or Goldsmith. But in his later years and more advanced studies, he fell into a Latin or German structure of sentence, foreign to the genius of the English language. He could not bear, for the sake of clearness and the reader's ease, to say, as ordinary men are content to do, a little more than the truth in one sentence and correct it in the next. The whole of the qualifying remarks which he intended to make, he insisted upon imbedding as parentheses in the very middle of the sentence itself. And thus the sense being so long suspended, and attention being required to the accessory ideas before the principal idea had been properly seized, it became difficult, without some practice, to make out the train of thought. It is fortunate that so many of the most important parts of his writings are free from this defect. We regard it as a *reductio ad absurdum* of his objection to poetry. In trying to write in a manner against which the same objection should not lie, he could stop nowhere short of utter unreadableness, and after all

attained no more accuracy than is compatible with opinions as imperfect and one-sided as those of any poet or sentimentalist breathing. Judge then in what state literature and philosophy would be, and what chance they would have of influencing the multitude, if his objection were allowed, and all styles of writing banished which would not stand his test.

We must here close this brief and imperfect view of Bentham and his doctrines; in which many parts of the subject have been entirely untouched, and no part done justice to, but which at least proceeds from an intimate familiarity with his writings, and is nearly the first attempt at an impartial estimate of his character as a philosopher, and of the result of his labours to the world.

After every abatement, and it has been seen whether we have made our abatements sparingly—there remains to Bentham an indisputable place among the great intellectual benefactors of mankind. His writings will long form an indispensable part of the education of the highest order of practical thinkers; and the collected edition of them ought to be in the hands of everyone who would either understand his age, or take any beneficial part in the great business of it.*

---

*Since the first publication of this paper, Lord Brougham's brilliant series of characters has been published, including a sketch of Bentham. Lord Brougham's view of Bentham's characteristics agrees in the main points, so far as it goes, with the result of our more minute examination, but there is an imputation cast upon Bentham, of a jealous and splenetic disposition in private life, of which we feel called upon to give at once a contradiction and an explanation. It is indispensable to a correct estimate of any of Bentham's dealings with the world, to bear in mind that in everything except abstract speculation he was to the last, what we have called him, essentially a boy. He had the freshness,

the simplicity, the confidingness, the liveliness and activity, all the delightful qualities of boyhood, and the weaknesses which are the reverse side of those qualities—the undue importance attached to trifles, the habitual mismeasurement of the practical bearing and value of things, the readiness to be either delighted or offended on inadequate cause. These were the real sources of what was unreasonable in some of his attacks on individuals, and in particular on Lord Brougham, on the subject of his Law Reforms; they were no more the effect of envy or malice, or any really unamiable quality, than the freaks of a pettish child, and are scarcely a fitter subject of censure or criticism.

Selected Essays

Ralph Waldo Emerson

Everyone knows Emerson, can recognize the handsome figure and the household name that have come down to us in history books; and everyone has read, if only because in school they had to read it, something he wrote—an essay or two, some poems. But most of us might have difficulty saying what his importance really was, historically speaking, and still fewer of us could say with assurance what it is now, or even if he has any. The man who for thirty years before the Civil War seemed both rich in ideas and a kind of sage in the way he expressed them has grown dim in our minds, is difficult to define. Of course this is the fate of many famous men. But in Emerson's case it suggests something about the kind of ideas he had, which were usually rarefied—Transcendental was the term then used to describe them—and it may reflect a certain limitation in his eloquence as well. His lack of systematic thinking is apparent, as is his tendency to wander in the discussion of whatever subject he happens in this or that essay to address.

The ideas he had in a sense were many—his brain was fertile and quick to see meaning in the lives of men, about whom he knew a great deal, having read much—but in another sense there was only one, which was that the soul is infinite in its power and that there is nothing we cannot make of ourselves if we try. In this he was critical of his contemporaries, who seemed to him to have lost faith in themselves. "Our age is retrospective," he wrote in his first published essay, *Nature* (1836). "It builds the sepulchers of the fathers. It writes biographies, histories, criticism. The foregoing generations beheld God and nature face to face; we, through their eyes. Why should we not enjoy an original relation to the universe? . . . There are new lands, new men, new thoughts. Let us demand our own works and laws and worship."

One can read this as the quintessentially American sentiment it was, but Emerson's statement of it caught the imagination of his countrymen as no one else's had, and we can hear it in the exhortation to step beyond the boundaries of the past that he had already delivered to himself. Neither in religion nor in politics nor in philosophical thought was he content to be traditional—certainly not as America already had become, in his opinion. The young man who spoke—he was thirty-three—had left the ministry, in which he found tired doctrines, was critical of republican complacencies, as being such, and spent his time on books of German philosophy and Oriental scripture that had far more to give the human spirit, as he thought, than the diet of politics and Christian orthodoxy on which his country mostly fed.

The medium in which Emerson said this was the lecture circuit, where after all he preached in layman's terms. His voice alone was worth attention. "I have heard some great speakers and some accomplished orators," James Russell Lowell remembered, "but never any that so moved and persuaded men as he. There is a kind of undertow in that rich baritone of his that sweeps our minds from their deeper waters with a drift we cannot and would not resist." Yet the words Emerson used were not preacher's words, if that means pious talk. He admired Plato, not least for his ability to cast philosophy in common speech. "From mares and puppies; from pitchers and soup-ladles; from cooks and criers; the shops of potters, horse doctors, butchers, and fishmongers"—these he said made Plato's illustrations, and so we listen as in turn Emerson wished men might listen to him. And listen they did. His audience was both large and loyal, though sometimes, as when he ventured west from Massachusetts, where he lived, he found his lack of folksiness and humor to be a disadvantage.

His talks were not always exhortational or programmatic. Many of them, like the three reprinted here, were merely disquisitions of a rather rambling if charming sort on subjects that happened to interest him—on which, like the teacher he really was, he realized he had something to say. His titles, such as "History," "Manners," "Politics," "The Comic," "The Tragic," "Farming," "Quotation and Originality," suggest the range of his always curious and catholic mind. Indeed, they show him to have been much like Montaigne, a writer he greatly admired and to whom he gave a fine tribute, fascinated as he was himself by everything in the complex, contradictory lives of human beings.

The years after the Civil War were difficult for Emerson. His own powers waned—he could not remember things or books as once he had, and his strength was no longer equal to the lecture circuit. By the time he died—in 1882, at the age of seventy-nine—he had become something of a relic. But his words, many of them, have lasted, and anyone who undertakes to read him will discover candid observations, on whatever subject, that are simply and wonderfully right. We cannot in many cases be certain how he knew such things, still less why he enjoyed the thought of them, but there is no doubting that he did, and did. The transcendental man was after all a trenchant one, and true.

Illusions

Flow, flow the waves hated,
Accursed, adored,
The waves of mutation:
No anchorage is.
Sleep is not, death is not;
Who seem to die live.
House you were born in,
Friends of your springtime,
Old man and young maid,
Day's toil and its guerdon,
They are all vanishing,
Fleeing to fables,
Cannot be moored.
See the stars through them,
Through treacherous marbles.
Know, the stars yonder,
The stars everlasting,
Are fugitive also,
And emulate, vaulted,
The lambent heat lightning,
And firefly's flight.
When thou dost return
On the wave's circulation,
Beholding the shimmer,
The wild dissipation,
And, out of endeavor
To change and to flow
The gas become solid,
And phantoms and nothings
Return to be things,
And endless imbroglio
Is law and the world—
Then first shalt thou know,
That in the wild turmoil,
Horsed on the Proteus,
Thou ridest to power,
And to endurance.

Some years ago, in company with an agreeable party, I spent a long summer day in exploring the Mammoth Cave in Kentucky. We traversed, through spacious galleries affording a solid masonry foundation for the town and county overhead, the six or eight black miles from the mouth of the cavern to the innermost recess which tourists visit—a niche or grotto made of one seamless stalactite, and called, I believe, Serena's Bower. I lost the light of one day. I saw high domes and bottomless pits; heard the voice of unseen waterfalls; paddled three-quarters of a mile in the deep Echo River, whose waters are peopled with the blind fish; crossed the streams "Lethe" and "Styx"; plied with music and guns the echoes in these alarming galleries; saw every form of stalagmite and stalactite in the sculptured and fretted chambers— icicle, orange-flower, acanthus, grapes, and snowball. We shot Bengal lights into the vaults and groins of the sparry cathedrals and examined all the masterpieces which the four combined engineers, water, limestone, gravitation, and time could make in the dark.

The mysteries and scenery of the cave had the same dignity that belongs to all natural objects, and which shames the fine things to which we foppishly compare them. I remarked especially the mimetic habit with which Nature, on new instruments, hums her old tunes, making night to mimic day, and chemistry to ape vegetation. But I then took notice and still chiefly remember that the best thing which the cave had to offer was an illusion. On arriving at what is called the "Star Chamber," our lamps were taken from us by the guide and extinguished or put aside, and, on looking upward, I saw or seemed to see the night heaven thick with stars glimmering more or less brightly over our heads, and even what seemed a comet flaming among them. All the party were touched with astonishment and pleasure. Our musical friends sung with much feeling a pretty song. "The stars are in the quiet sky," etc., and I sat down on the rocky floor to enjoy the serene picture. Some crystal specks in the black ceiling high overhead, reflecting the light of a half-hid lamp, yielded this magnificent effect.

I own I did not like the cave so well for eking out its sublimities with this theatrical trick. But I have had many experiences like it, before and since; and we must be content to be pleased without too curiously analyzing the occasions. Our conversation with Nature is not just what it seems. The cloud rack, the sunrise and sunset glories, rainbows and northern lights are not quite so spheral as our childhood thought them, and the part our organization plays in them is too large. The senses interfere everywhere and mix their own structure with all they report of. Once we fancied the earth a plane, and stationary. In admiring the sunset we do not yet deduct the rounding, coordinating, pictorial powers of the eye.

The same interference from our organization creates the most of our pleasure and pain. Our first mistake is the belief that the circumstance gives the joy which we give to the circumstance. Life is an ecstasy. Life is sweet as nitrous oxide; and the fisherman dripping all day over a cold pond, the switchman at the railway intersection, the farmer in the field, the Negro in the rice swamp, the fop in the street, the hunter in the woods, the barrister with the jury, the belle at the ball, all ascribe a certain pleasure to their employment, which they themselves give it. Health and appetite impart the sweetness to sugar, bread, and meat. We fancy that our civilization has got on far, but we still come back to our primers.

We live by our imaginations, by our admirations, by our sentiments. The child walks amid heaps of illusions, which he does not like to have disturbed. The boy, how sweet to him is his fancy! how dear the story of barons and battles! What a hero he is, while he feeds on his heroes! What a debt is his to imaginative books! He has no better friend or influence than Scott, Shakespeare, Plutarch, and Homer. The man lives to other objects, but who dare affirm that they are more real? Even the prose of the streets is full of refractions. In the life of the dreariest alderman, fancy enters into all details and colors them with rosy hue. He imitates the air and actions of people whom he admires, and is raised in his own eyes. He pays a debt quicker to a rich man than to a poor man. He wishes the bow and compliment of some leader in the state or in society; weighs what he says; perhaps he never comes nearer to him for that, but dies at last better contented for this amusement of his eyes and his fancy.

The world rolls, the din of life is never hushed. In London, in Paris, in Boston, in San Francisco, the carnival, the masquerade is at its height. Nobody drops his domino. The unities, the fictions of the piece it would be an impertinence to break. The chapter of fascinations is very long. Great is paint; nay, God is the painter; and we rightly accuse the critic who destroys too many illusions. Society does not love its unmaskers. It was wittily if somewhat bitterly said by d'Alembert, "*qu'un état de vapeur était un état très fâcheux, parcequ'il nous faisait voir les choses comme elles sont*" ["that an unsettled state was a very troublesome state, because it makes us see things as they are"]. I find men victims of illusion in all parts of life. Children, youths, adults, and old men, all are led by one bauble or another. Yoganidra, the goddess of illusion, Proteus, or Momus, or Gylfi's Mocking—for the Power [i.e., illusion, regarded as a divinity] has many names—is stronger than the Titans, stronger than Apollo. Few have overheard the gods or surprised their secret. Life is a succession of lessons which must be lived to be a understood. All is riddle, and the key to a riddle is another riddle. There are as many pillows of illusion as flakes in a snowstorm. We wake from one dream into another dream. The toys to be sure are various, and are graduated in refinement to the quality of

the dupe. The intellectual man requires a fine bait; the sots are easily amused. But everybody is drugged with his own frenzy, and the pageant marches at all hours, with music and banner and badge.

Amid the joyous troop who give in to the charivari [shivaree], comes now and then a sad-eyed boy whose eyes lack the requisite refractions to clothe the show in due glory, and who is afflicted with a tendency to trace home the glittering miscellany of fruits and flowers to one root. Science is a search after identity, and the scientific whim is lurking in all corners. At the State Fair a friend of mine complained that all the varieties of fancy pears in our orchards seem to have been selected by somebody who had a whim for a particular kind of pear, and only cultivated such as had that perfume; they were all alike. And I remember the quarrel of another youth with the confectioners, that when he racked his wit to choose the best comfits in the shops, in all the endless varieties of sweetmeat he could find only three flavors, or two. What then? Pears and cakes are good for something; and because you unluckily have an eye or nose too keen, why need you spoil the comfort which the rest of us find in them? I knew a humorist who in a good deal of rattle had a grain or two of sense. He shocked the company by maintaining that the attributes of God were two—power and risibility, and that it was the duty of every pious man to keep up the comedy. And I have known gentlemen of great stake in the community, but whose sympathies were cold—presidents of colleges and governors and senators—who held themselves bound to sign every temperance pledge, and act with Bible societies and missions and peacemakers, and cry *Hist-a-boy!* to every good dog. We must not carry comity too far, but we all have kind impulses in this direction. When the boys come into my yard for leave to gather horse chestnuts, I own I enter into Nature's game, and affect to grant the permission reluctantly, fearing that any moment they will find out the imposture of that showy chaff. But this tenderness is quite unnecessary; the enchantments are laid on very thick. Their young life is thatched with them. Bare and grim to tears is the lot of the children in the hovel I saw yesterday; yet not the less they hung it round with frippery romance, like the children of the happiest fortune, and talked of "the dear cottage where so many joyful hours had flown." Well, this thatching of hovels is the custom of the country. Women, more than all, are the element and kingdom of illusion. Being fascinated, they fascinate. They see through Claude Lorraines. And how dare any one, if he could, pluck away the coulisses, stage effects and ceremonies, by which they live? Too pathetic, too pitiable, is the region of affection, and its atmosphere always liable to mirage.

We are not very much to blame for our bad marriages. We live amid hallucinations; and this especial trap is laid to trip up our feet with, and all are tripped up first or last. But the mighty Mother who had been so sly with us, as if she felt that she owed us some indemnity, insinuates into the Pandora's box of marriage some deep and serious benefits and some great joys. We find a delight in the beauty and happiness of children that makes the heart too big for the body. In the worst-assorted connections there is ever some mixture of true marriage. Teague and his jade [ref. uncertain; perhaps the Irish immigrant, regarded as ill-mannered and impudent] get some just relations of mutual respect, kindly observation, and fostering of each other; learn something, and would carry themselves wiselier if they were now to begin.

'Tis fine for us to point at one or another fine madman, as if there were any exempts. The scholar in his library is none. I, who have all my life heard any number of orations and debates, read poems and miscellaneous books, conversed with many geniuses, am still the victim of any new page; and if Marmaduke, or Hugh,

or Moosehead, or any other, invent a new style or mythology, I fancy that the world will be all brave and right if dressed in these colors, which I had not thought of. Then at once I will daub with this new paint; but it will not stick. 'Tis like the cement which the peddler sells at the door; he makes broken crockery hold with it, but you can never buy of him a bit of the cement which will make it hold when he is gone.

Men who make themselves felt in the world avail themselves of a certain fate in their constitution which they know how to use. But they never deeply interest us unless they lift a corner of the curtain, or betray, ever so slightly, their penetration of what is behind it. 'Tis the charm of practical men that outside of their practicality are a certain poetry and play, as if they led the good horse Power by the bridle, and preferred to walk, though they can ride so fiercely. Bonaparte is intellectual, as well as Caesar; and the best soldiers, sea captains, and railway men have a gentleness when off duty, a good-natured admission that there are illusions, and who shall say that he is not their sport? We stigmatize the cast-iron fellows who cannot so detach themselves, as "dragon-ridden," "thunder-stricken," and "fools of fate," with whatever powers endowed.

Since our tuition is through emblems and indirections, it is well to know that there is method in it, a fixed scale and rank above rank in the phantasms. We begin low with coarse masks and rise to the most subtle and beautiful. The red men told Columbus "they had an herb which took away fatigue"; but he found the illusion of "arriving from the east at the Indies" more composing to his lofty spirit than any tobacco. Is not our faith in the impenetrability of matter more sedative than narcotics? You play with jackstraws, balls, bowls, horse and gun, estates and politics; but there are finer games before you. Is not time a pretty toy? Life will show you masks that are worth all your carnivals.

Yonder mountain must migrate into your mind. The fine stardust and nebulous blur in Orion, "the portentous year of Mizar and Alcor," must come down and be dealt with in your household thought. What if you shall come to discern that the play and playground of all this pompous history are radiations from yourself, and that the sun borrows his beams? What terrible questions we are learning to ask! The former men believed in magic, by which temples, cities, and men were swallowed up, and all trace of them gone. We are coming on the secret of a magic which sweeps out of men's minds all vestige of theism and beliefs which they and their fathers held and were framed upon.

There are deceptions of the senses, deceptions of the passions, and the structural, beneficent illusions of sentiment and of the intellect. There is the illusion of love, which attributes to the beloved person all which that person shares with his or her family, sex, age, or condition, nay, with the human mind itself. 'Tis these which the lover loves, and Anna Matilda [ref. unknown] gets the credit of them. As if one shut up always in a tower, with one window through which the face of heaven and earth could be seen, should fancy that all the marvels he beheld belonged to that window. There is the illusion of time, which is very deep; who has disposed of it? or come to the conviction that what seems the *succession* of thought is only the distribution of wholes into causal series? The intellect sees that every atom carries the whole of Nature; that the mind opens to omnipotence; that, in the endless striving and ascents, the metamorphosis is entire, so that the soul doth not know itself in its own act when that act is perfected. There is illusion that shall deceive even the elect. There is illusion that shall deceive even the performer of the miracle. Though he make his body, he denies that he makes it. Though the world exist from thought, thought is daunted in presence of the world. One after the other we accept the

mental laws, still resisting those which follow, which however must be accepted. But all our concessions only compel us to new profusion. And what avails it that science has come to treat space and time as simply forms of thought, and the material world as hypothetical, and withal our pretension of *property* and even of selfhood are fading with the rest, if, at last, even our thoughts are not finalities, but the incessant flowing and ascension reach these also, and each thought which yesterday was a finality, today is yielding to a larger generalization?

With such volatile elements to work in, 'tis no wonder if our estimates are loose and floating. We must work and affirm, but we have no guess of the value of what we say or do. The cloud is now as big as your hand, and now it covers a county. That story of Thor, who was set to drain the drinking horn in Asgard and to wrestle with the old woman and to run with the runner Lok, and presently found that he had been drinking up the sea, and wrestling with Time, and racing with Thought, describes us, who are contending, amid these seeming trifles, with the supreme energies of Nature. We fancy we have fallen into bad company and squalid condition, low debts, shoe bills, broken glass to pay for, pots to buy, butcher's meat, sugar, milk, and coal. "Set me some great task, ye gods! and I will show my spirit." "Not so," says the good Heaven; "plod and plough, vamp your old coats and hats, weave a shoestring; great affairs and the best wine by and by." Well, 'tis all phantasm; and if we weave a yard of tape in all humility and as well as we can, long hereafter we shall see it was no cotton tape at all but some galaxy which we braided, and that the threads were Time and Nature.

We cannot write the order of the variable winds. How can we penetrate the law of our shifting moods and susceptibility? Yet they differ as all and nothing. Instead of the firmament of yesterday, which our eyes require, it is today an eggshell which coops us in; we cannot even see what or where our stars of destiny are. From day to day the capital facts of human life are hidden from our eyes. Suddenly the mist rolls up and reveals them, and we think how much good time is gone that might have been saved had any hint of these things been shown. A sudden rise in the road shows us the system of mountains, and all the summits, which have been just as near us all the year, but quite out of mind. But these alternations are not without their order, and we are parties to our various fortune. If life seem a succession of dreams, yet poetic justice is done in dreams also. The visions of good men are good; it is the undisciplined will that is whipped with bad thoughts and bad fortunes. When we break the laws, we lose our hold on the central reality. Like sick men in hospitals, we change only from bed to bed, from one folly to another; and it cannot signify much what becomes of such castaways, wailing, stupid, comatose creatures, lifted from bed to bed, from the nothing of life to the nothing of death.

In this kingdom of illusions we grope eagerly for stays and foundations. There is none but a strict and faithful dealing at home and a severe barring out of all duplicity or illusion there. Whatever games are played with us, we must play no games with ourselves, but deal in our privacy with the last honesty and truth. I look upon the simple and childish virtues of veracity and honesty as the root of all that is sublime in character. Speak as you think, be what you are, pay your debts of all kinds. I prefer to be owned as sound and solvent, and my word as good as my bond, and to be what cannot be skipped, or dissipated, or undermined, to all the éclat in the universe. This reality is the foundation of friendship, religion, poetry, and art. At the top or at the bottom of all illusions, I set the cheat which still leads us to work and live for appearances; in spite of our conviction, in all sane hours, that it is what we really are that avails, with friends, with strangers, and with fate or fortune.

One would think from the talk of men that riches and poverty were a great matter; and our civilization mainly respects it. But the Indians say that they do not think the white man, with his brow of care, always toiling, afraid of heat and cold, and keeping within doors, has any advantage of them. The permanent interest of every man is never to be in a false position, but to have the weight of Nature to back him in all that he does. Riches and poverty are a thick or thin costume; and our life— the life of all of us—identical. For we transcend the circumstance continually and taste the real quality of existence; as in our employments, which only differ in the manipulations but express the same laws; or in our thoughts, which wear no silks and taste no ice creams. We see God face to face every hour, and know the savor of Nature.

The early Greek philosophers Heracleitus and Xenophanes measured their force on this problem of identity. Diogenes of Apollonia said that unless the atoms were made of one stuff, they could never blend and act with one another. But the Hindus, in their sacred writings, express the liveliest feeling, both of the essential identity and of that illusion which they conceive variety to be. "The notions, '*I am*,' and '*This is Mine*,' which influence mankind, are but delusions of the mother of the world. Dispel, O Lord of all creatures! the conceit of knowledge which proceeds from ignorance." And the beatitude of man they hold to lie in being freed from fascination.

The intellect is stimulated by the statement of truth in a trope, and the will by clothing the laws of life in illusions. But the unities of Truth and of Right are not broken by the disguise. There need never be any confusion in these. In a crowded life of many parts and performers, on a stage of nations, or in the obscurest hamlet in Maine or California, the same elements offer the same choices to each newcomer, and, according to his election, he fixes his fortune in absolute Nature. It would be hard to put more mental and moral philosophy than the Persians have thrown into a sentence—

Fooled thou must be, though wisest of the wise:
Then be the fool of virtue, not of vice.

There is no chance and no anarchy in the universe. All is system and gradation. Every god is there sitting in his sphere. The young mortal enters the hall of the firmament; there is he alone with them alone, they pouring on him benedictions and gifts, and beckoning him up to their thrones. On the instant, and incessantly, fall snowstorms of illusions. He fancies himself in a vast crowd which sways this way and that and whose movement and doings he must obey: he fancies himself poor, orphaned, insignificant. The mad crowd drives hither and thither, now furiously commanding this thing to be done, now that. What is he that he should resist their will, and think or act for himself? Every moment new changes and new showers of deceptions to baffle and distract him. And when, by and by, for an instant, the air clears and the cloud lifts a little, there are the gods still sitting around him on their thrones—they alone with him alone.

Education

A new degree of intellectual power seems cheap at any price. The use of the world is that man may learn its laws. And the human race have wisely signified their sense of this, by calling wealth, means— Man being the end. Language is always wise.

Therefore I praise New England because it is the country in the world where is the freest expenditure for education. We have already taken, at the planting of the Colonies (for aught I know for the first time in the world), the initial step, which for its importance might have been resisted as the most radical of revolutions, thus deciding at the start the destiny of this country—this, namely, that the poor man, whom the law does not allow to take an ear of corn when starving, nor a pair of shoes for his freezing feet, is allowed to put his hand into the pocket of the rich, and say, You shall educate me, not as you will, but as I will: not alone in the elements, but, by further provision, in the languages, in sciences, in the useful and in elegant arts. The child shall be taken up by the State, and taught, at the public cost, the rudiments of knowledge, and, at last, the ripest results of art and science.

Humanly speaking, the school, the college, society, make the difference between men. All the fairy tales of Aladdin or the invisible Gyges or the talisman that opens kings' palaces or the enchanted halls underground or in the sea, are only fictions to indicate the one miracle of intellectual enlargement. When a man stupid becomes a man inspired, when one and the same man passes out of the torpid into the perceiving state, leaves the din of trifles, the stupor of the senses, to enter into the quasi-omni science of high thought—up and down, around, all limits disappear. No horizon shuts down. He sees things in their causes, all facts in their connection.

One of the problems of history is the beginning of civilization. The animals that accompany and serve man make no progress as races. Those called domestic are capable of learning of man a few tricks of utility or amusement, but they cannot communicate the skill to their race. Each individual must be taught anew. The trained dog cannot train another dog. And Man himself in many races retains almost the unteachableness of the beast. For a thousand years the islands and forests of a great part of the world have been filled with savages who made no steps of advance in art or skill beyond the necessity of being fed and warmed. Certain nations with a better brain and usually in more temperate climates have made such progress as to compare with these as these compare with the bear and the wolf.

Victory over things is the office of man. Of course, until it is accomplished, it is the war and insult of things over him. His continual tendency, his great danger, is to overlook the fact that the world is only his teacher, and the nature of sun and moon, plant and animal only means of arousing his interior activity. Enamored of their beauty, comforted by their convenience, he seeks them as ends, and fast loses sight of the fact that they have worse than no values, that they become noxious, when he becomes their slave.

This apparatus of wants and faculties, this craving body, whose organs ask all the elements and all the functions of Nature for their satisfaction, educate the wondrous creature which they satisfy with light, with heat, with water, with wood, with bread, with wool. The necessities imposed by this most irritable and all-related texture have taught Man hunting, pasturage, agriculture, commerce, weaving, joining, masonry, geometry, astronomy. Here is a world pierced and belted with natural laws, and fenced and planted with civil partitions and properties, which all put new restraints on the young inhabitant. He too must come into this magic circle of relations, and know health and sickness, the fear of injury, the desire of external good, the charm of riches, the charm of power. The household is a school of power. There, within the door, learn the tragicomedy of human life. Here is the sincere thing, the wondrous composition for which day and night go round. In that routine are the sacred relations, the passions that bind and sever. Here is poverty and all the wisdom its hated necessities can teach, here labor drudges, here affections glow, here the secrets of character are told, the guards of man, the guards of woman, the compensations which, like angels of justice, pay every debt: the opium of custom, whereof all drink and many go mad. Here is Economy, and Glee, and Hospitality, and Ceremony, and Frankness, and Calamity, and Death, and Hope.

Everyone has a trust of power—every man, every boy a jurisdiction, whether it be over a cow or a rood of a potato field, or a fleet of ships, or the laws of a state. And what activity the desire of power inspires! What toils it sustains! How it sharpens the perceptions and stores the memory with facts. Thus a man may well spend many years of life in trade. It is a constant teaching of the laws of matter and of mind. No dollar of property can be created without some direct communication with nature, and of course some acquisition of knowledge and practical force. It is a constant contest with the active faculties of men, a study of the issues of one and another course of action, an accumulation of power, and, if the higher faculties of the individual be from time to time quickened, he will gain wisdom and virtue from his business.

As every wind draws music out of the Aeolian harp, so doth every object in Nature draw music out of his mind. Is it not true that every landscape I behold, every friend I meet, every act I perform, every pain I suffer, leaves me a different being from that they found me? That poverty, love, authority, anger, sickness, sorrow, success, all work actively upon our being and unlock for us the concealed faculties of the mind? Whatever private or petty ends are frustrated, this end is always answered. Whatever the man does, or whatever befalls him, opens another chamber in his soul—that is, he has got a new feeling, a new thought, a new organ. Do we not see how amazingly for this end man is fitted to the world?

What leads him to science? Why does he track in the midnight heaven a pure spark, a luminous patch wandering from age to age, but because he acquires thereby a majestic sense of power; learning that in his own constitution he can set the shining maze in order, and finding and carrying their law in his mind, can, as it were, see his simple idea realized up yonder in giddy distances and frightful periods of duration. If Newton come and first of men perceive that not alone certain bodies fall to the ground at a certain rate, but that all bodies in the Universe, the universe of bodies, fall always, and at one rate; that every atom in nature draws to every other atom—he extends the power of his mind not only over every cubic atom of his native planet, but he reports the condition of millions of worlds which his eye never saw. And what is the charm which every ore, every new plant, every new fact touching winds, clouds, ocean currents, the secrets of chemical composition and decomposition possess for Humboldt [1769–1859; classical figure in the development of the earth sciences]? What but that much revolving of similar facts in his mind has shown him that always the mind contains in its transparent chambers the means of classifying the most refractory phenomena, of depriving them of all casual and chaotic aspect, and subordinating them to a bright reason of its own, and so giving to man a sort of property—yea, the very highest property in every district and particle of the globe.

By the permanence of Nature, minds are trained alike, and made intelligible to each other. In our condition are the roots of language and communication, and these instructions we never exhaust.

In some sort the end of life is that the man should take up the universe into himself, or out of that quarry leave nothing unrepresented. Yonder mountain must migrate into his mind. Yonder magnificent astronomy he is at last to import, fetching away moon, and planet, solstice, period, comet, and binal [double] star, by comprehending their relation and law. Instead of the timid stripling he was, he is to be the stalwart Archimedes, Pythagoras, Columbus, Newton, of the physic, metaphysic, and ethics of the design of the world.

For truly the population of the globe has its origin in the aims which their existence is to serve; and so with every portion of them. The truth takes flesh in forms that can express it; and thus in history an idea always overhangs, like the moon, and rules the tide which rises simultaneously in all the souls of a generation.

While thus the world exists for the mind; while thus the man is ever invited inward into shining realms of knowledge and power by the shows of the world, which interpret to him the infinitude of his own consciousness—it becomes the office of a just education to awaken him to the knowledge of this fact.

We learn nothing rightly until we learn the symbolical character of life. Day creeps after day, each full of facts, dull, strange, despised things, that we cannot enough despise—call heavy, prosaic, and desert. The time we seek to kill: the attention it is elegant to divert from things around us. And presently the aroused intellect finds gold and gems in one of these scorned facts—then finds that the day of facts is a rock of diamonds; that a fact is an Epiphany of God.

We have our theory of life, our religion, our philosophy; and the event of each moment, the shower, the steamboat disaster, the passing of a beautiful face, the apoplexy of our neighbor, are all tests to try our theory, the approximate result we call truth, and reveal its defects. If I have renounced the search of truth, if I have come into the port of some pretending dogmatism, some new church or old church, some Schelling or Cousin [contemporary philosophers who had worked out all-embracing systems of thought], I have died to all use of these new events that are born out of prolific time into multitude of life every hour. I am as a bankrupt to whom brilliant opportunities offer in vain. He has just foreclosed his freedom, tied his hands, locked himself up and given the key to another to keep.

When I see the doors by which God enters into the mind; that there is no sot or fop, ruffian or pedant into whom thoughts do not enter by passages which the individual never left open, I can expect any revolution in character. "I have hope," said the great Leibniz, "that society may be reformed, when I see how much education may be reformed."

It is ominous, a presumption of crime, that this word *Education* has so cold, so hopeless a sound. A treatise on education, a convention for education, a lecture, a system, affects us with slight paralysis and a certain yawning of the jaws. We are not encouraged when the law touches it with its fingers. Education should be as broad as man. Whatever elements are in him that should foster and demonstrate. If he be dexterous, his tuition should make it appear; if he be capable of dividing men by the trenchant sword of his thought, education should unsheathe and sharpen it; if he is one to cement society by his all-reconciling affinities, oh! hasten their action! If he is jovial, if he is mercurial, if he is greathearted, a cunning artificer, a strong commander, a potent ally, ingenious, useful, elegant, witty, prophet, diviner—society has need of all these. The imagination must be addressed. Whey always coast on the surface and never open the interior of nature, not by science, which is surface still, but by poetry? Is not the Vast an element of the mind? Yet what teaching, what book of this day appeals to the Vast?

Our culture has truckled to the times— to the senses. It is not manworthy. If the vast and the spiritual are omitted, so are the practical and the moral. It does not make us brave or free. We teach boys to be such men as we are. We do not teach them to aspire to be all they can. We do not give them a training as if we believed in their noble nature. We scarce educate their bodies. We do not train the eye and the hand. We exercise their understandings to the apprehension and comparison of some facts, to a skill in numbers, in words; we aim to make accountants, attorneys, engineers; but not to make able, earnest, greathearted men. The great object of education should be commensurate with the object of life. It should be a moral one; to teach self-trust: to inspire the youthful man with an interest in himself; with a curiosity touching his own nature; to acquaint him with the resources of his mind, and to teach him that there is all his strength, and to inflame him with a piety toward the Grand Mind in which he lives. Thus would education conspire with the Divine Providence. A man is a little thing while he works by and for himself, but, when he gives voice to the rules of love and justice, is godlike, his word is current in all countries; and all men, though his enemies, are made his friends and obey it as their own.

In affirming that the moral nature of man is the predominant element and should therefore be mainly consulted in the arrangements of a school, I am very far from wishing that it should swallow up all the other instincts and faculties of man. It should be enthroned in his mind, but if it monopolize the man he is not yet sound, he does not yet know his wealth. He is in danger of becoming merely devout, and wearisome through the monotony of his thought. It is not less necessary that the intellectual and the active faculties should be nourished and matured. Let us apply to this subject the light of the same torch by which we have looked at all the phenomena of the time; the infinitude, namely, of every man. Everything teaches that.

One fact constitutes all my satisfaction, inspires all my trust, *viz.*, this perpetual youth, which, as long as there is any good in us, we cannot get rid of. It is very certain that the coming age and the departing age seldom understand each other. The old man thinks the young man has no distinct purpose, for he could never get anything intelligible and earnest out of him. Perhaps the young man does not think it worth his while to explain himself to so hard and inapprehensive a confessor. Let him be led up with a longsighted forbearance, and let not the sallies of his petulance or folly be checked with disgust or indignation or despair.

I call our system a system of despair, and I find all the correction, all the revolution that is needed and that the best spirits of this age promise, in one word, in Hope. Nature, when she sends a new mind into the world, fills it beforehand with a desire for that which she wishes it to know and do. Let us wait and see what is this new creation, of what new organ the great Spirit had need when it incarnated this new Will. A new Adam in the garden, he is to name all the beasts in the field, all the gods in the sky. And jealous provision seems to have been made in his constitution that you shall not invade and contaminate him with the worn weeds of your language and opinions. The charm of life is this variety of genius, these contrasts and flavors by which Heaven has modulated the identity of truth, and there is a perpetual hankering to violate this individuality, to warp his ways of thinking and behavior to resemble or reflect your thinking and behavior. A low self-love in the parent desires that this child should repeat his character and fortune; an expectation which the child, if justice is done him, will nobly disappoint. By working on the theory that this resemblance exists, we shall do what in us lies to defeat his proper promise and produce the ordinary and mediocre. I suffer whenever I see that common sight of a parent or senior imposing his opinion and way of thinking and being on a young soul to which they are totally unfit. Cannot we let people be themselves, and enjoy life in their own way? You are trying to make that man another *you*. One's enough.

Or we sacrifice the genius of the pupil, the unknown possibilities of his nature, to a neat and safe uniformity, as the Turks whitewash the costly mosaics of ancient art which the Greeks left on their temple walls. Rather let us have men whose manhood is only the continuation of their boyhood, natural characters still; such are able and fertile for heroic action; and not that sad spectacle with which we are too familiar, educated eyes in uneducated bodies.

I like boys, the masters of the playground and of the street—boys, who have the same liberal ticket of admission to all shops, factories, armories, town meetings, caucuses, mobs, target shootings, as flies have; quite unsuspected, coming in as naturally as the janitor—known to have no money in their pockets, and themselves not suspecting the value of this poverty; putting nobody on his guard, but seeing the inside of the show—hearing all the asides. There are no secrets from them, they know everything that befalls in the fire company, the merits of every engine and of every man at the brakes, how to work it, and are swift to try their hand at every part; so too the merits of every locomotive on the rails, and will coax the engineer to let them ride with him and pull the handles when it goes to the enginehouse. They are there only for fun, and not knowing that they are at school, in the courthouse, or the cattle show, quite as much and more than they were, an hour ago, in the arithmetic class.

They know truth from counterfeit as quick as the chemist does. They detect weakness in your eye and behavior a week before you open your mouth, and have given you the benefit of their opinion quick as a wink. They make no mistakes, have no pedantry, but entire belief on experience. Their elections at baseball or cricket are founded on merit, and are right. They don't pass for swimmers until they can swim, nor for stroke-oar until they can row: and I desire to be saved from their contempt. If I can pass with them, I can manage well enough with their fathers.

Everybody delights in the energy with which boys deal and talk with each other; the mixture of fun and earnest, reproach and coaxing, love and wrath, with which the game is played—the good-natured yet defiant independence of a leading boy's behavior in the school yard. How we envy in later life the happy youths to whom their boisterous games and rough exercise furnish the precise element which frames and sets off their school and college tasks, and teaches them, when least they think it, the use and meaning of these. In their fun and extreme freak [i.e., caprice] they hit on the topmost sense of Horace. The young giant, brown from his hunting tramp, tells his story well, interlarded with lucky allusions to Homer, to Virgil, to college songs, to Walter Scott; and Jove and Achilles, partridge and trout, opera and binomial theorem, Caesar in Gaul, Sherman in Savannah, and hazing in Holworthy [ref. unknown], dance through the narrative in merry confusion, yet the logic is good. If he can turn his books to such picturesque account in his fishing and hunting, it is easy to see how his reading and experience, as he has more of both, will interpenetrate each other. And everyone desires that this pure vigor of action and wealth of narrative, cheered with so much humor and street rhetoric, should be carried into the habit of the young man, purged of its uproar and rudeness, but with all its vivacity entire. His hunting and campings-out have given him an indispensable base: I wish to add a taste for good company through his impatience of bad. That stormy genius of his needs a little direction to games, charades, verses of society, song, and a correspondence year by year with his wisest and best friends. Friendship is an order of nobility; from its revelations we come more worthily into nature. Society he must have or he is poor indeed; he gladly enters a school which forbids conceit, affectation, emphasis, and dullness, and requires of each only the flower of his nature and experience; requires good will, beauty, wit, and select information; teaches by practice the law of conversation, namely, to hear as well as to speak.

Meantime, if circumstances do not permit the high social advantages, solitude has also its lessons. The obscure youth learns there the practice instead of the literature of his virtues; and, because of the disturbing effect of passion and sense, which by a multitude of trifles impede the mind's eye from the quiet search of the fine horizon line which truth keeps—the way to knowledge and power has ever been an escape from too much engagement with affairs and possessions; a way, not through plenty and superfluity, but by denial and renunciation, into solitude and privation; and, the more is taken away, the more real and inevitable wealth of being is made known to us. The solitary knows the essence of the thought, the scholar in society only its fair face. There is no want of example of great men, great benefactors, who have been monks and hermits in habit. The bias of mind is sometimes irresistible in that direction. The man is, as it were, born deaf and dumb, and dedicated to a narrow and lonely life. Let him study the art of solitude, yield as gracefully as he can to his destiny. Why cannot he get the good of his doom, and if it is from eternity a settled fact that he and society shall be nothing to each other, why need he blush so, and make wry faces to keep up a freshman's seat in the fine world? Heaven often protects valuable souls charged with great secrets, great ideas, by long shutting them up with their own thoughts. And the most genial and amiable of men must alternate society with solitude, and learn its severe lessons.

There comes the period of the imagination to each, a later youth; the power of beauty, the power of books, of poetry. Culture makes his books realities to him, their characters more brilliant, more effective on his mind, than his actual mates. Do not spare to put novels into the hands of young people as an occasional holiday and experiment; but, above all, good poetry in all kinds, epic, tragedy, lyric. If we can touch the imagination, we serve them, they will never forget it. Let him read *Tom Brown at Rugby,* read *Tom Brown at Oxford,* better yet, read *Hodson's Life*—Hodson who took prisoner the King of Delhi. They teach the same truth—a trust, against all appearances, against all privations, in your own worth, and not in tricks, plotting, or patronage.

I believe that our own experience instructs us that the secret of education lies in respecting the pupil. It is not for you to choose what he shall know, what he shall do. It is chosen and foreordained, and he only holds the key to his own secret. By your tampering and thwarting and too much governing he may be hindered from his end and kept out of his own. Respect the child. Wait and see the new product of Nature. Nature loves analogies, but not repetitions. Respect the child. Be not too much his parent. Trespass not on his solitude.

But I fear the outcry which replies to

this suggestion—Would you verily throw up the reins of public and private discipline; would you leave the young child to the mad career of his own passions and whimsies, and call this anarchy a respect for the child's nature? I answer—Respect the child, respect him to the end, but also respect yourself. Be the companion of his thought, the friend of his friendship, the lover of his virtue—but no kinsman of his sin. Let him find you so true to yourself that you are the irreconcilable hater of his vice and the imperturbable slighter of his trifling.

The two points in a boy's training are, to keep his *naturel* and train off all but that—to keep his *naturel*, but stop off his uproar, fooling, and horseplay—keep his nature and arm it with knowledge in the very direction in which it points. Here are the two capital facts, Genius and Drill. The first is the inspiration in the wellborn healthy child, the new perception he has of nature. Somewhat he sees in forms or hears in music or apprehends in mathematics, or believes practicable in mechanics or possible in political society, which no one else sees or hears or believes. This is the perpetual romance of new life, the invasion of God into the old dead world, when he sends into quiet houses a young soul with a thought which is not met, looking for something which is not there, but which ought to be there: the thought is dim but it is sure, and he casts about restless for means and masters to verify it; he makes wild attempts to explain himself and invoke the aid and consent of the bystanders. Baffled for want of language and methods to convey his meaning, not yet clear to himself, he conceives that though not in this house or town, yet in some other house or town is the wise master who can put him in possession of the rules and instruments to execute his will. Happy this child with a bias, with a thought which entrances him, leads him, now into deserts now into cities, the fool of an idea. Let him follow it in good and in evil report, in good or bad

company; it will justify itself; it will lead him at last into the illustrious society of the lovers of truth.

In London, in a private company, I became acquainted with a gentleman, Sir Charles Fellowes, who, being at Xanthus, in the Aegean Sea, had seen a Turk point with his staff to some carved work on the corner of a stone almost buried in the soil. Fellowes scraped away the dirt, was struck with the beauty of the sculptured ornaments, and, looking about him, observed more blocks and fragments like this. He returned to the spot, procured laborers and uncovered many blocks. He went back to England, bought a Greek grammar and learned the language; he read history and studied ancient art to explain his stones; he interested Gibson the sculptor; he invoked the assistance of the English government; he called in the succor of Sir Humphry Davy to analyze the pigments; of experts in coins, of scholars and connoisseurs; and at last in his third visit brought home to England such statues and marble reliefs and such careful plans that he was able to reconstruct, in the British Museum where it now stands, the perfect model of the Ionic trophy-monument, fifty years older than the Parthenon of Athens, and which had been destroyed by earthquakes, then by iconoclast Christians, then by savage Turks. But mark that in the task he had achieved an excellent education, and become associated with distinguished scholars whom he had interested in his pursuit; in short, had formed a college for himself; the enthusiast had found the master, the masters, whom he sought. Always genius seeks genius, desires nothing so much as to be a pupil and to find those who can lend it aid to perfect itself.

Nor are the two elements, enthusiasm and drill, incompatible. Accuracy is essential to beauty. The very definition of the intellect is Aristotle's: "that by which we know terms or boundaries." Give a boy accurate perceptions. Teach him the difference between the similar and the same.

Make him call things by their right names. Pardon in him no blunder. Then he will give you solid satisfaction as long as he lives. It is better to teach the child arithmetic and Latin grammar than rhetoric or moral philosophy, because they require exactitude of performance; it is made certain that the lesson is mastered, and that power of performance is worth more than the knowledge. He can learn anything which is important to him now that the power to learn is secured: as mechanics say, when one has learned the use of tools, it is easy to work at a new craft.

Letter by letter, syllable by syllable, the child learns to read, and in good time can convey to all the domestic circle the sense of Shakespeare. By many steps each just as short, the stammering boy and the hesitating collegian, in the school debate, in college clubs, in mock court, comes at last to full, secure, triumphant unfolding of his thought in the popular assembly, with a fullness of power that makes all the steps forgotten.

But this function of opening and feeding the human mind is not to be fulfilled by any mechanical or military method; is not to be trusted to any skill less large than Nature itself. You must not neglect the form, but you must secure the essentials. It is curious how perverse and intermeddling we are, and what vast pains and cost we incur to do wrong. While we all know in our own experience and apply natural methods in our own business—in education our common sense fails us, and we are continually trying costly machinery against nature, in patent schools and academies and in great colleges and universities.

The natural method forever confutes our experiments, and we must still come back to it. The whole history of the school is on the nurse's or mother's knee. The child is as hot to learn as the mother is to impart. There is mutual delight. The joy of our childhood in hearing beautiful stories from some skillful aunt who loves to tell them, must be repeated in youth.

The boy wishes to learn to skate, to coast, to catch a fish in the brook, to hit a mark with a snowball or a stone; and a boy a little older is just as well pleased to teach him these sciences. Not less delightful is the mutual pleasure of teaching and learning the secret of algebra, or of chemistry, or of good reading and good recitation of poetry or of prose, or of chosen facts in history or in biography.

Nature provided for the communication of thought, by planting with it in the receiving mind a fury to impart it. 'Tis so in every art, in every science. One burns to tell the new fact, the other burns to hear it. See how far a young doctor will ride or walk to witness a new surgical operation. I have seen a carriage maker's shop emptied of all its workmen into the street, to scrutinize a new pattern from New York. So in literature, the young man who has taste for poetry, for fine images, for noble thoughts, is insatiable for this nourishment, and forgets all the world for the more learned friend—who finds equal joy in dealing out his treasures.

Happy the natural college thus self-instituted around every natural teacher; the young men of Athens around Socrates; of Alexandria around Plotinus; of Paris around Abelard; of Germany around Fichte, or Niebuhr, or Goethe: in short the natural sphere of every leading mind. But the moment this is organized, difficulties begin. The college was to be the nurse and home of genius; but, though every young man is born with some determination in his nature, and is a potential genius; is at last to be one; it is, in the most, obstructed and delayed, and, whatever they may hereafter be, their senses are now opened in advance of their minds. They are more sensual than intellectual. Appetite and indolence they have, but no enthusiasm. These come in numbers to the college, few geniuses; and the teaching comes to be arranged for these many, and not for those few. Hence the instruction seems to require skillful tutors, of accurate and systematic mind, rather than ardent and inventive masters. Besides, the youth of genius are eccentric, won't drill, are irritable, uncertain, explosive, solitary, not men of the world, not good for everyday association. You have to work for large classes instead of individuals; you must lower your flag and reef your sails to wait for the dull sailors; you grow departmental, routine, military almost with your discipline and college police. But what doth such a school to form a great and heroic character? What abiding hope can it inspire? What reformer will it nurse? What poet will it breed to sing to the human race? What discoverer of Nature's laws will it prompt to enrich us by disclosing in the mind the statute which all matter must obey? What fiery soul will it send out to warm a nation with his charity? What tranquil mind will it have fortified to walk with meekness in private and obscure duties, to wait and to suffer? Is it not manifest that our academic institutions should have a wider scope; that they should not be timid and keep the ruts of the last generation, but that wise men thinking for themselves and heartily seeking the good of mankind, and counting the cost of innovation, should dare to arouse the young to a just and heroic life; that the moral nature should be addressed in the schoolroom, and children should be treated as the highborn candidates of truth and virtue?

So to regard the young child, the young man, requires, no doubt, rare patience: a patience that nothing but faith in the remedial forces of the soul can give. You see his sensualism; you see his want of those tastes and perceptions which make the power and safety of your character. Very likely. But he has something else. If he has his own vice, he has its correlative virtue. Every mind should be allowed to make its own statement in action, and its balance will appear. In these judgments one needs that foresight which was attributed to an eminent reformer, of whom it was said "his patience could see in the bud of

the aloe the blossom at the end of a hundred years." Alas for the cripple Practice when it seeks to come up with the bird Theory, which flies before it. Try your design on the best school. The scholars are of all ages and temperaments and capacities. It is difficult to class them, some are too young, some are slow, some perverse. Each requires so much consideration, that the morning hope of the teacher, of a day of love and progress, is often closed at evening by despair. Each single case, the more it is considered, shows more to be done; and the strict conditions of the hours, on one side, and the number of tasks, on the other. Whatever becomes of our method, the conditions stand fast— six hours, and thirty, fifty, or a hundred and fifty pupils. Something must be done, and done speedily, and in this distress the wisest are tempted to adopt violent means, to proclaim martial law, corporal punishment, mechanical arrangement, bribes, spies, wrath, main strength and ignorance, in lieu of that wise genial providential influence they had hoped, and yet hope at some future day to adopt. Of course the devotion to details reacts injuriously on the teacher. He cannot indulge his genius, he cannot delight in personal relations with young friends, when his eye is always on the clock, and twenty classes are to be dealt with before the day is done. Besides, how can he please himself with genius, and foster modest virtue? A sure proportion of rogue and dunce finds its way into every school and requires a cruel share of time, and the gentle teacher, who wished to be a Providence to youth, is grown a martinet, sore with suspicions; knows as much vice as the judge of a police court, and his love of learning is lost in the routine of grammars and books of elements.

A rule is so easy that it does not need a man to apply it; an automaton, a machine, can be made to keep a school so. It facilitates labor and thought so much that there is always the temptation in large schools to omit the endless task of meeting the wants of each single mind, and to govern by steam. But it is at frightful cost. Our modes of education aim to expedite, to save labor; to do for masses what cannot be done for masses, what must be done reverently, one by one: say rather, the whole world is needed for the tuition of each pupil. The advantages of this system of emulation and display are so prompt and obvious, it is such a time-saver, it is so energetic on slow and on bad natures, and is of so easy application, needing no sage or poet, but any tutor or schoolmaster in his first term can apply it—that it is not strange that this calomel of culture should be a popular medicine. On the other hand, total abstinence from this drug, and the adoption of simple discipline and the following of nature, involves at once immense claims on the time, the thoughts, on the life of the teacher. It requires time, use, insight, event, all the great lessons and assistances of God; and only to think of using it implies character and profoundness; to enter on this course of discipline is to be good and great. It is precisely analogous to the difference between the use of corporal punishment and the methods of love. It is so easy to bestow on a bad boy a blow, overpower him, and get obedience without words, that in this world of hurry and distraction, who can wait for the returns of reason and the conquest of self; in the uncertainty too whether that will ever come? And yet the familiar observation of the universal compensations might suggest the fear that so summary a stop of a bad humor was more jeopardous than its continuance.

Now the correction of this quack practice is to import into education the wisdom of life. Leave this military hurry and adopt the pace of Nature. Her secret is patience. Do you know how the naturalist learns all the secrets of the forest, of plants, of birds, of beasts, of reptiles, of fishes, of the rivers and the sea? When he goes into the woods the birds fly before him and he finds none; when he goes to the riverbank, the fish and the reptile swim away and leave him alone. His secret is patience; he sits down, and sits still; he is a statue; he is a log. These creatures have no value for their time, and he must put as low a rate on his. By dint of obstinate sitting still, reptile, fish, bird, and beast, which all wish to return to their haunts, begin to return. He sits still; if they approach, he remains passive as the stone he sits upon. They lose their fear. They have curiosity too about him. By and by the curiosity masters the fear, and they come swimming, creeping, and flying toward him; and as he is still immovable, they not only resume their haunts and their ordinary labors and manners, show themselves to him in their workday trim, but also volunteer some degree of advances toward fellowship and good understanding with a biped who behaves so civilly and well. Can you not baffle the impatience and passion of the child by your tranquillity? Can you not wait for him, as Nature and Providence do? Can you not keep for his mind and ways, for his secret, the same curiosity you give to the squirrel, snake, rabbit, and the sheldrake and the deer? He has a secret; wonderful methods in him; he is—every child—a new style of man; give him time and opportunity. Talk of Columbus and Newton! I tell you the child just born in yonder hovel is the beginning of a revolution as great as theirs. But you must have the believing and prophetic eye. Have the self-command you wish to inspire. Your teaching and discipline must have the reserve and taciturnity of Nature. Teach them to hold their tongues by holding your own. Say little; do not snarl; do not chide; but govern by the eye. See what they need, and that the right thing is done.

I confess myself utterly at a loss in suggesting particular reforms in our ways of teaching. No discretion that can be lodged with a school committee, with the overseers or visitors of an academy, of a college, can at all avail to reach these difficulties and perplexities, but they solve themselves when we leave institutions and address individuals. The will, the male power, organizes, imposes its own thought and wish on others, and makes that military eye which controls boys as it controls men; admirable in its results, a fortune to him who has it, and only dangerous when it leads the workman to overvalue and overuse it and precludes him from finer means. Sympathy, the female force—which they must use who have not the first—deficient in instant control and the breaking down of resistance, is more subtle and lasting and creative. I advise teachers to cherish mother wit. I assume that you will keep the grammar, reading, writing, and arithmetic in order; 'tis easy and of course you will. But smuggle in a little contraband wit, fancy, imagination, thought. If you have a taste which you have suppressed because it is not shared by those about you, tell them that. Set this law up, whatever becomes of the rules of the school: they must not whisper, much less talk; but if one of the young people says a wise thing, greet it, and let all the children clap their hands. They shall have no book but schoolbooks in the room; but if one has brought in a Plutarch or Shakespeare or Don Quixote or Goldsmith or any other good book, and understands what he reads, put him at once at the head of the class. Nobody shall be disorderly, or leave his desk without permission, but if a boy runs from his bench, or a girl, because the fire falls, or to check some injury that a little dastard is inflicting behind his desk

on some helpless sufferer, take away the medal from the head of the class and give it on the instant to the brave rescuer. If a child happens to show that he knows any fact about astronomy, or plants, or birds, or rocks, or history, that interests him and you, hush all the classes and encourage him to tell it so that all may hear. Then you have made your schoolroom like the world. Of course you will insist on modesty in the children, and respect to their teachers, but if the boy stops you in your speech, cries out that you are wrong and sets you right, hug him!

To whatsoever upright mind, to whatsoever beating heart I speak, to you it is committed to educate men. By simple living, by an illimitable soul, you inspire, you correct, you instruct, you raise, you embellish all. By your own act you teach the beholder how to do the practicable. According to the depth from which you draw your life, such is the depth not only of your strenuous effort, but of your manners and presence.

The beautiful nature of the world has here blended your happiness with your power. Work straight on in absolute duty, and you lend an arm and an encouragement to all the youth of the universe. Consent yourself to be an organ of your highest thought, and lo! suddenly you put all men in your debt, and are the fountain of an energy that goes pulsing on with waves of benefit to the borders of society, to the circumference of things.

Memory

Memory is a primary and fundamental faculty, without which none other can work; the cement, the bitumen, the matrix in which the other faculties are imbedded; or it is the thread on which the beads of man are strung, making the personal identity which is necessary to moral action. Without it all life and thought were an unrelated succession. As gravity holds matter from flying off into space, so memory gives stability to knowledge; it is the cohesion which keeps things from falling into a lump, or flowing in waves.

We like longevity, we like signs of riches and extent of nature in an individual. And most of all we like a great memory. The lowest life remembers. The sparrow, the ant, the worm, have the same memory as we. If you bar their path, or offer them somewhat disagreeable to their senses, they make one or two trials, and then once for all avoid it.

Every machine must be perfect of its sort. It is essential to a locomotive that it can reverse its movement, and run backward and forward with equal celerity. The builder of the mind found it not less needful that it should have retroaction, and command its past act and deed. Perception, though it were immense and could pierce through the universe, was not sufficient.

Memory performs the impossible for man by the strength of his divine arms; holds together past and present, beholding both, existing in both, abides in the flowing, and gives continuity and dignity to human life. It holds us to our family, to our friends. Hereby a home is possible; hereby only a new fact has value.

Opportunities of investment are useful only to those who have capital. Any piece of knowledge I acquire today, a fact that falls under my eyes, a book I read, a piece of news I hear, has a value at this moment exactly proportioned to my skill to deal with it. Tomorrow, when I know more, I recall that piece of knowledge and use it better.

The past has a new value every moment to the active mind, through the incessant purification and better method of its memory. Once it joined its facts by color and form and sensuous relations. Some fact that had a childish significance to your childhood and was a type in the nursery, when riper intelligence recalls it means more and serves you better as an illustration; and perhaps in your age has new meaning. What was an isolated, unrelated belief or conjecture, our later experience instructs us how to place in just connection with other views which confirm and expand it. The old whim or perception was an augury of a broader insight, at which we arrive later with securer conviction. This is the companion, this the tutor, the poet, the library, with which you travel. It does not lie, cannot be corrupted, reports to you not what you wish but what really befell. You say, "I can never think of some act of neglect, of selfishness, or of passion without pain." Well, that is as it should be. That is the police of the Universe: the angels are set to punish you, so long as you are capable of such crime. But in the history of character the day comes when you are incapable of such crime. Then you suffer no more, you look on it as heaven looks on it, with wonder at the deed, and with applause at the pain it has cost you.

Memory is not a pocket, but a living instructor, with a prophetic sense of the values which he guards; a guardian angel set there within you to record your life, and by recording to animate you to uplift it. It is a scripture written day by day from the birth of the man; all its records full of meanings which open as he lives on, explaining each other, explaining the world to him and expanding their sense as he advances, until it shall become the whole law of nature and life.

As every creature is furnished with teeth to seize and eat, and with stomach to digest its food, so the memory is furnished with a perfect apparatus. There is no book like the memory, none with such a good index, and that of every kind, alphabetic, systematic, arranged by names of persons, by colors, tastes, smells, shapes, likeness, unlikeness, by all sorts of mysterious hooks and eyes to catch and hold, and contrivances for giving a hint.

The memory collects and re-collects. We figure it as if the mind were a kind of looking glass, which being carried through the street of time receives on its clear plate every image that passes; only with this difference that our plate is iodized so that every image sinks into it, and is held there. But in addition to this property it has one more, this, namely, that of all the million images that are imprinted, the very one we want reappears in the center of the plate in the moment when we want it.

We can tell much about it, but you must not ask us what it is. On seeing a face I am aware that I have seen it before, or that I have not seen it before. On hearing a fact told I am aware that I knew it already. You say the first words of the old song, and I finish the line and the stanza. But where I have them, or what becomes of them when I am not thinking of them for months and years, that they should lie so still, as if they did not exist, and yet, so nigh that they come on the instant when they are called for, never any man was so sharp-sighted, or could turn himself inside out quick enough to find.

'Tis because of the believed incompatibility of the affirmative and advancing attitude of the mind with tenacious acts of recollection that people are often reproached with living in their memory. Late in life we live by memory, and in our solstices or periods of stagnation; as the starved camel in the desert lives on his humps. Memory was called by the schoolmen *vespertina cognitio*, evening knowledge, in distinction from the command of the future which we have by the knowledge of causes, and which they called *matutina cognitio*, or morning knowledge.

Am I asked whether the thoughts clothe themselves in words? I answer, Yes, always; but they are apt to be instantly forgotten. Never was truer fable than that of the Sibyl's writing on leaves which the wind scatters. The difference between men is that in one the memory with inconceivable swiftness flies after and re-collects the flying leaves—flies on wing as fast as that mysterious whirlwind, and the envious Fate is baffled.

This command of old facts, the clear beholding at will of what is best in our experience, is our splendid privilege. "He who calls what is vanished back again into being enjoys a bliss like that of creating," says Niebuhr. The memory plays a great part in settling the intellectual rank of men. We estimate a man by how much he remembers. A seneschal of Parnassus [Greek mountain sacred to the Muses] is Mnemosyne [mother of the Muses]. This power will alone make a man remarkable; and it is found in all good wits. Therefore the poets represented the Muses as the daughters of Memory, for the power exists in some marked and eminent degree in men of an ideal determination. Quintilian reckoned it the measure of genius: *"Tantum ingenii quantum memoriae."*

We are told that Boileau having recited to Daguesseau [ref. unknown; a forgotten prodigy] one day an epistle or satire he had just been composing, Daguesseau tranquilly told him he knew it already, and in proof set himself to recite it from end to end. Boileau, astonished, was much distressed until he perceived that it was only a feat of memory.

The mind disposes all its experience after its affection and to its ruling end; one man by puns and one by cause and effect, one to heroic benefit and one to wrath and animal desire. This is the high difference, the quality of the association by which a man remembers. In the minds of most men memory is nothing but a farm book or a pocket diary. On such a day I paid my note; on the next day the cow calved; on the next I cut my finger; on the next the banks suspended payment. But another man's memory is the history of science and art and civility and thought; and still another deals with laws and perceptions that are the theory of the world.

This thread or order of remembering, this classification, distributes men, one remembering by shop rule or interest; one by passion; one by trifling external marks, as dress or money. And one rarely takes an interest in how the facts really stand, in the order of cause and effect, without self-reference. This is an intellectual man. Nature interests him; a plant, a fish, time, space, mind, being, in their own method and law. Napoleon was such, and that saves him.

But this mysterious power that binds our life together has its own vagaries and interruptions. It sometimes occurs that memory has a personality of its own, and volunteers or refuses its informations at its will, not at mine. One sometimes asks himself, Is it possible that it is only a visitor, not a resident? Is it some old aunt who goes in and out of the house, and occasionally recites anecdotes of old times and persons which I recognize as having heard before, and she being gone again I search in vain for any trace of the anecdotes?

We can help ourselves to the *modus* of

mental processes only by coarse material experiences. A knife with a good spring, a forceps whose lips accurately meet and match, a steel trap, a loom, a watch, the teeth or jaws of which fit and play perfectly, as compared with the same tools when badly put together, describe to us the difference between a person of quick and strong perception, like Franklin or Swift or Webster or Richard Owen, and a heavy man who witnesses the same facts or shares experiences like theirs. 'Tis like the impression made by the same stamp in sand or in wax. The way in which Burke or Sheridan or Webster or any orator surprises us is by his always having a sharp tool that fits the present use. He has an old story, an odd circumstance, that illustrates the point he is now proving, and is better than an argument. The more he is heated, the wider he sees; he seems to remember all he ever knew; thus certifying us that he is in the habit of seeing better than other people; that what his mind grasps it does not let go. 'Tis the bulldog bite; you must cut off the head to loosen the teeth.

We hate this fatal shortness of memory, these docked men whom we behold. We gathered up what a rolling snowball as we came along—much of it professedly for the future, as capital stock of knowledge. Where is it now? Look behind you. I cannot see that your train is any longer than it was in childhood. The facts of the last two or three days or weeks are all you have with you—the reading of the last month's books. Your conversation, action, your face and manners report of no more, of no greater wealth of mind. Alas! you have lost something for everything you have gained, and cannot grow. Only so much iron will the lodestone draw; it gains new particles all the way as you move it, but one falls off for every one that adheres.

As there is strength in the wild horse which is never regained when he is once broken by training, and as there is a sound sleep of children and of savages, profound as the hibernation of bears, which never visits the eyes of civil gentlemen and ladies, so there is a wild memory in children and youth which makes what is early learned impossible to forget; and perhaps in the beginning of the world it had most vigor. Plato deplores writing as a barbarous invention which would weaken the memory by disuse. The rhapsodists in Athens it seems could recite at once any passage of Homer that was desired.

If writing weakens the memory, we may say as much and more of printing. What is the newspaper but a sponge or invention for oblivion? the rule being that for every fact added to the memory, one is crowded out, and that only what the affection animates can be remembered.

The mind has a better secret in generalization than merely adding units to its list of facts. The reason of the short memory is shallow thought. As deep as the thought, so great is the attraction. An act of the understanding will marshal and concatenate a few facts; a principle of the reason will thrill and magnetize and redistribute the whole world.

But defect of memory is not always want of genius. By no means. It is sometimes owing to excellence of genius. Thus men of great presence of mind who are always equal to the occasion do not need to rely on what they have stored for use, but can think in this moment as well and deeply as in any past moment, and if they cannot remember the rule they can make one. Indeed it is remarked that inventive men have bad memories. Sir Isaac Newton was embarrassed when the conversation turned on his discoveries and results; he could not recall them; but if he was asked why things were so or so he could find the reason on the spot.

A man would think twice about learning a new science or reading a new paragraph, if he believed the magnetism was only a constant amount, and that he lost a word or a thought for every word he gained. But the experience is not quite so bad.

In reading a foreign language, every new word mastered is a lamp lighting up related words and so assisting the memory. Apprehension of the whole sentence aids to fix the precise meaning of a particular word, and what familiarity has been acquired with the genius of the language and the writer helps in fixing the exact meaning of the sentence. So is it with every fact in a new science: they are mutually explaining, and each one adds transparency to the whole mass.

The damages of forgetting are more than compensated by the large values which new thoughts and knowledge give to what we already know. If new impressions sometimes efface old ones, yet we steadily gain insight; and because all nature has one law and meaning—part corresponding to part—all we have known aids us continually to the knowledge of the rest of nature. Thus, all the facts in this chest of memory are property at interest. And who shall set a boundary to this mounting value? Shall we not on higher stages of being remember and understand our early history better?

They say in Architecture, "An arch never sleeps"; I say, the Past will not sleep, it works still. With every new fact a ray of light shoots up from the long buried years. Who can judge the new book? He who has read many books. Who, the new assertion? He who has heard many the like. Who, the new man? He that has seen men. The experienced and cultivated man is lodged in a hall hung with pictures which every new day retouches, and to which every step in the march of the soul adds a more sublime perspective.

We learn early that there is great disparity of value between our experiences; some thoughts perish in the using. Some days are bright with thought and sentiment, and we live a year in a day. Yet these best days are not always those which memory can retain. This water once spilled cannot be gathered. There are more inventions in the thoughts of one happy day than ages could execute, and I suppose I speak the sense of most thoughtful men when I say, I would rather have a perfect recollection of all I have thought and felt in a day or a week of high activity than read all the books that have been published in a century.

The memory is one of the compensations which Nature grants to those who have used their days well; when age and calamity have bereaved them of their limbs or organs, then they retreat on mental faculty and concentrate on that. The poet, the philosopher, lamed, old, blind, sick, yet disputing the ground inch by inch against fortune, finds a strength against the wrecks and decays sometimes more invulnerable than the heyday of youth and talent.

I value the praise of Memory. And how does Memory praise? By holding fast the best. A thought takes its true rank in the memory by surviving other thoughts that were once preferred. Plato remembered Anaxagoras by one of his sayings. If we recall our own favorites we shall usually find that it is for one crowning act or thought that we hold them dear.

Have you not found memory an apotheosis or deification? The poor, short lone fact dies at the birth. Memory catches it up into her heaven, and bathes it in immortal waters. Then a thousand times over it lives and acts again, each time transfigured, ennobled. In solitude, in darkness, we tread over again the sunny walks of youth; confined now in populous streets you behold again the green fields, the shadows of the gray birches; by the solitary river hear again the joyful voices of early companions, and vibrate anew to the tenderness and dainty music of the poetry your boyhood fed upon. At this hour the stream is still flowing, though you hear it not; the plants are still drinking their accustomed life and repaying it with their beautiful forms. But you need not wander thither. It flows for you, and they grow for you, in the returning images of former summers. In low or bad company you fold yourself in your cloak, withdraw yourself entirely from all the doleful circumstance, recall and surround yourself with the best associates and the fairest hours of your life—

Passing sweet are the domains of tender memory.

You may perish out of your senses, but not out of your memory or imagination.

The memory has a fine art of sifting out the pain and keeping all the joy. The spring days when the bluebird arrives have usually only few hours of fine temperature, are sour and unlovely; but when late in autumn we hear rarely a bluebird's notes they are sweet by reminding us of the spring. Well, it is so with other tricks of memory. Of the most romantic fact the memory is more romantic; and this power of sinking the pain of any experience and of recalling the saddest with tranquillity, and even with a wise pleasure, is familiar. The memory is as the affection. Sampson Reed [1800–80; Swedenborgian philosopher highly regarded by Emerson] says, "The true way to store the memory is to develop the affections." A *souvenir* is a token of love. *Remember me* means, Do not cease to love me. We remember those things which we love and those things which we hate. The memory of all men is robust on the subject of a debt due to them, or of an insult inflicted on them. "They can remember," as Johnson said, "who kicked them last."

Every artist is alive on the subject of his art. The Persians say, "A real singer will never forget the song he has once learned." Michelangelo, after having once seen a work of any other artist, would remember it so perfectly that if it pleased him to make use of any portion thereof, he could do so, but in such a manner that none could perceive it.

We remember what we understand, and we understand best what we like; for this doubles our power of attention, and makes it our own. Captain John Brown, of Ossawatomie, said he had in Ohio three thousand sheep on his farm, and could tell a strange sheep in his flock as soon as he saw its face. One of my neighbors, a grazier, told me that he should know again every cow, ox, or steer that he ever saw. Abel Lawton knew every horse that went up and down through Concord to the towns in the county. And in higher examples each man's memory is in the line of his action.

Nature trains us on to see illusions and prodigies with no more wonder than our toast and omelet at breakfast. Talk of memory and cite me these fine examples of Grotius [a formidably learned scholar and jurist] and Daguesseau, and I think how awful is that power and what privilege and tyranny it must confer. Then I come to a bright schoolgirl who remembers all she hears, carries thousands of nursery rhymes and all the poetry in all the readers, hymnbooks, and pictorial ballads in her mind; and 'tis a mere drug. She carries it so carelessly, it seems like the profusion of hair on the shock heads of all the village boys and village dogs; it grows like grass. 'Tis a bushel-basket memory of all unchosen knowledge, heaped together in a huge hamper, without method, yet securely held, and ready to come at call; so that an old scholar, who knows what to do with a memory, is full of wonder and pity that this magical force should be squandered on such frippery.

He is a skillful doctor who can give me a recipe for the cure of a bad memory. And yet we have some hints from experience on this subject. And first, *health.* It is found that we remember best when the head is clear, when we are thoroughly awake. When the body is in a quiescent state in the absence of the passions, in the moderation of food, it yields itself a willing medium to the intellect. For the true river Lethe is the body of man, with its belly and uproar of appetite and mountains of indigestion and bad humors and quality of darkness. And for this reason, and observing some mysterious continuity of mental operation during sleep or when our will is suspended, 'tis an old rule of scholars, that which Fuller records, "'Tis best knocking in the nail overnight and clinching it next morning." Only I should give extension to this rule and say Yes, drive the nail this week and clinch it the next, and drive it this year and clinch it the next.

But Fate also is an artist. We forget also according to beautiful laws. Thoreau said, "of what significance are the things you can forget. A little thought is sexton to all the world."

We must be severe with ourselves, and what we wish to keep we must once thoroughly possess. Then the thing seen will no longer be what it was, a mere sensuous object before the eye or ear, but a reminder of its law, a possession for the intellect. Then we relieve ourselves of all task in the matter, we put the *onus* of being remembered on the object, instead of on our will. We shall do as we do with all our studies, prize the fact or the name of the person by the predominance it takes in our mind after near acquaintance. I have several times forgotten the name of Flamsteed [the Astronomer Royal in Newton's time], never that of Newton; and can drop easily many poets out of the Elizabethan chronology, but not Shakespeare.

We forget rapidly what should be forgotten. The *universal* sense of fables and anecdotes is marked by our tendency to forget name and date and geography. "How in the right are children," said Margaret Fuller [1810–50; writer and social reformer], "to forget name and date and place."

You cannot overstate our debt to the past, but has the present no claim? This past memory is the baggage, but where is the troop? The divine gift is not the old but the new. The divine is the instant life that receives and uses, the life that can well bury the old in the omnipotency with which it makes all things new.

The acceleration of mental process is equivalent to the lengthening of life. If a great many thoughts pass through your mind you will believe a long time has elapsed, many hours or days. In dreams a rush of many thoughts, of seeming experiences, of spending hours and going through a great variety of actions and companies, and when we start up and look at the watch, instead of a long night we are surprised to find it was a short nap. The opium eater says, "I sometimes seemed to have lived seventy or a hundred years in one night." You know what is told of the experience of some persons who have been recovered from drowning. They relate that their whole life's history seemed to pass before them in review. They remembered in a moment all that they ever did.

If we occupy ourselves long on this wonderful faculty, and see the natural helps of it in the mind, and the way in which new knowledge calls upon old knowledge— new giving undreamed-of value to old; everywhere relation and suggestion, so that what one had painfully held by strained attention and recapitulation now falls into place and is clamped and locked by inevitable connection as a planet in its orbit (every other orb, or the law or system of which it is a part, being a perpetual reminder)—we cannot fail to draw thence a sublime hint that thus there must be an endless increase in the power of memory only through its use; that there must be a proportion between the power of memory and the amount of knowables; and since the universe opens to us, the reach of the memory must be as large.

With every broader generalization which the mind makes, with every deeper insight, its retrospect is also wider. With every new insight into the duty or fact of today we come into new possession of the past.

When we live by principles instead of traditions, by obedience to the law of the mind instead of by passion, the Great Mind will enter into us, not as now in fragments and detached thoughts, but the light of today will shine backward and forward.

Memory is a presumption of a possession of the future. Now we are halves, we see the past but not the future, but in that day will the hemisphere complete itself and foresight be as perfect as aftersight.

Architectural Papers

Louis H. Sullivan

Editor's Introduction

There are two names that must appear on anyone's list of great American architects. One is Frank Lloyd Wright. The other is Louis Sullivan. Wright, who was Sullivan's student, built fine public buildings, but he is best known for the houses he designed, so striking in their horizontal lines, their perfect fitness to surroundings that seem part of them. Sullivan built houses, too, at least in early days—town houses, as they tended to be, in the city of Chicago, where he lived. But he was, par excellence, a designer of public and commercial structures—skyscrapers, as we might say, though none were of the height which that term signifies for us now. He is the great architect of urban spaces, of the city, and he made Chicago a symbol of the kind of architecture we still call modern, notwithstanding that all of his best work there was done a hundred years ago, in the decade of the 1890s. We could say—it is surely not too much to say—that Sullivan was the first man to see that the modern city needed an architecture of its own, as distinct from the mere enlargement of traditional forms. This at any rate is what he created, with a succession of buildings which are everywhere recognized, a little inconsistently, as classics of their kind.

Despite such distinction, Sullivan's productive career was brief. Born in Boston in 1856, he studied architecture briefly at the Massachusetts Institute of Technology, at that time the only school in the United States with a program in the subject, but withdrew after a year and in 1874 sailed to Paris, where he managed to pass the difficult entrance examination for the École des Beaux Arts. He was but a fitful student, though he took the opportunity to visit Florence and Rome. In 1875 he returned home to settle in Chicago. There, after working as a draftsman with several firms in that city, he got a job with one at which in 1879 he met Dankmar Adler, who in 1881, when Sullivan was 24, took him on as a partner.

This relationship, which lasted until 1895, was the making of Sullivan. Adler was a good businessman, which Sullivan was not; he was also an engineer, with special competence in acoustics. The combination of their talents produced the Auditorium Building in Chicago, a large pile of rough, gray stone which enclosed among other things a beautifully decorated concert hall, and which was completed in December 1889. It was Sullivan's first great triumph. Other commissions soon followed, notably the Wainwright Building in St. Louis. This is widely regarded as Sullivan's most important structure because, unlike the Auditorium, it has a steel frame, and because for the first time such a building was given an elegant and efficient form.

Perhaps his most influential work after that was the so-called Transportation Building he contributed to the World's Columbian Exposition, or World's Fair, at Chicago in 1893. Sullivan, like others, had hoped that this event would show America's commitment to a new kind of architecture, and he was bitterly disappointed when instead a series of neoclassic structures was decided upon. Sullivan knew that these would be widely influential, and that the setback they represented to the kind of architecture in which he believed—that is, modern architecture— would be severe. "The damage wrought by the World's Fair will last half a century from its date, if not longer," he predicted angrily. "It has penetrated deep into the constitution of the American mind, effecting there lesions significant of dementia." His Transportation Building (long since demolished), with its spreading structure and large, semicircular entrance—the so-called Golden Door of the Exposition—was an isolated and defiant statement of the direction he believed architecture ought to take in America, and which it did take, true to his prediction, only after the Second World War.

A period of poor business caused the breakup of Sullivan's partnership with Adler, and while Adler afterward proposed a renewal of their firm, Sullivan's touchy, irascible, tactless temper prevented this from happening. Unhappily, the same qualities made it hard for him to do business on his own—he alienated too many clients—and he was never really successful again. Indeed, after 1900 he had only about twenty commissions, many of which, though they contain much fine detail, were insignificant.

He remains important not only for his buildings, a fair number of which survive, but as a kind of prophet of modern architecture. The account he wrote of his own life, *The Autobiography of an Idea* (1924), is still valuable as a manifesto of the subject, as are some earlier short articles, dating mostly from the 1890s, which he collected with what he called his *Kindergarten Chats*—essays, articles, and talks he gave at various times—of which several are reprinted here. In them will be found the dictum he made famous, which was that in buildings, form should follow function—which may be traced in part to his American predecessor, Horatio Greenough (*GIT* 1984, 292–357). They contain as well a number of statements as to the unlimited resources of the human spirit which recall Emerson, some of whose writings appear elsewhere in this issue of *The Great Ideas Today*.

Architectural Papers

Characteristics and tendencies
of American architecture

Many who have commented upon the practice of architecture in this country have regarded the absence of a style, distinctively American, as both strange and deplorable; and with a view to betterment they have advanced theories as to the nature, and immediate realization, of such a style that evidence a lack of insight equally strange and deplorable. These theories have been for the greater part suggested by the feelings awakened in contemplating the matured beauty of Old World art, and imply a grafting or transplanting process. They have been proved empirical by the sufficient logic of time; their advocates having ignored the complex fact, that, like a new species of any class, a national style must be a growth, that slow and gradual assimilation of nutriment and a struggle against obstacles are necessary adjuncts to the purblind processes of growth, and that the resultant structure can bear only a chemical or metaphysical resemblance to the materials on which it has been nurtured.

We will, therefore, for the purposes of this paper disregard these dreams of a Minerva-like architectural splendor springing full-formed into being, and look rather for the early signs of a spontaneous architectural feeling arising in sympathy with the emotions latent or conspicuous in our people.

It is reasonable to believe that an unconquered country, peopled by colonization and natural increase, may bear in its younger and its coming generations a race whose birthright, implying freedom to receive and assimilate impressions, shall nurture emotions of rare quality and of a fruitfulness commensurate with the energy in an unexhausted soil.

It would be erroneous to assume that there will be no evidence of the activity of such emotions until as a large accumulation they break all bonds asunder. The individual is from day to day seeking expedients by means of which to shape his immediate surroundings into a realization of his desires, and we may assume it to be quite probable that the initial impelling force, operating through the individual, has already in many cases produced significant and valuable results. These results, if not thoroughly typical, must have in them much that is eminently characteristic, and that bear the stamp of internal origin.

To test this hypothesis we have therefore but to look into the daily life of our architecture and, in the complexion of its many fleeting phases, seek here and there for instances, some perhaps almost trivial, in which the existence of spontaneous and characteristic emotional feeling may be detected. Sometimes we shall find this impulse appearing as an element of warmth tingeing scholastic formalism; sometimes as a seemingly paradoxical inspiration in the works of the uncultivated. We may certainly expect to meet with it in the efforts of those upon whose imagination the chromatic eloquence of words and of music have taken strong hold; and above all, we are to look for it in the creations of the gifted ones whose souls are finely attuned to the touching beauty of nature and of humanity. To an apprehension of this subtle element, we may be happily guided by the suggestions of analogy. Our recent American literature comes aptly to this use. Glancing through its focusing substance, as through the lens of a camera, we may perceive an image of the abstraction we seek, and, by an extension of the process, we may fix an impression of its form and texture, to be developed at will.

Our literature is the only phase of our national art that has been accorded serious recognition, at home and abroad. The noticeable qualities of its present phases seem to be: excessive regard for minute detail, painful self-consciousness of finish, timidity and embarrassment in the delineation of all but the well-behaved and docile emotions, and a tacit fiction as to the passions: all beautifully executed with much patient, earnest labor, and diplomatically tempered to the understanding.

Exquisite, but not virile, our latter-day literature illustrates quite emphatically the quality of our tentative and provisional culture, which must ere long throw off these seedling leaves, when a higher temperature shall infuse glowing vitality into root and stem, and exuberant foliation give more certain assurance of the coming flower of our soil. Our literature, and in fact all that which we Americans complacently call our art, is too much a matter of heart and fingers, and too little an offspring of brain and soul. One must indeed have faith in the processes of nature to prophesy order eventuating upon so strange a chaos of luxuries. But to this end, transmitted knowledge must gradually be supplemented by the fresh impressions of the senses and the sensibilities, the fund so accumulated yielding richly of its own increase. This supplemental acquisition must of necessity be of slow growth, for we have all been educated to a dependence upon our artistic inheritance.

Our art is for the day, is suited to the day, and will also change as the day

changes. The law of variation is an ever-present force, and coordination is its goal. The first step toward a new order of things is accomplished when there appear minds receiving and assimilating fresh impressions, reaching new conclusions, and acting upon them. By this sign, we may know that such a movement is already upon us, and by the aid of the indicated literary analogy we may follow its erratic tendencies and note its increase in strength and individuality: we may see the germ of poetry which each man has within him, slowly awakening into life, and may feel the presence of an American romanticism.

This romanticism is, in the main, also exquisite but not virile. It seeks to touch all things with softened hand. Under the influence of its warmth of feeling, hard lines flow into graceful curves, angularities disappear in a mystical blending of surfaces.

One by one the completed styles of foreign climes are passing under this hand, each in turn being quietly divested of its local charm and clothed in a sentiment and mannerism unmistakably our own. Power laments, meanwhile, at the feet of a modern Omphale, his voice attuned to the domestic hum of the times.

Appreciation of the beauties of this romanticism is to some extent dependent upon the verbal explanation and comment of its exponents. A knowledge of their vocabulary is often of assistance in disclosing softness and refinement in many primitive expedients, and revealing beauty in barren places. Familiarity with the current phraseology of the allied arts is also useful in assisting the student to a comprehension of many things apparently incomprehensible. Metaphor and simile are rampant in this connection, a well-chosen word often serving to justify an architectural absurdity.

But overloaded as is this fabric of impulse with florid and complicated intertwinings of affection, when we examine the material thereof, we find it excellent and valuable.

Searching critically among the works executed in this feeling, we note in the varying examples, and indeed in parts of the same structure, a curious *mélange* of supersentimentalisms. Conspicuous at first glance, in some an offensive simplicity, in others a highly wrought charlatanism; further, we perceive ingenuity in device, or superb flow of spirits—all more or less leavened with stubborn common sense. After such an investigation, we may gladly become convinced that behind a somewhat uncertain vision resides a marvelous instinct.

National sensitiveness and pride, conjoined with fertility of resource, will aid as active stimuli in the development of this instinct toward a more rational and organic mode of expression, leading through many reactions to a higher sphere of artistic development.

We are now in the primary department, vaguely endeavoring to form a plastic alphabet by means of which to identify our beliefs. Progress in this respect has been very slow and results meager: for our beliefs have still within them too much of uncertainty and diffidence to take rank as convictions. Without these latter a sufficient creating power is lacking. The formation of an alphabet, and the simplest combinations of its terms, are matters of much importance; and easy progress in this respect is seriously impeded by complications of thought. To look at things simply and clearly is quite easy, until counterinfluences are set at work; then comes a struggle for survival, which now and then is successful—the result being an addition, however small, to our stock of elementary forms.

The ability to develop elementary ideas organically is not conspicuous in our profession. In this respect, the architect is inferior to the businessman and financier, whose capacity to expand a simple congenial idea, once fixed, into subtle, manifold and consistent ramifications is admirable, and a shining example which we have often

ignored, creating thereby an undesirable impression.

This view leads us on to a consideration of the element of power. Until this element is widely introduced into our work, giving it the impress of brilliancy, intuition, and great depth of feeling, that work, exhaustively considered, will remain but little more than a temporary expedient.

The presence of power, as a mental characteristic in one class of our people, augurs well for the belief that it may pervade our ranks. The beginnings of power are usually so crude and harsh as to be revolting to a refined taste, and hence it is instinctively shunned; but once subtilized, flushed with emotion, and guided by clear insight, it is a worker of miracles; responsive to its ardent wooings, Nature yields up her poetic secrets.

We surely have in us the germ of artistic greatness—no people on earth possessing more of innate poetic feeling, more of ideality, greater capacity to adore the beautiful, than our own people; but architects as a professional class have held it more expedient to maintain the traditions of their culture than to promulgate vitalizing thought. Here then we are weak, and should sentiment gain a pronounced ascendency, we may remain weak.

On us rests partially the responsibility, and partially on the public. We have at times individually sought to lead the public, when we more wisely should have followed it; and have, as a body, often followed, when with beneficent results we could have led. While we may compromise for a time, through a process of local adaptation, no architectural style can become a finality that runs counter to popular feeling. The desire at once to follow and to lead the public should be the initial attitude of our profession toward the formation of a national style. For while we conduct the technical operations, the shaping and controlling process is mainly in the hands of the public who are constantly keeping us within bounds. We cannot wholly escape this control, while we are without a national architecture fully representing the wishes of the public, and ministering to its conceptions of the beautiful and the useful. This can evidently not come to pass forthwith, for the public itself can only partially and imperfectly state its wants. Responding readily, however, to the intuition of those who anticipate its desires, it accepts provisionally year by year all the satisfaction it can get; so that while one recognized style after another shall pass through our hands to be tried and finally rejected in the search for permanent satisfaction, a modified residuum from each will doubtless be added to a fund representing our growth in emotional and spiritual wealth. The progress of this growth toward consummation in a national style involves the lives of many generations and need be of but little practical concern to us of today. We work at short range and for immediate results. Perhaps, however, there would be infused into our profession an abiding *esprit de corps*, should consideration of this subject and its associated themes lead to a substantial agreement upon our status, our tendencies, and our policy.

If the conclusions set forth in this paper be accepted as correct, it becomes clearly evident, however, that the formative beginnings of this national style, now in progress, are of the utmost immediate interest to us, in part through feelings of patriotism, in part because of a surmise that those who approach most nearly in the substance of their work and administration to the qualities inherent to [in] our race and potential to [of] a national style, will come nearest to the hearts of our people.

Harassed though the architect may be, by the cares and responsibilities of his daily life, there exists nevertheless within him, in the midst of this turmoil, an insuppressible yearning toward ideals. These delicate promptings should be both protected and nourished, that, like the flowering plants springing by the sun's gentle persuasion from little seeds buried in the coarser elements of the soil, they also, because of the warmth of human feeling, may bloom at times by the wayside, yielding refreshing odors and the joy of color to the plodding wayfarer.

The soft beams of the full-orbed moon fall with pathetic caress upon the slumbering life of the world; paling with the dawn, her tender vigil ended, she melts into the infinite depths when the ruddy herald of day proudly summons the workers. So does the soul watch over its greater ideals until the thrilling radiance of power shall awaken them to action.

Ideal thought and effective action should so compose the vital substance of our works that they may live, with us and after us, as a record of our fitness, and a memorial of the good we may have done. Then, in the affluence of time, when a rich burden of aspiring verdure may flourish in the undulating fields of thought, wrought into fertility through the bounty of nature and the energy of the race, the mellowed spontaneity of a national style reaching its full and perfect fruition shall have come from out the very treasury of nature.

"What is the just subordination, in architectural design, of details to mass?"

It is frequently difficult to understand that there may be two sides to a subject. It is proportionately difficult to imagine that there may be more than two, the number, indeed, mounting into the thousands. Therefore, while still in that placid and yielding state of mind, superinduced by distant and general considerations, I admit, once for all, that facets, without number, may be cut upon the rough gem which is presented as the subject of this symposium; and I further admit that each facet will reflect its share of light. I still further admit that the gem, as a whole, may be cut to suit the cutter; and taking advantage of this concession, broadly accorded to all, I shall proceed to fashion the stone after my own predilections, even as though it were the very jewel after which I longed. To approach a step nearer: If the question is a categorical one, demanding a similar reply, I can only answer, I do not know. For who shall say what is possible and what is impossible? Who shall fathom the infinite depths of creative art? Who drink up the sea, and say "all is now dry land?" I cannot do these things; I do not believe anyone can, or will ever be able. Therefore, I believe that in this regard the question is an open one, and will forever remain an open one. Assuming next that the question is not categorical, but rather general and optimistic, I may consider its scope limited within the confines of what has been done, what is for the moment uppermost in recollection, with also an underlying curiosity with regard to what may be done. This naturally makes prominent considerations of climate, locality, and temperament: climate, which is the arbiter of material things; locality, with its accidental variations, superadded to those of the seasons, and both creators of temperament, which is in turn the creator and the arbiter of art. All of which makes possible as a general and qualified answer: "That depends." Storms and frost would tend to influence a softening away of detail into the general mass; localities, more or less favorable, would intensify or relax this influence, while temperament would exert its just or morbid all-controlling sway of sentiment. Similarly, countries of sunshine and flowers, or the valleys, the mountains, the seacoast, the far-reaching plains, the preponderance of heat or cold, the lakes, rivers, bleak and fertile regions, regions of snow and ice, or sultry south winds, would each, according to its rhythmic nature, simple or qualified, awaken corresponding sympathies within the heart, which, if left untrammeled by ill-fitting theories, would spontaneously evolve a coordination of mass and detail, so normal, so indigenous, that it would instinctively be recognized as literally and poetically just.

Hence, this section may be closed with the broad sentiment that all is free and open, provided the general trend is in the direction of indigenous and sincere results; that when we become justly sympathetic, ward off extraneous and irrelevant influences, and make an earnest effort to reach real and intense results, we shall probably some day find a local answer to the question—an answer which none can gainsay. As for me, I do not yet know what that answer is to be, though I believe I share with others a premonition of its nature.

Finally, assuming that the question is local, and specific in its import, and calls for merely an individual expression of opinion as to what is today and here in Chicago the just subordination of details to mass, I willingly make such an explanation as I may.

Candidly, I do not especially believe in subordination of detail insofar as the word *subordination* conveys an idea of caste or rank, with the involved suggestion of a greater force suppressing a lesser; but I do believe in the differentiation of detail from mass (the idea of subordination occurring incidentally and as of no controlling import), because this word symbolizes to my mind an idea which is very congenial to it, namely, that of an expansive and rhythmic growth, in a building, of a single, germinal impulse or idea, which shall permeate the mass and its every detail with the same spirit, to such an extent, indeed, that it would be as difficult to determine (not, surely, as a matter of arithmetical ratio, but rather as a factor in the total complex impression on the beholder) which is the more important, which in fact subordinates, detail or mass, as it would be difficult to say of a tree, in its general impression upon us, "which is more to us, the leaves or the tree?"—a question which I believe has never arisen. For I do not know that it has occurred to anyone to ask what is the just subordination of leaves to mass in a tree? What are the just ratios of leaves, branches, and trunk? Should the leaves be large, and hide the branches, as in the horse chestnut, or should they be frivolous and dainty things, coquettishly exposing the branches? Should the trunk prevail, as in the proud and mournful southern pine, or should the trunk be short and sturdy, as the oak, with powerful gnarled and spreading branches, bared and grim before the tempest? It would be interesting if someone would kindly invent a precise formula for the growth of trees, so that we might forthwith declare any tree which grew at variance with the dictum to be altogether vulgar and devoid of savoir faire. For my part, I find their thousand ways all charming, and fruitful in suggestion. I graciously permit them to grow as they will, and look on with boundless admiration. For I know that they are simply trees; that they have no occasion to be ill at ease, or covert, or dyspeptic with introspection; therefore I trust them and regard them abidingly with love and veneration.

It may be said that I am at fault in comparing animate with inanimate things; but this is the very heart of a mysterious subject; for I insist strenuously that a building should live with intense, if quiescent, life, because it is sprung from the life of its architect. On no other basis are results of permanent value to be attained.

The more I ponder the title-question, the more I am at a loss for a precise answer; the possibilities, even within the limitations of climate, are so manifold, and so native. But for the moment it suits me to favor a very simple outline, particularly at the roof, which is the part most vulnerable to the elements.

Within this simple outline, then, I prefer such subdivision of the masses into detail as is strictly called for by the utilitarian requirements of the building; and that they should comport with its size, location, and purpose. That the materials of construction should largely determine the special form of details, and above all, that there shall effuse from the completed structure a single sentiment which shall be the spiritual result of a prior and perfect understanding and assimilation of all the data.

. . . .

In summing up the results of this sym posium,* I am at once impressed with th independence and the courtesy of my co laborers, as well as with the fact that thei comments bear out my preliminary state ment that each facet cut upon this gen would reflect its share of meaning an suggestion.

Mr. Pierce's statement, that a buildin with a soul is a work of architecture, an Mr. Cleveland's emphasis of the fact tha a building tells a wordless story, are pecu liarly agreeable to me, for they are state ments which carry sincerity of purpos within the words.

I substantially agree with all that thes gentlemen have said; though I gather tha Mr. Pierce attaches prime importance t mechanical and abstract explanations suc as are implied by the words *radiation, rep etition, unity in variety,* etc. His right to thi point of view I do not question, yet I can not accept it, for myself, as a finality. Hi "masculine" and "feminine" simile, how ever, seems to me far-reaching in its im plied analogies; recalling even the exquisit "correspondences" of Swedenborg.

Mr. Cleveland is upon catholic and hu mane ground when he calls for a recogni tion of the claims to poetic richness of th solemn and fateful work of the Druids— as indeed of the charms of story hid withi the silent stones of many ages. With him turn back thoughtfully to read the mysti and impressive volume of the past; leavin it as he does, with the heartfelt wish tha we in turn may tell our story as they o old told theirs, in a language of simple an majestic fervor.

The subject of our symposium seems a bound up with general and special con siderations of style—its causes and man

*A discussion at the regular meeting of th Illinois Association of Architects, held April 2 1887, in the form of a symposium, with talks b Louis H. Sullivan, L. D. Cleveland, and O. J Pierce, and a summary by Louis H. Sullivan.

ifestations—involving naturally enough a sentiment of solicitude regarding our future development in architectural art.

It is for this reason that I wish to add a word of my own, by way of conclusion, to forcibly emphasize that which I believe seems to us three to be the inherent suggestiveness of the theme.

This conclusion I shall mold under much heavier pressure of intensity than was given to the introduction, to wit:

I value spiritual results only. I say spiritual results precede all other results, and indicate them. I can see no efficient way of handling this subject on any other than a spiritual or psychic basis.

I say present theories of art are vanity. I say all past and future theories of art were and will be vanity. That the only substantial facts which remain after all the rubbish, dust, and scientific-analytic-aesthetic cobwebs are brushed away are these facts, which each man may take to himself, namely: That I am; that I am immersed in nature here with my fellowmen; that we are all striving after something which we do not now possess; that there is an inscrutable power permeating all, and the cause of all.

And I say that all we see and feel and know, without and within us, is one mighty poem of striving, one vast and subtle tragedy. That to remain unperturbed and serene within this turbulent and drifting flow of hope and sorrow, light and darkness, is the uttermost position and fact attainable to the soul, the only permanent link between the finite and infinite.

On this rock I would stand. And it is because I would stand here, that I say I value spiritual results only. It is for this reason that I say all mechanical theories of art are vanity, and that the best of rules are but as flowers planted over the graves of prodigious impulses which splendidly lived their lives, and passed away with the individual men who possessed these impulses. This is why I say that it is within the souls of individual men that art reaches culmi-

nations. This is why I say that each man is a law unto himself; and that he is a great or a little law insofar as he is a great or a little soul.

This is why I say that desire is the deepest of human emotions, and that prudence is its correlative; that it is the precursor, the creator, the arbiter of all the others. That great desire and great prudence must precede great results.

This is why I say that contemplation of nature and humanity is the only source of inspiration; this is why I say that without inspiration there can be no such thing as a just coordination of mass and details. That, as there may be countless inspirations profoundly vital, so, also, there may be countless coordinations of mass and details unspeakably just. That material results are to be measured by their contained inspiration; that these results will phase as the inspiration phases.

I say that the whole inquiry as to the just subordination of details to mass, insofar as it contains the implication of a fixed rule, is simply a pedagogical scarecrow.

Nor does this signify a plea for lawlessness. On the contrary, inspiration, such as I have indicated, has too much of pathos within it, too much of the calm of nature's mysterious decadence, to permit the forgetfulness, for more than a passing moment, of this deep-down conviction, that an idea lives according solely as by its power and prudence it compromises with death.

If cultivated mediocrity is what is wanted, the title-question can be answered readily and specifically for each historic style. If the culture of action is demanded, then indeed we have a task before us to find an answer, which shall at best be painfully and laboriously worked out. For every problem is for us, as yet, unsolved; we are merely as pioneers in a primeval forest. Yet while our results can be but relative, they may be the fruit of great desires and hence may speak of greatness.

Therefore I say that each one must

perforce answer the question for himself; and that his answer will be profound or superficial according to the reach of his inspiration, and the gentleness and power of his sympathy; and that this answer can be found, in tangible form, only in his works; for it is here that he records his life, and it is by his works, and not his words, that he shall be judged; for here he can hide nothing—standing to the spiritual as one naked.

Therefore, again I say, I value spiritual results only, and regard all else as vanity. It is needless, I trust, for me to say my feet are upon the ground; though Mr. Pierce seems to hold the placing this discussion upon a psychic basis as a species of ballooning. Here I differ with him radically, for I regard spiritual or psychic facts as the only permanent and reliable facts—the only solid ground. And I believe that until we shall walk securely upon this ground we can have but little force or directness or purpose, but little insight, but little fervor, but little faith in material results.

Emotional architecture as compared with intellectual:

A study in subjective and objective

How strange it seems that education, in practice, so often means suppression: that instead of leading the mind outward to the light of day it crowds things in upon it that darken and weary it. Yet evidently the true object of education, now as ever, is to develop the capabilities of the head and of the heart. He, therefore, who possesses a sound head and a responsive heart is worthy of enlightened guidance, is amenable to educational influence.

Let us now imagine a simple youth so equipped, so gifted, I am almost forced to say, an inborn poet, untaught, unschooled, and living an outdoor life. So familiarly has he fared with sunshine and air and the living things, that they seem, as indeed they are, everyday and common to him.

Yet the mere community of their lives the similarity in the experiences of the boy the plants, and the animals in that native simple, naïf, unsullied state that we who are perhaps unduly artificial call by contrast natural, this state has drawn him very near to them all.

Breathing the same air as they, maturing in the same glowing sunshine, sustained by the same satisfying moisture, he and they expand side by side, defining themselves intimately to each other; and the boy growing always, after a while feels himself to be not only with them but of them. His is a brotherhood with the trees; a wistful eye he softens to the flowers; he has a comely friendship for them all.

He knows that the young leaves love the dew; that the tendril reaches quietly for the twig it may cling to. He has seen the fern unfolding its brown spiral to become anon green and regular. He has splashed knee-deep in the marsh; he knows the dank fragrance very well; he parts his friends the rushes to make a way for his eyes that seek what they may devour—his eyes with a keen and endless appetite. His hands touch the warmish water: sniffing the active air, he lives as only a boy can live—his lively sensibilities always in physical touch with his surroundings, in the full and irrepressible enjoyment of his five senses.

These five senses, and they only, stand between him and Nature. It is they that interpret her affection; and the ready language that they deal in keeps him in such a natural sympathy, so well in touch, so intimately at ease, that he does not for a moment realize that he is then and there doing that which education, so called, once having made inoperative in him, he will in afteryears, poet though he be, reacquire only with the utmost difficulty the power to do.

This something that he is doing, and the physical and psychic state that it implies we call *Touch:* meaning not the touch of the painter, not the touch of the sculptor not the mechanical and technical touch of the fingers only, not quite their negligent contact with things, but the exquisite touch of the sensibilities, the warm physical touch of the body, the touch of a sound head and a responsive heart, the touch of the native one, the poet, out of doors, in spontaneous communion with Nature.

So has our youngster started easily and naturally, all alone without premeditation or guidance, upon the road to knowledge, to leadership and power. For this sensibility, this healthfulness, this touch, this directness of apprehension, this natural clearness of eyesight that is his, is the first essential prerequisite in the early analytical strivings of the mind: it is that perfect concrete analysis by the senses and the sympathies which serves as a basis for the abstract analyses of the intellect.

Let us not forget our little man, for he is to companion me in spirit through this discourse. I believe he exists somewhere, has in his breast the true architectural afflatus, and will some day come forth the Messiah of our art. For he has that early and sure understanding by the eyes that will survive the future uncertainties of the brain. He has that exalted animal sense which alone can discern the pathway to hidden knowledge; that acute and instant scent in matters objective leading to matters subjective that we call *Intuition*.

This physical endowment, this sense of touch, is, decidedly, wherever found, a generous gift of nature, but it is potent for results insofar only as it is urged into sustained and decisive action by a certain appetite or desire.

This desire, this insistence, this urgency which will not be denied; this uncomfortable hunger, this uneasy searching, this profound discontent, oh! so deep; this cry for more; this appetite, this yearning, ever unsatisfied, is not of the body alone but of the soul, and, always and everywhere, in all times and in all places, high or low, wherever found, it is the dominant characteristic of man's eminence in nature—it is

the justification of the eminence of a few men among their fellows.

For appetite, in a state of nature, implies not only a keen desire and a search for the food wanted but, as well, a rejection of all else, thus insuring a wonderful singleness of purpose, a concentration of action, a definiteness of end in the selection of that nourishment of the faculties which, when assimilated, is to become in turn thought and expression through the agency of a second desire equally great, equally intense, equally insistent, namely, the desire to act. This desire to act we call *Imagination*.

These two great desires, which are in essence the desire to absorb and the desire to emit, the desire to know and the desire to test, the desire to hear and the desire to utter, are the basis not only of a true and effective education, not only are they the wholesome body and the enchanting voice of art, but they are greater than these, for they are the animating quality of that higher purpose and significance of art that we call poetry.

Now the desire to act that in due time follows upon nutrition can assert itself tangibly and fully only by means of three agencies, the which, by virtue of its life-giving qualities, this nutritive power has called into being. All three of them must cooperate in turn in order to produce a fully rounded result. They are first, the *Imagination*, which is the very beginning of action because it is a sympathy that lives both in our senses and our intellect— the flash between the past and the future, the middle link in that living chain or sequence leading from nature unto art, and that lies deep down in the emotions and the will. It is this divine faculty which, in an illumined instant, in that supreme moment when ideas are born, reveals the end with the beginning, and liberates, as an offspring of man, that which before had rested, perhaps for untold centuries, dormant but potential in the inmost heart of Nature. This is the supreme crisis. This is

The Auditorium Building in Chicago (1886–89). Designed during the midpoint of the period (1879–95) when Louis H. Sullivan worked in association with Dankmar Adler, this 10-story-high building with a 17-story tower housed a hotel, offices, and a 3,982-seat auditorium.

the summit of the soul, the fertile touch of the spirit, the smile of nature's bounty—the moment of *Inspiration!* All else is from this moment on a foregone conclusion, an absolute certainty to the mastermind: a task surely, but not a doubt.

Second in this trinity comes *Thought*, the faculty that doubts and inquires, that recognizes time and space and the material limitations, that slowly systemizes, that works by small increments and cumulation, that formulates, that concentrates, works, reworks and reviews, that goes slowly, deliberately, that makes very firm and sure, and that eventually arrives at a science of logical statement that shall shape and define the scheme and structure that is to underlie, penetrate, and support the form of an artwork. It is the hard, the bony structure, it is the tough, tendinous fiber; it may be at times perhaps as limber as the

lips that move, yet it is never the need of smiling—never the smile.

Third, last, and the winsome one, exuberant in life and movement, copious in speech, comes *Expression*, open-armed and free, supple, active, dramatic, changeable, beautifully pensive, persuasive, and wonderful. Hers it is to clothe the structure of art with a form of beauty; for she is the perfection of the physical, she is the physical itself, and the uttermost attainment of emotionality. Hers is an infinite tenderness, an adorable and sweet fascination. In her companionship, imaginative Thought, long searching, has found its own and lives anew, immortal, filled with sensibility, graciousness, and the warm blood of a fully rounded maturity.

Thus Art comes into Life! Thus Life comes into Art!

And thus by reason of a process of elab

404

oration and growth, through the natural storage and upbuilding of the products of nutrition lifting themselves higher and higher into organization, the physical and spiritual experiences of our lives, seeking reproduction, shall find imaginative utterance, in their own image, in a *harmonious system of thinking and an equally harmonious method of expressing the thought.*

And so it shall come that when our nourishment shall be natural, our imagination therefore fervid, intense, and visionlike; when our thinking and our speech shall have become as processes of nature; when, in consequence, from its mysterious abode in visible things, the invisible and infinitely fluent spirit of the universe passing to us shall have made our tongues eloquent, our utterance serene, then, and not till then, shall we possess, individually and as a people, the necessary elements of a great *Style.*

For otherwise and without this unitary impulse our expression, though delicate as a flower, our thinking as abstract as the winds that blow, our imagination as luminous as the dawn, are useless and unavailing to create: they may set forth, they cannot create.

Man, by means of his physical power, his mechanical resources, his mental ingenuity, may set things side by side. A composition, literally so called, will result, but not a great artwork, not at all an artwork in fact, but merely a more or less refined exhibition of brute force exercised upon helpful materials. It may be as a noise in lessening degrees of offensiveness, it can never become a musical tone. Though it shall have ceased to be vulgar in becoming sophistic, it will remain to the end what it was in the beginning: impotent to inspire—dead, absolutely dead.

The interior of the Auditorium Building shows Sullivan's great talent for designing ornamentation.

It cannot for a moment be doubted that an artwork to be alive, to awaken us to its life, to inspire us sooner or later with its purpose, must indeed be animate with a soul, must have been breathed upon by the spirit and must breathe in turn that spirit. It must stand for the actual, vital firsthand experiences of the one who made it, and must represent his deep-down impression not only of physical nature but more especially and necessarily his understanding of the outworking of that *Great Spirit* which makes nature so intelligible to us that it ceases to be a phantasm and becomes a sweet, a superb, a convincing *Reality*.

It absolutely must be the determination and the capacity of the artist that his work shall be as real and convincing as is his own life: as suggestive as his own eyesight makes all things to him; and yet as unreal, as fugitive, as inscrutable, as subjective, as the why and wherefore of the simplest flower that blows.

It is the presence of this unreality that makes the artwork real: it is by virtue of this silent subjectivity that the objective voice of an art song becomes sonorous and thrilling.

Unless, therefore, subjectivity permeate an artwork, that work cannot aspire to greatness; for whatever of imagination, of thought, and of expression it may possess, these as much will remain three separate things—not three phases of one thing.

An artist must necessarily, therefore, remain a more or less educated hand worker, a more or less clever sophisticator, a more or less successful framer of compromises, unless, when he was born, there was born with him a hunger for the spiritual; for all other craving avails as naught. Unless, as a child, with that marvelous instinct given only to children, he has heard the voice of Nature murmuring in the woodland or afield or seaward, no after hearing can avail to catch this revelation.

And thus it is that subjectivity and objectivity, not as two separate elements but as two complementary and harmonious phases of one impulse, have always constituted and will always constitute the embodied spirit of art.

No phase of human nature can contain greater interest for the student of psychology than the history, natural, political, religious, and artistic, of the successive phases for good and for ill of Objectivity and Subjectivity. *They are the two controlling elements of human endeavor.* They have caused in their internecine warfare misery and perturbation. They are ordinarily known and spoken of as the intellectual and the emotional, but they lie deeper, much deeper than these: they lie in the very heart of Nature. Coming into man's being, they have been antagonistic because of the fanaticism and one-sidedness of human nature, because of its immobility. Because from the beginning man has been beset by beautiful, by despicable, illusions. Because one set of men have believed in what they could see and another set have believed in what they could not see. Because it has too often happened that the man who could see with the outer eye could not see with the inner eye; because the other man, rhapsodizing with the clear insight of faith, had no thought for the things of this world. Neither has believed in the virtue of the other. Neither has inferred from the presence of the other, the necessary existence of a balancing but hidden power. Now and then through the ages they have come twin-born in the bosom of an individual man—upon whose brow the generations have placed the wreath of immortality.

So vast, so overwhelming is the power of a great, a properly balanced subjectivity, so enormously does it draw on the spiritual nutrition and stored-up vitality of the world, that, soon sapping this up, and still craving, the man possessed of it, urged by it, goes straight to the unfailing bounty of nature, and there, by virtue of his passionate adoration, passing the portals of the objective, he enters that extraordinary communion that the sacred writers called "to walk with God."

There can be no doubt that the most profound desire that fills the human soul, the most heartfelt hope, is the wish to be at peace with Nature and the Inscrutable Spirit; nor can there be a doubt that the greatest Artwork is that which most nearly typifies a realization of this ardent, patient longing. All efforts of the body, all undertakings of the mind, tend, consciously or unconsciously, toward this consummation, tend toward this final peace: the peace of perfect equilibrium, the repose of absolute unity, the serenity of a complete identification.

When, therefore, turning from this our contemplation we compare the outworking of the vital processes of nature with the so-called creative activity of the average man of education and culture, we wonder at the disparity, we seek its cause.

When, after having with joy observed the quality of identity and singleness that Nature imparts to her offspring, when with aroused expectancy, with a glowing sense of the richness, fullness, and variety that might and should come from the man's brain with the impulse of nature's fecundity flowing through it, we seek—we are amazed to find in this man's work no such thing.

When we, in place of a fertile unity which we had hoped for, come suddenly upon miscellany and barrenness, we are deeply mortified, we are rudely shocked.

We are dismayed at this: that man, Nature's highest product, should alone have gone awry, that with remarkable perversity he should have strayed—that for the simple and obvious he should substitute the factitious, the artificial.

The cause needs not a long searching, it is near at hand. It lies precisely in that much glorified, much abused word *education.*

To my view no word in the entire vocabulary of the English language contains so much of pathos, so much of tragedy as this one pitiful word *education,* for it typifies a fundamental perversity of the human soul, a willful blindness of the mind, a poverty of the heart.

For one brain that education has stimulated and strengthened, it has malformed, stupefied, and discouraged thousands. Only the strongest, only the masterful, can dominate it, and return to the ownership of their souls.

For it is education's crime that it has removed us from Nature. As tender children it took us harshly away with stern words, and the sweet face of our natural mother has faded in the unspeakable past, whence it regards us at times, dimly and flittingly, causing in us uneasy and disturbing emotion.

And thus it is through a brutish and mean system of guidance, through the density of atmosphere that we have breathed, that we are not what our successors may easily become, a race filled with spiritual riches in addition to the vast material wealth.

That in place of a happy people, open-eyed children of Nature teeming with beautiful impulses, we are a people lost in darkness, groping under a sooty and lurid sky sinister with clouds that shut out the sunshine and the clear blue heavens.

Yet the murky materialism—the fierce objectivity, the fanatical selfishness—of this dark age of ours, in this sense the darkest of all dark ages, is so prodigious, so grotesque, so monstrous, that in its very self it contains the elements of change: from its own intensity, its own excess, its complex striving, it predetermines the golden age of the world.

The human mind in all countries having gone to the uttermost limit of its own capacity, flushed with its conquests, haughty after its self-assertion upon emerging from the prior dark age, is now nearing a new phase, a phase inherent in the nature and destiny of things.

The human mind, like the silkworm oppressed with the fullness of its own accumulation, has spun about itself gradually and slowly a cocoon that at last has shut out the light of the world from which it drew the substance of its thread. But this darkness has produced the chrysalis, and we within the darkness feel the beginning of our throes. The inevitable change, after centuries upon centuries of preparation, is about to begin.

Human development, through a series of vast attractions and perturbations, has now arrived at a materialism so profound, so exalted as to prove the fittest basis for a coming era of spiritual splendor.

To foresee this necessity, consider but a moment the richness of our heritage from the past, its orderly sequence, its uplifting wave of power, its conservation of force.

Think of the Hindu, with folded hands, soaring in contemplation, thousands of years ago—think of what he has left us. Think of the Hebrew man coming out of Ur of the Chaldees, to find for us the One Great Spirit. Think of the somber Egyptians, those giants who struggled so courageously with fate—think of the stability they have given to us. Think of the stars of Israel, singing in the morning's dawn. Think of the lonely man of Nazareth breathing a spirit of gentleness of which the world had never heard before. Think of the delicately objective Greeks, lovers of the physical, accurate thinkers, the worshipers of beauty. Think that in them the Orient, sleeping, was born anew. Think of the Goth, and with him the birth of emotion as we know it. Think of modern Science which has taught us not to fear. Think of modern Music, arising in glory as the heart took wings—*a new thing under the sun*. Think deeply of the French Revolution and Democracy—the utterance of freedom, the beginning of the Individual Man. Think now of our own age with its machinery, its steam power, its means of communication, its annihilation of distance. Think of the humanitarianism of our day. Think, as we stand here, now, in a new land, a Promised Land that at last is ours, think how passionately latent, how marvelous to contemplate is America, our

country. *Think that here destiny has decreed there shall be enacted the final part in the drama of man's emancipation—the redemption of his soul!*

Think of these things, think of what they signify, of what they promise for us, and think then that as architects it peculiarly behooves us to review our own special past, to forecast our future, to realize somewhat our present status.

Summoned to answer before an enlightened judgment seat, how shall we now give other, alas, than a wretched accounting of our stewardship! How shall we excuse our sterility? We surely need to inquire, for we must need explain the emaciation of our art in the midst of plenty, its weakness in the midst of strength, its beggarly poverty in the midst of abundance.

By what glamour or speciousness of words shall we persuade a wrathful judgment toward kindness? How can our vapid record be made to plead for us?

Shall we summon the clear-eyed, intellectual Greek or the emotional and introspective Goth to bear witness that we stand as ambassadors in their names—we would surely be repudiated.

Shall we call to the fateful Egyptian or the dashing, polished Assyrian—one would scorn us, the other would flout us.

Who are we then, and how shall we explain our sinister condition, our mere existence?

Shall we claim we are second cousins to Europe, or must we, before we can ourselves behold the truth, so far abase our heads in the ashes as to acknowledge that we of the great and glorious ending of the nineteenth century are the direct lineal descendants of the original bastards and indiscretions of architecture?

Or, still seeking excuses in our fin-de-siècle pocket, shall we plead in the language of myth that our art, like Brunhild, lies sleeping: that she awaits a son of Nature, one without fear, to penetrate the wall of flame, to lift her helmet's visor?

Dreading the storm, shall we seek shelter under the spreading plea that poets are born, not made; that, if Nature for all these centuries has not brought forth a great master-spirit in the architectural art, it must be for very good reasons of her own—for reasons definitely interwrought with the beneficence of her own rhythmical movements? That, with her endless fecundity, there must be a profoundly significant reason for this barrenness.

Or, perhaps, shall we simply say that men have now turned to other gods, that they have forgotten the ancient deities?

That there has arisen in our land a new king who knows not Joseph; that he has set o'er us taskmasters to afflict us with burdens.

All these pleadings may be true, yet after all they do not explain why we make easy things very difficult, why we employ artificial instead of natural processes, why we walk backward instead of forward, why we see cross-eyed instead of straight-eyed, why we turn our minds inside out instead of letting them alone; they do not explain why we are so vulgarly self-conscious, so pitifully bashful, so awkward in our art, so explanatory, so uncertain that we know anything at all or are anybody in particular, so characterless, so insipid, so utterly without savor. They do not explain why the intellectual and emotional phases of the architectural mind do precisely the wrong thing when the right thing is quite attainable.

No! I pretend to advocate the real, the true cause of my generation, of my art. I do not wish to abase them except insofar as he who loveth chasteneth. I know that the secret of our weakness lies not only in our plethoric dyspepsia, in our lack of desire, in our deficiency of gumption and moral courage, but that it lies primarily in the utterly purposeless education we have received.

I know that the architectural schools teach a certain art or method of study in which one is made partly familiar with the objective aspects and forms of architec-

ture. I know that this, as far as it goes, is conscientiously and thoroughly done. But I also know that it is doubtful, in my mind, if one student in a thousand emerges from his school possessed of a fine conception of what architecture really is in form, in spirit, and in truth: and I say this is not primarily the student's fault. I know that before entering his architectural school he has passed through other schools, and that they began the mischief: that they had told him grammar was a book, algebra was a book, geometry another book, geography, chemistry, physics, still others: they never told him, never permitted him, to guess for himself how these things were actually intense symbols, complex ratios, representing man's relation to Nature and his fellowman; they never told him that his mathematics, etc., etc., came into being in response to a *desire* in the human breast to come nearer to Nature—that the full moon looked round to the human eye ages before the circle was dreamed of.

Our student knows, to be sure, as a result of his teaching that the Greeks built certain-shaped buildings, that the Goths built certain-shaped buildings, and that other peoples built other buildings of still other shapes. He knows, moreover, if he has been a conscientious hewer of wood and drawer of water, a thousand and one specific facts concerning the shapes and measurements and ratios of the whole and the parts of said buildings, and can neatly and deftly draw and color them to scale. He moreover has read in the philosophies or heard at lectures that the architecture of a given time gives one an excellent idea of the civilization of that time.

This, roughly speaking, is the sum total of his education, and he takes his architectural instruction literally, just as he has taken every other form of instruction literally from the time he was a child—because he has been told to do so, because he has been told that architecture is a fixed, a real, a specific, a definite thing, that it's all done, that it's all known, arranged, tabulated, and put away neatly in handy packages called books. He is allowed to believe, though perhaps not distinctly so taught, that, to all intents and purposes, when his turn comes, if he wishes to make some architecture for Americans or for this generation at large, he can dip it out of his books with the same facility that dubs a grocer dipping beans out of a bin. He is taught by the logic of events that architecture in practice is a commercial article, like a patent medicine, unknown in its mixture and sold to the public exclusively on the brand.

He has seriously been told at the school, and has been encouraged in this belief by the endorsement of people of culture, that he can learn all about architecture if he but possess the attributes of scholarship and industry. That architecture is the name of a system of accredited, historical facts as useful, as available, and as susceptible to inspection as the books of a mercantile house.

Everything literal, formal, and smart in his nature has been encouraged—the early and plastic glow to emotion and sensibility has been ignored.

He has been taught many cold and dead things, but the one warm living thing that he has not been taught and apparently never will be taught is the stately and all-comprehending truth that architecture, wherever it has appeared and reached a spontaneous culmination, is not at all what we so stupidly call a reality, but, on the contrary, it is a most complex, a glowing and gloriously wrought metaphor, embodying as no other form of language under the sun can do, the pure, clean, and deep inspiration of the race flowing as a stream of living water from its wellspring to the sea.

He has not been taught that an architect, to be a true exponent of his time, must possess first, last, and always the sympathy, the intuition of a poet; that this is the one real, vital principle that survives through all places and all times.

This seeking for a natural expression

of our lives, of our thoughts, our meditations, our feelings, is the architectural art as I understand it: and it is because I so understand it, that, ignoring the viciousness of the past, I gladly make an appeal to the good that is in human nature—that goodness of heart and soundness of head, that ready and natural response of the soul in which I have always trusted and shall always trust. It is to this sane and wholesome quality that I plead for the abiding sincerity and nobility of our art. It is to this *manliness* that I call to come before the judgment seat and make an answer for us.

I know very well that our country will in due time possess a most interesting, varied, characteristic, and beautiful architecture; that the time will begin whenever we take as our point of the departure the few and simple elements of architecture and not its complex forms. That this time will come just as soon as the young are relieved of the depressing weight of a factitious education, the benumbing influence of an instruction that insulates them from the vitalizing currents of nature. Just so soon as those having them in charge, coming to the full sense of the fact, realizing how truly dangerous a thing is a little knowledge, a partial knowledge, dreading to assume the responsibility for stunted, for imperfectly developed natures, feeling how deeply necessary it is that a technical or intellectual training be supplemented by a full, a rich, a chaste development of the emotions, shall say to the young that they are free, that from the musty school they may fly to the open air, to the sunshine, to the birds, the flowers, and, wanton and joyous in their own fancies, face to face with the integrity of nature, they shall substitute for the arbitrary discipline of the school the natural, the easy self-control of a dignified manhood, to the end that not books but personal feeling, personal character, and personal responsibility shall form the true foundation of their art.

It has, alas, for centuries been taught that the intellect and the emotions were two separate and antagonistic things. This teaching has been firmly believed, cruelly lived up to.

How depressing it is to realize that it might have been taught that they are two beautifully congenial and harmonious phases of that single and integral essence that we call the soul. That no nature in which the development of either is wanting can be called a completely rounded nature.

That, therefore, classical architecture, so called (meaning the Greek), was one-sided and incomplete because it was almost exclusively intellectual. That the emotional architecture (meaning especially the Gothic) was likewise one-sided and incomplete, however great and beautiful its development of feeling, because of the almost total absence of mentality. That no complete architecture has yet appeared in the history of the world because men, in this form of art alone, have obstinately sought to express themselves solely in terms either of the head or of the heart.

I hold that architectural art, thus far, has failed to reach its highest development, its fullest capability of imagination, of thought and expression, because it has not yet found a way to become truly plastic: it does not yet respond to the poet's touch. That it is today the only art for which the multitudinous rhythms of outward nature, the manifold fluctuations of man's inner being have no significance, no place.

That the Greek Architecture, unerring as far as it went—and it went very far indeed in one direction—was but one radius within the field of a possible circle of expression. That, though perfect in its eyesight, definite in its desires, clear in its purpose, it was not resourceful in forms: that it lacked the flexibility and the humanity to respond to the varied and constantly shifting desires of the heart.

It was a pure, it was a noble art, wherefore we call it classic; but after all it was an apologetic art, for, while possessing serenity, it lacked the divinely human element of mobility: the Greek never caught the secret of the changing of the seasons, the orderly and complete sequences of their rhythm within the calmly moving year. Nor did this selfsame Greek know what we now know of Nature's bounty, for music in those days had not been born: this lovely friend, approaching man to man, had not yet begun to bloom as a rose, to exhale its wondrous perfume.

That the Gothic architecture, with somber ecstatic eye, with its thought far above with Christ in the heavens, seeing but little here below, feverish and over-wrought, taking comfort in gardening and plant life, sympathizing deeply with Nature's visible forms, evolved a copious and rich variety of incidental expressions but lacked the unitary comprehension, the absolute consciousness and mastery of pure form that can come alone of unclouded and serene contemplation, of perfect repose and peace of mind.

I believe, in other words, that the Greek knew the statics, the Goth the dynamics, of the art, but that neither of them suspected the mobile equilibrium of it: neither of them divined the movement and the stability of nature. Failing in this, both have forever fallen short, and must pass away when the true, the *Poetic Architecture* shall arise—that architecture which shall speak with clearness, with eloquence, and with warmth, of the fullness, the completeness of man's intercourse with Nature and with his fellowmen.

Moreover, we know, or should by this time know, that human nature has now become too rich in possessions, too well equipped, too magnificently endowed, that [for] any hitherto architecture can [to] be said to have hinted at its resources, much less to have exhausted them by anticipation.

It is this consciousness, this price, that shall be our motive, our friend, philosopher, and guide in the beautiful country that stretches so invitingly before us.

In that land, the schools, having found the object of their long, blind searching, shall teach directness, simplicity, naturalness: they shall protect the young against palpable illusion. They shall teach that, while man once invented a process called composition, Nature has forever brought forth organisms. They shall encourage the love of Nature that wells up in every childish heart, and shall not suppress, shall not stifle, the teeming imagination of the young.

They shall teach, as the result of their own bitter experience, that conscious mental effort, that conscious emotionality, are poor mates to breed from, and that true parturition comes of a deep, instinctive, subconscious desire. That true art, springing fresh from Nature, must have in it, to live, much of the glance of an eye, much of the sound of a voice, much of the life of a life.

That Nature is strong, generous, comprehensive, fecund, subtile: that in growth and decadence she continually sets forth the drama of man's life.

That, thro' the rotating seasons, thro' the procession of the years, thro' the march of the centuries, permeating all, sustaining all, there murmurs the still, small voice of a power that holds us in the hollow of its hand.

The tall office building artistically considered

The architects of this land and generation are now brought face to face with something new under the sun—namely, that evolution and integration of social conditions, that special grouping of them, that results in a demand for the erection of tall office buildings.

It is not my purpose to discuss the social conditions; I accept them as the fact, and say at once that the design of the tall office building must be recognized and confronted at the outset as a problem to be solved—a vital problem, pressing for a true solution.

Let us state the conditions in the plainest manner. Briefly, they are these: offices are

necessary for the transaction of business; the invention and perfection of the high-speed elevators make vertical travel, that was once tedious and painful, now easy and comfortable; development of steel manufacture has shown the way to safe, rigid, economical constructions rising to a great height; continued growth of population in the great cities, consequent congestion of centers and rise in value of ground, stimulate an increase in number of stories; these, successfully piled one upon another, react on ground values—and so on, by action and reaction, interaction and inter-reaction. Thus has come about that form of lofty construction called the "modern office building." It has come in answer to a call, for in it a new grouping of social conditions has found a habitation and a name.

Up to this point all in evidence is materialistic, an exhibition of force, of resolution, of brains in the keen sense of the word. It is the joint product of the speculator, the engineer, the builder.

Problem: How shall we impart to this sterile pile, this crude, harsh, brutal agglomeration, this stark, staring exclamation of eternal strife, the graciousness of those higher forms of sensibility and culture that rest on the lower and fiercer passions? How shall we proclaim from the dizzy height of this strange, weird, modern housetop the peaceful evangel of sentiment, of beauty, the cult of a higher life?

This is the problem; and we must seek the solution of it in a process analogous to its own evolution—indeed, a continuation of it—namely, by proceeding step by step from general to special aspects, from coarser to finer considerations.

It is my belief that it is of the very essence of every problem that it contains and suggests its own solution. This I believe to be natural law. Let us examine, then, carefully the elements, let us search out this contained suggestion, this essence of the problem.

The practical conditions are, broadly speaking, these:

Wanted—1st, a story belowground, containing boilers, engines of various sorts, etc.—in short, the plant for power, heating, lighting, etc. 2nd, a ground floor, so called, devoted to stores, banks, or other establishments requiring large area, ample spacing, ample light, and great freedom of access. 3rd, a second story readily accessible by stairways—this space usually in large subdivisions, with corresponding liberality in structural spacing and expanse of glass and breadth of external openings. 4th, above this an indefinite number of stories of offices piled tier upon tier, one tier just like another tier, one office just like all the other offices—an office being similar to a cell in a honeycomb, merely a compartment, nothing more. 5th, and last, at the top of this pile is placed a space or story that, as related to the life and usefulness of the structure, is purely physiological in its nature—namely, the attic. In this the circulatory system completes itself and makes its grand turn, ascending and descending. The space is filled with tanks, pipes, valves, sheaves, and mechanical etcetera that supplement and complement the force-originating plant hidden belowground in the cellar. Finally, or at the beginning rather, there must be on the ground floor a main aperture or entrance common to all the occupants or patrons of the building.

This tabulation is, in the main, characteristic of every tall office building in the country. As to the necessary arrangements for light courts, these are not germane to the problem, and as will become soon evident, I trust need not be considered here. These things, and such others as the arrangement of elevators, for example, have to do strictly with the economics of the building, and I assume them to have been fully considered and disposed of to the satisfaction of purely utilitarian and pecuniary demands. Only in rare instances does the plan or floor arrangement of the tall office building take on an æsthetic value, and this usually when the lighting court is external or becomes an internal feature of great importance.

As I am here seeking not for an individual or special solution, but for a true normal type, the attention must be confined to those conditions that, in the main, are constant in all tall office buildings, and every mere incidental and accidental variation eliminated from the consideration, as harmful to the clearness of the main inquiry.

The practical horizontal and vertical division or office unit is naturally based on a room of comfortable area and height, and the size of this standard office room as naturally predetermines the standard structural unit, and, approximately, the size of window openings. In turn, these purely arbitrary units of structure form in an equally natural way the true basis of the artistic development of the exterior. Of course the structural spacings and openings in the first or mercantile story are required to be the largest of all; those in the second or quasi-mercantile story are of a somewhat similar nature. The spacings and openings in the attic are of no importance whatsoever (the windows have no actual value), for light may be taken from the top, and no recognition of a cellular division is necessary in the structural spacing.

Hence it follows inevitably, and in the simplest possible way, that if we follow our natural instincts without thought of books, rules, precedents, or any such educational impediment to a spontaneous and "sensible" result, we will in the following manner design the exterior of our tall office building—to wit:

Beginning with the first story, we give this a main entrance that attracts the eye to its location, and the remainder of the story we treat in a more or less liberal, expansive, sumptuous way—a way based exactly on the practical necessities, but expressed with a sentiment of largeness and freedom. The second story we treat in a similar way, but usually with milder pretension. Above this, throughout the indefinite number of typical office tiers, we take our cue from the individual cell, which requires a window with its separating pier, its sill and lintel, and we, without more ado, make them look all alike because they are all alike. This brings us to the attic, which, having no division into office cells, and no special requirement for lighting, gives us the power to show by means of its broad expanse of wall, and its dominating weight and character, that which is the fact—namely, that the series of office tiers has come definitely to an end.

This may perhaps seem a bald result and a heartless, pessimistic way of stating it, but even so we certainly have advanced a most characteristic stage beyond the imagined sinister building of the speculator-engineer-builder combination. For the hand of the architect is now definitely felt in the decisive position at once taken, and the suggestion of a thoroughly sound, logical, coherent expression of the conditions is becoming apparent.

When I say the hand of the architect, I do not mean necessarily the accomplished and trained architect. I mean only a man with a strong, natural liking for buildings, and a disposition to shape them in what seems to his unaffected nature a direct and simple way. He will probably tread an innocent path from his problem to its solution, and therein he will show an enviable gift of logic. If he have some gift for form in detail, some feeling for form purely and simply as form, some love for that, his result in addition to its simple straightforward naturalness and completeness in general statement, will have something of the charm of sentiment.

However, thus far the results are only partial and tentative at best; relatively true, they are but superficial. We are doubtless right in our instinct but we must seek a fuller justification, a finer sanction, for it.

I assume now that in the study of our problem we have passed through the various stages of inquiry, as follows: 1st, the social basis of the demand for tall office buildings; 2nd, its literal material satisfaction; 3rd, the elevation of the question from considerations of literal planning, construction, and equipment, to the plane of elementary architecture as a direct outgrowth of sound, sensible building; 4th, the question again elevated from an elementary architecture to the beginnings of true architectural expression, through the addition of a certain quality and quantity of sentiment.

But our building may have all these in a considerable degree and yet be far from that adequate solution of the problem I am attempting to define. We must now heed the imperative voice of emotion.

It demands of us, what is the chief characteristic of the tall office building? And at once we answer, it is lofty. This loftiness is to the artist-nature its thrilling aspect. It is the very open organ-tone in its appeal. It must be in turn the dominant chord in his expression of it, the true excitant of his imagination. It must be tall, every inch of it tall. The force and power of altitude must be in it, the glory and pride of exaltation must be in it. It must be every inch a proud and soaring thing, rising in sheer exultation that from bottom to top it is a unit without a single dissenting line—that it is the new, the unexpected, the eloquent peroration of most bald, most sinister, most forbidding conditions.

The man who designs in this spirit and with the sense of responsibility to the generation he lives in must be no coward, no denier, no bookworm, no dilettante. He must live of his life and for his life in the fullest, most consummate sense. He must realize at once and with the grasp of inspiration that the problem of the tall office building is one of the most stupendous, one of the most magnificent opportunities that the Lord of Nature in His beneficence has ever offered to the proud spirit of man.

That this has not been perceived—indeed, has been flatly denied—is an exhibition of human perversity that must give us pause.

One more consideration. Let us now lift this question into the region of calm, philosophical observation. Let us seek a comprehensive, a final solution: let the problem indeed dissolve.

Certain critics, and very thoughtful ones, have advanced the theory that the true prototype of the tall office building is the classical column, consisting of base, shaft, and capital—the molded base of the column typical of the lower stories of our building, the plain or fluted shaft suggesting the monotonous, uninterrupted series of office-tiers, and the capital the completing power and luxuriance of the attic.

Other theorizers, assuming a mystical symbolism as a guide, quote the many trinities in nature and art, and the beauty and conclusiveness of such trinity in unity. They aver the beauty of prime numbers, the mysticism of the number three, the beauty of all things that are in three parts— to wit, the day, subdividing into morning, noon, and night; the limbs, the thorax, and the head, constituting the body. So they say, should the building be in three parts vertically, substantially as before, but for different motives.

Others, of purely intellectual temperament, hold that such a design should be in the nature of a logical statement; it should have a beginning, a middle, and an ending, each clearly defined—therefore again a building, as above, in three parts vertically.

Others, seeking their examples and justification in the vegetable kingdom, urge that such a design shall above all things be organic. They quote the suitable flower with its bunch of leaves at the earth, its long graceful stem, carrying the gorgeous single flower. They point to the pine tree, its massy roots, its lithe, uninterrupted trunk, its tuft of green high in the air. Thus, they say, should be the design of the tall office building: again in three parts vertically.

Others still, more susceptible to the power of a unit than to the grace of a trinity, say that such a design should be struck out at a blow, as though by a blacksmith or by mighty Jove, or should be thought-born, as was Minerva, full grown. They accept the notion of a triple division as permissible and welcome, but nonessential. With them it is a subdivision of their unit: the unit does not come from the alliance of the three; they accept it without murmur, provided the subdivision does not disturb the sense of singleness and repose.

All of these critics and theorists agree, however, positively, unequivocally, in this, that the tall office building should not, must not, be made a field for the display of architectural knowledge in the encyclopedic sense; that too much learning in this instance is fully as dangerous, as obnoxious, as too little learning; that miscellany is abhorrent to their sense; that the sixteen-story building must not consist of sixteen separate, distinct, and unrelated buildings piled one upon the other until the top of the pile is reached.

To this latter folly I would not refer were it not the fact that nine out of every ten tall office buildings are designed in precisely this way in effect, not by the ignorant, but by the educated. It would seem indeed, as though the "trained" architect, when facing this problem, were beset at every story, or at most, every third or fourth story, by the hysterical dread lest he be in "bad form"; lest he be not bedecking his building with sufficiency of quotation from this, that, or the other "correct" building in some other land and some other time; lest he be not copious enough in the display of his wares; lest he betray, in short, a lack of resource. To loosen up the touch of this cramped and fidgety hand, to allow the nerves to calm, the brain to cool, to reflect equally, to reason naturally, seems beyond him; he lives, as it were, in a waking nightmare filled with the *disjecta membra* of architecture. The spectacle is not inspiriting.

As to the former and serious views held by discerning and thoughtful critics, I shall,

The Guaranty (now Prudential) Building (above) in Buffalo, New York (1894–95), is a classic tall office building designed by Sullivan and Adler. The Golden Door (opposite, top) was the archway entrance of the Transportation Building, the Adler and Sullivan contribution to the 1893 Columbian Exposition in Chicago. The National Farmers' (now Security) Bank (opposite, bottom) in Owatonna, Minnesota (1908), was the first of seven banks designed by Sullivan for a number of small Midwestern towns.

with however much of regret, dissent from them for the purpose of this demonstration, for I regard them as secondary only, nonessential, and as touching not at all upon the vital spot, upon the quick of the entire matter, upon the true, the immovable philosophy of the architectural art.

This view let me now state, for it brings to the solution of the problem a final, comprehensive formula.

All things in nature have a shape, that is to say, a form, an outward semblance, that tells us what they are, that distinguishes them from ourselves and from each other.

Unfailingly in nature these shapes express the inner life, the native quality, of the animal, tree, bird, fish, that they present to us; they are so characteristic, so recognizable, that we say, simply, it is "natural" it should be so. Yet the moment we peer beneath this surface of things, the moment we look through the tranquil reflection of ourselves and the clouds above us, down into the clear, fluent, unfathomable depth of nature, how startling is the silence of it, how amazing the flow of life, how absorbing the mystery. Unceasingly the essence of things is taking shape in the matter of things, and this unspeakable process we call birth and growth. Awhile the spirit and the matter fade away together, and it is this that we call decadence, death. These two happenings seem jointed and interdependent, blended into one like a bubble and its iridescence, and they seem borne along upon a slowly moving air. This air is wonderful past all understanding.

Yet to the steadfast eye of one standing upon the shore of things, looking chiefly and most lovingly upon that side on which the sun shines and that we feel joyously to be life, the heart is ever gladdened by the beauty, the exquisite spontaneity, with which life seeks and takes on its forms in an accord perfectly responsive to its needs. It seems ever as though the life and the form were absolutely one and inseparable, so adequate is the sense of fulfillment.

Whether it be the sweeping eagle in his flight or the open apple blossom, the toiling workhorse, the blithe swan, the branching oak, the winding stream at its base, the drifting clouds, over all the coursing sun, form ever follows function, and this is the law. Where function does not change form does not change. The granite rocks, the ever-brooding hills, remain for ages; the lightning lives, comes into shape, and dies in a twinkling.

It is the pervading law of all things organic and inorganic, of all things physical and metaphysical, of all things human and all things superhuman, of all true manifestations of the head, of the heart, of the soul, that the life is recognizable in its expression, that form ever follows function. This is the law.

Shall we, then, daily violate this law in our art? Are we so decadent, so imbecile, so utterly weak of eyesight, that we cannot perceive this truth so simple, so very simple? Is it indeed a truth so transparent that we see through it but do not see it? Is it really then a very marvelous thing, or is it rather so commonplace, so everyday, so near a thing to us, that we cannot perceive that the shape, form, outward expression, design, or whatever we may choose, of the tall office building should in the very nature of things follow the functions of the building, and that where the function does not change, the form is not to change?

Does this not readily, clearly, and conclusively show that the lower one or two stories will take on a special character suited to the special needs, that the tiers of typical offices, having the same unchanging function, shall continue in the same unchanging form, and that as to the attic, specific and conclusive as it is in its very nature, its function shall equally be so in force, in significance, in continuity, in conclusiveness of outward expression? From this results, naturally, spontaneously, unwittingly, a three-part division, not from any theory, symbol, or fancied logic.

And thus the design of the tall office building takes its place with all other architectural types made when architecture, as has happened once in many years, was a living art. Witness the Greek temple, the Gothic cathedral, the medieval fortress.

And thus, when native instinct and sensibility shall govern the exercise of our beloved art; when the known law, the respected law, shall be that form ever follows function; when our architects shall cease struggling and prattling handcuffed and vainglorious in the asylum of a foreign school; when it is truly felt, cheerfully accepted, that this law opens up the airy sunshine of green fields, and gives to us a freedom that the very beauty and sumptuousness of the outworking of the law itself as exhibited in nature will deter any sane, any sensitive man from changing into license, when it becomes evident that we are merely speaking a foreign language with a noticeable American accent, whereas each and every architect in the land might, under the benign influence of this law, express in the simplest, most modest, most natural way that which it is in him to say; that he might really and would surely develop his own characteristic individuality, and that the architectural art with him would certainly become a living form of speech, a natural form of utterance, giving surcease to him and adding treasures small and great to the growing art of his land; when we know and feel that Nature is our friend, not our implacable enemy— that an afternoon in the country, an hour by the sea, a full open view of one single day, through dawn, high noon, and twilight, will suggest to us so much that is rhythmical, deep, and eternal in the vast art of architecture, something so deep, so true, that all the narrow formalities, hard-and-fast rules, and strangling bonds of the schools cannot stifle it in us—then it may be proclaimed that we are on the high road to a natural and satisfying art, an architecture that will soon become a fine art in the true, the best sense of the word, an art that will live because it will be of the people, for the people, and by the people.

What is architecture:

A study in the American people of today

The intellectual trend of the hour is toward simplification. The full powers of the modern scientific mind are now directed, with a common consent, toward searching out the few and simple principles that are believed to underlie the complexity of Nature, and such investigation is steadily revealing a unitary impulse underlying all men and all things.

This method of analysis reveals a curious aspect of Man, namely: that as he thinks, so he acts; and, conversely, one may read in his acts what he thinks—his real thoughts, be it understood, not what he avows he thinks. For all men think, all men act. To term a man unthinking is a misuse of words; what really is meant is that he does not think with accuracy, fitness, and power. If, then, it be true that as a man thinks so must he act in inevitable accordance with his thought, so is it true that society, which is but a summation of individuals, acts precisely as it thinks. Thus are the thoughts of a people to be read in the acts of a people, as clearly as words are read upon the printed page.

If, in like manner, we apply this method of analysis to the complex spread of historical and contemporaneous architecture, we perceive, clearly revealed in their simplicity, its three elementary forms, namely, the pier, the lintel, and the arch. These are the three, the only three letters, from which has expanded the Architectural Art as a great and superb language wherewith Man has expressed, through the generations, the changing drift of his thoughts. Thus, throughout the past and the present, each building stands as a social act. In such act we read that which cannot escape our analysis, for it is indelibly fixed in the building, namely, the nature of the thoughts of the individual and the people whose image the building is or was.

Perhaps I should not leave the three elements, pier, lintel, and arch, thus baldly set forth. It may not appear to the reader that the truth concerning them is as clear and simple as I state it. He may think, for example, that there was a marked difference between the Egyptian and the Greek Architectures, even though both were based on pier and lintel only. There was a marked difference. The difference that existed between the Egyptian and the Greek minds. The Egyptian animated pier and lintel with his thought—he could not do otherwise; and the Egyptian temple took form as an Egyptian act—it could not be otherwise. So Greek thought, clearly defined, took form in the Greek temple, clearly defined, and the Greek temple stood clearly forth as a Greek act. Yet both were as simply pier-and-lintel as I, in setting one brick upon two separated other bricks, simply expose the principles of pier and lintel.

Similarly the Roman aqueduct and the medieval cathedral were both in the pier-and-arch form. But what a far cry from Roman thought to medieval thought! And how clearly is that difference in thought shown in the differences in form taken on in each case by pier and arch, as each structure in its time stood forth as an act of the people. How eloquently these structures speak to us of the militant and simple power of Roman thought, of the mystic yearning of medieval thought.

But, you may say, these structures were not acts of the people, rather, in one case the act of an emperor, in the other case an act of the church. Very well; but what really was the emperor but an act of the people—expressing the thought of the people; and what was the church but similarly the thought of the people in action? When the thought of the Roman people changed, the vast Roman fabric disintegrated; when the thought of the medieval people changed, the vitality of the church subsided exactly in proportion as the supporting thought of the people was withdrawn. Thus every form of government, every social institution, every undertaking, however great, however

small, every symbol of enlightenment or degradation, each and all have sprung and are still springing from the life of the people, and have ever formed and are now as surely forming images of their thought. Slowly by centuries, generations, years, days, hours, the thought of the people has changed; so with precision have their acts responsively changed; thus thoughts and acts have flowed and are flowing ever onward, unceasingly onward, involved within the impelling power of Life. Throughout this stream of human life, and thought, and activity, men have ever felt the need to build; and from the need arose the power to build. So, as they thought, they built; for, strange as it may seem, they could build in no other way. As they built, they made, used, and left behind them records of their thinking. Then, as through the years new men came with changed thoughts, so arose new buildings in consonance with the change of thought—the building always the expression of the thinking. Whatever the character of the thinking, just so was the character of the building. Pier, lintel, and arch changed in form, purpose, and expression, following, with the fidelity of Life, Man's changing thoughts as he moved in the flow of his destiny—as he was moved ever onward by a drift unseen and unknown—and which is now flowing and is still unseen and unknown.

This flow of building we call Historical Architecture. At no time and in no instance has it been other than an index of the flow of the thought of the people—an emanation from the inmost life of the people.

Perhaps you think this is not so; perhaps you think the feudal lord built the fortified castle. So he did, ostensibly. But where did his need and power so to build come from? From his retainers. And whence came the power of his retainers? From the people. As the people thought, so they acted. And thus the power of the feudal lord rested upon the thought, the belief of the people; upon their need and upon their power.

Thus all power rests upon the consent of the people, that is, upon their thought. The instant their thought begins to change, that instant the power, resting upon it and sanctioned by it, begins its waning. Thus the decay of the old and the formation of the new are synchronous effects of one cause. That single cause is: Thought. Thus we perceive that the simplest aspect of all human activity is change.

To analyze the influences that cause thought to change would take me, now, too far afield. Suffice it to say that thought, once having undergone change, does not again become the same—however great the lapse in time. Thus is there ever new birth, never rebirth.

It may now become clear to my reader that we ought, in viewing historic Architecture, to cease to regard it under the artificial classification of styles, as is now the accepted way, and to consider (as is more natural and more logical) each building of the past and the present as a product and index of the civilization of the time, also, as the product and index of the thought of the people of the time and place. In this way we shall develop in our minds a much broader, clearer panorama of the actual living flow of Architecture through the ages; and grasp the clear, simple, accurate notion, that Architecture always has been, and still is, a simple impulse of which the manifestation in varied form is continuously changing.

I should add, perhaps, that, in speaking of the people, I do not use the word in the unhappy sense of the lower classes, so called. I mean all the people; and I look upon all the people as constituting a social organism.

I am quite aware that these are views not generally held among architects. Indeed you will not find a thesis of this kind set forth in books or taught in schools. For the prevailing view concerning Architecture is strangely artificial and fruitless, as indeed are the current American ideas concerning almost any phase of the welfare of all the people. That is to say; in our democratic land, ideas, thoughts, are weirdly, indeed destructively, undemocratic—an aspect of our current civilization which, later, I shall consider.

I therefore ask my reader, for the time being at least, to repose sufficient confidence in my statements, that he may lay aside his existing notions concerning Architecture, which are of necessity traditional, and, as such, acquired habits of thinking, unanalyzed by him; and thus lay his mind open to receive and consider the simple and more natural views which make up my paper, to the end that he may perceive how far astray we are from an Architecture natural, truthful, and wholesome, such as should characterize a truly democratic people. I ask this because the welfare of democracy is my chief concern in life; and because I have always regarded Architecture, and still so regard it, as merely one of the activities of a people, and as such, necessarily in harmony with all the others. For as a people thinks concerning Architecture, so it thinks concerning everything else; and as it thinks concerning any other thing, so it thinks concerning Architecture; for the thought of a people, however complicated it may appear, is all of-a-piece, and represents the balance of heredity and environment at the time.

I trust, further, that a long disquisition is not necessary in order to show that the attempt at imitation, by us of this day, of the bygone forms of building, is a procedure unworthy of a free people; and that the dictum of schools, that Architecture is finished and done, is a suggestion humiliating to every active brain, and, therefore, in fact, a puerility and a falsehood when weighed in the scales of truly democratic thought. Such dictum gives the lie, in arrogant fashion, to healthful human experience. It says, in a word: The American people are not fit for democracy. Perhaps they are not. If so, we shall see how and why. We shall see if this alleged unfitness is really normal and natural, or if it is a feudal condition imposed upon the people by a traditional system of inverted thinking. We shall see if those whom we have entrusted with leadership in our matters educational have or have not misled us. We shall see, in a larger sense, if we, as a people, not only have betrayed each other, but have failed in that trust which the world-spirit of democracy placed in our hands, as we, a new people, emerged to fill a new and spacious land.

All of this we shall presently read in our current Architecture, and we shall test the accuracy of that reading by a brief analysis of the thought and activities of the American people as they are expressed in other ways. For, be sure, what we shall find in our Architecture, we shall as surely find elsewhere and everywhere.

If it is assumed that the art of reading is confined to the printed page, we cannot go far. But if we broaden and quicken our sense of reading until it appears to us, in its more vital aspect, as a science, an art of interpretation, we shall go very far indeed. In truth, there will be no ending of our journey; for the broad field of nature, of human thought and endeavor, will open to us as a book of life, wherein the greatest and the smallest, the most steadfast and the most fleeting, will appear in their true value. Then will our minds have escaped slavery to WORDS and be at liberty, in the open air of reality, freely and fully to deal with THINGS.

Indeed, most of us have, in less or greater measure, this gift of reading things. We come into it naturally; but, curiously enough, many are ashamed because it does not bear the sanction of authority, because it does not bear the official stamp of that much misunderstood word *scholarship*, a stamp, by the way, which gives currency to most of the notions antagonistic to the development of our common thinking powers. It is this same scholastic fetishism, too, that has caused an illogical gap between the theoretical and the practical. In right thinking such gap cannot ex-

ist. A true method of education, therefore, should consist in a careful and complete development of our common and natural powers of thinking, which, in reality, are vastly greater, infinitely more susceptible to development than is generally assumed. Indeed, the contumacy in which we habitually underrate the latent powers of the average human mind is greatly to our discredit. It constitutes, in fact, a superstition. A superstition whose origin is readily traceable to the scholasticism of past centuries, and to the tenacious notion of social caste. It is definitely the opposite of the modern and enlightened view now steadily gaining ground, that the true spirit of democratic education consists in searching out, liberating, and developing the splendid but obscured powers of the average man, and particularly those of his children.

It is disquieting to note that the system of education on which we lavish funds with such generous, even prodigal, hand, falls short of fulfilling its true democratic function; and that particularly in the so-called higher branches its tendency appears daily more reactionary, more feudal.

It is not an agreeable reflection that so many of our university graduates lack the trained ability to see clearly, and to think simply, concisely, constructively; that there is perhaps more showing of cynicism than good faith, seemingly more distrust of men than confidence in them, and, withal, no consummate ability to interpret things.

In contrast, we have the active-minded but "uneducated" man, he who has so large a share in our activities. He reads well those things that he believes concern him closely. His mind is active, practical, superficial; and, whether he deals with small things or large, its quality is nearly the same in all cases. His thoughts almost always are concerned with the immediate. His powers of reflection are undeveloped, and thus he ignores those simple, vital things which grow up beside him, and with which, as a destiny, he will some day have to reckon, and will then find himself unprepared.

he constructive thinking power of such men, the imaginative reach, the incisive intuition, the forceful will, sometimes amaze us. But when we examine closely we find that all this is but a brilliant superstructure, that the hidden foundation is weak because the foundation-thought was not sought to be placed broad, deep, and secure in the humanities. Thus we have at the poles of our thinking two classes of men, each of which believes it is dealing with realities, but both in fact dealing with phantoms; for between them they have studied everything but the real thoughts and the real hearts of the people. They have not sufficiently reckoned with the true and only source both of social stability and of social change. If, in time, such divergence of thought, as it grows in acuteness, shall lead to painful readjustments, such will be but the result, natural and inexorable, of a fatal misunderstanding, the outgrowth of that fatal defect in our system of thinking which is leading us away from our fellows.

If I say that these aspects of our thought are readable in our current Architecture, I am not saying too much, for acts point surely to the parent thoughts, and in everything that men do they leave an indelible imprint of their minds. If this suggestion be followed out, it will become surprisingly clear how each and every building reveals itself naked to the eye; how its every aspect, to the smallest detail, to the lightest move of the hand, reveals the workings of the mind of the man who made it, and who is responsible to us for it. Everything is there for us to read, to interpret; and this we may do at our leisure. The building has not means of locomotion, it cannot hide itself, it cannot get away. There it is, and there it will stay—telling more truths about him who made it, who thought it, than he in his fatuity imagines; revealing his mind and his heart exactly for what they are worth, not a whit more, not a whit less; telling, plainly, the lies he thinks; telling with almost cruel truthfulness of his bad faith, his feeble, wobbly mind, his

impudence, his selfish egoism, his mental irresponsibility, his apathy, his disdain for real things. Is it cruelty to analyze thus clearly? Is it vivisection thus to pursue, step by step, to uncover nerve after nerve, dispassionately to probe and test and weigh act after act, thought after thought, to follow every twist and turn of the mind that made the building, sifting and judging it until at last the building says to us: "I am no more a real building than the thing that made me is a real man!"

If so, then it must, correspondingly, be a pleasure and a genuine beneficence to recognize and note, in some other building, the honest effort of an honest man, the kindly willingness and frankness of a sincere mind to give expression to simple, direct, natural thinking, to produce a building as real as the man who made it.

And is it not, as naturally, helpful to recognize and note in still another building a mind perhaps not too well trained, perhaps not very sure of itself, but still courageously seeking a way; the building showing where the mind stumbles and tries again, showing just where the thought is not immanent, not clear, not self-centered?

Is it not the part of wisdom to cheer, to encourage such a mind, rather than to dishearten it with ridicule? To say to it: Learn that the mind works best when allowed to work naturally; learn to do what your problem suggests when you have reduced it to its simplest terms; you will thus find all problems, however complex, taking on a simplicity you had not dreamed of; accept this simplicity, boldly, and with confidence, do not lose your nerve and run away from it, or you are lost, for you are here at the point men so heedlessly call genius— as though it were necessarily rare; for you are here at the point no living brain can surpass in essence, the point all truly great minds seek—the point of vital simplicity— the point of view which so illuminates the mind that the art of expression becomes spontaneous, powerful, and unerring, and achievement a certainty; so, if you would seek and express the best that is in yourself, you must search out the best that is in your people; for they are your problem, and you are indissolubly a part of them; it is for you to affirm that which they really wish to affirm, namely, the best that is in them, and they as truly wish you to express the best that is in yourself; if the people seem to have but little faith it is because they have been tricked so long; they are weary of dishonesty, much more weary than you know, and in their hearts they seek honest and fearless men, men simple and clear of mind, loyal to their own manhood and to the people. The American people are now in a stupor; be on hand at the awakening. The lion is now in the net, or the larva in the cocoon—take the simile you prefer.

But to simplify the mind is, in fact, not so easy. Everything is against you. You are surrounded by a mist of tradition which you, alone, must dispel. The schools will not help you, for they too are in a mist. So, you must develop your mind as best you can. The only safe method is to take nothing for granted, but to analyze, test, and examine all things, for yourself, and determine their true values; to sift the wheat from the chaff, and to reduce all thoughts, all activities, to the simple test of honesty. You will be surprised, perhaps, to see how matters that you once deemed solid, fall apart; and how things that you once deemed inconsequential take on a new and momentous significance. But in time your mind will clarify and strengthen, and you will have moved into that domain of intellectual power wherein thought discriminates, with justice and clarity, between those things which make for the health, and those which make for the illness of a people. When you have done this, your mind will have reached its balance; you will have something to say, and you will say it with candor.

In the light of the preceding statements, the current mannerisms of architectural criticism must often seem trivial. For of what avail is it to say that this is too small, that too large, this too thick, that too thin, or to quote this, that, or the other precedent, when the real question may be: Is not the entire design a mean evasion, a parasitic growth? Why magnify this, that, or the other little thing, if the entire scheme of thinking, that the building stands for, is false, and puts a mask upon the people who want true buildings, but do not know how to get them so long as architects betray them with architectural phrases?

Why have we not more of vital architectural criticism? Is it because our professional critics lack penetration? Because they lack courage? Is it because they, who should be free, are not free? Is it because they who should know, do not know? Do they not see, or will they not? Do they know such buildings to be lies, and refrain from saying so? Or are they, too, inert of mind? Are their minds, too, benumbed with culture, and their hearts, thus, made faint?

How is a people to know what, for them, a real and fitting Architecture may mean, if it is not first made clear to them that the current and accepted Architecture with which their minds are rapidly being distorted—is false to them! To whom are we to look if not to our trusted critics? And if these fail us, what then?

But—the cynic may observe—what if they do fail us! They write merely in the fashion. For everybody else betrays everybody else. We are all false: and why should a false people expect other than a false Architecture? A people always gets what it deserves, neither more or less. It's up to the people, anyway. If they want a real Architecture, let them become real, themselves. If they do not wish to be betrayed let them quit betraying. If they really wish loyalty, let them be loyal. If they really wish thinkers, let them so think. If they really do not wish humbug Architecture let them cease being humbugs themselves. There is so much of truth in this discouraging view, that I shall later clarify it.

For the moment, however, it is significant in passing to note, concerning our architectural periodicals. They float along, aimlessly enough, drifting in the tide of heedless commercialism—their pages filled with views of buildings, buildings, like "words, words, words." Building in this "style," that, and the other; false always, except now and then and here and there in spots, where the "style" has been dropped in spots, and where, in consequence, the real building appears in spots; or where the architect, under "compulsion," has had to let the "style" go—and do something sensible; or, rarely, where the architect, of his own free will, has chosen to be clean, and has expressed himself with feeling and simple, direct eloquence. The publishers may well say: Make the Architecture and we will publish it; we are but mirrors of the times. If our pages are filled with pretentious trash, it is because architects make it. We publish what our critics write, such as it is, and what architects write, such as it is. We give our readers, who are mostly architects, what they give us. If they want better, they will let us know. We are willing.

And a word concerning "Handbooks on Architecture." All that need be said of them is that they are the blind leading the blind.

Concerning more ambitious works: while they contain certain, or rather uncertain, attempts at philosophy, such discussion is left in the air as a vapor; it is not condensed into terms of vital, present use.

Thus, it happens that the would-be searcher after architectural reality finds no air, no comfort. He is led into a jungle within whose depths his guides are lost, and he is left without compass and without a star. And why is this so? The answer is at hand: Because it has long and tacitly been assumed, by our would-be mentors, that the Architectural Art is a closed book, that the word FINIS was written centuries ago, and that all, obviously, that is left for us moderns is the humble privilege to select, copy, and adapt. Because it has not been assumed that ALL buildings have arisen, have stood, and stand as physical symbols of the psychic state of the people. Because no distinction has been made between WAS and IS. And—what is most dispiriting—this lunacy continues its erratic parade in plain open view of the towering fact that modern science, with devoted patience of research, has evolved, is perfecting, and has placed freely at our service the most comprehensive, accurate, and high-powered system of organic reasoning that the world has known. These methods and powers, the breadth and fertility of this supreme search for the all-life-process, this most fruitful function of democracy, is, by those connected with the Architectural Art and its teaching, today regarded vacantly. Strangely they undervalue that which for us all, in all truth, in the serenity of human hope, heralds a sunrise for the race. Truly, procreant modern thought, clothed in all its radiance of good will, is a poet, a teacher, and a prophet not known in the land of these.

Confronting this ignoble apathy of those we have trusted, let us assume, if it be but in fancy, a normal student of Nature and of Man. Let us assume a virile critic, human and humane, sensitive to all, and aware of this modern daybreak. He will have been a lifelong seeker of realities. His compass pointing ever to the central fact that all is life; his drinking water, the knowledge that act and thought are fatefully the same; his nourishing food, the conviction that pure democracy is the deepest-down, the most persistent, while the most obscured desire within the consciousness of man—so equipped, he will have traversed the high seas and the lands, from poles to equator, all latitudes and longitudes of the prolific world of repressed but aspiring humanity. He will hold history, as a staff, in his hand. He will weigh the Modern Man in a just balance, wherein he will set against that man his accountability to all the people. He, as dispassionately, will weigh the people, collectively, against their manifest responsibility and accountability to the child and to the man.

Let us suppose him, now, in his wandering, to have come into Our Land. That he views our Architecture, weighs it, evaluates it; then, turning in thought, looks out upon us, as a people, analyzes us, weighs us, takes our measure, appraises us; that he then places People and Architecture in the great balance of History, and thoughtfully weighs, carefully appraises; then places the people, with all their activities, in the new balance of Democracy, again to weigh, again to appraise; and then puts us with our self-called Common Sense into the serene balance of Nature; and, at the last, weighs Us and Our All, in the fateful balance of All-Encompassing Life—and makes the last appraisement! What, think you, will be his revaluing of our valuations of things, of thoughts, of men? What, in the sifting, would prove wheat, what, in the weighing, would have substance, what in this refiner's fire would be the dross? After his reflections, what will he say? What will he say, after weighing us against our broad, fertile land, with its many waters, its superb and simulating air, its sumptuous and placid beauty? How will he define us when he shall have searched our minds and hearts? For we cannot hide! What will he say when he shall come to hold us in a close accounting of our stewardship of the talent, Liberty, the treasure that the world has paid so dear in sorrow to transmit to us?

What he might say, would prove a new and most dramatic story.

But surely he might, in part, speak thus: As you are, so are your buildings; and, as are your buildings, so are you. You and your Architecture are the same. Each is the faithful portrait of the other. To read the one is to read the other. To interpret the one is to interpret the other. Arising from both, as a miasma: What falsity! What betrayal of the present and the past! Arising from both, as the most thrilling, the more heart-piercing of refrains, as the murmur of a crowd, I hear the cry: "What is the use?" that cry begun in frivolity, passing into cynicism, and, now, deepening into pessimism. That cry which in all time and in all peoples became the cry of death or of revolution, when from frivolity it had merged through pessimism—into an utterance of despair! Your buildings, good, bad and indifferent, arise as warning hands in the faces of all—for they are what you are. Take heed! Did you think Architecture a thing of books—of the past? No! Never! IT WAS, ALWAYS, OF ITS PRESENT AND ITS PEOPLE! IT, NOW, IS OF THE PRESENT, AND OF YOU! This Architecture is ashamed to be natural but is not ashamed to lie; so, you, as a people, are ashamed to be natural but are not ashamed to lie. This Architecture is ashamed to be honest, but it is not ashamed to steal; so, then, by the unanswerable logic of Life, you are ashamed to be honest but are not ashamed to steal. This Architecture is filled with hypocrisy and cant. So, likewise, are you, but you say you are not. This Architecture is neurasthenic; so have you burned the candle at both ends. Is then this Democracy? This Architecture shows, ah, so plainly, the decline of Democracy, and a rank new growth of Feudalism—sure sign of a people in peril! This Architecture has no serenity—sure symbol of a people out of balance. This Architecture reveals no lucid guiding principle—nor have you yet evolved a lucid guiding principle, sorely though you now need it! This Architecture shows no love of Nature—you despise Nature. In it is no joy of living—you know not what the fullness of life signifies—you are unhappy, fevered, and perturbed. In these buildings the Dollar is vulgarly exalted—and the Dollar you place above Man. You adore it twenty-four hours each day: it is your God! These buildings show lack of great thinkers, real men, among your architects and, as a people, you are poor in great thinkers, real men—though you now, in your extremity, are in dire need of great thinkers, real men. These buildings show no love of country, no affection for the people. So have you no affection for each

ther, but secretly will ruin each and any,
so much do you love gold, so wantonly
will you betray not only your neighbor but
yourselves and your own children, for it!

Yet, here and there, a building bespeaks
integrity—so have you that much of integrity. All is not false—so are you not
wholly false. What leaven is found in your
buildings—such leaven is found in you.
Weight for weight, measure for measure,
sign for sign—as are your buildings, so are
you!

A colossal energy is in your buildings,
but not true power—so is found in you a
frenzied energy, but not the true power of
equipoise. Is this an indictment? Not unless
you yourselves are an indictment of yourselves. There stand the buildings, they have
their unchanging physiognomy. Look! See!
Thus, this is a reading, an interpretation.

Here and there are buildings, modest,
truthful, and sincere: products of a genuine
feeling existing in you. They are not truly
shamed where you are not ashamed; they
are natural where you are natural; they
are democratic where you are democratic.
Side by side they stand against the false
and feudal—all intermixed. So are your
thoughts and acts intermixed, democratic
and feudal, in a strange and sinister drift.

Your buildings show no philosophy. So
have you no philosophy. You pretend a philosophy of common sense. Weighed in the
balance of your acts, your common sense
is light as folly: a patent-medicine folly;
an adulterated-food folly, a dyspeptic folly,
the folly of filth and smoke in your cities,
and innumerable everyday follies quite the
reverse of that common sense which you
assume to mean clear-cut and sturdy thinking in the affairs of daily life. You boast
a philosophy of Success. It has long been
your daily harangue. But, weighed in the
balance of Democracy, your successes are
but too clearly, in the main, feudal. They
are pessimisms, not optimisms. You did not
think to count the cost; but you are beginning now to catch a corner of its masked
visage. The sight of the true full cost

will stagger you—when the mask is fully
drawn aside, and it stands clearly revealed!
You would not foresee a crisis, BUT CRISIS
FORESAW YOU, AND NOW IS UPON YOU.

You tacitly assumed philosophy to be an
empty word, not a vital need; you did not
inquire; and in so blindfolding your minds,
you have walked straight to the edge of
an abyss.

For a Sound Philosophy is the Saving
Grace of a Democratic People! It means,
very simply, a balanced system of thinking,
concerning the vital relations of a people.
It is intensely practical. Nothing can be
more so. For it saves waste. It looks far
behind and far ahead. It forestalls Crisis.
It nurtures, economizes, and directs the
vitality of a people. It has for its sole and
abiding objective, their equilibrium, hence
their happiness.

Thus, foibles and follies have usurped
in your minds the vacant seat of Wisdom.
Thus, has your Dollar betrayed you, as it
must. And thus, has NOT been given to
the World that which was and still remains
your highest office, and your noblest privilege to give, in return for that Liberty
which was once yours, and which the world
gave to you: A sane and pure accounting
of Democracy; a philosophy founded upon
Man—thereby setting forth, in clear and
human terms, the integrity, the responsibility, and the accountability of the individual—in short, a new, a real Philosophy
of the People.

It is not yet too late.

Let such philosophy be the spiritual
firstfruit of your fair and far-flung land.
For you must now think quickly, and
with a penetration, concentration, simplicity, accuracy, and nerve, the necessity of
which you have hitherto belittled and denied. Your one splendid power and reserve
lies in your resourceful intelligence when
forced by your distress into a crisis. Your
Architecture hints at this in its many-sided
practicalities. Your history in this land has
proved it. Use this power at once!

Again, this Architecture, in the large

sense, is barren of poetry; yet, strangely enough it faintly contains in its physiognomy a latent suggestion, which bespeaks dramatic, lyric, eloquent, and appealing possibilities. In fine, it expresses obscurely the most human qualities you as a people possess, and which, such is your awkward mental bashfulness, you are ashamed to acknowledge, much less to proclaim. One longs to wash from this dirty face its overlay of timidity and abasement; to strip from its form the rags of neglect and contumely, and to see if indeed there be not beneath its forlorn and pitiful aspect, the real face and form of unsuspected Cinderella.

I surmise—or is it a hope born of visible possibilities? A sense of not negligible probabilities? For, truly, what in all the world is more sweet, in the last analysis, however fickle and at times childishly cruel, than is the American heart!

On this foundation, deeper and stronger than you suspect, I would, if I were you, build a new superstructure, really truer to yourselves, and more enduring, than that which now is crumbling upon its weak support of over-smartness and fundamental untruth.

Fortunate, indeed, are you, that your corruption has been so crude; for you can still survive the surgery of its eradication.

It is on this sound heart, and that still better part of it as yet unmatured and unrevealed to your own consciousness, that I would build anew and aright.

For he who knows even a genuinely little of Mankind knows this truth: The heart is greater than the head. For, in the heart, is Desire; and, from it, comes forth Courage and Magnanimity.

To be sure, you had assumed that poetry meant verses; and that reading such was an unworthy weakness for men of brains and hardheaded business. You have held to a fiction, patterned upon your farcical common sense, that sentiment has no place in affairs. Again you did not inquire; you assumed, took for granted—as is your heedless way. You have not looked into

your own hearts. You have looked only at the vacancy of convention from which realities have long since departed. Only the husks remain there, like the shells of beetles upon the bark of a living tree.

You have not thought deeply enough to know that the heart in you is the woman in man. You have derided your femininity, where you have suspected it; whereas, you should have known its power, cherished and utilized it, for it is the hidden wellspring of Intuition and Imagination. What can the brain accomplish without these two! They are the man's two inner eyes; without them, he is stone-blind. For the mind sends forth their powers both together. One carries the light, the other searches; and between them they find treasures. These they bring to the brain, which first elaborates them, then says to the will "Do"—and Action follows.

Poetically considered, as far as the huge disordered resultant mass of your Architecture is concerned, Intuition and Imagination have not gone forth to illuminate and search the hearts of the people. Thus are its works stone-blind. If such works be called masculine, this term will prove but a misuse of neuter. For they are empty of procreant powers. They do not inspire the thoughtful mind, but much do they depress it; they are choked with inarticulate cries which evoke pathos in the hearer.

Consider, now, that poetry is not verse—although some verse may be poetic. Consider, now, poetry as apart from words and as resident in things, in thoughts, in acts. For if you persist in regarding print or language as the only readable or hearable things—you must, indeed, remain dull interpreters of the voices of Nature, and of the acts and thoughts of the men of the present and the past, in their varied, but fundamentally alike activities. No; poetry rightly considered, stands for the highest form of intellectual scope and activity. Indeed, it were truer to say psychic activity, if it be known what realities lie behind the mask of that word.

And, be it said in passing, most words are masks. Habit has accustomed you to this company of masks, beautiful some of them, repellent others, but you seldom draw aside a word-mask to see, for yourselves, the countenance of reality which it may both reveal and conceal. For, as I have said, you do not inquire, you are prone to take things for granted. You have seen masks since childhood, and have assumed and still assume them to be real, because, since childhood, you have been told they were, and are, real, by those to whose selfish interest it was, and is, that you cherish the illusion. Latterly, however, you have sufficiently awakened to draw aside the mask-word *Respectability.*

You dearly love the mask-word *Brains,* which means physical action; and sniff at the word *Intellect,* which stands for clear, powerfully constructive reflection. Therefore, as this is your thought, naturally enough, you are the victims of your impulsive acts, and of your apathy toward far-reaching, inevitable, yes, inexorable, consequences.

It is vitally with realities that poetry deals. But you say it does not; so that settles the matter as far as you are concerned—at least you think it does—in reality it settles you—it keeps you self-bound.

You say that poetry deals only with metaphor and figures of speech. What is your daily talk but metaphor and figures of speech! Every word, genuinely used, is a picture; whether used in conversation or in literary production. Mental life, indeed physical life, is almost entirely a matter of eyesight.

Now poetry, properly understood, means the most highly efficient form of mental eyesight. That is to say, it is that power of seeing and doing which reveals to Man's inner self the fullness and the subtle power of Life.

Poetry, as a living thing, therefore, stands for the most telling quality that man can impart to his thoughts and his acts. Judged by this test, your buildings are dreary, empty places.

Further, these buildings reveal no genuine art of expression—and neither have you as a people genuinely expressed yourselves. You have sniffed at this, too; for you are very cynical, and very pert, and very cocksure. The leer is not long absent from your eyes. You have said in substance: "What do we want of an art of expression? We cannot sell it!" Perhaps not. But you can and have sold yourselves.

You have assumed that an art of expression is a fiction, something apart from yourselves; as you have assumed almost all things, of genuinely preservative value, to be fictions, apart from yourselves—things negligible, to be put on or off like a coat.

Therefore look at your body of laws—complicated, grotesque, and inefficient, spiked with "jokers," as guns are spiked. Look at your Constitution. Does that now really express the sound life in you, or is there a "joker" in that, too, that is surely strangling you? Look at your business. What is it become but a war of extermination among cannibals? Does it express Democracy? Are you, as a People, now really a Democracy? Do you still possess the power of self-government of a people, by a people, for a people? Or is it now perished, as your Abraham Lincoln, on the field of Gettysburg, hoped it might not, and as hoped a weary and heartsick people at the close of an awful struggle to preserve Democracy in its integrity, to preserve that fundamental art of expression whereby a people may, unhampered, give voice and form to the aspiration of their lives, their hopes, as they press onward toward the enjoyment of their birthright, the birthright of every man—the right to happiness!

Do you realize with what caustic accuracy this stupor is shown in your buildings? They, too, stand for the spiked laws of an art of expression. For what is there to express but the true life of a people? What is there, in a Democracy, but All the People? By what right does any man say: "I am! I own! I am therefore a law unto myself! How quickly among you has I LEAD! BECOME—I POSSESS! I BETRAY! How glibly have you acquiesced! With what awful folly have you assumed selfish egotism to be the basis of Democracy!

How significant is it that, now, a few rough hands are shaking you, a few sharp shrill voices calling: "Awake before it is too late!"

"But," I hear you say, testily, "we are too young to consider these accomplishments. We have been so busy with our material development that we have not found the time to consider them."

Know then that, to begin with, they are not accomplishments but necessaries. And, to end with, you are old enough, and have found the time to succeed in nearly making a fine art of—Betrayal, and a science of—Graft!

Know that you are as old as the race. That each man among you has in him the accumulated power of the race, ready at hand for use, in the right way, when he shall conclude it better to think straight and hence act straight, rather than, as now, to act crooked and pretend to be straight.

Know that the test, plain, simple HONESTY (and you all know, every man of you knows, exactly what that means), is always at your hand.

Know that as all complex manifestations have a simple basis of origin, so the vast complexity of your national unrest, ill health, inability to think clearly and accurately concerning simple things, really vital things, is easily and swiftly traceable to the single, actual, active cause—Dishonesty; and that this points with unescapable logic and in just measure to each INDIVIDUAL MAN!

The Remedy: INDIVIDUAL HONESTY.

A conclusion as logical and as just!

"But," you may say, "how absurdly simple."

Doubtless it is absurd, if you think it is, and will so remain, as far as you are concerned, just so long as you think it is—and no longer. But just so long will your social

pains and aches and unrest continue; and these you do not consider absurd.

When Newton saw the apple fall, he saw what you might likewise call an absurdly simple thing. Yet with this simple thing he connected up the Universe.

Moreover, this simple thing, Honesty, stands in the Universe of Human Thought and Action, as its very Center of Gravity, and is our human mask-word behind which abides all the power of Nature's Integrity, the profoundest FACT which modern thinking has persuaded Life to reveal.

What folly, then, for Man to buck against the stupendous FLOW of LIFE; instead of voluntarily and gladly placing himself in harmony with it, and thus transferring to himself Nature's own creative energy and equipoise.

"But," you say, "All this is above our heads."

No it is not! IT IS CLOSE BESIDE YOUR HAND! And therein lies its power.

Again you say: "How can honesty be enforced?"

It cannot be enforced.

"Then how will the remedy go into effect?"

It cannot GO into effect. It can only COME into effect.

"Then how can it come?"

Ask Nature.

"And what will Nature say?"

Nature is always saying: "I center at each man, woman, and child. I knock at the door of each heart, and I wait. I wait in patience—ready to enter with my gifts."

"And is that all that Nature says?"

That is all.

"Then how are we to receive Nature?"

By opening wide the door of your minds! For your greatest crime against yourselves is that you have locked the door in Her face and have thrown away the key! Now you say: "There is no key!"

"Then how shall we make a key?"

First: Care scrupulously for your individual and collective physical health. Beware of those who are undermining it; they are your deadliest danger. Beware of yourselves if you are undermining it, for you are then your own deadliest enemy. Thus will you achieve the first vital preliminary—a quiet, strong, and resilient nervous system. Thus will your five senses become accurate interpreters of your physical surroundings; and thus, quite naturally, will the brain resume, in you, its normal power to act and react.

Second: Begin at once the establishment of a truly democratic system of education. The basis of this must be CHARACTER; and the mind must be so trained in the sense of reality that it may reach the fullness of its power to weigh all things, and to realize that the origin and sustenance of its power comes from without, and is Nature's bounteous, unstinted gift to all men.

Such system of education will result in equilibrium of body, mind, and heart. It will therefore develop real men and women—as is Nature's desire.

It will produce social equilibrium in every aspect of human affairs. It will so clearly reveal the follies that have cursed you, that you will abandon them forever. For you will then recognize and gladly accept the simple, central truth that the individual grows in power only as he grows in integrity, and that the unfailing source of that integrity lies in the eternal integrity of Nature and of that Infinite Serenity of which Nature is but a symbol.

Thus will you make of Democracy a religion—the only one the world will have developed—befitting freemen—free in the integrity of their bodies, free in the integrity of their thought.

So doing, all aspects of your activities will change, because your thoughts will have changed. All of your activities will then take on organic and balanced coherence, because all of your thoughts will have a common center of gravity in the integrity of individual Man.

And, as the oak tree is ever true to the acorn from which it sprang, and propagates true acorns in its turn, so will you then give true expression and form to the seed of Democracy that was planted in your soil, and so spread in turn the seeds of true Democracy.

Thus, as your thoughts change, will your civilization change. And thus, as Democracy takes living and integral shape within your thought, will the Feudalism, now tainting you, disappear. For its present power rests wholly upon your acquiescent and supporting thought. Its strength lies wholly in you, not in itself. So, inevitably, as the sustaining power of your thought is withdrawn, this Feudalism will crumble and vanish!

So have you no need of Force, for force is a crude and inefficient instrument. THOUGHT is the fine and powerful instrument. Therefore, HAVE THOUGHT FOR THE INTEGRITY OF YOUR OWN THOUGHT. For all social power, for good, or for ill, rests upon the thought of the People. THIS IS THE SINGLE LESSON IN THE HISTORY OF MANKIND THAT IS REALLY WORTH THE WHILE.

Naturally, then, as your thoughts thus change, your growing Architecture will change. Its falsity will depart; its reality will gradually appear. For the integrity of your thought, as a People, will then have penetrated the minds of your architects.

THEN, TOO, AS YOUR BASIC THOUGHT CHANGES WILL EMERGE A PHILOSOPHY, A POETRY, AND AN ART OF EXPRESSION IN ALL THINGS: FOR YOU WILL HAVE LEARNED THAT A CHARACTERISTIC PHILOSOPHY, POETRY, AND ART OF EXPRESSION ARE VITAL TO THE HEALTHFUL GROWTH AND DEVELOPMENT OF A DEMOCRATIC PEOPLE.

As a People you have enormous latent, unused power.

Awaken it.

Use it.

Use it for the common good.

Begin now!

For it is as true today as when one of your wise men said it:—"THE WAY TO RESUME IS TO RESUME!"

Selected Stories

Guy de Maupassant

Editor's Introduction

If the ideas of Emerson sometimes seemed high and thin, and if those of Louis Sullivan were on occasion impossibly grand—to speak only of figures whose works appear in this issue of *The Great Ideas Today*—the views of Maupassant were so low that no one has ever been able to see them over the heads of the persons who populate his many stories; nor do they seem to have been larger than the lives that appear in these tales. He is the kind of storyteller—Chekhov, his contemporary, is another—whose art consists in rendering human existence without stopping to tell us what they think about it, still less asking *us* to think, to take sides, to judge of its merit. Possibly for Maupassant it had no merit. His mentor was Gustave Flaubert, whose pessimism was profound and who despised the hypocrisy, the vital lies he detected in the French bourgeoisie of his time—that is, the nineteenth century. It is easy to imagine that Maupassant's depiction of prostitutes and other lowlifes reflected a scorn he felt of human pretensions. But he never says so. On the contrary he seems wholly charitable, as the greatest writers always do seem, knowing better than to quarrel with their material. He is content to let people be as they are, and he is only at pains, so far as we can tell, to be sure we know what that is.

His own life was unremarkable, except that it was short—too short, we might suppose, for his prodigious output, which comprises some 300 tales along with half a dozen novels and many articles, the whole *oeuvre,* or most of it, produced in a single decade. He was born in 1850 in Normandy, a province that figures in many of his stories. As a young man he served with the French army during the disastrous Franco-German War of 1870, and then, after an interval in the civil service, which he did not like, he moved to Paris. There, Flaubert, who was a family friend, kept a kindly eye on him, taking him to lunch, lecturing him on style, and reading the work that Maupassant had begun to produce with the intention of becoming a writer. Flaubert also introduced him to his literary friends, among them Émile Zola, Ivan Turgenev, and Henry James, who came to visit on Sunday afternoons. "He's my disciple and I love him like a son," Flaubert said of Maupassant, who was much grieved when a decade later, in 1880, Flaubert died suddenly of a stroke.

That year was the beginning of Maupassant's career in the sense that, while he had written a good deal previously, he had until then published nothing under his own name; Flaubert was a severe taskmaster, never satisfied with his own work and demanding of the young man he regarded as his pupil. The tale that launched Maupassant was *Boule de Suif* (Ball-of-Fat), one of the ones reprinted here and always cited as among his best. Other stories followed quickly. His subjects, besides the recent war, were the Norman peasantry, the civil service, and Bohemian life on the banks of the river Seine in Paris—things he knew from his own experience. A common presence in the tales is a womanizing man, usually the chief character, who may be taken as a depiction of Maupassant himself, whose own affairs with women, many of them prostitutes, were frequent, open, and exuberant. This did not prevent him from other energetic activity, chiefly rowing, which he sometimes did for as far as fifty miles a day. Unhappily, it did have mortal consequences. One of the women with whom he slept in the 1870s infected him with syphilis that his doctors failed to treat, or that he refused to have treated, depending on which account of the matter is believed. The first indications of the disease appeared in the late 1870s. Gradually he developed symptoms—eye trouble, migraine headaches— at odds with his outwardly robust physique. Then his mental state deteriorated. In 1892 he attempted suicide by cutting his throat. Committed to an asylum, hopelessly insane, he died the following year.

Widely read as his work has always been, it has not received great critical attention; there is no school of interpretation devoted to Maupassant. Yet he was nothing if not a conscious and careful artist. "Whatever you want to say," he once quoted Flaubert as having told him, "there is only one word to express it, only one verb to give it movement, only one adjective to qualify it. You must search for that word, that verb, that adjective, and never be content with an approximation, never resort to tricks, even clever ones, and never have recourse to verbal sleight-of-hand to avoid a difficulty." That Maupassant took this advice seriously is suggested by the fact that he recalled it. But there is no proof of it in what he wrote, as there is with Flaubert himself, in whose perfect sentences we sometimes sense the polish. Maupassant's words do not reveal the effort, if there was any, that they cost him. This may be what criticism finds hard to forgive, this lack of any handle to grab him by, any sign that he wished to mean more than his stories, as such, seem to be. What that amounts to, judging by the many readers he has had, is enough.

Ball-of-Fat

For many days now the fag end of the army had been straggling through the town. They were not troops, but a disbanded horde. The beards of the men were long and filthy, their uniforms in tatters, and they advanced at an easy pace without flag or regiment. All seemed worn-out and back-broken, incapable of a thought or a resolution, marching by habit solely, and falling from fatigue as soon as they stopped. In short, they were a mobilized, pacific people, bending under the weight of the gun; some little squads on the alert, easy to take alarm and prompt in enthusiasm, ready to attack or to flee; and in the midst of them, some red breeches, the remains of a division broken up in a great battle; some somber artillery men in line with these varied kinds of foot soldiers; and sometimes the brilliant helmet of a dragoon on foot who followed with difficulty the shortest march of the lines.

Some legions of free-shooters, under the heroic names of "Avengers of the Defeat," "Citizens of the Tomb," "Partakers of Death," passed in their turn with the air of bandits.

Their leaders were former cloth or grain merchants, ex-merchants in tallow or soap, warriors of circumstance, officers elected on account of their escutcheons and the length of their mustaches, covered with arms and with braid, speaking in constrained voices, discussing plans of campaign and pretending to carry agonized France alone on their swaggering shoulders, but sometimes fearing their own soldiers, prison-birds, that were often brave at first and later proved to be plunderers and debauchees.

It was said that the Prussians were going to enter Rouen.

The National Guard, who for two months had been carefully reconnoitering in the neighboring woods, shooting sometimes their own sentinels, and ready for a combat whenever a little wolf stirred in the thicket, had now returned to their firesides. Their arms, their uniforms, all the murderous accoutrements with which they had lately struck fear into the national heart for three leagues in every direction, had suddenly disappeared.

The last French soldiers finally came across the Seine to reach the Audemer bridge through Saint-Sever and Bourg-Achard; and, marching behind, on foot, between two officers of ordnance, the General, in despair, unable to do anything with these incongruous tatters, himself lost in the breaking-up of a people accustomed to conquer, and disastrously beaten, in spite of his legendary bravery.

A profound calm, a frightful, silent expectancy had spread over the city. Many of the heavy citizens, emasculated by commerce, anxiously awaited the conquerors, trembling lest their roasting spits or kitchen knives be considered arms.

All life seemed stopped; shops were closed, the streets dumb. Sometimes an inhabitant, intimidated by this silence, moved rapidly along next the walls. The agony of waiting made them wish the enemy would come.

In the afternoon of the day which followed the departure of the French troops, some uhlans [mounted cavalry], coming from one knows not where, crossed the town with celerity. Then, a little later, a black mass descended the side of St. Catharine, while two other invading bands appeared by the way of Darnetal and Boisguillaume. The advance guard of the three bodies joined one another at the same moment in Hotel de Ville square and, by all the neighboring streets, the German army continued to arrive, spreading out its battalions, making the pavement resound under their hard, rhythmic step.

Some orders of the commander, in a foreign, guttural voice, reached the houses which seemed dead and deserted, while behind closed shutters, eyes were watching these victorious men, masters of the city, of fortunes, of lives, through the "rights of war." The inhabitants, shut up in their rooms, were visited with the kind of excitement that a cataclysm, or some fatal upheaval of the earth, brings to us, against which all force is useless. For the same sensation is produced each time that the established order of things is overturned, when security no longer exists, and all that protect the laws of man and of nature find themselves at the mercy of unreasoning, ferocious brutality. The trembling of the earth crushing the houses and burying an entire people; a river overflowing its banks and carrying in its course the drowned peasants, carcasses of beeves, and girders snatched from roofs, or a glorious army massacring those trying to defend themselves, leading others prisoners, pillaging in the name of the sword and thanking God to the sound of the cannon, all are alike frightful scourges which disconnect all belief in eternal justice, all the confidence that we have in the protection of Heaven and the reason of man.

Some detachments rapped at each door, then disappeared into the houses. It was occupation after invasion. Then the duty commences for the conquered to show themselves gracious toward the conquerors.

After some time, as soon as the first terror disappears, a new calm is established. In many families, the Prussian officer eats at the table. He is sometimes well bred and, through politeness, pities France and speaks of his repugnance in taking part in this affair. One is grateful to him for this sentiment; then, one may be, some day or other, in need of his protection. By treating him well, one has, perhaps, a less number of men to feed. And why should we wound anyone on whom we are entirely dependent? To act thus would be less bravery than temerity. And temerity is no longer a fault of the commoner of Rouen, as it was at the time of the heroic defense, when their city became famous. Finally, each told himself that the highest judgment of French urbanity required that they be allowed to be polite to the strange soldier in the house, provided they did not show themselves familiar with him in public. Outside they would not make themselves known to each other, but at home they could chat freely, and the German might remain longer each evening warming his feet at their hearthstones.

The town even took on, little by little, its ordinary aspect. The French scarcely went out, but the Prussian soldiers grumbled in the streets. In short, the officers of the Blue Hussars, who dragged with arrogance their great weapons of death up and down the pavement, seemed to have no more grievous scorn for the simple citizens than the officers or the sportsmen who, the year before, drank in the same *cafés*.

There was nevertheless something in the air, something subtle and unknown, a strange, intolerable atmosphere like a penetrating odor, the odor of invasion. It filled the dwellings and the public places, changed the taste of the food, gave the impression of being on a journey, far away, among barbarous and dangerous tribes.

The conquerors exacted money, much money. The inhabitants always paid, and they were rich enough to do it. But the richer a trading Norman becomes the more he suffers at every outlay, at each part of his fortune that he sees pass from his hands into those of another.

Therefore, two or three leagues below

he town, following the course of the river toward Croisset, Dieppedalle, or Biessart, mariners and fishermen often picked up the swollen corpse of a German in uniform from the bottom of the river, killed by the blow of a knife, the head crushed with a stone, or perhaps thrown into the water by a push from the high bridge. The slime of the riverbed buried these obscure vengeances, savage but legitimate unknown heroisms, mute attacks more perilous than the battles of broad day and without the echoing sound of glory.

For hatred of the foreigner always arouses some intrepid ones, who are ready to die for an idea.

Finally, as soon as the invaders had brought the town quite under subjection with their inflexible discipline, without having been guilty of any of the horrors for which they were famous along their triumphal line of march, people began to take courage, and the need of trade put new heart into the commerce of the country. Some had large interests at Havre, which the French army occupied, and they wished to try and reach this port by going to Dieppe by land and there embarking.

They used their influence with the German soldiers with whom they had an acquaintance, and finally, an authorization of departure was obtained from the General-in-chief.

Then, a large diligence, with four horses, having been engaged for this journey, and ten persons having engaged seats in it, it was resolved to set out on Tuesday morning before daylight, in order to escape observation.

For some time before, the frost had been hardening the earth and on Monday, toward three o'clock, great black clouds coming from the north brought the snow which fell without interruption during the evening and all night.

At half past four in the morning, the travelers met in the courtyard of Hotel Normandie, where they were to take the carriage.

They were still full of sleep, and shivering with cold under their wraps. They could only see each other dimly in the obscure light, and the accumulation of heavy winter garments made them all resemble fat curates in long cassocks. Only two of the men were acquainted; a third accosted them and they chatted: "I'm going to take my wife," said one. "I too," said another. "And I," said the third. The first added: "We shall not return to Rouen, and if the Prussians approach Havre, we shall go over to England." All had the same projects, being of the same mind.

As yet the horses were not harnessed. A little lantern, carried by a stable boy, went out one door from time to time, to immediately appear at another. The feet of the horses striking the floor could be heard, although deadened by the straw and litter, and the voice of a man talking to the beasts, sometimes swearing, came from the end of the building. A light tinkling of bells announced that they were taking down the harness; this murmur soon became a clear and continuous rhythm by the movement of the animal, stopping sometimes, then breaking into a brusque shake which was accompanied by the dull stamp of a sabot upon the hard earth.

The door suddenly closed. All noise ceased. The frozen citizens were silent; they remained immovable and stiff.

A curtain of uninterrupted white flakes constantly sparkled in its descent to the ground. It effaced forms and powdered everything with a downy moss. And nothing could be heard in the great silence. The town was calm, and buried under the wintry frost, as this fall of snow, unnameable and floating, a sensation rather than a sound (trembling atoms which only seem to fill all space), came to cover the earth.

The man reappeared with his lantern, pulling at the end of a rope a sad horse which would not come willingly. He placed him against the pole, fastened the traces, walked about a long time adjusting the

437

harness, for he had the use of but one hand, the other carrying the lantern. As he went for the second horse, he noticed the travelers, motionless, already white with snow, and said to them: "Why not get into the carriage? You will be under cover, at least."

They had evidently not thought of it, and they hastened to do so. The three men installed their wives at the back and then followed them. Then the other forms, undecided and veiled, took in their turn the last places without exchanging a word.

The floor was covered with straw, in which the feet ensconced themselves. The ladies at the back having brought little copper foot stoves, with a carbon fire, lighted them and, for some time, in low voices, enumerated the advantages of the appliances, repeating things that they had known for a long time.

Finally, the carriage was harnessed with six horses instead of four, because the traveling was very bad, and a voice called out: "Is everybody aboard?"

And a voice within answered: "Yes."

They were off. The carriage moved slowly, slowly for a little way. The wheels were imbedded in the snow; the whole body groaned with heavy cracking sounds; the horses glistened, puffed, and smoked; and the great whip of the driver snapped without ceasing, hovering about on all sides, knotting and unrolling itself like a thin serpent, lashing brusquely some horse on the rebound, which then put forth its most violent effort.

Now the day was imperceptibly dawning. The light flakes, which one of the travelers, a Rouenese by birth, said looked like a shower of cotton, no longer fell. A faint light filtered through the great dull clouds, which rendered more brilliant the white of the fields, where appeared a line of great trees clothed in whiteness, or a chimney with a cap of snow.

In the carriage, each looked at the others curiously, in the sad light of this dawn.

At the back, in the best places, Mr. Loiseau, wholesale merchant of wine, of Grand-Pont street, and Mrs. Loiseau were sleeping opposite each other. Loiseau had bought out his former patron, who failed in business, and made his fortune. He sold bad wine at a good price to small retailers in the country and passed among his friends and acquaintances as a knavish wag, a true Norman full of deceit and joviality.

His reputation as a sharper was so well established that one evening at the residence of the prefect, Mr. Tournel, author of some fables and songs, of keen, satirical mind, a local celebrity, having proposed to some ladies, who seemed to be getting a little sleepy, that they make up a game of "Loiseau tricks," the joke traversed the rooms of the prefect, reached those of the town, and then, in the months to come made many a face in the province expand with laughter.

Loiseau was especially known for his love of farce of every kind, for his jokes, good and bad; and no one could ever talk with him without thinking: "He is invaluable, this Loiseau." Of tall figure, his balloon-shaped front was surmounted by a ruddy face surrounded by gray whiskers.

His wife, large, strong, and resolute, with a quick, decisive manner, was the order and arithmetic of this house of commerce, while he was the life of it through his joyous activity.

Beside them, Mr. Carré-Lamadon held himself with great dignity, as if belonging to a superior caste; a considerable man, in cottons, proprietor of three mills, officer of the Legion of Honor, and member of the General Council. He had remained, during the Empire, chief of the friendly opposition, famous for making the Emperor pay more dear for rallying to the cause than if he had combated it with blunted arms, according to his own story. Madame Carré-Lamadon, much younger than her husband, was the consolation of officers of good family sent to Rouen in garrison. She sat opposite her husband, very dainty, petite, and pretty, wrapped closely in furs, and looking with sad eyes at the interior of the carriage.

Her neighbors, the Count and Countess Hubert de Breville, bore the name of one of the most ancient and noble families of Normandy. The Count, an old gentleman of good figure, accentuated, by the artifices of his toilette, his resemblance to King Henry IV, who, following a glorious legend of the family, had impregnated one of the De Breville ladies, whose husband, for this reason, was made a count and governor of the province.

A colleague of Mr. Carré-Lamadon in the General Council, Count Hubert represented the Orléans party in the Department.

The story of his marriage with the daughter of a little captain of a privateer had always remained a mystery. But as the Countess had a grand air, received better than anyone, and passed for having been loved by the son of Louis-Philippe, all the nobility did her honor, and her salon remained the first in the country, the only one which preserved the old gallantry, and to which the *entrée* was difficult. The fortune of the Brevilles amounted, it was said, to five hundred thousand francs in income, all in good securities.

These six persons formed the foundation of the carriage company, the society side, serene and strong, honest, established people, who had both religion and principles.

By a strange chance, all the women were upon the same seat; and the Countess had for neighbors two sisters who picked at long strings of beads and muttered some *Paters* and *Aves*. One was old and as pitted with smallpox as if she had received a broadside of grapeshot full in the face. The other, very sad, had a pretty face and a disease of the lungs, which, added to their devoted faith, illumined them and made them appear like martyrs.

Opposite these two devotees were a man and a woman who attracted the notice of all. The man, well known, was Cornudet the democrat, the terror of respectable people.

For twenty years he had soaked his great red beard in the *bocks* [glasses of beer] of all the democratic *cafés*. He had consumed with his friends and *confrères* [colleagues] a rather pretty fortune left him by his father, an old confectioner, and he awaited the establishing of the Republic with impatience, that he might have the position he merited by his great expenditures. On the fourth of September, by some joke perhaps, he believed himself elected prefect, but when he went to assume the duties, the clerks of the office were masters of the place and refused to recognize him, obliging him to retreat. Rather a good bachelor, on the whole, inoffensive and serviceable, he had busied himself with incomparable ardor in organizing the defense against the Prussians. He had dug holes in all the plains, cut down young trees from the neighboring forests, sown snares over all routes and, at the approach of the enemy, took himself quickly back to the town. He now thought he could be of more use in Havre where more entrenchments would be necessary.

The woman, one of those called a coquette, was celebrated for her *embonpoint* [plumpness], which had given her the nickname of "Ball-of-Fat." Small, round, and fat as lard, with puffy fingers choked at the phalanges, like chaplets of short sausages; with a stretched and shining skin, an enormous bosom which shook under her dress, she was, nevertheless, pleasing and sought after, on account of a certain freshness and breeziness of disposition. Her face was a round apple, a peony bud ready to pop into bloom, and inside that opened two great black eyes, shaded with thick brows that cast a shadow within; and below, a charming mouth, humid for kissing, furnished with shining, microscopic baby teeth. She was, it was said, full of admirable qualities.

As soon as she was recognized, a whisper went around among the honest women, and the words "prostitute" and "public shame" were whispered so loud that she raised her head. Then she threw at her neighbors such a provoking, courageous look that a great silence reigned, and everybody looked down except Loiseau, who watched her with an exhilarated air.

And immediately conversation began among the three ladies, whom the presence of this girl had suddenly rendered friendly, almost intimate. It seemed to them they should bring their married dignity into union in opposition to that sold without shame; for legal love always takes on a tone of contempt for its free *confrère*.

The three men, also drawn together by an instinct of preservation at the sight of Cornudet, talked money with a certain high tone of disdain for the poor. Count Hubert talked of the havoc which the Prussians had caused, the losses which resulted from being robbed of cattle and from destroyed crops, with the assurance of a great lord, ten times millionaire, whom these ravages would scarcely cramp for a year. Mr. Carré-Lamadon, largely experienced in the cotton industry, had had need of sending six hundred thousand francs to England, as a trifle in reserve if it should be needed. As for Loiseau, he had arranged with the French administration to sell them all the wines that remained in his cellars, on account of which the State owed him a formidable sum, which he counted on collecting at Havre.

And all three threw toward each other swift and amicable glances.

Although in different conditions, they felt themselves to be brothers through money, that grand freemasonry of those who possess it and make the gold rattle by putting their hands in their trousers' pockets.

The carriage went so slowly that at ten o'clock in the morning they had not gone four leagues. The men had got down three times to climb hills on foot. They began to be disturbed because they should be now taking breakfast at Tôtes, and they despaired now of reaching there before night. Each one had begun to watch for an inn along the route, when the carriage foundered in a snowdrift and it took two hours to extricate it.

Growing appetites troubled their minds, and no eating-house, no wineshop showed itself, the approach of the Prussians and the passage of the troops having frightened away all these industries.

The gentlemen ran to the farms along the way for provisions, but they did not even find bread, for the defiant peasant had concealed his stores for fear of being pillaged by the soldiers who, having nothing to put between their teeth, took by force whatever they discovered.

Toward one o'clock in the afternoon, Loiseau announced that there was a decided hollow in his stomach. Everybody suffered with him, and the violent need of eating, ever increasing, had killed conversation.

From time to time someone yawned; another immediately imitated him; and each, in his turn, in accordance with his character, his knowledge of life, and his social position, opened his mouth with carelessness or modesty, placing his hand quickly before the yawning hole from whence issued a vapor.

Ball-of-Fat, after many attempts, bent down as if seeking something under her skirts. She hesitated a second, looked at her neighbors, then sat up again tranquilly. The faces were pale and drawn. Loiseau affirmed that he would give a thousand francs for a small ham. His wife made a gesture, as if in protest; but she kept quiet. She was always troubled when anyone spoke of squandering money and could not comprehend any pleasantry on the subject. "The fact is," said the Count, "I cannot understand why I did not think to bring some provisions with me." Each reproached himself in the same way.

However, Cornudet had a flask full of rum. He offered it; it was refused coldly. Loiseau alone accepted two swallows, and then passed back the flask saying, by way of thanks: "It is good all the same; it is warming and checks the appetite." The alcohol put him in good humor and he proposed that they do as they did on the little ship in the song, eat the fattest of the passengers. This indirect allusion to Ball-of-Fat choked the well-bred people. They said nothing. Cornudet alone laughed. The two good sisters had ceased to mumble their rosaries and, with their hands enfolded in their great sleeves, held themselves immovable, obstinately lowering their eyes, without doubt offering to Heaven the suffering it had brought upon them.

Finally at three o'clock, when they found themselves in the midst of an interminable plain, without a single village in sight, Ball-of-Fat bending down quickly drew from under the seat a large basket covered with a white napkin.

At first she brought out a little china plate and a silver cup; then a large dish in which there were two whole chickens, cut up and imbedded in their own jelly. And one could still see in the basket other good things, some *pâtés*, fruits, and sweetmeats, provisions for three days if they should not see the kitchen of an inn. Four necks of bottles were seen among the packages of food. She took a wing of a chicken and began to eat it delicately, with one of those little biscuits called "Regence" in Normandy.

All looks were turned in her direction. Then the odor spread, enlarging the nostrils and making the mouth water, besides causing a painful contraction of the jaw behind the ears. The scorn of the women for this girl became ferocious, as if they had a desire to kill her and throw her out of the carriage into the snow, her, her silver cup, her basket, provisions and all.

But Loiseau with his eyes devoured the dish of chicken. He said: "Fortunately Madame had more precaution than we. There are some people who know how to think ahead always."

She turned toward him, saying: "If you would like some of it, sir? It is hard to go without breakfast so long."

He saluted her and replied: "Faith, I frankly cannot refuse; I can stand it no longer. Everything goes in time of war, does it not, Madame?" And then casting a comprehensive glance around, he added: "In moments like this, one can but be pleased to find people who are obliging."

He had a newspaper which he spread out on his knees, that no spot might come to his pantaloons, and upon the point of a knife that he always carried in his pocket, he took up a leg all glistening with jelly, put it between his teeth and masticated it with a satisfaction so evident that there ran through the carriage a great sigh of distress.

Then Ball-of-Fat, in a sweet and humble voice, proposed that the two sisters partake of her collation. They both accepted instantly and, without raising their eyes, began to eat very quickly, after stammering their thanks. Cornudet no longer refused the offers of his neighbor, and they formed with the sisters a sort of table, by spreading out some newspapers upon their knees.

The mouths opened and shut without ceasing, they masticated, swallowed, gulping ferociously. Loiseau in his corner was working hard and, in a low voice, was trying to induce his wife to follow his example. She resisted for a long time; then, when a drawn sensation ran through her body, she yielded. Her husband, rounding his phrase, asked their "charming companion" if he might be allowed to offer a little piece to Madame Loiseau.

She replied: "Why, yes, certainly, sir," with an amiable smile, as she passed the dish.

An embarrassing thing confronted them when they opened the first bottle of Bordeaux: they had but one cup. Each passed it after having tasted. Cornudet alone, for politeness without doubt, placed his lips at the spot left humid by his fair neighbor.

Then, surrounded by people eating, suffocated by the odors of the food, the Count and Countess de Breville, as well as Madame and Mr. Carré-Lamadon, were suffering that odious torment which has

reserved the name of Tantalus. Suddenly the young wife of the manufacturer gave forth such a sigh that all heads were turned in her direction; she was as white as the snow without; her eyes closed, her head drooped; she had lost consciousness. Her husband, much excited, implored the help of everybody. Each lost his head completely, until the elder of the two sisters, holding the head of the sufferer, slipped Ball-of-Fat's cup between her lips and forced her to swallow a few drops of wine. The pretty little lady revived, opened her eyes, smiled, and declared in a dying voice that she felt very well now. But, in order that the attack might not return, the sister urged her to drink a full glass of Bordeaux, and added: "It is just hunger, nothing more."

Then Ball-of-Fat, blushing and embarrassed, looked at the four travelers who had fasted and stammered: "Goodness knows! If I dared to offer anything to these gentlemen and ladies, I would—" Then she was silent, as if fearing an insult. Loiseau took up the word: "Ah! certainly, in times like these all the world are brothers and ought to aid each other. Come, ladies, without ceremony; why the devil not accept? We do not know whether we shall even find a house where we can pass the night. At the pace we are going now, we shall not reach Tôtes before noon tomorrow—"

They still hesitated, no one daring to assume the responsibility of a "Yes." The Count decided the question. He turned toward the fat, intimidated girl and, taking on a grand air of condescension, he said to her:

"We accept with gratitude, Madame."

It is the first step that counts. The Rubicon passed, one lends himself to the occasion squarely. The basket was stripped. It still contained a *pâté de foie gras, a pâté of larks,* a piece of smoked tongue, some preserved pears, a loaf of hard bread, some wafers, and a full cup of pickled gherkins and onions, of which crudities Ball-of-Fat, like all women, was extremely fond.

They could not eat this girl's provisions without speaking to her. And so they chatted, with reserve at first; then, as she carried herself well, with more abandon. The ladies De Breville and Carré-Lamadon, who were acquainted with all the ins and outs of good breeding, were gracious with a certain delicacy. The Countess, especially, showed that amiable condescension of very noble ladies who do not fear being spoiled by contact with anyone and was charming. But the great Madame Loiseau, who had the soul of a plebeian, remained crabbed, saying little and eating much.

The conversation was about the war, naturally. They related the horrible deeds of the Prussians, the brave acts of the French; and all of them, although running away, did homage to those who stayed behind. Then personal stories began to be told, and Ball-of-Fat related, with sincere emotion, and in the heated words that such girls sometimes use in expressing their natural feelings, how she had left Rouen:

"I believed at first that I could remain," she said. "I had my house full of provisions, and I preferred to feed a few soldiers rather than expatriate myself, to go I knew not where. But as soon as I saw them, those Prussians, that was too much for me! They made my blood boil with anger, and I wept for very shame all day long. Oh! if I were only a man! I watched them from my windows, the great porkers with their pointed helmets, and my maid held my hands to keep me from throwing the furniture down upon them. Then one of them came to lodge at my house; I sprang at his throat the first thing; they are no more difficult to strangle than other people. And I should have put an end to that one then and there had they not pulled me away by the hair. After that, it was necessary to keep out of sight. And finally, when I found an opportunity, I left town and—here I am!"

They congratulated her. She grew in the estimation of her companions, who had not shown themselves so hot-brained, and Cornudet, while listening to her, took on the approving, benevolent smile of an apostle, as a priest would if he heard a devotee praise God, for the long-bearded democrats have a monopoly of patriotism, as the men in cassocks have of religion. In his turn he spoke, in a doctrinal tone, with the emphasis of a proclamation such as we see pasted on the walls about town, and finished by a bit of eloquence whereby he gave that "scamp of a Badinguet" a good lashing.

Then Ball-of-Fat was angry, for she was a Bonapartist. She grew redder than a cherry and, stammering with indignation, said:

"I would like to have seen you in his place, you other people. Then everything would have been quite right; oh, yes! It is you who have betrayed this man! One would never have had to leave France if it had been governed by blackguards like you!"

Cornudet, undisturbed, preserved a disdainful, superior smile, but all felt that the high note had been struck, until the Count, not without some difficulty, calmed the exasperated girl and proclaimed with a manner of authority that all sincere opinions should be respected. But the Countess and the manufacturer's wife, who had in their souls an unreasonable hatred for the people that favor a Republic, and the same instinctive tenderness that all women have for a decorative, despotic government, felt themselves drawn, in spite of themselves, toward this prostitute so full of dignity, whose sentiments so strongly resembled their own.

The basket was empty. By ten o'clock they had easily exhausted the contents and regretted that there was not more. Conversation continued for some time, but a little more coldly since they had finished eating.

The night fell, the darkness little by little became profound, and the cold, felt more during digestion, made Ball-of-Fat shiver in spite of her plumpness. Then Madame de Breville offered her the little foot stove, in which the fuel had been renewed many times since morning; she accepted it immediately, for her feet were becoming numb with cold. The ladies Carré-Lamadon and Loiseau gave theirs to the two religious sisters.

The driver had lighted his lanterns. They shone out with a lively glimmer showing a cloud of foam beyond the sweat of the horses; and, on both sides of the way, the snow seemed to roll itself along under the moving reflection of the lights.

Inside the carriage one could distinguish nothing. But a sudden movement seemed to be made between Ball-of-Fat and Cornudet; and Loiseau, whose eye penetrated the shadow, believed that he saw the big-bearded man start back quickly as if he had received a swift, noiseless blow.

Then some twinkling points of fire appeared in the distance along the road. It was Tôtes. They had traveled eleven hours, which, with the two hours given to resting and feeding the horses, made thirteen. They entered the town and stopped before the Hotel of Commerce.

The carriage door opened! A well-known sound gave the travelers a start; it was the scabbard of a sword hitting the ground. Immediately a German voice was heard in the darkness.

Although the diligence was not moving no one offered to alight, fearing someone might be waiting to murder them as they stepped out. Then the conductor appeared, holding in his hand one of the lanterns, which lighted the carriage to its depth and showed the two rows of frightened faces whose mouths were open and whose eyes were wide with surprise and fear.

Outside beside the driver, in plain sight stood a German officer, an excessively tall young man, thin and blond, squeezed into his uniform like a girl in a corset, and wearing on his head a flat, oilcloth cap which made him resemble the porter of an English hotel. His enormous mustache, of long straight hairs, growing gradually thin at each side and terminating in a single blond thread so fine that one could not perceive where it ended, seemed to weigh heavily on the corners of his mouth and, drawing down the cheeks, left a decided wrinkle about the lips.

In Alsatian French, he invited the travelers to come in, saying in a suave tone: "Will you descend, gentlemen and ladies?"

The two good sisters were the first to obey, with the docility of saints accustomed ever to submission. The Count and Countess then appeared, followed by the manufacturer and his wife; then Loiseau, pushing ahead of him his larger half. The last-named, as he set foot on the earth, said to the officer: "Good evening, sir," more as a measure of prudence than politeness. The officer, insolent as all powerful people usually are, looked at him without a word.

Ball-of-Fat and Cornudet, although nearest the door, were the last to descend, grave and haughty before the enemy. The fat girl tried to control herself and be calm. The democrat waved a tragic hand and his long beard seemed to tremble a little and grow redder. They wished to preserve their dignity, comprehending that in such meetings as these they represented in some degree their great country; moreover, somewhat disgusted with the docility of her companions, the fat girl tried to show more pride than her neighbors, the honest women, and as she felt that someone should set an example, she continued her attitude of resistance assumed at the beginning of the journey.

They entered the vast kitchen of the inn, and the German, having demanded their traveling papers signed by the General-in-chief (in which the name, the description, and profession of each traveler was mentioned), and having examined them all critically, comparing the people and their signatures, said: "It is quite right," and went out.

Then they breathed. They were still hungry and supper was ordered. A half hour was necessary to prepare it, and while two servants were attending to this they went to their rooms. They found them along a corridor which terminated in a large glazed door.

Finally, they sat down at table, when the proprietor of the inn himself appeared. He was a former horse merchant, a large, asthmatic man, with a constant wheezing and rattling in his throat. His father had left him the name of Follenvie. He asked:

"Is Miss Elizabeth Rousset here?"

Ball-of-Fat started as she answered: "It is I."

"The Prussian officer wishes to speak with you immediately."

"With me?"

"Yes, that is, if you are Miss Elizabeth Rousset."

She was disturbed, and reflecting for an instant, declared flatly:

"That is my name, but I shall not go."

A stir was felt around her; each discussed and tried to think of the cause of this order. The Count approached her, saying:

"You are wrong, Madame, for your refusal may lead to considerable difficulty, not only for yourself, but for all your companions. It is never worthwhile to resist those in power. This request cannot assuredly bring any danger; it is, without doubt, about some forgotten formality."

Everybody agreed with him, asking, begging, beseeching her to go, and at last they convinced her that it was best; they all feared the complications that might result from disobedience. She finally said:

"It is for you that I do this, you understand."

The Countess took her by the hand, saying: "And we are grateful to you for it."

She went out. They waited before sitting down at table.

Each one regretted not having been sent for in the place of this violent, irascible girl, and mentally prepared some platitudes, in case they should be called in their turn.

But at the end of ten minutes she reappeared, out of breath, red to suffocation, and exasperated. She stammered: "Oh! the rascal; the rascal!"

All gathered around to learn something, but she said nothing; and when the Count insisted, she responded with great dignity: "No, it does not concern you; I can say nothing."

Then they all seated themselves around a high soup tureen, whence came the odor of cabbage. In spite of alarm, the supper was gay. The cider was good, the beverage Loiseau and the good sisters took as a means of economy. The others called for wine; Cornudet demanded beer. He had a special fashion of uncorking the bottle, making froth on the liquid, carefully filling the glass and then holding it before the light to better appreciate the color. When he drank, his great beard, which still kept some of the foam of his beloved beverage, seemed to tremble with tenderness; his eyes were squinted, in order not to lose sight of his tipple, and he had the unique air of fulfilling the function for which he was born. One would say that there was in his mind a meeting, like that of affinities, between the two great passions that occupied his life—Pale Ale and Revolutions; and assuredly he could not taste the one without thinking of the other.

Mr. and Mrs. Follenvie dined at the end of the table. The man, rattling like a cracked locomotive, had too much trouble in breathing to talk while eating, but his wife was never silent. She told all her impressions at the arrival of the Prussians, what they did, what they said, reviling them because they cost her some money, and because she had two sons in the army. She addressed herself especially to the Countess, flattered by being able to talk with a lady of quality.

When she lowered her voice to say some delicate thing, her husband would interrupt, from time to time, with: "You had better keep silent, Madame Follenvie." But she paid no attention, continuing in this fashion:

"Yes, Madame, those people there not only eat our potatoes and pork, but our pork and potatoes. And it must not be believed that they are at all proper—oh, no! such filthy things they do, saving the respect I owe to you! And if you could see them exercise for hours in the day! They are all there in the field, marching ahead, then marching back, turning here and turning there. They might be cultivating the land, or at least working on the roads of their own country! But no, Madame, these military men are profitable to no one. Poor people have to feed them, or perhaps be murdered! I am only an old woman without education, it is true, but when I see some endangering their constitutions by raging from morning to night, I say: 'When there are so many people found to be useless, how unnecessary it is for others to take so much trouble to be nuisances!' Truly, is it not an abomination to kill people, whether they be Prussian, or English, or Polish, or French? If one man revenges himself upon another who has done him some injury, it is wicked and he is punished; but when they exterminate our boys, as if they were game, with guns, they give decorations to the one who destroys the most! Now, you see, I can never understand that, never!"

Cornudet raised his voice: "War is a barbarity when one attacks a peaceable neighbor, but a sacred duty when one defends his country."

The old woman lowered her head:

"Yes, when one defends himself, it is another thing; but why not make it a duty to kill all the kings who make these wars for their pleasure?"

Cornudet's eyes flashed. "Bravo, my countrywoman!" said he.

Mr. Carré-Lamadon reflected profoundly. Although he was prejudiced as a Captain of Industry, the good sense of this peasant woman made him think of the opulence that would be brought into the country were the idle and consequently mischievous hands, and the troops which were now maintained in unproductiveness, employed in some great industrial work that it would require centuries to achieve.

Loiseau, leaving his place, went to speak with the innkeeper in a low tone of voice. The great man laughed, shook, and squeaked, his corpulence quivered with joy at the jokes of his neighbor, and he bought of him six cases of wine for spring, after the Prussians had gone.

As soon as supper was finished, as they were worn out with fatigue, they retired.

However, Loiseau, who had observed things, after getting his wife to bed, glued his eye and then his ear to a hole in the wall, to try and discover what are known as "the mysteries of the corridor."

At the end of about an hour, he heard a groping, and, looking quickly, he perceived Ball-of-Fat, who appeared still more plump in a blue cashmere negligee trimmed with white lace. She had a candle in her hand and was directing her steps toward the great door at the end of the corridor. But a door at the side opened, and when she returned at the end of some minutes Cornudet, in his suspenders, followed her. They spoke low, then they stopped. Ball-of-Fat seemed to be defending the entrance to her room with energy. Loiseau, unfortunately, could not hear all their words, but finally, as they raised their voices, he was able to catch a few. Cornudet insisted with vivacity. He said:

"Come, now, you are a silly woman; what harm can be done?"

She had an indignant air in responding: "No, my dear, there are moments when such things are out of place. Here it would be a shame."

He doubtless did not comprehend and asked why. Then she cried out, raising her voice still more:

"Why? you do not see why? When there are Prussians in the house, in the very next room, perhaps?"

He was silent. This patriotic shame of the harlot, who would not suffer his caress so near the enemy, must have awakened the latent dignity in his heart, for after simply kissing her, he went back to his own door with a bound.

Loiseau, much excited, left the aperture, cut a caper in his room, put on his pajamas, turned back the clothes that covered the bony carcass of his companion, whom he awakened with a kiss, murmuring: "Do you love me, dearie?"

Then all the house was still. And immediately there arose somewhere, from an uncertain quarter, which might be the cellar but was quite as likely to be the garret, a powerful snoring, monotonous and regular, a heavy, prolonged sound, like a great kettle under pressure. Mr. Follenvie was asleep.

As they had decided that they would set out at eight o'clock the next morning, they all collected in the kitchen. But the carriage, the roof of which was covered with snow, stood undisturbed in the courtyard, without horses and without a conductor. They sought him in vain in the stables, in the hay, and in the coach house. Then they resolved to scour the town and started out. They found themselves in a square, with a church at one end and some low houses on either side, where they perceived some Prussian soldiers. The first one they saw was paring potatoes. The second, further off, was cleaning the hairdresser's shop. Another, bearded to the eyes, was tending a troublesome brat, cradling it and trying to appease it; and the great peasant women, whose husbands were "away in the army," indicated by signs to their obedient conquerors the work they wished to have done: cutting wood, cooking the soup, grinding the coffee, or what not. One of them even washed the linen of his hostess, an impotent old grandmother.

The Count, astonished, asked questions of the beadle who came out of the rectory. The old man responded:

"Oh! those men are not wicked; they are not the Prussians we hear about. They are from far off, I know not where; and they have left wives and children in their country; it is not amusing to them, this war, I can tell you! I am sure they also weep for their homes, and that it makes as much sorrow among them as it does among us. Here, now, there is not so much unhappiness for the moment, because the soldiers do no harm and they work as if they were in their own homes. You see, sir, among poor people it is necessary that they aid one another. These are the great traits which war develops."

Cornudet, indignant at the cordial relations between the conquerors and the conquered, preferred to shut himself up in the inn. Loiseau had a joke for the occasion: "They will repeople the land."

Mr. Carré-Lamadon had a serious word: "They try to make amends."

But they did not find the driver. Finally, they discovered him in a *café* of the village, sitting at table fraternally with the officer of ordinance. The Count called out to him:

"Were you not ordered to be ready at eight o'clock?"

"Well, yes; but another order has been given me since."

"By whom?"

"Faith! the Prussian commander."

"What was it?"

"Not to harness at all."

"Why?"

"I know nothing about it. Go and ask him. They tell me not to harness, and I don't harness. That's all."

"Did he give you the order himself?"

"No, sir, the innkeeper gave the order for him."

"When was that?"

"Last evening, as I was going to bed."

The three men returned, much disturbed. They asked for Mr. Follenvie, but the servant answered that that gentleman, because of his asthma, never rose before ten o'clock. And he had given strict orders not to be wakened before that, except in case of fire.

They wished to see the officer, but that was absolutely impossible, since, while he lodged at the inn, Mr. Follenvie alone was authorized to speak to him upon civil affairs. So they waited. The women went up to their rooms again and occupied themselves with futile tasks.

Cornudet installed himself near the great chimney in the kitchen, where there was a good fire burning. He ordered one of the little tables to be brought from the *café*, then a can of beer, he then drew out his pipe, which plays among democrats a part almost equal to his own, because in serving Cornudet it was serving its country. It was a superb pipe, an admirably colored meerschaum, as black as the teeth of its master, but perfumed, curved, glistening, easy to the hand, completing his physiognomy. And he remained motionless, his eyes as much fixed upon the flame of the fire as upon his favorite tipple and its frothy crown; and each time that he drank, he passed his long, thin fingers through his scanty, gray hair, with an air of satisfaction, after which he sucked in his mustache fringed with foam.

Loiseau, under the pretext of stretching his legs, went to place some wine among the retailers of the country. The Count and the manufacturer began to talk politics. They could foresee the future of France. One of them believed in an Orléans, the other in some unknown savior for the country, a hero who would reveal himself when all were in despair: a Guesclin, or a Joan of Arc, perhaps, or would it be another Napoleon First? Ah! if the Prince Imperial were not so young!

Cornudet listened to them and smiled like one who holds the word of destiny. His pipe perfumed the kitchen.

As ten o'clock struck, Mr. Follenvie appeared. They asked him hurried questions; but he could only repeat two or three times without variation, these words:

"The officer said to me: 'Mr. Follenvie, you see to it that the carriage is not harnessed for those travelers tomorrow. I do not wish them to leave without my order. That is sufficient.' "

Then they wished to see the officer. The Count sent him his card, on which Mr. Carré-Lamadon wrote his name and all his titles. The Prussian sent back word that he would meet the two gentlemen after he had breakfasted, that is to say, about one o'clock.

The ladies reappeared and ate a little something, despite their disquiet. Ball-of-Fat seemed ill and prodigiously troubled.

They were finishing their coffee when the word came that the officer was ready to meet the gentlemen. Loiseau joined them; but when they tried to enlist Cornudet, to give more solemnity to their proceedings, he declared proudly that he would have nothing to do with the Germans; and he betook himself to his chimney corner and ordered another liter of beer.

The three men mounted the staircase and were introduced to the best room of the inn, where the officer received them, stretched out in an armchair, his feet on the mantelpiece, smoking a long, porcelain pipe, and enveloped in a flamboyant dressing gown, appropriated, without doubt, from some dwelling belonging to a common citizen of bad taste. He did not rise, nor greet them in any way, not even looking at them. It was a magnificent display of natural blackguardism transformed into the military victor.

At the expiration of some moments, he asked: "What is it you wish?"

The Count became spokesman: "We desire to go on our way, sir."

"No."

"May I ask the cause of this refusal?"

"Because I do not wish it."

"But, I would respectfully observe to you, sir, that your General-in-chief gave us permission to go to Dieppe; and I know of nothing we have done to merit your severity."

"I do not wish it—that is all; you can go."

All three, having bowed, retired.

The afternoon was lamentable. They could not understand this caprice of the German; and the most singular ideas would come into their heads to trouble them. Everybody stayed in the kitchen and discussed the situation endlessly, imagining all sorts of unlikely things. Perhaps they would be retained as hostages—but to what end?—or taken prisoners—or rather a considerable ransom might be demanded. At this thought a panic prevailed. The richest were the most frightened, already seeing themselves constrained to pay for their lives with sacks of gold poured into the hands of this insolent soldier. They racked their brains to think of some acceptable falsehoods to conceal their riches and make them pass themselves off for poor people, very poor people. Loiseau took off the chain to his watch and hid it away in his pocket. The falling night increased their apprehensions. The lamp was lighted, and as there was still two hours before dinner, Madame Loiseau proposed a game of Thirty-one. It would be a diversion. They accepted. Cornudet himself, having smoked out his pipe, took part for politeness.

The Count shuffled the cards, dealt, and Ball-of-Fat had thirty-one at the outset; immediately the interest was great enough to appease the fear that haunted their minds. Then Cornudet perceived that the house of Loiseau was given to tricks.

As they were going to the dinner table, Mr. Follenvie again appeared, and, in wheezing, rattling voice, announced:

"The Prussian officer orders me to ask Miss Elizabeth Rousset if she has yet changed her mind."

Ball-of-Fat remained standing and was pale; then suddenly becoming crimson, such a stifling anger took possession of her that she could not speak. But finally she flashed out: "You may say to the dirty beast, that idiot, that carrion of a Prussian, that I shall never change it; you understand, never, never, never!"

The great innkeeper went out. Then Ball-of-Fat was immediately surrounded, questioned, and solicited by all to disclose the mystery of his visit. She resisted, at first, but soon becoming exasperated, she said: "What does he want? You really want to know what he wants? He wants to sleep with me."

Everybody was choked for words, and indignation was rife. Cornudet broke his glass, so violently did he bring his fist down upon the table. There was a clamor of censure against this ignoble soldier, a blast of anger, a union of all for resistance, as if a demand had been made on each one of the party for the sacrifice exacted of her. The Count declared with disgust that those people conducted themselves after the fashion of the ancient barbarians. The women, especially, showed to Ball-of-Fat a most energetic and tender commiseration. The good sisters, who only showed themselves at mealtime, lowered their heads and said nothing.

They all dined, nevertheless, when the first *furore* had abated. But there was little conversation; they were thinking.

The ladies retired early, and the men, all smoking, organized a game at cards to which Mr. Follenvie was invited, as they intended to put a few casual questions to him on the subject of conquering the resistance of this officer. But he thought of nothing but the cards and, without listening or answering, would keep repeating: "To the game, sirs, to the game." His attention was so taken that he even forgot to expectorate, which must have put him some points to the good with the organ in his breast. His whistling lungs ran the whole asthmatic scale, from deep, profound tones to the sharp rustiness of a young cock essaying to crow.

He even refused to retire when his wife, who had fallen asleep previously, came to look for him. She went away alone, for she was an "early bird," always up with the sun, while her husband was a "night owl," always ready to pass the night with his friends. He cried out to her: "Leave my creamed chicken before the fire!" and then went on with his game. When they saw that they could get nothing from him, they declared that it was time to stop, and each sought his bed.

They all rose rather early the next day, with an undefined hope of getting away, which desire the terror of passing another day in that horrible inn greatly increased.

Alas! the horses remained in the stable and the driver was invisible. For want of better employment, they went out and walked around the carriage.

The breakfast was very doleful; it became apparent that a coldness had arisen toward Ball-of-Fat, and that the night, which brings counsel, had slightly modified their judgments. They almost wished now that the Prussian had secretly found this girl, in order to give her companions a pleasant surprise in the morning. What could be more simple? Besides, who would know anything about it? She could save appearances by telling the officer that she took pity on their distress. To her, it would make so little difference!

No one had avowed these thoughts yet.

In the afternoon, as they were almost perishing from *ennui*, the Count proposed that they take a walk around the village. Each wrapped up warmly and the little party set out, with the exception of Cornudet, who preferred to remain near the fire, and the good sisters, who passed their time in the church or at the curate's.

The cold, growing more intense every day, cruelly pinched their noses and ears; their feet became so numb that each step was torture; and when they came to a field it seemed to them frightfully sad under this limitless white, so that everybody returned immediately, with hearts hard pressed and souls congealed.

The four women walked ahead, the three gentlemen followed just behind. Loiseau, who understood the situation, asked suddenly if they thought that girl there was going to keep them long in such a place as this. The Count, always courteous, said that they could not exact from a woman a sacrifice so hard, unless it should come of her own will. Mr. Carré-Lamadon remarked that if the French made their return through Dieppe, as they were likely to, a battle would surely take place at

Tôtes. This reflection made the two others anxious.

"If we could only get away on foot," said Loiseau.

The Count shrugged his shoulders: "How can we think of it in this snow? and with our wives?" he said. "And then, we should be pursued and caught in ten minutes and led back prisoners at the mercy of these soldiers."

It was true, and they were silent.

The ladies talked of their clothes, but a certain constraint seemed to disunite them. Suddenly at the end of the street, the officer appeared. His tall, wasp-like figure in uniform was outlined upon the horizon formed by the snow, and he was marching with knees apart, a gait particularly military, which is affected that they may not spot their carefully blackened boots.

He bowed in passing near the ladies and looked disdainfully at the men, who preserved their dignity by not seeing him, except Loiseau, who made a motion toward raising his hat.

Ball-of-Fat reddened to the ears, and the three married women resented the great humiliation of being thus met by this soldier in the company of this girl whom he had treated so cavalierly.

But they spoke of him, of his figure and his face. Madame Carré-Lamadon, who had known many officers and considered herself a connoisseur of them, found this one not at all bad; she regretted even that he was not French, because he would make such a pretty hussar, one all the women would rave over.

Again in the house, no one knew what to do. Some sharp words, even, were said about things very insignificant. The dinner was silent, and almost immediately after it, each one went to his room to kill time in sleep.

They descended the next morning with weary faces and exasperated hearts. The women scarcely spoke to Ball-of-Fat.

A bell began to ring. It was for a baptism. The fat girl had a child being brought up among the peasants of Yvetot. She had not seen it for a year, or thought of it; but now the idea of a child being baptized threw into her heart a sudden and violent tenderness for her own, and she strongly wished to be present at the ceremony.

As soon as she was gone, everybody looked at each other, then pulled their chairs together, for they thought that finally something should be decided upon. Loiseau had an inspiration: it was to hold Ball-of-Fat alone and let the others go.

Mr. Follenvie was charged with the commission, but he returned almost immediately, for the German, who understood human nature, had put him out. He pretended that he would retain everybody so long as his desire was not satisfied.

Then the commonplace nature of Mrs. Loiseau burst out with:

"Well, we are not going to stay here to die of old age. Since it is the trade of this creature to accommodate herself to all kinds, I fail to see how she has the right to refuse one more than another. I can tell you she has received all she could find in Rouen, even the coachmen! Yes, Madame, the prefect's coachman! I know him very well, for he bought his wine at our house. And to think that today we should be drawn into this embarrassment by this affected woman, this minx! For my part, I find that this officer conducts himself very well. He has perhaps suffered privations for a long time; and doubtless he would have preferred us three; but no, he is contented with common property. He respects married women. And we must remember too that he is master. He has only to say 'I wish,' and he could take us by force with his soldiers."

The two women had a cold shiver. Pretty Mrs. Carré-Lamadon's eyes grew brilliant and she became a little pale, as if she saw herself already taken by force by the officer.

The men met and discussed the situation. Loiseau, furious, was for delivering "the wretch" bound hand and foot to the enemy. But the Count, descended through three generations of ambassadors, and endowed with the temperament of a diplomatist, was the advocate of ingenuity.

"It is best to decide upon something," said he. Then they conspired.

The women kept together, the tone of their voices was lowered, each gave advice and the discussion was general. Everything was very harmonious. The ladies especially found delicate shades and charming subtleties of expression for saying the most unusual things. A stranger would have understood nothing, so great was the precaution of language observed. But the light edge of modesty, with which every woman of the world is barbed, only covers the surface; they blossom out in a scandalous adventure of this kind, being deeply amused and feeling themselves in their element, mixing love with sensuality as a greedy cook prepares supper for his master.

Even gaiety returned, so funny did the whole story seem to them at last. The Count found some of the jokes a little off-color, but they were so well told that he was forced to smile. In his turn, Loiseau came out with some still bolder tales, and yet nobody was wounded. The brutal thought, expressed by his wife, dominated all minds: "Since it is her trade, why should she refuse this one more than another?" The genteel Mrs. Carré-Lamadon seemed to think that in her place, she would refuse this one less than some others.

They prepared the blockade at length, as if they were about to surround a fortress. Each took some rôle to play, some arguments he would bring to bear, some maneuvers that he would endeavor to put into execution. They decided on the plan of attack, the ruse to employ, the surprise of assault, that should force this living citadel to receive the enemy in her room.

Cornudet remained apart from the rest and was a stranger to the whole affair.

So entirely were their minds distracted that they did not hear Ball-of-Fat enter. The Count uttered a light "Ssh!" which turned all eyes in her direction. There she was. The abrupt silence and a certain embarrassment hindered them from speaking to her at first. The Countess, more accustomed to the duplicity of society than the others, finally inquired:

"Was it very amusing, that baptism?"

The fat girl, filled with emotion, told them all about it, the faces, the attitudes and even the appearance of the church. She added: "It is good to pray sometimes."

And up to the time for luncheon these ladies continued to be amiable toward her in order to increase her docility and her confidence in their counsel. At the table they commenced the approach. This was in the shape of a vague conversation upon devotion. They cited ancient examples: Judith and Holophernes, then, without reason, Lucrece and Sextus, and Cleopatra obliging all the generals of the enemy to pass by her couch and reducing them in servility to slaves. Then they brought out a fantastic story, hatched in the imagination of these ignorant millionaires, where the women of Rome went to Capua for the purpose of lulling Hannibal to sleep in their arms, and his lieutenants and phalanxes of mercenaries as well. They cited all the women who have been taken by conquering armies, making a battlefield of their bodies, making them also a weapon, and a means of success; and all those hideous and detestable beings who have conquered by their heroic caresses, and sacrificed their chastity to vengeance or a beloved cause. They even spoke in veiled terms of that great English family which allowed one of its women to be inoculated with a horrible and contagious disease in order to transmit it to Bonaparte, who was miraculously saved by a sudden illness at the hour of the fatal rendezvous.

And all this was related in an agreeable, temperate fashion, except as it was enlivened by the enthusiasm deemed proper to excite emulation.

One might finally have believed that the sole duty of woman here below was a sacrifice of her person, and a continual abandonment to soldierly caprices.

The two good sisters seemed not to hear, lost as they were in profound thought. Ball-of-Fat said nothing.

During the whole afternoon they let her reflect. But, in the place of calling her "Madame" as they had up to this time, they simply called her "Mademoiselle" without knowing exactly why, as if they had a desire to put her down a degree in their esteem, which she had taken by storm, and make her feel her shameful situation.

The moment supper was served, Mr. Follenvie appeared with his old phrase: "The Prussian officer orders me to ask if Miss Elizabeth Rousset has yet changed her mind."

Ball-of-Fat responded dryly: "No, sir."

But at dinner the coalition weakened. Loiseau made three unhappy remarks. Each one beat his wits for new examples but found nothing; when the Countess, without premeditation, perhaps feeling some vague need of rendering homage to religion, asked the elder of the good sisters to tell them some great deeds in the lives of the saints. It appeared that many of their acts would have been considered crimes in our eyes; but the Church gave absolution of them readily, since they were done for the glory of God, or for the good of all. It was a powerful argument; the Countess made the most of it.

Thus it may be by one of those tacit understandings, or the veiled complacency in which anyone who wears the ecclesiastical garb excels; it may be simply from the effect of a happy unintelligence, a helpful stupidity; but in fact the religious sister lent a formidable support to the conspiracy. They had thought her timid, but she showed herself courageous, verbose, even violent. She was not troubled by the chatter of the casuist; her doctrine seemed a bar of iron; her faith never hesitated; her conscience had no scruples. She found the sacrifice of Abraham perfectly simple, for she would immediately kill father or

mother on an order from on high. And nothing, in her opinion, could displease the Lord, if the intention was laudable. The Countess put to use the authority of her unwitting accomplice and added to it the edifying paraphrase and axiom of Jesuit morals: "The need justifies the means."

Then she asked her: "Then, my sister, do you think that God accepts intentions and pardons the deed when the motive is pure?"

"Who could doubt it, Madame? An action blamable in itself often becomes meritorious by the thought it springs from."

And they continued thus, unraveling the will of God, foreseeing his decisions, making themselves interested in things that, in truth, they would never think of noticing. All this was guarded, skillful, discreet. But each word of the saintly sister in a cap helped to break down the resistance of the unworthy courtesan. Then the conversation changed a little, the woman of the chaplet speaking of the houses of her order, of her Superior, of herself, of her dainty neighbor, the dear sister Saint-Nicephore. They had been called to the hospitals of Havre to care for the hundreds of soldiers stricken with smallpox. They depicted these miserable creatures, giving details of the malady. And while they were stopped, *en route*, by the caprice of this Prussian officer, a great number of Frenchmen might die whom perhaps they could have saved! It was a specialty with her, caring for soldiers. She had been in the Crimea, in Italy, in Austria, and in telling of her campaigns, she revealed herself as one of those religious aids to drums and trumpets who seem made to follow camps, pick up the wounded in the thick of battle, and, better than an officer, subdue with a word great bands of undisciplined recruits. A true, good sister of the rataplan, whose ravaged face, marked with innumerable scars, appeared the image of the devastation of war.

No one could speak after her, so excellent seemed the effect of her words.

As soon as the repast was ended they quickly went up to their rooms, with the purpose of not coming down the next day until late in the morning.

The luncheon was quiet. They had given the grain of seed time to germinate and bear fruit. The Countess proposed that they take a walk in the afternoon. The Count, being agreeably inclined, gave an arm to Ball-of-Fat and walked behind the others with her. He talked to her in a familiar, paternal tone, a little disdainful, after the manner of men having girls in their employ, calling her "my dear child," from the height of his social position, of his undisputed honor. He reached the vital part of the question at once:

"Then you prefer to leave us here, exposed to the violences which follow a defeat, rather than consent to a favor which you have so often given in your life?"

Ball-of-Fat answered nothing.

Then he tried to reach her through gentleness, reason, and then the sentiments. He knew how to remain "The Count," even while showing himself gallant or complimentary, or very amiable if it became necessary. He exalted the service that she would render them, and spoke of her appreciation; then suddenly became gaily familiar, and said:

"And you know, my dear, it would be something for him to boast of that he had known a pretty girl; something it is difficult to find in his country."

Ball-of-Fat did not answer but joined the rest of the party. As soon as they entered the house she went to her room and did not appear again. The disquiet was extreme. What were they to do? If she continued to resist, what an embarrassment!

The dinner hour struck. They waited in vain. Mr. Follenvie finally entered and said that Miss Rousset was indisposed, and would not be at the table. Everybody pricked up his ears. The Count went to the innkeeper and said in a low voice:

"Is he in there?"

"Yes."

For convenience, he said nothing to his companions but made a slight sign with his head. Immediately a great sigh of relief went up from every breast and a light appeared in their faces. Loiseau cried out:

"Holy Christopher! I pay for the champagne, if there is any to be found in the establishment." And Mrs. Loiseau was pained to see the proprietor return with four quart bottles in his hands.

Each one had suddenly become communicative and buoyant. A wanton joy filled their hearts. The Count suddenly perceived that Mrs. Carré-Lamadon was charming, the manufacturer paid compliments to the Countess. The conversation was lively, gay, full of touches.

Suddenly Loiseau, with anxious face and hand upraised, called out: "Silence!" Everybody was silent, surprised, already frightened. Then he listened intently and said: "S-s-sh!" his two eyes and his hand raised toward the ceiling, listening, and then continuing, in his natural voice: "All right! All goes well!"

They failed to comprehend at first, but soon all laughed. At the end of a quarter of an hour he began the same farce again, renewing it occasionally during the whole afternoon. And he pretended to call to someone in the story above, giving him advice in a double meaning, drawn from the fountainhead—the mind of a commercial traveler. For some moments he would assume a sad air, breathing in a whisper "Poor girl!" then he would murmur between his teeth, with an appearance of rage: "Ugh! That scamp of a Prussian." Sometimes, at a moment when no more was thought about it, he would say, in an affected voice, many times over: "Enough, enough!" and add, as if speaking to himself, "If we could only see her again, it isn't necessary that he should kill her, the wretch!"

Although these jokes were in deplorable taste, they amused all and wounded no one, for indignation, like other things, depends upon its surroundings, and the atmosphere which had been gradually created around them was charged with sensual thoughts.

At the dessert the women themselves made some delicate and discreet allusions. Their eyes glistened; they had drunk much. The Count, who preserved, even in his flights, his grand appearance of gravity, made a comparison, much relished, upon the subject of those wintering at the pole and the joy of shipwrecked sailors who saw an opening toward the south.

Loiseau suddenly arose, a glass of champagne in his hand, and said: "I drink to our deliverance." Everybody was on his feet; they shouted in agreement. Even the two good sisters consented to touch their lips to the froth of the wine which they had never before tasted. They declared that it tasted like charged lemonade, only much nicer.

Loiseau resumed: "It is unfortunate that we have no piano, for we might make up a quadrille."

Cornudet had not said a word, nor made a gesture; he appeared plunged in very grave thoughts, and made sometimes a furious motion, so that his great beard seemed to wish to free itself. Finally, toward midnight, as they were separating, Loiseau, who was staggering, touched him suddenly on the stomach and said to him in a stammer: "You are not very funny, this evening; you have said nothing, citizen!" Then Cornudet raised his head brusquely and, casting a brilliant, terrible glance around the company, said: "I tell you all that you have been guilty of infamy!" He rose, went to the door, and again repeated: "Infamy, I say!" and disappeared.

This made a coldness at first. Loiseau, interlocutor, was stupefied; but he recovered immediately and laughed heartily as he said: "He is very green, my friends. He is very green." And then, as they did not comprehend, he told them about the "mysteries of the corridor." Then there was a return of gaiety. The women behaved like lunatics. The Count and Mr. Carré-

Lamadon wept from the force of their laughter. They could not believe it.

"How is that? Are you sure?"

"I tell you I saw it."

"And she refused—"

"Yes, because the Prussian officer was in the next room."

"Impossible!"

"I swear it!"

The Count was stifled with laughter. The industrial gentleman held his sides with both hands. Loiseau continued:

"And now you understand why he saw nothing funny this evening! No, nothing at all!" And the three started out half ill, suffocated.

They separated. But Mrs. Loiseau, who was of a spiteful nature, remarked to her husband as they were getting into bed, that "that grisette" of a little Carré-Lamadon was yellow with envy all the evening. "You know," she continued, "how some women will take to a uniform, whether it be French or Prussian! It is all the same to them! Oh! what a pity!"

And all night, in the darkness of the corridor, there were to be heard light noises, like whisperings and walking in bare feet, and imperceptible creakings. They did not go to sleep until late, that is sure, for there were threads of light shining under the doors for a long time. The champagne had its effect; they say it troubles sleep.

The next day a clear winter's sun made the snow very brilliant. The diligence, already harnessed, waited before the door, while an army of white pigeons, in their thick plumage, with rose-colored eyes, with a black spot in the center, walked up and down gravely among the legs of the six horses, seeking their livelihood in the manure scattered there.

The driver, enveloped in his sheepskin, had a lighted pipe under the seat, and all the travelers, radiant, were rapidly packing some provisions for the rest of the journey. They were only waiting for Ball-of-Fat. Finally she appeared.

She seemed a little troubled, ashamed.

And she advanced timidly toward her companions, who all, with one motion, turned as if they had not seen her. The Count, with dignity, took the arm of his wife and removed her from this impure contact.

The fat girl stopped, half stupefied; then, plucking up courage, she approached the manufacturer's wife with "Good morning, Madame," humbly murmured. The lady made a slight bow of the head which she accompanied with a look of outraged virtue. Everybody seemed busy and kept themselves as far from her as if she had had some infectious disease in her skirts. Then they hurried into the carriage, where she came last, alone, and where she took the place she had occupied during the first part of the journey.

They seemed not to see her or know her; although Madame Loiseau, looking at her from afar, said to her husband in a half-tone: "Happily, I don't have to sit beside her."

The heavy carriage began to move and the remainder of the journey commenced. No one spoke at first. Ball-of-Fat dared not raise her eyes. She felt indignant toward all her neighbors, and at the same time humiliated at having yielded to the foul kisses of this Prussian, into whose arms they had hypocritically thrown her.

Then the Countess, turning toward Mrs. Carré-Lamadon, broke the difficult silence:

"I believe you know Madame d'Etrelles?"

"Yes, she is one of my friends."

"What a charming woman!"

"Delightful! A very gentle nature, and well educated, besides; then she is an artist to the tips of her fingers, sings beautifully, and draws to perfection."

The manufacturer chatted with the Count, and in the midst of the rattling of the glass, an occasional word escaped such as "coupon—premium—limit—expiration."

Loiseau, who had pilfered the old pack of cards from the inn, greasy through five years of contact with tables badly cleaned, began a game of bezique with his wife.

The good sisters took from their belt the long rosary which hung there, made together the sign of the cross, and suddenly began to move their lips in a lively murmur, as if they were going through the whole of the "Oremus." And from time to time they kissed a medal, made the sign anew, then recommenced their muttering which was rapid and continued.

Cornudet sat motionless, thinking.

At the end of three hours on the way, Loiseau put up the cards and said: "I am hungry."

His wife drew out a package from whence she brought a piece of cold veal. She cut it evenly in thin pieces and they both began to eat.

"Suppose we do the same," said the Countess.

They consented to it and she undid the provisions prepared for the two couples. It was in one of those dishes whose lid is decorated with a china hare, to signify that a *pâté* of hare is inside, a succulent dish of pork, where white rivers of lard cross the brown flesh of the game, mixed with some other viands hashed fine. A beautiful square of Gruyère cheese, wrapped in a piece of newspaper, preserved the imprint "divers things" upon the unctuous plate.

The two good sisters unrolled a big sausage which smelled of garlic; and Cornudet plunged his two hands into the vast pockets of his overcoat, at the same time, and drew out four hard eggs and a piece of bread. He removed the shells and threw them in the straw under his feet; then he began to eat the eggs, letting fall on his vast beard some bits of clear yellow, which looked like stars caught there.

Ball-of-Fat, in the haste and distraction of her rising, had not thought of provisions, and she looked at them exasperated, suffocating with rage, at all of them eating so placidly. A tumultuous anger swept over her at first, and she opened her mouth to cry out at them, to hurl at them a flood of injury which mounted to her lips; but she could not speak, her exasperation strangled her.

No one looked at her or thought of her. She felt herself drowned in the scorn of these honest scoundrels, who had first sacrificed her and then rejected her, like some improper or useless article. She thought of her great basket full of good things which they had greedily devoured, of her two chickens shining with jelly, of her *pâtés*, her pears, and the four bottles of Bordeaux; and her fury suddenly falling, as a cord drawn too tightly breaks, she felt ready to weep. She made terrible efforts to prevent it, making ugly faces, swallowing her sobs as children do, but the tears came and glistened in the corners of her eyes, and then two great drops, detaching themselves from the rest, rolled slowly down like little streams of water that filter through rock, and, falling regularly, rebounded upon her breast. She sat erect, her eyes fixed, her face rigid and pale, hoping that no one would notice her.

But the Countess perceived her and told her husband by a sign. He shrugged his shoulders, as much as to say:

"What would you have me do, it is not my fault."

Mrs. Loiseau indulged in a mute laugh of triumph and murmured:

"She weeps for shame."

The two good sisters began to pray again, after having wrapped in a paper the remainder of their sausage.

Then Cornudet, who was digesting his eggs, extended his legs to the seat opposite, crossed them, folded his arms, smiled like a man who is watching a good farce, and began to whistle the "Marseillaise."

All faces grew dark. The popular song assuredly did not please his neighbors. They became nervous and agitated, having an appearance of wishing to howl, like dogs, when they hear a barbarous organ. He perceived this but did not stop. Sometimes he would hum the words:

> *"Sacred love of country*
> *Help, sustain th' avenging arm;*
> *Liberty, sweet Liberty*
> *Ever fight, with no alarm."*

They traveled fast, the snow being harder. But as far as Dieppe, during the long, sad hours of the journey across the jolts in the road, through the falling night, in the profound darkness of the carriage, he continued his vengeful, monotonous whistling with a ferocious obstinacy, constraining his neighbors to follow the song from one end to the other, and to recall the words that belonged to each measure.

Ball-of-Fat wept continually; and sometimes a sob, which she was not able to restrain, echoed between the two rows of people in the shadows.

Mademoiselle Fifi

The Major Graf [Count] von Farlsberg, the Prussian commandant, was reading his newspaper, lying back in a great armchair, with his booted feet on the beautiful marble fireplace, where his spurs had made two holes, which grew deeper every day, during the three months that he had been in the château of Urville.

A cup of coffee was smoking on a small, inlaid table, which was stained with liquors, burnt by cigars, notched by the penknife of the victorious officer, who occasionally would stop while sharpening a pencil, to jot down figures or to make a drawing on it, just as it took his fancy.

When he had read his letters and the German newspapers, which his baggage-master had brought him, he got up, and after throwing three or four enormous pieces of green wood onto the fire—for these gentlemen were gradually cutting down the park in order to keep themselves warm—he went to the window. The rain was descending in torrents, a regular Normandy rain, which looked as if it were being poured out by some furious hand, a slanting rain, which was as thick as a curtain, which formed a kind of wall with oblique stripes, and which deluged everything—a regular rain, such as one frequently experiences in the neighborhood of Rouen, which is the watering-pot of France.

For a long time the officer looked at the sodden turf and at the swollen Andelle beyond it, which was overflowing its banks, and he was drumming a waltz from the Rhine on the windowpanes, with his fingers, when a noise made him turn round; it was his second in command, Captain Baron von Kelweinstein.

The major was a giant, with broad shoulders and a long, fair beard, which hung like a cloth onto his chest. His whole solemn person suggested the idea of a military peacock, a peacock who was carrying his tail spread out onto his breast. He had cold, gentle, blue eyes, and the scar from a sword-cut, which he had received in the war with Austria; he was said to be an honorable man as well as a brave officer.

The captain, a short, red-faced man, who was tightly girthed in at the waist, had his red hair cropped quite close to his head, and in certain lights almost looked as if he had been rubbed over with phosphorus. He had lost two front teeth one night, though he could not quite remember how. This defect made him speak so that he could not always be understood, and he had a bald patch on the top of his head, which made him look rather like a monk, with a fringe of curly, bright, golden hair round the circle of bare skin.

The commandant shook hands with him and drank his cup of coffee (the sixth that morning) at a draught, while he listened to his subordinate's report of what had occurred; and then they both went to the window and declared that it was a very unpleasant outlook. The major, who was a quiet man, with a wife at home, could accommodate himself to everything; but the captain, who was rather fast, being in the habit of frequenting low resorts, and much given to women, was mad at having been shut up for three months in the compulsory chastity of that wretched hole.

There was a knock at the door, and when the commandant said, "Come in," one of their automatic soldiers appeared and by his mere presence announced that breakfast was ready. In the dining room, they met three other officers of lower rank: a lieutenant, Otto von Grossling, and two sublieutenants, Fritz Scheunebarg and Count Wilhelm von Eyrick, a very short, fair-haired man, who was proud and brutal toward men, harsh toward prisoners, and very violent.

Since he had been in France, his comrades had called him nothing but "Mademoiselle Fifi." They had given him that nickname on account of his dandified style and small waist, which looked as if he wore stays; from his pale face, on which his budding mustache scarcely showed; and on account of the habit he had acquired of employing the French expression, *fi, fi donc,* which he pronounced with a slight whistle, when he wished to express his sovereign contempt for persons or things.

The dining room of the château was a magnificent long room whose fine old mirrors, now cracked by pistol bullets, and Flemish tapestry, now cut to ribbons and hanging in rags in places from sword-cuts, told too well what Mademoiselle Fifi's occupation was during his spare time.

There were three family portraits on the walls; a steel-clad knight, a cardinal, and a judge, who were all smoking long porcelain pipes, which had been inserted into holes in the canvas, while a lady in a long, pointed waist proudly exhibited an enormous pair of mustaches, drawn with a piece of charcoal.

The officers ate their breakfast almost in silence in that mutilated room, which looked dull in the rain and melancholy under its vanquished appearance, although its old oak floor had become as solid as the stone floor of a public house.

When they had finished eating and were smoking and drinking, they began as usual to talk about the dull life they were leading. The bottle of brandy and of liquors passed from hand to hand, and all sat back in their chairs, taking repeated sips from their glasses and scarcely removing the long, bent stems, which terminated in china bowls painted in a manner to delight a Hottentot, from their mouths.

As soon as their glasses were empty, they filled them again, with a gesture of resigned weariness, but Mademoiselle Fifi emptied his every minute, and a soldier immediately gave him another. They were enveloped in a cloud of strong tobacco smoke; they seemed to be sunk in a state of drowsy, stupid intoxication, in that dull state of drunkenness of men who have nothing to do, when suddenly, the baron sat up, and said: "By heavens! This cannot go on; we must think of something to do." And on hearing this, Lieutenant Otto and Sublieutenant Fritz, who preeminently possessed the grave, heavy German countenance, said: "What, Captain?"

He thought for a few moments, and then replied: "What? Well, we must get up some entertainment, if the commandant will allow us."

"What sort of an entertainment, captain?" the major asked, taking his pipe out of his mouth.

"I will arrange all that, commandant," the baron said: "I will send *Le Devoir* to Rouen, who will bring us some ladies. I know where they can be found. We will have supper here, as all the materials are at hand, and, at least, we shall have a jolly evening."

Graf von Farlsberg shrugged his shoulders with a smile: "You must surely be mad, my friend."

But all the other officers got up, surrounded their chief, and said: "Let captain have his own way, commandant; it is terribly dull here."

And the major ended by yielding. "Very well," he replied, and the baron immediately sent for *Le Devoir*.

The latter was an old corporal who had never been seen to smile, but who carried out all orders of his superiors to the letter, no matter what they might be. He stood there with an impassive face while

he received the baron's instructions and then went out; five minutes later a large wagon belonging to the military train, covered with a miller's tilt, galloped off as fast as four horses could take it under the pouring rain, and the officers all seemed to awaken from their lethargy, their looks brightened, and they began to talk.

Although it was raining as hard as ever, the major declared that it was not so dull, and Lieutenant von Grossling said with conviction that the sky was clearing up, while Mademoiselle Fifi did not seem to be

able to keep in his place. He got up, and sat down again, and his bright eyes seemed to be looking for something to destroy. Suddenly, looking at the lady with the mustaches, the young fellow pulled out his revolver, and said: "You shall not see it." And without leaving his seat he aimed, and with two successive bullets cut out both the eyes of the portrait.

"Let us make a mine!" he then exclaimed, and the conversation was suddenly interrupted, as if they had found some fresh and powerful subject of interest. The mine was his invention, his method of destruction, and his favorite amusement.

When he left the château, the lawful owner, Count Fernand d'Amoys d'Urville, had not had time to carry away or to hide anything except the plate, which had been stowed away in a hole made in one of the walls, so that, as he was very rich and had good taste, the large drawing room, which opened into the dining room, had looked like the gallery in a museum, before his precipitate flight.

Expensive oil paintings, watercolors, and drawings hung upon the walls, while on the tables, on the hanging shelves, and in elegant glass cupboards, there were a thousand knickknacks: small vases, statuettes, groups in Dresden china, grotesque Chinese figures, old ivory, and Venetian glass, which filled the large room with their precious and fantastical array.

Scarcely anything was left now; not that the things had been stolen, for the major would not have allowed that, but Mademoiselle Fifi *would have a mine,* and on that occasion all the officers thoroughly enjoyed themselves for five minutes. The little marquis went into the drawing room to get what he wanted, and he brought back a small, delicate china teapot, which he filled with gunpowder, and carefully introduced a piece of German tinder into it, through the spout. Then he lighted it, and took this infernal machine into the next room; but he came back immediately, and shut the door. The Germans all stood expectantly, their faces full of childish, smiling curiosity, and as soon as the explosion had shaken the château, they all rushed in at once.

Mademoiselle Fifi, who got in first, clapped his hands in delight at the sight of a terra-cotta Venus, whose head had been blown off, and each picked up pieces of porcelain, and wondered at the strange shape of the fragments, while the major was looking with a paternal eye at the large drawing room which had been wrecked in such a Neronic fashion, and which was strewn with the fragments of works of art. He went out first, and said, with a smile: "He managed that very well!"

But there was such a cloud of smoke in the dining room, mingled with the tobacco smoke, that they could not breathe, so the commandant opened the window, and all the officers, who had gone into the room for a glass of cognac, went up to it.

The moist air blew into the room and brought a sort of spray with it, which powdered their beards. They looked at the tall trees, which were dripping with the rain, at the broad valley which was covered with mist, and at the church spire in the distance, which rose up like a gray point in the beating rain.

The bells had not rung since their arrival. That was the only resistance which the invaders had met with in the neighborhood. The parish priest had not refused to take in and to feed the Prussian soldiers; he had several times even drunk a bottle of beer or claret with the hostile commandant, who often employed him as a benevolent intermediary; but it was no use to ask him for a single stroke of the bells; he would sooner have allowed himself to be shot. That was his way of protesting against the invasion, a peaceful and silent protest, the only one, he said, which was suitable to a priest, who was a man of mildness, and not of blood; and everyone, for twenty-five miles round, praised Abbé Chantavoine's firmness and heroism in venturing to proclaim the public mourning by the obstinate silence of his church bells.

The whole village grew enthusiastic over his resistance, and was ready to back up their pastor and to risk anything, as they looked upon that silent protest as the safeguard of the national honor. It seemed to the peasants that thus they had deserved better of their country than Belfort and Strassburg, that they had set an equally valuable example, and that the name of their little village would become immortalized by that; but with that exception, they refused their Prussian conquerors nothing.

The commandant and his officers laughed among themselves at that inoffensive courage, and as the people in the whole country round showed themselves obliging and compliant toward them, they willingly tolerated their silent patriotism. Only little Count Wilhelm would have liked to have forced them to ring the bells. He was very angry at his superior's politic compliance with the priest's scruples, and every day he begged the commandant to allow him to sound "ding-dong, ding-dong," just once, only just once, just by way of a joke. And he asked it like a wheedling woman, in the tender voice of some mistress who wishes to obtain something, but the commandant would not yield, and to console *herself,* Mademoiselle Fifi made a *mine* in the château.

The five men stood there together for some minutes, inhaling the moist air, and at last Lieutenant Fritz said, with a laugh: "The ladies will certainly not have fine weather for their drive." Then they separated, each to his own duties, while the captain had plenty to do in seeing about the dinner.

When they met again, as it was growing dark, they began to laugh at seeing each other as dandified and smart as on the day of a grand review. The commandant's hair did not look as gray as it did in the morning, and the captain had shaved—had only kept his mustache on, which made him look as if he had a streak of fire under his nose.

In spite of the rain they left the window open, and one of them went to listen from time to time. At a quarter past six the baron said he heard a rumbling in the distance. They all rushed down, and soon the wagon drove up at a gallop with its four horses, splashed up to their backs, steaming and panting. Five women got out at the bottom of the steps, five handsome girls whom a comrade of the captain, to whom *Le Devoir* had taken his card, had selected with care.

They had not required much pressing, as they were sure of being well treated, for they had got to know the Prussians in the three months during which they had had to do with them. So they resigned themselves to the men as they did to the state of affairs. "It is part of our business, so it must be done," they said as they drove along; no doubt to allay some slight, secret scruples of conscience.

They went into the dining room immediately, which looked still more dismal in its dilapidated state, when it was lighted up; while the table covered with choice dishes, the beautiful china and glass, and the plate, which had been found in the hole in the wall where its owner had hidden it, gave to the place the look of a bandits' resort, where they were supping after committing a robbery. The captain was radiant; he took hold of the women as if he were familiar with them, appraising them, kissing them, valuing them for what they were worth as *ladies of pleasure;* and when the three young men wanted to appropriate one each, he opposed them authoritatively, reserving to himself the right to apportion them justly, according to their several ranks, so as not to wound the hierarchy. Therefore, so as to avoid all discussion, jarring, and suspicion of partiality, he placed them all in a line according to height, and addressing the tallest, he said in a voice of command:

"What is your name?"

"Pamela," she replied, raising her voice.

Then he said: "Number One, called Pamela, is adjudged to the commandant."

Then, having kissed Blondina, the second, as a sign of proprietorship, he proffered stout Amanda to Lieutenant Otto, Eva, "the Tomato," to Sublieutenant Fritz, and Rachel, the shortest of them all, a very young, dark girl, with eyes as black as ink, a Jewess, whose snub nose confirmed by exception the rule which allots hooked noses to all her race, to the youngest officer, frail Count Wilhelm von Eyrick.

They were all pretty and plump, without any distinctive features, and all were very much alike in look and person, from their daily dissipation and the life common to houses of public accommodation.

The three younger men wished to carry off their women immediately, under the pretext of finding them brushes and soap; but the captain wisely opposed this, for he said they were quite fit to sit down to dinner and that those who went up would wish for a change when they came down, and so would disturb the other couples, and his experience in such matters carried the day. There were only many kisses; expectant kisses.

Suddenly Rachel choked, and began to cough until the tears came into her eyes, while smoke came through her nostrils. Under pretense of kissing her, the count had blown a whiff of tobacco into her mouth. She did not fly into a rage, and did not say a word, but she looked at her possessor with latent hatred in her dark eyes.

They sat down to dinner. The commandant seemed delighted; he made Pamela sit on his right, and Blondina on his left, and said, as he unfolded his table napkin: "That was a delightful idea of yours, captain."

Lieutenants Otto and Fritz, who were as polite as if they had been with fashionable ladies, rather intimidated their neighbors, but Baron von Kelweinstein gave the reins to all his vicious propensities, beamed, made doubtful remarks, and seemed on fire with his crown of red hair. He paid them compliments in French from the other side of the Rhine, and sputtered out gallant remarks, only fit for a low pothouse, from between his two broken teeth.

They did not understand him, however, and their intelligence did not seem to be awakened until he uttered nasty words and broad expressions, which were mangled by his accent. Then all began to laugh at once, like mad women, and fell against each other, repeating the words, which the baron then began to say all wrong, in order that he might have the pleasure of hearing them say doubtful things. They gave him as much of that stuff as he wanted, for they were drunk after the first bottle of wine, and, becoming themselves once more, and opening the door to their usual habits, they kissed the mustaches on the right and left of them, pinched their arms, uttered furious cries, drank out of every glass, and sang French couplets and bits of German songs, which they had picked up in their daily intercourse with the enemy.

Soon the men themselves, intoxicated by that which was displayed to their sight and touch, grew very amorous, shouted and broke the plates and dishes, while the soldiers behind them waited on them stolidly. The commandant was the only one who put any restraint upon himself.

Mademoiselle Fifi had taken Rachel onto his knees, and, getting excited, at one moment kissed the little black curls on her neck, inhaling the pleasant warmth of her body and all the savor of her person through the slight space there was between her dress and her skin, and at another pinched her furiously through the material and made her scream, for he was seized with a species of ferocity, and tormented by his desire to hurt her. He often held her close to him, as if to make her part of himself, and put his lips in a long kiss on the Jewess's rosy mouth, until she lost her breath; and at last he bit her until a stream of blood ran down her chin and onto her bodice.

For the second time, she looked him full in the face, and as she bathed the wound, she said: "You will have to pay for that!"

But he merely laughed a hard laugh, and said: "I will pay."

At dessert, champagne was served, and the commandant rose, and in the same voice in which he would have drunk to the health of the Empress Augusta, he drank: "To our ladies!" Then a series of toasts began, toasts worthy of the lowest soldiers and of drunkards, mingled with filthy jokes, which were made still more brutal by their ignorance of the language.

They got up, one after the other, trying to say something witty, forcing themselves to be funny, and the women, who were so drunk that they almost fell off their chairs, with vacant looks and clammy tongues, applauded madly each time.

The captain, who no doubt wished to impart an appearance of gallantry to the orgy, raised his glass again, and said: "To our victories over hearts!" Thereupon Lieutenant Otto, who was a species of bear from the Black Forest, jumped up, inflamed and saturated with drink, and seized by an access of alcoholic patriotism, cried: "To our victories over France!"

Drunk as they were, the women were silent, and Rachel turned round with a shudder and said: "Look here, I know some Frenchmen in whose presence you would not dare to say that." But the little count, still holding her on his knees, began to laugh, for the wine had made him very merry, and said: "Ha! ha! ha! I have never met any of them, myself. As soon as we show ourselves, they run away!"

The girl, who was in a terrible rage, shouted into his face: "You are lying, you dirty scoundrel!"

For a moment, he looked at her steadily, with his bright eyes upon her, as he had looked at the portrait before he destroyed it with revolver bullets, and then he began to laugh: "Ah! yes, talk about them, my dear! Should we be here now, if they were brave?" Then getting excited, he exclaimed: "We are the masters! France belongs to us!" She jumped off his knees with a bound and threw herself into her chair, while he rose, held out his glass over the table, and repeated: "France and the French, the woods, the fields, and the houses of France belong to us!"

The others, who were quite drunk, and who were suddenly seized by military enthusiasm, the enthusiasm of brutes, seized their glasses, and shouting, "Long live Prussia!" emptied them at a draught.

The girls did not protest, for they were reduced to silence and were afraid. Even

Rachel did not say a word, as she had no reply to make, and then the little count put his champagne glass, which had just been refilled, onto the head of the Jewess, and exclaimed: "All the women in France belong to us, also!"

At that she got up so quickly that the glass upset, spilling the amber-colored wine onto her black hair as if to baptize her, and broke into a hundred fragments as it fell onto the floor. With trembling lips, she defied the looks of the officer, who was still laughing, and she stammered out, in a voice choked with rage: "That—that—that—is not true, for you shall certainly not have any French women."

He sat down again, so as to laugh at his ease, and trying effectually to speak in the Parisian accent, he said: "That is good, very good! Then what did you come here for, my dear?"

She was thunderstruck, and made no reply for a moment, for in her agitation she did not understand him at first; but as soon as she grasped his meaning, she said to him indignantly and vehemently: "I! I! am not a woman; I am only a strumpet, and that is all that Prussians want."

Almost before she had finished, he slapped her full in her face; but as he was raising his hand again, as if he would strike her, she, almost mad with passion, took up a small dessert knife from the table and stabbed him right in the neck, just above the breastbone. Something that he was going to say was cut short in his throat, and he sat there, with his mouth half open, and a terrible look in his eyes.

All the officers shouted in horror and leaped up tumultuously; but throwing her chair between Lieutenant Otto's legs, who fell down at full length, she ran to the window, opened it before they could seize her, and jumped out into the night and pouring rain.

In two minutes, Mademoiselle Fifi was dead. Fritz and Otto drew their swords and wanted to kill the women, who threw themselves at their feet and clung to their knees.

With some difficulty the major stopped the slaughter and had the four terrified girls locked up in a room under the care of two soldiers. Then he organized the pursuit of the fugitive, as carefully as if he were about to engage in a skirmish, feeling quite sure that she would be caught.

The table, which had been cleared immediately, now served as a bed on which to lay Fifi out, and the four officers made for the window, rigid and sobered with the stern faces of soldiers on duty, and tried to pierce through the darkness of the night amid the steady torrent of rain. Suddenly a shot was heard, and then another a long way off; and for four hours they heard, from time to time, near or distant reports and rallying cries, strange words uttered as a call, in guttural voices.

In the morning they all returned. Two soldiers had been killed and three others wounded by their comrades in the ardor of that chase, and in the confusion of such a nocturnal pursuit, but they had not caught Rachel.

Then the inhabitants of the district were terrorized, the houses were turned topsy-turvy, the country was scoured and beaten up, over and over again, but the Jewess did not seem to have left a single trace of her passage behind her.

When the general was told of it, he gave orders to hush up the affair, so as not to set a bad example to the army, but he severely censured the commandant, who in turn punished his inferiors. The general had said: "One does not go to war in order to amuse oneself, and to caress prostitutes." And Graf von Farlsberg, in his exasperation, made up his mind to have his revenge on the district, but as he required a pretext for showing severity, he sent for the priest and ordered him to have the bell tolled at the funeral of Count von Eyrick.

Contrary to all expectation, the priest showed himself humble and most respectful, and when Mademoiselle Fifi's body left the Château d'Urville on its way to the cemetery, carried by soldiers, preceded, surrounded, and followed by soldiers who marched with loaded rifles, for the first time the bell sounded its funereal knell in a lively manner, as if a friendly hand were caressing it. At night it sounded again, and the next day and every day; it rang as much as anyone could desire. Sometimes, even, it would start at night and sound gently through the darkness, seized by strange joy, awakened, one could not tell why. All the peasants in the neighborhood declared that it was bewitched, and nobody except the priest and the sacristan would now go near the church tower, but they went because a poor girl was living there in grief and solitude, secretly nourished by those two men.

She remained there until the German troops departed, and then one evening the priest borrowed the baker's cart and himself drove his prisoner to Rouen. When they got there, he embraced her, and she quickly went back on foot to the establishment from which she had come, where the proprietress, who thought that she was dead, was very glad to see her.

A short time afterward, a patriot who had no prejudices, who liked her because of her bold deed, and who afterward loved her for herself, married her, and made a lady of her.

Toine

Everybody for ten leagues round knew Toine, fat Toine, "Toine-my-Fine," Antoine Mâcheblé, the landlord of Tournevent.

He had made famous this village, buried in the depths of the valley that descended to the sea. It was a poor peasant hamlet composed of a dozen Norman houses surrounded by ditches and encircled by trees. The houses were huddled together in this shrub-covered ravine, behind the curve of the hill, which had caused the village to be called Tournevent [*tourne-vent:* chimney-cowl]. As birds conceal themselves in the furrows during a storm, they seemed to have sought a shelter in this hollow, a shelter against the fierce salt winds of the sea, which gnawed and burned like fire and withered and destroyed like the blasts of winter.

The whole hamlet seemed to be the property of Antoine Mâcheblé, who was besides often called Toine, and Toine-my-Fine, on account of a manner of speech of which he constantly availed himself. "My Fine is the best in France," he would say. His *fine* was his cognac, be it understood. For twenty years he had watered the country with his cognac, and in serving his customers he was in the habit of saying: "It warms the stomach and clears the head; there is nothing better for your health, my son." He called everybody "my son," although he had never had a son of his own.

Ah, yes, everyone knew old Toine, the biggest man in the canton, or even in the *arrondissement.* His little house seemed too ridiculously small to contain him, and when he was seen standing in his doorway, where he spent the greater part of every day, one wondered how he could enter his dwelling. But he did enter each time a customer presented himself, for Toine-my-Fine was invited by right to levy a little glass on all who drank in his house.

His *café* bore on its sign the legend "The Rendezvous of Friends," and old Toine was truly the friend of all the country round. People came from Fécamp and Montivilliers to see him and tipple with him and to hear his stories—for this great, good-natured man could make a tombstone laugh. He could joke without giving offense, wink an eye to express what he dare not utter, and punch one's ribs in a fit of gaiety, so as to force a laugh in spite of oneself. And then it was a curiosity just to see him drink. He drank all that was offered him by everybody, with a joy in his wicked eye, a joy which came from a double pleasure: the pleasure of regaling himself first, and the pleasure of heaping up money at the expense of his friends afterward. The blackguards of the community wondered why Toine had no children, and one day asked him as much. With a wicked wink he replied: "My wife is not attractive enough for such a fine fellow as I am."

The quarrels of Toine and his homely wife were as much enjoyed by the tipplers as was their favorite cognac, for they had squabbled through the whole thirty years of their married life. Only Toine was good-natured over it, while his wife was furious. She was a tall peasant woman who walked with long stilt-like strides and carried on her thin, flat body the head of an ugly screech owl. She spent her whole time in rearing poultry in the little yard behind the public house, and was renowned for the success with which she fattened her fowls.

When any of the great ladies of Fécamp gave a feast to the people of quality, it was necessary to the success of the repast that it should be garnished with the celebrated fowls from mother Toine's poultry yard.

But she was born with a vile temper and had continued to be dissatisfied with everything. Angry with everybody, she was particularly so with her husband. She jeered at his gaiety, his popularity, his good health, and his *embonpoint;* she treated him with the utmost contempt because he got his money without working for it, and because, as she said, he ate and drank as much as ten ordinary men. She declared every day that he was only fit to be littered in the stable with the naked swine, whom he resembled, and that he was only a mass of fat that made her sick at her stomach. "Wait a little, wait a little," she would shriek in his face, "we shall soon see what is going to happen! This great windbag will burst like a sack of grain!"

Toine laughed till he shook like a bowl of jelly and, tapping his enormous belly, replied: "Ah, my old hen, let us see you try to make your chickens as fat as this."

And rolling up his sleeve he showed his brawny arm. "Do you not see the feathers growing already?" he cried. And the customers would strike their fists on the table and fairly writhe with joy, and would stamp their feet and spit upon the floor in a delirium of delight.

The old woman grew more furious than ever, and shouted at the top of her lungs: "Just wait a bit, we shall see what will happen. Your Toine-my-Fine will burst like a sack of grain."

And she rushed out, maddened with rage at the laughter of the crowd of drinkers.

Toine, in fact, was a wonder to see, so fat and red and short of breath had he grown. He was one of those enormous creatures with whom Death seems to amuse himself by tricks, gaieties, and fatal buffooneries, making irresistibly comic the slow work of destruction. Instead of showing himself, as toward others, in white hairs, shrunken limbs, wrinkles, and general feebleness which make one say with a shiver: "Heavens, how he has changed!" he took pleasure in fattening Toine; in making a droll monster of him, in reddening his face and giving him the appearance of superhuman health; and the deformities which he inflicted on other beings became in Toine's case laughable and diverting instead of sinister and pitiable.

"Wait a little, wait a little," muttered mother Toine, as she scattered the grain about her poultry yard, "we are going to see what will happen!"

II

It happened that Toine had a seizure and fell smitten with a paralytic stroke. They carried the giant to the little chamber partitioned off at the rear of the *café* in order that he might hear what was going on on the other side of the wall, and converse with his friends, for his brain remained clear while his enormous body was prone and helpless. They hoped for a time that his mighty limbs would recover some of their energy, but this hope disappeared very soon, and Toine-my-Fine was forced to pass his days and nights in his bed, which was made up but once a week, with the help of four friends who lifted him by his four limbs while his mattress was turned. He continued cheerful, but with a different kind of gaiety; more timid, more humble, and with the pathetic fear of a little child in the presence of his wife, who scolded and raged all the day long. "There he lies, the great glutton, the good-for-nothing idler, the nasty thing!" she cried. Toine replied nothing, only winking his eye behind the old woman's back, and turned over in the bed, the only movement he was able to make. He called this change "making a move to the north, or a move to the south." His only entertainment now was to listen to the conversation in the *café* and to join in the talk across the wall, and when he recognized the voice of a friend he would cry: "Hello, my son; is it thou, Célestin?"

And Célestin Maloisel would reply: "It is me, father Toine. How do you gallop today, my great rabbit?"

"I cannot gallop yet, Célestin," Toine would answer, "but I am not growing thin, either. The shell is good." Soon he invited his intimates into his chamber for company, because it pained him to see them drinking without him. He told them it grieved him not to be able to take his cognac with them. "I can stand everything else," he said; "but not to drink with you makes me sad, my sons."

Then the screech owl's head of mother Toine would appear at the window, and she would say: "Look, look at him! this great hulking idler, who must be fed and washed and scoured like a pig!"

And when she disappeared a red-plumaged rooster sometimes perched on the windowsill, and, looking about with his round and curious eye, gave forth a shrill crow. And sometimes two or three hens flew in and scratched and pecked about the floor, attracted by the crumbs, which fell from father Toine's plate.

The friends of Toine-my-Fine very soon deserted the *café* for his chamber, and every afternoon they gossiped around the bed of the big man. Bedridden as he was, this rascal of a Toine still amused them; he would have made the devil himself laugh, the jolly fellow! There were three friends who came every day: Célestin Maloisel, a tall, spare man with a body twisted like the trunk of an apple tree; Prosper Horslaville, a little dried-up old man with a nose like a ferret, malicious and sly as a fox; and Césaire Paumelle, who never uttered a word, but who enjoyed himself all the same. These men brought in a board from the yard which they placed across the bed and on which they played dominoes from two o'clock in the afternoon until six. But mother Toine soon interfered: she could not endure that her husband should amuse

himself by playing dominoes in his bed, and each time she saw the play, she bounded into the room in a rage, overturned the board, seized the dominoes, and carried them into the *café*, declaring that it was enough to feed this great lump of tallow without seeing him divert himself at the expense of hard-working people. Célestin Maloisel bent his head before the storm, but Prosper Horslaville tried to further excite the old woman, whose rages amused him. Seeing her one day more exasperated than usual, he said: "Hello, mother Toine. Do you know what I would do if I were in your place?"

She waited for an explanation, fixing her owl-like eyes upon him. He continued: "Your husband, who never leaves his bed, is as hot as an oven. I should set him to hatching out eggs."

She remained stupefied, thinking he was jesting, watching the meager and sly face of the peasant, who continued:

"I would put five eggs under each arm the same day that I set the yellow hen; they would all hatch out at the same time; and when they were out of their shells, I would put your husband's chicks under the hen for her to bring up. That would bring you some poultry, mother Toine."

The old woman was amazed. "Can that be?" she asked.

Prosper continued: "Why can't it? Since they put eggs in a warm box to hatch, one might as well put them in a warm bed."

She was greatly impressed with this reasoning and went out composed and thoughtful.

Eight days later she came into Toine's chamber with her apron full of eggs and said: "I have just put the yellow hen to set with ten eggs under her; here are ten for you! Be careful not to break them!"

Toine was astonished. "What do you mean?" he cried.

"I mean that you shall hatch them, good-for-nothing."

Toine laughed at first, then as she insisted he grew angry, he resisted and obstinately refused to allow her to put the eggs under his great arms, that his warmth might hatch them. But the baffled old woman grew furious and declared: "You shall have not a bite to eat so long as you refuse to take them—there, we'll see what will happen!"

Toine was uneasy, but he said nothing till he heard the clock strike twelve; then he called to his wife, who bawled from the kitchen: "There is no dinner for you today, you great idler!"

He thought at first she was joking, but when he found she was in earnest he begged and prayed and swore by fits; turned himself to the north and the south, and growing desperate under the pangs of hunger and the smell of the viands, he pounded on the wall with his great fists, until at last worn out and almost famished, he allowed his wife to introduce the eggs into his bed and place them under his arms. After that he had his soup.

When his friends arrived as usual, they believed Toine to be very ill; he seemed constrained and in pain.

Then they began to play dominoes as formerly, but Toine appeared to take no pleasure in the game, and put forth his hand so gingerly and with such evident precaution that they suspected at once something was wrong.

"Hast thou thy arm tied?" demanded Horslaville.

Toine feebly responded: "I have a feeling of heaviness in my shoulder."

Suddenly someone entered the *café,* and the players paused to listen. It was the mayor and his assistant, who called for two glasses of cognac and then began to talk of the affairs of the country. As they spoke in low tones, Toine tried to press his ear against the wall; and forgetting his eggs, he gave a sudden lunge "to the north," which made an omelet of them in short order. At the oath he uttered, mother Toine came running in, and divining the disaster she uncovered him with a jerk. She stood a moment too enraged and breathless to

speak, at the sight of the yellow poultice pasted on the flank of her husband. Then, trembling with fury, she flung herself on the paralytic and began to pound him with great force on the body, as though she were pounding her dirty linen on the banks of the river. She showered her blows upon him with the force and rapidity of a drummer beating his drum.

The friends of Toine were choking with laughter, coughing, sneezing, uttering exclamations, while the frightened man parried the attacks of his wife with due precaution in order not to break the five eggs he still had on the other side.

III

Toine was conquered. He was compelled to hatch eggs. He had to renounce the innocent pleasure of dominoes, to give up any effort to move to the north or south, for his wife deprived him of all nourishment every time he broke an egg. He lay on his back, with his eyes fixed on the ceiling, his arms extended like wings, warming against his immense body the incipient chicks in their white shells. He spoke only in low tones as if he feared a noise as much as a movement, and he asked often about the yellow hen in the poultry yard, who was engaged in the same task as himself. The old woman went from the hen to her husband, and from her husband to the hen, possessed and preoccupied with the little broods which were maturing in the bed and in the nest. The country people, who soon learned the story, came in, curious and serious to get the news of Toine. They entered on tiptoe as one enters a sick-chamber and inquired with concern:

"How goes it, Toine?"

"It has to go," he answered; "but it is so long, I am tired of waiting. I get excited and feel cold shivers galloping all over my skin."

One morning his wife came in very much elated and exclaimed: "The yellow

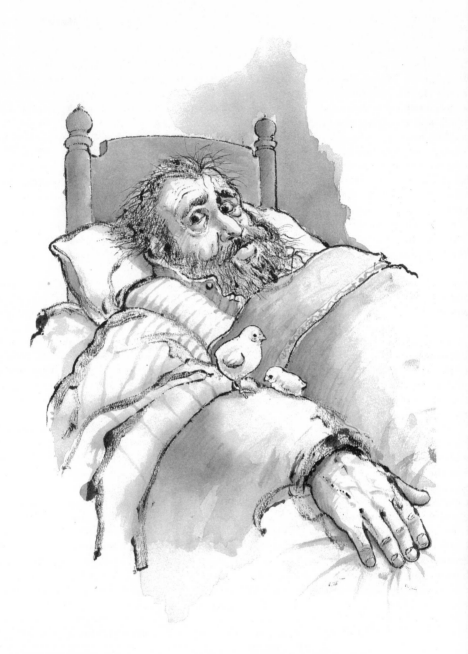

hen has hatched seven chicks; there were but three bad eggs!"

Toine felt his heart beat. How many would he have?

"Will it be soon?" he asked, with the anguish of a woman who is about to become a mother.

The old woman, who was tortured by the fear of failure, answered angrily:

"It is to be hoped so!"

They waited.

The friends, seeing that Toine's time was approaching, became very uneasy themselves. They gossiped about it in the house, and kept all the neighbors informed of the progress of affairs. Toward three o'clock Toine grew drowsy. He slept now half the time. He was suddenly awakened by an unusual tickling under his left arm. He put his hand carefully to the place and seized a little beast covered with yellow down, which struggled between his fingers. His emotion was so great that he cried out and let go the chick, which ran across his breast. The *café* was full of people. The customers rushed into the room and circled around the bed, while mother Toine, who had arrived at the first sound, carefully caught the fledgling as it nestled in her husband's beard. No one uttered a word. It was a warm April day; one could hear through the open window the clucking of the yellow hen calling to her newborn. Toine, who perspired with emotion and agony, murmured: "I feel another one under my left arm."

His wife plunged her great, gaunt hand under the bedclothes and drew forth a second chick with all the precautions of a midwife.

The neighbors wished to see it and passed it from hand to hand, regarding it with awe as though it were a phenomenon. For the space of twenty minutes no more were hatched, then four chicks came out of their shells at the same time. This caused a great excitement among the watchers.

Toine smiled, happy at his success, and began to feel proud of this singular paternity. Such a sight had never been seen before. This was a droll man, truly! "That makes six," cried Toine. "*Sacre bleu,* what a christening there will be!" and a great laugh rang out from the public. Other people now crowded into the *café* and filled the doorway, with outstretched necks and curious eyes.

"How many has he?" they inquired.

"There are six."

Mother Toine ran with the new fledglings to the hen, who, clucking distractedly, erected her feathers and spread wide her wings to shelter her increasing flock of little ones.

"Here comes another one!" cried Toine. He was mistaken—there were three of them. This was a triumph! The last one chipped its shell at seven o'clock in the evening. All Toine's eggs were good! He was delivered, and delirious with joy, he seized and kissed the frail little creature on the back. He could have smothered it with caresses. He wished to keep this little one in his bed until the next day, moved by the tenderness of a mother for this being to whom he had given life; but the old woman carried it away, as she had done the others, without listening to the supplications of her husband.

The friends of Toine went home delighted, conversing of the event by the way.

Horslaville remained after the others had gone, and approaching the ear of Toine whispered: "You will invite me to the first fricassee, will you not?"

At the idea of a fricassee, the visage of Toine brightened and he answered:

"Certainly I will invite thee, my son."

PICTURE CREDITS

THE
GREAT IDEAS

Volumes 1 and 2